Human Resource Management

Ninth Edition

Human Resource Management

R. Wayne Mondy, SPHR
McNeese State University

Robert M. Noe, SPHR
Texas A&M University–Commerce

In collaboration with

Judy Bandy Mondy
McNeese State University

Upper Saddle River, New Jersey 07458

Library of Congress Cataloging-in-Publication Data

Mondy R, Wayne,
Human resource management.—9th ed. / R. Wayne Mondy, Robert M. Noe.
p. cm.
"A new feature to the ninth edition ... is the inclusion of a CD-ROM entitled Human resource management skills by Mary Gowan"—Pref.
Includes bibliographical references and index.
ISBN 0-13-144716-5
1. Personnel management—United States. 2. Personnel management. I. Noe, Robert M. II. Gowan, Mary. Human resource management skills. III. Title.

HF5549.2.U5M66 2005
658.3—dc22 2003066172

Acquisitions Editor: Michael Ablassmeir
Editor-in-Chief: Jeff Shelstad
Assistant Editor: Melissa Yu
Media Project Manager: Jessica Sabloff
Marketing Manager: Anke Braun
Senior Managing Editor (Production): Judy Leale
Production Editor: Marcela Boos
Production Assistant: Joseph DeProspero
Permissions Coordinator: Virginia Somma
Associate Director, Manufacturing: Vincent Scelta
Production Manager: Arnold Vila
Manufacturing Buyer: Diane Peirano
Design Manager: Maria Lange
Interior Design: John Romer
Cover Design: John Romer
Cover Illustration: Todd Davidson/Stock Illustration Source, Inc.
Manager, Print Production: Christy Mahon
Composition: Carlisle Communications
Full-Service Project Management: Ann Imhof, Carlisle Communications
Printer/Binder: Courier-Kendallville

Credits and acknowledgments borrowed from other sources and reproduced, with permission, in this textbook appear on appropriate page within text.

Pearson Education LTD.
Pearson Education Singapore, Pte. Ltd
Pearson Education, Canada, Ltd
Pearson Education–Japan
Pearson Education Australia PTY, Limited
Pearson Education North Asia Ltd
Pearson Educación de Mexico, S.A. de C.V.
Pearson Education Malaysia, Pte. Ltd

10 9 8 7 6 5 4 3
ISBN 0-13-144716-5

To my daughters, granddaughter, and grandson

Alyson Lynn and Marianne Elizabeth,
Madison Jon, and Matthew Bryce

RWM

To my grandchildren

Michael, Lillie, Robert, Vaughan, and Anna

RMN

Brief Contents

Contents

Preface

HUMAN RESOURCE MANAGEMENT is arguably the most exciting area within the field of business. Much has changed in the world since the writing of the eighth edition of this book: the election of a new president, 9/11, two wars, and much more. The major technological changes that have occurred within the past few years continue to accelerate and no end appears in sight. The value of the human resource management function is gaining increasing importance in managing organizations. Today, with companies having access to the same technology, it is the human resources that make the real difference in achieving organizational goals. In fact, an organization's unique advantage has become increasingly dependent upon a firm's most valuable asset, its employees.

The ninth edition of Human Resource Management reveals this strategic function in a practical, realistic manner yet maintains its balance of pragmatism and theoretical concepts. The interrelationship of human resource management functions and the increasing utilization of technology is reflected throughout this book. And, the strategic role of HR in planning and operating organizations is apparent as each major human resource function is discussed. This book is designed primarily for students who are being exposed to human resource management for the first time. It will help to put them in touch with the field through the use of numerous examples and company material and will reinforce the notion that, by definition, all managers are necessarily involved with human resources. The book provides helpful insights for those students who desire to make human resource management their career choice and for all others who aspire to management positions.

KEY FEATURES OF THE NINTH EDITION

NEW **Chapter 2** New chapter on Social Responsibility and Business Ethics sets the stage for an integrated presentation of Ethical Dilemmas, which confront students in Chapters 2- 15.

Ethical Dilemmas These unique exercises are included in the body of chapters 2 - 15 to permit students to practice making ethical decisions regarding real-world situations. Instructors will find a debriefing guide in the Instructor Manual that accompanies this text.

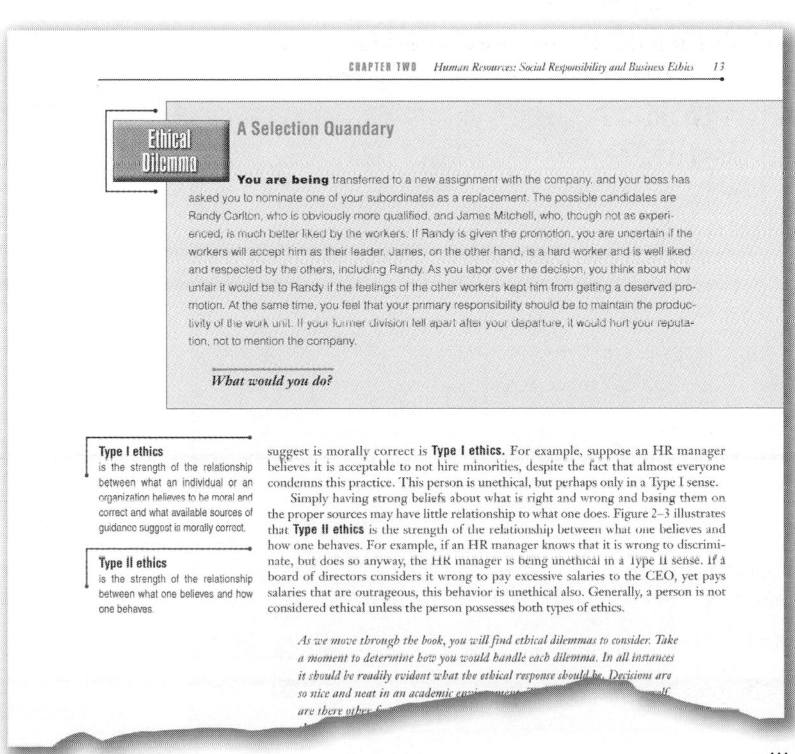

CHAPTER TWO *Human Resources: Social Responsibility and Business Ethics* 13

Ethical Dilemma

A Selection Quandary

You are being transferred to a new assignment with the company, and your boss has asked you to nominate one of your subordinates as a replacement. The possible candidates are Randy Carlton, who is obviously more qualified, and James Mitchell, who, though not as experienced, is much better liked by the workers. If Randy is given the promotion, you are uncertain if the workers will accept him as their leader. James, on the other hand, is a hard worker and is well liked and respected by the others, including Randy. As you labor over the decision, you think about how unfair it would be to Randy if the feelings of the other workers kept him from getting a deserved promotion. At the same time, you feel that your primary responsibility should be to maintain the productivity of the work unit. If your former division fell apart after your departure, it would hurt your reputation, not to mention the company.

What would you do?

Type I ethics is the strength of the relationship between what an individual or an organization believes to be moral and correct and what available sources of guidance suggest is morally correct.

Type II ethics is the strength of the relationship between what one believes and how one behaves.

suggest is morally correct is **Type I ethics.** For example, suppose an HR manager believes it is acceptable to not hire minorities, despite the fact that almost everyone condemns this practice. This person is unethical, but perhaps only in a Type I sense.

Simply having strong beliefs about what is right and wrong and basing them on the proper sources may have little relationship to what one does. Figure 2–3 illustrates that **Type II ethics** is the strength of the relationship between what one believes and how one behaves. For example, if an HR manager knows that it is wrong to discriminate, but does so anyway, the HR manager is being unethical in a Type II sense. If a board of directors considers it wrong to pay excessive salaries to the CEO, yet pays salaries that are outrageous, this behavior is unethical also. Generally, a person is not considered ethical unless the person possesses both types of ethics.

As we move through the book, you will find ethical dilemmas to consider. Take a moment to determine how you would handle each dilemma. In all instances it should be readily evident what the ethical response should be. Decisions are so nice and neat in an academic

CHAPTER 2

Human Resources: Social Responsibility and Business Ethics

HRM IN *Action:*

Changing Attitudes Toward Social Responsibility and Business Ethics

Harlan Teller, president of Hill and Knowlton's, said, "Corporate social responsibility (CSR) has moved from a 'nice-to-do' to a 'must-do.'"[1] Apparently, socially responsible behavior pays off on the bottom line. That is the conclusion of new research based on business ethics' 100 best corporate citizens list, which shows that the financial performance of these companies was "significantly better" than others in the Standard & Poor's 500. ... service to the follow...

1 OBJECTIVE

Describe the changing attitudes toward social responsibility and business ethics

NEW **HRM in Action** These new chapter-opening vignettes introduce students to current, stimulating topics that peak their interest in the materials that follow. Topics covered include: *Changing Attitudes Toward Social Responsibility and Business Ethics* (Chapter 2), *Internet Recruiting* (Chapter 5), *Credential Fraud* (Chapter 6), *Career Security* (Chapter 7), *Are Top Executives Paid Too Much?* (Chapter 9).

NEW **Human Resource Management Skills** Skills modules at the end of appropriate chapters integrate the Gowan, Human Resource Management Skills CD-ROM with the chapter content. Each module contains an introduction, a skills section that allows the student to apply his or her knowledge and gain additional insights through interactive exercises, and finally a quiz that tests students on the material covered in the module.

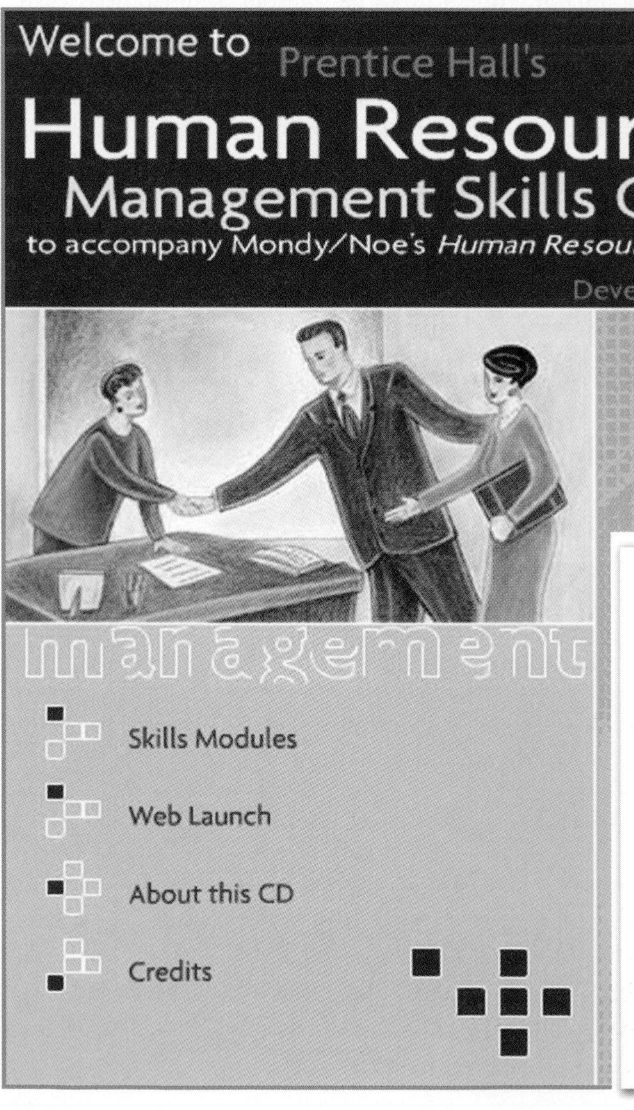

20 PART TWO *HR Social, Ethical, and Legal Considerations*

HRM Incident 1

An Ethical Flaw

Amber Davis had recently graduated from college with a degree in general business. Amber was quite bright, although her grades did not reflect this. She had thoroughly enjoyed school—dating, tennis, swimming—but few academic endeavors. When she graduated from the university, she had not found a job. Her dad was extremely upset when he discovered this, and he took it upon himself to see that Amber became employed.

Amber's father, Allen Davis, was executive vice president of a medium-sized manufacturing firm. One of the people he contacted in seeking employment for Amber was Bill Garbo, the president of another firm in the area. Mr. Davis purchased many of his firm's supplies from Garbo's company. After telling Bill his problem, Allen was told to send Amber to Bill's office for an interview. Amber went, as instructed by her father, and before she left Bill's firm, she was surprised to learn that she had a job in the accounting department. Amber may have been lazy, but she certainly was not stupid. She realized that Bill had hired her because he hoped that his action would lead to future business from her father's company. Although Amber's work was not challenging, it paid better than the other jobs in the accounting department.

It did not take long for the employees in the department to discover the reason she had been hired; Amber told them. When a difficult job was assigned to Amber, she normally got one of the other employees to do it, implying that Mr. Garbo would be pleased with that person if he or she helped her out. She developed a pattern of coming in late, taking long lunch breaks, and leaving early. When the department manager attempted to reprimand her for these unorthodox activities, Amber would bring up the close relationship that her father had with the president of the firm. The department manager was at the end of his rope

Questions

1. From an ethical standpoint, how would you evaluate the merits of Mr. Garbo's employing Amber? Discuss.
2. Now that she is employed, what course would you follow to address her on-the-job behavior?
3. Do you feel that a firm should have policies regarding practices such as hiring people like Amber? Discuss.

"You Can'...

NEW **Global Perspectives** This new feature included in each chapter highlights for students the differences in the cultures of various countries and the need for recognizing the need for varying approaches to HRM. Some topics include: *When In Rome, Do As the Romans Do Does Not Work Today, A Database of Repatriate Skills, Outsourcing Goes Offshore*, and *One Type of Pay Plan Does Not Fit All.*

NEW **HR Trends & Innovations** These sections highlight changing conditions and advancements in the field of human resource management. All of the Trends and Innovations are new to this edition. Some topics discussed include: *Dual-Career Families, Evolution of Jobs, Teaching Through Interactive Satellite Broadcasts*, and *Unique Benefits.*

NEW **New and/or Updated Cutting-Edge Topics** The dynamic field of HR Management continues to create new and exciting concepts. In the ninth edition of Human Resource Management, we present students with the latest innovative topics to keep them abreast of developments in the field. Some of these avant-garde topics include:

- Accelerated Succession Planning: An Alternative to Traditional Approaches (Chapter 4)
- The Global Labor Market: Outsourcing Goes Offshore (Chapter 5)
- Credential Fraud (Chapter 6)
- Reverse Mentoring; Teaching Through Interactive Satellite Broadcasts (Chapter 7)
- Two Cultures' View of Performance Appraisal (Chapter 8)
- Top Executive Pay (Is it Too Much?); HR's Role in Executive Compensation; Cash Balance Plans (Chapter 9)
- Unique Benefits (Chapter 10)
- Safety and Security Strategies for a Post-September 11 World; OSHA's Changing Role; The Stress of an International Assignment (Chapter 11)
- Homeland Security Act of 2002; Unions Today (Chapter 12)
- Layoffs in Today's Environment (Chapter 14)

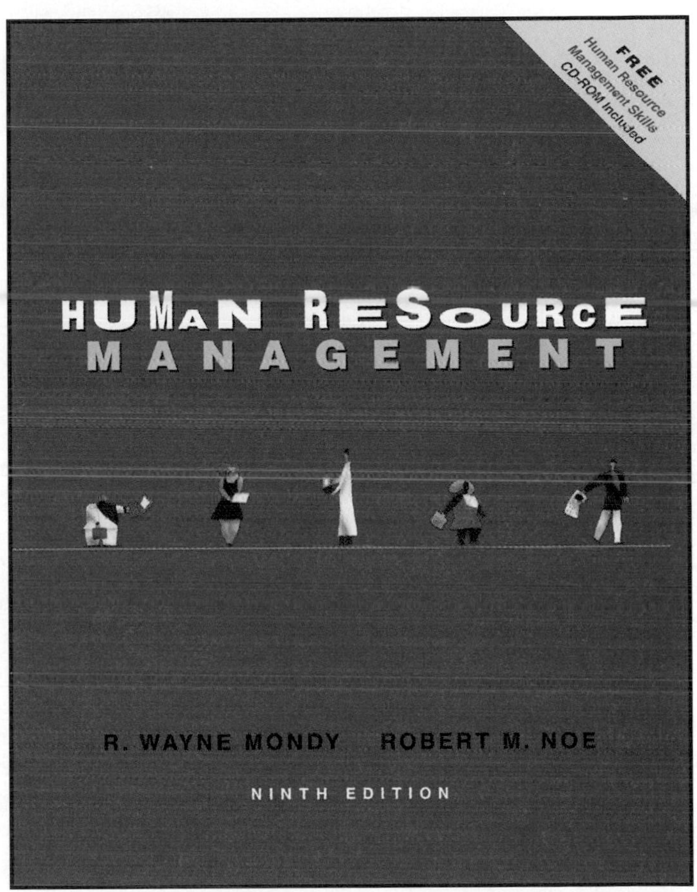

Other noteworthy topics that have been substantially updated in the ninth edition include:

- HR's Changing Role: Who Performs the Human Resource Management Tasks?; HR as a Strategic Partner (Chapter 1)
- Social Responsibility and Business Ethics as related to the field of human resource management (Chapter 2 – an all new chapter)
- Diversity and Diversity Management (Chapter 3)

- The Expanded Job Description; Strategic Planning and the Human Resource Planning Process (Chapter 4)
- Internet Recruiting; Outsourcing; Applicant Tracking Systems (Chapter 5)
- The Significance of Employee Selection; Personality Tests; Genetic Testing; Behavioral Interviews; Negligent Hiring (Chapter 6)
- Mentoring and Coaching; Management Development (Chapter 7)
- 360-Degree Evaluation; Forced Distribution (Chapter 8)
- Fair Labor Standards Act of 1938; Executive Compensation (Chapter 9)
- Health Care; Defined Benefit Plans; Defined Contribution Plans; Flextime; Telecommuting (Chapter 10)
- The Occupational Health and Safety Act; Repetitive Stress Injuries; Congress and OSHA; Workplace Violence (Chapter 11)
- The Public Sector; Union Growth Strategies (Chapter 12)
- Breakdowns in Negotiations; Collective Bargaining In the Public Sector (Chapter 13)
- Approaches to Disciplinary Action; Alternative Dispute Resolution; Employment at Will (Chapter 14)
- Global Human Resource Management, has been extensively revised to reflect current HRM challenges (Chapter 15).

TEACHING AND LEARNING RESOURCES

- **HUMAN RESOURCE MANAGEMENT CD-ROM**
  Developed by Mary Gowan of George Washington University, this student CD-ROM focuses on essential HR skills such as Strategic Planning and Recruitment, Job Analysis, and Total Rewards. Each module contains an introduction, a skills section that allows the student to apply his or her knowledge though interactive exercises, and finally a quiz that tests students on the material covered in the module.

- **STUDY GUIDE**
  This study guide assists students in learning human resource management. The guide includes chapter descriptions, key terms, chapter study outlines, exercises, "You and HR" memos, and study quizzes.

- **COMPANION WEBSITE AT WWW.PRENHALL.COM/MONDY**

- **INSTRUCTOR'S MANUAL**
  This helpful Instructor's Manual includes sample syllabi, lecture outlines, Ethical Dilemma exercises, and answers to all end-of-chapter and case questions.

- **TEST ITEM FILE**

- **INSTRUCTOR'S RESOURCE CENTER CD-ROM**
  A brand new interface plus searchable database means accessing and finding resources has never been easier. Resources included on this CD: Instructor's Manual, Test Item File, PowerPoints, and TestGen electronic test manager software.

- **Human Resource Management Skills Video**
  In these compelling part-ending video segments, students will watch a panel of real-life HR executives from companies like BMG and hotjobs discuss current human resource issues like sexual harassment and discrimination, recruiting, the complexities of restructuring, incentives and benefits, labor relations, and the successes and failures of expatriate employees.

- **Course Management Content in WebCT, Blackboard, and CourseCompass**

ACKNOWLEDGEMENTS

The assistance and encouragement of many people is normally required in the writing of any book. It is especially true in the writing of *Human Resource Management, ninth edition.* Although it would be virtually impossible to list each person who assisted in this project, we feel that certain people must be credited because of the magnitude of their contribution. Dr. Judy Bandy Mondy developed the HR Web Wisdoms and PowerPoint presentation for this edition. Judy is a true professional.

We would also like to thank Marthanne Lamansky, Kendra Ingram, and Sue Weatherbee, all very competent and professional individuals, who were always available to ensure that our deadlines were met. As with the previous editions, the support and encouragement of many practicing HRM professionals has made this book possible.

We especially appreciate the efforts of the professionals who reviewed this edition. These individuals are:

THOMAS TIMMERMAN, *Tennessee Technological University*

ANNE FIEDLER, *Barry University*

JOHN CRAGIN, *Oklahoma Baptist University*

NORMAN HANSEN, *Newbury College*

SCOTT BOYAR, *University of Southern Alabama*

WESLEY PAYNE, *Southwester Tennessee Community College*

STEPHEN HIATT, *Catawba College*

MICHAEL HORST, *York College of Pennsylvania*

LOUIS PREYSZ III, *Flagler College*

SAVANNAH CLAY, *Central Piedmont Community College*

LEE WEYANT, *Eastern New Mexico University*

JACK PARTLOW, *Northern Virginia Community College*

PART ONE

Introduction

CHAPTER OBJECTIVES

After completing this chapter, students should be able to

1. Explain human capital management.
2. Define human resource management.
3. Identify the human resource management functions.
4. Identify the external environmental factors that affect human resource management.
5. Explain who performs the human resource management tasks.
6. Explain the need for human resources to be a strategic partner.
7. Describe the various human resource classifications, including executives, generalists, and specialists.
8. Describe the changes that occur in the human resource function as a firm grows larger and more complex, and the evolving HR organization.

CHAPTER

Strategic Human Resource Management: An Overview

HRM IN *Action:*

Human Capital Management—A Strategic Role for Human Resources

 **OBJECTIVE**

Explain human capital management.

Human capital management (HCM): The task of measuring the cause and effect relationship of various HR programs and policies on the bottom line of the firm.

Even though employees account for as much as 80 percent of the worth of a corporation, it is difficult to measure and understand how they contribute to the bottom line.[1] "I can put a value on everything in my office: my clock, my desk. But I can't put a value on people," says Jac Fitzenz, founder and chairman of the Saratoga Institute, a human capital management consulting firm in Santa Clara, California.[2] Executives are coming under pressure from boards, investors, and analysts to show how they manage human capital in their companies.[3]

According to a recent *HRMagazine* article, "A company's human capital asset is the collective sum of the attributes, life experience, knowledge, inventiveness, energy, and enthusiasm that its people choose to invest in their work."[4] **Human capital management (HCM)** is the task of measuring the cause and effect relationship of various HR programs and policies on the bottom line of the firm.[5,6] HCM attempts to obtain additional productivity from workers; it is in this area that HR can truly play a significant role.[7] Human capital assessment "leads to a different kind of role for HR," says David Norton of the Balanced Scorecard Collaborative. HR executives can help a corporation build a strategy map, and "suddenly they start talking a different language," one that puts HR at the table and helps senior management view the complex roles of HR and human capital in a different light.[8] Starting to measure and manage human capital requires a change in philosophy for organizations.[9]

The hospitality industry provides two examples of the strategic role of human resources. An analysis of the relationship between compensation level and total annual employee turnover yielded statistically significant results. The data suggest that compensation does have an effect on employee intentions to stay in or leave their organizations. The second example is based on an analysis of training and employee turnover. The results suggest that since training and employee turnover influence sales, long-range plans for growth must consider the consequences of HR decisions regarding employee development and retention.[10]

With human capital management, an attempt is made to determine the relationships that exist between certain HR actions and the bottom line. Instead of assuming that all employees react in the same way, a profile of each employee may be developed and analyzed for cause and effect. For example, could the firm pay a certain worker less but give this individual a sabbatical every so often? Or for another person, if the firm eliminated a worker's 401(k) match, would he or she quit or would the change be barely noticed? Analyses such as these are not science fiction but are present today in the form of human capital management.[11] Companies have begun to realize that the productivity of workers in an organization is closely related to determining employees' "competencies and preferences."[12] However, HCM decisions must be tailored to fit the culture of each company. It is not a one-size-fits-all situation.[13]

A big difference between human capital management (HCM) and old-era HR is that instead of trying to emulate what other companies are doing, a manager attempts to discover what is best for his or her company. For instance, First Tennessee realized that bank customers reacted far more favorably to experienced employees than they did to new hires. Increasing retention of current workers had a major effect on annual sales. As another example, "a blue-chip technology company learned that its pay structure was penalizing the highest performers and rewarding the weakest; lackluster employees were clustered in a cash-cow unit, while superstars were toiling in a still-profitless upstart division."[14] Much work remains to see if HCM is the wave of the future or merely another fad that fails to live up to its projected potential.[15]

In the first part of this chapter, we discussed human capital management as it relates to strategic human resource management. Next we describe human resource management and the human resource management functions. We then describe the dynamic human resource management environment. Next, we address the changing role of HR, the development of the human resource manager into a strategic partner with upper management. The various titles of the human resource manager are then discussed. A description of the scope of this book concludes the chapter.

Define human resource management.

Human Resource Management

Human resource management (HRM) is the utilization of individuals to achieve organizational objectives. Consequently, managers at every level must concern themselves with HRM. Basically, all managers get things done through the efforts of others; this requires effective HRM. Individuals dealing with human resource matters face a multitude of challenges, ranging from a constantly changing workforce to ever-present government regulations, a major technological revolution, and the effects of 9/11 and its aftermath. Furthermore, global competition has forced both large and small organizations to be more conscious of costs and productivity. Because of the critical nature of human resource issues, these matters must receive major attention from upper management.

Human resource management (HRM):
The utilization of a firm's human resources to achieve organizational objectives.

 OBJECTIVE

Identify the human resource management functions.

Staffing:
The process through which an organization ensures that it always has the proper number of employees with the appropriate skills in the right jobs at the right time to achieve the organization's objectives.

Human Resource Management Functions

People who are engaged in the management of human resources develop and work through an integrated HRM system. As Figure 1-1 shows, five functional areas are associated with effective HRM: staffing, human resource development, compensation and benefits, safety and health, and employee and labor relations. These functional areas mirror the human resource certification examination format, which is shown in the appendix to Chapter 2.[16] We discuss these functions next.

Staffing

Staffing is the process through which an organization ensures that it always has the proper number of employees with the appropriate skills in the right jobs, at the right time, to achieve the organization's objectives. Staffing involves job analysis, human resource planning, recruitment, and selection, all of which are discussed in this text.

Job analysis is the systematic process of determining the skills, duties, and knowledge required for performing jobs in an organization. It impacts virtually every aspect of HRM including planning, recruitment, and selection. *Human resource planning (HRP)* is the process of comparing human resource requirements with their availability and determining whether the firm has a shortage or excess of personnel. The data provided set the stage for recruitment or other HR actions. *Recruitment* is the process of attracting qualified individuals and encouraging them to apply for work with the organization. *Selection* is the process through which the organization chooses, from a group of applicants, those individuals best suited both for open positions and for the company. Successful accomplishment of these three tasks is vital if the organization is to effectively accomplish its mission. Chapters 4, 5, and 6 are devoted to these topics, which we collectively refer to as *staffing*. The appendix to Chapter 5, Internet Recruiting, will likely be of interest to students, especially when they begin their job search upon graduation.

Human resource development (HRD):
A major HRM function that consists not only of T&D but also individual career planning and development activities and performance appraisal.

Human Resource Development

Human resource development (HRD) is a major HRM function that consists not only of training and development but also of individual career planning and development activities, organization development, and performance appraisal, an activity that emphasizes training and development (T&D) needs. *Training* is designed to provide learners with the knowledge and skills needed for their present jobs. *Development* involves learning that goes beyond today's job; it has a more long-term focus. Training and development is covered in Chapter 7.

Human Resource Links

www.lir.msu.edu/hotlinks/

This Web site provides a link to numerous human resource sites.

Career planning is an ongoing process whereby an individual sets career goals and identifies the means to achieve them. This is a continuing and difficult process because the average person graduating from college today may face five to seven career changes (career, not employer) in his or her working years.[17] *Career development* is a formal approach used by the organization to ensure that people with the proper qualifications and experiences are available when needed. Individual careers and organizational needs are not separate and distinct. Organizations should assist employees in career planning so the needs of both can be satisfied. Career planning and development is discussed in the appendix to Chapter 7. Students may find that the information provided is useful in evaluating their careers.

Organization development (OD) is the planned process of improving an organization by developing its structures, systems, and processes to improve effectiveness and achieving desired goals. OD applies to an entire system, such as a company or a plant. In this section we discuss a number of interventions that serve to improve a firm's performance.

Performance appraisal is a formal system of review and evaluation of individual or team task performance. It affords employees the opportunity to capitalize on their

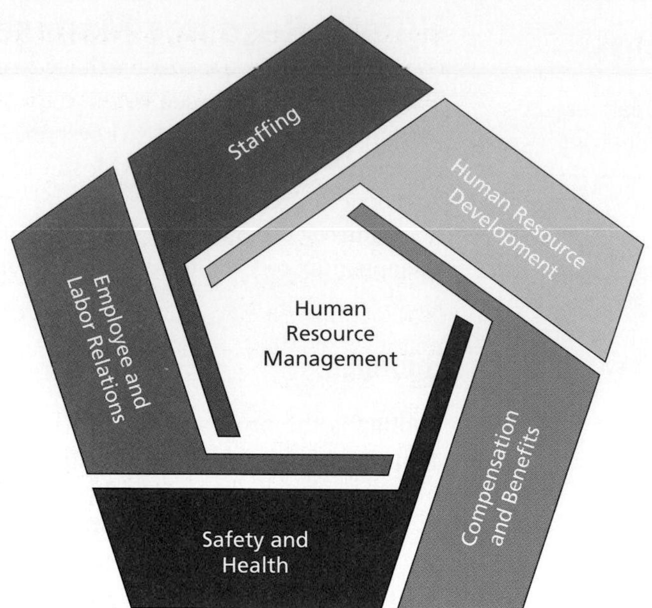

Figure 1-1 The Human Resource Management System

strengths and overcome identified deficiencies, thereby helping them to become more satisfied and productive employees. Performance appraisal is discussed in Chapter 8.

Operative employees: All workers in a firm except managers and professionals, such as engineers, accountants, and professional secretaries.

Throughout this text, but especially in the HRD chapters, we use the term "operative employees". **Operative employees** are all of the workers in an organization except managers and professionals, such as engineers, accountants, or professional secretaries. Steelworkers, truck drivers, retail clerks, and waiters are examples of operative employees.

Compensation and Benefits

The question of what constitutes a fair day's pay has plagued management, unions, and workers for a long time. A well-thought-out compensation system provides employees with adequate and equitable rewards for their contributions to the meeting of organizational goals. As used in this book, the term *compensation* includes the total of all rewards provided employees in return for their services. The reward may be one or a combination of the following:

- *Pay:* The money that a person receives for performing a job.
- *Benefits:* Additional financial rewards, other than base pay, including paid vacations, sick leave, holidays, and medical insurance.
- *Nonfinancial rewards:* Nonmonetary rewards, such as enjoyment of the work performed or a satisfactory workplace environment that provides flexibility.

We discuss compensation in Chapter 9 and address benefits and other compensation issues in Chapter 10.

Safety and Health

Safety involves protecting employees from injuries caused by work-related accidents. *Health* refers to the employees' freedom from physical or emotional illness. These aspects of the job are important because employees who work in a safe environment and enjoy good health are more likely to be productive and yield long-term benefits to the organization. Today, because of federal and state legislation that reflects societal concerns, most organizations have become attentive to their employees' safety and health.[18] Chapter 11 is devoted to the topic of safety and health.

Employee and Labor Relations

Private-sector union membership has fallen from 39 percent in 1958 to 9 percent today, the lowest percentage since 1901.[19] Even so, a business firm is required by law to recognize a union and bargain with it in good faith if the firm's employees want the union to represent them. In the past, this relationship was an accepted way of life for many employers. But most firms today would like to have a union-free environment. When a labor union represents a firm's employees, the human resource activity is often referred to as *industrial relations*, which handles the job of collective bargaining. Chapters 12 and 13 relate strictly to unions. Chapter 14 relates to both union and nonunion internal employee relations.

SHRM HR Links

www.shrm.org/hrlinks/default.asp

This SHRM Web site has a series of links to topics of particular interest to HR professionals and students.

Human Resource Research

Although human resource research is not a distinct HRM function, it pervades all functional areas, and the researcher's laboratory is the entire work environment. For instance, a study related to recruitment may suggest the type of worker most likely to succeed in a particular firm. Research on job safety may identify the causes of certain work-related accidents. The reasons for problems such as excessive absenteeism or excessive grievances may not be readily apparent. However, when such problems occur, human resource research can often shed light on their causes and possible solutions. Human resource research is clearly an important key to developing the most productive and satisfied workforce possible.

Interrelationships of HRM Functions

All HRM functional areas are highly interrelated. Management must recognize that decisions in one area will affect other areas. For instance, a firm that emphasizes recruiting top-quality candidates but neglects to provide satisfactory compensation is wasting time, effort, and money. In addition, a firm's compensation system will be inadequate unless employees are provided a safe and healthy work environment. The interrelationships among the HRM functional areas will become more obvious as we address these topics throughout the book.

4 OBJECTIVE

Identify the external environmental factors that affect human resource management.

The Dynamic Human Resource Management Environment

External environment: The factors that affect a firm's human resources from outside the organization's boundaries.

Many interrelated factors affect the five previously identified HRM functions. Factors outside its boundaries that affect a firm's human resources make up the **external environment**. The firm often has little, if any, control over how the external environment affects management of its human resources. As illustrated in Figure 1-2, external factors include the labor force, legal considerations, society, unions, shareholders, competition, customers, technology, and the economy. Each factor, either separately or in combination with others, can place constraints on how HRM tasks are accomplished.

The Labor Force

The labor force is a pool of individuals external to the firm from which the organization obtains its workers. The capabilities of a firm's employees determine to a large

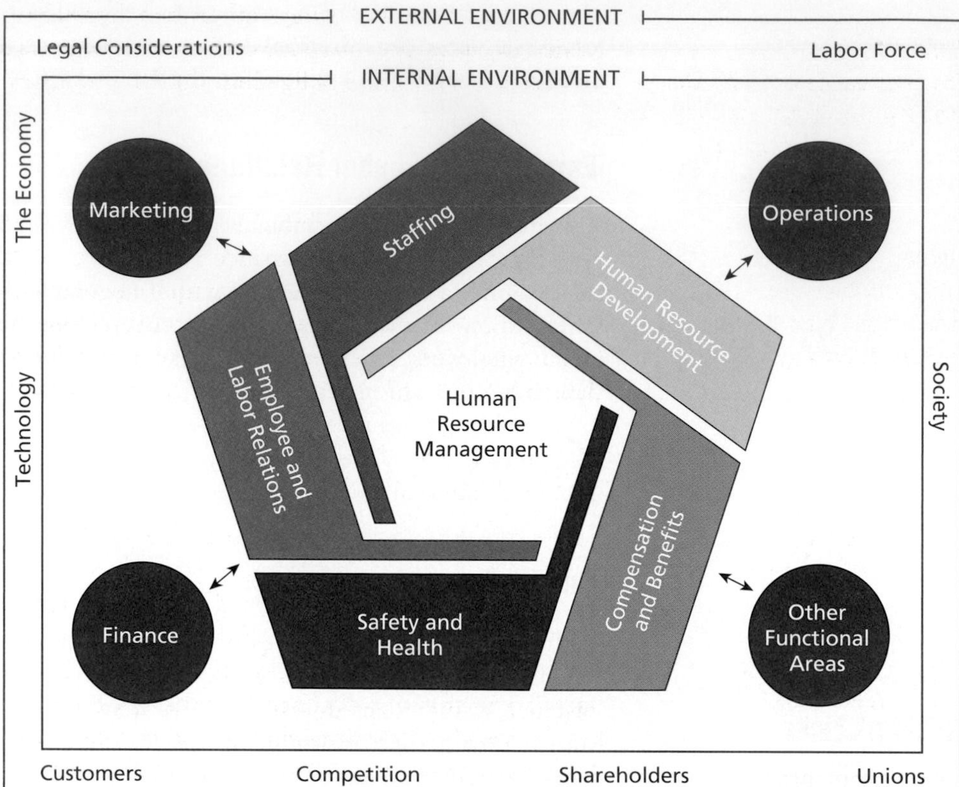

Figure 1-2 The Environments of Human Resource Management

Employment Management Association Forum

www.shrm.org/ema/

Online community for recruiting and employment professionals.

extent how well the organization can perform its mission. Since new employees are hired from outside the firm, the labor force is considered an external environmental factor. The labor force is always changing, and these shifts inevitably cause changes in the workforce of an organization. In turn, changes in individuals within an organization affect the way management must deal with its workforce. This topic will be discussed later in Chapter 3 under the heading, "Managing the Diverse Workforce."

Legal Considerations

Another significant external force affecting HRM relates to federal, state, and local legislation and the many court decisions interpreting this legislation. In addition, many presidential executive orders have had a major impact on HRM. These legal considerations affect virtually the entire spectrum of human resource policies. We highlight in Chapter 3 the most significant of these considerations, which affect equal employment opportunity. Laws, court decisions, and executive orders affecting other HRM activities will be described in the appropriate chapters.

Society

Society may also exert pressure on HRM. The public is no longer content to accept, without question, the actions of business. This was forcefully brought to the forefront with the failures of such large companies such as Enron, WorldCom, Arthur Andersen, and others. To remain acceptable to the general public, a firm must accomplish its purpose while complying with societal norms.

Social responsibility: The implied, enforced, or felt obligation of managers, acting in their official capacity, to serve or protect the interests of groups other than themselves.

A new chapter has been added to the ninth edition entitled "Human Resources: Social Responsibility and Business Ethics." When a firm responds effectively to social interests, it is said to be socially responsible. **Social responsibility** is the implied, enforced, or felt obligation of managers, acting in their official capacity, to serve or protect the interests of groups other than themselves.[20] Social responsibility is closely related to **ethics**: the discipline dealing with what is good and bad, or right and wrong, or with moral duty and obligation. Both are topics of Chapter 2.

Ethics:
The discipline dealing with what is good and bad, or right and wrong, or with moral duty and obligation.

Unions

Union:
Comprised of employees who have joined together for the purpose of dealing with their employer.

Wage levels, benefits, and working conditions for millions of employees reflect decisions made jointly by unions and management. A **union** is comprised of employees who have joined together for the purpose of dealing with their employer. Unions are treated as an environmental factor because, essentially, they become a third party when dealing with the company. In a unionized organization, the union rather than the individual employee negotiates an agreement with management.

Shareholders

Shareholders:
The owners of a corporation.

The owners of a corporation are called **shareholders**. Because shareholders, or stockholders, have invested money in the firm, they may at times challenge programs considered by management to be beneficial to the organization. Managers may be forced to justify the merits of a particular program in terms of how it will affect future projects, costs, revenues, profits, and even benefits to society as a whole. Stockholders are wielding increasing influence. We discuss in Chapter 2 how stockholders' interests have been violated in such high-profile failures as Enron, WorldCom, Arthur Andersen, and others.

Competition

Firms may face intense competition in both their product or service and labor markets. Unless an organization is in the unusual position of monopolizing the market it serves, other firms will be producing similar products or services. A firm also must maintain a supply of competent employees if it is to succeed, grow, and prosper. But other organizations are also striving for that same objective. A firm's major task is to ensure that it obtains and retains a sufficient number of employees in various career fields to allow it to compete effectively. A bidding war often results when competitors attempt to fill certain critical positions in their firms. Because of the strategic nature of their needs, firms are sometimes forced to resort to unusual means to recruit and retain such employees. The poster shown in Figure 1-3 exemplifies the approach some organizations have used to recruit qualified workers.

Customers

The people who actually use a firm's goods and services also are part of its external environment. Because sales are crucial to the firm's survival, management has the task of ensuring that its employment practices do not antagonize the customers it serves. Customers constantly demand high-quality products and after-purchase service. Therefore, a firm's workforce should be capable of providing top-quality goods and services. These conditions relate directly to the skills, qualifications, and motivations of the organization's employees.

Technology

It has been estimated that there will be more technological change in the next 50 years than in the last 1,000 years.[21] As previously mentioned, the average person graduating from college today may face five to seven *career* changes in his or her working years. These advances affect every area of a business, including HRM. For example, Internet

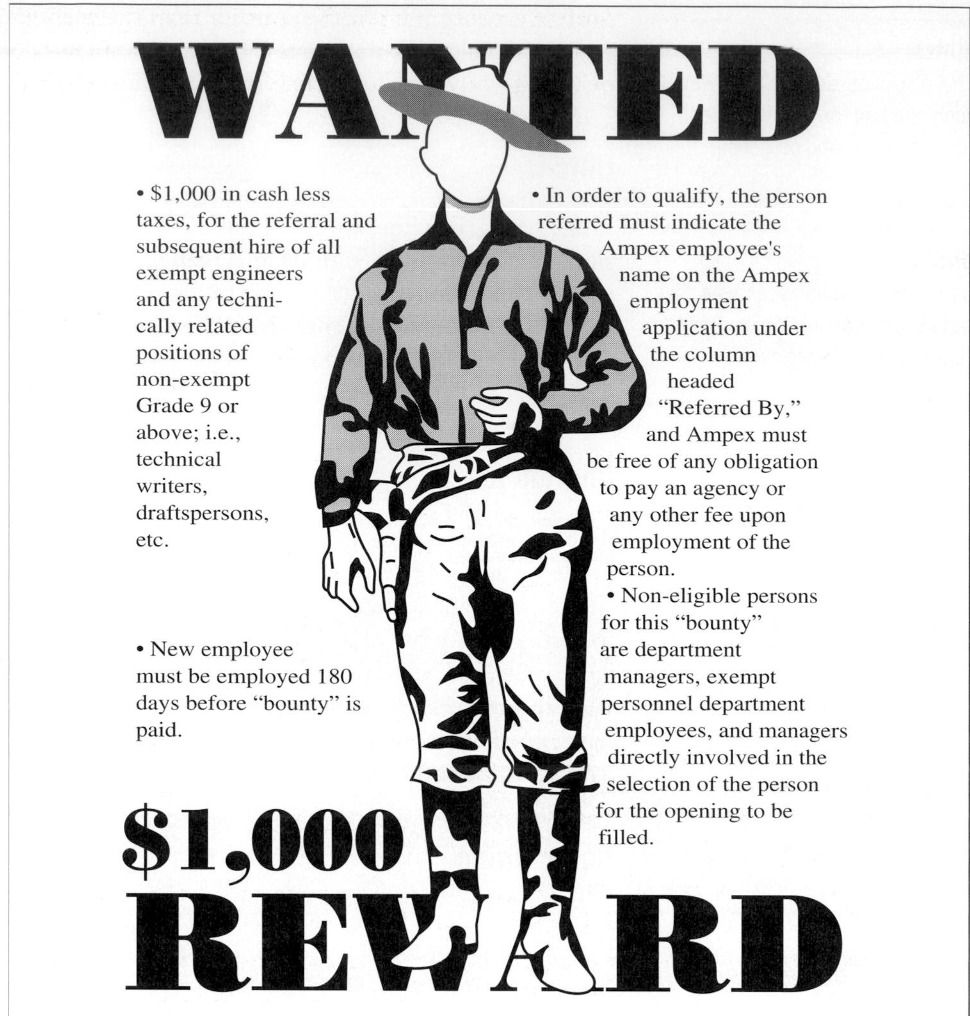

Figure 1-3 A Recruitment Poster

recruiting, the topic of the appendix to Chapter 5 is now being used by virtually all organizations.

The world has never before seen technological changes occur as rapidly as they are presently happening. According to a recent survey by the Society for Human Resource Management, the top workplace trend identified was technology.[22] HR technology has the potential to either increase or decrease an organization's worth.[23] HR professionals who realize and embrace the new technology are the ones who will succeed.[24] Some of the top HR technology trends include: increased Web-connected workplaces, outsourcing of functions to individuals and firms throughout the world, virtual workplaces (such as online meetings, Web conferences, and videoconferencing), using analytical tools to measure the success of HR practices and to predict future results, and contingency planning such as planning for disasters.[25] A major commitment among organizations is being made to increase the use of e-HR.[26] Certainly, HR must become a technology enabler.[27] The impact of technology on these practices is noted throughout this book.

HR Web Wisdom

Bureau of Labour Statistics

stats.bls.gov/

The government Web site provides information regarding the economy.

The Economy

The economy of the nation, on the whole and in its various segments, is a major environmental factor affecting HRM. As a generalization, when the economy is booming, recruiting qualified workers is more difficult. On the other hand, when a downturn is experienced, more applicants are typically available. To complicate this situation even further, one segment of the country may be experiencing a downturn, another a slow recovery, and another a boom. The Bureau of Labor Statistics forecasts that the information and services industry will account for more than 90 percent of the workforce growth in the coming decade.[28]

How Human Resource Management Is Practiced in the Real World

At the beginning of each chapter, there is an "HRM in Action" that focuses on an important topic related to the chapter. Sections entitled "Ethical Dilemmas" are included in all but the first chapter to see how you would react to an ethical situation. A "Trends and Innovations" feature is included in each section to highlight current developments in the field of human resource management. "A Global Perspective" is included at the end of each chapter that highlights HRM in the global environment. Finally, two "HRM Incidents" are provided at the end of each chapter to highlight material covered in the chapter. A new feature to the ninth edition of Human Resource Management is the inclusion of a CD-ROM entitled *Human Resource Management Skills* by Mary Gowan that provides additional insight into selected HRM topics. A description of each Skill Module is included at the end of the appropriate chapter.

5 OBJECTIVE

Explain who performs the human resource management tasks.

HR's Changing Role: Who Performs the Human Resource Management Tasks?

The person or units who perform the HRM tasks have changed dramatically in recent years. This restructuring has often resulted in a shift in who carries out each function, not an elimination of the previously identified HR functions.[29] Some organizations continue to perform the majority of HR functions within the firm. However, as internal operations are reexamined, questions are raised, such as: Can some HR tasks be performed more efficiently by line managers or outside vendors? Can some HR tasks be centralized or eliminated altogether? One apparent fact is that all functions within today's organizations are being scrutinized for cost cutting, including HR. All units must operate under a lean budget in this competitive global environment and HR is no exception.[30]

As a shift is made in allocating who will perform the human resource function, many HR departments continue to get smaller because others are now accomplishing certain functions. Shared service centers, outsourcing, and line managers now assist in the accomplishment of human resource activities. This shift permits HR to shed its administrative image and focus on more strategic and mission-oriented activities (to be discussed later). Let us first look at the traditional human resource manager.

The Human Resource Manager

Human resource manager: An individual who normally acts in an *advisory* or *staff* capacity, working with other managers regarding human resource matters.

A human resource manager performs each of the five HR functions. While this position has disappeared in some companies, the HRM tasks remain. A **human resource manager** is an individual who normally acts in an *advisory* or *staff* capacity, working with other managers regarding human resource matters. Historically, the HR department performed the five functions internally.[31] Often, large HR departments were created, with the central figure being the HR manager or executive. The human resource manager was primarily responsible for coordinating the management of human resources to help the organization achieve its goals. There was a shared responsibility between line managers and human resource professionals. Often the line manager goes to HR for guidance in topics such as promotion, hiring, discipline, or discharge.[32] The distinction between human resource management and the human resource manager is illustrated by the following account:

> *Bill Brown, the production supervisor for Ajax Manufacturing, has just learned that one of his machine operators has resigned. He immediately calls Sandra Williams, the human resource manager, and says, "Sandra, I just had a Class A machine operator quit down here. Can you find some qualified people for me to interview?" "Sure, Bill," Sandra replies. "I'll send two or three down to you within the week, and you can select the one that best fits your needs."*

In this instance, both Bill and Sandra are concerned with accomplishing organizational goals, but from different perspectives. As a human resource manager, Sandra identifies applicants who meet the criteria specified by Bill. Yet, Bill will make the final decision as to the person who is hired because he is responsible for the machine operators' performance. His primary responsibility is production; hers is human resources. As a human resource manager, Sandra must constantly deal with the many problems related to human resources that Bill and the other managers face. Her job is to help them meet the human resource needs of the entire organization. Today, many of the tasks the HR manager traditionally performed have been reduced or eliminated and it is estimated that the present HR structure and service delivery costs need to be reduced by 30 to 40 percent.[33]

Shared Service Centers

Shared service center (SSC): A center that takes routine, transaction-based activities dispersed throughout the organization and consolidates them in one place.

A shared service center (SSC), also known as a center of expertise,[34] takes routine, transaction-based activities dispersed throughout the organization and consolidates them in one place. For example, a company with 20 strategic business units could consolidate routine HR tasks and perform them in one location. The increased volume makes the tasks more suitable for automation, which in turn results in the need for fewer HR personnel. The most common HR functions that use SSCs are benefits and pension administration, payroll, relocation assistance and recruitment support, global training and development, succession planning, and talent retention.[35]

Outsourcing Firms

Outsourcing: The process of transferring responsibility for an area of service and its objectives to an external provider.

Outsourcing is the process of transferring responsibility for an area of service and its objectives to an external provider.[36] The increased use of outsourcing has been pushed by the need to reduce costs caused by sluggish earnings or tighter budgets, mergers, and acquisitions that have created many redundant systems.[37] Also, employees today are increasingly literate in the use of the Web. The key to outsourcing success is to determine which functions to outsource, the extent to which they should be outsourced, and which ones to keep in house.[38,39] The type of work being outsourced can range from payroll and benefits administration to entire HR service lines encompassing recruitment and retention, employee relationship management, benefits administration, relocation and expatriation, knowledge management, and reporting.[40] HR outsourcing, which was a roughly $60 billion business in 2001, could soon top $100 billion per year.[41] In a recent survey of HR executives, it was found that nearly 7 out of 10 employers outsource some aspect of HR to outside vendors or consultants.[42] HR professionals are moving toward focusing their time and resources on their core businesses and are trying to outsource any function that they consider nonstrategic.[43] For instance, Procter & Gamble is studying outsourcing noncore competencies in business administration, such as human resources, accounting, and information technology.[44]

Even the government has begun to outsource more. The federal government is pressuring federal agencies to review which tasks are inherently governmental and which should be put up for competitive bid.[45] The Transportation Security Administration (TSA) and the Coast Guard have joined several agencies that outsource their human resource operations. TSA has contracted out all of its human resources operations except for those involving executive personnel.[46]

Line Managers

Line managers: Individuals directly involved in accomplishing the primary purpose of the organization.

Individuals directly involved in accomplishing the primary purpose of the organization are **line managers**. As the traditional work of HR managers diminishes, line managers are stepping up and performing duties often done by the human resource manager.[47] Line managers often perform many of the staffing functions previously accomplished by HR, such as interviewing. The quality of people hired will make or break any manager. All managers understand that their workers must be continuously trained and developed. Compensation and benefits are important to every member of the workforce. And, if the organization is unionized, the line manager must know how to deal effectively with the union.

OBJECTIVE

Explain the need for human resources to be a strategic partner.

HR as a Strategic Partner

HR as a Strategic Partner

www.hr-guide.com

This Web site contains general information related to human resources.

During the corporate scandals of recent years, some say that HR played a seemingly invisible role, and that attention to corporate governance and executive compensation was sadly neglected.[48] Perhaps the HR executives were themselves too weak politically to be champions of organization transformation.[49] The inference being made was that if HR professionals in these firms had been more strategically focused, perhaps the scandals could have been avoided or the impact lessened. Some believe that HR should have questioned the salaries, stock options, and related perks received by some corporate executives even as the company was reduced to penny stock.

There has been much discussion in recent years about how HR professionals must assume a strategic role when it comes to the management of human resources.[50] But, what exactly should they be doing? Richard Pinola, chair and CEO of Right Management Consultants, Inc. (Philadelphia), during a session at SHRM's annual conference in Philadelphia, listed the following tasks that CEOs want from HR:

- Make workforce strategies integral to company strategies and goals.
- Leverage HR's role in major change initiatives such as:
  —Strategic planning.
  —Mergers and acquisitions.
  —Systems implementation.
  —Reorganizing/downsizing.
- Earn the right to a seat at the corporate table.
- Develop awareness and/or an understanding of the business.
- Understand finance and profits.
- Help line managers achieve their goals.[51]

The above list is a sharp deviation from what has traditionally been an administrative type role for HR.[52] The HR professional must now integrate the goals of HR with the goals of the organization.[53] HR must continue to focus on expanding its strategic and high-level corporate participation with an emphasis on adding value.

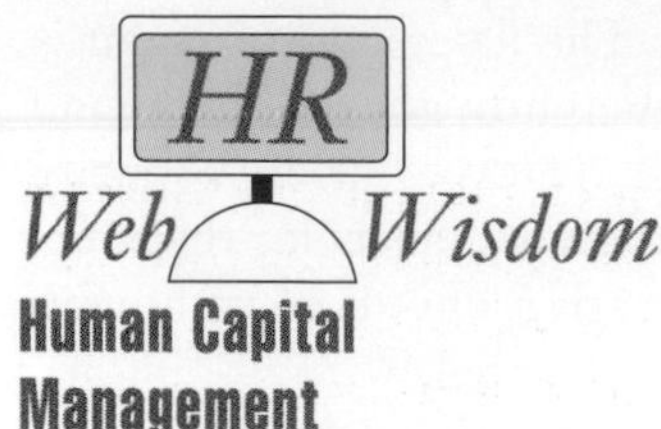

Human Capital Management

www.bettermanagement.com/businessTopicHome.aspx?FilterID=709

This Web site explores information on human talent, knowledge, advancement, and management of an organization's employees.

In doing so, HR must demonstrate that it can produce a return on investment for its programs.[54] The CEO needs help in matters that human resource professionals are qualified to handle. As HR expert and author David Bratton said, "They (HR) are the enablers, they are the ones who should know about change and develop strategies to make it work."[55] Human resource professionals can give the CEO and CFO a powerful understanding of the role human capital plays in the organization and the way it combines with business processes to expand or shrink shareholder value.[56]

Part of HR becoming a strategic business partner includes writing a measurable business plan and following through on its implementation. And just like its counterparts in finance, IT, operations, and sales and marketing, HR must be held accountable to its plan.[57] Jeffrey Christian, chairman and CEO of Christian & Timbers, a New York–based executive recruitment firm, said, "as talent becomes universally accepted as a core element of critical business strategy, the HR function will become more closely identified with strategic activities than with administrative ones."[58] Clearly, the HR executives at high-performing companies are making strategic contributions to their organizations.[59]

CEOs want an HR partner who understands the operational side of the business. To succeed, HR executives must comprehend the complex organizational design and be able to determine the capabilities of the company's workforce, both today and in the future. HR must ensure that human resources support the firm's mission. Harold W. Burlingame, longtime AT&T HR executive, has been hailed as a model HR executive for his continued emphasis on HR involvement in the business end of an organization.[60] Michael Maccoby, an executive consultant, said this about Mr. Burlingame: "He was before his time. A generation ago many HR people were more like policemen than managers of human capital, but Burlingame was always very strategic. He had a deep understanding of how to connect HR to business strategy."[61]

To answer the question of whether the HR executive is involved strategically, William Schiemann, chair and CEO of Metrus Group, suggests that the following questions be asked:

1. Is HR present at mergers and acquisitions planning meetings, strategy reviews, and restructuring discussions?
2. Does HR provide an annual report on its ROI?
3. Does HR lead the people strategy? Has it developed performance indicators for the success of that strategy?
4. Is HR rated by its customers?
5. Does the organization conduct strategic versus entitlement employee surveys?
6. Are employee and other survey initiatives linked to customer and financial metrics?
7. Is there an ROI process to evaluate HR initiatives connected to the business strategy?[62]

P. O. Mak, head of HR for GE Capital Asia-Pacific, said, "You have to think in terms of a business leader and understand the big picture. Either you confine yourself in a room and work on policy, or you can get out in front of what's going on globally in business."[63] If today's HR managers are to become strategic partners in their organizations, they must run their departments according to the same rigid criteria that apply to other units. They must be able to use data available in their unit to forecast outcomes and become real partners with upper management. HR units must be able to show how they add value to the company.[64] Tied closely to strategic HR is the emerging field of human capital management, which we featured at the beginning of this chapter.

OBJECTIVE

Describe the various human resource classifications, including executives, generalists, and specialists.

Executive:
A top-level manager who reports directly to a corporation's chief executive officer or to the head of a major division.

Generalist:
A person who performs tasks in a variety of human resource–related areas.

Specialist:
An individual who may be a human resource executive, a human resource manager, or a nonmanager, and who is typically concerned with only one of the five functional areas of human resource management.

Human Resource Designations

Various designations are used within the human resource profession; among these are HR executives, generalists, and specialists. An **executive** is a top-level manager who reports directly to the corporation's chief executive officer (CEO) or to the head of a major division. A **generalist**, who often is an executive, performs tasks in a variety of HR-related areas. The generalist is involved in several, or all, of the five HRM functions. A change is taking place in some companies. They are assigning an HR generalist to each line organization and maintaining a smaller core of centralized staff. These individuals then serve the HR needs of a specific department. A **specialist** may be an HR executive, manager, or nonmanager who is typically concerned with only one of the five functional areas of HRM. Figure 1-4 helps clarify these distinctions.

The vice president of industrial relations shown in Figure 1-4 specializes primarily in union-related matters. This person is both an executive and a specialist. The HR vice president is both an executive and a generalist, having responsibility for a wide variety of functions. The manager of compensation and benefits is a specialist, as is the benefits analyst. Whereas a position level in the organization identifies an executive, the breadth of such positions distinguishes generalists and specialists.

OBJECTIVE

Describe the changes that occur in the human resource function as a firm grows larger and more complex, and the evolving HR organization.

The Human Resource Functions in Organizations of Various Sizes

As firms grow and become more complex, the HR function also becomes more complex and achieves greater importance. The basic purpose of HRM remains the same; the difference is in the approach used to accomplish its objectives.

Human Resource Functions in Small Businesses

Small businesses seldom have a formal HR unit and HRM specialists, as Figure 1-5 shows. Rather, other managers in the company handle HR functions. The focus of their activities is generally on hiring and retaining capable employees. Some aspects of HR functions may actually be more significant in smaller firms than in larger ones.

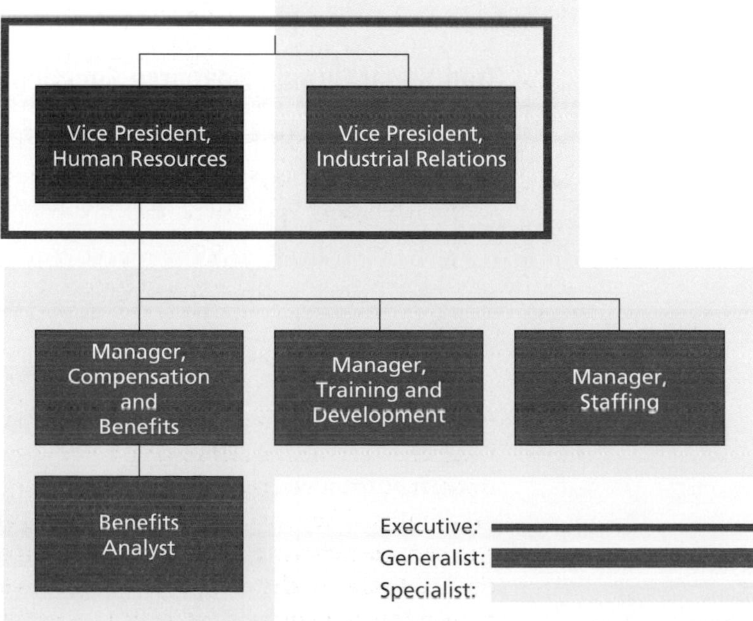

Figure 1-4 Human Resource Executives, Generalists, and Specialists

Trends & Innovations

A Change in HR Job Titles

There is no doubt that the job of HR professionals is changing. Certainly, job descriptions will have to be rewritten. The use of the terms "generalists" and "specialists" may become less common.[65] Here is one person's view of the types of future jobs for HR professionals.

The *CFO for HR* is the numbers expert who determines the value of HR and analyzes the cost-effectiveness of various HR practices. Remember we discussed human capital earlier in this chapter.

The *internal consultant* assists managers to recruit, interview, hire, and retain the talent that is needed and advises managers on legal and ethical matters such as EEO laws.

The *talent manager* is responsible for finding, developing, and keeping the employees who will best accomplish the firm's objectives. This individual is answerable for moving workers through the organization from hiring until they leave the organization.

The *vendor manager* determines which functions can be handled better and less expensively outside the organization.

The *self-service leader* works with the many functions that have been centralized, such as benefits and pension administration, that employees can access from their desktop computers.[66]

Whether any of this entire list will ultimately evolve is debatable. The only certainty is that HR jobs are in a state of flux.

For example, a staffing mistake in hiring an incompetent employee who *turns off* customers may cause the business to fail. In a larger firm, such an error might be much less harmful.

Human Resource Management Functions in Medium-Sized Firms

As a firm grows, a separate staff function may be required to coordinate HR activities. In a medium-sized firm, the person chosen to fill this role will be expected to handle most of the HR activities, as Figure 1-6 implies. For these firms, there is little specialization. A secretary may be available to handle correspondence, but the HR manager is essentially the entire department.

Traditional Human Resource Functions in a Large Firm

When the firm's HR function becomes too complex for one person, separate sections have historically been created and placed under a human resource executive. These sections typically performed tasks involving training and development, compensation

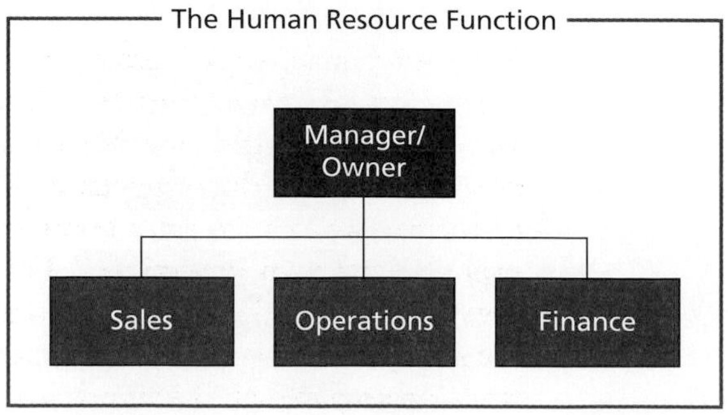

Figure 1-5 The Human Resource Function in a Small Business

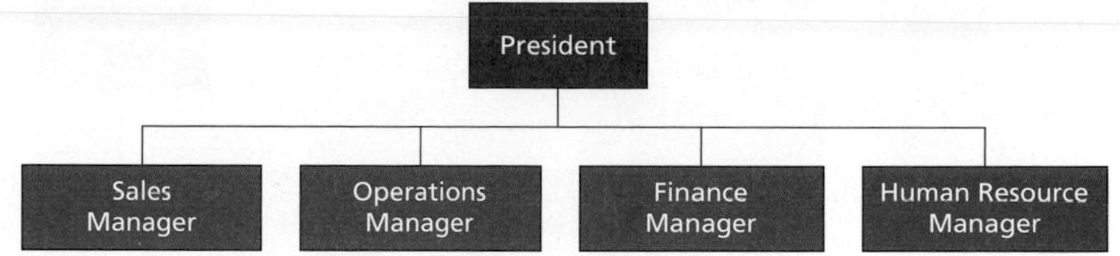

Figure 1-6 The Human Resource Function in a Medium-Sized Business.

and benefits, staffing, safety and health, and labor relations (if the firm is unionized), as depicted in Figure 1-7. Each HR function may have a manager and staff reporting to the HR executive. The HR vice president works closely with top management in formulating corporate policy.

An Evolving HR Organization

The HR organizational structure of firms changes as they outsource, use company service centers, and involve line managers more in traditional HR tasks. Regardless of an organization's design, the five previously identified HR functions must still be accomplished. An example of an evolving HR organization is presented in Figure 1-8. Here, the company has outsourced executive development, a function previously performed by the training department. Employee benefits have been placed with a shared service center. Safety and health has been removed from HR and, because of its importance in this particular firm, reports directly to the CEO. In this example, the other HR tasks remain under the control of the HR vice president but line managers are more involved in the employee selection process.

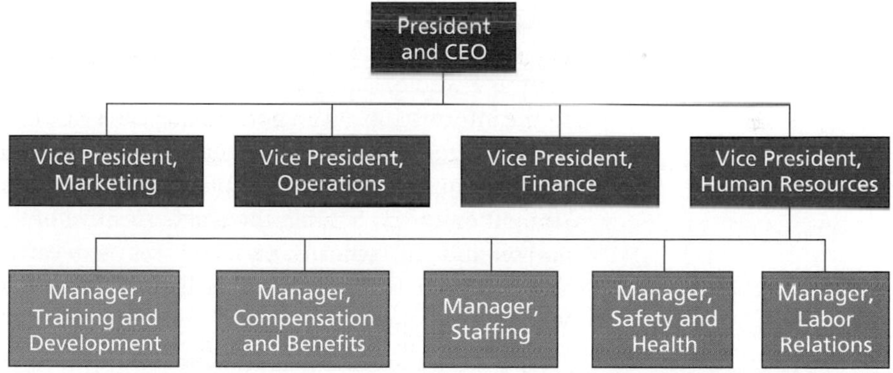

Figure 1-7 The Human Resource Function in a Large Firm

A Global Perspective: Everything Else Is Quantified, Why Not Human Capital?

Superior human capital practices can more than double the shareholder value of organizations, according to Watson Wyatts Human Capital Index studies in Europe, Asia-Pacific, and North America.[67] Wan Ainun Radzi and Patricia Chua both agree about the importance of quantifying human capital. "Everything else is quantified as an item on a company's balance sheet," says Chua. "But not human capital. That is an intangible." They believe that quantifying human capital will be the next big trend among companies aiming for a competitive advantage ahead of the sweeping changes that are expected in the wake of globalization and liberalizing trade arrangements. They are marketing a Web-based application called Human Capital Information Online and hope it will provide the largest human resources

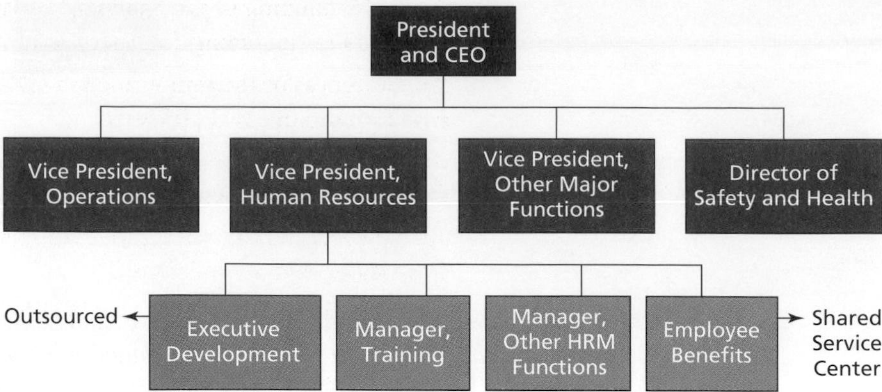

Figure 1-8 A New HR Organizational Variation for Large Firms

database available in Asia. They have information from over 65 Malaysian companies, data that have been broken down into various performance indicators from factors like sick leave and absenteeism to turnover, training, and health-care costs. They have information on manufacturing as a whole, which is then broken down into subcategories such as cement or the packaging industry. The program, now priced at $4,500 a year, is continuously updated so that managers can, from their desktops, find out how their companies are faring against the competition. "It allows companies to benchmark themselves in their particular industry," says Ainun.[68]

The application is the brainchild of Kuala Lumpur–based Organization Renewal Inc., or ORI, and its founder Rahim Majid. "It's innovative in that it precipitates a change in thought," says Rahim. Over 10 years, ORI built up a database which had been previously available to clients on a monthly basis, but it only went to the HR department and the chief executive. The application simply folded the database into the Web, making it instantaneously available to all levels of management and increasing accountability all around. But now, the marketed version of the product is available to a company as a whole, and it can be determined who within the company should have access to the information. "It's a good management tool," says Mohamad Sidek Ahmad, a vice president for corporate affairs at national utility Tenaga Nasional, Malaysia's second-largest company in terms of capitalization. "We can identify our sources of inefficiency straight away." T. S. Ong, the chief executive of Genting Sanyen, a power, packaging, and oil-and-gas company, says, "It gives us an early warning. Sometimes we can't fulfill orders for one reason or another. Is there too much medical leave being taken? Or, are we looking at our spending on training compared to our competition? Are we spending too little?"[69]

Scope of This Book

Effective HRM is crucial to the success of every organization. To be effective, managers must understand and competently practice HRM. We designed this book to give you the following:

- An insight into the evolving role of strategic HRM in today's organizations, the strategic role of HR functions, and the impact of technology and global competition.
- An awareness of the importance of social responsibility and business ethics in HRM.

- An understanding of job analysis, human resource planning, recruitment (including Internet recruiting), and selection.
- An awareness of the importance of HRD (training and developing) for employees at all levels.
- An understanding of performance appraisal and its role in performance management.
- An appreciation of how compensation and benefits programs are formulated and administered.
- An understanding of safety and health factors as they affect the firm's profitability.
- An opportunity to understand employee and labor relations.
- An appreciation of the global dimension of HRM.

Students often question whether the content of a book corresponds to the realities of the business world. In writing and revising this book, we have drawn heavily on the comments, observations, and experiences of HR practitioners as well as our own extensive research efforts. We cite the HR practices of leading business organizations to illustrate how theory can be applied in the real world. Our intent is to enable you to experience HRM in action.

This book is organized under eight parts, as shown in Figure 1-9; combined, they provide a comprehensive view of human resource management. As you read it, we hope you will be stimulated to increase your knowledge in this rapidly changing, expanding, and challenging field.

Figure 1-9 Organization of This Book

PART I. INTRODUCTION
Chapter 1: Strategic Human Resource Management: An Overview

PART II. HR ETHICAL, LEGAL, AND SOCIAL CONSIDERATIONS
Chapter 2: Human Resources: Social Responsibility and Business Ethics
Chapter 3: Workforce Diversity, Equal Employment Opportunity, and Affirmative Action

PART III. STAFFING
Chapter 4: Job Analysis and Human Resource Planning
Chapter 5: Recruitment
Appendix Chapter 5: Internet Recruiting
Chapter 6: Selection

PART IV. HUMAN RESOURCE DEVELOPMENT
Chapter 7: Training and Development
Appendix Chapter 7: Career Planning and Development
Chapter 8: Performance Appraisal

PART V. COMPENSATION AND BENEFITS
Chapter 9: Compensation
Chapter 10: Benefits and Other Compensation Issues

PART VI. SAFETY AND HEALTH
Chapter 11: A Safe and Healthy Work Environment

PART VII. EMPLOYEE AND LABOR RELATIONS
Chapter 12: The Evolution of Labor Union
Chapter 13: Collective Bargaining
Chapter 14: Internal Employee Relations

PART VIII. OPERATING IN A GLOBAL ENVIRONMENT
Chapter 15: Global Human Resource Management

Summary

1. Explain human capital management (HCM).
HCM is the task of measuring the cause and effect relationship of various HR programs and policies on the bottom line of the firm.

2. Define human resource management (HRM).
HRM is the utilization of individuals to achieve organizational objectives. Consequently, all managers at every level must concern themselves with HRM.

3. Identify the HRM functions.
The HRM functions include staffing, human resource development, compensation and benefits, safety and health, and employee and labor relations.

4. Identify the external environmental factors that affect HRM.
External factors include the labor force, legal considerations, society, unions, shareholders, competition, customers, technology, and the economy. Each factor, either separately or in combination with others, can place constraints on how HRM tasks are accomplished.

5. Explain who performs the HRM tasks.
Shared service centers take routine, transaction-based activities that are dispersed throughout the organization and consolidate them in one place. Outsourcing is the process of transferring responsibility for an area of service and its objectives to an external provider. Line managers in certain firms are being used more frequently than before to deliver HR services.

6. Explain the need for HR to be a strategic partner.
The increasing recognition of HR as a legitimate business unit has made it highly strategic in nature and increasingly critical to achieving corporate objectives. HR involvement in strategy is necessary to ensure that human resources support the firms mission.

7. Describe the various HR classifications including executives, generalists, and specialists.
Executives are top-level managers, who report directly to the corporation's CEO or the head of a major division. Generalists (who are often executives) are persons who perform tasks in a wide variety of HR-related areas. A specialist may be a human resource executive, manager, or nonmanager who typically is concerned with only one of the functional areas of HRM.

8. Describe the changes that occur in the HR function as a firm grows larger and more complex, and the evolving HR organization.
As firms grow and become more complex, the HR functions become more complex and achieve greater importance. The basic functions remain essentially the same, but the company changes the approach it uses to accomplish its objectives.

Key Terms

- **Human capital management (HCM), 3**
- **Human resource management (HRM), 4**
- **Staffing, 5**
- **Human resource development (HRD), 5**
- **Operative employees, 6**
- **External environment, 7**
- **Social responsibility, 8**
- **Ethics, 9**
- **Union, 9**
- **Shareholders, 9**
- **Human resource manager, 11**
- **Shared service center (SSC), 12**
- **Outsourcing, 12**
- **Line managers, 13**
- **Executive, 15**
- **Generalist, 15**
- **Specialist, 15**

Questions for Review

1. Define *human capital management* and *human resource management*.
2. What human resource management functions must be performed regardless of the organization's size?
3. What are the external environmental factors that affect human resource management? Describe each.
4. This chapter describes HR's changing role in business. Describe each component that is involved in human resource management.
5. How should HR act as a strategic partner?
6. What are the various titles associated with human resource management?
7. How does the implementation of human resource functions change as a firm grows? Briefly describe each stage of development.

HRM Incident 1

HRM Incident 1: It Sure Is Different Now!

Maxine Vincent is the new HR manager of Developmental Technologies, Inc., which was once the research and development division of a large, long-distance service provider located in Philadelphia. Developmental Technologies, Inc., became a separate business entity so the long-distance provider could prepare for the competitive changes resulting from the deregulation of telecommunication services. Maxine was the assistant to the vice president of HR for the long-distance carrier before the reorganization, so she believed she was well prepared to deal with her new responsibilities as manager. However, the new company does not have the unlimited resources of the older one; therefore, reducing operating costs is a necessity.

Although Maxine was not totally enthusiastic about the idea, outsourcing of certain HR functions appeared to be a solution. Even though Maxine had no previous experience with outsourcing, she believed that it would be one way of relieving the burden on her rather small staff. Just as she was to meet with potential outsourcing providers, her boss called to set up a meeting to discuss her role as a strategic partner in upper-level planning. This was the first Maxine had heard of being a strategic partner and she was both apprehensive and somewhat excited about the opportunity to influence the future direction of Developmental Technologies. Evidently, there would now be a new way of doing things.

Questions

1. What human resource management function might Maxine outsource? Explain your answer.
2. What should be Maxine's role as a strategic partner?

HRM Incident 2

HRM Incident 2: Downsizing

As the largest employer in Ouachita County, Arkansas, International Forest Products Company (IFP) is an important part of the local economy. Ouachita County is a mostly rural area of south-central Arkansas. It employs almost 10 percent of the local workforce, and few alternative job opportunities are available in the area.

Scott Wheeler, the human resource director at IFP, tells of a difficult decision he once had to make. According to Scott, everything was going along pretty well despite the economic recession, but he knew that sooner or later the company would be affected. "I got the word at a private meeting with the president, Mr. Deason, that we would have to cut the workforce by 30 percent on a crash basis. I was to get back to him within a week with a suggested plan. I knew that my plan would not be the final one, since the move was so major, but I knew that Mr. Deason was depending on me to provide at least a workable approach.

"First, I thought about how the union would react. Certainly, workers would have to be let go in order of seniority. The union would try to protect as many jobs as possible. I also knew that all of management's actions during this period would be intensely scrutinized. We had to make sure that we had our act together.

"Then there was the impact on the surrounding community to consider. The economy of Ouachita County had not been in good shape recently. Aside from the influence on the individual workers who were laid off, I knew that our cutbacks would further depress the area's economy. I knew that there would be a number of government officials and civic leaders who would want to know how we were trying to minimize the harm done to the public in the area.

"We really had no choice but to make the cuts, I believed. First of all, I had no choice because Mr. Deason said that we were going to do it. Also, I had recently read a news account that one of our competitors, Johns Manville Corporation in West Monroe, Louisiana, had laid off several hundred workers in a cost-cutting move. To keep our sales from being further depressed, we had to ensure that our costs were just as low as those of our competitors. The wood products market is very competitive and a cost advantage of even 2 or 3 percent would allow competitors to take many of our customers.

"Finally, a major reason for the cutbacks was to protect the interests of our shareholders. A few years ago a shareholder group disrupted our annual meeting to insist that IFP make certain antipollution changes. In general, though, the shareholders seem to be more concerned with the returns on their investments than with social responsibility. At our meeting, the president reminded me that, just like every other manager in the company, I should place the shareholders' interests above all else. I really was quite overwhelmed as I began to work up a personnel plan that would balance all of the conflicting interests that I knew about."

Questions

1. List the elements in the company's environment that will affect Scott's suggested plan. How legitimate is the interest of each of these?
2. Is it true that Scott should be concerned first and foremost with protecting the interests of shareholders? Discuss.

We invite you to visit the Mondy homepage on the Prentice Hall Web site at

www.prenhall.com/mondy

for updated information, Web-based exercises, and links to other HR-related sites.

Notes

1. Steve Bates, "Accounting for People: HR Executives and Academics Are Searching for the Holy Grail of HR—Measurements of the Value of Human Capital," *HRMagazine* 47 (October 2002): 30.
2. Ibid.
3. Stephen Taub, "Majority of Finance Chiefs Say They Should Play Major Role in Human Capital Management; Few Actually Do," *CFO.com* (February 19, 2003): 1.
4. Leslie A. Weatherly, "Human Capital—The Elusive Asset," *HRMagazine* 48 (March 2003): S1–S9.
5. Michelle Conlin, "Now It's Getting Personal: Companies Drill Down on Employees' Data to Zero in on Perks that Spur the Most Productivity," *BusinessWeek* 3812 (December 16, 2002): 90–92.
6. Susan Meisinger, "Taking the Measure of Human Capital," *HRMagazine* 48 (January 2003): 10.
7. "Preparing to Measure HR Success," *HR Focus* 79 (December 2002): 1.
8. Bates, "Accounting for People," 30–37.
9. Ibid.
10. J. Bruce Tracey and Arthur E. Nathan, "The Strategic and Operational Roles of Human Resources: An Emerging Model," *Cornell Hotel and Restaurant Administration Quarterly* 43 (August 2002): 17–26.
11. Conlin, "Now It's Getting Personal," 90–92.
12. Jeanie Caison, "A Workers Worth?" *Incentive* 177 (March 2003): 30–33.
13. Robert Colman, "Dangerous HR Fads," *CMA Management* 77 (March 2003): 8.
14. Conlin, "Now It's Getting Personal."
15. Colman, "Dangerous HR Fads," 8.
16. David Forman and Debra J. Cohen, "The SHRM Learning System," *Human Resource Management* 38 (Summer 1999): 155.
17. Russ Westcott, "Has Your Work Life Plateaued?" *Quality Progress* 34 (October 2001): 60.
18. The key law in the area of health and safety is the Occupational Safety and Health Act of 1970. This act is discussed in Chapter 11.
19. Thomas B. Edsall, "For AFL-CIO and White House, the Great Divide Is Deepening," *Washington Post* (September 2, 2002): A10.
20. Kenneth E. Goodpaster and John B. Matthews, Jr., "Can a Corporation Have a Conscience?" *Harvard Business Review* 60 (January–February 1982): 132–141.
21. Richard L. Knowdell, "The 10 New Rules for Strategizing Your Career," *The Futurist* 32 (June 1998): 1.
22. "What's Ahead for HR? SHRM Research Identifies Top Trends," *HR Focus* 79 (September 2002): 8.
23. Julie Britt, "Focused HR Technology Can Add Value," *HRMagazine* 47 (March 2002): 24.
24. Bill Leonard, "Straight Talk," *HRMagazine* 47 (January 2002): 46–51.
25. 2002's HR Tech Trends," *Canadian HR Reporter* 15 (January 28, 2002): 7.

26. "Three New Surveys Track the Growth of e-HR," *HR Focus* 79 (April 2002): 4–6.
27. "Trends to Watch in HRs Future," *HR Focus* 79 (December 2002): 7.
28. Dave Patel, "Managing Talent," *HRMagazine* 47 (March 2002): 112.
29. "HR's New Role: Creating Value," *HR Focus* 77 (January 2000): 14.
30. Richard Pinola, "What CEOs Want from HR," *HR Focus* 79 (September 2002): 1.
31. Reyer A. Swaak, "Are We Saying Good-bye to HR?" *Compensation & Benefits Review* 28 (September/October 1996): 32+.
32. Paul Falcone, "Understanding the HR Mind-set," *HRMagazine* 47 (October 2002): 117–122.
33. "Preparing to Measure HR Success," *HR Focus* 79 (December 2002): 1, 11.
34. Ibid.
35. Barbara Quinn, "Consolidating the Business of HR," *Canadian HR Reporter* 15 (February 25, 2002): 17.
36. Steven L. Goldman, "Today's Business: Think Value, Not Dollars," *Journal of Accountancy* 194 (August 2002): 55–57.
37. "HR Outsourcing Statistics: Large Company Strategies," *HR Focus* 80 (April 2003): S2.
38. Tom Andel, "P&G Outsources to Cut Costs," *Material Handling Management* 57 (April 2002): 7.
39. "HR Focus Readers Share Good, Bad, and Ugly Outsourcing Experiences," *HR Focus* 80 (April 2003): S1, S3+.
40. Denise Pelham, "Is It Time to Outsource HR?" *Training* 39 (April 2002): 50–52.
41. Steve Bates, "Facing the Future," *HRMagazine* 47 (July 2002): 26–32.
42. Joel Schettler, "Human Resources Belt-Tightening," *Training* 40 (February 2003): 17.
43. Bates, "Facing the Future."
44. Andel, "P&G Outsources to Cut Costs," 7.
45. Mark Matthews, Tom Ichnowski, and Debra K. Rubin, "Feds Get Ready to Outsource More," *ENR* 249 (December 23, 2002): 10.
46. Dipka Bhambhani, "HR Outsourcing Catches On," *Government Computer News* 22 (March 24, 2003): 54.
47. Stephanie Perkins and Mark Terman, "Avoiding Employment Practice Hazards," *Strategic Finance* 81 (October 1999): 64–70.
48. Susan Meisinger "Trust in the Top," *HRMagazine* 47 (October 2002): 8.
49. "7 Steps Before Strategy," *Workforce* 81 (November 2002): 40–44.
50. Allan Harcrow, "A 360-degree View of HR," *Workforce* 81 (June 2002): 28–34.
51. Pinola, "What CEOs Want from HR."
52. Diane Faulkner, "25th Anniversary: HR Yesterday, Today and Tomorrow," *Credit Union Management* 25 (November 2002): 32–33.
53. Susan Meisinger, "Strategic HR Means Translating Plans into Action," *HRMagazine* 48 (March 2003): 8.
54. "Addressing 2003s Top Issues for HR," *HR Focus* 80 (January 2003): 1, 14+.
55. David Brown, "The Future Is Nigh for Strategies HR," *Canadian HR Reporter* 15 (June 17, 2002): 7.
56. Barbara Davison, "The Difference Between Rightsizing and Wrongsizing," *The Journal of Business Strategy* 23 (July/August 2002): 31–35.
57. Kathryn Tyler, "Evaluate Your Next Move," *HRMagazine* 46 (November 2001): 66–71.
58. Steve Bates, "Demand for HR Executives Rising Sharply This Year," *HRMagazine* 47 (November 2002): 12.
59. "More on What CEOs Want from HR," *HR Focus* 80 (April 2003): 5.
60. Steve Bates, "His True Calling," *HRMagazine* 47 (August 2002): 38–43.
61. Ibid.
62. "Trends to Watch in HRs Future," *HR Focus* 79 (December 2002): 7.
63. Kevin Voigt, "The New Face of HR," *Far Eastern Economic Review* 165 (September 5, 2002): 61.
64. Bates, "His True Calling."
65. Ibid.
66. Ibid.
67. "Better HR Improves Shareholder Value for Global Companies," *HR Focus* 80 (March 2003): 8–9.
68. S. Jayasankaran, "Valuing Human Capital," *Far Eastern Economic Review* 165(August 8, 2002): 53.
69. Ibid.

PART TWO

HR Social, Ethical, and Legal Considerations

CHAPTER OBJECTIVES

After completing this chapter, students should be able to

1. Describe the changing attitudes toward social responsibility and business ethics.
2. Describe the concept of corporate social responsibility.
3. Explain the attempts at legislating ethics and social responsibility.
4. Explain what is meant by stakeholder analysis and the social contact.
5. Describe how a corporate social responsibility program is implemented.
6. Understand the model of ethics and describe human resource ethics.
7. Understand the importance of a code of ethics and describe ethics and the HR manager.
8. Describe the professionalization of human resource management.

CHAPTER 2

Human Resources: Social Responsibility and Business Ethics

HRM IN *Action:*

Changing Attitudes Toward Social Responsibility and Business Ethics

 **OBJECTIVE**

Describe the changing attitudes toward social responsibility and business ethics.

Harlan Teller, president of Hill and Knowlton's, said, "Corporate social responsibility (CSR) has moved from a 'nice-to-do' to a 'must-do.'"[1] Apparently, socially responsible behavior pays off on the bottom line. That is the conclusion of new research based on *Business Ethics'* 100 best corporate citizens list, which shows that the financial performance of these companies was "significantly better" than others in the Standard & Poor's 500. The rankings were based on corporate service to the following stakeholder groups: stockholders, employees, customers, the community, the environment, overseas stakeholders, and women and minorities. The top companies for 2002 were IBM, Fannie Mae, St. Paul Companies, and Procter & Gamble.[2]

In PricewaterhouseCoopers' recent Global CEO's Survey of more than 1,100 CEOs from around the world, 68 percent agreed CSR is vital to the profitability of any company and 24 percent said they currently issue public reports on CSR within their firms.[3] In order to meet the expectations of society, future managers will need to be more socially responsible. New data released by the Social Investment Forum show that being socially responsible pays off, even in difficult economic times. The performance ratings of socially and environmentally responsible mutual funds remain strong, the report said, suggesting that many people are attracted to socially responsible investing.[4] Socially responsible investment (SRI) amounted to more than $2 trillion by the end of 2001, up from $639 billion in 1995, according to the Social Investment Forum.[5]

With regard to ethics, most of the 500 largest corporations in the United States now have a code of ethics, which encompasses written conduct standards, internal education, formal agreements on industry standards, ethics offices, social accounting, and social projects. Even so, business ethics scandals continue to be headline news stories today.[6] Lying on resumes, obstruction of justice, destruction of records, stock price manipulation, earnings management, cutting corners to meet Wall Street's expectations, fraud, waste, and abuse, unfortunately, are occurring all too often when those in business go ethically wrong.[7] However, business is not alone. There is virtually no occupation that has not had its own painful ethical crises in recent years. Think about what has occurred in the judicial system, the health profession, the academic realm, and even religion. We even had a president who lied under oath.[8] But certainly a devastating blow to society was dealt by business.

According to ExecuNet.com, a career-development Web site for executives, nearly 60 percent of the executives responding to an ExecuNet survey said they believe there has been an erosion of corporate ethics in the past five years. Almost 70 percent of the respondents said they will review potential employers more closely, and nearly 65 percent said they will investigate the culture and value system of any prospective employer more thoroughly. Approximately 40 percent of those who took part in the survey said that at least once in their career they quit a job because of their employer's unethical business practices.[9]

We began this chapter by examining the changing attitudes toward social responsibility and business ethics. Then we describe the concept of corporate social responsibility and explain the attempts to legislate ethics and social responsibility. This is followed by an explanation of what is meant by stakeholder analysis and the social contract. Next, we describe how a corporate social responsibility program is implemented. This is followed by the presentation of a model of ethics and a presentation of human resource ethics. We then stress the importance of a code of ethics and describe ethics and the HR manager. Finally, we describe the professionalization of human resource management.

2 OBJECTIVE

Describe the concept of corporate social responsibility.

Corporate social responsibility (CSR): The implied, enforced, or felt obligation of managers, acting in their official capacity, to serve or protect the interests of groups other than themselves. It is how a company as a whole behaves toward society.

Business for Social Responsibility

www.bsr.org/

This Web site is for a global organization that helps member companies achieve success in ways that respect ethical values, people, communities, and the environment.

Corporate Social Responsibility

When a corporation behaves as if it has a conscience, it is said to be socially responsible. **Corporate social responsibility (CSR)** is the implied, enforced, or felt obligation of managers, acting in their official capacity, to serve or protect the interests of groups other than themselves. It is how a company as a whole behaves toward society.[10] It is certainly more than words being said.[11] At Enron, for example, the firm's stated values—respect, integrity, communication, and excellence—were once proudly etched on paperweights.[12] General Norman Schwarzkopf, hero of Desert Storm, has a piece of advice that all CEOs should follow. He calls it Rule 14: "When in doubt, do what's right."[13] The image of the business world would be in much better shape if this simple advice had been followed.

An organization's top executives usually determine a corporation's approach to social responsibility. However, recently corporate leadership has been under fire.[14] Seemingly daily, corporate leaders are in the news for unscrupulous acts. According to a recent issue of *BusinessWeek*, "Faith in Corporate America hasn't been so strained since the early 1900s, when the public's furor over the monopoly powers of big business led to years of trust busting by Theodore Roosevelt."[15] Headlines have exposed the far-from-socially responsible exploits of Enron, Arthur Andersen, WorldCom, Global Crossing, Xerox, Adelphia Communications, Tyco, and others. The ruthless self-interest that motivates the leaders of some large corporations has been revealed. Often corporate executives made decisions that did not parallel the expectations of society. The same seems to be true of boards of directors with their often used *rubber-stamp* approach. Evidently, shareholders also need to keep an eye on the boards. The image of Enron is now a vital presence in every boardroom. To have served on the Enron board literally has become a badge of shame.[16]

Intel, a company that continues to rank high in social responsibility issues, has established a set of core values that drive its actions, both internally and externally. It has created an impression of being a great place to work and of the company as an asset to the communities where it operates. Following these principles, its employees volunteer time (more than 230,000 hours last year) and Intel contributes a great deal of money (about $120 million in global education support).[17]

3 OBJECTIVE

Explain the attempts at legislating ethics and social responsibility.

Legislating Ethics and Social Responsibility

In 1907, Teddy Roosevelt said, "Men can never escape being governed. If from lawlessness or fickleness, from folly or self-indulgence, they refuse to govern themselves, then in the end they will be governed [by others]."[18] Many contend that ethics and social responsibility cannot be legislated. However, much of the current legislation was passed because of social responsibility and business ethics breakdowns. There have been three attempts to legislate social responsibility and business ethics since the late 1980s. The first, the Procurement Integrity Act of 1988, was passed after there were reports of military contracts for $500 toilet seats. There was also a $5,000 hammer.[19]

The second attempt occurred with the passage of the 1992 Federal Sentencing Guidelines for Organizations (FSGO) that outlined an effective ethics program. It promised softer punishments for wayward corporations that already had ethics programs in place. In the law were recommendations regarding standards, ethics training, and a system to report misconduct anonymously. Executives were supposed to be responsible for the misconduct of those lower in the organization. If executives were proactive in their efforts to prevent white-collar crime it would lessen a judgment against them and reduce the liability. Organizations responded by creating ethics officer positions, installing ethics hotlines, and developing codes of conduct. At least 90 percent of companies now have a written code of ethics and conduct.[20] But, it is one thing to have a code of ethics and quite another to have this code instilled in all employees from top to bottom. For example, the Enron debacle was not supposed to happen. Although this firm publicly referred to its "Code of Ethics," it was not a member of the Ethics Officer Association and did not have an ethics officer to administer compliance with its code.[21] It became apparent that top management pursued business as usual. One study even suggested the possibility that ethics programs may serve as window dressing to deflect attention or culpability resulting from illegal actions.[22]

The third attempt at legislating social responsibility and business ethics was due not only to Enron and others but also to the way the public viewed the world after September 11.[23] The Corporate and Auditing Accountability, Responsibility and Transparency Act (CAART) was signed into law in 2002 and criminalizes many corporate acts that were previously relegated to various regulatory structures. Known as the Sarbanes-Oxley Act, its primary focus is to redress accounting and financial reporting abuses in light of recent corporate scandals. The Act contains broad employee whistle-blower protections that subject corporations and their managerial personnel to significant civil and criminal penalties for retaliating, harassing, or discriminating against employees who report suspected corporate wrongdoing. The whistle-blower protections of the Act apply to corporations listed on U.S. stock exchanges, companies otherwise obligated to file reports under the Securities and Exchange Act, and officers, employees, contractors, subcontractors, and agents of those companies. The Act states that management may not "discharge, demote, suspend, threaten, harass or in any other manner discriminate" against an employee protected by the Act. It protects any employee who lawfully provides information to governmental authorities concerning conduct he or she reasonably believes constitutes mail, wire, or securities fraud; violations of any rule or regulation issued by the Securities and Exchange Commission (SEC); or violations of any other federal law relating to fraud against shareholders.[24] The law prohibits loans to executives and directors.[25] The Sarbanes-Oxley Act does not require SEC reporting banks and bank

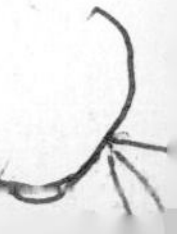

holding companies to have a code of ethics, but if an SEC reporting company does not have one, it must explain why.[26] But, as former Securities and Exchange Commission Chairman Arthur Levitt said, "While the Sarbanes-Oxley Act has brought about significant change, the greatest change is being brought about not by regulation or legislation, but by humiliation and embarrassment and private rights of action."[27]

While many of the of Sarbanes-Oxley tasks fall outside of the responsibilities of human resources, HR professionals will need to take action with regard to the act's nonretaliation provisions. In addition, if HR is to be a strategic partner in corporate affairs, HR professional must understand where the Act's corporate mandates intersect with existing HR policies and practices so they can fit them together with corporate compliance efforts.[28]

Even with the passage of the Corporate Reform Bill, the Blue Ribbon Conference Board Commission on Public Trust and Private Enterprise has recommended additional executive compensation reforms designed to restore trust in America's publicly traded corporations. Among the suggestions are:

- Any outside compensation consultants should be retained by the board's compensation committee and should report solely to the committee.
- Stock options should be expensed on a uniform and broadly accepted basis.
- Senior managers and executives should be required to own a meaningful amount of company stock on a long-term basis.
- Executive officers should be required to give public notice before selling company stock.[29]

Social Investment Forum

www.socialinvest.org/

This Web site offers comprehensive information on contacts, and resources for socially responsible investing.

In retrospect, Congress itself may have caused many of the problems leading to the passage of the (CAART). In 1997, it blocked an attempt by the SEC and the AICPA (American Institute of Certified Public Accountants) to pass a rule banning auditors from doing most kinds of lucrative consulting work for the same companies they audited. Some 46 members of Congress from both parties sent letters opposing the measure.[30]

OBJECTIVE

Explain what is meant by stakeholder analysis and the social contact.

Stakeholder Analysis and the Social Contract

Organizational stakeholder: An individual or group whose interests are affected by organizational activities. Although all stakeholders are affected by the organization, managers may not acknowledge responsibility to all of them.

Most organizations, whether profit or nonprofit, have a large number of stakeholders. An **organizational stakeholder** is an individual or group whose interests are affected by organizational activities. Although all stakeholders are affected by the organization, managers may not acknowledge responsibility to all of them.[31] Society is increasingly holding corporate boards of directors and management accountable for putting the interest of stakeholders first. Some of the stakeholders for Crown Metal Products, a fictitious manufacturer of metal, are shown in Figure 2-1. But only a few, identified by bold arrows, are viewed as constituencies by Crown management. Each firm will have different stakeholders based on the organization's mission and the focus of social responsibility efforts.

The actions of many corporate executives are designed to serve interests other than those of the common shareholder. For example, a number of managements have placed large amounts of company stock in employee stock ownership trusts for the purpose of avoiding takeover attempts that were clearly in the interests of common shareholders. This benefited the employees, of course, but it also helped the managers keep their jobs. Other companies make gifts of company resources, often cash, to universities, churches, clubs, and so forth, knowing that any possible benefit to shareholders is remote. Some authorities favor this trend and suggest that members of the public should be placed on major corporate boards to protect the interests of nonowner stakeholders.

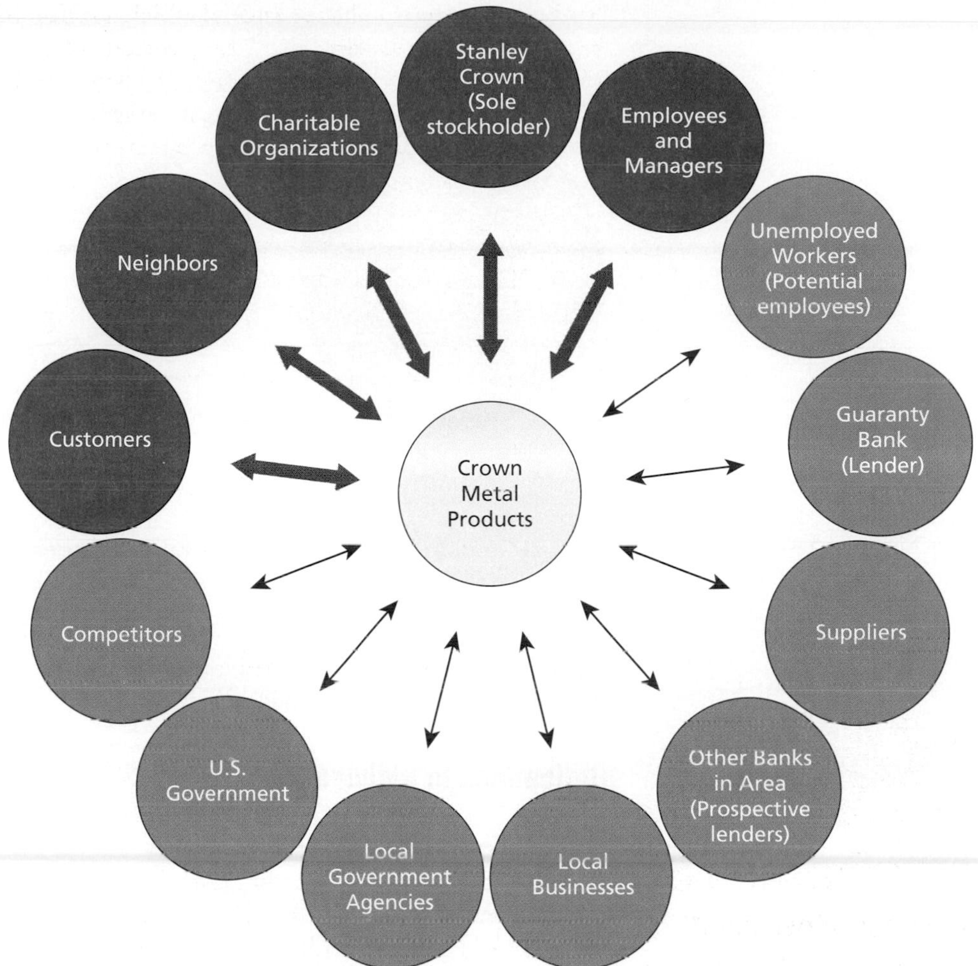

Figure 2-1 Stakeholders of Crown Metal Products
Source: R. Wayne Mondy and Shane R. Premeaux *Management: Concepts, Practices and Skills*, 7th ed. (Upper Saddle River, NJ: Prentice Hall, 1995), p. 80.

Social contract:
The set of written and unwritten rules and assumptions about acceptable interrelationships among the various elements of society. Much of the social contract is embedded in the customs of society.

One approach to stakeholder analysis involved consideration of the social contract. The **social contract** is the set of written and unwritten rules and assumptions about acceptable interrelationships among the various elements of society. Much of the social contract is embedded in the customs of society. For example, in integrating minorities into the workforce, society has come to expect companies to do more than the law requires. "Shareholder activism has focused on HR issues since the mid–1970s," says Timothy Smith, a senior vicepresident at Walden Asset Management in Boston and president of the Social Investment Forum, a trade association. He says HR should actually feel supported, rather than irritated by shareholders, "especially if they find executive management isn't paying enough attention to certain workplace issues. This is a chance for shareholders to actually help."[32]

Some of the *contract provisions* result from practices of the parties to the contract. Like a legal contract, the social contract often involves a *quid pro quo*. One party to the contract behaves in a certain way and expects a certain pattern of behavior from the other. For example, a relationship of trust may have developed between a manufacturer and the community in which it operates. Because of this, each will inform the other well in advance of any planned action that might cause harm, such as the phasing down of a plant's operations by the company. The widespread belief that such a relationship was rare prompted Congress to pass the Worker Adjustment and Retraining Notification Act of 1988. That law requires firms employing 100 or more workers to give 60 days' notice to employees and local government officials when a plant closing or layoff affecting 50 or more employees for a 90-day period is planned.

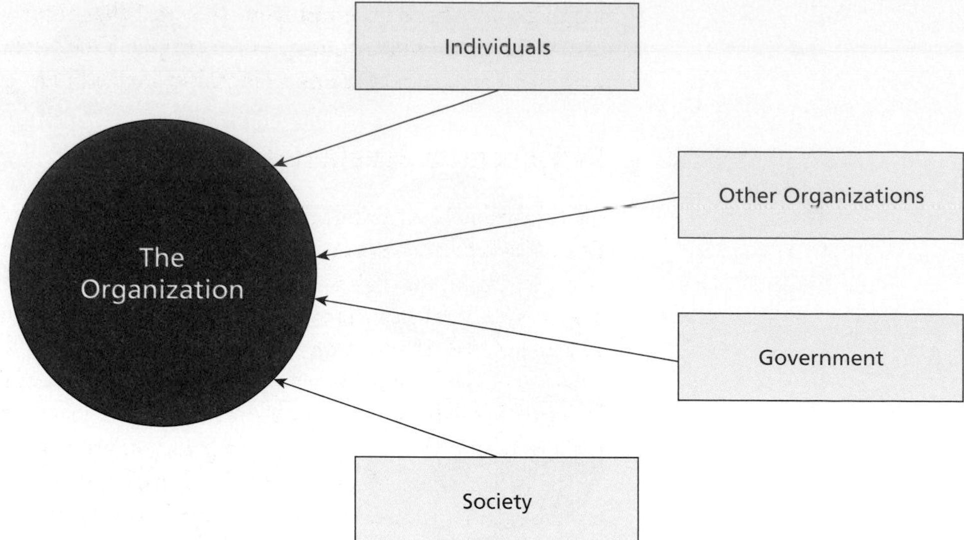

Figure 2-2 The Social Contract
Source: R. Wayne Mondy and Shane R. Premeaux, *Management: Concepts, Practices, and Skills*, 7th ed. (Upper Saddle River, NJ: Prentice Hall, 1995), p. 82.

The social contract concerns relationships with individuals, government, other organizations, and society in general as Figure 2-2 illustrates. Each of these relationships will be considered individually in the following sections.

Obligations to Individuals

Organizations have certain obligations to their employees. Individuals often find healthy outlets for their energies through joining organizations. From their employers, they expect a fair day's pay for a fair day's work—and perhaps much more. Many expect to be paid for time off to vote, perform jury service, and so forth. To the extent that individuals' expectations are acknowledged as responsibilities by the organization, they become part of the social contract. Many individuals are now voicing their opinions by purchasing stock from firms that have a reputation for being socially responsible. The Internet has made it much easier for them to check out companies' records on environmental, social, and ethical issues.[33]

Obligations to Other Organizations

Managers must be concerned with relationships involving other organizations—both organizations that are like their own, such as competitors, and very different ones. Commercial businesses are expected to compete with one another on an honorable basis, without subterfuge or reckless unconcern for their mutual rights. However, some organizations appear to have a certain amount of disdain for competitors, especially when it comes to recruiting. Dr. Ferdinand Piech, chairman of Volkswagen AG, hired Jose Ignacio Lopez de Arriortua from General Motors to head manufacturing and purchasing at Volkswagen. Lopez took seven GM co-workers with him in the move. He made contact with 40 others, and may have taken trade secrets with him.[34] If this is true, it is fairly obvious that Volkswagen AG was not competing on an honorable basis with General Motors. Charities such as the United Way expect support from business, often including the loan of executives to help with annual fund drives. At the same time, such institutions are expected to come, hat in hand, to business managers, requesting rather than demanding assistance.

In the traditional view of social responsibility, business best meets its obligations through pursuit of its own interests. Some companies view the social contract mainly in terms of the company's interests. For example, FMC Corporation, a major diversified manufacturer, has firm policies about how it will direct its contributions. The basic criteria FMC applies are that contributions must help areas around company facilities or where its employees live and that their gifts must improve the corporation's business environment. For example, FMC might contribute to a business college in an area where it has a plant, but it would not give gifts to distant universities.

Obligations to Government

Government is an important party to the social contract for every kind of organization. Under the auspices of government, companies have a license to do business, along with patent rights, trademarks, and so forth. Churches are often incorporated under state laws and given nonprofit status. Many quasi-governmental agencies, such as the Federal Deposit Insurance Corporation (FDIC), regional planning commissions, and local school boards, have been given special missions by government.

In addition, organizations are expected to recognize the need for order rather than anarchy and to accept some government intervention in organizational affairs. They are expected to work with the guidelines of governmental organizations such as the Equal Employment Opportunity Commission and the Office of Federal Contract Compliance Programs (to be discussed in Chapter 3).

Obligations to Society in General

The traditional view of business responsibility has been that businesses should produce and distribute goods and services in return for a profit. Businesses have performed this function effectively, giving the United States one of the highest overall standards of living in the world. A high percentage of the population has its basic needs for food, clothing, shelter, health, and education reasonably well satisfied. And most citizens are afforded some leisure time. Profitable firms are able to pay taxes to the government and make donations to charities. All this should be a matter of some pride for business owners and managers.

Businesses operate by public consent with the basic purpose of satisfying the needs of society. As those needs are more fully met, society demands more of all of its institutions, particularly large business firms. Some of the goals businesses are expected to help society meet are presented next.

- Elimination of poverty.
- Provision of quality health care.
- Preservation of the environment by reductions in the level of pollution.
- Provision of a sufficient number of jobs and career opportunities for all members of society.
- Improvement in the quality of working life of employees.
- Provision of safe, livable communities with good housing and efficient transportation.[35]

At the same time, remember that in order to survive, businesses must make a profit over the long run. If they fail, they will not be able to contribute. As responsible corporate citizens, businesses should follow the spirit of the law as well as the letter. As previously mentioned, there is a major difference in adhering to equal employment laws and being an equal opportunity employer.

In the sixteenth century, Sir Thomas More said, "If virtue were profitable, common sense would make us good and greed would make us saintly."[36] More knew that virtue is not profitable, so people must make hard ethical choices from time to time. Common sense hardly makes one good. In the United States today, the consensus is clear. Corporate strategists are being held to a higher standard than just pursuing their own interests, or even those of stockholders; they must consider the interests of other groups too.

Sir Thomas More (1478–1535)

English saint and diplomat, More was the author of Utopia and lord chancellor from 1529 to 1532.

More had been one of Henry VIII's primary councilors. He began to fall out of favor with the king when he did not sign a letter urging the pope to declare Henry's marriage to Catherine void.

In 1533 the Act of Restraint of Appeals cut judicial ties between England and Rome. Thomas Cranmer, the archbishop of Cantenbury, declared the king's marriage to Catherine void on May 23, 1533. Anne Boleyn was crowned June 1.

More was called to Lambeth on April 13, 1534, to confirm by oath the Act of Succession (March 1534) which, in part, declared the king's marriage to Catherine void and the one to Anne valid. More was willing to accept this. But he refused the oath because it also entailed a repudiation of papal supremacy.

On April 17 he was imprisoned in the Tower of London.

In 1534 the Act of Supremacy established the king as the supreme head of the Church of England. Denying this authority was considered high treason.

More was tried in Westminster hall on July 1, 1535. He was convicted of treason for his refusal to affirm the king's supremacy. He was beheaded on Tower Hill July 6.

More was beatified on December 29, 1886, and was canonized on May 19, 1935.

In 1966, a film by Fred Zinnemann was made based on Robert Bolt's play about Sir Thomas More. The film featured Paul Scofield and Peter O'Toole, with contributions by Wendy Hiller and Robert Shaw. Cinematography was by Ted Moore.

5 OBJECTIVE

Describe how a corporate social responsibility program is implemented.

Implementing a Corporate Social Responsibility Program[37]

Social audit:
A systematic assessment of a company's activities in terms of its social impact.

To overcome the negative publicity of corporate misdeeds and to restore trust, businesses are now conducting more audits of their social responsibility activities, not just financial ones.[38] Some of the topics included in the audit focus on such core values as social responsibility, open communication, treatment of employees, confidentiality, and leadership.[39] Firms are now acknowledging responsibilities to various stakeholder groups other than corporate owners. Some even set specific objectives in social areas. They are attempting to formally measure their contributions to various elements of society and to society as a whole. An increasing number of companies, as well as public and voluntary sector organizations, are trying to assess their social performance systematically.[40] A **social audit** is a systematic assessment of a company's activities in terms of its social impact. Three possible types of social audits are currently being utilized: (1) simple inventory of activities, (2) compilation of socially relevant expenditures, and (3) determination of social impact. The inventory is generally a good starting place. It consists of a listing of socially oriented activities undertaken by the firm. Here are some examples: (1) minority employment and training, (2) support of minority enterprises, (3) pollution control, (4) corporate giving, (5) involvement in selected community projects by executives, and (6) a hardcore unemployment program. The ideal social audit would go well beyond a simple listing and involve determining the true benefits to society of any socially oriented business activity.

The following steps are recommended for establishing and implementing a corporate social responsibility (CSR) program. First, a person should be assigned the

Trends & Innovations

A Change In Ethical Standards?

Everyone is not as ethical as Leonard Roberts, the former CEO of Arby's, the fast-food restaurant chain. He took over the chain when it was losing money and made Arby's profitable, but then resigned from the board of directors when Arby's owner threatened to withhold bonuses for Roberts's staff and not to give promised help to Arby's franchisees in order to further increase profits. In retaliation for his ethical stand, Roberts was fired. He was then hired as CEO of the Shoney's restaurant chain. Soon after arriving he discovered that the company was the subject of the largest racial discrimination suit in history. After investigating and discovering that the company was, in fact, in the wrong, Mr. Roberts promised the suit would be settled fairly. Shoney's owner agreed to pay and settle, but only if Roberts would resign afterward. "My stand on integrity was getting a little hard on my wife and kids," Mr. Roberts said. "However, I knew it had to be done. There was no other way. You cannot fake it. You must stand up for what is right regardless. You cannot maintain your integrity 90 percent and be a leader. It's got to be one hundred percent." Later Mr. Roberts became CEO of Radio Shack and a year after that, CEO of Tandy's, which owns Radio Shack. Because of his work at Radio Shack, *Brandweek* magazine named him Retailor of the Year.[41]

responsibility for the program and a structure should be developed. This individual should at a very minimum report to senior management or a board member. Second, a review of what the company is presently doing with regard to CSR should be determined. The difference between where the company is at present and where it wants to be should be determined (a gap analysis). Third, shareholders' expectations and perspectives are determined. Fourth, a policy statement is written covering CSR areas such as environmental, social, and community issues. Fifth, a set of corporate objectives and an action plan to implement the policies should be developed. Sixth, company-wide quantitative and qualitative targets and key performance indicators over a two- to five-year period, together with the necessary measurement, monitoring, and auditing mechanisms should be created. These actions and strategies should focus on core business of the organization. Seventh, communicate to stakeholders and fund managers the direction of CSR with this company. Eighth, the progress of the CSR program should be determined. Finally, the progress of the CSR program should be reported.[42] The CSR program should not be a one-time-only attempt, but rather a continuing effort to monitor and report the firm's achievements in the area of social responsibility.

6 OBJECTIVE

Understand the model of ethics and describe human resource ethics.

A Model of Ethics

It was not long ago that many organizations paid only lip service to ethics. Then the world witnessed the fall of companies such as Enron and WorldCom. Even the practices of giants such as IBM, General Electric, and Xerox have been called into question.[43] Some believe that there will be other major business-related scandals. If this occurs, additional pensions and jobs would be wiped out.[44] In one study of 300 large public companies, the firms that made an explicit commitment to follow an ethics code provided more than twice the value to shareholders in comparison to companies that did not.[45]

According to Kenneth D. Lewis, Chairman and Chief Executive Officer, Bank of America, "There is a difference between what's legal and what's ethical. But we don't

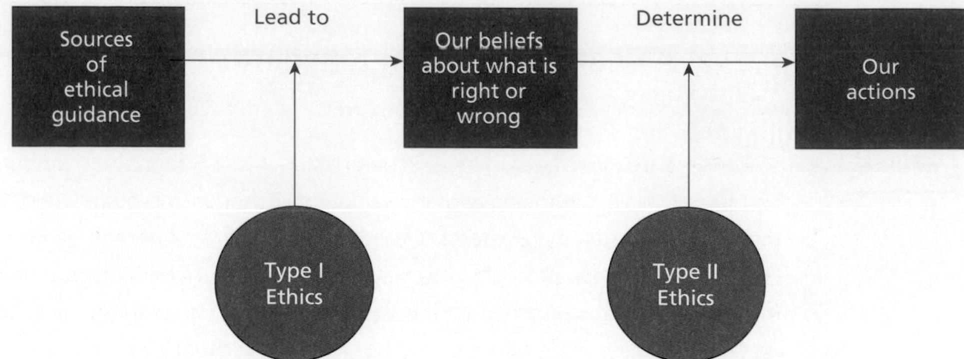

Figure 2-3 A Model of Ethics
Source: R. Wayne Mondy and Shane R. Premeaux, *Management: Concepts, Practices, and Skills*, the 7th ed. (Upper Saddle River, NJ: Prentice Hall, 1995), p. 91.

often talk about it, and I've wondered why. Maybe people think it's too soft . . . too hard to define . . . or, in corporate language, not 'actionable.' Maybe it's easier for us to defer to new laws and regulations as the solution. But new laws are only part of the solution. And, in my view, they don't get to the heart of the problem."[46] Remember that earlier in this chapter we discussed three laws that had been passed in an attempt to curtail ethical lapses.

Ethics:
The discipline dealing with what is good and bad, or right and wrong, or with moral duty and obligation.

Ethics is the discipline dealing with what is good and bad, or right and wrong, or with moral duty and obligation. Ethics is about deciding whether an action is good or bad and what to do about it if it is "bad." Ethics is a philosophical discipline that describes and directs moral conduct.[47] Those in HR make ethical (or unethical) decisions every day. Do you send the best-qualified person, who is a minority, to be interviewed knowing that the person making the selection does not want minorities in the department? Do you "forget" to tell a prospect about the dangerous aspect of a certain job? Some ethical decisions are major and some are minor. But decisions in small matters often set a pattern for the more important decisions a manager makes.

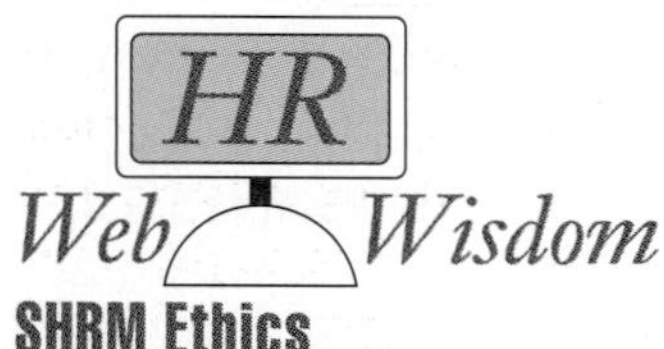

SHRM Ethics

www.shrm.org/hrlingks/default.asp

This SHRM Web site provides management practices information related to ethics.

A model of ethics is presented in Figure 2-3. As can be seen, ethics consists mainly of two relationships, indicated by the bold horizontal arrows. A person or organization is ethical if these relationships are strong and positive. Notice that the first element in the model is sources of ethical guidance. One might use a number of sources to determine what is right or wrong, good or bad, moral or immoral. These sources include the Bible and other holy books. They also include the *still, small voice* that many refer to as conscience. Millions believe that conscience is a gift of God or the voice of God. Others see it as a developed response based on the internalization of societal mores. Another source of ethical guidance is the behavior and advice of the people psychologists call *significant others*—our parents, friends, and role models and members of our churches, clubs, and associations. For most professionals, there are codes of ethics that proscribe certain behavior. Without this conscience that has developed it might be easy to say, "Everyone does it," "Just this once won't hurt," or "No one will ever know."[48]

Laws also offer guides to ethical behavior, prohibiting acts that can be especially harmful to others. If a certain behavior were illegal, most would consider it to be unethical as well. There are exceptions, of course. For example, through the 1950s, laws in most southern states relegated black persons to the backs of buses and otherwise assigned them inferior status. Martin Luther King, Jr., resisted such laws and, in fact, engaged in civil disobedience and other nonviolent forms of resistance to their enforcement. King won the Nobel Peace Prize for his efforts.

Notice in Figure 2-3 that the sources of ethical guidance should lead to our beliefs or convictions about what is right or wrong. Most would agree that people have a responsibility to avail themselves of these sources of ethical guidance. In short, individuals should care about what is right and wrong and not just be concerned with what is expedient. The strength of the relationship between what an individual or an organization believes to be moral and correct and what available sources of guidance sug-

Ethical Dilemma

A Selection Quandary

You are being transferred to a new assignment with the company, and your boss has asked you to nominate one of your subordinates as a replacement. The possible candidates are Randy Carlton, who is obviously more qualified, and James Mitchell, who, though not as experienced, is much better liked by the workers. If Randy is given the promotion, you are uncertain if the workers will accept him as their leader. James, on the other hand, is a hard worker and is well liked and respected by the others, including Randy. As you labor over the decision, you think about how unfair it would be to Randy if the feelings of the other workers kept him from getting a deserved promotion. At the same time, you feel that your primary responsibility should be to maintain the productivity of the work unit. If your former division fell apart after your departure, it would hurt your reputation, not to mention the company.

What would you do?

Type I ethics:
The strength of the relationship between what an individual or an organization believes to be moral and correct and what available sources of guidance suggest is morally correct.

Type II ethics:
The strength of the relationship between what one believes and how one behaves.

gest is morally correct is **Type I ethics.** For example, suppose an HR manager believes it is acceptable to not hire minorities, despite the fact that almost everyone condemns this practice. This person is unethical, but perhaps only in a Type I sense.

Simply having strong beliefs about what is right and wrong and basing them on the proper sources may have little relationship to what one does. Figure 2-3 illustrates that **Type II ethics** is the strength of the relationship between what one believes and how one behaves. For example, if an HR manager knows that it is wrong to discriminate, but does so anyway, the HR manager is being unethical in a Type II sense. If a board of directors considers it wrong to pay excessive salaries to the CEO, yet pays salaries that are outrageous, this behavior is unethical also. Generally, a person is not considered ethical unless the person possesses both types of ethics.

As we move through the book, you will find ethical dilemmas to consider. Take a moment to determine how you would handle each dilemma. In all instances it should be readily evident what the ethical response should be. Decisions are so nice and neat in an academic environment. Then, you should ask yourself, are there other factors that some would consider in making a decision? Often there is considerable evidence that might sway a person to make a less-than-ethical decision.

 **OBJECTIVE**

Understand the importance of a code of ethics and describe ethics and the HR manager.

Human Resource Ethics

Human resource ethics:
The application of ethical principles to human resource relationships and activities.

Human resource ethics is the application of ethical principles to human resource relationships and activities. As previously noted, reading the newspaper or watching the evening news provides ample illustration of illegal or unethical practices of individuals in large corporations. Deciding what is ethical is often difficult. Some believe that those in human resources have a great deal to do with establishing an organization's conscience.[49] Certainly, some of the ethical lapses of recent years occurred in the field referred to as human resource management.

For organizations to grow and prosper, good people must be employed. Today college job-seekers believe that corporate leadership ethics is important in their search for the "right" firm to work for. In a recent survey, 82 percent said that finding an ethical firm was important in their job search.[50] Some companies are searching for new employees who have a sound ethical base because they have discovered that a person who is ethical tends to be more successful. Catherine H. Gates, training coordinator for Montgomery Mutual Insurance Co. in Sandy Spring, Maryland, said, "People who score high on ethics tests tend to do better from a long-term professional standpoint."[51]

Of late, a large amount of talk regarding ethics relates to the excessive amount of compensation some executives receive. Many forms of executive compensation such as stock options and separation packages have been called into question. Twenty years ago, Lee Iacocca, then chairman of Chrysler, was the highest-paid corporate executive in America at $20 million per year. CEOs of large corporations in 2001 made 411 times as much as the average factory worker. In the past decade, as rank-and-file wages increased 36 percent, CEO pay climbed 340 percent, to an average of $11 million.[52] Jack Welch, once a business school and GE corporate icon, is now known for corporate excess. His former wife revealed his $9 million annual pension plan payout, plus outrageous perks such as lifetime use of GE's $80,000-per-month Manhattan apartment with free food and free maid service; lifetime use of the GE fleet of corporate jets, including a Boeing 737 business jet; a new Mercedes plus a limousine and driver; and assorted free sports and opera box tickets.[53] Bruce Ellig, an executive compensation expert and author of *The Complete Guide to Executive Compensation*, said, "Compensation committees should be focused on pay-for-performance plans. Perks are pay-for-position, and do nothing to create shareholder value."[54] "Excessive CEO pay is the mad-cow disease of American boardrooms," says J. Richard Finlay, chairman of Canada's Center for Corporate & Public Governance. "It moves from company to company, rendering directors incapable of applying common sense."[55]

A Code of Ethics

Most companies have codes of ethics. Many industry associations adopt such codes, which are then recommended to members. Some consultants specialize in helping companies embed ethical principles in their corporate cultures. And most business schools now teach business ethics in their courses. There are many kinds of ethical codes. An excellent example of a code of ethics was developed by the Society for Human Resource Management (SHRM). Major provisions in the SHRM code of ethics include professional responsibility, professional development, ethical leadership, fairness and justice, conflicts of interests, and use of information. With regard to conflict of interest, the code states, "As HR professionals, we must maintain a high level of trust with our stakeholders. We must protect the interests of our stakeholders as well as our professional integrity and should not engage in activities that create actual, apparent, or potential conflicts of interest."[56] It is vitally important that those who work with human resource management understand those practices that are unacceptable and ensure that organizational members behave ethically in dealing with others.

A code of ethics establishes the rules by which the organization lives. But as Samuel A. DiPiazza, Jr., Global CEO of PricewaterhouseCoopers, said, "It is easy to talk about ethics but it is a lot harder to create an ethical, effective, diverse organization that stands for truth and integrity."[57] Once these rules are published, everyone within and outside the firm knows the rules that company employees should live by.[58] A broad-based participation of those subject to the code is important. Michael Coates, CEO of Hill and Knowlton Canada, said, "For a company to behave ethically, it must live and breathe its code of conduct, train its personnel and communicate its code through its visioning statements. It cannot just print a manual that sits on a corporate shelf."[59] Just what should be included in a code of ethics? Topics typically covered might be business conduct, fair competition, and workplace and HR issues.[60] Employees should be given realistic examples of ethical behavior. For example, at Wal-Mart, it is considered unethical to accept gifts from suppliers. It either destroys the gifts or gives them to charity.[61]

To keep the code on the front burner for employees, larger firms appoint an ethics officer. This individual should be a person who understands the work environment. A likely candidate for this position might be the vice president of HR. To obtain the involvement of others within the organization an ethics committee should be established. Often representatives from legal, human resources, corporate compliance, corporate communications, external affairs, and training departments are included.[62]

There are reasons to encourage industry associations to develop and promote improved codes of ethics. It is difficult for a single firm to pioneer ethical practices if its competitors take advantage of unethical shortcuts. For example, U.S. companies must comply with the Foreign Corrupt Practices Act, which prohibits bribes of foreign government officials or business executives.[63] Obviously, the law does not prevent foreign competitors from bribing government or business officials to get business, and such practices are common in many countries. This sometimes puts U.S. companies at a disadvantage. A growing number of international organizations have developed guidelines to help curb corruption in the future. Several multinationals, including Switzerland's Ciba-Geigy, have encouraged other multinationals to band together and adopt policies on corrupt practices that will resemble those in U.S. law. Perhaps such voluntary codes will be effective in upgrading the standards of ethics practiced in international business.

Even the criteria for winning the Baldrige National Quality Award have recently changed. They now place an increased emphasis on ethics in leadership. As of 2003, the criteria say senior leaders should serve as role models to the rest of their organizations. Baldrige applicants are asked questions as to how senior leaders create an environment that fosters and requires legal and ethical behavior and how the leaders address such governance matters as fiscal accountability and independence in audits.[64]

Ethics and the HR Manager

HR Web Wisdom

International Business Ethics Institute

www.business-ethics.org/index.asp

This Web site was founded in 1994 in response to the growing need for transnationalism in the field of business ethics.

During the recent corporate scandals, human resource professionals appeared to have been *virtually invisible*. Some believe that HR could have done much more to diminish corporate wrongdoing and improve the corporate image. That being said, many believe that it is now the duty of the HR professional to help restore trust in organizations.[65] In fact, one of the core principles of the SHRM Code of Ethical and Professional Standards in HR Management states that "As HR professionals, we are responsible for adding value to the organizations we serve and contributing to the ethical success of those organizations."[66]

The HR manager can help foster an ethical culture, but that means more than just hanging the codes-of-conduct posters on walls. Instead, since the HR professionals' primary job is dealing with people, they must help to instill ethical practices into the corporate culture. They need to help establish an environment where employees throughout the organization work to reduce ethical lapses. The ethical bearing of those in HR goes a long way in establishing the credibility of the entire organization. In a recent study, in companies where employees believe that the HR department is effective, 62 percent of workers also believe that the organization is trustworthy. However, in companies where HR was deemed ineffective, only 8 percent of employees believe that management can be trusted. Certainly, top management must be the focal point for building trust, but HR goes a long way in maintaining trust.[67] Apparently there has been some change involving HR executives. In a survey of HR executives, 79 percent said they would blow the whistle over a legal violation at their company. Eighty-three percent said they would take strong action if they learned of a violation of professional or ethical standards.[68]

There are two areas where HR professionals can have a major impact on ethics and therefore corporate culture. These areas are corporate governance and executive compensation. HR should review and enforce organizational governance policies and implementation methods to ensure a high level of executive integrity and effectiveness. All employees should know what is ethical and unethical in their specific area of operations. It is insufficient to say that everyone should be ethical. Dialogue should be developed so that workers in different areas know what is ethical. For example, ethical questions confronting a salesperson will be different from that of research or production.

The second area HR should focus on is executive compensation. It is perhaps in the area of compensation that HR executives could have the greatest impact on corporate behavior. If top-level HR professionals know the strategic nature of the organization and know the company thoroughly they can play a major supporting role in establishing and adjusting compensation for the CEO and other top managers. Obviously, the present method of determining executive compensation is under close public examination including stock options, success-to-reward equations, and equity of separation packages. "HR can make sure that the compensation committee has relevant, fair and accurate information for decision making, in collaboration with consultants and management," says Edward Graskamp, national practice leader for executive compensation at consulting firm Watson Wyatt. HR executives must become recognized in their organizations as being able to contribute to strategic deliberations. The HR executive can provide the needed guidance and information so that informed compensation decisions can be made. It is the duty of HR professionals to promote ethical compensation practices.[69]

OBJECTIVE

Describe the professionalization of human resource management.

Professionalization of Human Resource Management

A **profession** is a vocation characterized by the existence of a common body of knowledge and a procedure for certifying members of the profession. Performance standards are established by members of the profession rather than by outsiders; that is, the profession is self-regulated. Most professions also have effective representative organizations that permit members to exchange ideas of mutual concern. These characteristics apply to the field of human resources, and several well-known organizations serve the profession. Among the more prominent are the Society for Human Resource Management (SHRM); Human Resource Certification Institute (HRCI); American Society for Training and Development (ASTD); and WorldatWork, The Professional Association for Compensation, Benefits, and Total Rewards (formerly the American Compensation Association).

Profession:
A vocation characterized by the existence of a common body of knowledge and a procedure for certifying members of the profession.

Society for Human Resource Management

The largest national professional organization for individuals involved in all areas of human resource management is the Society for Human Resource Management (SHRM). The name reflects the increasingly important role that human resource management plays in the overall bottom line of organizations. The basic goals of the society include defining, maintaining, and improving standards of excellence in the practice of human resource management. Membership consists of 175,000 professionals with more than 500 affiliated chapters within the United States and members in more than 120 countries. There are also numerous student chapters on university campuses across the country.[70] SHRM publishes a monthly journal, *HRMagazine*, and a monthly newspaper, *HR News*. A major subsidiary of SHRM, the Employment Management Association (EMA) offers in-depth information on issues addressing employment and retention issues, whereas SHRM offers a broader coverage of HR issues. EMA focuses on all these aspects of the employment process—from hiring to exit interviews and beyond.[71]

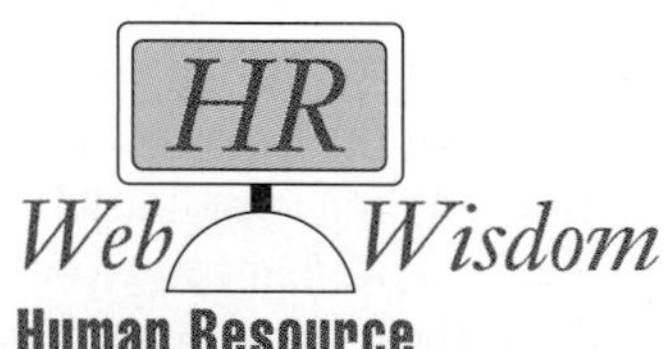

Human Resource Certification Institute (HRCI)

www.hrci.org

This Web site provides information on the Professional Certification Program in HR Management for individuals seeking to expand their formal HR training.

Human Resource Certification Institute

One of the more significant developments in the field of HRM has been the establishment of the Human Resource Certification Institute (HRCI), an affiliate of SHRM. Founded in 1976, HRCI's goal is to recognize human resource professionals through a certification program.[72] Since 1976, more than 60,000 HR professionals have been certified.[73] This program encourages human resource professionals to update their knowledge and skills continuously. Certification indicates that they have mastered a validated common body of knowledge. A number of years ago,

Wiley Beavers, a former national president of SHRM, stated that human resource certification would:

- Allow students to focus on career directions earlier in their education.
- Provide sound guidelines for young practitioners in important HR areas.
- Encourage senior practitioners to update their knowledge.

The appendix to this chapter contains the requirements to obtain certification through the Human Resource Certification Institution.

American Society for Training and Development

Founded in 1944, the American Society for Training and Development (ASTD) has grown to become the largest specialized professional organization in human resources. Its membership numbers more than 70,000, and it has more than 150 local chapters. ASTD members work in more than 15,000 multinational corporations, small and medium-sized businesses, government agencies, and colleges and universities.[74] The membership consists of individuals who are concerned specifically with training and development. The society publishes a monthly journal, *T+D* magazine. Numerous other publications are also available to help its members remain current in the field.[75]

A Global Perspective

"When In Rome, Do As the Romans Do" Does Not Work Today

The old adage, "When in Rome do as the Romans do," made ethical decisions easy. The new one, yet to be written, will make ethical decisions harder. Dennis Bakke, CEO of AES Corporation, the world's largest independent power producer, based in Arlington, Virginia, is a proclaimed "cultural imperialist." He will not lower the ethical standards for his $9.3 billion corporation in any of the 31 nations in which it owns or invests in 184 power plants. That includes countries like corruption-plagued Uganda. Recently, AES gained final approval to build a 250-megawatt hydroelectric dam on Uganda's upper Nile River. Bakke says that in a decade of project development, so far he has forbidden the paying of bribes. Outsiders hearing about the $550 million project say that resisting corruption must have been impossible. But Bakke maintains otherwise. He says he would not even approve of paying Ugandan reporters fees for writing positive stories, a routine Ugandan practice, despite heavy criticism leveled at AES for destroying the Bujagali rapids, for displacing poor farmers, and for backroom political dealing. Bakke deals regularly with an issue facing all firms that do business globally. He must decide what is ethically acceptable when home and host country practices conflict. But the dilemmas he and other CEOs handle have become much more complex and more quickly attract the media spotlight.[76]

If we believe that the nation-state has some moral responsibility," says Rushwood Kidder, president of the Institute for Global Ethics in Camden, Maine, "then we have to extend [the same to the multinational corporation] the entity that is taking the nation-state's place in more and more parts of society." John Browne, CEO of BP, feels similarly. "If globalization marks the end of sovereignty for national governments," he said in a speech at Cambridge University last year, "it should equally end any sense of splendid isolation that exists in the corporate world." The old adage that was once accepted in many quarters—"When in Rome, do as the Romans do"—has become ever more unacceptable. Anti globalization protesters have taken to the streets to remind CEOs of that. The new CEO challenge is to act like an ethical leader for society as a whole, to act before crises demand it, to engage outsiders in decision making, and to adhere to standards of behavior that locals embrace.[77]

WorldatWork: The Professional Association for Compensation, Benefits, and Total Rewards

WorldatWork was founded in 1955 as the American Compensation Association (ACA) and currently has a membership that exceeds 25,000.[78] This organization consists of managerial and human resource professionals who are responsible for the establishment, execution, administration, or application of compensation practices and policies in their organizations. The WorldatWork's quarterly journal contains information related to compensation issues. Its certification program is well known for its quality. WorldatWork offers three professional certifications to members: Certified Compensation Professional (CCP), Certified Benefits Professional (CBP), and Global Remuneration Professional (GRP).[79]

Summary

1. Describe the changing attitudes toward social responsibility and business ethics.

Apparently, socially responsible behavior pays off on the bottom line. That is the conclusion of new research based on business ethics' 100 best corporate citizens list which shows the financial performance of these companies was "significantly better" than others in the Standard & Poor's 500. With regard to ethics, most of the 500 largest corporations in the United States now have a code of ethics.

2. Describe the concept of corporate social responsibility.

Corporate social responsibility (CSR) is the implied, enforced, or felt obligation of managers, acting in their official capacity, to serve or protect the interests of groups other than themselves. It is how a company as a whole behaves toward society.

3. Explain the attempts at legislating social responsibility.

There have been three attempts to legislate social responsibility and business ethics since the late 1980s. The first, the Procurement Integrity Act of 1988, was passed after there were reports of military contracts for such things as $500 toilet seats. The second attempt occurred with the passage of the 1992 Federal Sentencing Guidelines for Organizations that outlined an effective ethics program. The third attempt at legislating social responsibility and business ethics was the Corporate and Auditing Accountability, Responsibility and Transparency Act, which focused on the accounting and financial reporting abuses in light of recent corporate scandals.

4. Explain what is meant by stakeholder analysis and the social contact.

Protecting the diversity of stakeholder interests requires answering questions regarding how you will treat the various stakeholders. Answering such questions is termed *stakeholder analysis*. The social contract is the set of written and unwritten rules and assumptions about acceptable interrelationships among the various elements of society.

5. Describe how a corporate social responsibility program is implemented.

First, a person should be assigned the responsibility for the program and a structure should be developed. Second, a review of what the company is presently doing with regard to CSR should be determined. Third, shareholders' expectations and perspectives are determined. Fourth, a policy statement is written covering CSR areas such as environmental, social, and community issues. Fifth, a set of corporate objectives and an action plan to implement the policies should be developed. Sixth, company-wide quantitative and qualitative targets and key performance indicators should be created. Seventh, communicate to stakeholders and fund managers the direction of CSR with this company. Eighth, the progress of the CSR program should be determined. Finally, the progress of the CSR program should be reported.

6. Understand the model of ethics and describe human resource ethics.

Ethics is the discipline dealing with what is good and bad, or right and wrong, or with moral duty and obligation. Ethics consists mainly of two relationships. The first element in the model is sources of ethical guidance. The strength of the relationship between what an individual or an organization believes to be moral and correct and what available sources of guidance suggest is morally correct is Type I ethics. Type II ethics is the strength of the relationship between what one believes and how one behaves. Generally, a person is not considered ethical unless the person possesses both types of ethics. Human resource ethics is the application of ethical principles to human resource relationships and activities.

7. Understand the importance of a code of ethics and describe ethics and the HR manager.
A code of ethics establishes the rules that the organization lives by. The HR manager can help foster an ethical culture.

8. Describe the professionalization of human resource management.
Several well-known organizations serve the profession. Among the more prominent are the Society for Human Resource Management (SHRM); Human Resource Certification Institute (HRCI); American Society for Training and Development (ASTD); and the WorldatWork, The Professional Association for Compensation, Benefits, and Total Rewards (formerly the American Compensation Association).

Key Terms

- **Corporate social responsibility (CSR), 26**
- **Organizational stakeholder, 28**
- **Social contract, 29**
- **Social audit, 32**
- **Ethics, 34**
- **Type I ethics, 35**
- **Type II ethics, 35**
- **Human resource ethics, 35**
- **Profession, 38**

Questions for Review

1. What has been the changing attitude toward social responsibility and business ethics?
2. What is corporate social responsibility?
3. What laws have been passed in an attempt to legislate social responsibility?
4. What is meant by the terms *stakeholder analysis* and *social contract*?
5. What are the steps that are involved in implementing a corporate social responsibility program?
6. Describe the model of ethics presented in your text. Distinguish between Type I and Type II ethics.
7. What are human resource ethics?
8. Why is it important to have a code of ethics?
9. What are the areas where HR professionals can have a major impact on ethics?
10. Define *profession*. Do you believe that the field of human resource management is a profession? Explain your answer.

An Ethical Flaw

Amber Davis had recently graduated from college with a degree in general business. Amber was quite bright, although her grades did not reflect this. She had thoroughly enjoyed school—dating, tennis, swimming—but few academic endeavors. When she graduated from the university, she had not found a job. Her dad was extremely upset when he discovered this, and he took it upon himself to see that Amber became employed.

Amber's father, Allen Davis, was executive vice president of a medium-sized manufacturing firm. One of the people he contacted in seeking employment for Amber was Bill Garbo, the president of another firm in the area. Mr. Davis purchased many of his firm's supplies from Garbo's company. After telling Bill his problem, Allen was told to send Amber to Bill's office for an interview. Amber went, as instructed by her father, and before she left Bill's firm, she was surprised to learn that she had a job in the accounting department. Amber may have been lazy, but she certainly was not stupid. She realized that Bill had hired her because he hoped that his action would lead to future business from her father's company. Although Amber's work was not challenging, it paid better than the other jobs in the accounting department.

It did not take long for the employees in the department to discover the reason she had been hired; Amber told them. When a difficult job was assigned to Amber, she normally got one of the other employees to do it, implying that Mr. Garbo would be pleased with that person if he or she helped her out. She developed a pattern of coming in late, taking long lunch breaks, and leaving early. When the department manager attempted to reprimand her for these unorthodox activities, Amber would bring up the close relationship that her father had with the president of the firm. The department manager was at the end of his rope

Questions

1. From an ethical standpoint, how would you evaluate the merits of Mr. Garbo's employing Amber? Discuss.
2. Now that she is employed, what course would you follow to address her on-the-job behavior?
3. Do you feel that a firm should have policies regarding practices such as hiring people like Amber? Discuss.

HRM Incident 2

"You Can't Fire Me"

Norman Blankenship came in the side door of the office at Consolidation Coal Company's Rowland mine, near Clear Creek, West Virginia. He told the mine dispatcher not to tell anyone he was there. Norman was general superintendent of the Rowland operation. He had been with Consolidation for 23 years, having started out as a mining machine operator.

Norman had heard that one of his section bosses, Tom Serinsky, had been sleeping on the job. Tom had been hired two months earlier and assigned to the Rowland mine by the regional personnel office. He had gone to work as section boss, working the midnight to 8:00 A.M. shift. Because of his age and experience, Serinsky was the senior person in the mine on his shift.

Norman took one of the battery-operated jeeps used to transport personnel and supplies in and out of the mine and proceeded to the area where Tom was assigned. Upon arriving, he saw Tom lying on an emergency stretcher. Norman stopped his jeep a few yards away from where Tom was sleeping and approached him. "Hey, you asleep?" Norman asked. Tom awakened with a start and said, "No, I wasn't sleeping."

Norman waited for Tom to collect his senses and then said, "I could tell that you *were* sleeping. But that's beside the point. You weren't at your workstation. You know that I have no choice but to fire you." After Tom had left, Norman called his mine foreman and asked him to come in and complete the remainder of Tom's shift.

The next morning, Norman had the mine personnel officer officially terminate Tom. As part of the standard procedure, the personnel officer notified the regional personnel director that Tom had been fired and gave the reasons for firing him. The regional personnel director asked the personnel officer to get Norman on the line. The regional personnel director said, "Norm, you know Tom is Eustus Frederick's brother-in-law, don't you?" Frederick was a regional vice president. "No, I didn't know that," replied Norman, "but it doesn't matter. The rules are clear. I wouldn't care if he was Frederick's son."

The next day, the regional personnel director showed up at the mine just as Norman was getting ready to make a routine tour of the mine. "I guess you know what I'm here for," said the personnel director. "Yeah, you're here to take away my authority," replied Norman. "No, I'm just here to investigate," said the personnel director.

By the time Norman returned to the mine office after his tour, the personnel director had finished his interviews. He told Norman, "I think we're going to have to put Tom back to work. If we decide to do that, can you let him work for you?" "No, absolutely not," said Norman. "In fact, if he works here, I go." A week later, Norman learned that Tom had gone to work as section boss at another Consolidation coal mine in the region.

Questions

1. What would you do now if you were Norman?
2. Do you believe the personnel director handled the matter in an ethical manner? Explain.

Take it to the Net

We invite you to visit the Mondy homepage on the Prentice Hall Web site at

www.prenhall.com/mondy

for updated information, Web-based exercises, and links to other HR-related sites.

Notes

1. Beth Snyder Bulik, "Can CEOs Defend Corporate America's Image?" *Chief Executive* 180 (July 2002): 56.
2. Elizabeth Murphy, "Best Corporate Citizens Have Better Financial Performance," *Strategic Finance* 83 (January 2002): 20.
3. John Hobel, "Should Companies Have a Conscience?" *Canadian HR Reporter* (February 25, 2002): 4.
4. "Socially Responsible Funds Rank Highly with Investors," *Investor Relations Business* (January 28, 2002): 1.
5. Ellyn Spragins, "Put a Halo on Your Portfolio," *Fortune Small Business* 12 (April 2002): 84.
6. Stan Lomax, "Cooking the Books," *Business and Economic Review* 49 (April-June 2003): 3–8.
7. Joan E. Dubinsky, "Business Ethics: A Set of Practical Tools," *Internal Auditing* 17 (July/August 2002): 39–45.
8. Knight Kiplinger, "Ethics on the Ropes," *Kiplinger's Personal Finance* 56 (May 2002): 66–68.
9. Bill Leonard, "Corporate Scandals Will Slow the Pace of Executive Recruitment," *HRMagazine* 47 (October 2002): 27–28.
10. Lance Moir, " What Do We Mean by Corporate Social Responsibility?" *Corporate Governance* 1 (2001): 2.
11. Dubinsky, "Business Ethics."
12. Carroll Lachnit, "Why Ethics Is HR's Issue," *Workforce* 81 (March 2002): 10.
13. Robert C. Hazard, Jr., "Corporate Ethics, Corporate Pay and the Lodging Industry," *Lodging Hospitality* 58 (November 2002): 65.
14. Joel Schettler, "Leadership in Corporate America," *Training* 39 (September 2002): 66–77.
15. John A. Byrne, Louis Lavelle, Nanette Byrnes, Marcia Vickers, and Amy Borrus, "How to Fix Corporate Governance," *BusinessWeek* (May 6, 2002): 68.
16. Murray Weidenbaum, "Business Ethics: Everybody's Favorite Oxymoron," *Executive Speeches* 17 (April/May 2003): 15.
17. Bulik, "Can CEOs Defend Corporate America's Image?"
18. Kenneth D. Lewis, "The Responsibility of the CEO: Providing Ethical and Moral Leadership," *Vital Speeches of the Day* (October 15, 2002): 6–9.
19. Alynda Wheat, "Keeping an Eye on Corporate America," *Fortune* 146 (November 25, 2002): 44–46.
20. Rebecca Barnett, "Character Leadership," *Executive Excellence* 19 (October 2002): 20.
21. Curtis C. Verschoor, "Were Enron's Ethical Missteps a Major Cause of Its Downfall?" *Strategic Finance* 83 (February 2002): 22.
22. Marie McKendall, "Ethical Compliance Programs and Corporate Illegality: Testing the Assumptions of the Corporate Sentencing Guidelines," *Journal of Business Ethics* 37 (June 2002): 367–383.
23. Rushworth M. Kidder and Curtis C. Verschoor, "Entering the Third Age of Ethics," *Strategic Finance* 84 (October 2002): 20, 22.
24. Gerlad L. Mattman, Jr., "Sarbanes-Oxley Creates New Exposures," *National Underwriter* (November 11, 2002): 27–28.
25. New ERISA and Pension Rules Come with Sarbanes-Oxley Act," *HR Focus* 79 (October 2002): 8–9.
26. Jeffrey C. Gerrish, "Ten New Commandments for Corporate Governance," *ABA Banking Journal* 94 (November 2002): 16–20.
27. Howard Stock, "Ethics Trump Rules, Levitt Says," *Investor Relations Business* (April 7, 2003): 1.
28. Jonathan A. Segal, "The 'Joy' of Uncooking," *HRMagazine* (November 2002): 52–57.
29. Steve Bates, "Tough Reforms Suggested for Executive Compensation," *HRMagazine* 47 (November 2002): 12–14.
30. Congress' Own Corporate Scandals," *BusinessWeek* (September 30, 2002): 126.
31. Jesse F. Dillard and Kristi Yuthas, "Ethical Audit Decisions: A Structuration Perspective," *Journal of Business Ethics* 36 (March 2002): 49–64.
32. Eilene Zimmerman, "Shareholders Are Watching HR," *Workforce* 81 (October 2002): 18.
33. Susan Scharreik, "Following Your Conscience Is Just a Few Clicks Away," *BusinessWeek* (May 13, 2002): 116–118.
34. Alex Taylor III, "VW's Rocky Road Ahead," *Fortune* 128 (August 23, 1993): 64–68.
35. Adapted from the Committee for Economic Development and from Sandra L. Holmes, "Corporate Social Performance and Present Areas of Commitment," *Academy of Management Journal* 20 (September 1977): 435.
36. Quoted in Robert Bolt, *A Man for All Seasons* (New York: Random House, 1962).
37. Andreas King, "How to Get Started in Corporate Social Responsibility," *Financial Management* (October 2002): 5.
38. Myra Stark, "The Get-Real World," *Brandweek* (October 7, 2002): 16–17.
39. Arthur Gross Schaefer and Anthony J. Zaller, "Why Ethics Tools Don't Work," *Nonprofit World* 17 (March/April 1999): 42–50.
40. Adrian Henriques, "Social Audit and Quality," *Quality Focus* 4 (Second Quarter 2000): 60–64.
41. Andreas King, "How to Get Started in Corporate Social Responsibility," *Financial Management* (October 2002): 5.
42. Victor M. Parachin, "Integrity—The Most Important Trait to Cultivate," *Supervision* 63 (February 2002): 3.
43. Jeffrey Marshall, "Setting a New Route for Corporate Governance," *Financial Executive* 18 (June 2002): 32–36.
44. Ellsworth Quarrels, "Covering Ethical Cover-Ups: Media Focus on Shining CEO Stars Leaves Us in the Dark About Their Practices," *Across the Board* 39 (September/October 2002): 49–50.
45. Janet Wiscombe, "Don't Fear Whistle-blowers," *Workforce* 81 (July 2002): 26–32.
46. Kenneth D. Lewis, "The Responsibility of the CEO: Providing Ethical and Moral Leadership," *Vital Speeches of the Day* (October 15, 2002): 6–9.
47. Dubinsky, "Business Ethics."
48. Patricia Wallington, "Honestly! Ethical Behavior Isn't Easy, Just Essential. Here's How to Run an Honest Organization and Be an Ethical Leader," *CIO* (March 15, 2003): 41–41.
49. John Hobel, "Ethics, Enron and Intrigue," *Canadian HR Reporter* (June 3, 2002): 4.

50. Steve Bates, "Corporate Ethics Important to Today's Job Seekers," *HRMagazine* 47 (November 2002): 12.
51. Rodd Zolkos, "Unethical Behavior Tarnishes Image of Insurance Industry," *Business Insurance* (November 18, 2002): 20E.
52. Byrne, Lavelle, Byrnes, Vickers, and Borrus, "How to Fix Corporate Governance," 71.
53. Robert C. Hazard, Jr., "Corporate Ethics, Corporate Pay and the Lodging Industry," *Lodging Hospitality* 58 (November 2002): 65.
54. Compensation Expert: More Action Needed," *Financial Executive* 18 (November 2002): 10.
55. Byrne, Lavelle, Byrnes, Vickers, and Borrus, "How to Fix Corporate Governance," 70.
56. http://www.shrm.org/ethics/code-of-ethics.asp, August 1, 2003.
57. Samuel A. DiPiazza, "Ethics In Action," *Executive Excellence* 19 (January 2002): 15–16.
58. Peter de Jager, "Ethics: Good, Evil, and Moral Duty," *Information Management Journal* (September/October 2002): 82–85.
59. Peter R. Kensicki, "Create Your Own Ethical Statement," *National Underwriter* (October 21, 2002): 33–34.
60. Ethical Corporate Behavior Begins With a Code of Conduct," *HR Focus* 79 (July 2002): 8–9.
61. Ben Chapman, "Kickback Controversy," *Successful Meetings* 52 (April 2003): 17.
62. Ibid.
63. Judith Scott, Debora Gilliard, and Richard Scott, "Eliminating Bribery as a Transnational Marketing Strategy," *International Journal of Commerce & Management* 12 (2002): 1.
64. Debbie Phillips-Donaldson, "Corporate Ethics Rule," *Quality Progress* 36 (April 2003): 6.
65. "Will HR Lead in Developing Corporate Ethics Programs?" *HR Focus* 80 (January 2003): 8–9.
66. Susan Meisinger, "Trust in the Top," *HRMagazine* 47 (October 2002): 8.
67. Shari Caudron, "Rebuilding Employee Trust," *Workforce* 81 (October 2002): 28–34.
68. Steve Bates, "HR Seen as Willing to 'Blow the Whistle'," *HRMagazine* 48 (January 2003): 14–16.
69. Meisinger, "Trust in the Top."
70. http://www.shrm.org/about/, August 1, 2003.
71. http://www.shrm.org/ema/faqs/faqs.htm, August 1, 2003
72. Details of the HRCI are shown in the Appendix to this chapter.
73. http://www.hrci.org/about/history.html, August 1, 2003.
74. http://www.astd.org/virtual_community/about_astd/index.html, August 1, 2003.
75. http://www1.astd.org/publications/, August 1, 2003.
76. http://www.WorldatWork.org, August 1, 2003.
77. http://www.WorldatWork.org, August 1, 2003.
78. Bill Birchard, "Global Profits, Ethical Perils," *Chief Executive* 179 (June 2002): 48–54.
79. Ibid.

APPENDIX CHAPTER 2 Human Resource Certification Institute (HRCI)

PROFESSIONAL CERTIFICATION

The Human Resource Certification Institute (HRCI) is an affiliate of the Society for Human Resource Management (SHRM). Since its founding in 1976, HRCI has granted certification to many HR professionals. Today, more than 60,000 HR professionals are PHR or SPHR certified through the Institute.

EXAM OVERVIEW

There are two levels of certification, the Professional in Human Resources (PHR) and the Senior Professional in Human Resources (SPHR). Both exams are generalist (i.e., they assess all the functional areas of the HR field) but differ in terms of focus and the cognitive level of questions. PHR questions tend to be at an operational/technical level. SPHR questions tend to be more at the strategic and/or policy level.

Test questions on both exams reflect the most recently published test specifications. The exams are multiple-choice and consist of 200 scoreable questions plus 25 pre-test questions randomly distributed throughout the exam (total of 225 questions). Each question lists four possible answers, only one of which is correct or "the best possible answer." The answer to each question can be derived independently of the answer to any other question. Four hours are allotted to complete the exam.

Pre-test questions are not counted in scoring. They are, however, essential in building the PHR and SPHR item (or test question) banks and are on the exam to statistically assess their difficulty level and effectiveness at discriminating between candidates who meet the passing standard and those who do not. The information gathered in the pre-test process determines whether or not the question will be included on a future exam. Pre-test questions are indistinguishable from scoreable questions.

Questions represent the following functional areas in HR. The percentages indicate the extent to which each functional area is emphasized at either exam level.

	PHR	SPHR
Strategic Management	12%	26%
Workforce Planning and Employment	26%	16%
Human Resource Development	15%	13%
Compensation and Benefits	20%	16%
Employee and Labor Relations	21%	24%
Occupational Health, Safety and Security	6%	5%

Exams are designed to reflect the percentages listed above and are reviewed by a panel of certified professionals with subject matter expertise to ensure that the questions are up-to-date and reflect the published test specifications.

ELIGIBILITY

PHR and SPHR certification is intended for HR professionals who have at least two years of exempt-level HR work experience. To be eligible to take either exam, candidates must demonstrate that:

- At least 51 percent of their daily activities are within the human resource function.
- Those activities are at the exempt-level as defined under the Fair Labor Standards Act (FLSA).

The exams reflect today's HR practices. Although two years of exempt-level HR work experience need not be current or sequential, the more recent the experience the more likely it will

[1]*Used with the permission of the Human Resource Certification Institute.*

coincide with the exam's content. HRCI also offers a special student/recent graduate category. For more information about taking the exam as a student/recent graduate, please visit the HRCI homepage at www.hrci.org

To qualify for either exam, candidates must demonstrate work experience in an exempt-level HR position. The Fair Labor Standards Act (FLSA) and its amendments define "Exempt." All managers and supervisors have some HR responsibilities as part of their jobs, but it is generally not the dominant work function on a daily basis and therefore would not make them eligible to take the exam.

In the HR field, exempt-level positions are categorized as:

- HR practitioners (those whose job duties are normally found in the typical HR function).
- HR educators (those whose principal areas of instruction are in the HR field in an accredited institution of higher learning).
- HR researchers (those whose research activities are restricted primarily to the HR field).
- HR consultants (those whose consulting activities are primarily in the HR field).

CHOOSING THE APPROPRIATE EXAM LEVEL

With this in mind, HRCI strongly recommends that PHR candidates have two to four years of exempt-level HR work experience and SPHR candidates have six to eight years of exempt-level HR work experience.

CHOOSING AN EXAM LEVEL	PHR	SPHR
Minimum required exempt-level HR experience	2 YEARS	2 YEARS
Recommended exempt-level HR experience	2–4 YEARS	6–8 YEARS

RECERTIFICATION

Passing the PHR or SPHR exam means that you have demonstrated mastery of the HR body of knowledge. This is just the first step, however. The HR field is constantly changing and challenges HR professionals to stay abreast of key issues and increased workplace demands. Recertification is the means by which certified professionals demonstrate their currency and maintain their professional edge. Recertification is required every three years by the expiration date of your current recertification cycle (indicated on passing candidates' certificates). PHR and SPHR certified professionals can recertify by either participating in sixty (60) contact hours of updating HR experience and/or professional development activities or by successfully retesting. For more information about recertification through professional development opportunities, please visit the HRCI home page at www.hrci.org/recertification.

CHAPTER OBJECTIVES

After completing this chapter, students should be able to

1. Describe the projected future diverse workforce.
2. Describe diversity and diversity management.
3. Explain the various components of the present diverse workforce.
4. Identify the major laws affecting equal employment opportunity.
5. Explain presidential Executive Orders 11246 and 11375.
6. Identify some of the major Supreme Court decisions that have had an impact on equal employment opportunity.
7. Describe the Equal Employment Opportunity Commission.
8. Explain the purpose of the *Uniform Guidelines on Employee Selection Procedures.*
9. Explain adverse impact.
10. Describe the *Uniform Guidelines* related to sexual harassment, national origin, and religion.
11. Explain affirmative action programs.

CHAPTER 3

Workforce Diversity, Equal Employment Opportunity, and Affirmative Action

HRM IN *Action:*

The Projected Future Diverse Workforce

OBJECTIVE

Describe the projected future diverse workforce.

Diversity aims to create workforces that mirror the populations and customers that organizations serve.[1] R. Roosevelt Thomas Jr., president of the American Institute for Managing Diversity, clarified some misconceptions about diversity in corporate America when he said, "People vary along an infinite number of possibilities." Thomas also believes, "They vary according to race and gender, but they also vary according to age, sexual orientation, and when they joined the company. Some workers are union members; some are not. Some are exempt; some are nonexempt. The variety is endless. Your definition has to be sufficiently broad to encompass everyone."[2] Many believe that a firm with a diverse workforce can have a competitive advantage.[3] Diversity has been achieved in some areas, but perhaps other areas have a way to go.[4]

In 2000, the U.S. labor force was 141 million.[5] By 2010 the civilian labor force is projected to increase by 17 million, or 12 percent, to 158 million. In the future, the U.S. workforce will become more diverse. According to the U.S. Bureau of Labor Statistics, four out of every ten people entering the workforce from 1998 to 2008 will be members of minority groups.[6] White, non-Hispanic persons will continue to make up a decreasing share of the labor force. Hispanics, non-Hispanic blacks, Asian, and other ethnic groups are projected to account for an increasing share by 2010. By 2010, for the first time, Hispanics will constitute a greater share of the labor force than will blacks. The numbers of men and women in the labor force will grow, but the number of men will grow at a slower rate than the number of women. As a result, men's share of the labor force is expected to decrease while women's share is expected to increase.[7] The youth labor force, aged 16 to 24, is expected to increase its share, growing more rapidly than the overall labor force. The large group, 25 to 54 years old, is projected to decline by 2010. Workers 55 and older are projected to increase between 2000 and 2010, due to the aging of the baby-boom generation.[8] The labor force now includes more women and older persons than ever before. The Bureau of Labor Statistics predicts that by the year 2010, the

SHRM HR Links

www.shrm.org/hrlinks/default.asp

This SHRM Web site provides numerous links related to diversity and legal issues.

median age of the labor force will be over 40, women will make up nearly half of the workforce (48 percent), and they will be the majority (59 percent) of the new additions to the labor force.[9]

Employees with disabilities are being included in increasing numbers. Many immigrants from developing areas, especially Southeast Asia and Latin America, have joined the labor force. The challenge for managers in the coming decades will be to recognize that people with common, but different characteristics from the mainstream, often think, act, learn, and communicate differently. Because every person, culture, and business situation is unique, there are no simple rules for managing diversity, but diversity experts say that employers need to develop patience, open-mindedness, acceptance, and cultural awareness. Only by such measures can productivity be maximized.

Workforce Diversity

www.doi.gov/diversity/

This government Web site provides current diversity news.

OBJECTIVE

Describe diversity and diversity management.

First, we described the projected future diverse workforce. Then we describe diversity and diversity management and explain the various components of the present diverse workforce. But, developing this diverse workforce did not just happen. Major laws, executive orders, and Supreme Court decisions have had a major impact in formulating this new work environment. Therefore, the second part of this chapter provides an overview of the major EEO legislation that has impacted human resource management and helped to create this diverse workforce. Toward this end, we discuss the significant equal employment opportunity laws affecting human resource management. Then, we describe the importance of presidential Executive Orders 11246 and 11375. Next, we review significant Supreme Court decisions and describe the Equal Employment Opportunity Commission. We then discuss the *Uniform Guidelines on Employee Selection Procedures* and address the issues of adverse impact, and additional guidelines. We devote the remainder of this chapter to affirmative action programs.

Diversity and Diversity Management

Diversity:
Any perceived difference among people: age, functional specialty, profession, sexual orientation, geographic origin, lifestyle, tenure with the organization, or position.

Diversity management:
Ensuring that factors are in place to provide for and encourage the continued development of a diverse workforce by melding these actual and perceived differences among workers to achieve maximum productivity.

Diversity refers to any perceived difference among people: age, race, religion, functional specialty, profession, sexual orientation, geographic origin, lifestyle, tenure with the organization, or position, and any other perceived difference.[10] Diversity is more than equal employment and affirmative action,[11] a topic to be discussed later in this chapter. **Diversity management** is ensuring that factors are in place to provide for and encourage the continued development of a diverse workforce by melding these actual and perceived differences among workers to achieve maximum productivity.[12] Diversity management involves creating a supportive culture where all employees can be effective.[13] In creating this culture it is important that top management strongly support workplace diversity as a company goal and include diversity initiatives in their companies' business strategies.[14] It has grown out of the need for organizations to recognize the changing workforce and other social pressures that often result.[15] Diversity is more than being politically correct; it is about fostering a culture that values individuals and their wide array of needs and contributions.[16] Components that combine to make up the diverse workforce will be discussed next.

 OBJECTIVE

Explain the various components of the present diverse workforce.

Single Parents and Working Mothers

The number of single-parent households in the United States is growing.[17] Although the divorce rate peaked in the early 1980s,[18] the number of divorces remains around 50 percent. Often, one or more children are involved. Of course, there are always widows and widowers who have children, and there are some men and women who choose to raise children outside of wedlock.

According to *Workforce*, breakdowns in primary child-care arrangements cost U.S. companies more than $3 billion in lost productivity each year.[19] Traditionally, child-care needs were viewed as being outside the realm of the business world, a responsibility workers had to bear and manage alone. This situation was particularly difficult for single parents, but even working-parent couples often could not afford a full-time, live-in housekeeper. For many workers, child care has been managed with the help of family or friends. The need for alternative arrangements is evidenced by the fact that in 1950, only 12 percent of women with children under age six were in the labor force. However, today 71 percent of mothers work.[20]

Many women who formerly remained at home to care for children and the household now need and want to work outside the home. If this valuable segment of the workforce is to be effectively utilized, organizations must fully recognize the importance of addressing work/family issues. Business has begun to see that providing child-care services and workplace flexibility may influence workers' choice of employers. At SAS Institute Inc., one of the world's largest private software company, the company's 4,000 employees bring 700 children to day care each day and next year the same children will be able to enroll in SAS kindergarten.[21] Some companies provide joint day-care service in the same building where the offices are. Other companies, such as IBM, provide day-care referral services. In an AFL-CIO poll of its members, almost 80 percent of men as well as women named affordable child care a high priority.[22] More and more companies provide paid maternity leave, and some offer paternity leave. Still other firms give time off for children's visits to doctors, which can be charged against the parents' sick leave or personal time. Managers need to be sensitive to the needs of working parents. At times, management also needs to be creative in accommodating this most valuable segment of the workforce.

HR Web Wisdom

DOL Women's Bureau

www.dol.gov/wb/

This government Web site provides information regarding women in business.

Women in Business

Numerous factors have contributed to the growth and development of the U.S. labor force. However, nothing has been more prominent than the rise in the number of women in the labor force.[23] Therefore, the base of building a diverse workforce rests on an employer's ability to attract and retain females.[24] The number of women in the labor force rose from 18 million in 1950 to 66 million in 2000, an annual growth rate of 2.6 percent.[25] Women represent 11.9 percent of corporate officers (1,386 out of 11,681) at America's 500 largest companies.[26] However, the number of women in entry- and mid-level managerial positions has risen from 34 percent in 1983 to 46 percent in 1998, meaning many more women are in the pipeline to executive spots.There are more than nine million women-owned businesses, up from 400,000 in 1972.[27]

Because of the number of women who are entering the workforce, there is an increasing number of nontraditional households in the United States. These households include those headed by single parents and those in which both partners work full time.

Workers of Color

Workers of color (including Hispanics, African Americans, and Asians) are at times stereotyped. They may encounter misunderstandings and expectations based on ethnic or cultural differences. Members of ethnic or racial groups are socialized within their particular cultures. Many are socialized as members of two cultural groups—the dominant culture and their racial or ethnic culture. Ella Bell, professor of organizational behavior at MIT, refers to this dual membership as *biculturalism*. In her study of African-American women, Bell identifies the stress of coping with membership in two cultures simultaneously as *bicultural stress*. She indicates that role conflict, competing roles from two cultures, and role overload, too many expectations to comfortably fulfill, are common characteristics of bicultural stress. Although these issues can be applied to other minority groups, they are particularly intense for women of color. This is because this group experiences dynamics affecting *both* minorities and women.[28]

Socialization in one's culture of origin can lead to misunderstandings in the workplace. This is particularly true when the manager relies solely on the cultural norms of the majority group. According to these norms, within the American culture it is acceptable, even considered positive, to publicly praise an individual for a job well done. However, in cultures that place primary value on group harmony and collective achievement, this method of rewarding an employee may cause emotional discomfort. Some employees feel that, if praised publicly, they will lose face within their group.

Older Workers

It is estimated that by the year 2010 more than half of all U.S. workers will be age 40 or more and legally protected by the Age Discrimination in Employment Act (to be discussed later).[29] The population of the United States is growing older and will have a tremendous impact on workplace issues, largely because 11 percent fewer Americans were born in the two decades between 1966 and 1985 than were born in the 20 years following World War II.[30] The nation's workforce is hitting middle age, and the threat of a long-term labor shortage is developing. The growing segment of Americans 65 and older is widely considered to be one of the most important groups in the labor force.

Older workers not only provide a largely untapped hiring pool, but there are now more of them who want—or need—to work longer. Over the past year or so, many almost-retired individuals or recent retirees have had to stretch their earning years because their stock portfolios lost significant value.[31] As the workforce grows older, its needs and interests may change. Many will become bored with their present careers and desire different challenges. The *graying* of the workforce has required some adjustments. Some older workers favor less demanding full-time jobs, others choose semiretirement, and still others prefer part-time work. Many of these individuals require retraining.

People with Disabilities

One in five disabled adults has not graduated from high school, and more than 70 percent of disabled people between the ages of 18 and 55 are unemployed.[32] Common disabilities include limited hearing or sight, limited mobility, mental or emotional deficiencies, and various nerve disorders. Such disabilities limit the amount or kind of work a person can do or make its achievement unusually difficult. In jobs for which they are qualified, however, disabled workers do as well as the unimpaired in terms of productivity, attendance, and average tenure. In fact, in certain high-turnover occupations, disabled workers have had lower turnover rates.

A serious barrier to effective employment of disabled persons is bias, or prejudice. Managers should examine their own biases and preconceived attitudes toward such individuals. Many individuals experience anxiety around workers with disabilities, especially if the disabilities are severe. Fellow workers may show pity or feel that a disabled worker is fragile. Some even show disgust. The manager can set the tone for proper treatment of workers with disabilities. If someone is unsure about how to act or how much help to offer, the disabled person should be asked for guidance. Managers must always strive to treat employees with disabilities as they treat other employees and must hold them accountable for achievement.

Immigrants

Large numbers of immigrants from Asia and Latin America have settled in many parts of the United States. Some are highly skilled and well educated and others are only minimally qualified and have little education. They have one thing in common: an eagerness to work. They have brought with them attitudes, values, and mores particular to their home country cultures.

After the end of hostilities in Vietnam, Vietnamese immigrants settled along the Mississippi and Texas Gulf Coast. At about the same time, thousands of Thais fleeing the upheaval in Thailand came to the Boston area to work and live. New York's Puerto Rican community has long been an economic and political force there. Cubans who fled Castro's regime congregated in southern Florida, especially Miami. A flood of Mexicans and other Hispanics continue across the southern border of the United States. The Irish, the Poles, the Italians, and others who came here in past decades have long since assimilated into, and indeed become, the culture. Newer immigrants require time to adapt. Meanwhile, they generally take low-paying and menial jobs, live in substandard housing, and form enclaves where they cling to some semblance of the cultures they left.

Wherever they settle, members of these ethnic groups soon begin to become part of the regular workforce in certain occupations and break out of their isolation. They begin to adopt the English language and American customs. They learn new skills and adapt old skills to their new country. Human resource managers can place these individuals in jobs appropriate to their skills, with excellent results for the organization. As corporations employ more foreign nationals in this country, managers must work to understand the different cultures of their employees.

Young Persons with Limited Education or Skills

Each year, thousands of young, unskilled workers are hired, especially during peak periods, such as holiday buying seasons. These workers generally have limited education, sometimes even less than a high school diploma. Those who have completed high school often find that their education hardly fits the work they are expected to do. Many of these young adults and teenagers have poor work habits; they tend to be tardy or absent more often than experienced or better-educated workers.

Although the negative attributes of these workers at times seem to outweigh the positive ones, they are a permanent part of the workforce. Certainly, when teenagers are hired, an organization is not hiring maturity or experience; but young people possess many qualities such as energy, enthusiasm, excitement, and eagerness to prove themselves.[33] There are many jobs they can do well. More jobs can be *de-skilled*, making it possible for lower-skilled workers to do them. A well-known example of de-skilling is McDonald's substitution of pictures for numbers on its cash register keys. Managers should also look for ways to train unskilled workers and to further their formal education. Because of the training needs of unskilled workers, corporate universities have been established (a topic discussed in Chapter 7).

Dual-Career Families

www.sloan.org/programs/stndrd_dualcareer.html.

The goal of this Web site is to enhance scholarly, business, and public understanding of the interaction of family and workplace and of how the workplace can be restructured to provide more choice in work hours to meet the needs of an increasingly diverse workforce, particularly working parents and older workers.

Educational Level of Employees

Another form of diversity now found in the workplace concerns the educational level of employees. The United States is becoming a bipolar country with regard to education, with a growing number of very educated people on one side and an alarming increase in the illiteracy rate on the other. These functionally illiterate people want to join the workforce.[34] Complicating this situation even more is the estimate that more than half of the new jobs created through 2005 will require some education beyond high school.[35] Adding even more complexity is the trend in the workplace to empower

Trends & Innovations

Dual-Career Families

The increasing number of **dual-career families,** where both the husband and wife have jobs and family responsibilities, presents both challenges and opportunities for organizations. In fact, approximately half of marriages are dual career.[37] Approximately 63 percent of these marriages have children under 19 years of age.[38] In a study by the Conference Board, a New York business research group, more than 50 percent of employers said employees in their organizations have turned down relocations because of spouses' jobs and concerns about their children.[39] As a result of this trend, some firms have revised their policies against nepotism to allow both partners to work for the same company. Other firms have developed polices to assist the spouse of an employee who is transferred. When a firm wishes to transfer an employee to another location, the employee's spouse may be unwilling to give up a good position or may be unable to find an equivalent position in the new location. Some companies are offering assistance in finding a position for the spouse of a transferred employee.[40]

As the number of dual-career families increases, organizations must become even more flexible. For example, cafeteria benefit plans may need to be more flexible for today's workers. With dual-career families, only one of the spouses might pick up a health-care plan, and the second spouse might select additional vacation. Some companies are actually designing their buildings to help dual-career families. At Procter & Gamble, the company specifically incorporated into the plant a dry cleaner, a shoe repair shop, and a cafeteria that prepares food that employees can take home at night, relieving them of the need to prepare an evening meal.[41] According to one survey, more than anything, dual-career families want flexibility in their workplaces and careers. Flexible hours topped the list, with cafeteria-style benefits, family leave, customizable career paths, the ability to telecommute from a home office, formal flexible work programs, and company-supported child care, also being important.[42]

Some dual-career families have established long-distance jobs to ensure that both couples are able to advance in their careers. The shift is coming as job relocations create a mobile workforce, leaving many professional couples grappling with career tracks that diverge. More are choosing to live in separate cities so both partners can get ahead. No one knows how many couples sustain long-distance relationships, but researchers at Loyola University in Chicago estimate about 6 to 8 percent of all job relocations today result in commuting relationships.[43]

Dual-career family:
A situation in which both husband and wife have jobs and family responsibilities.

workers. Empowerment is possible because of the advanced educational level required of the new workforce; however, those with limited education will be left out of this empowerment effort.[36]

Equal Employment Opportunity: An Overview

As was seen from the above discussion, the workforce of today has become truly diverse. But, this was not the case in the early 1960s. In fact, little in the workforce of those days remotely resembles that of today. Then, few mainstream opportunities were available to women and minorities. If this were so today, our economy would certainly grind to a halt. But diversity did not just happen. Legislation (federal, state, and local), Supreme Court decisions, and executive orders have encouraged both public and private organizations to tap the abilities of a workforce that was largely underutilized before the mid-1960s. The concept of equal employment opportunity has undergone much modification and fine-tuning since the passage of the Civil Rights Act of 1964. Numerous amendments to that act have been passed, as well as other acts in response to oversights in the initial legislation. Major Supreme Court decisions interpreting the provisions of the act have also been handed down. Executive orders were signed into law that further strengthened equal employment opportunity. Over four decades have passed since the introduction of the first legislation, and equal employment opportunity has become an integral part of the workplace.

Although equal employment opportunity has come a long way since the early 1960s, continuing efforts are required. While perfection is elusive, the majority of businesses today do attempt to make employment decisions based on who is the best qualified, as opposed to whether an individual is of a certain gender, race, religion, color, national origin, age, or is disabled. Let us look now at some of the laws, executive orders, and Supreme Court decisions that had such a major impact in creating this diverse workforce.

OBJECTIVE

Identify the major laws affecting equal employment opportunity.

Laws Affecting Equal Employment Opportunity

Numerous national laws have been passed that have had an impact on equal employment opportunity. The passage of these laws reflects society's attitude toward the changes that should be made to give everyone an equal opportunity for employment. We briefly describe the most significant of these laws in the following sections.

Civil Rights Act of 1866

The oldest federal legislation affecting staffing is the Civil Rights Act of 1866, which is based on the Thirteenth Amendment to the U.S. Constitution. Specifically, this act provides that all citizens have the same right "as enjoyed by white citizens . . . to inherit, purchase, . . . hold, and convey . . . property, [and that] all persons . . . shall have the same right to make and enforce contracts . . . as enjoyed by white citizens." As interpreted by the courts, employment as well as membership in a union is a contractual arrangement. Blacks and Hispanics are covered by this act if they are discriminated against on the basis of race. Until 1968, it was assumed that the act was applicable only when action by a state or state agency, and not by private parties, was involved. That year the Supreme Court overruled this assumption and broadened the interpretation of the act to cover all contractual arrangements. There is no statute of limitation to the act as evidenced by the fact that it continues to be used today in race discrimination in housing cases.[44]

EEOC

www.eeoc.gov

This government Web site is the home page for the Equal Employment Opportunity Commission.

Title VII of the Civil Rights Act of 1964—Amended 1972

The statute that has had the greatest impact on human resource management is Title VII of the Civil Rights Act of 1964, as amended by the Equal Employment Act of 1972. Under Title VII, it is illegal for an employer to discriminate in hiring, firing, promoting, compensating, or in terms, conditions, or privileges of employment on the basis of race, color, sex, religion, or national origin.[45]

Title VII covers employers engaged in or affecting interstate commerce who have 15 or more employees for each working day in each of 20 calendar weeks in the current or preceding calendar year. Also included in the definition of employers are state and local governments, schools, colleges, unions, and private employment agencies that procure employees for an employer with 15 or more employees.

Three notable exceptions to discrimination as covered by Title VII are bona fide occupational qualifications (BFOQs), seniority and merit systems, and testing and educational requirements. According to the act it is not:

> *an unlawful employment practice for an employer to hire and employ employees . . . on the basis of his religion, sex, or national origin in those certain instances where religion, sex, or national origin is a bona fide occupational qualification reasonably necessary to the normal operation of the particular business or enterprise.*

Thus, for example, religious institutions, such as churches or synagogues, may legally refuse to hire professors whose religious persuasion is different from that of the hiring institution. Likewise, a maximum-security correctional institution housing only male inmates may decline to hire females as security guards. The concept of bona fide occupational qualification was designed to be narrowly, not broadly, interpreted and has been so construed by the courts in a number of cases. The burden of proving the necessity for a BFOQ rests entirely on the employer.

The second exception to discrimination under Title VII is a bona fide seniority system such as the type normally contained in a union contract. Differences in employment conditions among workers are permitted "provided that such differences are not the result of an intention to discriminate because of race, color, religion, sex, or national origin." Even if a bona fide seniority system has an adverse impact on those individuals protected by Title VII (i.e., it affects a class or group), the system can be invalidated only by evidence that the actual motives of the parties to the agreement were to discriminate.

In the matter of testing and educational requirements, Title VII states that it is not "an unlawful employment practice for an employer to give, and to act upon, the results of any professionally developed ability test provided that such test, its administration, or action upon the results is not designed, intended or used to discriminate because of race, color, religion, sex, or national origin." Employment testing and educational requirements must be job related, and the burden of proof is on the employer when adverse impact is shown to establish that a demonstrable relationship exists between actual job performance and the test or educational requirement.

Persons not covered by Title VII include aliens not authorized to work in the United States and members of the communist party. Homosexuals are also not protected under Title VII. The courts have consistently ruled that where the term "sex" is used in any federal statute that term refers to biological gender and not to sexual preference.

The Civil Rights Act of 1964 also created the Equal Employment Opportunity Commission (EEOC) and assigned enforcement of Title VII to this agency. Consisting of five members appointed by the president, the EEOC is empowered to investigate, conciliate, and litigate charges of discrimination arising under provisions of Title VII. Additionally, the commission has the responsibility of issuing procedural regulations and interpretations of Title VII and the other statutes it enforces. The most significant regulation issued by EEOC is the *Uniform Guidelines on Employee Selection Procedures*.

Age Discrimination in Employment Act of 1967—Amended in 1978 and 1986

Age discrimination suits are now the fastest-growing category of discrimination complaints filed with the U.S. Equal Employment Opportunity Commission. According to the EEOC, age-based discrimination suits accounted for 21.5 percent of all claims filed with the agency in 2001, up from 20.0 percent the prior year, the largest increase of any category of claims. In 2001, 17,405 age discrimination claims were filed with the agency, up from 16,008 in 2000.[46] They are also the most expensive.[47] Recently, the nation's largest public retirement fund, California Public Employees Retirement System, agreed to pay a record $250 million to settle charges that it shortchanged firefighters and law enforcement officers on disability benefits because of their age.[48] As originally enacted, the Age Discrimination in Employment Act (ADEA) prohibited employers from discriminating against individuals who were 40 to 65 years old. The 1978 amendment provided protection for individuals who were at least 40, but less than 70 years old. In a 1986 amendment, employer discrimination against anyone over 40 years old became illegal. The EEOC is responsible for administering this act.

The act pertains to employers who have 20 or more employees for 20 or more calendar weeks (either in the current or preceding calendar year); unions with 25 or more members; employment agencies; and federal, state, and local government subunits. The Supreme Court continues to refine the law. An exception was created when the Supreme Court ruled that states cannot be sued for violating a federal age discrimination law. State employees claimed in their suit that a state Board of Regents' failure to adjust professors' and librarians' salaries was aimed at them, since it had a *disproportionate impact* on those over 40. An appeals court eventually rejected that claim, citing the state's sovereign immunity. The Supreme Court decision affirmed the appeal.[49]

Enforcement procedures begins when a charge is filed, but the EEOC can review compliance even if no charge is filed. The Age Discrimination in Employment Act differs from Title VII of the Civil Rights Act in providing for a trial by jury and carrying a possible criminal penalty for violation of the act. The trial-by-jury provision is important because juries are thought to have great sympathy for older people who may have been discriminated against. The criminal penalty provision means that a person may receive more than lost wages if discrimination is proved. The 1978 amendment also makes class action suits possible.

The Older Workers Benefit Protection Act (OWBPA), an amendment to the Age Discrimination in Employment Act, prohibits discrimination in the administration of benefits on the basis of age, but also permits early retirement incentive plans as long as they are voluntary.[50] The act establishes wrongful termination waiver requirements as a means of protecting older employees by ensuring that fully informed and willful personnel make that waiver acceptance.[51]

Age can actually be a bona fide occupational qualification where it is reasonably necessary to the essence of the business, and the employer has a rational or factual basis for believing that all, or substantially all, people within the age class would not be able to perform satisfactorily. In 1997, the U.S. Federal Court of Appeals ruled that the Federal Aviation Administration adequately explained its longstanding rule that it can force pilots to retire at age 60. The age 60 rule was first imposed in 1959 and had long been controversial.[52]

This ruling supported the 1974 Seventh Circuit Court decision that Greyhound did not violate the ADEA when it refused to hire persons 35 years of age or older as intercity bus drivers. Again, the likelihood of risk or harm to its passengers was involved. Greyhound presented evidence concerning degenerative physical and sensory changes that humans undergo at about age 35 that have a detrimental effect upon driving skills, and that the changes are not detectable by physical tests.[53]

Rehabilitation Act of 1973

The Rehabilitation Act prohibits discrimination against disabled workers who are employed by certain government contractors and subcontractors and organizations that receive federal grants in excess of $2,500. Individuals are considered disabled if they have a physical or mental impairment that substantially limits one or more major life activities or if they have a record of such impairment. Protected under the act are diseases and conditions such as epilepsy, cancer, cardiovascular disorders, AIDS, blindness, deafness, mental retardation, emotional disorders, and dyslexia.

There are two primary levels of the act. All federal contractors or subcontractors exceeding the $2,500 base are required to post notices that they agree to take affirmative action to recruit, employ, and promote qualified disabled individuals. If the contract or subcontract exceeds $50,000, or if the contractor has 50 or more employees, the employer must prepare a written affirmative action plan for review by the Office of Federal Contract Compliance Programs (OFCCP), which administers the act. In it, the contractor must specify that reasonable steps are being taken to hire and promote disabled persons.

In a recent interpretation of Section 8 of the Rehabilitation Act, federal technology buyers are forced to think about people who are blind, deaf, paralyzed, or have other disabilities before they buy software, computers, printers, copiers, fax machines, kiosks, telecommunications devices, or video and multimedia products. Federal Web site designers also have to make their sites accessible to disabled users, and anyone in government who develops or maintains technology products has to make sure those technologies are accessible.[54] Thus far, federal law exempts corporate America from complying with the guidelines. However, companies wanting to obtain government business must fully comply.[55]

Pregnancy Discrimination Act of 1978

Passed as an amendment to Title VII of the Civil Rights Act, the Pregnancy Discrimination Act prohibits discrimination in employment based on pregnancy, childbirth, or related medical conditions. The basic principle of the act is that women affected by pregnancy and related conditions must be treated the same as other applicants and employees on the basis of their ability or inability to work.[56] A woman is therefore protected against such practices as being fired or refused a job or promotion merely because she is pregnant or has had an abortion. She usually cannot be forced to take a leave of absence as long as she can work. If other employees on disability leave are entitled to return to their jobs when they are able to work again, so too are women who have been unable to work because of pregnancy. Also, passing over a person for promotion while she is pregnant may be a violation of the Act.[57]

The same principle applies in the benefits area, including disability benefits, sick leave, and health insurance. A woman unable to work for pregnancy-related reasons is entitled to disability benefits or sick leave on the same basis as employees unable to work for medical reasons. Also, any health insurance provided must cover expenses for pregnancy-related conditions on the same basis as expenses for other medical conditions. However, health insurance for expenses arising from an abortion is not required except where the life of the mother would be endangered if the fetus were carried to term or where medical complications have arisen from an abortion.

In a class action suit originally filed in 1978, but not settled until July 1991, American Telephone & Telegraph Company (AT&T) agreed to settle a pregnancy discrimination suit with the EEOC for $66 million. This suit was the largest cash recovery in the agency's history and involved more than 13,000 then-present and former female AT&T workers. The 1978 suit charged that Western Electric required pregnant workers to leave their jobs at the end of their sixth month of pregnancy, denied them seniority credit, and refused to guarantee them a job when they returned.[58]

Immigration Control Acts

Some researchers place the number of illegal immigrants at up to 11 million.[59] It is because of this that two immigration control acts are discussed as related to human resource management. These are the Immigration Reform and Control Act of 1986 and the Illegal Immigration Reform and Immigrant Responsibility Act of 1996.

Immigration Reform and Control Act. The 1986 Immigration Reform and Control Act (IRCA) granted amnesty to approximately 1.7 million long-term unauthorized workers in an effort to bring them "out of the shadows" and improve their labor market opportunities.[60] It also established criminal and civil sanctions against employers who knowingly hire unauthorized aliens. The act also makes unlawful the hiring of anyone unless the person's employment authorization and identity are verified. When dealing with the national origin provision of the Civil Rights Act, IRCA reduces the threshold coverage from 15 to 4 employees. The effect of this extension of the 1964 law is to curtail hiring actions of some businesses. They often choose to hire only U.S. citizens and, thereby, avoid any potential violation of IRCA. However, many foreign nationals are in this country legally (many are legal immigrants awaiting citizenship); refusing to hire them would violate their civil rights.[61]

Illegal Immigration Reform and Immigrant Responsibility Act. The Illegal Immigration Reform and Immigrant Responsibility Act was signed into law in 1996.[62] The legislation was passed partly in response to the fact that at least one of the terrorists who blew up the World Trade Center in 1993, killing six people and wounding 1,000, had legally entered on a student visa.[63] The law places severe limitations on persons who come to the United States and remain in the country longer than permitted by their visas and/or persons who violate their nonimmigrant status. Anyone unlawfully present in the United States for 180 days, but less than one year, will be subject to a three-year ban for admission to the United States. Anyone unlawfully present in the United States for one year or more is subject to a ten-year ban from admission to the United States. There are certain exceptions, however, such as extreme hardship.[64]

Americans with Disabilities Act

The Americans with Disabilities Act (ADA), passed in 1990, prohibits discrimination against *qualified individuals with disabilities*.[65] The ADA prohibits discrimination in all employment practices, including job application procedures, hiring, firing, advancement, compensation, training; and other terms, conditions, and privileges of employment. It applies to recruitment, advertising, tenure, layoffs, leaves, fringe benefits, and all other employment-related activities. The employment provisions apply to private employers, state and local governments, employment agencies, and labor unions. Persons discriminated against because they have a known association or relationship with a disabled individual are also protected. Employers with 15 or more employees are covered.

The ADA defines an *individual with a disability* as a person who has, or is regarded as having, a physical or mental impairment that substantially limits one or more major life activities, and has a record of such an impairment, or is regarded as having such an impairment. However, the Supreme Court ruled that people with correctable physical limitations, like poor eyesight or high blood pressure, may not seek the protection of the Americans with Disabilities Act. The ruling means more than 100 million Americans with correctable impairments are not covered by anti-discrimination law.[66] In the recent *Toyota Motor Manufacturing, Kentucky, Inc. v Williams* decision, the unanimous Court held that an employee failed to demonstrate a disability under the ADA based on her inability to perform certain tasks associated with her assembly line job. The Court concluded that for an employee's inability to perform certain aspects of her job to constitute a substantial impairment of the major life activity of performing manual tasks, the employee must show that the "impairments prevented or restricted her from performing tasks that are of central importance to most people's daily lives."[67]

The EEOC guidelines on pre-employment inquiries and tests regarding disabilities clarify provisions in the ADA that prohibit inquiries and medical examinations intended to gain information about applicants' disabilities before a conditional job offer. The guiding principle is to ask only about potential employees' ability to do the job, and not about their disabilities.[68] Lawful inquiries include those regarding performance of specific functions or possession of training, while illegal inquiries include those that ascertain previous medical conditions or extent of prior drug use. The ADA does not protect people currently using illegal drugs. It does protect those in rehabilitation programs who are not currently using illegal drugs, those who have been rehabilitated, and those erroneously labeled as drug users.[69]

Civil Rights Act of 1991

During 1988–1989, the Supreme Court rendered six employment discrimination decisions of such magnitude that a congressional response was provoked.[70] The result was passage of the Civil Rights Act of 1991. The act amended five statutes: (1) the Civil Rights Act of 1866; (2) Title VII of the Civil Rights Act of 1964, as Amended; (3) the Age Discrimination in Employment Act of 1967, as Amended; (4) the Rehabilitation Act of 1973; and (5) the Americans with Disabilities Act of 1990.

The Civil Rights Act of 1991 had the following purposes:

- To provide appropriate remedies for intentional discrimination and unlawful harassment in the workplace.
- To codify the concepts of *business necessity* and *job related* pronounced by the Supreme Court in *Griggs v Duke Power Co.*
- To confirm statutory authority and provide statutory guidelines for the adjudication of disparate impacts under Title VII of the Civil Rights Act of 1964. *Disparate impact* occurs when certain actions in the employment process work to the disadvantage of members of protected groups. The concept of disparate impact will be discussed later under the topic of *adverse impact*.
- To respond to recent decisions of the Supreme Court by expanding the scope of relevant civil rights statutes in order to provide adequate protection to victims of discrimination.

Under this act, a complaining party may recover punitive damages if the complaining party demonstrates that the company engaged in a discriminatory practice with malice or with reckless indifference to the law. However, the following limits, based on the number of people employed by the company, were placed on the amount of the award:

- Between 15 and 100 employees—$50,000
- Between 101 and 200 employees—$100,000
- Between 201 and 500 employees—$200,000
- More than 500 employees—$300,000

In each case, aggrieved employees must be with the firm for 20 or more calendar weeks in the current or preceding calendar year.

With regard to burden of proof, a complaining party must show that a particular employment practice causes a *disparate impact* on the basis of race, color, religion, sex, or national origin. It must also be shown that the company is unable to demonstrate that the challenged practice is job related for the position in question and consistent with business necessity. The act also extends the coverage of the Civil Rights Act of 1964 to extraterritorial employment. However, the act does not apply to U.S. companies operating in other countries if it would violate the law or the customs of the foreign country. The act also extends the nondiscrimination principles to Congress and other government agencies, such as the General Accounting Office and the Government Printing Office.

Glass ceiling:
The invisible barrier in organizations that impedes women and minorities from career advancement.

Also included in the Civil Rights Act of 1991 is the Glass Ceiling Act. The **glass ceiling** is the invisible barrier in organizations that impedes women and minorities from career advancement.[71] This act established a Glass Ceiling Commission to study the manner in which businesses fill management and decision-making positions, the developmental and skill-enhancing practices used to foster the necessary qualifications for advancement to such positions, and the compensation programs and reward structures currently utilized in the workplace. It was also to study the limited progress made by minorities and women. It established an annual award for excellence in promoting a more diverse skilled workforce at the management and decision-making levels in business. Some industries, such as hospitality, appear to have broken the glass ceiling.[72] Although the glass ceiling in corporate America may be showing a few cracks, some believe more work needs to be done to effectively break the ceiling for women and minorities.[73]

State and Local Laws

Numerous state and local laws also affect equal employment opportunity. A number of states and some cities have passed fair employment practice laws prohibiting discrimination on the basis of race, color, religion, gender, or national origin. Even prior to federal legislation, several states had anti-discrimination legislation relating to age and gender. For instance, New York protected individuals between the ages of 18 and 65 prior to the 1978 and 1986 ADEA amendments, and California had no upper limit on protected age. Recently, San Francisco voted to ban weight discrimination. The Board of Supervisors added body size to city laws that already bar discrimination based on race, color, religion, age, ancestry, sex, sexual orientation, disability, place of birth or gender identity.[74] When EEOC regulations conflict with state or local civil rights regulations, the legislation more favorable to women and minorities applies.

 **OBJECTIVE**

Explain presidential Executive Orders 11246 and 11375.

Executive Order 11246, as Amended by Executive Order 11375

Executive order (EO): Directive issued by the president that has the force and effect of law enacted by the Congress.

Affirmative action: Stipulated by Executive Order 11246, it requires employers to take positive steps to ensure employment of applicants and treatment of employees during employment without regard to race, creed, color, or national origin.

An **executive order (EO)** is a directive issued by the president and has the force and effect of a law enacted by Congress as they apply to federal agencies and federal contractors. In 1965, President Lyndon B. Johnson signed EO 11246, which establishes the policy of the U.S. government as providing equal opportunity in federal employment for all qualified people. It prohibits discrimination in employment because of race, creed, color, or national origin. The order also requires promoting the full realization of equal employment opportunity through a positive, continuing program in each executive department and agency. The policy of equal opportunity applies to every aspect of federal employment policy and practice.

A major provision of EO 11246 requires adherence to a policy of nondiscrimination in employment as a condition for the approval of a grant, contract, loan, insurance, or guarantee. Every executive department and agency that administers a program involving federal financial assistance must include such language in its contracts. Contractors must agree not to discriminate in employment because of race, creed, color, or national origin during performance of a contract.

Affirmative action, stipulated by EO 11246, requires covered employers to take positive steps to ensure employment of applicants and treatment of employees during employment without regard to race, creed, color, or national origin. Covered human

Ethical Dilemma

What Was the Real Message?

You were recently hired as information technology manager and one of your first tasks was to pre-screen candidates for an IT position with a subsidiary. After interviewing 20 candidates, you recommend an individual you consider the most qualified for upper management for the second interview. A day later, you are taken aside by a "friend" and told in vague phrases, accompanied by less ambiguous body language, that you should not waste management's time by sending certain "types" (nudge-nudge-wink-wink).[75] The intent of the message was clear, if you want to be accepted as a team player with this company, you had better get with the program.

What would you do?

resource practices relate to employment, upgrading, demotion, transfer, recruitment or recruitment advertising, layoffs or termination, rates of pay or other forms of compensation; and selection for training, including apprenticeships. Employers are required to post notices explaining these requirements in conspicuous places in the workplace. In the event of contractor noncompliance, contracts can be canceled, terminated, or suspended in whole or in part, and the contractor may be declared ineligible for future government contracts. In 1968, EO 11375, which changed the word "creed" to "religion" and added sex discrimination to the other prohibited items, amended EO 11246. These EOs are enforced by the Department of Labor through the Office of Federal Contract Compliance Programs (OFCCP).

OBJECTIVE

Identify some of the major Supreme Court decisions that have had an impact on equal employment opportunity.

Supreme Court of the United States

www.supremecourtus.gov/

This government Web site provides past and present rulings of the Supreme Court of the United States.

Significant U.S. Supreme Court Decisions

Knowledge of the law is obviously important for human resource managers; however, they must be aware of and understand much more than the words in the law itself. The manner in which the courts interpret the law is also vitally important. Also, interpretation continuously changes, even though the law may not have been amended. Discussions of some of the more significant U.S. Supreme Court decisions affecting equal employment opportunity follow.

Griggs v Duke Power Company

A major decision affecting the field of human resource management was rendered in 1971. A group of black employees at Duke Power Company had charged job discrimination under Title VII of the Civil Rights Act of 1964. Prior to Title VII, the Duke Power Company had two workforces, separated by race. After passage of the act, the company required applicants to have a high school diploma and pass a paper-and-pencil test to qualify for certain jobs. The plaintiff was able to demonstrate that, in the relevant labor market, 34 percent of the white males but only 12 percent of the black males had a high school education. The plaintiff was also able to show that people already in those jobs were performing successfully even though they did not have high school diplomas. No business necessity could be shown for this educational requirement.

In an 8–0 vote, the Supreme Court ruled against Duke Power Company and stated, "If an employment practice which operates to exclude Negroes cannot be shown to be related to job performance, the practice is prohibited." A major implication of the decision is that when human resource management practices eliminate substantial numbers of minority or women applicants (prima facie evidence), the burden of proof is on the employer to show that the practice is job related. This court decision significantly affected the human resource practices of many firms. Questions in employment procedures that should be avoided if not job related include credit record, arrest record, conviction record, garnishment record, and education. Even work experience requirements that are not job related should be avoided.

Albermarle Paper Company v Moody

In 1966, a class action suit was brought against Albermarle Paper Company and the plant employees' labor union. A permanent injunction was requested against any policy, practice, custom, or usage at the plant that violated Title VII. In 1975, the Supreme Court, in *Albermarle Paper Co. v Moody*, reaffirmed the idea that any test used in the selection process or in promotion decisions must be validated if it is found its use has had an adverse impact on women and minorities. The employer has the burden of proof for showing that the test is valid. Subsequently, the employer must show that any selection or promotion device actually measures what it is supposed to measure.

Phillips v Martin Marietta Corporation

In 1971, the Court ruled that Martin Marietta had discriminated against a woman because she had young children. The company had a rule prohibiting the hiring of women with school-age children. The company argued that it did not preclude all women from job consideration, only those women with school-age children. Martin Marietta contended that this was a business requirement. The argument was obviously based on stereotypes and was rejected. A major implication of this decision is that a firm cannot impose standards for employment only on women. For example, a firm cannot reject divorced women if it does not also reject divorced men. Neither application forms nor interviews should contain questions for women that do not also apply to men. Therefore, questions concerning *marital status* ("Do you wish to be addressed as Ms., Miss, or Mrs.?") should not be asked.

Espinoza v Farah Manufacturing Company

In 1973, the Court ruled that Title VII does not prohibit discrimination on the basis of lack of citizenship. The EEOC had previously said that refusing to hire anyone who was a noncitizen was discriminatory as this selection standard was likely to have an adverse impact on individuals of foreign national origin. Because 92 percent of the employees at the Farah facility in question were Hispanics who had become American citizens, the Court held that the company had not discriminated on the basis of national origin when it refused to hire a Hispanic who was not a U.S. citizen.

Weber v Kaiser Aluminum and Chemical Corporation

In 1974, the United Steelworkers of America and Kaiser Aluminum and Chemical Corporation entered into a master collective bargaining agreement covering terms and conditions of employment at 15 Kaiser plants. The agreement contained an affirmative action plan designed to eliminate conspicuous racial imbalances in Kaiser's then almost exclusively white craft workforce. Black craft hiring goals equal to the percentage of blacks in the respective local labor forces were set for each Kaiser plant. To enable the plants to meet these goals, on-the-job training programs were established to teach unskilled black and white production workers the skills necessary to become craft workers. The plan reserved 50 percent of the openings in the newly created in-plant training programs for black employees.

In 1974, only 1.83 percent (5 out of 273) of the skilled craft workers at the Gramercy, Louisiana, plant were black, even though the labor force in the Gramercy area was approximately 39 percent black. Thirteen craft trainees, of whom seven were black and six were white, were selected from Gramercy's production workforce. The most junior black selected for the program had less seniority than several white production workers whose bids for admission were rejected. Brian Weber subsequently instituted a class action suit alleging that the action by Kaiser and USWA discriminated against him and other similarly situated white employees in violation of Title VII. Although the lower courts ruled that Kaiser's actions were illegal because they fostered reverse discrimination, the Supreme Court reversed that decision, stating that Title VII does not prohibit race-conscious affirmative action plans. Because the company and the union voluntarily agreed to the affirmative action plan, it did not violate Title VII.

Dothard v Rawlingson

At the time Rawlingson applied for a position as correctional counselor trainee, she was a 22-year-old college graduate whose major course of study had been correctional psychology. She was refused employment because she failed to meet the minimum height and weight requirements. In this 1977 case, the Supreme Court upheld the U.S. District Court's decision that Alabama's statutory minimum height requirement of five feet two inches and minimum weight requirement of 120 pounds for the position of correctional counselor had a discriminatory impact on women applicants. The contention was that minimum height and weight requirements for the position of correctional counselor were job related. However, the Court stated that this argument does not rebut *prima facie* evidence showing these requirements have a discriminatory impact on women, whereas no evidence was produced correlating these requirements with a requisite amount of strength thought essential to good performance.

University of California Regents v Bakke

This Supreme Court decision dealt with the first major test involving reverse discrimination. The University of California had reserved 16 places in each beginning medical school class for minorities. Allen Bakke, a white man, was denied admission even though he scored higher on the admission criteria than some minority applicants who were admitted. The Supreme Court ruled 5–4 in Bakke's favor. As a result, Bakke was admitted to the university and later received his degree. But, at the same time, the Court reaffirmed that race may be taken into account in admission decisions.

American Tobacco Company v Patterson

This 1982 Supreme Court decision allows seniority and promotion systems established since Title VII to stand, although they unintentionally hurt minority workers. Under *Griggs v Duke Power Co.*, a *prima facie* violation of Title VII may be established by policies or practices that are neutral on their face and in intent, but that nonetheless discriminate against a particular group. A seniority system would fall under the *Griggs* rationale if it were not for Section 703(h) of the Civil Rights Act, which provides:

> *Notwithstanding any other provision of this subchapter, it shall not be an unlawful employment practice for an employer to apply standards of compensation, or different terms, conditions, or privileges of employment pursuant to a bona fide seniority or merit system . . . provided that such differences are not the result of an intention to discriminate because of race, color, religion, sex, or national origin, nor shall it be an unlawful employment practice for an employer to give and to act upon the results of any professionally developed ability test provided that such test, its administration or action upon the results is not designed, intended or used to discriminate because of race, color, religion, sex, or national origin. . . .*

Thus, the court ruled that a seniority system adopted after Title VII may stand even though it has an *unintended* discriminatory impact.

City of Richmond v J. A. Croson Co.

The City of Richmond adopted a Minority Business Utilization Plan requiring prime contractors awarded city construction contracts to subcontract at least 30 percent of the dollar amount of each contract to one or more Minority Business Enterprises (MBEs). The plan defined MBEs to include a business from anywhere in the country that was at least 51 percent owned and controlled by black, Spanish-speaking, Oriental, Native American, Eskimo, or Aleut citizens. After J. A. Croson Co. was denied a waiver and lost its contract, it brought suit alleging that the plan was unconstitutional under the Fourteenth Amendment's Equal Protection Clause. The Supreme Court affirmed a Court of Appeals ruling that the city's plan was not justified by a compelling governmental interest because the record revealed no prior discrimination by the city itself in awarding contracts, and the 30 percent set-aside was not narrowly tailored to accomplish a remedial purpose. The decision forced 36 states and many cities and counties to review their policies.

O'Connor v Consolidated Coin Caterers Corp.

The U.S. Supreme Court unanimously ruled that an employee does not have to show that he or she was replaced by someone younger than 40 to bring suit under the ADEA. The Court declared that discrimination is illegal even when all the employees are members of the protected age group. The case began in 1990 when James O'Connor's job as a regional sales manager was eliminated. The company did not select O'Connor, age 56, to manage either of its two remaining sales territories. He later was fired. His replacement was 40 years old. O'Connor was evidently doing so well that he earned a bonus of $37,000 the previous year. Apparently, O'Connor's new boss told him he was "too damn old" for the kind of work he was doing and that what the company needed was "new blood."

Writing for the Court, Justice Scalia stated, "The ADEA does not ban discrimination against employees because they are aged 40; it bans discrimination against employees because of their age, but limits the protected class to those who are 40 or older." Thus, it is not relevant that one member in the protected class has lost out to another member in that class, so long as the person lost out because of his or her age. The Court also found that being replaced by someone substantially younger was a more reliable indicator of age discrimination than being replaced by someone outside the protected class.[76]

Adarand Constructors v Pena

In a 5–4 decision, the U.S. Supreme Court in 1995 criticized the moral justification for affirmative action, saying that race-conscious programs can amount to unconstitutional reverse discrimination and even harm those they seek to advance. The *Adarand* case concerned a Department of Transportation policy that gave contractors a bonus if they hired minority subcontractors. A white contractor challenged the policy in court after losing a contract to build guardrails, despite offering the lowest bid. A federal appeals court upheld the program as within the proper bounds of affirmative action. The Supreme Court decision did not uphold or reject that ruling, but instead sent the case back for further review under new, tougher rules. As a result, the ruling seems to invite legal challenges to other federal affirmative action programs.[77] However, since the 2003 rulings in the case of *Grutter v Bollinger* and *Gratz v Bollinger* (discussed next) organizations are unsure how the Supreme Court will address affirmative action in the private sector.[78]

Affirmative Action—2003

In June 2003, the Supreme Court appeared to support the *Bakke* decision. In the case of *Grutter v Bollinger*, the Court ruled in a 5–4 decision that colleges and universities have a "compelling interest" in achieving diverse campuses. Schools may favor black, Hispanic, and other minority students in admissions as long as administrators take the time to assess each applicant's background and potential. Justice Sandra Day O'Connor, in writing for the majority opinion, said, "Effective participation by members of all racial and ethnic groups in the civic life of our nation is essential if the dream of one nation, indivisible, is to be realized."[79]

In another recent case, *Gratz v Bollinger*, the Court, in a 6–3 decision, said that in trying to achieve diversity, colleges and universities could not use point systems that blindly give extra credit to minority applicants.[80] The university used a point system to determine admissions criteria in its College of Literature, Science and the Arts, with minority applicants receiving bonus points. The court determined that Michigan's 150-point index for screening applicants, which gave an automatic 20 points to minority applicants, was not the proper way to achieve racial diversity.[81]

OBJECTIVE

Describe the Equal Employment Opportunity Commission.

Equal Employment Opportunity Commission

Title VII of the Civil Rights Act, as amended, created the Equal Employment Opportunity Commission that is charged with administering the act. Under Title VII, filing a discrimination charge initiates EEOC action. The EEOC continually receives complaints. In 1998, 79,591 employees filed complaints with the Equal Employment Opportunity Commission. Employers paid more than $169 million in damages to employees who won claims.[82] Charges may be filed by one of the presidentially appointed EEOC commissioners, by any aggrieved person, or by anyone acting on behalf of an aggrieved person. Charges must be filed within 180 days of the alleged act; however, the time is extended to 300 days if a state or local agency is involved in the case.

Notice in Figure 3-1 that when a charge is filed, the EEOC first attempts a no-fault settlement. Essentially, the organization charged with the violation is invited to settle the case with no admission of guilt. Most charges are settled at this stage.

Failing settlement, the EEOC investigates the charges. Once the employer is notified that an investigation will take place, no records relating to the charge may be destroyed. During the investigative process, the employer is permitted to present a position statement. After the investigation has been completed, the district director of the EEOC will issue a *probable cause* or a *no probable cause* statement.

In the event of a probable cause statement, the next step involves attempted conciliation. In the event this effort fails, the case will be reviewed for litigation potential. Some of the factors that determine whether the EEOC will pursue litigation are (1) the number of people affected by the alleged practice; (2) the amount of money involved in the charge; (3) other charges against the employer; and (4) the type of

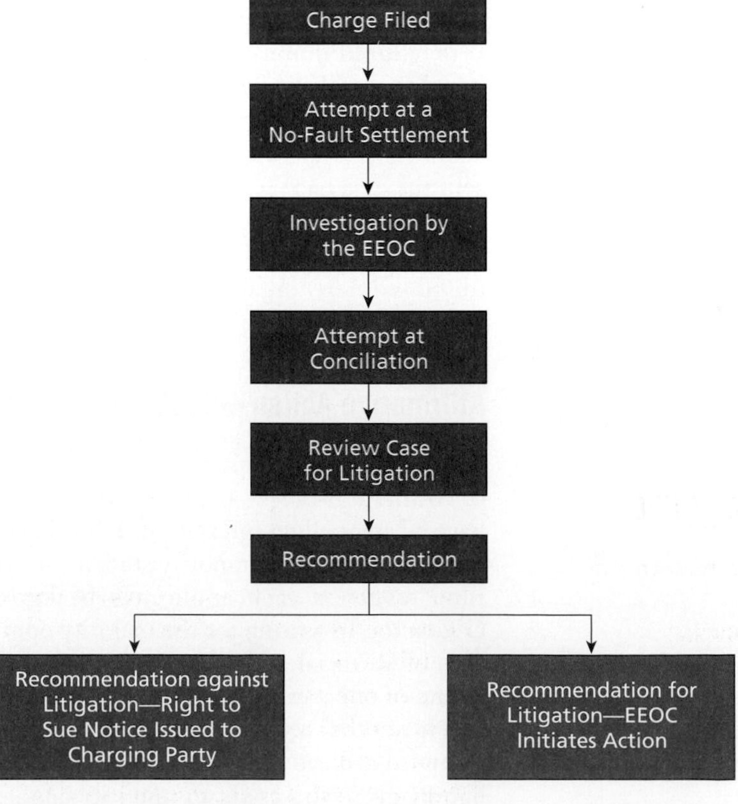

Figure 3-1 EEOC Procedure Once a Charge Is Filed

charge. Recommendations for litigation are then passed on to the general counsel of the EEOC. If the recommendation is against litigation, a right to sue notice will be issued to the charging party. The EEOC files suit in only about 1 percent of all charges.[83] Note that the Civil Rights Act of 1964 prohibits retaliation against employees who have opposed an illegal employment practice. The act also protects those who have testified, assisted, or participated in the investigation of discrimination.

Recently, the EEOC began a new strategy. Burdened with thousands of backlogged employment-discrimination cases, it is trying a new approach. The enforcement agency formally launched a voluntary mediation program in cities around the country. The goal is to resolve a significant number of disputes before the EEOC even begins its investigation by bringing the contesting parties together in a neutral forum.[84] Chair Cari Dominguez said, during her keynote address at SHRM's Employment Law and Legislative Conference in Washington, D.C., that the Equal Employment Opportunity Commission (EEOC) will implement a plan focusing primarily on prevention, strategic enforcement, and litigation.[85]

8 OBJECTIVE

Explain the purpose of the *Uniform Guidelines on Employee Selection Procedures.*

Uniform Guidelines on Employee Selection Procedures

Prior to 1978, employers were faced with complying with several different selection guidelines. In 1978, the Equal Employment Opportunity Commission, the Civil Service Commission, the Department of Justice, and the Department of Labor adopted the *Uniform Guidelines on Employee Selection Procedures*. These guidelines cover several federal equal employment opportunity statutes and executive orders, including Title VII of the Civil Rights Act, EO 11246, and the Equal Pay Act. They do not apply to the Age Discrimination in Employment Act or the Rehabilitation Act.

The *Uniform Guidelines* provide a single set of principles that were designed to assist employers, labor organizations, employment agencies, and licensing and certification boards in complying with federal prohibitions against employment practices that discriminate on the basis of race, color, religion, gender, and national origin. The *Uniform Guidelines* provide a framework for making legal employment decisions about hiring, promotion, demotion, referral, retention, licensing and certification, the proper use of tests, and other selection procedures. Under the *Uniform Guidelines*, recruiting procedures are not considered selection procedures and therefore are not covered.

Regarding selection procedures, the *Uniform Guidelines* state that a test is

> *any measure, combination of measures, or procedures used as a basis for any employment decision. Selection procedures include the full range of assessment techniques from traditional paper and pencil tests, performance tests, testing programs or probationary periods and physical, education, and work experience requirement through informal or casual interviews and unscored application forms.*

Using this definition, virtually any instrument or procedure used in the selection decision is considered a test.

9 OBJECTIVE

Explain adverse impact.

Adverse impact:
A concept established by the *Uniform Guidelines*; it occurs if women and minorities are not hired at the rate of at least 80 percent of the best-achieving group.

The Concept of Adverse Impact

Prior to the issuance of the *Uniform Guidelines*, the only way to prove job relatedness was to validate each test. The *Uniform Guidelines* do not require validation in all cases. Essentially, it is required only in instances where the test or other selection device produces an adverse impact on a minority group. Under the *Uniform Guidelines*, adverse impact has been defined in terms of selection rates, the selection rate being the number of applicants hired or promoted, divided by the total number of applicants. **Adverse impact,** a concept established by the *Uniform Guidelines*, occurs if women and minorities are not hired at the rate of at least 80 percent of the best-achieving group. This has also been called the four-fifths rule, which is actually a guideline subject to interpretation by the EEOC. The groups identified for analysis under the guidelines are (1) blacks, (2) Native Americans (including Alaskan natives), (3) Asians, (4) Hispanics, (5) women, and (6) men.

The following formula is used to compute adverse impact for hiring:

$$\frac{\text{Success rate for women and minority applicants}}{\text{Success rate for best} - \text{achieving group applicants}} = \text{Determination of adverse impact}$$

The success rate for women and minority applicants is determined by dividing the number of members of a specific group *employed* in a period by the number of women and minority *applicants* in a period. The success rate of best-achieving group applicants is determined by dividing the number of people in the best-achieving group *employed* by the number of the best-achieving group *applicants* in a period.

Using the formula, let us determine whether there has been an adverse impact in the following case. During 2003, 400 people were hired for a particular job. Of the total, 300 were white and 100 were black. There were 1,500 applicants for these jobs, of whom 1,000 were white and 500 were black. Using the adverse formula, we have:

$$\frac{100/500}{300/1,000} = \frac{0.2}{0.3} = 66.67\%$$

We conclude that adverse impact exists.

Evidence of adverse impact involves more than the total number of minority workers *employed*. Also considered is the total number of qualified *applicants*. For instance, assume that 300 blacks and 300 whites were hired. But there were 1,500 black applicants and 1,000 white applicants. Putting these figures into the adverse impact formula, we conclude that adverse impact still exists.

$$\frac{300/1,500}{300/1,000} = \frac{0.2}{0.3} = 66.67\%$$

Thus, it is clear that firms must monitor their recruitment efforts very carefully. Obviously, firms should attempt to recruit qualified individuals because once in the applicant pool, they will be used in computing adverse impact.

Assuming that adverse impact is shown, employers have two avenues available to them if they still desire to use a particular selection standard. First, the employer may validate a selection device by showing that it is indeed a predictor of success. The employer can show a strong relationship between the selection device and job performance, and that if it did not use this procedure, the firm's training costs would become prohibitive. If the device has proved to be a predictor of job performance, business necessity has been established. If the firm's selection device has not been validated, business necessity may be demonstrated in another manner.

The second avenue available to employers should adverse impact be shown is the *bona fide occupational qualification* (BFOQ) defense. The BFOQ defense means that only one group is capable of performing the job successfully. Courts have narrowly interpreted this defense because it almost always relates to sex discrimination. For instance, courts have rejected the concept that because most women cannot lift 50 pounds, all women should be eliminated from consideration for a job requiring heavy lifting.

Creators of the *Uniform Guidelines* adopted the bottom-line approach in assessing whether a firm's employment practices are discriminatory. For example, if a number of separate procedures are used in making a selection decision, the enforcement agencies will focus on the end result of these procedures to determine whether adverse impact has occurred. Essentially, the EEOC is more concerned with what is occurring than how it occurred. It admits that discriminatory employment practices that cannot be validated may exist; however, the net effect, or the bottom line, of the selection procedures is the focus of the EEOC attention.

 OBJECTIVE

Describe the *Uniform Guidelines* related to sexual harassment, national origin, and religion.

Additional Guidelines

Since the *Uniform Guidelines* were published in 1978, they have been modified several times. Some of these changes reflect Supreme Court decisions; others clarify implementation procedures. The three major changes discussed are the *Interpretative Guidelines on Sexual Harassment*, *Guidelines on Discrimination Because of National Origin*, and *Guidelines on Discrimination Because of Religion*.

Interpretative Guidelines on Sexual Harassment

One of the most fervently pursued civil rights issues today relates to sexual harassment.[86] From 1990 to 1998, the number of sexual harassment complaints filed with the Equal Employment Opportunity Commission more than doubled, climbing from 6,100 to 15,500.[87] As we previously mentioned, Title VII of the Civil Rights Act generally prohibits discrimination in employment on the basis of gender. The EEOC has also issued interpretative guidelines that state that employers have an affirmative duty to maintain a workplace free from sexual harassment. The OFCCP has also issued similar guidelines. Managers in both for-profit and not-for-profit organizations must be particularly alert to the issue of sexual harassment. The EEOC issued the guidelines because of the belief that sexual harassment continued to be a widespread problem. Table 3-1 contains the EEOC's definition of sexual harassment. As you see, there are two distinct types of sexual harassment; (1) where a hostile work environment is created, and (2) when there is a *quid pro quo*, for example, an offer of promotion or pay raise in exchange for sex.

According to these guidelines, employers are totally liable for the acts of their supervisors, regardless of whether the employer is aware of the sexual harassment act.[88] Where co-workers are concerned, the employer is responsible for such acts if the employer knew, or should have known, about them. The employer is not responsible when it can show that it took immediate and appropriate corrective action on learning of the problem.

Another important aspect of these guidelines is that employers may be liable for acts committed by nonemployees in the workplace if the employer knew, or should have known, of the conduct and failed to take appropriate action. Firms are responsible for developing programs to prevent sexual harassment in the workplace.[89] They must also investigate all formal and informal complaints alleging sexual harassment. After investigating, a firm must take immediate and appropriate action to correct the situation.[90] Failure to do so constitutes a violation of Title VII, as interpreted by the EEOC. To prevail in court, companies must have clear procedures for handling sexual harassment complaints. Typically, employers choose an impartial ombudsperson to hear and investigate charges before lawyers get involved. If the sexual harassment complaint appears legitimate, the company must take *immediate* and *appropriate action*.

There have been numerous sexual harassment court cases. In *Miller v Bank of America*, a U.S. Circuit Court of Appeals held an employer liable for the sexually harassing acts of its supervisors, even though the company had a policy prohibiting

Table 3-1 EEOC Definition of Sexual Harassment

Unwelcome sexual advances, requests for sexual favors, and verbal or physical conduct of a sexual nature that occur under any of the following situations:

1. When submission to such conduct is made either explicitly or implicitly a term or condition of an individual's employment
2. When submission to or rejection of such contact by an individual is used as the basis for employment decisions affecting such individual
3. When such conduct has the purpose or effect of unreasonably interfering with an individual's work performance or creating an intimidating, hostile, or offensive working environment

such conduct, and even though the victim did not formally notify the employer of the problem. Another U.S. Circuit Court of Appeals ruled that sexual harassment, in and of itself, is a violation of Title VII. The court ruled that the law does not require the victim to prove that she or he resisted harassment and was penalized for that resistance. The first sexual harassment case to reach the U.S. Supreme Court was the case of *Meritor Savings Bank v Vinson*. In the *Vinson* decision, the Supreme Court recognized for the first time that Title VII could be used for offensive environment claims.[91] According to the EEOC, specific actions that could create a hostile workplace include a pattern of threatening, intimidating or hostile acts and remarks, negative sexual stereotyping, or the display of written or graphic materials considered degrading. The Supreme Court decision in *Harris v Forklift Systems, Inc.* expanded the hostile workplace concept and made it easier to win sexual harassment claims. In a unanimous decision, the Supreme Court held that "to be accountable as abusive work environment harassment, conduct need not seriously affect . . . the psychological well-being or lead the plaintiff to suffer injury." No longer does severe psychological injury have to be proved. Under this ruling, plaintiffs needs to show only that their employer allowed a hostile to abusive work environment to exist.[92] In a recent Seventh U.S. Circuit Court of Appeals ruling, a company president's one-time sexual proposition to a subordinate was sufficient to constitute a hostile work environment. The decision was made in light of the president's position of significant authority and the closeness in which the individual worked.[93]

Complaints still occur all too regularly. Dial Corporation recently agreed to pay $10 million to settle a class action sexual harassment lawsuit brought by the EEOC. The move could have implications for employers around the country. The case, which involved lurid allegations about male employees' behavior at the Aurora factory, was filed on behalf of 90 female employees who worked at the plant. Some believe the settlement could move employers across the United States to take tougher steps to prevent sexual harassment.[94]

For a long time an unresolved question in employment law has been whether same-sex harassment (for example, males harassing males) is unlawful under Title VII of the Civil Rights Act of 1964. The Supreme Court, in the case of *Oncale v Sundowner Offshore Services*, held that same-sex sexual harassment may be unlawful under Title VII. The Court emphasized that Title VII does not prohibit all verbal or physical harassment in the workplace, only that which constitutes discrimination because of sex.[95] The Supreme Court decided that a plaintiff could make out a claim for sexual harassment as long as the harassing conduct was "because of sex."[96] In 1999, an El Paso jury awarded $7.3 million to shoe salesman David Gonzalez, who claimed his male supervisor sexually harassed him. The decision against Little Rock–based Dillard's Inc., department store, is believed to be one of the largest sums returned in a same-sex harassment case.[97]

Guidelines on Discrimination Because of National Origin

Both EEOC and the courts have interpreted national origin protection under Title VII as extending far beyond discrimination against individuals who came from, or whose forebears came from, a particular country. National origin protection also covers (1) marriage or association with a person of a specific national origin; (2) membership in, or association with, an organization identified with, or seeking to promote the interests of national groups; (3) attendance at, or participation in, schools, churches, temples, or mosques generally used by persons of a national origin group; and (4) use of an individual's or spouse's name that is associated with a national origin group.[98] As Table 3-2 shows, the EEOC has identified certain selection procedures that may be discriminatory.

Harassment on the basis of national origin is a violation of Title VII. Employers have an affirmative duty to maintain a working environment free from

Table 3-2 Selection Procedures That May Be Discriminatory with Regard to National Origin

1. Fluency in English requirements: One questionable practice involves denying employment opportunities because of an individual's foreign accent or inability to communicate well in English. When this practice is continually followed, the Commission will presume that such a rule violates Title VII and will study it closely. However, a firm may require that employees speak only in English at certain times if business necessity can be shown.
2. Training or education requirements: Denying employment opportunities to an individual because of his or her foreign training or education, or practices that require an individual to be foreign trained or educated may be discriminatory.

such harassment. Ethnic slurs and other verbal or physical conduct relating to an individual's national origin constitute harassment when this conduct (1) has the purpose or effect of creating an intimidating, hostile, or offensive working environment; (2) has the purpose or effect of unreasonably interfering with an individual's work performance; or (3) otherwise adversely affects an individual's employment opportunity.

Of current interest with regard to national origin is the English-only rule. Courts have generally ruled in the employer's favor if the rule would promote safety and product quality and stop harassment. For example, suppose a company has a rule that only English must be spoken except during breaks. That rule must be justified by a compelling business necessity. In *Garcia v Spun Steak*, the Ninth Circuit Court of Appeals (the Supreme Court refused to review) concluded that the rule did not necessarily violate Title VII. Spun Steak's management implemented the policy after some workers complained they were being harassed and insulted in a language they could not understand. The rule allowed workers to speak Spanish during breaks and lunch periods.[99] However, English-only policies that are not job related have been challenged and eliminated.[100]

Guidelines on Discrimination Because of Religion

The number of religion-related discrimination complaints filed with the Equal Employment Opportunity Commission (EEOC) has increased by 24 percent in the past five years.[101] Employers have an obligation to accommodate religious practices unless they can demonstrate a resulting hardship. The most common claims filed under the religious accommodation provisions involve employees objecting to either Sabbath employment or membership in or financial support of labor unions.[102] Consideration is given to identifiable costs in relation to the size and operating costs of the employer and the number of individuals who actually need the accommodation. These guidelines recognize that regular payment of premium wages constitutes undue hardship, whereas these payments on an infrequent or temporary basis do not. Undue hardship would also exist if an accommodation required a firm to vary from its bona fide seniority system.

These guidelines identify several means of accommodating religious practices that prohibit working on certain days. Some of the methods suggested included voluntary substitutes, flexible scheduling, lateral transfer, and change of job assignments. Some collective bargaining agreements include a provision that each employee must join the union or pay the union a sum equivalent to dues. When an employee's religious beliefs prevent compliance, the union should accommodate the employee by permitting that person to make an equivalent donation to a charitable organization.

 OBJECTIVE

Explain affirmative action programs.

Affirmative action program (AAP):
An approach developed by organizations with government contracts to demonstrate that workers are employed in proportion to their representation in the firm's relevant labor market.

Affirmative Action Programs

An **affirmative action program (AAP)** is an approach developed by organizations with government contracts to demonstrate that workers are employed in proportion to their representation in the firm's relevant labor market. As previously mentioned, EO 11246, as amended by EO 11375, created the need for affirmative action programs. An affirmative action program may also be voluntarily implemented by an organization. In such an event, goals are established and action is taken to hire and move minorities and women up in the organization. In other situations, an AAP may be mandated by the OFCCP. The degree of control the OFCCP will impose depends on the size of the contract, with contracts of $10,000 or less not covered. The first level of control involves contracts that exceed $10,000 but are less than $50,000. These contractors are governed by the equal opportunity clause, as shown in Table 3-3.

Table 3-3 Equal Opportunity Clause—Government Contracts

1. The contractor will not discriminate against any employee or applicant for employment because of race, color, religion, sex, or national origin. The contractor will take affirmative action to ensure that applicants are employed, and that employees are treated during employment, without regard to their race, color, religion, sex, or national origin. Such action shall include, but not be limited to the following: employment, upgrading, demotions, or transfer; recruitment or recruitment advertising, layoff or termination; rates of pay or other forms of compensation; and selection for training, including apprenticeship. The contractor agrees to post in conspicuous places, available to employees and applicants for employment, notices to be provided by the contracting officer setting forth the provisions for this nondiscrimination clause.
2. The contractor will in all solicitations or advertisements for employees placed by or on behalf of the contractor, state that all qualified applicants will receive consideration for employment without regard to race, color, religion, sex, or national origin.
3. The contractor will send to each labor union or representative of workers with which he or she has a collective bargaining agreement or other contract or understanding, a notice to be provided by the agency contracting officer, advising the labor union or workers' representative of the contractor's commitments under section 202 of Executive Order 11246 of September 24, 1965, and shall post copies of the notice in conspicuous places available to employees and applicants for employment.
4. The contractor will comply with all provisions of Executive Order 11246 of September 24, 1965, and the rules, regulations, and relevant orders of the Secretary of Labor.
5. The contractor will furnish all information and reports required by Executive Order 11246 of September 24, 1965, and by the rules, regulations, and orders of the Secretary of Labor, or pursuant thereto, and will permit access to his or her books, records, and accounts by the contracting agency and the Secretary of Labor for purposes of investigation to ascertain compliance with such rules, regulations, and orders.
6. In the event of the contractor's noncompliance with the nondiscrimination clauses of this contract or with any of such rules, regulations, or orders, this contract may be canceled, terminated, or suspended in whole or in part and the contractor may be declared ineligible for further Government contracts in accordance with procedures authorized in Executive Order 11246 of September 24, 1965, or by rule, regulation, or order of the Secretary of State, or as otherwise provided by law.
7. The contractor will include the provisions of paragraphs (1) through (7) in every subcontract or purchase order unless exempted by rules, regulations, or orders of the Secretary of Labor issued pursuant to section 204 of Executive Order 11246 of September 24, 1965, so that such provisions will be binding upon each subcontractor or vendor. The contractor will take such action with respect to any subcontract or purchase order as may be directed by the Secretary of Labor as a means of enforcing such provisions including sanctions for noncompliance: Provided, however, that in the event the contractor becomes involved in, or is threatened with litigation with a subcontractor or vendor as a result of such direction, the contractor may request the United States to enter into such litigation to protect the interests of the United States.

Source: Federal Register, 45, no. 251 (Tuesday, December 30, 1980): 86230.

Joint Reporting Committee

- Equal Employment Opportunity Commission
- Office of Federal Contract Compliance Programs (Labor)

EQUAL EMPLOYMENT OPPORTUNITY

EMPLOYER INFORMATION REPORT EEO—1

1997

Standard Form 100 (Rev. 4-92)

O.M.B. No. 3048-0007
EXPIRES 12/31/93
100-213

Section A—TYPE OF REPORT
Refer to instructions for number and types of reports to be filed.

1. Indicate by marking in the appropriate box the type of reporting unit for which this copy of the form is submitted (MARK ONLY ONE BOX).

(1) ☐ Single-establishment Employer Report

Multi-establishment Employer:
(2) ☐ Consolidated Report (Required)
(3) ☐ Headquarters Unit Report (Required)
(4) ☐ Individual Establishment Report (submit one for each establishment with 50 or more employees)
(5) ☐ Special Report

2. Total number of reports being filed by this Company (Answer on Consolidated Report only) ______

Section B—COMPANY IDENTIFICATION *(To be answered by all employers)* — OFFICE USE ONLY

1. Parent Company
   a. Name of parent company (owns or controls establishment in item 2) omit if same as label — a.

Address (Number and street) — b.

City or town | State | ZIP code — c.

2. Establishment for which this report is filed. (Omit if same as label)
   a. Name of establishment — d.

Address (Number and street) | City or town | County | State | ZIP code — e.

b. Employer Identification No. (IRS 9-DIGIT TAX NUMBER) — f.

Was an EEO–1 report filed for this establishment last year? ☐ Yes ☐ No

Section C—EMPLOYERS WHO ARE REQUIRED TO FILE *(To be answered by all employers)*

☐ Yes ☐ No 1. Does the entire company have at least 100 employees in the payroll period for which you are reporting?

☐ Yes ☐ No 2. Is your company affiliated through common ownership and/or centralized management with other entities in an enterprise with a total employment of 100 or more?

☐ Yes ☐ No 3. Does the company or any of its establishments (1) have 50 or more employees AND (b) is not exempt as provided by 41 CFR 60–1.5, AND either (1) is a prime government contractor or first-tier subcontractor, and has a contract, subcontract, or purchase order amounting to $50,000 or more, or (2) serves as a depository for Government funds in any amount or is a financial institution which is an issuing and paying agent for U.S. Savings Bonds and Savings Notes?

If the response to question C–3 is yes, please enter your Dun and Bradstreet Identification number (if you have one):

NOTE: If the answer is yes to questions 1, 2, or 3, complete the entire form, otherwise skip to Section G.

NSN 7540–00–180–6384

Figure 3-2 Equal Opportunity Employer Information Report

Office of Federal Contract Compliance Programs

www.dol.gov/esa/ofccp/index.htm

This government Web site is the homepage for the Office of Federal Contract Compliance Programs.

The second level of control occurs if the contractor (1) has 50 or more employees; (2) has a contract of $50,000 or more; (3) has contracts which, in any 12-month period, total $50,000 or more or reasonably may be expected to total $50,000 or more; or (4) is a financial institution that serves as a depository for government funds in any amount, acts as an issuing or redeeming agent for U.S. savings bonds and savings notes in any amount, or subscribes to federal deposit or share insurance. Contractors meeting these criteria must develop a written affirmative action program for each of their establishments and file an annual EEO-1 report (see Figure 3-2). Affirmative action programs require specific steps to guarantee equal employment opportunity. Prerequisite to development of a satisfactory AAP is identification and analysis of problem areas inherent in employment of

Section D EMPLOYMENT DATA

Employment at this establishment—Report all permanent full-time and part-time employees including apprentices and on-the-job trainees unless specifically excluded as set forth in the instructions. Enter the appropriate figures on all lines and in all columns. Blank spaces will be considered as zeros.

JOB CATEGORIES		OVERALL TOTALS (SUM OF COL. B THRU K)	MALE					FEMALE				
			WHITE (NOT OF HISPANIC ORIGIN)	BLACK (NOT OF HISPANIC ORIGIN)	HISPANIC	ASIAN OR PACIFIC ISLANDER	AMERICAN INDIAN OR ALASKAN NATIVE	WHITE (NOT OF HISPANIC ORIGIN)	BLACK (NOT OF HISPANIC ORIGIN)	HISPANIC	ASIAN OR PACIFIC ISLANDER	AMERICAN INDIAN OR ALASKAN NATIVE
		A	B	C	D	E	F	G	H	I	J	K
Officials and Managers	1											
Officials and Managers	2											
Officials and Managers	3											
Officials and Managers	4											
Officials and Managers	5											
Officials and Managers	6											
Officials and Managers	7											
Officials and Managers	8											
Service Workers	9											
TOTAL	10											
Total employment reported in previous EEO-1 report	11											

NOTE: Omit questions 1 and 2 on the Consolidated Report.

1. Date(s) of payroll period used:

2. Does this establishment employ apprentices?
1 ☐ Yes 2 ☐ No

Section E—ESTABLISHMENT INFORMATION (*Omit on the Consolidated Report*)

1. What is the major activity of this establishment? (Be specific, i.e., manufacturing steel castings, retail grocer, wholesale plumbing supplies, title insurance, etc. Include the specific type of product or type of service provided, as well as the principal business or industrial activity.)

OFFICE USE ONLY

g.

Section F—REMARKS

Use this item to give any identification data appearing on last report which differs from that given above, explain major changes in composition or reporting units and other pertinent information.

Section G—CERTIFICATION (*See Instructions G*)

Check one
1 ☐ All reports are accurate and were prepared in accordance with the instructions. (Check on consolidated only)
2 ☐ This report is accurate and was prepared in accordance with the instructions.

Name of Certifying Official	Title	Signature	Date

Name of person to contact regarding this report (Type or print)	Address (Number and Street)			
Title	City and State	ZIP code	Telephone Number (including Area Code)	Extension

All reports and information obtained from individual reports will be kept confidential as required by Section 709(e) of Title VII.
WILLFULLY FALSE STATEMENTS ON THIS REPORT ARE PUNISHABLE BY LAW, U.S. CODE, TITLE 18, SECTION 1001.

Figure 3-2 *(continued)*

minorities and women and an evaluation of opportunities for utilizing minority and women employees.

The third level of control on contractors is in effect when contracts exceed $1 million. All previously stated requirements must be met, and in addition, the OFCCP is authorized to conduct pre-award compliance reviews. The purpose of a compliance review is to determine whether the contractor is maintaining nondiscriminatory hiring and employment practices. The review also ensures that the contractor is utilizing affirmative action to guarantee that applicants are employed, placed, trained, upgraded, promoted, terminated, and otherwise treated fairly without regard to race, color, religion, gender, national origin, veteran status, or disability during employment. In determining whether to conduct a pre-award review, the OFCCP may consider, for example, the items presented in Table 3-4.

If an investigation indicates a violation, the OFCCP first tries to secure compliance through persuasion. If persuasion fails to resolve the issue, the OFCCP serves a

Table 3-4 Factors That the OFCCP May Consider in Conducting a Pre-Award Review

1. The past EEO performance of the contractor, including its current EEO profile and indications of underutilization.
2. The volume and nature of complaints filed by employees or applicants against the contractor.
3. Whether the contractor is in a growth industry.
4. The level of employment or promotional opportunities resulting from the expansion of, or turnover in, the contractor's workforce.
5. The employment opportunities likely to result from the contract in issue.
6. Whether resources are available to conduct the review.

notice to show cause or a notice of violation. A show cause notice contains a list of the violations, a statement of how the OFCCP proposes that corrections be made, a request for a written response to the findings, and a suggested date for a conciliation conference. The firm usually has 30 days to respond. Successful conciliation results in a written contract between the OFCCP and the contractor. In a conciliation agreement, the contractor agrees to take specific steps to remedy noncompliance with an EO. Firms that do not correct violations can be passed over in the awarding of future contracts. The procedures for developing affirmative action plans were published in the *Federal Register* of December 4, 1974. These regulations are referred to as Revised Order No. 4. The OFCCP guide for compliance officers, outlining what to cover in a compliance review, is known as Order No. 14.

The OFCCP is very specific about what should be included in an affirmative action program. A policy statement has to be developed that reflects the CEO's attitude regarding equal employment opportunity, assigns overall responsibility for preparing and implementing the affirmative action program, and provides for reporting and monitoring procedures. The policy should state that the firm intends to recruit, hire, train, and promote persons in all job titles without regard to race, color, religion, gender, or national origin, except where gender is a *bona fide organizational qualification* (BFOQ). The policy should guarantee that all human resource actions involving such areas as compensation, benefits, transfers, layoffs, return from layoffs, company-sponsored training, education, tuition assistance, and social and recreational programs will be administered without regard to race, color, religion, gender, or national origin. Revised Order No. 4 is quite specific with regard to dissemination of a firm's EEO policy, both internally and externally. An executive should be appointed to manage the firm's equal employment opportunity program. This person should be given the necessary support by top management to accomplish the assignment. Revised Order No. 4 specifies the minimum level of responsibility associated with the task of EEO manager.

An acceptable AAP must include an analysis of deficiencies in the utilization of minority groups and women. The first step in conducting a utilization analysis is to make a workforce analysis. The second step involves an analysis of all major job groups. An explanation of the situation is required if minorities or women are currently being underutilized. A job group is defined as one or more jobs having similar content, wage rates, and opportunities. Underutilization is defined as having fewer minorities or women in a particular job group than would reasonably be expected by their availability. The utilization analysis is important because the calculations determine whether underutilization exists. For example, if the utilization analysis shows that the availability of blacks for a certain job group is 30 percent, the organization should have at least 30 percent black employment in that group. If actual employment is less than 30 percent, underutilization exists, and the firm should set a goal of 30 percent black employment for that job group.

The primary focus of any affirmative action program is on goals and timetables, with the issue being how many and by when. Goals and timetables developed by the firm should cover its entire affirmative action program, including correction of deficiencies. These goals and timetables should be attainable; that is, they should be based on results that the firm, making good-faith efforts, could reasonably expect to achieve. Goals should be significant and measurable, as well as attainable. Two types of goals must be established regarding underutilization: annual and ultimate. The annual goal is to move toward elimination of underutilization, whereas the ultimate goal is to correct all underutilization. Goals should be specific in terms of planned results, with timetables for completion. However, goals should not establish inflexible quotas that must be met. Rather, they should be targets that are reasonably attainable.

Employers should also conduct a detailed analysis of job descriptions to ensure that they accurately reflect job content. Job specifications should be validated, with special attention given to academic, experience, and skill requirements. If a job specification screens out a disproportionate number of minorities or women, the requirements must be professionally validated in relation to job performance. Thus, a comprehensive job analysis program is required.

When an opening occurs, everyone involved in human resource recruiting, screening, selection, and promotion should be aware of the opening. In addition, the firm should evaluate the entire selection process to ensure freedom from bias. Individuals involved in the process should be carefully selected and trained to minimize bias in all human resource actions.

Firms should observe the requirements of the *Uniform Guidelines*. Selection techniques other than paper-and-pencil tests can also be used improperly, and thus discriminate against minorities and women. Such techniques include unscored interviews, unscored or casual application forms, use of conviction records and credit checks, and consideration of marital status, dependency, and minor children. Where data suggest that discrimination or unfair exclusion of minorities and women exists, the firm should analyze its unscored procedures and eliminate them if they are not objective and valid. Some techniques that can be used to improve recruitment and increase the flow of minority and women applicants are shown in Table 3-5.

Table 3-5 Techniques to Improve Recruitment of Minorities and Women

- Identify referral organizations for minorities and women.
- Hold formal briefing sessions with representatives of referral organizations.
- Encourage minority and women employees to refer applicants to the firm.
- Include minorities and women on the Personnel Relations staff.
- Permit minorities and women to participate in Career Days, Youth Motivation Programs, and related activities in their community.
- Actively participate in job fairs and give company representatives the authority to make on-the-spot-commitments.
- Actively recruit at schools having predominant minority or female enrollments.
- Use special efforts to reach minorities and women during school recruitment drives.
- Undertake special employment programs whenever possible for women and minorities. These might include technical and nontechnical co-op programs, after-school and/or work-study jobs, summer jobs for underprivileged individuals, summer work-study programs, and motivation, training, and employment programs for the hardcore unemployed.
- Pictorially present minorities and women in recruiting brochures.
- Include the minority news media and women's interest media when expending help wanted advertising.

Source: Federal Register, 45, no. 251 (Tuesday, December 30, 1980): 86243.

A Global Perspective

Equal Employment Opportunity

The global assignment of women and members of racial/ethnic minorities can involve legal issues, as these individuals may be protected by EEO regulations. American workers employed by American-controlled businesses operating overseas are still protected under the American employment laws.[103] Presently, it is estimated that women constitute 18 to 20 percent of the U.S. expatriate managerial workforce. Unfortunately, these gains in female expatriate participation rates have not been equally distributed worldwide.[104] There are some countries in which the sexist culture is so ingrained that women would have extreme difficulty participating on equal footing with the majority population in the workforce.

Sexual harassment is also a global problem. A disproportionate number of cross-cultural sexual harassment complaints involve perpetrators and victims from different ethnic, racial, or national origin groups. When individuals from two different cultures interact, there is a potential for sexual harassment problems. Some behaviors that violate U.S. cultural norms may not be perceived as a problem in another culture. In many Mediterranean and Latin countries, physical contact and sensuality are a common part of socializing. For example, one Brazilian senior HR executive was surprised when he was admonished for calling the women at work "girls." While this label was appropriate and acceptable in his native culture, it was insulting to American women and could contribute to a hostile or intimidating work environment by U.S. standards.[105]

Australia, Canada, the Netherlands, Sweden, and the United Kingdom are among jurisdictions that have laws specifying prohibited conduct and allowing employees to seek individual remedies. Italy, the Philippines, Taiwan, and Venezuela define sexual harassment as a criminal offense, and penalties and remedies are provided in special statutory penal codes. In Germany, Spain, and Thailand, sexual discrimination law is based on the concept of termination indemnity that allows employees to terminate their employment relationships due to discrimination or harassment. In turn, termination indemnity laws require employers to pay employees substantial severance pay if the cause of their termination is due to discrimination or harassment. In Japan, recent legislative initiatives are bolstered by U.S.-style regulations prohibiting sexual harassment.[106]

Summary

1. Describe the projected future diverse workforce.

The U.S. workforce will become more diverse by 2010.

2. Describe diversity and diversity management.

Diversity refers to any perceived difference among people: age, race, religion, functional specialty, profession, sexual orientation, geographic origin, lifestyle, tenure with the organization, or position, and any other perceived difference. Diversity management is ensuring that factors are in place to provide for and encourage the continued development of a diverse workforce by melding these actual and perceived differences among workers to achieve maximum productivity.

3. Explain the various components of the present diverse workforce.

The workforce is made up of the following: dual-career families, workers of color, older workers, people with disabilities, immigrants, young persons with limited education or skills, and employees with varying educational levels.

4. Identify the major laws affecting equal employment opportunity.

Major laws include the Civil Rights Act of 1866; Title VII of the Civil Rights Act of 1964, as Amended in 1972; Age Discrimination in Employment Act of 1967, as Amended in 1978 and 1986; Rehabilitation Act of 1973; Pregnancy Discrimination Act of 1978; Immigration Reform and Control Act (IRCA) of 1986; Immigration Act of 1990; Illegal Immigration Reform and Immigrant Responsibility Act of 1996; and the Civil Rights Act of 1991.

5. Explain Presidential Executive Orders 11246 and 11375.

By EO 11246, the policy of the government of the United States was expanded to provide equal opportunity in federal employment for all qualified persons. The order prohibited discrimination in employment because of race, creed, color, or national origin. EO 11375, which changed the word "creed" to "religion" and added sex discrimination to the other prohibited items, amended EO 11246.

6. Identify some of the major Supreme Court decisions that have had an impact on equal employment opportunity.

Major decisions include *Griggs v Duke Power Company*, *Albermarle Paper Company v Moody*, *Phillips v Martin Marietta Corporation*, *Espinoza v Farah Manufacturing Company*, *Weber v Kaiser Aluminum and Chemical Corporation*, *Dothard v Rawlingson*, *University of California Regents v Bakke*, *American Tobacco Company v Patterson*, *Meritor Savings Bank v Vinson*, *City of Richmond v J. A. Croson Company*, *Adarand Constructors v Pena*, *Grutter v Bollinger*, *Gratz v Bollinger*, and *O'Connor v Consolidated Coin Caterers Corporation*.

7. Describe the Equal Employment Opportunity Commission.

Title VII of the Civil Rights Act, as amended, created the Equal Employment Opportunity Commission. It was initially charged with administering the act.

8. Explain the purpose of the *Uniform Guidelines on Employee Selection Procedures*.

The guidelines adopted a single set of principles that were designed to assist employers, labor organizations, employment agencies, and licensing and certification boards to comply with requirements of federal law prohibiting employment practices that discriminated on the basis of race, color, religion, sex, and national origin. They were designed to provide a framework for determining the proper use of tests and other selection procedures.

9. Explain adverse impact.

Adverse impact is a concept established by the *Uniform Guidelines* and occurs if women and minorities are not hired at the rate of at least 80 percent of the best-achieving group.

10. Describe the *Uniform Guidelines* related to sexual harassment, national origin, and religion.

The EEOC has also issued interpretive guidelines that state that employers have an affirmative duty to maintain a workplace free from sexual harassment. The EEOC broadly defined discrimination on the basis of national origin as the denial of equal employment opportunity because of an individual's ancestors or place of birth or because an individual has the physical, cultural, or linguistic characteristics of a national origin group. Employers have an obligation to accommodate religious practices unless they can demonstrate a resulting hardship.

11. Explain affirmative action programs.

An affirmative action program (AAP) is an approach that an organization with government contracts develops to demonstrate that women or minorities are employed in proportion to their representation in the firm's relevant labor market.

Key Terms

- **Diversity, 50**
- **Diversity management, 50**
- **Dual-career families, 54**
- **Glass ceiling, 60**
- **Executive order (EO), 61**
- **Affirmative action, 61**
- **Adverse impact, 67**
- **Affirmative action program (AAP), 72**

Questions for Review

1. What is the expected composition of the future diverse workforce?
2. Define *diversity* and *diversity management*.
3. What are the components that combine to make up the present diverse workforce? Briefly describe each.
4. Briefly describe the following laws:
   a. Civil Rights Act of 1866
   b. Title VII of the Civil Rights Act of 1964, as amended in 1972
   c. Age Discrimination in Employment Act of 1967, as amended in 1978 and 1986
   d. Rehabilitation Act of 1973
   e. Pregnancy Discrimination Act of 1978
   f. Immigration Control Acts
   g. Americans with Disabilities Act of 1990
   h. Civil Rights Act of 1991.
5. What is a presidential executive order? Describe the major provisions of EO 11246, as amended by EO 11375.
6. What is the purpose of the Office of Federal Contract Compliance Programs?
7. What are the significant U.S. Supreme Court decisions that have had an impact on equal employment opportunity?
8. What is the purpose of the *Uniform Guidelines on Employee Selection Procedures*?
9. Distinguish between adverse impact and affirmative action programs.
10. How does the Equal Employment Opportunity Commission (EEOC) define sexual harassment?

HRM Incident 1

I Feel Great

Les Partain, supervisor of the training and development department for Gazelle Corporation, was 64 years old and had been with the firm for over 30 years. For the past 12 years he had served as Gazelle's training and development manager and felt that he had been doing a good job. This belief was supported by the fact that during the last five years he had received excellent performance reports from his boss, Bennie Helton, director of personnel.

Six months before Les's birthday, he and Bennie were enjoying a cup of coffee together. "Les," said Bennie, "I know that you're pleased with the progress our T&D section has made under your leadership. We're really going to miss you when you retire this year. You'll certainly live the good life because you'll receive the maximum retirement benefits. If I can be of any assistance to you in developing the paperwork for your retirement, please let me know."

"Gee, Bennie," said Les. "I really appreciate the good words, but I've never felt better in my life, and although our retirement plan is excellent, I figure that I have at least five more good years. There are many other things I would like to do for the department before I retire. I have some excellent employees, and we can get many things done within the next five years."

After finishing their coffee, both men returned to their work. As Bennie left, he was thinking, "My gosh, I had no idea that character intended to hang on. The only reason I gave him those good performance appraisals was to make him feel better before he retired. He was actually only an average worker and I was anxious to move a more aggressive person into that key job. We stand to lose several good people in that department if Les doesn't leave. From what they tell me, he's not doing too much of a job."

Questions

1. From a legal viewpoint, what do you believe Bennie can do regarding this situation? Discuss.
2. What actions should Bennie have taken in the past to avoid his current predicament?

HRM Incident 2

So, What's Affirmative Action?

Supreme Construction Company began as a small commercial builder located in Baytown, Texas. Until the late 1990s, Alex Boyd, Supreme's founder, concentrated his efforts on small, freestanding shops and offices. Up to that time, Alex had never employed more than 15 people.

In 1997, Alex's son Michael graduated from college with a degree in construction management and immediately joined the company full time. Michael had worked on a variety of Supreme jobs while in school, and Alex felt his son was really cut out for the construction business. Michael was given increasing responsibility, and the company continued its success, although with a few more projects and a few more employees than before. In 2002, Michael approached his father with a proposition: "Let's get into some of the bigger projects now. We have the capital to expand and I really believe we can do it." Alex approved, and Supreme began doing small shopping centers and multistory office buildings in addition to work in its traditional area of specialization. Soon, employment had grown to 75 employees.

In 2003, the National Aeronautics and Space Administration (NASA) released construction specifications for two aircraft hangars to be built southeast of Houston. Although Supreme had never done any construction work for the government, Michael and Alex considered the job within the company's capabilities. Michael worked up the $1,982,000 bid and submitted it to the NASA procurement office.

Several weeks later the bids were opened. Supreme had the low bid. However, the acceptance letter was contingent on submission of a satisfactory affirmative action program.

Questions

1. Explain why Supreme must submit an affirmative action program.
2. Generally, what should the program be designed to accomplish?

Human Resource Management Skills

Chapter 3: Workforce Diversity, Equal Employment Opportunity, and Affirmative Action

As previously mentioned in Chapter 1, a new feature to the ninth edition of *Human Resource Management* is the inclusion of a CD-ROM entitled *Human Resource Management Skills* by Mary Gowan that provides additional insight into selected HRM topics.

A Skills Module entitled *Equal Employment Opportunity and the Legal Environment* is presented to provide additional insight into topics in this chapter. The Module focuses on ensuring legal complance while hiring qualified applicants and managing employees, and addresses topics including: the *Griggs v Duke Power Company* case, disparate treatment and adverse impact, affirmative action, the four-fifths rule, *prima facie* evidence, BFOQs, and sexual harassment. Several scenarios are presented to give students realistic experience in dealing with the topics.

A test is provided at the end of the module to determine mastery of the material in the Skills Module. Also, directions are given for assignments that can be used in class or assigned as homework.

Take it to the Net

We invite you to visit the Mondy homepage on the Prentice Hall Web site at

www.prenhall.com/mondy

for updated information, Web-based exercises, and links to other HR-related sites.

Notes

1. Robert J. Grossman, "Is Diversity Working?" *HR Magazine* 45 (March, 2000): 46–50.
2. Barbara Ettorre, Donald J. McNerne, and Bob Smith, "HR's Shift to a Center of Influence" (American Management Association's 67th Annual Human Resources Conference and Exposition), *HR Focus* 73 (June 1996): 12.
3. Roderick Hudson, "Workplace Diversity a Competitive Advantage," *Business Insurance* (March 17, 2003): 14F.
4. "How to Determine Whether Your Diversity Program Is Succeeding," *HR Focus* 79 (September 2002): 9.
5. Mitra Toossi, "A Century of Change: The U.S. Labor Force, 1950–2050," *Monthly Labor Review* 125 (May 2002): 15–28.
6. Todd Campbell, "Diversity in Depth," *HRMagazine* 48 (March 2003): 152.
7. Toossi, "A Century of Change."
8. Occupational Outlook 2002–2003, www.bls.gov/oco/oco2003.htm, January 24, 2003.
9. Peter Francese, "The American Work Force," *American Demographics* 24 (February 2002): 40–41.
10. Matti F. Dobbs, "Managing Diversity: Lessons from the Private Sector," *Public Personnel Management* 25 (September 1996): 351.
11. Lin Grensing-Pophal, "Welcoming Diversity," *Credit Union Management* 25 (October 2002): 28–31.
12. "Diversity: A 'New' Tool for Retention," *HR Focus* 77 (June 2000): 14.
13. C. W. Von Bergen, Barlow Soper, and Teresa Foster, "Unintended Negative Effects of Diversity Management," *Public Personnel Management* 31(Summer 2002): 239–251.
14. "Communications, Funding, Affinity Groups Fuel Diversity Programs," *HR Focus* 80 (April 2003): 9.
15. Von Bergen, Soper, and Foster, "Unintended Negative Effects of Diversity Management."
16. Melissa Solomon, "Create Diversity in Culture, Ideas," *Computerworld* 36 (May 6, 2002): 42–43.
17. "Don't Forget the 9.8 Million Single Moms This Mother's Day; Match.Com Invites Friends and Family to 'Give a Single Mom a Break' on Saturday, May 8," *Business Wire* (April 29, 1999): 1.
18. Rose Gutierrez, "Living Arrangements and Housing Demand," *Housing Economics* 50 (June 2002): 10–13.
19. "Oh, baby! Now what?" *Workforce* 79 (June 2000): 32.
20. Catherine Arnst, "Women Work. The Support System Doesn't," *BusinessWeek* (November 4, 2002): 46.
21. Diane Brady, "Rethinking the Rat Race Technology Is Making 'All Work and No Play' a Real Possibility: How Will We Strike the Proper Balance of Work and Life?" *BusinessWeek* (August 26, 2002): 142.
22. Arnst, "Women Work. The Support System Doesn't," 46.
23. Toossi, "A Century of Change."
24. Fay Hansen, "Truth and Myths About Work/Life Balance," *Workforce* 81 (December 2002): 34–39.
25. Toossi, "A Century of Change."
26. "Few Women Corporate Officers Hold Key Line Officer Posts," *HR Focus* 77 (February 2000): 8.
27. Leah K. Glasheen and Susan L. Crowley, "More Women in Driver's Seat; But Barriers Hinder Many in Midcareer," *AARP Bulletin* (November 1999): 3.
28. Ella Bell, "The Bicultural Life Experience of Career Oriented Black Women," *Journal of Organizational Behavior* 11 (November 1990): 459–478.
29. Michael Barrier, "An Age-old Problem," *HRMagazine* 47 (March 2002): 34–37.
30. Steven Van Yoder, "Coping with the Graying Workforce," *Financial Executive* 18 (January/February 2002): 26–29.
31. "Retirees Offer New Workforce Options," *HR Focus* 79 (December 2002): 3.
32. Joel Schettler, "Equal Access to All," *Training* 39 (January 2002): 44–48.
33. Robert D. Ramsey, "Should You Hire Today's Teenagers?" *Supervision* 62 (January 2001): 8–10.
34. Patricia Buhler, "Managing in the 90s," *Supervision* 58 (March 1997): 24.
35. Laurie J. Bassi, George Benson, and Scott Cheney, "The Top Ten Trends," *Training & Development* 50 (November 1996): 28.
36. Ibid.
37. Carol Kleiman, "Dual-Career Couples Can't Get Together Without Outside Help," *Tampa Tribune* (March 2, 2003): 3.
38. Ibid.
39. Amy Saltzman, "A Family Transfer," *U.S. News & World Report* 122 (February 10, 1997): 60–62.
40. Donna Bergles and Lisa Da Rocha, "Putting Work-Life Balance into Relocation Planning," *Canadian HR Reporter* (September 23, 2002): 9–10.
41. Joan Hamilton, Stephen Baker, and Bill Vlasic, "The New Workplace," *BusinessWeek* (April 29, 1996): 106.
42. Robert Bellinger, "The Profession: New Survey Finds Men and Women Embrace Common Goals—Dual-Career Couples Crave Flexible Hours and Jobs," *Electronic Engineering Times* (October 1998): 121.
43. Stephanie Armour, "Married . . . with Separation More Couples Live Apart as Careers Put Miles Between Them," *USA Today* (November 23, 1998): 01B.
44. Robert J. Aalberts, "Can Tenants in Privately Owned Apartments Be Drug Tested?" *The Journal of Real Estate Research* 23 (January-April 2002): 201–214.
45. Mary-Kathryn Zachary, "When Does Liability End in Discrimination Suits?" *Supervision* 63 (December 2002): 23–26.

46. Michael Price, "Anti-Discrimination Training Useful to Prevent Bias Claims," *Business Insurance* 37 (January 27, 2003): 12.
47. Ira Carnaham, "Removing the Scarlet A," *Forbes* 170 (August 12, 2002): 78.
48. Marjorie Valbrun and Nick Wingfield, "Calpers Settles EEOC Lawsuit on Disability Pay," *Wall Street Journal* (January 31, 2003): A2.
49. "Court Says Age Bias Law Doesn't Affect States," *United Press International* (January 11, 2000): 1.
50. Robert J. Noble, Esq., "To Waiver or Not to Waiver Is the Question of OWPWA," *Personnel* 68 (June 1991): 11.
51. Kate Colborn, "You Want Me to Sign What?" *EDN* 38 (March 11, 1993): 69.
52. Carol J. Castaneda, "Panel Backs FAA on Retire-at-60 Rule," *USA Today* (July 16, 1997): 6A.
53. Donald L. Caruth, Robert M. Noe III, and R. Wayne Mondy, *Staffing the Contemporary Organization* (New York: Quorum Books, 1988): 49.
54. Brian Friel, "Access Granted," *Government Executive* 34 (June 2002): 45–52.
55. Joel Schettler, "Equal Access to All," *Training* 39 (January 2002): 44–48.
56. Gillian Flynn, "Watch Out for Pregnancy Discrimination," *Workforce* 81 (November 2002): 84–85.
57. Ibid.
58. John J. Keller, "AT&T Will Settle EEOC Lawsuit for $66 Million," *Wall Street Journal* 88, no. 13 (July 18, 1991): B8.
59. Dan Seligman, "Illegals with Legal Rights," *Forbes* 169 (January 7, 2002): 128.
60. Sherrie A. Kossoudji and Deborah A. Cobb-Clark, "Coming Out of the Shadows: Learning About Legal Status and Wages from the Legalized Population," *Journal of Labor Economics* 20 (July 2002): 598–628.
61. Art L. Bethke, "The IRCA: What's an Employer to Do?" *Wisconsin Small Business Forum* 6 (Fall 1987): 26.
62. Jonathan L. Hafetz, "The Untold Story of Noncriminal Habeas Corpus and the 1996 Immigration Acts," *Yale Law Journal* 107 (June 1998): 2509–2544.
63. "Common Sense and Student Visas," *Washington Times* (January 1, 2003): 1.
64. Dan P. Danilow, "New Immigration Law Signed," *Northwest Asian Weekly* (November 15, 1996): PG.
65. Jathan W. Janove, "Skating Through the Minefield," *HRMagazine* 48 (March 2003): 107.
66. Susan E. Long, "Supreme Court Issues Several Key ADA Decisions," *HR Focus* 76 (September 1999): 3.
67. William J. Kilberg, "Review of the Supreme Court's October 2001 Term," *Employee Relations Law Journal* 28 (Winter 2002): 1–5.
68. Gary H. Anthes, "The Invisible Workforce," *Computerworld* 34 (May 2000): 50–54.
69. Eric Minton, "The ADA and Records Management," *Records Management Quarterly* 28 (January 1994): 12.
70. The six cases are *Ward Cove Packing Co., Inc., v Antonio*; *Price Waterhouse v Hopkins*; *Patterson v McClean Credit Union*; *Martin v Wilks*; *West Virginia Hospitals v Casey*; and *Lorence v AT&T*.
71. Bud Baker and Susan S. Lightle, "Cracks in the Glass Ceiling: An Analysis of Gender Equity in the Federal Government Auditing Career Field," *The Journal of Government Financial Management* 50 (Fall 2001): 18–26.
72. Irma S. Mann and Stephanie Seacord, "What Glass Ceiling?" *Lodging Hospitality* 59 (March 15, 2003): 38–40.
73. Alan Hughes, "More Work, Less Pay," *Black Enterprise* 33 (December 2002): 32.
74. Andrew Quinn, "San Francisco Comes Down Hard on Weightism," *Reuters* (May 8, 2000): 1.
75. Peter de Jager, "Ethics: Good, Evil, and Moral Duty," *Information Management Journal* (September/October 2002): 82–85.
76. Constance B. DiCesare, "Age Discrimination (*O'Connor v Consolidated Coin Caterers Corp.*)," *Monthly Labor Review* 119 (July 1996): 51.
77. Lyle Denniston, "1978 *Bakke* Decision Resurrected in Ruling," *Boston Globe* (June 24, 2003): A13.
78. Alison B. Marshall, "U.S. Supreme Court Tackles Affirmative Action in University Admissions: Will the Outcome Affect Corporate Diversity Efforts?" *Employee Relations Law Journal* 29 (Summer 2003): 99.
79. Charles Proctor, "Supreme Court Votes to Uphold Affirmative Action in U. Michigan Case," *University Wire* (June 24, 2003): 1.
80. Lorraine Woellert, "Anger on the Right, Opportunity for Bush: Ire over Affirmative Action Makes the President Look More Centrist," *BusinessWeek* (July 7, 2003): 32.
81. Proctor, "Supreme Court Votes to Uphold Affirmative Action in U. Michigan Case."
82. Donald Caruth and Gail Handlogten, "Avoiding HR Lawsuits," *Credit Union Executive Journal* 39 (November/December 1999): 25.
83. Nancy J. Arencibia, "Is Arbitration Right for Your Company?" *Financial Executive* 18 (December 2002): 46–47.
84. Diana Kunde, "Heading Off Trouble: EEOC Turns to Mediation to Resolve Backlog of Cases,"*Dallas Morning News* (February 24, 1999): 1D.
85. "Faster, Better Service and EEOC Enforcement on the Way," *HR Focus* 79 (June 2002): 8.
86. "Job Bias Suits and Jury Awards Are Souring," *HR Focus* 77 (March 2000): 2.
87. Susan E. Long and Catherine G. Leonard, "The Changing Face of Sexual Harassment," *HR Focus* 76 (October 1999): S1.
88. Complying with EEOC Anti-Harassment Guidelines: Supervisor Training and Communications Prove Crucial," *PR Newswire* (June 23, 1999): 1.
89. Debbie Rodman Sandler, "Sexual Harassment Rulings Less Than Meets the Eye," *HRMagazine* 43 (October 1, 1998): 136–143.
90. Theresa Brady, "Added Liability: Third-Party Sexual Harassment," *Management Review* 86 (April 1997): 45–47.
91. Stacey J. Garvin, "Employer Liability for Sexual Harassment," *HRMagazine* 36 (June 1991): 107.
92. David S. Shenvyn, Ezekiel A. Kaufman, and Adam A. Klausner, "Same-Sex Sexual Harassment," *Cornell Hotel*

and Restaurant Administration Quarterly 41(December 2000): 75–80.

93. Maria Greco Danaher, "Exec's Isolated Come-On Supports Hostile Environment Claim," *HRMagazine* 48 (February 2003): 105.
94. Sarah Ellison and Joann S. Lublin, "Dial to Pay $10 Million to Settle a Sexual-Harassment Lawsuit," *Wall Street Journal* (April 30, 2003): B4.
95. Mary-Kathryn Zachary, "Supreme Court Clarifies Same-Sex Harassment," *Supervision* 59 (July 1998): 20–21.
96. Shenvyn, Kaufman, and Klausner, "Same-Sex Sexual Harassment."
97. Jennifer Laabs, "News Digest," *Workforce* 78 (July 1999): 22.
98. Barbara Lindemann Schlei and Paul Grossman, *Employment Discrimination Law*, 2nd ed. (Washington, D.C.: Bureau of National Affairs, 1983): 423.
99. Theresa Brady, "The Downside of Diversity," *Management Review* 85 (June 1996): 29.
100. "EEOC Guidance on National Origin Bias," *HR Focus* 80 (January 2003): 2.
101. "The Growing Importance of Tolerance in the Workplace," *HR Focus* 78 (November 2001): 3–5.
102. Ibid.
103. David Drickhamer, "Employment Laws Apply Abroad: Americans Overseas Have Same Rights as U.S. Counterparts," 251 (May 2002): 12.
104. Nathan D. Kling, Joe F. Alexander, Denny E. McCorkle, and Rutilio Martinez, "Preparing for Careers in Global Business: Strategies for U.S. Female Students," *American Business Review* 17 (June 1999): 34–42.
105. Wendy Hardman and Jacqueline Heidelberg, "When Sexual Harassment is a Foreign Affair," *Personnel Journal* 75 (April 1996): 91.
106. Gerald L. Maatmann, Jr., "Harassment, Discrimination Laws Go Global," *National Underwriter* (September 11, 2000): 34–35.

PART THREE

Staffing

CHAPTER OBJECTIVES

After completing this chapter, students should be able to

1. Describe the importance of succession planning.
2. Explain why job analysis is a basic human resource tool.
3. Explain the reasons for conducting job analysis.
4. Describe the types of information required for job analysis.
5. Describe the various job analysis methods.
6. Describe the components of a well-designed job description.
7. Identify the other methods available for conducting job analysis.
8. Describe how job analysis helps satisfy various legal requirements.
9. Explain strategic planning and the human resource planning process.
10. Describe human resource forecasting techniques.
11. Define *requirements* and *availability forecasts*.
12. Identify what a firm can do when either a surplus or a shortage of workers exists.
13. Describe accelerated succession planning as an alternative to traditional approaches.
14. Explain the importance of planning for disasters.
15. Explain the importance of a human resource information system.
16. Describe some job design concepts.

CHAPTER 4

Job Analysis and Human Resource Planning

HRM IN *Action:*

Succession Planning

OBJECTIVE

Describe the importance of succession planning.

Succession planning:
The process of ensuring that qualified persons are available to assume key managerial positions once the positions are vacant.

The fatal crash of Commerce Secretary Ron Brown's plane in 1996 with 16 corporate executives on board suddenly brought major attention to succession planning across the nation.[1] Were replacements ready to assume these leadership positions? But it does not take something as rare as a plane crash to cause a company's sudden loss. A month later, Texas Instruments CEO Jerry Junkins, with no history of heart disease, died suddenly of a heart attack at age 58. Fortunately, Junkins had personally groomed his successor, and continuity was assured.[2] More recently, the events of 9/11 reinforced the uncertainty of today's business world and the need for succession planning. Merrill Lynch, Morgan Stanley, Bank of New York, and Deutsche Bank, among others, activated their comprehensive disaster plans and were back up and running almost immediately after the World Trade Center tragedy.[3] **Succession planning** is the process of ensuring that qualified persons are available to assume key managerial positions once the positions are vacant. This definition includes untimely deaths, resignations, terminations, or the orderly retirements of company officials. The goal is to help ensure a smooth transition and operational efficiency.[4]

Because of the tremendous changes that will confront management in this century, succession planning is taking on more importance than ever before. It is not only deaths that have created an increased focus on succession planning. The premature firing of CEOs is no longer a rare event. CEOs are being terminated faster than in the past. Recently, only 47 percent of corporate chiefs who departed did so under terms of a so-called regular transition, compared with 72 percent in 1995.[5] Jill Barad's hasty departure from Mattel came just three years after she had ascended to the top. Shortly after that announcement, Douglas Ivester left Coca-Cola after two and a half years at the helm. Two weeks later, Robert Annunziata was gone from Global Crossing after only 53 weeks. The following week Robert Ayling was abruptly ousted from British Airways after only four

SHRM HR Links

www.shrm.org/hrlinks/default.asp

This SHRM Web site provides management practices information related to succession planning.

years on the job. Then, Dale Morrison of Campbell Soup was out after less than three years. A weak CEO succession plan hurts not only staff morale and business performance, but also stock price.[6] Many expect the tenure for CEOs to continue to grow shorter.[7]

Studies show that executives hired from outside the company are more expensive than those chosen through a formal internal succession process. But, outsiders perform no better on average. Although at times there are justifications for going external for top-level executives, an internal succession process is best.[8] Effective succession planning concerns itself with building a series of feeder groups up and down the entire leadership pipeline.[9]

We began this chapter by discussing the importance of succession planning. Next, we show why job analysis is a basic human resource management tool and explain the reasons for conducting job analysis. Then we review the types of job analysis information required and discuss job analysis methods. Following this, we explain the components of a well-designed job description and discuss other methods for conducting job analysis and the ways job analysis helps to satisfy various legal requirements. We then examine the human resource planning process and some human resource forecasting techniques. Next, we discuss forecasting human resource requirements and availability, and describe what actions could be taken should either a surplus or a shortage of workers exist. Then a succession plan example is provided followed by a discussion of accelerated succession planning and the importance of planning for disasters. Next, a section is devoted to human resource information systems (HRIS). This chapter ends with a discussion of some job design concepts.

2 OBJECTIVE

Explain why job analysis is a basic human resource tool.

Job Analysis: A Basic Human Resource Management Tool

Job analysis:
The systematic process of determining the skills, duties, and knowledge required for performing specific jobs in an organization.

Job:
A group of tasks that must be performed if an organization is to achieve its goals.

Position:
The collection of tasks and responsibilities performed by one person.

Job analysis is the systematic process of determining the skills, duties, and knowledge required for performing jobs in an organization.[10] Traditionally, it is an essential and pervasive human resource technique and the starting point for other human resource activities.[11] In today's rapidly changing work environment, the need for a sound job analysis system is critical. New jobs are being created, and old jobs are being redesigned or eliminated. A job analysis that was conducted only a few years ago quite probably includes obsolete data. Some have even suggested that changes are occurring too fast to maintain an effective job analysis system.

A **job** consists of a group of tasks that must be performed for an organization to achieve its goals. A job may require the services of one person, such as that of the president, or the services of 75, as might be the case with data entry operators in a large firm. A **position** is the collection of tasks and responsibilities performed by one person; there is a position for every individual in an organization. In a work group consisting of a supervisor, two senior clerks, and four word processing operators, there are three jobs and seven positions. For instance, a small company might have 25 jobs for its 75 employees, whereas in a large company 2,000 jobs may exist for 50,000 employees. In some firms, as few as 10 jobs may make up 90 percent of the workforce.

The purpose of job analysis is to obtain answers to six important questions:

1. What physical and mental tasks does the worker accomplish?
2. When is the job to be completed?

3. Where is the job to be accomplished?
4. How does the worker do the job?
5. Why is the job done?
6. What qualifications are needed to perform the job?

Job analysis provides a summary of a job's duties and responsibilities, its relationship to other jobs, the knowledge and skills required, and working conditions under which it is performed. Job facts are gathered, analyzed, and recorded, as the job exists, not as the job should exist. Determining how the job should exist is most often assigned to industrial engineers, methods analysts, or others. Job analysis is conducted after the job has been designed, the worker has been trained, and the job is being performed.

Job analysis is performed on three occasions. First, it is done when the organization is founded and a job analysis program is initiated for the first time. Second, it is performed when new jobs are created. Third, it is used when jobs are changed significantly as a result of new technologies, methods, procedures, or systems. Job analysis is most often performed because of changes in the nature of jobs. Job analysis information is used to prepare both job descriptions and job specifications.

Job description:
A document that provides information regarding the tasks, duties, and responsibilities of a job.

Job specification:
A document that outlines the minimum acceptable qualifications a person should possess to perform a particular job.

The **job description** is a document that provides information regarding the essential tasks, duties, and responsibilities of the job. The minimum acceptable qualifications that a person should possess in order to perform a particular job are contained in the **job specification**. We discuss both types of documents in greater detail later in this chapter.

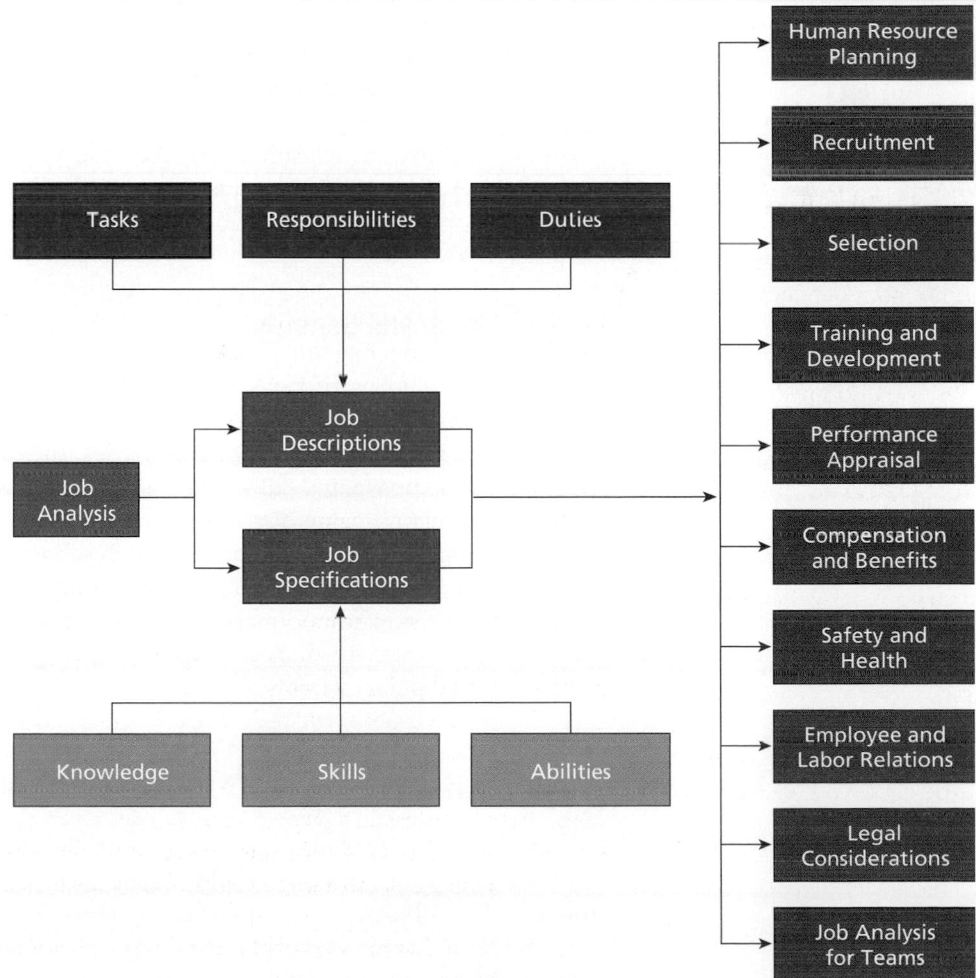

Figure 4-1 Job Analysis: A Basic Human Resource Management Tool

3 **OBJECTIVE**

Explain the reasons for conducting job analysis.

Reasons for Conducting Job Analysis

As Figure 4-1 shows, data derived from job analysis can have an impact on virtually every aspect of human resource management. A major use of job analysis data is found in the area of human resource planning (to be discussed in this chapter). Merely knowing that the firm will need 1,000 new employees to produce goods or services to satisfy sales demand is insufficient. Each job requires different knowledge, skills, and ability levels (KSAs). Obviously, effective human resource planning must take these job requirements into consideration.

Staffing

All areas of staffing would be haphazard if the recruiter did not know the qualifications needed to perform the various jobs. Lacking up-to-date job descriptions and specifications, a firm would have to recruit and select employees for jobs without having clear guidelines; this practice could have disastrous consequences. Such a practice is virtually unheard of when firms procure raw materials, supplies, or equipment. Surely, the same logic should apply when recruiting and selecting a firm's most valuable asset!

Training and Development

Job specification information often proves beneficial in identifying training and development needs. If the specification suggests that the job requires a particular knowledge, skill, or ability—and the person filling the position does not possess all the qualifications required, training and/or development are probably in order. They should be directed at assisting workers in performing duties specified in their present job descriptions or preparing them for broader responsibilities. With regard to performance appraisal, employees should be evaluated in terms of how well they accomplish the duties specified in their job descriptions and any specific goals that may have been established. A manager who evaluates an employee on factors not clearly predetermined is left wide open to allegations of discrimination.

Compensation and Benefits

In the area of compensation, it is helpful to know the relative value of a particular job to the company before a dollar value is placed on it. From an internal perspective, the more significant its duties and responsibilities, the more the job is worth. Jobs that require greater knowledge, skills, and abilities should be worth more to the firm. For example, the relative value of a job calling for a master's degree normally would be higher than that of a job that requires a high school diploma. This might not be the case if the market value of the job requiring only a high school diploma was higher, however. Such a situation occurred in a major West Coast city a number of years ago. It came to light that city *sanitation engineers* (garbage collectors) were paid more than better-educated public schoolteachers.

Safety and Health

Information derived from job analysis is also valuable in identifying safety and health considerations. For example, employers are required to state whether a job is hazardous.[12] The job description/specification should reflect this condition. In addition, in certain hazardous jobs, workers may need specific information about the hazards in order to perform the jobs safely.

Employee and Labor Relations

Job analysis information is also important in employee and labor relations. When employees are considered for promotion, transfer, or demotion, the job description provides a standard for evaluation and comparison of talent. Regardless of whether the firm is unionized, information obtained through job analysis can often lead to more objective human resource decisions.

Legal Considerations

A proper prepared job analysis is particularly important for supporting the legality of employment practices. In fact, the importance of job analysis is well documented in the *Uniform Guidelines on Employee Selection Procedures.*[13] Job analysis data are needed to defend decisions involving promotion, transfers, and demotions, for example. Job analysis provides the basis for tying the functional areas together and the foundation for developing a sound human resource program.

Job Analysis for Teams

Historically, companies have established permanent jobs and filled these jobs with people who best fit the job description. The jobs then continued in effect for years to come.[14] In some firms today, people are being hired as team members. Whenever someone asks a team member, "What is your job description?" the reply might well be "Whatever." What this means is that if a project has to be completed, individuals do what has to be done to complete the task.[15]

With team design, there are no narrow jobs. Today, the work that departments and functional domains have is often bundled into teams. The members of these teams have a far greater depth and breadth of skills than would have been required in traditional jobs. Formerly, there might have been 100 separate job classifications in a facility. With team design, there may be just 10 or fewer broadly defined roles of teams.[16] Another dimension is added to job analysis when teams are considered: Job analysis may determine how important it is for employees to be team players and work well in group situations. Other traits that might be discovered through job analysis include the ability to work in more than one system.[17]

OBJECTIVE

Describe the types of information required for job analysis.

Types of Job Analysis Information

Considerable information is needed for the successful accomplishment of job analysis. The job analyst identifies the job's actual duties and responsibilities and gathers the other types of data shown in Table 4-1. Essential functions of the job are determined in this process. Note that work activities, worker-oriented activities, and the types of machines, tools, equipment, and work aids used in the job are important. This information is used later to help determine the job skills needed. In addition, the job analyst looks at job-related tangibles and intangibles, such as the knowledge needed, the materials processed, and the goods made or services performed.

Some job analysis systems identify job standards. Work measurement studies may be needed to determine how long it takes to perform a task. With regard to job content, the analyst studies the work schedule, financial and nonfinancial incentives, and physical working conditions. Specific education, training, and work experience pertinent to the job are identified. Because many jobs are often performed in conjunction with others, organizational and social contexts are also noted. Subjective skills required, such as *strong interpersonal skills,* should be identified if the job requires that the jobholder be personable.[18]

Table 4-1 Types of Data Collected in Job Analysis

Summary of Types of Data Collected through Job Analysis[a]

1. **Work activities**
   a. Work activities and processes
   b. Activity records (in film form, for example)
   c. Procedures used
   d. Personal responsibility
2. **Worker-oriented activities**
   a. Human behaviors, such as physical actions and communicating on the job
   b. Elemental motions for methods analysis
   c. Personal job demands, such as energy expenditure
3. **Machines, tools, equipment, and work aids used**
4. **Job-related tangibles and intangibles**
   a. Knowledge dealt with or applied (as in accounting)
   b. Materials processed
   c. Products made or services performed
5. **Work performance[b]**
   a. Error analysis
   b. Work standards
   c. Work measurements, such as time taken for a task
6. **Job context**
   a. Work schedule
   b. Financial and nonfinancial incentives
   c. Physical working conditions
   d. Organizational and social contexts
7. **Personal requirements for the job**
   a. Personal attributes such as personality and interests
   b. Education and training required
   c. Work experience

[a]This information can be in the form of qualitative, verbal, narrative descriptions or quantitative measurements of each item, such as error rates per unit of time or noise level.
[b]All job analysis systems do not develop the work performance aspects.
Source: Reprinted by permission of Marvin D. Dunnette.

OBJECTIVE

Describe the various job analysis methods.

Job Analysis Methods

Job analysis has traditionally been conducted in a number of different ways because organizational needs and resources for conducting job analysis differ. Selection of a specific method should be based on the purposes for which the information is to be used (job evaluation, pay increases, development, and so on) and the approach that is most feasible for a particular organization. We describe the most common methods of job analysis in the following sections.

Questionnaires

Questionnaires are typically quick and economical to use. The job analyst may administer a structured questionnaire to employees, who identify the tasks they perform. In some cases, employees may lack verbal skills, a condition that makes this method less useful. Also, some employees may tend to exaggerate the significance of their tasks, suggesting more responsibility than actually exists.

Trends & Innovations

Evolution of Jobs

Not too long ago, there were no personal computers for cars, so there were no jobs designing them. And many companies had no Web site, so they had no need for a Web designer. All that has changed quickly. Intel product line engineer Patrick Johnson helped design Intel's Connected Car PC and the company's Internet appliances, computing devices designed specifically for the Internet. Now he's working on a chip to process images and other media for a future generation of copy machines, computerized cash registers, ATMs, and other appliances.

A 12-year Intel employee, Johnson was part of the small group that came up with the idea of a PC for the car. The group was then given the job of designing it. According to Johnson, "We had never built a computer for the car before. We had to decide what goes into it, how it gets packaged." After spending three years on the car computer, Johnson worked for nine months overseeing development of two Internet appliances. One is a set-top box to bring the Internet to television. The other is a countertop appliance, essentially a PC optimized for Internet access. "Five years ago, only a handful of people would have predicted how important the Internet would become," he said. "Not too many people know how it's going to evolve over the next five."

As another example, the title of marketing director has also existed for years, but today's Internet marketers have little in common with their analog counterparts. Robert Danoff, senior vice president of marketing for Tempe-based NeoPlanet, has worked on both sides of the digital divide and says they are very different. In traditional marketing, research would lead to meetings with an advertising agency in a six- to eight-week process before ads are published. On the Internet, the process can happen in 48 hours. According to Danoff, "There's been a dramatic time compression." As these jobs have evolved, so will others in the future, and probably the not-too-distant future.[19]

Observation

When using the observation method, the job analyst watches the worker perform job tasks and records his or her observations. This method is used primarily to gather information on jobs emphasizing manual skills, such as those of a machine operator. It can also help the analyst identify interrelationships between physical and mental tasks. Observation alone is usually an insufficient means of conducting job analysis, however, particularly when mental skills are dominant in a job. Observing a financial analyst at work would not reveal much about the requirements of the job.

Interviews

An understanding of the job may also be gained through interviewing both the employee and the supervisor. Usually, the analyst interviews the employee first, helping him or her describe the duties performed. Then, the analyst normally contacts the supervisor for additional information, to check the accuracy of the information obtained from the employee, and to clarify certain points.

Employee Recording

In some instances, job analysis information is gathered by having employees describe their daily work activities in a diary or log. With this method, the problem of employees exaggerating job importance may have to be overcome. Even so, valuable understanding of highly specialized jobs, such as, for example, recreational therapist, may be obtained in this way.

Combination of Methods

Usually, an analyst does not use one job analysis method exclusively. A combination of methods is often more appropriate. In analyzing clerical and administrative jobs, the analyst might use questionnaires supported by interviews and limited observation. In studying production jobs, interviews supplemented by extensive work observations may provide the necessary data. Basically, the analyst should employ the combination of techniques needed for accurate job descriptions/specifications.

Conducting Job Analysis

The person who conducts job analysis is interested in gathering data on what is involved in performing a particular job. The people who participate in job analysis should include, at a minimum, the employee and the employee's immediate supervisor. Large organizations may have one or more job analysts, but in small organizations line supervisors may be responsible for job analysis. Organizations that lack the technical expertise often use outside consultants to perform job analysis.

Regardless of the approach taken, before conducting job analysis, the analyst should learn as much as possible about the job by reviewing organizational charts and talking with individuals acquainted with the jobs to be studied. Before beginning, the supervisor should introduce the analyst to the employees and explain the purpose of the job analysis. Although employee attitudes about the job are beyond the job analyst's control, the analyst must attempt to develop mutual trust and confidence with those whose jobs are being analyzed. Failure in this area will detract from an otherwise technically sound job analysis. Upon completion of the job analysis, two basic human resource documents, job descriptions and job specifications, can be prepared.

Timeliness of Job Analysis

The rapid pace of technological change makes the need for accurate job analysis even more important now and in the future. Historically, job analyses could be conducted and then set aside for several years. Today, however, job requirements are changing so rapidly that they must be constantly reviewed to keep them relevant. Recall from Chapter 1 that the average person graduating from college today may face five to seven career changes in his or her working years. If this projection is accurate, the need for accurate and timely job analysis is becoming even more important.

On the downside, because of rapid technological changes, companies that do not constantly monitor their job analysis program will be placed in a difficult position. Recruiting for a position with an inaccurate job description may result in a poor match of skills possessed and skills needed. Also, training may be irrelevant and the compensation system may be flawed. Thus, job analysis is likely to be even more important in today's environment.

Describe the components of a well-designed job description.

Job Description

Information obtained through job analysis is crucial to the development of job descriptions. Earlier, *job description* was defined as a document that states the tasks, duties, and responsibilities of the job. It is vitally important that job descriptions are both relevant and accurate. Interviewers would be hard pressed to select the best-qualified worker if this information were not available.[20] They should provide concise statements of what employees are expected to do on the job and indicate what employees do, how they do it, and the conditions under which the duties are performed.[21] Concise job descriptions put an end to the possibility of hearing "that's not my job."[22] They are valuable to keep a firm focused in hiring.[23]

Job descriptions take on an even greater importance under the Americans with Disabilities Act (ADA) because the identification of *essential job functions* may be critical to a defense regarding reasonable accommodation.[24] Although there is no legal mandate to do so, some firms present essential job functions in a separate section of the job description. However, Peggy Mastroianni, the Equal Employment Opportunity Commission's associate legal counsel, predicts that reasonable accommodation of workers with disabilities will be the next hot issue in ADA employment litigation.[25]

Among the items frequently included in a job description are these:

- Major duties performed
- Percentage of time devoted to each duty
- Performance standards to be achieved
- Working conditions and possible hazards
- Number of employees performing the job, and to whom they report
- The machines and equipment used on the job

The contents of the job description vary somewhat with the purpose for which it will be used. The next sections address the parts of a job description.

HR Web Wisdom

O*NET – Beyond Information — Intelligence

www.doleta.gov/programs/onet

This Department of Labor Web site provides information on O*NET, which is a unique, powerful source for continually updated occupational information and labor market research.

Job Identification

The job identification section includes the job title, the department, the reporting relationship, and a job number or code. A good title will closely approximate the nature of the work content and will distinguish that job from others. Unfortunately, job titles are often misleading. An executive secretary in one organization may be little more than a highly paid clerk, whereas a person with the same title in another firm may practically run the company. For instance, one former student's first job after graduation was with a major tire and rubber company as an *assistant district service manager*. Because the primary duties of the job were to unload tires from trucks, check the tread wear, and stack the tires in boxcars, a more appropriate title would probably have been *tire checker and stacker*.

Historically, the *Dictionary of Occupational Titles* (*DOT*) has been an information source that assists in standardizing job titles.[26] An example of a *DOT* definition for a *branch manager*, occupational code 183.137-010, is provided in Figure 4-2. The first digit of the code identifies one of the following major occupations:

0 Professional, technical, and managerial
2 Clerical and sales
3 Service
4 Farming, fishing, forestry, and related
5 Processing
6 Machine trade
7 Bench work
8 Structural work
9 Miscellaneous

For the branch manager, the major classification would be *managerial* occupations. Thus, this example has a code 1.

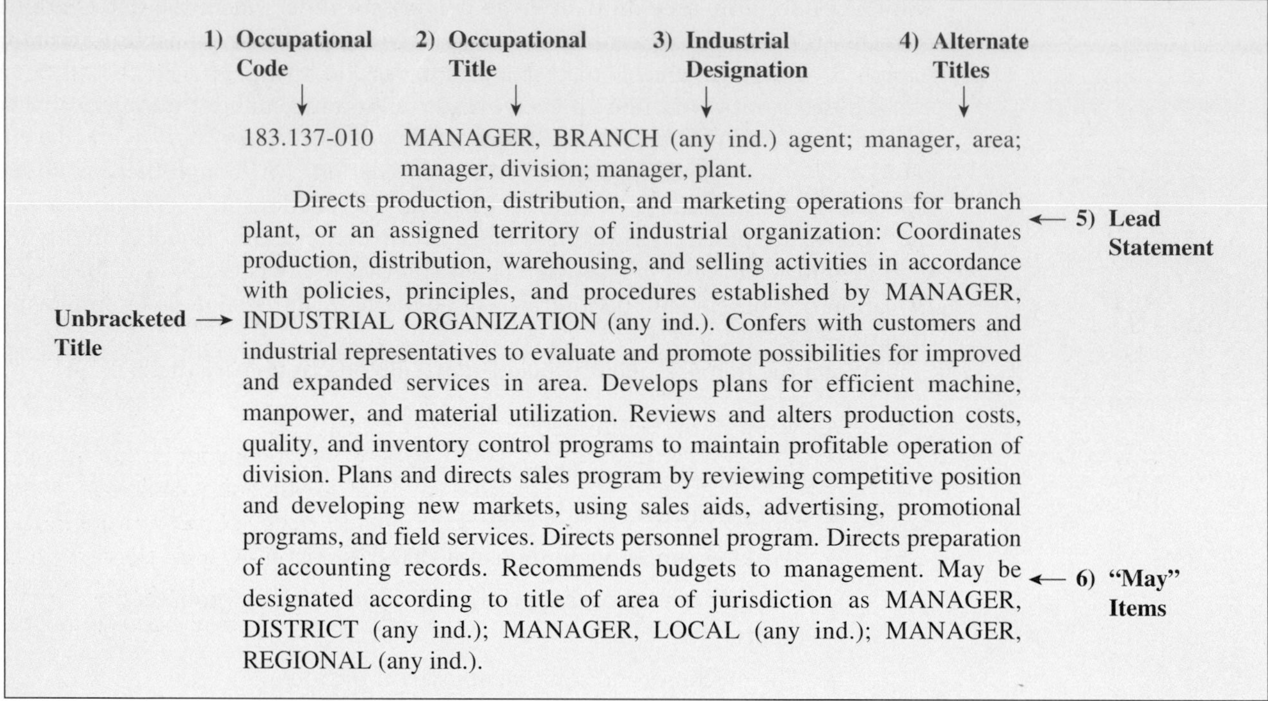

183.137-010 MANAGER, BRANCH (any ind.) agent; manager, area; manager, division; manager, plant.

Directs production, distribution, and marketing operations for branch plant, or an assigned territory of industrial organization: Coordinates production, distribution, warehousing, and selling activities in accordance with policies, principles, and procedures established by MANAGER, INDUSTRIAL ORGANIZATION (any ind.). Confers with customers and industrial representatives to evaluate and promote possibilities for improved and expanded services in area. Develops plans for efficient machine, manpower, and material utilization. Reviews and alters production costs, quality, and inventory control programs to maintain profitable operation of division. Plans and directs sales program by reviewing competitive position and developing new markets, using sales aids, advertising, promotional programs, and field services. Directs personnel program. Directs preparation of accounting records. Recommends budgets to management. May be designated according to title of area of jurisdiction as MANAGER, DISTRICT (any ind.); MANAGER, LOCAL (any ind.); MANAGER, REGIONAL (any ind.).

Figure 4-2 The Parts of the *Dictionary of Occupational Titles* Definition
Source: U.S. Department of Labor. *Dictionary of Occupational Titles.*

The *Dictionary of Occupational Titles* was recently replaced by the U.S. Department of Labor's O'NET OnLine network (www.online.onetcenter.org). The database is designed to replace the older and lengthier *Dictionary of Occupational Titles.* In addition to the standard occupational classification titles and codes, it offers detailed information on earnings, education, job growth, required skills, and related jobs. The new *DOT* included standardized and related jobs.[27]

The next two digits represent breakdowns of the general occupation category. Digits four through six describe the job's relationship to data, people, and things. For the branch manager, a code 1 for data would be *coordinating*, a code 3 for people would be *supervising*, and a code 7 for things would be *handling*.

The final three digits indicate the alphabetical order of titles within the six-digit code group. These codes assist in distinguishing a specific occupation from other similar ones. The digits 010 indicate the alphabetical order for branch manager.

Date of the Job Analysis

The job analysis date is placed on the job description to aid in identifying job changes that would make the description obsolete. Some firms have found it useful to place an expiration date on the document. This practice ensures periodic review of job content and minimizes the number of obsolete job descriptions.

Job Summary

The job summary provides a concise overview of the job. It is generally a short paragraph that states job content.

Duties Performed

The body of the job description delineates the major duties to be performed. Usually, one sentence beginning with an action verb such as receives, performs, establishes, or *assembles* adequately explains each duty. As stated earlier, essential functions may be shown in a separate section to aid in complying with the Americans with Disabilities Act. Recently, the EEOC said that working at home can be a reasonable accommodation for a person that qualifies as a disability under the Americans with Disabilities Act (ADA).[28]

Job Specification

Recall that we defined *job specification* as a document containing the minimum acceptable qualifications that a person should possess in order to perform a particular job. Items typically included in the job specification are factors that can be shown to be job related, such as educational requirements, experience, personality traits, and physical abilities. In practice, job specifications are often included as a major section of job descriptions.

Figure 4-3 is an actual job description provided by Conoco for an Administrative Support position. Some of the critical skills needed for the job include interpersonal skills/team player, ability to influence others, and knowledge of software applications. This type of information is extremely valuable in the recruiting and selection process.

After jobs have been analyzed and the descriptions written, the results should be reviewed with the supervisor and the worker to ensure that they are accurate, clear,

Position Title: Administrative Support	Code:	Salary Grade:
Work Location:	Report To:	Function:

Basic Purpose/Accountabilities:
Responsible for providing and coordinating administrative support to assigned functional groups. Focus is on aligning contributions to department needs and company goals.

Primary Functions/Responsibilities:	Critical Skills/Leadership Criteria:
—Preparation of time sheets —Track employee attendance —Manage fixtures, furniture, and equipment necessary to support the function —Process invoices, monitor expenditures —Coordinate and support meetings —Participate in planning process on projects —Type documentation to individuals external to Conoco —Assist with presentation preparation and planning —Coordinate large scale documentation reproduction —External mailing/facsimile transmission —Coordinate central office supplies —Resource computer software applications —Coordinate work activities with other functions —Generate alternatives and make recommendations on improving area work process —Record retention/filing	CRITICAL SKILLS —Interpersonal skills/team player —Ability to influence others —Knowledge of business software applications —Confidentiality —Planning, organizing, and time management —Written and oral communication —Customer orientation —Knowledge of operations and organization LEADERSHIP CRITERIA —Able to lead others —Engenders trust —Understands and uses functional expertise to contribute —Accepts ownership, is accountable, and delivers on commitments —Oriented towards continuous learning

Quantitative Factors/Business Model Activities:

Quantitative	Business Model

Figure 4-3 A Conoco Job Description
Source: Conoco Inc.

and understandable. The courtesy of reviewing results with employees also helps to gain their acceptance.

The Expanded Job Description

When first hearing false reports that he had died, Mark Twain responded, "Reports of my death have been greatly exaggerated." As we hear report after report about the demise of the *job*, we have a similar response.[29] After talking with managers representing literally scores of business firms, we have yet to locate an organization void of jobs.

Nevertheless, it cannot be denied that jobs are changing by getting bigger and more complex. The last duty shown on the proverbial job description, "And any other duty that may be assigned," is increasingly becoming *THE* job description. This enlarged, flexible, complex job changes the way many tasks are performed. Managers cannot simply look for individuals who possess narrow skills required to perform a job. They must go deeper and seek competencies, intelligence, ability to adjust, and ability and willingness to work in teams. Today more than ever, people go from project to project and from team to team. Job definitions become blurred, and titles become almost meaningless as job descriptions have become even more all-encompassing.[30] Basically, what matters is what you know and how well you apply it to the business.

 **OBJECTIVE**

Identify the other methods available for conducting job analysis.

Other Job Analysis Methods

Over the years, attempts have been made to provide more systematic methods of conducting job analysis. We describe several of these approaches next.

Department of Labor Job Analysis Schedule

Job analysis schedule (JAS): A systematic method of studying jobs and occupations; developed by the U.S. Department of Labor.

The U.S. Department of Labor established a method of systematically studying jobs and occupations called the **job analysis schedule (JAS)**. When the JAS method is used, a trained analyst gathers information. A major component of the JAS is the Work Performed Ratings section. Here, what workers do in performing a job with regard to data (D), people (P), and things (T) is evaluated. Each is viewed as a hierarchy of functions, with the items higher in the category being more difficult. The codes in the worker functions section represent the highest level of involvement in each of the three categories.

The JAS component "Worker Traits Ratings" relates primarily to job requirement data. The topics general education designation (GED), specific vocational preparation (SVP), aptitudes, temperaments, interests, physical demands, and environmental conditions are included. The Description of Tasks section provides a specific description of the work performed. Both routine tasks and occasionally performed tasks are included.

Functional Job Analysis

Functional job analysis (FJA): A comprehensive approach to formulating job descriptions that concentrates on the interactions among the work, the worker, and the work organization.

Functional job analysis (FJA) is a comprehensive job analysis approach that concentrates on the interactions among the work, the worker, and the organization. This approach is a modification of the job analysis schedule. It assesses specific job outputs and identifies job tasks in terms of task statements.[31] The fundamental elements of FJA follow:

1. A major distinction is made between what gets done and what workers do to get things done. It is more important in job analysis to know the latter. For instance, a word processing

Table 4-2 Worker Function Scale for Job Analysis Schedule

Data (4th digit)		People (5th digit)		Things (6th digit)	
0	Synthesizing	0	Monitoring	0	Setting up
1	Coordinating	1	Negotiating	1	Precision working
2	Analyzing	2	Instructing	2	Operating—controlling
3	Compiling	3	Supervising	3	Driving—operating
4	Computing	4	Diverting	4	Manipulating
5	Copying	5	Persuading	5	Tending
6	Comparing	6	Speaking—signaling	6	Feeding—offbearing
7	No significant relationship	7	Serving	7	Handling
		8	No significant relationship	8	No significant relationship

Source: U.S. Department of Labor, *Dictionary of Occupational Titles.*

operator does not just keep the system running; a number of tasks must be performed in accomplishing the job.

2. Each job is concerned with data, people, and things.
3. Workers function in unique ways as they relate to data, people, and things.
4. Each job requires the worker to relate to data, people, and things in some way.
5. Only a few definite and identifiable functions are involved with data, people, and things (refer to Table 4-2).
6. These functions proceed from the simple to the complex. The least complex form of data would be comparing, and the most complex would be synthesizing. In addition, the assumption is that if an upper-level function is required, all the lower-level functions are also required.
7. The three hierarchies for data, people, and things provide two measures for a job.[32] First, there is a measure of relative complexity in relation to data, people, and things, in essence, the amount of interrelationship among the three functions. Second, there is a measure of proportional involvement for each function. For instance, 50 percent of a person's time may be spent in analyzing, 30 percent in supervising, and 20 percent in operating.

Position Analysis Questionnaire

Position analysis questionnaire (PAQ): A structured job analysis questionnaire that uses a checklist approach to identify job elements.

The **position analysis questionnaire (PAQ)** is a structured job analysis questionnaire that uses a checklist approach to identify job elements. It focuses on general worker behaviors instead of tasks. Some 194 job descriptors relate to job-oriented elements. Advocates of the PAQ believe that its ability to identify job elements, behaviors required of job incumbents, and other job characteristics makes this procedure applicable to the analysis of virtually any type of job. Each job descriptor is evaluated on a specified scale such as extent of use, amount of time, importance of job, possibility of occurrence, and applicability.

Each job being studied is scored relative to the 32 job dimensions. The score derived represents a profile of the job; this can be compared with standard profiles to group jobs into known job families, that is, jobs of a similar nature. In essence, the PAQ identifies significant job behaviors and classifies jobs. Using the PAQ, job descriptions can be based on the relative importance and emphasis placed on various job elements. The PAQ has been called one of the most useful job analysis methods.[33]

Management position description questionnaire (MPDQ):
A method of job analysis designed for management positions that uses a checklist to analyze jobs.

Management Position Description Questionnaire

The **management position description questionnaire (MPDQ)** is a method of job analysis designed for management positions; it uses a checklist to analyze jobs. The MPDQ has been used to determine the training needs of individuals who are slated to move into managerial positions. It has also been used to evaluate and set compensation rates for managerial jobs and to assign the jobs to job families.

Guidelines-oriented job analysis (GOJA):
A method of job analysis that involves a step-by-step procedure for describing the work of a particular job classification.

Guidelines-Oriented Job Analysis

The **guidelines-oriented job analysis (GOJA)** responds to the legislation affecting staffing and involves a step-by-step procedure for describing the work of a particular job classification.[34] It is also used for developing selection tools, such as application forms, and for documenting compliance with various legal requirements. The GOJA obtains the following types of information: (1) machines, tools, and equipment; (2) supervision; (3) contacts; (4) duties; (5) knowledge, skills, and abilities; (6) physical and other requirements; and (7) differentiating requirements.

8 OBJECTIVE

Describe how job analysis helps satisfy various legal requirements.

Job Analysis and the Law

Effective job analysis is essential to sound human resource management as an organization recruits, selects, and promotes employees. In particular, human resource management has focused on job analysis because selection methods need to be clearly job related.[35] Legislation requiring thorough job analysis includes the following acts.

- *Fair Labor Standards Act:* Employees are categorized as exempt or nonexempt, and job analysis is basic to this determination. Nonexempt workers must be paid time and a half when they work more than 40 hours per week. Overtime pay is not required for exempt employees.
- *Equal Pay Act:* Men are often paid higher salaries than women, even though they perform essentially the same job. If jobs are not substantially different, the employees performing them must receive similar pay. When pay differences exist, job descriptions can be used to show whether jobs are substantially equal in terms of skill, effort, responsibility, or working conditions.
- *Civil Rights Act:* As with the Equal Pay Act, job descriptions may provide the basis for an equitable compensation system and an adequate defense against unfair discrimination charges in initial selection, promotion, and all other areas of human resource administration. When job analysis is not performed, defending certain qualifications established for the job is usually difficult. For instance, stating that a high school diploma is required without having determined its necessity through job analysis makes the firm vulnerable in discrimination suits.
- *Occupational Safety and Health Act:* Job descriptions are required to specify elements of the job that endanger health or are considered unsatisfactory or distasteful by the majority of the popula-

tion. Showing the job description to the employee in advance is a good defense.

- *Americans with Disabilities Act (ADA):* Employers are required to make reasonable accommodations for workers with disabilities who are able to perform the *essential functions* of a job. It is important that organizations distinguish these essential functions from those that are marginal. The EEOC defines *reasonable accommodation* as any modification or adjustment to a job, an employment practice, or the work environment that makes it possible for an individual with a disability to enjoy an equal employment opportunity. What constitutes reasonable accommodation depends on the disability and the skills of the person in question.[36]

OBJECTIVE

Explain strategic planning and the human resource planning process.

Strategic Planning and the Human Resource Planning Process

Strategic planning:
The determination of overall organizational purposes and goals and how they are to be achieved.

In Chapter 1, we stressed that HR executives are now focusing their attention on how human resources can help the organization achieve its strategic objectives. Thus, HR must now be highly involved in the strategic planning process. **Strategic planning** is the process by which top management determines overall organizational purposes and objectives and how they are to be achieved.

When a firm's mission is clearly defined and its guiding principles understood, employees and managers are likely to put forth maximum effort in pursuing company objectives. Top management expects HR activities to be closely aligned to this mission and strategic goals and to add value toward achieving these goals.[37] The advantage of strategic planning is most evident as firms respond to rapidly changing environments. As Larry Bossidy and Ram Charan, in their book *Execution: The Discipline of Getting Things Done*, wrote, "If executives do not get the people process right, they will never fulfill the potential of the business."[38]

Human resource planning (HRP):
The process of systematically reviewing human resource requirements to ensure that the required numbers of employees, with the required skills, are available when and where they are needed.

Human resource planning (HRP), the process of systematically reviewing human resource requirements to ensure that the required numbers of employees, with the required skills, are available when and where they are needed. Effective staffing decisions begin with human resource planning.[39] Human resource planning involves matching the internal and external supply of people with job openings anticipated in the organization over a specified period of time. The human resource planning process is illustrated in Figure 4-4. Note that strategic planning precedes human resource planning. Leading strategic HR expert and author David Bratton said, "The whole issue of managing change, that is where HR is converging with organizational strategy."[40]

HR Planning Organization

www.hrps.org

This Web site is the homepage for the Human Resource Planning Society.

Specific quantitative and qualitative human resource plans are determined from the organizational plans. Note in Figure 4-4 that human resource planning has two components: requirements and availability. Forecasting human resource requirements involves determining the number and types of employees needed, by skill level and location. These projections will reflect various factors, such as production plans and changes in productivity. In order to forecast availability, the human resource manager looks to both internal sources (presently employed employees) and external sources (the labor market). When employee requirements and availability have been analyzed, the firm can determine whether it will have a surplus or shortage of employees. Ways must be found to reduce the number of employees if a surplus is projected. Some of these methods include restricted hiring, reduced hours, early retirements, and layoffs. If a worker shortage is forecast, the firm must obtain the proper quantity and quality of workers from outside the organization. In this case, external recruitment and selection are required.

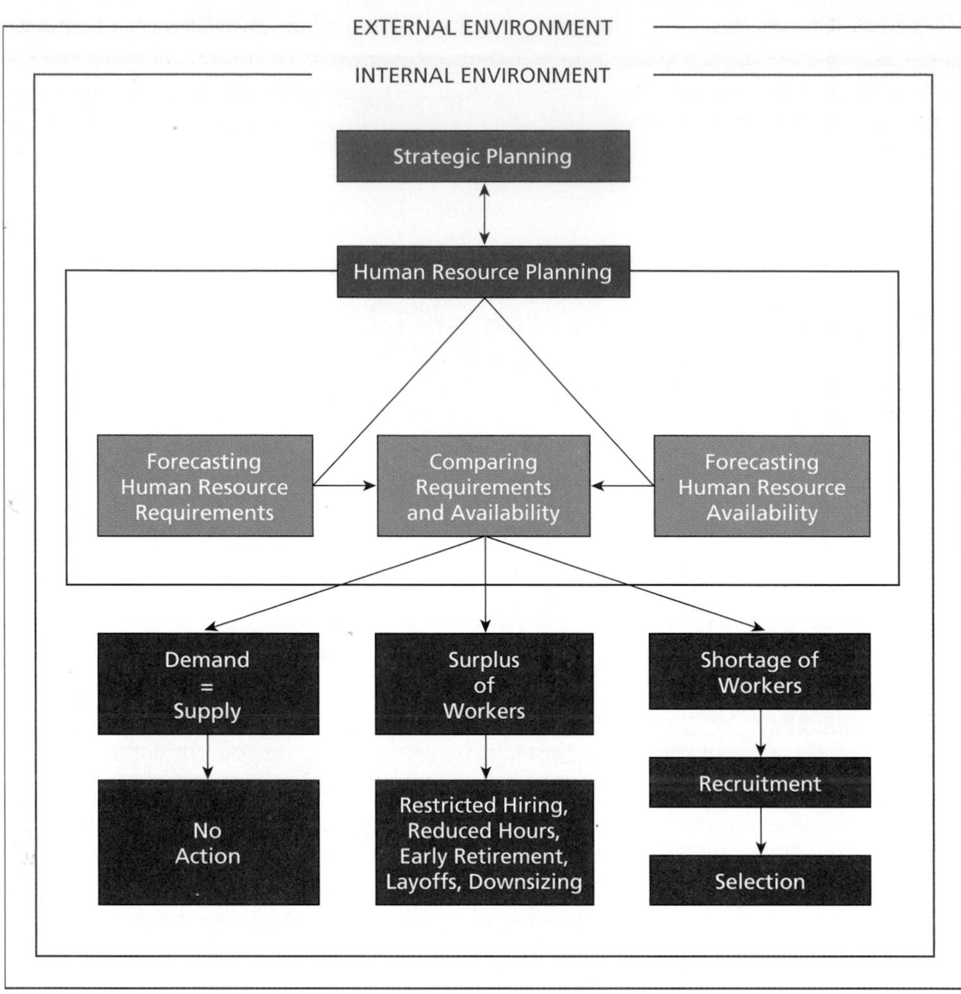

Figure 4-4 The Human Resource Planning Process

Because conditions in the external and internal environments can change quickly, the human resource planning process must be continuous. Changing conditions could affect the entire organization, thereby requiring extensive modification of forecasts. Planning, in general, enables managers to anticipate and prepare for changing conditions, and HR planning in particular allows flexibility in the area of human resource management.

Describe human resource forecasting techniques.

Human Resource Forecasting Techniques

Several techniques for forecasting human resource requirements and availability are currently used by HR professionals. Some of the techniques are qualitative in nature, and others are quantitative. Several of the better-known methods are described in this section.

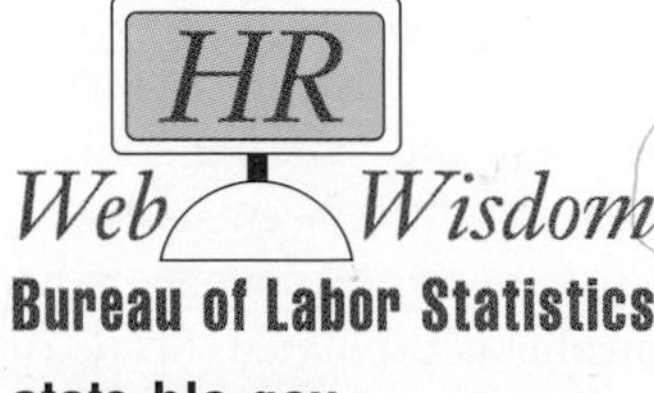

Bureau of Labor Statistics

stats.bls.gov

This government Web site provides information related to human resource planning

Zero-Base Forecasting

The **zero-base forecasting** approach uses the organization's current level of employment as the starting point for determining future staffing needs. Essentially, the same procedure is used for human resource planning as for zero-base budgeting, whereby each budget must be justified each year. If an employee retires, is fired, or leaves the firm for any other reason, the position is not automatically filled. Instead, an analysis is made to determine whether the firm can justify filling it. Equal concern is shown for

Zero-base forecasting: A method for estimating future employment needs using the organization's current level of employment as the starting point.

creating new positions when they appear to be needed. The key to zero-base forecasting is a thorough analysis of human resource needs. In today's globally competitive environment, an open position is thoroughly analyzed before a replacement is approved. Frequently, the position is not filled and the work is spread out among remaining employees.

Bottom-Up Approach

Bottom-up approach: A forecasting method beginning with the lowest organizational units and progressing upward through an organization ultimately to provide an aggregate forecast of employment needs.

In the **bottom-up approach**, each successive level in the organization, starting with the lowest, forecasts its requirements, ultimately providing an aggregate forecast of employees needed. It is based on the reasoning that the manager in each unit is most knowledgeable about employment requirements. Human resource forecasting is often most effective when managers periodically project their human resource needs, comparing their current and anticipated levels, and giving the human resource department adequate lead time to explore internal and external sources.

Use of Mathematical Models

Another means of forecasting human resource requirements is to use mathematical models to predict future requirements. One of the most useful predictors of employment levels is sales volume. The relationship between demand and the number of employees needed is a positive one. As you can see in Figure 4-5, a firm's sales volume is depicted on the horizontal axis, and the number of employees actually required is shown on the vertical axis. In this illustration, as sales decrease, so does the number of employees. Using such a method, managers can approximate the number of employees required at different demand levels.

Simulation

Simulation: A technique for experimenting with a real-world situation by means of a mathematical model that represents the actual situation.

Simulation is a technique for experimenting with a real-world situation through a mathematical model representing that situation. A model is an abstraction of the real world. Thus, a simulation model is an attempt to represent a real-world situation through mathematical logic to predict what will occur. Simulation assists managers by permitting them to ask many *what if* questions without having to make a decision resulting in real-world consequences. In human resource management, a simulation model might be developed to represent the interrelationships among employment

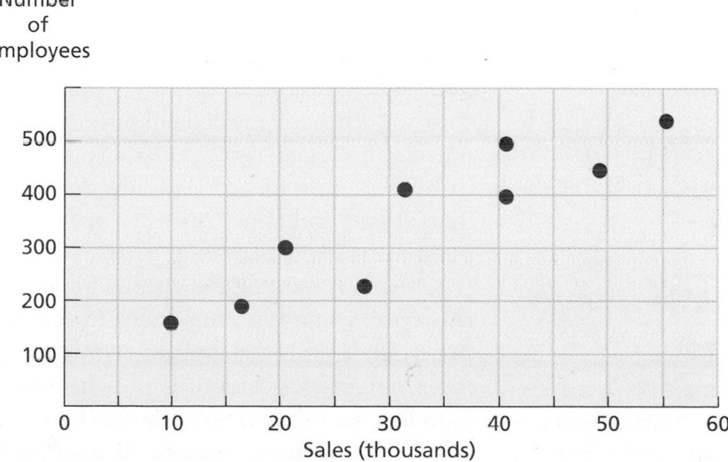

Figure 4-5 The Relationship of Sales Volume to Number of Employees

levels and many other variables. The manager could then ask *what if* questions such as these:

- What would happen if we put 10 percent of the present workforce on overtime?
- What would happen if the plant utilized two shifts? Three shifts?

The purpose of the model is to permit managers to gain considerable insight into a particular problem before making an actual decision.

11 OBJECTIVE

Define *requirements* and *availability* forecasts.

Forecasting Human Resource Requirements

Requirements forecast:
An estimate of the numbers and kinds of employees an organization will need at future dates to realize its stated objectives.

A **requirements forecast** is an estimate of the numbers and kinds of employees the organization will need at future dates in order to realize its stated goals. Before human resource requirements can be projected, demand for the firm's goods or services must be forecasted. This forecast is then converted into people requirements for the activities necessary to meet this demand. For a firm that manufactures personal computers, activities might be stated in terms of the number of units to be produced, number of sales calls to be made, number of vouchers to be processed, or a variety of other activities. For example, manufacturing 1,000 laptop computers each week might require 10,000 hours of work by assemblers during a 40-hour week. Dividing the 10,000 hours by the 40 hours in the workweek gives 250 assembly workers needed. Similar calculations are performed for the other jobs needed to produce and market the personal computers.

Forecasting Human Resource Availability

Forecasting requirements provides managers with the means of estimating how many and what types of employees will be required. But there is another side to the coin, as this example illustrates:

> *A large manufacturing firm on the West Coast was preparing to begin operations in a new plant. Analysts had already determined there was a large long-term demand for the new product. Financing was available and equipment was in place. But production did not begin for two years! Management had made a critical mistake: It had studied the demand side of human resources but not the supply side. There were not enough qualified workers in the local labor market to operate the new plant. New workers had to receive extensive training before they could move into the newly created jobs.*

Availability forecast:
A process of determining whether the firm will be able to secure employees with the necessary skills, and from what sources.

The determination of whether the firm will be able to secure employees with the necessary skills, and from what sources, is called an **availability forecast.** It helps to show whether the needed employees may be obtained from within the company, from outside the organization, or from a combination of the two sources. Another possibility is that the required skills are not immediately available from any feasible source. The illustration above provides one more instance of the importance of HR involvement in strategic planning.

Many of the workers needed for future positions may already work for the firm. If the firm is small, management probably knows all the workers sufficiently well to match their skills and aspirations with the company's needs. Suppose the firm is creating a new sales position. It may be common knowledge in the company that Mary Garcia, a five-year employee, has both the skills and the desire to take over the new job. This unplanned process of matching people and positions may be sufficient for smaller firms. As organizations grow, however, the matching process becomes increasingly difficult. Databases are being used by organizations that take human resources seriously. Also, succession planning helps to ensure an internal supply of highly qualified management personnel.

Databases include information on all managerial and nonmanagerial employees. Information generally provided for nonmanagerial employees includes the following:

- Background and biographical data
- Work experience
- Specific skills and knowledge
- Licenses or certifications held
- In-house training programs completed
- Previous performance appraisal evaluations
- Career goals

Information generally provided for managerial employees includes the following:

- Work history and experience
- Educational background
- Assessment of strengths and weaknesses
- Developmental needs
- Promotion potential at present, and with further development
- Current job performance
- Field of specialization
- Job preferences
- Geographic preferences
- Career goals and aspirations
- Anticipated retirement date
- Personal history, including psychological assessments

Identify what a firm can do when either a surplus or a shortage of workers exists.

Surplus of Employees Forecasted

When a comparison of requirements and availability indicates a worker surplus will result, restricted hiring, reduced hours, early retirements, and layoffs may be required to correct the situation. Downsizing, one result of worker surpluses, will be discussed as a separate topic in Chapter 14.

Restricted Hiring

When a firm implements a restricted hiring policy, it reduces the workforce by not replacing employees who leave. New workers are hired only when the overall performance of the organization may be affected. For instance, if a quality control department that consisted of four inspectors lost one to a competitor, this individual might not be replaced. If the firm lost all its inspectors, however, it would probably replace at least some of them to ensure continued operation.

Reduced Hours

A company can also react to a reduced workload requirement by reducing the total number of hours worked. Instead of continuing a 40-hour week, management may decide to cut each employee's time to 30 hours. This cutback normally applies only to hourly employees because management and other professionals typically are exempt employees and therefore not paid on an hourly basis.

Early Retirement

Early retirement of some present employees is another way to reduce the number of workers. Some employees will be delighted to retire, but others will be somewhat reluctant. However, the latter may be willing to accept early retirement if the total retirement package is made sufficiently attractive.

Layoffs

At times, a firm has no choice but to lay off part of its workforce.[41] Layoffs have become a way of life since the economic downturn began in 2000, and will be discussed in greater detail in Chapter 14.

Shortage of Workers Forecasted

When firms are faced with a shortage of workers, organizations will have to intensify their efforts to recruit the necessary people to meet the needs of the firm. Some possible actions will be discussed next.

Creative Recruiting

A shortage of personnel often means that new approaches to recruiting must be used. The organization may have to recruit in different geographic areas than in the past, explore new methods, and seek different kinds of candidates.

Compensation Incentives

Firms competing for workers in a high-demand situation may have to rely on compensation incentives. Premium pay is one obvious method; however, this approach may trigger a bidding war that the organization cannot sustain for an extended period. More subtle forms of rewards may be required to attract employees to a firm, such as four-day workweeks, flexible working hours, telecommuting, part-time employment, and child-care centers. These are discussed in Chapter 10.

Training Programs

Special training programs may be needed to prepare previously unemployable individuals for positions with a firm. Remedial education and skills training are two types of programs that may help attract individuals to a particular company.

Different Selection Standards

Another approach for dealing with shortages of workers is the lowering of employment standards. Selection criteria that screen out certain workers may have to be altered to ensure that enough people are available to fill jobs. For instance, instead of desiring extensive work experience, a firm may be willing to hire an inexperienced worker and train the individual to do the job.

Ethical Dilemma

Which "Thinker" Should Go?

Your company is a leading producer of advanced microchips. You are the chief researcher in your firm's "think tank," which consists of eight people with various specialties. Your group has generated most of the ideas and product innovations that have kept the company an industry leader for 10 years. In fact, the think tank has been so successful that another one has been organized to support the company's newest manufacturing operation on the coast. The individuals to be included in the new think tank have already been selected, but your boss has just assigned you the task of deciding who from your group of thinkers will head the new organization.

The person best qualified for the job is Tim Matherson. Tim is an MIT graduate, the informal team leader, and the individual who personally spearheaded three of the team's five most successful product advancements. However, if Tim is given the promotion, the void created by his leaving will be difficult to fill. On the other hand, the boss forced his nephew, Robert Jones, into the group. He is a sharp graduate of the local state university, but he is not a team player and he is always trying to push you around. You can either recommend Tim, illustrating that those who produce the most benefit the most, or you can recommend Robert, making the boss happy, getting rid of a problem, and, most important of all, keeping your best performer.

What would you do?

A Succession Plan Example

In the HRM in Action at the beginning of this chapter we highlighted the importance of succession planning. The succession plan of Detroit Edison is provided with its Career Planning Inventory Organization Review Chart in Figure 4-6. The chart

Confidential ***CPI Organization Review Chart—Information as of Feb 03 2005***
Chart Number: DO-B01

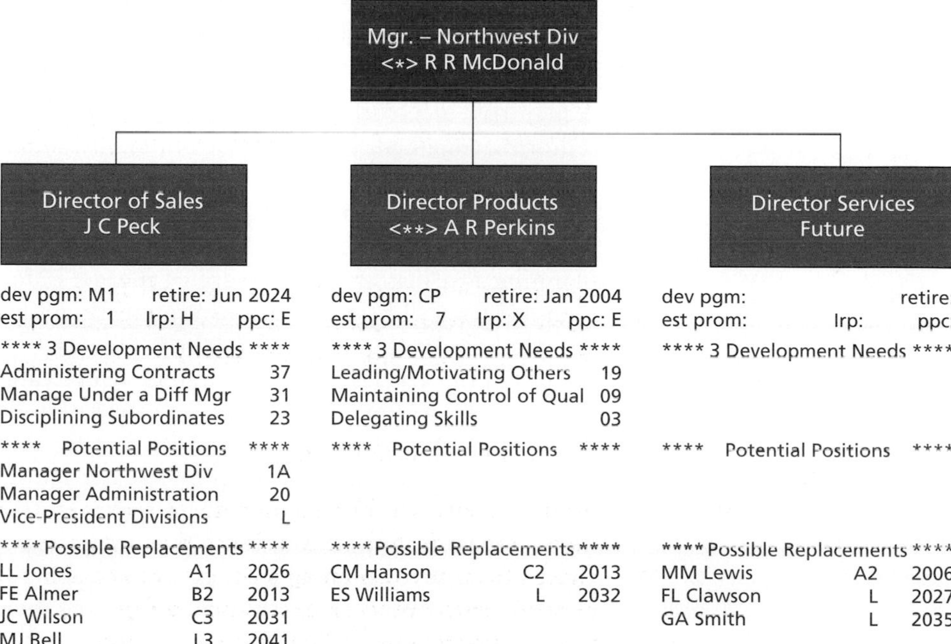

Figure 4-6 Career Planning Inventory Organization Review Chart

shows a manager in the top box, with immediate subordinates in the lower boxes. Information shown on the chart includes the following:

- *Position Box:* Each box shows the position title and the incumbent's name. The symbol * preceding the name identifies incumbents who will retire between 2003 and 2010, indicating that short-range planning is required. The symbol ** preceding the name identifies incumbents who will retire between 2007 and 2014, indicating that long-range planning is required. If the word *open* appears in the box, the position is unfilled. If *future* appears, the position is anticipated but does not yet exist.
- *dev pgm:* Identifies the particular development program in which the employee participates.
- *retire:* Indicates the month and year of the employee's planned retirement.
- *est prom:* Indicates the employee's estimated potential for promotion.
- *lrp:* Indicates the employee's long-range career potential with the company.
- *ppc:* Indicates the incumbent's current organizational level.
- *3 Development Needs:* Describes three priority development needs that have been identified.
- *Potential Positions:* Shows the title of each position to which the incumbent is potentially promotable, along with codes that indicate an estimate of when the employee would be ready.
- *Possible Replacements:* Lists the names of up to 10 possible replacements for the incumbent, with codes indicating when the replacements would be ready for promotion to this position.

13 OBJECTIVE

Describe accelerated succession planning as an alternative to traditional approaches.

Accelerated Succession Planning: An Alternative to Traditional Approaches

A majority of North American firms want to fill 80 percent or more of their senior management positions with internal candidates. However, few are coming near that goal. A major reason for this situation is the breakdown in traditional management succession programs. Management succession programs typically focus on placement rather than skill development. In many firms, succession planning is a lost art—a casualty of mergers, downsizing, reorganizations, and reengineering. These conditions are creating a leadership deficit at a time when the need to develop internal talent is greatest.[42] One answer to this dilemma is the use of the acceleration pool system. **Acceleration pools** is management succession planning system that develops a group of high potential candidates for undefined executive jobs and focus on increasing their skills and knowledge rather than targeting one or two people for each senior management position. These pool members receive "stretch" assignments that offer the best learning and highest visibility opportunities. They spend less time in these assignments, but receive exposure to more special developmental experiences such as university executive programs and in-company learning sessions. They also get more feedback and coaching.[43]

Acceleration pools: A management succession planning system that develops a group of high-potential candidates for undefined executive jobs and focus on increasing their skills and knowledge rather than targeting one or two people for each senior management position.

14 OBJECTIVE

Explain the importance of planning for disasters.

The Importance of Planning for Disasters

The 9/11 attack on the World Trade Center pointed out vividly the need for disaster planning.[44] When disaster strikes business, there are always significant human resource issues to address.[45] Plans should focus on catastrophes that range from natural calamities such as earthquakes and floods to man-made crises such as bomb attacks. They should also cover day-to-day occurrences such as power failures, server malfunctions, and virus attacks. These plans need to address how the company will respond when employees who play a critical role or possess unique skills and knowledge suddenly become incapacitated or unavailable for some extended period of time.

To fill these voids, it is necessary to identify which positions and personnel within the company are critical to the organization's continued ability to accomplish its primary mission. Critical positions are those that cannot be left vacant even briefly without disastrous results, and which would be very difficult to fill. Databases are valuable here also. For critical positions the company should identify the name of the person, key responsibilities, required competencies, classification, pool of candidates for progression, candidate's existing competencies, and training required for candidates. That information should serve as the basis for the contingency plan, which should document those who could potentially step in to fulfill that role, the person with the authority to invoke that contingency, and other information required to ensure a smooth transition.[46]

Succession planning, acceleration pools, and disaster plans all require a human resource information system (HRIS). We will now describe the importance of an HRIS.

15 OBJECTIVE

Explain the importance of a human resource information system.

Human resource information system (HRIS):
Any organized approach for obtaining relevant and timely information on which to base human resource decisions.

People Soft

www.peoplesoft.com/corp/en/public_index.jsp

This Web site is the homepage for PeopleSoft, a major developer of human resource management systems.

Human Resource Information Systems

Earlier in this chapter we discussed how databases include information on managerial and nonmanagerial employees to be used to identify talent presently existing within a company. We also discussed human resource planning and succession planning. These and virtually all human resource management functions can be enhanced through the use of a **human resource information system (HRIS)**, any organized approach for obtaining relevant and timely information on which to base human resource decisions. It must also be cost-effective.[47] An HRIS should be designed to provide information that is

- *Timely.* A manager must have access to up-to-date information.
- *Accurate.* A manager must be able to rely on the accuracy of the information provided.
- *Concise.* A manager can absorb only so much information at any one time.
- *Relevant.* A manager should receive only the information needed in a particular situation.
- *Complete.* A manager should receive complete, not partial information.

The absence of even one of these characteristics reduces the effectiveness of an HRIS and complicates the decision-making process. Conversely, a system possessing all these characteristics enhances the ease and accuracy of the decision-making process. An effective HRIS also provides online data and forecasts related to business operations.

- *Exception Reports.* Exception reports highlight variations in operations that are serious enough to require management's attention. One type of exception report is the quality-exception report, completed when the number of product defects exceeds a predetermined maximum. The human resource manager may be interested in this type of information in order to identify additional training needs.

- *On-Demand Reports.* An on-demand report provides information in response to a specific request. The number of engineers with five years' work experience who speak fluent Spanish is an example of an on-demand report that the human resource manager could request from the database.
- *Forecasts.* A forecast applies predictive models to specific situations. Managers need forecasts of the number and types of employees required to satisfy projected demand for the firm's product.

Firms realize that a properly developed HRIS can provide tremendous benefits to the organization. While many HR directors and managers at small organizations shoulder HRIS in addition to their many other responsibilities, larger organizations have specific staff to address technology issues.[48] Figure 4-7 presents an overview of the human resource information system designed for one organization. Utilizing numerous types of input data, the HRIS makes available many types of output data that have far-reaching human resource planning and operational value. The HRIS ties together all human resource information into a system.

Throughout this book, we will stress how HR is shedding routine administering tasks. The HRIS provides an excellent means to reduce the burden of these tasks. Many medium-sized and large companies have added self-service capabilities to their HRIS. Self-service puts the responsibility for many information-management tasks, such as filing change-of-address forms and completing benefits enrollment, in the hands of employees.[49] This dramatically reduces the amount of time that HR staffers

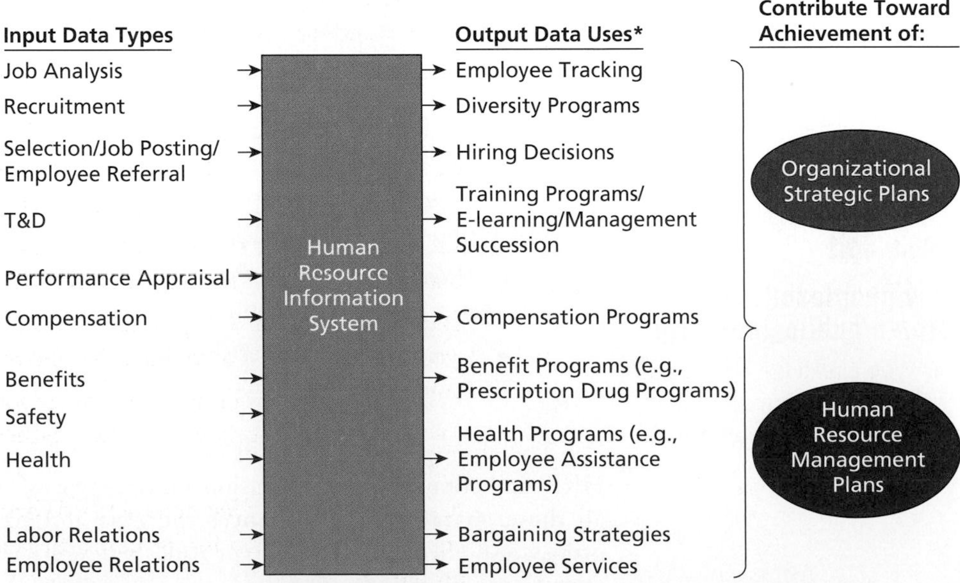

Figure 4-7 A Human Resource Information System

spend on administrative tasks and frees them to focus their attention on more strategic company goals.[50]

Data from various input sources are integrated to provide the needed outputs. Information needed in the firm's human resource decision-making process is readily available when the system is properly designed. For instance, many firms are now studying historical trends to determine the best means of securing qualified applicants. In addition, complying with statutes and government regulations would be extremely difficult were it not for the modern HRIS.

There are numerous firms that provide Human Resource Information Systems. One of the more significant of these is PeopleSoft, the largest HRIS software provider. The system lets a company manage HR business processes—from recruitment to retirement—with pure Internet applications that are built on a best-practices performance record of more than ten years. PeopleSoft HRMS applications are used every day by nine out of the top ten *Fortune* 500 companies, including Exxon-Mobil, Wal-Mart, General Motors, Ford, Citigroup, IBM, AT&T, and Verizon Communications.[51]

16 OBJECTIVE

Describe some job design concepts.

Job Design Concepts

We previously said that new jobs were being created at a rapid pace. If this is so, jobs have to be designed. **Job design** is the process of determining the specific tasks to be performed, the methods used in performing these tasks, and how the job relates to other work in the organization. Several concepts related to job design will be discussed next.

Job design:
A process of determining the specific tasks to be performed, the methods used in performing these tasks, and how the job relates to other work in an organization.

Job Enrichment

Strongly advocated by Frederick Herzberg, **job enrichment** consists of basic changes in the content and level of responsibility of a job so as to provide greater challenge to the worker. Job enrichment provides a vertical expansion of responsibilities.[52] The worker has the opportunity to derive a feeling of achievement, recognition, responsibility, and personal growth in performing the job. Although job enrichment programs do not always achieve positive results, they have often brought about improvements in job performance, and in the level of worker satisfaction in many organizations.

Job enrichment:
The restructuring of the content and level of responsibility of a job to make it more challenging, meaningful, and interesting to a worker.

According to Herzberg, five principles should be followed when implementing job enrichment:

1. *Increasing job demands:* The job should be changed in such a way as to increase the level of difficulty and responsibility.
2. *Increasing the worker's accountability:* More individual control and authority over the work should be allowed, while the manager retains ultimate accountability.
3. *Providing work scheduling freedom:* Within limits, individual workers should be allowed to schedule their own work.
4. *Providing feedback:* Timely periodic reports on performance should be made directly to workers rather than to their supervisors.
5. *Providing new learning experiences:* Work situations should encourage opportunities for new experiences and personal growth.[53]

Today, job enrichment is moving toward the team level, as more teams become autonomous, or self-managed.[54]

Job Enlargement

Job enlargement:
The process of increasing the number of tasks a worker performs without increasing the level of responsibility.

There is a clear distinction between job enrichment and job enlargement. **Job enlargement** is defined as increasing the number of tasks a worker performs, with all of the tasks at the same level of responsibility.[55] Job enlargement involves providing greater variety to the worker. For example, instead of knowing how to operate only one machine, a person is taught to operate two or even three, but no higher level of responsibility is required. Both job enrichment and job enlargement can be used with workers who have progressed as far as they can in their present jobs or are victims of burnout.[56]

Reengineering

Reengineering:
The fundamental rethinking and radical redesign of business processes to achieve dramatic improvements in critical, contemporary measures of performance such as cost, quality, service, and speed.

Reengineering is "the fundamental rethinking and radical redesign of business processes to achieve dramatic improvements in critical contemporary measures of performance, such as cost, quality, service, and speed."[57] Reengineering essentially involves the firm rethinking and redesigning its business system to become more competitive. When Hewlett-Packard developed its new product line of low-cost printers, engineers were told to ignore the models then being sold and start from scratch. Through reengineering, CEO Vyomesh Joshi wanted an entire product line to be brought out at one time. He also wanted to take it from concept to store shelves in less than three years, 18 months faster than HP had ever accomplished a product launch. Radical design had to be considered and engineers had to "think outside the box," but the task was accomplished.[58]

Reengineering emphasizes the radical redesign of work in which companies organize around process instead of by functional departments. Incremental change is not what is desired; instead, radical changes are wanted that will alter entire operations at one time. Essentially, the firm must rethink and redesign its business system from the ground up.

Reengineering focuses on the overall aspects of job designs, organizational structures, and management systems. It stresses that work should be organized around outcomes as opposed to tasks or functions. Reengineering should never be confused with downsizing (discussed in Chapter 14), even though a workforce reduction often results from this strategy.[59] Naturally, job design considerations are of paramount concern because as the process changes, so do essential elements of jobs.

A Global Perspective

A Database of Repatriate Skills

Brenda Fender, director of international initiatives for the Employee Relocation Council in Washington, D.C., believes that many organizations still have a long way to go in taking advantage of the experience and knowledge of repatriates. "Many companies just don't track it," she says. J. Stewart Black, president of the Center for Global Assignments, a research and consulting organization in Alpine, Utah, says that "the vast majority" of U.S. companies have failed to realize the importance of creating databases of repatriate skills. If an employee leaves the company, her skills and knowledge will be lost for good. The resultant cost of losing a valuable employee, Black says, can be "staggering." Black says that the $2 million cost of a four-year overseas assignment becomes even higher when the usual 25 percent attrition rate is factored in.[60]

Colgate-Palmolive Company recognized the wealth of information it already had on expatriate skills in a system not originally designed for that purpose. Coleen Smith, New York–based vice president for global people development, says that the company began putting together a global succession-planning database almost 10 years ago. "It has taken a variety of forms over the years," she says. While Colgate-Palmolive's database is primarily for succession planning, it also contains data on each manager's experience with an awareness of particular cultures. The information is made available throughout the company's worldwide network. "Senior leaders," Smith says, "have come to expect a certain level of information, which we really manage through our global succession-planning database."[61]

Colgate-Palmolive sees a foreign assignment as part of an extended overseas career track rather than as a one off assignment. A successful foreign assignment tends to lead to another and another. "Our top priority is to identify, develop and retain the next two to three generations of leaders," Smith says. And part of that strategy includes directly using the knowledge of the company's current and former expatriates. Seventy-five percent of Colgate-Palmolive's $9.5 billion in annual sales comes from outside North America. The company has a global expatriate population of about 300, a figure that has remained steady over the past decade. Forty percent of these expatriates have had four or more global assignments. Seventy-five percent have had two or more. The system has gained upper-level support given that the company's senior executives, Smith says, "have all worked in multiple locations around the world." Colgate-Palmolive's wide geographical spread puts enormous emphasis on detailed knowledge of local markets. In Europe, the company must respond to pressure from both consumers and governments for environmentally friendly packaging. In Latin America, managers might have to cope with the complexities growing out of recurrent hyperinflation or periodic currency devaluations. Such swings can affect both product pricing and business planning. All this knowledge about local markets must reach every corner of Colgate-Palmolive's global operations. And this is where a database of expatriate knowledge comes into play.[62]

Summary

1. Describe the importance of succession planning.
Succession planning is the process of ensuring that qualified persons are available to assume key managerial positions once the positions are vacant. This definition includes untimely deaths, resignations, terminations, or the orderly retirements of company officials.

2. Explain why job analysis is a basic human resource tool.
Job analysis is the systematic process of determining the skills, duties, and knowledge required for performing jobs in an organization. It is an essential and pervasive human resource technique. In today's rapidly changing work environment, the need for a sound job analysis system is extremely critical. New jobs are being created, and old jobs are being redesigned or eliminated.

3. Explain the reasons for conducting job analysis.
Without a properly conducted job analysis, it would be difficult, if not impossible, to satisfactorily perform the other human resource–related functions.

4. Describe the types of information required for job analysis.
Work activities, worker-oriented activities, and the types of machines, tools, equipment, and work aids used in the job are important. This information is used to help determine the job skills needed. In addition, the job analyst looks at job-related tangibles and intangibles.

5. Describe the various job analysis methods.
The job analyst may administer a structured questionnaire, witness the work being performed, interview both the employee and the supervisor, or ask them to describe their daily work activities in a diary or log. A combination of methods is often used.

6. Describe the components of a well-designed job description.
Components include the job identification section, which includes the job title, department, reporting relationship, and a job number or code; the job analysis date; the job summary; and the body of the job description that delineates the major duties to be performed.

7. Identify the other methods available for conducting job analysis.
The U.S. Department of Labor job analysis schedule (JAS); functional job analysis (FJA); the position analysis questionnaire (PAQ); the management position description questionnaire (MPDQ); and guidelines-oriented job analysis (GOJA).

8. Describe how job analysis helps satisfy various legal requirements.
Legislation requiring thorough job analysis includes the following acts: Fair Labor Standards Act, Equal Pay Act, Civil Rights Act, Occupational Safety and Health Act, and the Americans with Disabilities Act.

9. Explain strategic planning and the human resource planning process.
After strategic plans have been formulated, human resource planning can be undertaken. Human resource planning has two components: requirements and availability.

10. Describe some human resource forecasting techniques.
Forecasting techniques include zero-base forecasting, the bottom-up approach, and the use of predictor variables.

11. Define *requirements* and *availability* forecasts.
A requirements forecast is an estimate of the numbers and kinds of employees the organization will need at future dates in order to realize its goals. Determining whether the firm will be able to secure employees with the necessary skills and from what sources these individuals may be obtained is called an availability forecast.

12. Identify what a firm can do when either a surplus or a shortage of workers exists.
When a surplus of workers exists a firm may implement one or more of the following: restricted hiring, reduced hours, early retirement, and layoffs. When a shortage of

workers exists, creative recruiting, compensation incentives, training programs, and different selection standards are possible.

13. Describe accelerated succession planning as an alternative to traditional approaches.
There has been a breakdown in traditional management succession programs. One answer to this dilemma is the use of the acceleration pool system. Acceleration pools, rather than targeting one or two people for each senior management position, develop a group of high-potential candidates for undefined executive jobs and focus on increasing their skills and knowledge.

14. Explain the importance of planning for disasters.
The 9/11 attack on the World Trade Center pointed out vividly the need for disaster planning. When disaster strikes your business, there are always significant human resource issues to address. Plans should focus on catastrophes that range from natural calamities, such as earthquakes and floods to man-made crises such as bomb attacks. They should also cover day-to-day occurrences such as power failures, server malfunctions, and virus attacks.

15. Describe some job design concepts.
Job design is the process of determining the specific tasks to be performed, the methods used in performing the tasks, and how the job relates to other work in the organization. Job enrichment consists of basic changes in the content and level of responsibility of a job so as to provide greater challenge to the worker. Job enrichment provides a vertical expansion of responsibilities. Job enlargement is defined as increasing the number of tasks a worker performs, with all of the tasks at the same level of responsibility. Reengineering is the fundamental rethinking and radical redesign of business processes to achieve dramatic improvements in critical contemporary measures of performance, such as cost, quality, service, and speed.

Key Terms

- **Succession planning, 85**
- **Job analysis, 86**
- **Job, 86**
- **Position, 86**
- **Job description, 87**
- **Job specification, 87**
- **Job analysis schedule (JAS), 96**
- **Functional job analysis (FJA), 96**
- **Position analysis questionnaire (PAQ), 97**
- **Management position description questionnaire (MPDQ), 98**
- **Guidelines-oriented job analysis (GOJA), 98**
- **Strategic planning, 99**
- **Human resource planning (HRP), 99**
- **Zero-base forecasting, 101**
- **Bottom-up approach, 101**
- **Simulation, 101**
- **Requirements forecast, 102**
- **Availability forecast, 102**
- **Acceleration pools, 106**
- **Human Resource Information System (HRIS), 107**
- **Job design, 109**
- **Job enrichment, 109**
- **Job enlargement, 110**
- **Reengineering, 110**

Questions for Review

1. Define *succession planning*. Why is it important?
2. What is the distinction between a job and a position? Define *job analysis*.
3. Why is job analysis considered to be a basic human resource tool?
4. When is job analysis performed?
5. What are the types of information required for job analysis?
6. What are the traditional methods used to conduct job analysis? Describe each type.
7. What are the basic components of a job description? Briefly describe each.

8. Briefly define each of the following: (a) the U.S. Department of Labor job analysis schedule (JAS); (b) functional job analysis (FJA); (c) the position analysis questionnaire (PAQ); (d) the management position description questionnaire (MPDQ); and (e) guidelines-oriented job analysis (GOJA).
9. Describe how effective job analysis can be used to satisfy each of the following statutes: (a) Fair Labor Standards Act, (b) Equal Pay Act, (c) Civil Rights Act, (d) Occupational Safety and Health Act, and (e) Americans with Disabilities Act.
10. What are the steps involved in the human resource planning process?
11. What are the human resource forecasting techniques?
12. Distinguish between forecasting human resource requirements and availability.
13. What actions could a firm take if it had a worker surplus?
14. What actions could a firm take if it forecasted a shortage of workers?
15. What is accelerated succession planning? Why are firms beginning to use this as an alternative to traditional succession planning?
16. Why is disaster planning important?
17. Define *human resource information system (HRIS)*. Why is a human resource information system needed?
18. Define each of the following: (a) job design, (b) job enrichment, (c) job enlargement, and (d) reengineering.

A Degree for Meter Readers

Judy Anderson was assigned as a recruiter for South Illinois Electric Company (SIE), a small supplier of natural gas and electricity for Cairo, Illinois, and the surrounding area. The company had expanded rapidly during the last half of the 1990s, and this growth was expected to continue. In January 2003, SIE purchased the utilities system serving neighboring Mitchell County. This expansion concerned Judy. The company workforce had increased by 30 percent the previous year, and Judy had found it a struggle to recruit enough qualified job applicants. She knew that new expansion would intensify the problem.

Judy is particularly concerned about meter readers. The tasks required in meter reading are relatively simple. A person drives to homes served by the company, finds the gas or electric meter, and records its current reading. If the meter has been tampered with, it is reported. Otherwise, no decision-making of any consequence is associated with the job. The reader performs no calculations. The pay was $8.00 per hour, high for unskilled work in the area. Even so, Judy had been having considerable difficulty keeping the 37 meter reader positions filled.

Judy was thinking about how to attract more job applicants when she received a call from the human resource director, Sam McCord. "Judy," Sam said, "I'm unhappy with the job specification calling for only a high school education for meter readers. In planning for the future, we need better-educated people in the company. I've decided to change the education requirement for the meter reader job from a high school diploma to a college degree."

But, Mr. McCord," protested Judy, "the company is growing rapidly. If we are to have enough people to fill those jobs we just can't insist on finding college applicants to perform such basic tasks. I don't see how we can meet our future needs for this job with such an unrealistic job qualification."

Sam terminated the conversation abruptly by saying, "No, I don't agree. We need to upgrade all the people in our organization. This is just part of a general effort to do that. Anyway, I cleared this with the president before I decided to do it."

Questions

1. Should there be a minimum education requirement for the meter reader job? Discuss.
2. What is your opinion of Sam's effort to upgrade the people in the organization?
3. What legal ramifications, if any, should Sam have considered?

HRM Incident 2

Strategic HR?

Brian Charles, the vice president of marketing for Sharpco Manufacturing, commented at the weekly executive directors' meeting, "I have good news. We can get the large contract with Medord Corporation. All we have to do is complete the project in one year instead of two. I told them we could do it."

Charmagne Powell, vice president of human resources, brought Brian back to reality by reminding him, "Remember the strategic plan we were involved in developing and we all agreed to? Our present workers do not have the expertise required to produce the quality that Medord's particular specifications require. Under the two-year project timetable, we planned to retrain our present workers gradually. With this new time schedule, we will have to go into the job market and recruit workers who are already experienced in this process. We all need to study your proposal further. Human resource costs will rise considerably if we attempt to complete the project in one year instead of two. Sure, Brian, we can do it, but with these constraints, will the project be cost-effective?"

Questions

1. Was Charmagne considering the strategic nature of human resource planning when she challenged Brian's "good news" forecast? Discuss.
2. How did the involvement in developing the corporate strategic plan assist Charmagne in challenging Brian?

Human Resource Management Skills

Chapter 4: Job Analysis and Human Resource Planning

A Skills Module entitled *Job Analysis* is presented to provide additional insight into topics in this chapter. The module addresses the following topics: importance of job analysis; process of job analysis, and using job analysis information to develop job descriptions for recruitment, selection, training, performance management, and compensation. The module includes information on identifying KSAOCs (knowledge, skills, abilities, and other characteristics) and competencies as well as presenting information on job design and contingent workers.

The first portion of the *Strategic Planning and Recruitment* Skills Module pertains to human resource planning. Topics include an overview of the importance of strategic planning including discussion of the role of employees in achieving a competitive advantage and when human resource planning should take place. Also covered are types of labor markets, conditions that can exist relative to labor demand and labor supply, and what HR strategies should be used under varying labor market conditions.

Several job analysis and human resource planning scenarios are presented to give students realistic experience in dealing with the topic.

A test is provided at the end of the module to determine mastery of the material included in the Skills Module. Also, directions are given for assignments that can be used in class or assigned as homework.

Take it to the Net

We invite you to visit the Mondy homepage on the Prentice Hall Web site at

www.prenhall.com/mondy

for updated information. Web-based exercises, and links to other HR-related sites.

Notes

1. Robert J. Grossman, "Heirs Unapparent as the Next Millennium Begins, Leaders Will Have to Be Made Because Not Enough Have Been Born," *HRMagazine* 44 (February 1999): 36–44.
2. Gale Dutton, "Future Shock: Who Will Run the Company?" *Management Review* 85 (August 1996): 19.
3. Dean R. O'Hare, "RMs Have What It Takes in War Against Terrorism," *National Underwriter* (April 15, 2002): 10–11.
4. Joe Tripalin "Passing the Torch," *Credit Union Management* 25 (September 2002): 10–12.
5. David Gabriel, "Lost Leaders," *Telephony* (September 16, 2002): 44.
6. Des Dearlove and Stuart Crainer, "Help Wanted: Superhero," *Chief Executive* 182 (October 2002): 26–29.
7. Ibid.
8. Ram Charan and Jerry Useen, "The 5 Pitfalls of CEO Succession," *Fortune* (November 18, 2002): 78.
9. Gregory C. Kesler, "Why the Leadership Bench Never Gets Deeper: Ten Insights About Executive Talent Development," *Human Resource Planning* 25 (2002): 32–34.
10. R. Wayne Mondy, Robert M. Noe, and Robert E. Edwards, "What the Staffing Function Entails," *Personnel* 63 (April 1986): 55–58.
11. Ivan T. Robertson and Mike Smith "Personnel Selection," *Journal of Occupational and Organizational Psychology* (74 November 2001): 441–472.
12. Michael J. Blotzer, "Job Hazard Analysis and More," *Occupational Hazards* (July 1, 1998): 25(3).
13. *Uniform Guidelines on Employee Selection Procedures*, *Federal Register* (August 25, 1978): Part IV.
14. IBM Human Resources Conference, "IT Should Support HR Changes," October 23, 1996.
15. Mary Molina Fitzer, "Managing from Afar: Performance and Rewards in a Telecommmuting Environment," *Compensation & Benefits Review* 29 (January/February 1997): 65–73.
16. N. Fredric Crandall and Marc J. Wallace Jr., "Inside the Virtual Workplace: Forging a New Deal for Work and Rewards," *Compensation & Benefits Review* 29 (January/February 1997): 27–36.
17. Gilbert B. Siegel, "Job Analysis in the TQM Environment," *Public Personnel Management* 25 (December 1996): 493.
18. Jonathan A. Segal, "Brains in a Jar," *HRMagazine* 44 (April 1999): 130.
19. Jonathan Sidener, "Pace of Net Technology Means Redefining Jobs Quickly," *Arizona Republic* (May 14, 2000): S13.
20. Brenda George, "Need a Recruiter? Here's Your 'To Do' List," *AFP Exchange* 22 (September/October 2002): 36–38.
21. Nancy Doucette, "Preventing 'Bad Hire' Days," *Rough Notes* 145 (July 2002): 36–39.
22. Nancy Doucette, "That's Not My Job," *Rough Notes* 145 (August 2002): 40–42.
23. Alison Rice, "Revolving Door," *Builder* 25 (August 2002): 130–132.
24. Stuart Silverstein, "Guidelines for Disability Cases," *Newsday* (May 11, 1997): F12.
25. Accommodation Will Be the Next ADA Issue," *HR Focus* 79 (March 2000): 2.
26. U.S. Department of Labor, *Dictionary of Occupational Titles*, 4th ed. (Washington, DC: U.S. Government Printing Office, 1977).
27. Marilyn Rosenthal, "O*NET Dictionary of Occupational Titles 2001–2002," *Library Journal* (October 1, 2002): 68.
28. EEOC Says Telework Is a Reasonable Accommodation," *Compensation & Benefits Report* 17 (April 2003): 12.
29. Howard Risher, "The End of Jobs: Planning and Managing Rewards in the New Work Paradigm," *Compensation & Benefits Review* 29 (January/February 1997): 13–17.
30. Diane Brady, "Rethinking the Rat Race: Technology Is Making 'All Work and No Play' a Real Possibility: How Will We Strike the Proper Balance of Work and Life?" *BusinessWeek* (August 26, 2002): 142–143.
31. Jodi Barnes Nelson, "The Boundaryless Organization: Implications for Job Analysis, Recruitment, and Selection," *Human Resource Planning* 20 (1997): 39–49.
32. Robert J. Harvey, "Functional Job Analysis," *Personnel Psychology* 55 (Spring 2002): 202–205.
33. Ibid.
34. Stephen E. Bemis, Ann Holt Belenky, and Dee Ann Soder, *Job Analysis: An Effective Management Tool* (Washington, DC: The Bureau of National Affairs, 1983): 42.
35. James P. Clifford, "Job Analysis: Why Do It, and How Should It Be Done?" *Public Personnel Management* 23 (Summer 1994): 324.
36. Eric Minton, "The ADA and Records Management," *Records Management* 28 (January 1994): 12.
37. Melody Jones, "Four Trends to Reckon With," *HR Focus* 73 (July 1996): 22.
38. Larry Bossidy and Ram Charan, "Finding the Leaders Within ; Making Sure You Have the Right People in the Right Job Is More Important to Your Company Than Strategic Direction or Decisions," *CIO* (October 15, 2002): 111.
39. Patricia M. Buhler, "Tips to Improved Staffing Decisions," *Supervision* 63 (October 2002): 20–22.
40. David Brown, "The Future Is Nigh for Strategies HR," *Canadian HR Reporter* (June 17, 2002): 7.
41. Daniel Eisenberg, "Firms Brace for a Worker Shortage," *Time* (May 6, 2002): 44.
42. William C. Byhan, "Bench Strength: Succession Planning, As We Know It, Is Dead. Long Live Acceleration Pools," *Across the Board* 37 (February 2000): 34.
43. William C. Byham, "How to Create a Reservoir of Ready-Made Leaders," *Training & Development* 54 (March 2000): 29.
44. Stan Lomax, "When Disaster Strikes: A Primer for Managers," *Business and Economic Review* 48 (January-March 2002): 11–15.
45. Jeffrey I. Pasek, "Crisis Management for HR," *HRMagazine* 47 (August 2002): 111–116.
46. Selvaraju Balaji, "Could Key Personnel Losses Create Chaos?" *Security Management* 46 (July 2002): 184.
47. "How Employers Save on HRIS Costs," *HR Focus* 79 (December 2002): 10–11.

48. HR and HRIS: Who Does What?" *HR Focus* 79 (October 2002): S2.
49. Alyson Behr, "HRMS Made Easy," *InfoWorld* (April 7, 2003): 30–31.
50. Sarah Gale, "Three Stories of Self-Service Success," *Workforce* (January 1, 2003): 60.
51. http://www.peoplesoft.com/corp/en/public_index.jsp, July 28, 2003.
52. James J. Kirk, Bridget Downey, Steve Duckett, and Connie Woody, "Name Your Career Development Intervention," *Journal of Workplace Learning* 12 (2000): 205–216.
53. Frederick Herzberg, "One More Time: How Do You Motivate Employees?" *Harvard Business Review* 65 (September/October 1987): 109–120.
54. Patricia M. Buhler, "Managers: Out with the Old and in with the New — Skills That Is," *Supervision* 59 (June 1998): 22–26.
55. Kirk, Downey, Duckett, and Woody, "Name Your Career Development Intervention," 205–216.
56. Ibid.
57. Michael Hammer and James Champy, *Reengineering the Corporation: A Manifesto for Business Revolution* (New York: HarperCollins Publishers, 1993): 32.
58. Noshua Watson, "What's Wrong with This Printer?" *Fortune* (February 17, 2003): 120.
59. "The Malapropian 'R' Word," *Industry Forum*, prepared by the American Management Association (September 1993): 1.
60. Robert O'Connor, "Plug the Expat Knowledge Drain," *HRMagazine* 47 (October 2002): 101–107.
61. Ibid.
62. Ibid.

CHAPTER OBJECTIVES

After completing this chapter, students should be able to

1. Explain the importance of Internet recruiting.
2. Explain alternatives to recruitment.
3. Explain the external and internal environment of recruitment.
4. Describe the recruitment process.
5. Describe internal recruitment methods.
6. Explain external sources of recruitment.
7. Identify external recruitment methods.
8. Describe an applicant tracking system.
9. Describe how recruitment methods and sources are tailored to each other.
10. Explain recruitment for diversity.

CHAPTER 5

Recruitment

HRM IN *Action:*

Internet Recruiting

OBJECTIVE

Explain the importance of Internet recruiting.

Recruitment:
The process of attracting individuals on a timely basis, in sufficient numbers, and with appropriate qualifications, and encouraging them to apply for jobs with an organization.

Recruitment is the process of attracting individuals on a timely basis, in sufficient numbers, and with appropriate qualifications, and encouraging them to apply for jobs with an organization. Finding the appropriate way of encouraging qualified candidates to apply for employment is extremely important when a firm needs to hire employees, and the Internet can be a valuable recruiting tool. The speed and expanded talent pool offered by the Web make the recruitment process more efficient and cost-effective for both employer and job candidate. Initiating contact with prospective employers by telephone or through the U.S. Postal Service is fast becoming an outmoded technique for candidates looking for a job. Basically, recruiting on the Web expands individual employment options, and improves the recruitment process for businesses. The age-old task of matching candidates with jobs is being revolutionized.

Internet recruiting has gone from a hot, but unproven, recruiting approach to an integral, measurable part of the recruiter's toolbox, says David Manaster, president of Electronic Recruiting Exchange.[1] "Using the Internet has become a fundamental part of recruiting. It's difficult to do without it," he says.[2] According to the Search Tactics Poll conducted by the *Society for Human Resources Management Career Journal,* "Eighty-eight percent of HR professionals use Internet job postings to find job candidates and 96 percent of job seekers use them to find jobs."[3] This figure includes those firms that use their homepage for job listings. Recently, an estimated 52 million Americans used the Internet to search for employment.[4] IDC, a Framingham, Massachusetts, research firm, says the market for online e-recruiting services worldwide will be worth almost $15.7 billion by 2006, with a compound annual growth rate of 40.9 percent.[5]

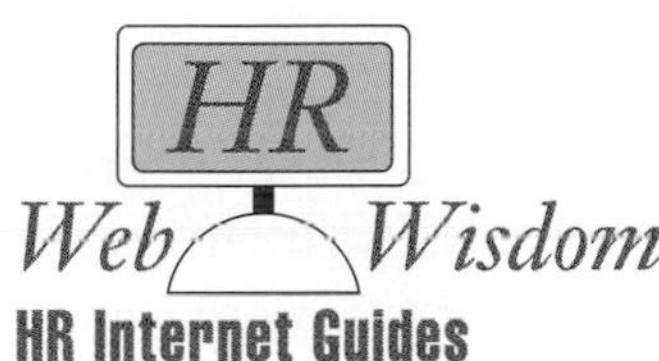

HR Internet Guides

www.hr-guide.com

This Web site contains links to other Internet-based resources for HR professionals such as recruitment, selection, and EEO.

The Internet will likely be a most effective recruiting and staffing tool in the future. Although Internet recruiting has not replaced traditional recruiting, it has become an essential aid for today's recruiters. To maximize recruiting success, HR managers must:

- Research Internet employment sites and become familiar with the options available.
- Be upbeat and informative on the company Web site and use it as a selling device that promotes the company to prospective job candidates.[6] HR professionals must be heavily involved in developing the recruiting section of the corporate homepage. They must provide all the data that candidates need, including information about the job, company, work environment, and how candidates may apply online.
- Remember that writing effective recruitment ads on the Internet is different from the short, one-column-inch ads in the Sunday newspaper. The Internet provides enough space to fully describe the job, location, and company. It is important to include the company Web address in job ads placed in other media.
- Experiment with various advertising approaches by placing ads in several relevant sites across the Internet, including the company homepage, state and federal job-posting services (free), and/or several of the commercial online employment sites.
- Monitor both traditional and Internet advertisements to judge the cost-effectiveness of each approach.
- Experiment with various Web sites to determine which sites contain pools of the skills necessary for open positions.[7]

Do not neglect traditional recruiting methods.[8] Internet recruiting should not be treated as a standalone HR tool but should be integrated into an overall recruiting and selection strategy. Internet recruitment is an innovative and effective means for attracting applicants. However, as with other recruitment methods, it is not a selection tool. It does not replace conducting background checks, face-to-face interviews, and other steps required to assess attitudes and behavior that are vital to finding qualified employees. Detailed treatment of Internet recruitment and the essentials of an online résumé are presented in the appendix to this chapter.

OBJECTIVE

Explain alternatives to recruitment.

SHRM HR Links

www.shrm.org/hrlinks/default.asp

This SHRM Web site provides information related to temporary workers.

We began this chapter by defining the recruitment process and describing the importance of Internet recruiting. Next, we explain alternatives to recruitment followed by the external and internal environments of recruitment. A description of the recruitment process precedes a discussion of internal recruitment methods. Then we examine external sources of recruitment and identify external recruitment methods. Next, an applicant tracking system is described. Then we explain how recruitment methods and sources are tailored to each other. The final portion of this chapter is devoted to recruitment for diversity.

Alternatives to Recruitment

Even when human resource planning indicates a need for additional or replacement employees, a firm may decide against increasing the size of its workforce. Recruitment and selection costs are significant when you consider all the related expenses: the search process, interviewing, agency fees, relocation and processing of a new employee. Although selection decisions are not necessarily permanent, once applicants are on the payroll, they may be difficult to remove even if their performance is marginal. Therefore, a firm should consider its alternatives carefully before engaging in recruitment. Alternatives to recruitment commonly include outsourcing, use of contingent workers, employee leasing, and overtime.

Outsourcing

As defined in Chapter 1, *outsourcing* is the process of transferring responsibility for an area of service and its objectives to an external provider. Subcontracting of various functions to other firms has been a common practice in industry for decades. This decision may make sense when the subcontractor can perform a given function, such as maintenance, with perhaps even greater efficiency and effectiveness. Management should understand, however, that there may be no retreat. Once a decision to outsource is made and internal systems disassembled, it may be difficult or even impossible to reverse the practice. Therefore, a sound outsource contract is vital.[9]

Within the past few years, outsourcing has become a widespread and increasingly popular alternative involving virtually every business area, including human resources. For example, several years ago, Kellogg, which has 14,000 employees worldwide, revamped its recruiting function by outsourcing the hiring of all employees except those working on an hourly basis. A vendor now works directly with hiring managers in each phase of the process and uses its own recruitment technology to track all data and details. Staffing professionals at each location continue to hire hourly employees.[10]

During 2002, Bank of America slashed 3,700 of its 25,000 technical and back-office jobs. Reduced demand was not the sole cause of these layoffs. Former Bank of America managers and contractors state that India will receive one-third of those jobs where work that costs $100 an hour in the United States is accomplished for $20. Globalization is definitely causing the outsourcing of upscale information technology jobs offshore to places such as India, Eastern Europe, and parts of South America.[11] These jobs include chip design, software engineering, programming, Web development, basic research, financial analysis, computer technical support, and even insurance claims processing. The cost of performing these tasks abroad is significantly lower than in the United States.[12]

Contingent Workers

Contingent workers: Described as the "disposable American workforce" by a former Secretary of Labor, work as part-timers, temporaries, or independent contractors.

Contingent workers, described as the "disposable American workforce" by a former secretary of labor, work as part-timers, temporaries, or independent contractors. According to the American Staffing Association (ASA), the temporary workforce has doubled in size over the last decade. The number of workers in the United States who do not have a contract for ongoing employment is about 5.4 million people, roughly 4 percent of the workforce. Millions more are employed in alternative work arrangements and serve as on-call employees, temporary help agency workers, and contract workers.[13] Contingent workers clearly comprise a large and important component of the U.S. workforce. Some observers go further and predict that the temporary workforce will grow faster than its permanent counterpart for years to come. Manpower, a temporary staffing company, provides additional evidence of the growing importance of the temporary workforce. This firm is now one of the largest employers in the United States.[14]

As the economy has slowed, however, the number of temporary jobs available dropped 15 percent, nearly a half a million positions. This suggests that temporary employees were among the first workers laid off when the economy slowed. To a degree, it appears that flexible employment was successful in preventing regular job losses.[15]

Rationale for Using Contingent Workers

According to a Conference Board survey, over 80 percent of the respondents indicated the primary reason for the rapid growth of jobs for these workers was to achieve *flexibility*. Global competition and changing technology prevent employers from accurately forecasting their employment needs months in advance. To avoid hiring people one day and resorting to layoffs the next, firms look to the benefits of flexible employment strategies.[16]

In addition to the need for flexibility, another factor is *cost*. The total cost of a permanent employee is about 30 to 40 percent above gross pay. This figure does not include, among other things, the costs of recruitment. To avoid some of these expenses and to maintain flexibility as workloads vary, many organizations utilize part-time or temporary employees. Companies that provide temporary workers assist their clients in handling excess or special workloads. These companies assign their own employees to their customers and fulfill all the obligations normally associated with an employer. Client firms avoid the expenses of recruitment, absenteeism, turnover, and employee benefits. At least this is the idea. However, the costs of contingent staffing may be underestimated.[17]

Contingent workers are the human equivalents of just-in-time inventory. These *disposable workers* permit distinct advantages; maximum flexibility for the employer and lower labor costs. The main unanswered question is whether this approach to staffing is healthy for our society in the long run. In the shorter term, the advantages gained by using contingent workers may be essential for success or even survival of many companies.

Professional Employer Organizations (Employee Leasing)

Professional employer organization (PEO):
Firms that work with company clients in a co-employment relationship to provide human resource administration, comprehensive employee benefit programs, assumption of employer risk, tax filing, and compliance with employment laws.

StaffMarket.com

www.staffmarket.com/smdevmaster2/smpeoabout2.asp

This Web site is a major professional employer organization.

Professional employer organizations (PEOs) are firms that work with company clients in a co-employment relationship to provide human resource administration, comprehensive employee benefit programs, assumption of employer risk, tax filing, and compliance with employment laws.[18] PEOs typically charge from 1 to 4 percent of the customer's gross wages, with percentages based on the number of leased employees. The organization handles the company's payroll, benefits, human resources, and risk management.[19] Small and medium-sized firms are the primary users of PEOs.

Advantages for Employees. Leasing also has advantages for employees. Because leasing companies provide workers for many companies, they often enjoy economies of scale that permit them to offer a wider selection of benefits at considerably lower cost, due to the large numbers of employees in their pools.[20] In addition, workers frequently have greater opportunities for job mobility. Some leasing firms operate throughout the nation. The relocation of one employed spouse in a dual-career family may be more satisfactory if the leasing company offers the other spouse a job in the new location, too. In addition, if a client organization's business suffers a downturn, the leasing company offers job security. The PEO can transfer employees to another client, avoiding both layoffs and loss of seniority.[21]

Potential Disadvantages. A potential disadvantage to the client is erosion of employee loyalty because workers receive pay and benefits from the leasing company. Regardless of any shortcomings, use of employee leasing is growing. By 2005, the industry could have $185 billion in revenues and more than 9 million employees.[22]

Overtime

Perhaps the most commonly used method of meeting short-term fluctuations in work volume is overtime. Overtime may help both employer and employee. The employer benefits by avoiding recruitment, selection, and training costs. The employees gain from increased income during the overtime period.

There are potential problems with overtime, however. Some managers believe that when employees work for unusually long periods, the company pays more and receives less in return. Employees may become fatigued and lack the energy to perform at a normal rate. Two additional possible problems relate to the use of prolonged overtime. Consciously or not, employees may pace themselves to ensure overtime. They may also become accustomed to the added income resulting from overtime pay. Employees may even elevate their standard of living to the level permitted by this additional income. Then, when a firm tightens its belt and overtime is limited, employee morale may deteriorate along with their pay. This possibility has become reality to an increasing number of employees as many companies are reducing bonuses and overtime.[23]

3 OBJECTIVE

Explain the external and internal environment of recruitment.

External Environment of Recruitment

Like other human resource functions, the recruitment process does not occur in a vacuum. Factors external to the organization can significantly affect the firm's recruitment efforts. Of particular importance is the demand for and supply of specific skills in the labor market. If demand for a particular skill is high relative to supply, an extraordinary recruiting effort may be required.

Labor Market Conditions

As competition for the best employees continues, even when the economy is sputtering, some business firms have implemented creative approaches to recruitment. In addition, as firms seek to reduce labor costs, many have outsourced jobs to qualified individuals in foreign countries as discussed in a later section.

Domestic Labor Market. A firm's recruitment process may be simplified when the unemployment rate in an organization's labor market is high. The number of unsolicited applicants is usually greater, and the increased size of the labor pool provides a better opportunity for attracting qualified applicants. Conversely, as the unemployment rate drops, recruitment efforts must be increased and new sources explored. Although the recruiter's day-to-day activities provide a *feel* for the labor market, accurate employment data, found in professional journals and U.S. Department of Labor reports, can be useful.

Local labor market conditions are of primary importance in recruitment for most nonmanagerial, many supervisory, and even some middle-management positions. However, recruitment for executive, professional, and technical positions often extends to national or even global markets.

Organizations may employ various tactics to enhance or enlarge their labor market for certain jobs. For example, a small firm in Los Angeles expanded its market by hiring people with few, if any, qualifications. The firm is willing to spend the necessary time and money needed to provide even basic training. In another organization, the corporate manager of recruiting had a special T-shirt made that had an ad printed on the front for a director of sales and marketing and his firm's name and address on the back. He wore the shirt to a professional meeting and the effort resulted in a couple of hires for sales managers. Another senior vice president of HR went into the community and posted notices in churches, grocery stores, and bus stops. These efforts followed a more traditional recruitment approach that was unsuccessful.[24]

Global Labor Market. Today, the labor market for many professional and technical positions is much broader and truly global. Specialists in Bangalore, India, for example, develop information technology applications for American customers as others process home loans. Radiologists interpret 30 CT scans a day there and specialists design mobile-phone chips. In New Delhi, young college-educated men and women are busy processing claims for a major U.S. insurance company and others provide help-desk support for a big U.S. Internet service provider. Other employees providing various tasks are available in locations throughout the world such as Manila, Shanghai, Budapest, and Costa Rica.[25] India, in particular, is a good match for U.S. business firms. After the United States, India has the world's largest English-speaking population. The country has about 200,000 information technology graduates and postgraduates each year and labor costs are just a fraction of U.S. labor costs. In addition, the difference in time zones permits firms to position their employees to work around the clock.[26]

You can readily see how the labor market for numerous jobs has expanded tremendously. The Internet, efficient communications systems, and increased education of the world's population have all contributed to this growth. Some sources feel that in the long run, there will be a critical shortage of professionals in the United States, Europe, and Japan. If this is the case, the solutions may be an increase in immigration or moving businesses overseas. The concern stems from birthrates that have been declining for decades. For example, in the United States, 11,000 people a day turn 50; by 2020, 50 percent of Europe's population will be over 50; and in Japan, the population will fall from 126 million today to less than 100 million in the next 50 years.[27] If these data prove to be correct, the staffing challenges to HR will become quite different from those of today.

Air Products & Chemicals, Inc.

www.airproducts.com/

This Web site is for the company mentioned in this book that solved the problem to the satisfaction of both the EEOC and the OFCCP regarding who was an applicant.

Legal Considerations

Legal matters also play a significant role in recruitment practices in the United States. This is not surprising since the candidate and the employer first make contact during the recruitment process. One survey found that about one-fourth of all discrimination claims resulted from employers' recruitment and selection actions.[28] Therefore, it is essential for organizations to emphasize nondiscriminatory practices at this stage. EEOC guidelines suggest that companies with more than 100 employees keep staffing records for a minimum of two years.[29] This information enables a compilation of demographic data—including age, race, and gender—based on that applicant pool.[30] The EEOC uses these data to determine if a company's hiring practices are discriminatory.

Dramatic increases in firms using the Internet for recruiting has added to management's challenge. Critics of the EEOC guidelines contended that given the sheer volume of résumés they receive through the Internet, compiling demographic data based on each résumé is costly and time-consuming.[31] Three questions required addressing:

- Who is an applicant?
- Is everyone in the résumé database an applicant for each opening?
- How do you deal fairly and consistently with all résumés, especially those that are unsolicited?

These questions were largely unanswered until a Pennsylvania firm developed a unique solution. Air Products and Chemicals Inc., of Allentown, Pennsylvania, solved the problem to the satisfaction of both the EEOC and the OFCCP. Through forced choices on its Web site, the company shifted the burden of declaring candidacy for a specific job to the résumé submitter. The system allowed anyone to view openings on the company's Web site. However, it would not accept résumés unless they were attached to a specific position and the applicant alone would make the position selection. Air Products defines an applicant as anyone who has filled out a profile and attached it to a specific opening. To try the system, visit the Career Center portion of Air Products' Web site at www.airproducts.com.[32]

The OFCCP bought off on the system and particularly liked one other aspect. Air Products requires the submitter to respond to questions about race and gender. But, one option for each question is, "I don't want to give this information," a choice only 14 percent make. This enables Air Products recruiters to collect voluntary affirmative action data for 86 percent of applicants before they meet them. Previously, recruiters had no legal way to determine race or gender until they met an applicant in person. This allows the company and government to access the EEO posture of the company. It allows Air Products to find problems and fix them long before the government becomes involved.[33]

Corporate Image

The firm's corporate image is another factor that affects recruitment. If employees believe that their employer deals with them fairly, the positive word-of-mouth support they provide is of great value to the firm. It assists in establishing credibility with prospective employees. Good reputations earned in this manner may help attract more and better-qualified applicants. A firm's positive public image encourages prospective employees to respond to its recruitment efforts and enhances its recruitment success.

In the aftermath of Enron, many firms have become increasingly aware of complying *effectively* with the countless laws they must follow. A formal compliance program cannot only protect an organization; it can also enhance employee morale and its corporate image.[34]

Internal Environment of Recruitment

The labor market and the government exert powerful external influences on the recruitment process. In addition, the organization's practices and policies have an impact.

Human Resource Planning

In most cases, a firm cannot attract prospective employees in sufficient numbers and with the required skills overnight. Examining alternative sources of recruits and determining the most productive sources and methods for obtaining them often requires planning time. After identifying the best alternatives, managers can make better recruitment decisions.

Promotion Policies

An organization's promotion policy can have a significant impact on recruitment. A firm can stress a policy of promotion from within its own ranks or one where positions are generally filled from outside the organization. Depending on specific circumstances, either approach may have merit.

Promotion from within (PFW): The policy of filling vacancies above entry-level positions with employees presently employed by a company.

Promotion from within (PFW) is the policy of filling vacancies above entry-level positions with current employees. When an organization emphasizes promotion from within, its workers have an incentive to strive for advancement. When employees see co-workers promoted, they become more aware of their own opportunities. Motivation provided by this practice often improves employee morale. Today's *flatter* organizational structures, with fewer levels of management, restrict upward mobility to a degree. However, the opportunity to move up in an organization will continue to serve as a motivating factor for some employees.

It is unlikely, however, that a firm can (or would even desire to) adhere rigidly to a practice of promotion from within. The vice president of human resources for a major automobile manufacturer offers this advice: "A strictly applied 'PFW' policy eventually leads to inbreeding, a lack of cross-fertilization, and a lack of creativity. A good goal, in my opinion, is to fill 80 percent of openings above entry-level positions from within." David Powell, vice president of marketing for 3M, states, "We have always had a very strong culture of promotion from within. So people who have been successful in jobs have moved up to the next level, and they've taken their knowledge and their skills and their experiences to that level. That's helped to provide a lot of stability also."[35]

Frequently, new blood provides new ideas and innovation that must take place for firms to remain competitive. In such cases, even organizations with promotion from within policies may opt to look outside the organization for new talent. In any event, a promotion policy that first considers insiders is great for employee morale and motivation and is often beneficial to the organization.

The Firm's Knowledge of Employees

HR Web Wisdom

FedEx

www.fedex.com

This Web site is the site mentioned in your text that helps candidates identify their ideal job.

Another advantage of internal recruitment is that the organization is usually well aware of its employees' capabilities. An employee's job performance, by itself, may not be a reliable criterion for promotion. Nevertheless, management will know many of the employee's personal and job-related qualities. The employee has a track record, as opposed to being an *unknown entity*. Also, the company's investment in the individual may yield a higher return. Still another positive factor is the employee's knowledge of the firm, its policies, and its people.

FedEx has a philosophy that employees should be doing the kind of work they want to do. To assist in this, the firm has a Web site (www.fedex.com) that helps candidates identify their ideal job. Using drop-down lists, it prompts them to enter data about desires; location, type of work, and so forth; and to describe their skills. When jobs open, these electronic résumés are sorted. Hiring managers have instant access to a database in which the candidates have profiled themselves and specified what they want and can do.[36]

Nepotism

Company policies related to the employment of relatives may also affect a firm's recruitment efforts. The content of such policies varies greatly, but it is common for firms to have anti-nepotism policies that discourage the employment of close relatives, especially when related employees would work in the same department, under the same supervisor, or in supervisor-subordinate roles. Still, when the labor market is tight, a firm may decide that it makes more sense to keep relatives on board than to lose them to a competitor.[37]

When internal alternatives to hiring additional employees are considered, but determined to be inappropriate, organizations, with due consideration to environmental factors, turn to recruitment to attract potential employees and encourage them to apply for open positions.

4 OBJECTIVE

Describe the recruitment process.

The Recruitment Process

As previously defined, *recruitment* is the process of attracting individuals on a timely basis, in sufficient numbers and with appropriate qualifications, and encouraging them to apply for jobs with an organization. The firm may then select those applicants with qualifications most closely related to job specifications. Labor availability rises as the economy cools. Still, competition for the most-qualified candidates can still be intense.[38]

Finding the appropriate way of encouraging qualified candidates to apply for employment is extremely important when a firm needs to hire employees. Some firms, such as General Motors, centralized their recruitment at corporate headquarters. The rationale was a need for consistency in their message to potential hires. Other advantages seen for this approach include minimizing duplication of work and the resulting increased productivity. Naturally, this approach is not appropriate for all firms. Some prefer at least some degree of decentralization that enables the firm to be fluid and flexible in meeting business needs.[39]

How many times do we hear CEOs state, "Our most important assets are human"? While this adage has probably always been true, some executives are actually

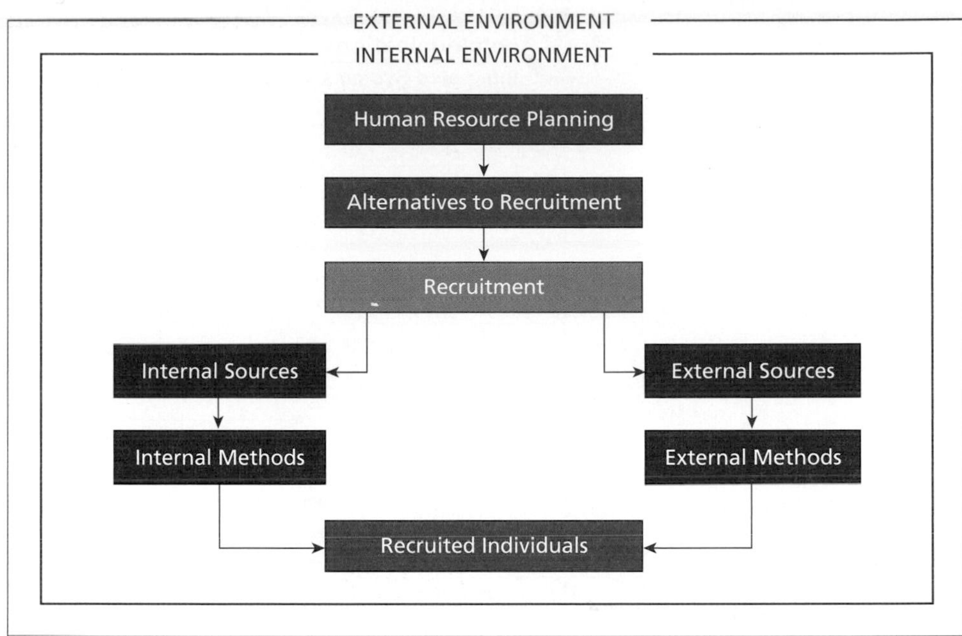

Figure 5-1 The Recruitment Process

beginning to believe it. Hiring the best people available has never been more critical than it is today because of global competition. Furthermore, hiring decisions can be no better than the alternatives presented through recruitment efforts.

Figure 5-1 shows that when human resource planning indicates a need for employees, the firm may evaluate alternatives to hiring. If these alternatives prove to be inappropriate, the recruitment process starts. Frequently, recruitment begins when a manager initiates an **employee requisition,** a document that specifies job title, department, the date the employee is needed for work, and other details. Figure 5-2 shows L3 Communication's employee requisition.[40] With this information, managers can refer to the appropriate job description to determine the qualifications the recruited person needs. These qualifications, however, are becoming less clear-cut. Job descriptions often lack clarity because of the additional duties assigned. Also, they frequently focus heavily, if not exclusively, on minimum objective requirements, such as education and job experience.[41] However, these documents often pay little or no attention to the more subjective behavioral competencies essential to a job, such as flexibility, agility, and strategic insight. When you recruit and hire for one task, it will not be long before the firm asks the employee to do several others as well. With such wide ranging expectations from the company, the employee will obviously need a broader variety of skills and abilities. Some firms are dealing with this situation by striving to employ individuals who are bright, adaptable, and can work effectively in teams. Hiring for organizational *fit* is discussed in Chapter 6.

Employee requisition:
A document that specifies job title, department, the date the employee is needed for work, and other details.

The next step in the recruitment process is to determine whether qualified employees are available within the firm (the internal source) or if it's necessary to look to external sources, such as colleges, universities, and other organizations. Because of the high cost of recruitment, organizations need to employ the most productive recruitment sources and methods available. According to the Saratoga Institute Human Capital Report for 2000, the total cost per hire (internal and external hires) for surveyed participants averaged $4,588. The exempt cost per hire averaged $12,032 and nonexempt $989.[42]

Recruitment sources:
Various locations in which qualified individuals are sought as potential employees.

Recruitment methods:
The specific means by which potential employees are attracted to an organization.

Recruitment sources are where qualified individuals are located, such as colleges or competitors. **Recruitment methods** are the specific means used to attract potential employees to the firm, such as newspaper ads. Tapping productive sources of applicants and using suitable recruitment methods are essential to maximizing recruiting efficiency and effectiveness. As Jim Goodnight, CEO of the software giant SAS

L3 communications
Integrated Systems

PERSONNEL REQUISITION FORM

Requisition Number:		Date:	
Dept No.		Dept Name:	
Job Type: Full Time ☐	Part Time ☐	Need Date:	
Job Title:	Req. Type:	Direct ☐	Indirect ☐
Job Code:	Grade:	No. Openings:	
Year(s) of Experience:		Project Name:	
Additional ☐	Replacement ☐	Replacing:	
Hiring Supervisor:		E-Mail:	
Telephone:		Fax:	
Dept. Manager:		Telephone:	
Job Location:		Job Building:	
Security Clearance:	None ☐ Confidential ☐ Secret ☐ Top Secret ☐	Existing Clearance:	Yes ☐ No ☐

Minimum Education Level: None ☐ High School ☐ Associate ☐ Bachelor ☐ Master ☐ Ph.D. ☐
Certification: Yes ☐ No ☐ If yes, specify:

Degree Fields: May substitute related experience for education? Yes ☐ No ☐

Shift: First ☐ Second ☐ Third ☐ Rotating ☐ Overtime Required: Yes ☐ No ☐

Job Description:

Required Skills (specialized experience/knowledge/skills for this job):

Desired Skills (other skills/abilities which will be helpful):

Describe the physical requirements of the job (e.g. Bending, lifting, overhead work):

	Name/Title	Signature	Date
Manager:			
Director:			
Vice President:			
Finance:			
HR:			

Figure 5-2 An Employee Requisition Form for L3 Communications

Institute Inc., stated, "Ninety-five percent of our assets drive out the gate every afternoon at five. I want them to come back in the morning. I need them to come back in the morning."[43] In one survey, nearly two-thirds of respondents said that recruiting, selecting, and placing employees are among their top three priorities.[44]

When a firm identifies the sources of candidates, it employs appropriate methods for either internal or external recruitment to accomplish recruitment objectives. A candidate responds to the firm's recruitment efforts by submitting professional and personal data on either an application for employment form or a résumé, depending upon the company's policy. We discuss these two instruments in the following chapter.

Companies may discover that some recruitment sources and methods are superior to others for locating and attracting potential talent. For instance, one large equipment manufacturer determined that medium-sized, state-supported colleges and universities located in rural areas were good sources of potential managers. Other firms may arrive at different conclusions. To maximize recruiting effectiveness, utilizing recruitment sources and methods tailored to specific needs is vitally important.

 **OBJECTIVE**

Describe internal recruitment methods.

Internal Recruitment Methods

Management should be able to identify current employees who are capable of filling positions as they become available. Helpful tools used for internal recruitment include employee databases, job posting, and job bidding procedures. As we mentioned in Chapter 4, employee databases permit organizations to determine whether current employees possess the qualifications for filling open positions. As a recruitment device, these databases have proved to be extremely valuable to organizations when they are current. Databases can be valuable in locating talent internally and supporting the concept of promotion from within.

Job Posting and Job Bidding

Job posting:
A procedure for communicating to company employees the fact that a job opening exists.

Job bidding:
A technique that permits individuals in an organization who believe that they possess the required qualifications to apply for a posted job.

Job posting is a procedure for informing employees that job openings exist. **Job bidding** is a procedure that permits employees who believe that they possess the required qualifications to apply for a posted job. In years past, jobs were typically posted on a bulletin board. Today, at least in larger firms, it is more likely that the posting is done on the firm's intranet or the Internet.

The job posting and bidding procedures can help minimize the commonly heard complaint that insiders never hear of a job opening until it is filled. The procedure reflects an openness that most employees value highly. Now, if a worker does not know about a vacancy, it's because he or she did not check the online posting regularly. Yet, even with an online system, a job posting and bidding system has some negative features. For one thing, an effective system requires the expenditure of time and money. Also, when bidders are unsuccessful, someone must explain to them why they were not selected. Management must choose the most qualified applicant or else the system will lack credibility. Of course, the chosen applicant must also be perceived by peers as the most qualified. Management may have little control over this factor. The key to success in this and many other managerial actions is the degree of trust and confidence that employees have in their supervisors and company. Still, complaints may occur even in a well-designed and implemented system.

Employee Referrals

A recent study of 22 large firms found that employee referrals were the single most productive internal recruitment method and accounted for 30 to 40 percent of new hires.[45] Many organizations have found that their employees can serve an important role in the recruitment process by actively soliciting applications from their friends and associates. Kellogg is one firm that has implemented a Web-based recruitment management system including online internal job posting and employee referral programs. The technology allows hiring managers to see on their computer monitors a list of names and qualifications of the referred applicants.[46]

Employee enlistment is a unique form of employee referral where every employee becomes a company recruiter. This is not the same as merely asking employees to refer friends to the company. The firm supplies employees with simple business cards that do not contain names or positions. Instead, these cards have a message similar to: "We are always looking for great __________. For additional information, log onto our Web site." Employees then distribute the cards wherever they go; to parties, sports events, family gatherings, picnics, or the park. The purpose is to let people know that the company really does want people to apply.

OBJECTIVE

Explain external sources of recruitment.

External Recruitment Sources

At times, a firm must look beyond its own borders to find employees, particularly when expanding its workforce. The following needs require external recruitment: (1) to fill entry-level jobs; (2) to acquire skills not possessed by current employees; and (3) to obtain employees with different backgrounds to provide a diversity of ideas. As Figure 5-3 shows, even with internal promotions, firms fill entry-level jobs from the outside. Thus, after the president of a firm retires, a series of internal promotions follows. Ultimately, however, the firm has to recruit externally for the entry-level position of salary analyst. If an outside candidate were selected for the president's position, the chain reaction of promotions from within would not have occurred. If no current employee has the desired qualifications, candidates may be attracted from a number of outside sources.

High Schools and Vocational Schools

Organizations concerned with recruiting clerical and other entry-level operative employees often depend on high schools and vocational schools. Many of these institutions have training programs for specific occupational skills, such as home appliance repair and small engine mechanics. Some companies work with schools to ensure a constant supply of trained individuals with specific job skills. In some areas, companies even loan employees to schools to assist in the training programs. We discuss business support of education in Chapter 7.

Community Colleges

Many community colleges are sensitive to the specific employment needs in their local labor markets and graduate highly sought-after students with marketable skills. Typically, community colleges have two-year programs designed for both a terminal education and preparation for a four-year university degree program. Many community colleges also have excellent mid-management programs combined with training for specific trades. In addition, career centers often provide a place for employers to contact students, thereby facilitating the recruitment process. We provide additional information on the role of community colleges in our society in Chapter 7.

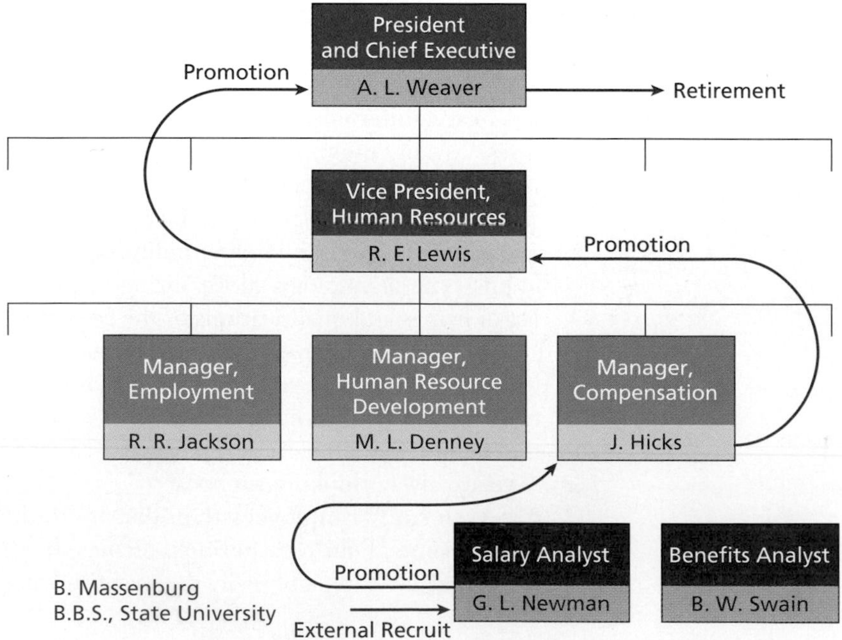

Figure 5-3 Internal Promotion and External Recruitment

Colleges and Universities

Colleges and universities also represent a major recruitment source for many organizations. Organizations typically find potential professional, technical, and management employees in these institutions. Placement directors, faculty, and administrators can be helpful to organizations in their search for recruits. Because on-campus recruitment is mutually beneficial, both employers and universities should take steps to develop and maintain close relationships. When a company establishes recruitment programs with educational institutions, it should continue those programs year after year to maintain an effective relationship with each school. It is important that the firm knows the school and that the school knows the firm.[47]

Competitors in the Labor Market

When recent experience is required, competitors and other firms in the same industry or geographic area may be the most important source of recruits. In fact, the most highly qualified applicants often come directly from competitors in the same labor market, as people typically do not enter the workforce loaded with experience and job skills. There is one caveat, however. Employers should check to see if such applicants are bound by noncompete or nondisclosure agreements. While these agreements may not be 100 percent ironclad, there is no point in taking a chance.[48]

The fact that approximately 5 percent of the working population is, at any one time, either actively seeking or receptive to a change of position emphasizes the importance of these sources. If a firm promises the opportunity to do something meaningful, that promise will be a powerful magnet for many individuals looking for employment.[49] Even organizations that have policies of promotion from within occasionally look elsewhere to fill positions. Hardly a day goes by that we do not read about an executive leaving one company for another, often at a huge salary increase. Although the ethics of corporate raiding may be debatable, it is apparent that competitors and other firms do serve as external sources of recruitment for high-quality talent.

Smaller firms in particular look for employees trained by larger organizations that have greater developmental resources. For instance, an optical firm located in the Midwest believes that its own operation is not large enough to provide extensive training and development programs. Therefore, a person recruited by this firm for a significant management role is likely to have held at least two previous positions with a competitor.

Ethical Dilemma

Unfair Advantage?

You are the vice president for human resources for a high-tech company that is competing for a major government project. You believe that one of your key competitors is ahead of you in project development and you would like to recruit some of their engineers who are knowledgeable about the project. You receive an anonymous e-mail that includes the names and phone numbers of key people involved in your competitor's project. If you use the information and are able to hire some of the competitor's key people, your company has a chance to beat the competitor and you will become a hero. If you do not use the information, your company may lose a great deal of money.[50]

What would you do?

Former Employees

At one time, when employees quit a company, their managers and peers tended to view them as being disloyal, ungrateful, and they were "punished" with no-return policies. A common attitude was that if you left your firm, you did not appreciate what the company had done for you. Today, smart employers try to get their best ex-employees to come back. Former employees are definitely an important potential recruitment source. The advantage of tracking former employees is that the firm knows their strengths and weaknesses. And, the ex-employees know the company. Recruiting and hiring a former employee can be a tremendous benefit and can encourage others to stay with the firm.[51] It sends the message that things are not always greener on the other side of the fence.

The Unemployed

The unemployed often provide a valuable source of recruits. Qualified applicants join the unemployment rolls every day for various reasons. Companies may downsize their operations, go out of business, or merge with other firms, leaving qualified workers without jobs. Employees are also fired sometimes merely because of personality differences with their bosses. Not infrequently, employees become frustrated with their jobs and simply quit.

Persons with Disabilities

Individuals with disabilities have historically faced stigmas and stereotyping and this was reflected in recruitment and hiring. The Americans with Disabilities Act has helped change this situation. Attitudes also change as our population ages and the likelihood of disability increases. You can always identify more closely with the problems of a given group when you become part of that group, and the graying of our society will add to the numbers of disabled persons.

Society benefits when people with disabilities are recruited and hired. The economy becomes stronger and the government supports fewer people. Disabled individuals can be valuable because, forced to learn new or different ways to do things, they are often able to apply these skills to their work. Their presence in a workgroup can add to its diversity and increase the flow of new ideas.[52]

Older Individuals

Older workers, including those who are retired, may also represent a valuable source of employees. Although these workers are often victims of negative stereotyping, the facts support the notion that older people can perform many jobs extremely well. When Kentucky Fried Chicken Corporation had difficulty recruiting younger employees, it turned to older individuals and those with disabilities. The results included a dramatically reduced turnover rate. Management surveys indicate that most employers have high opinions of their older workers. They value them for many reasons. Compared to younger workers, many older employees have more positive work habits, lower absenteeism rates, and higher levels of commitment to the organization.[53]

HR Web Wisdom

Defense Outplacement Referral System (DORS)

www.dmdc.osd.mil/

This Web site is the résumé and referral system for the military that allows employers to request résumés for open positions.

Military Personnel

Operation Transition is a program that offers employers two vehicles for tapping into the military labor pool at no cost: the Defense Outplacement Referral System (DORS) and the Transition Bulletin Board (TBB). DORS is an automated résumé and referral system that allows employers to request résumés for open positions. Companies can register for the program at www.dmdc.osd.mil. The TBB, www.dmdc.osd.mil/tbb, is a bulletin board where companies can post jobs online. Job seekers at military bases around the world see these listings.[54]

Hiring of former service members may make sense to many employers because many of these individuals typically have a proven work history and are flexible, motivated, and drug free. Another valuable characteristic of veterans is their goal and team orientation. General Electric found an endless supply of talent in junior military officers. Many were graduates of U.S. military academies who had spent four to five years in the service. They were found to be hardworking, smart, and intense; they had leadership experience and were flexible. GE was so impressed with the quality of this recruitment source that it put in place a plan to hire 200 of these former officers each year. The firm now has more than 1,400 on the payroll.[55]

Self-Employed Workers

Finally, the self-employed worker may also be a good potential recruit. These individuals may be true entrepreneurs who are ingenious and creative. For many firms, these qualities are essential for continued competitiveness.[56] Such individuals may constitute a source of applicants for any number of jobs requiring technical, professional, administrative, or entrepreneurial expertise within a firm.

OBJECTIVE

Identify external recruitment methods.

External Recruitment Methods

By examining recruitment sources, a firm determines the location of potential job applicants. It then seeks to attract these applicants by specific recruitment methods. According to a recent study, the most popular external recruitment method is newspaper and magazine want ads, used by 89 percent of the respondents. The next most popular method is the Internet, utilized by 67 percent of participants in the survey.[57] Newspaper advertising remains the dominant choice for filling local positions and enhancing corporate brand in a local market. Internet advertising allows the penetration of new markets and develops a wider range of qualified applicants.[58] "Internet recruiting has revolutionized the way organizations of all sizes seek new applicants," said SHRM Vice President of Knowledge Development Debra Cohen. "It has proven to be a cost-effective recruiting tool that complements newspaper advertising and other methods."[59]

Advertising

Advertising:
A way of communicating the firm's employment needs to the public through media such as radio, newspaper, or industry publications.

Advertising communicates the firm's employment needs to the public through media such as newspapers, radio, television, and industry publications. The Internet is the newest and fastest growing external recruitment method. Regardless of the advertising method utilized, in determining the content of an advertising message, a firm must decide on the corporate image it wants to project. Obviously, the firm should give prospective employees an accurate picture of the job and the organization.

Newspaper Advertising. The firm's previous experience with various media should suggest the most effective approach for specific types of jobs. A common form of advertising that provides broad coverage at a relatively low cost is the newspaper ad. Such ads tend to generate a vast number of candidates, most of whom aren't qualified, and these inquiries are costly to process.[60] This situation increases the likelihood of poor selection decisions. At the same time, the firm should attempt to appeal to the self-interest of prospective employees, emphasizing the job's unique qualities. The ad must tell potential employees why they should be interested in that particular job and

Are you spending the best years of your life with an organization that has your best interest at heart?

If not, check us out!

Our mid-sized electronics firm is looking for a professional recruiter with at least two years' experience in HR or a bachelor's degree in that field. Must have extensive knowledge in recruitment sources and methods used in recruiting professional employees. General knowledge of human resources and performance management is a definite plus.

Consider these company practices:

- ✷ Three weeks of paid vacation
- ✷ Ten paid holidays each year
- ✷ Five personal days each year
- ✷ Professional education opportunities
- ✷ Performance-based pay and excellent benefits
- ✷ Casual dress every day

If interested, you may apply online at www.prenhall.com/mondy or FAX to 337-475-0161

Cyber Electronics, Inc.

We are an Equal Opportunity Employer

Figure 5-4 A Job Advertisement

organization. The message should also indicate how an applicant is to respond: apply in person, apply by telephone, or submit a résumé by fax or e-mail. Figure 5-4 shows an advertisement that encourages applicants to apply for a position.

Although few individuals base their decision to change jobs on advertising, an ad creates awareness, generates interest, and encourages a prospect to seek more information about the firm and the job opportunities that it provides. Examination of the Sunday edition of any major newspaper reveals the extensive use of newspaper advertising in recruiting.

Advertising in Professional and Trade Journals. Certain media attract audiences that are more homogeneous in terms of employment skills, education, and orientation. Advertisements placed in such publications as the *Wall Street Journal* relate primarily to managerial, professional, and technical positions. The readers of these publications are generally individuals qualified for many of the positions advertised. Focusing on a specific labor market minimizes the likelihood of receiving marginally qualified or even totally unqualified applicants.

Virtually every professional group publishes a journal that is widely read by its members. Advertising for a marketing executive position in *Marketing Forum*, for example, would hit the target market because marketing professionals are virtually the exclusive readers. Trade journals are also widely utilized. However, using journals does present problems. For example, they lack scheduling flexibility; their publishing deadlines may be weeks prior to the issue. Because firms cannot always anticipate staffing far in advance, journals have obvious limitations for recruitment.

Advertising in Other Media. Qualified prospects who read job ads in newspapers and professional and trade journals may not be so dissatisfied with their present jobs that they will pursue opportunities advertised. Therefore, in high-demand situations, a firm needs to consider all available media resources. Such resources include radio, billboards, and television. These methods are likely to be more expensive than newspapers or journals, but, in specific situations, they may prove successful. For instance, a regional medical center used billboards successfully to attract registered nurses. One large manufacturing firm had considerable luck in advertising for production trainees by means of spot advertisements on the radio. A large electronics firm used television to attract experienced engineers when it opened a new facility and needed more engineers immediately. Thus, in situations where hiring needs are urgent, television and radio may provide good results even though these media may not be sufficient by themselves. Broadcast messages can let people know that an organization is seeking recruits. A primary limitation is the amount of information they can transmit.

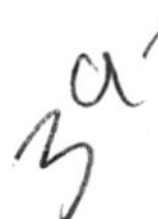

Employment Agencies

Employment agency: An organization that helps firms recruit employees and at the same time aids individuals in their attempt to locate jobs.

America's Job Bank

www.jobsearch.org

This Web site is a partnership between the U.S. Department of Labor and the state-operated Public Employment Service.

An **employment agency** is an organization that helps firms recruit employees and at the same time aids individuals in their attempt to locate jobs. These agencies perform recruitment and selection functions that have proven quite beneficial to many organizations.

Private Employment Agencies. *Private employment agencies*, known best for recruiting white-collar employees, offer an important service in bringing qualified applicants and open positions together. However, firms utilize private employment agencies for virtually every type of position. Neither the organization nor the job applicant should overlook this method. The one-time fees that some agencies charge often turn off candidates, although many private employment agencies deal primarily with firms that pay the fees. Employment agencies often have their own Web sites to show prospective employees the array of jobs that are available through their agency.

Public Employment Agencies. *Public employment agencies*, operated by each state, receive overall policy direction from the U.S. Employment Service. Public employment agencies, best known for recruiting and placing individuals in operative jobs, have become increasingly involved in matching people with technical, professional, and managerial positions. Some public agencies use computerized job-matching systems to aid in the recruitment process. Public employment agencies provide their services without charge to either the employer or the prospective employee.

America's Job Bank is a partnership between the U.S. Department of Labor and the state-operated Public Employment Service (http://www.ajb.dni.us/). It is the largest online source for national and international employment. It offers job posting for employers and résumé posting and job searching by occupation, keyword, and zip code for job-hunters.[61]

Recruiters

Recruiters most commonly focus on technical and vocational schools, community colleges, colleges, and universities. Employers rank on-campus recruiting as the number-one method for recruiting students.[62] The key contact for recruiters on college and university campuses is often the student placement director. This administrator is in an excellent position to arrange interviews with students possessing the qualifications desired by the firm. Placement services help organizations utilize their recruiters efficiently. They identify qualified candidates, schedule interviews, and provide suitable rooms for interviews.

The company recruiter plays a vital role in attracting applicants. The interviewee often perceives the recruiter's actions as a reflection of the character of the firm. If the recruiter is dull, the interviewee may think the company dull; if the recruiter is apathetic, discourteous, or vulgar, the interviewee may well attribute all these negative characteristics to the firm. Recruiters must always be aware of the image they present at the screening interview because it makes a lasting impression. Recruitment success comes down to good personal selling, appealing to the candidate's priorities and

Trends & Innovations

The Cyber Recruiter

The Internet recruiter, also called *cyber recruiter,* is a person whose primary responsibility is to use the Internet in the recruitment process.[63] Most companies currently post jobs on their organization's Web site. Individuals must be in place to monitor and coordinate these activities. The more a company recruits on the Internet, the greater the need for Internet recruiters. Currently, high-tech firms have the greatest needs, and Internet recruiters can sometimes be quite aggressive. Dan Harris, CEO and senior trainer at Recruiters Dream Network in Arlington, Texas, says, "Good Internet recruiters can match a potential candidate to a position and present it as a dream job. If the recruiter doesn't come across like a used-car salesman, a reasonable person will listen to a reasonable offer."[64]

At Texas Instruments (TI), once you hit the "Submit Your Résumé "button on its recruiting site, TI has a cyber recruiting team that actually reads the résumés sent to them via the Web. They read a résumé and do a quick comparison with the positions currently open. Depending upon the number of résumés received, it is possible that someone from TI will contact an applicant the same day. If a strong match to one of the openings exists, they will either call or e-mail the applicant to establish contact. According to TI, the number of people hired via the Internet has tripled within the last year. Once contact is established, an applicant will likely talk by phone to a recruiter who will ask more questions. Then, the applicant might talk to the program manager or someone else in the department with the job opening. Once a match is determined, the applicant may be invited to visit TI. However, the company can often work with applicants over the phone or use e-mail to make a hiring decision. Everything is done to facilitate the hiring process. TI could hire a person within days or a couple of weeks after receiving a résumé.[65]

Internet recruiter:
Also called cyber recruiter, is a person whose primary responsibility is to use the Internet in the recruitment process.

addressing his or her concerns. The recruiter should underscore the job's opportunities and keep the lines of communication open.[66]

Some American firms have discovered an innovative use of recruiters. All it takes is a computer system with equipment at both corporate headquarters and on a college campus. Recruiters can communicate with college career counselors and interview students through a videoconferencing system without leaving the office. Connie Thanasoulis-Cerrachio of Citibank stated that $1,000 versus the cost of $12 or $13 an interview was an amazing savings.[67]

Job Fairs

Job fair:
A recruiting method engaged in by a single employer or group of employers to attract a large number of applicants for interviews.

A **job fair** is a recruiting method engaged in by a single employer or group of employers to attract a large number of applicants for interviews. From an employer's viewpoint, a primary advantage of job fairs is the opportunity to meet a large number of candidates in a short time. Conversely, applicants may have convenient access to a number of employers. More than a dozen commercial firms operate job fairs, but government agencies, charitable organizations, and business alliances frequently sponsor them. As a recruitment method, job fairs offer the potential for a much lower cost per hire than traditional approaches. General job fairs, however, are likely to attract a large number of unqualified individuals. The answer to this will probably be more industry- or skill-specific events and those that focus on diversity.[68]

Virtual Job Fairs

A virtual job fair is an online event.[69] An online job fair was recently held for students from 22 colleges and universities throughout Maine. The event allowed students to visit virtual employer booths and submit their résumés online 24 hours a day, seven days a week. It has the potential to open up a larger job market to Maine students and graduates. For employers, the virtual job fair reveals a wider range of students than might attend a live fair. "This venue is less expensive for employers and more convenient for students," said Sherry Treworgy, associate director of the Career Center at the University of Maine.[70]

Internships

Internship:
A special form of recruitment that involves placing a student in a temporary job with no obligation either by the company to hire the student permanently or by the student to accept a permanent position with the firm following graduation.

An **internship** is a special form of recruitment that involves placing a student in a temporary job with no obligation either by the company to hire the student permanently or by the student to accept a permanent position with the firm following graduation. More companies are now using internships as a recruiting technique and many are recruiting students through internships in their sophomore and junior years. However, employers are becoming selective. Most of the students hired these days are high achievers. They have good grades, plus professional experience from summer jobs and internships.[71]

An internship typically involves a temporary job for the summer months or a part-time job during the school year. It may also take the form of working full-time one semester and going to school full-time the next.

Basic Benefits of Internships

During the internship, the student gets to view business practices firsthand. At the same time, the intern contributes to the firm by performing needed tasks. Through this relationship, a student can determine whether a company would be a desirable employer. Similarly, having a relatively lengthy time to observe the student's job performance, the firm can make a better judgment regarding the person's qualifications. Studies show that students with internship and co-op experience are able to find jobs more easily and they progress much further and faster in the business world than those without.[72]

In addition to other benefits, internships provide opportunities for students to bridge the gap from business theory to practice. Many employers feel that internships enhance an application by demonstrating a solid commitment to a career choice. More than half the employers surveyed by the National Association of Colleges and Employers say their recent hires out of college had internship experience.[73] Firms have learned that student interns can also serve as effective recruiters. If the intern has a good experience, he or she will tell other students about it.

Internships also serve as an effective public relations tool that provides visibility for the company and assists in recruitment. Tim Toland, senior vice president for Savage and Associates of Toledo, Ohio, praises the benefits of his firm's internship program. He states that his company is able to get a good look at candidates for 12 weeks, and the same for them. They get a taste for the industry and for his firm. One payoff: about 50 to 60 percent of these interns are hired.[74]

Students' professors may be an additional potentially beneficial source for internships. Faculty members may bring expertise to the firm and then return to the classroom with real-world experience to augment their teaching. In addition, the relationship with faculty members may give the company a recruiting edge.[75]

Futurestep.com

www.futurestep.com

This Web site is the homepage of a global leader in middle management recruitment.

Executive Search Firms

Executive search firms:
Organizations used by some firms to locate experienced professionals and executives when other sources prove inadequate.

Executive search firms are organizations used by some firms to locate experienced professionals and executives when other sources prove inadequate. At one time, there was a bias against executive search firms because they were thought to be raiders.

However, in time it became apparent that bringing in outside talent was often healthy and a means to add new capabilities for the firm.[76] The key benefit of executive search firms is the targeting of ideal candidates. In addition, the search firm can find those not actively looking for a job.[77] Searches now often take weeks instead of months. Futurestep.com, a Korn/Ferry International company, is a global leader in middle management recruitment. Futurestep provides customized recruitment solutions to employers, and offers candidates access to exclusive job opportunities around the world. The company combines traditional search expertise with the reach and speed of the Internet.[78] There are two types of executive search firms: contingency and retained.

Contingency search firms: A search firm that receives fees only upon successful placement of a candidate in a job opening.

Contingency Firms. **Contingency search firms** receive fees only upon successful placement of a candidate in a job opening. The search firm's fee is generally a percentage of the individual's compensation for the first year. The client pays expenses, as well as the fee. A contingency recruiter goes to work when there is an urgent need to fill a position, an opening exists for a difficult position, or when a hiring executive wants to know about top-notch talent as those people surface, regardless of whether there is an opening.[79]

Retained search firms: Search firms that are considered as consultants to their client organizations, serve on an exclusive contract basis, and typically recruit top business executives.

Retained Firms. **Retained search firms,** considered as consultants to their client organizations, serve on an exclusive contract basis, and typically recruit top business executives. The executive search industry has evolved from a basic recruitment service to a highly sophisticated profession serving a greatly expanded role. These firms assist organizations in determining their human resource needs, establishing compensation packages, and revising organizational structures.

Search Firm Procedures. An executive search firm's representatives often visit the client's offices and interview the company's management. This enables them to gain a clear understanding of the company's goals and the job qualifications required. After obtaining this information, they contact and interview potential candidates, check references, and refer the best-qualified person to the client for the selection decision. Search firms maintain databases of résumés for this process. Other sources used include networking contacts, files from previous searches, specialized directories, personal calls, previous clients, colleagues, and unsolicited résumés. The search firm's task is to present candidates that are eminently qualified to do the job and it is the company's decision whom to hire.[80]

The relationship between a client company and a search firm should be based on mutual trust and understanding. Both parties gain most from their relationship when they interact often and maintain good communication. To ensure success, the search firm must understand in detail the nature of the client's operations, the responsibilities of the open position, and the client's corporate culture. Similarly, the client must understand the search process, work with the consultant, and provide continuous, honest feedback.

Professional Associations

Many professional associations in business areas including finance, marketing, accounting, and human resources provide recruitment and placement services for their members. The Society for Human Resource Management, for example, operates a job referral service for members seeking new positions and employers with positions to fill. SHRM has a first-rate Web site for human resource professionals.[81]

Walk-In Applicants

If an organization has the reputation of being a good place to work, it may be able to attract qualified prospects even without extensive recruitment efforts. Acting on their own initiative, well-qualified workers may seek out a specific company to apply for a job. Unsolicited applicants who apply because they are favorably impressed with the firm's reputation often prove to be valuable employees.

Open Houses

Open houses are a valuable recruiting tool, especially during days of low unemployment. Here, firms pair potential hires and recruiters in a warm, casual environment that encourages on-the-spot job offers. Open houses are cheaper and faster than hiring through recruitment agencies, and they are also more popular than job fairs. There are pros and cons to holding a truly *open* house. If the event is open, it may draw a large turnout, but it also may attract a number of unqualified candidates. Some companies prefer to control the types of candidates they host, and so they conduct invitation-only sessions. In this scenario, the HR staff screens résumés in response to ads, then invites only pre-selected candidates. Advertising of open houses may be through both conventional media and the Internet, where a firm might feature its open house on its homepage.

Event Recruiting

Cisco Systems pioneered event recruiting as a recruitment approach and it has been successful. The concept is simple—have recruiters attend the same events as the people you are seeking. In the case of programmers in the Silicon Valley, the choice spots have been microbreweries, marathons, and bike races. Companies that participate in these events should become involved in some way that promotes their name and cause. For example, they might sponsor or co-sponsor an event, pass out refreshments, and give away prizes. Individuals should know that the company is recruiting and the type of workers it seeks.

Event recruiting gives a company the opportunity to reflect its image. For example, Cisco quickly developed the reputation as the company with *cool* recruiters and, therefore, it must be a *cool* place to work. Everyone was aware of it. Even if a participant was not interested, he or she probably knew someone who was. It became obvious to lots of people that companies such as IBM and Hewlett-Packard were not there, and therefore might not be *cool* places to work. And, *cool* is big for some employees who want an atmosphere of youth, excitement, growth, and perhaps most of all, permission to experiment and make mistakes.[82]

Sign-On Bonuses

Some firms are following the sports industry practice by offering sign-on bonuses to high-demand prospects. A Towers Perrin survey indicated that more than 56 percent of employers still use sign-on bonuses in all employee categories except clerical staff. Thirty-six percent give a \$1,000 to \$4,999 sign-on bonus, and at the executive level, 37 percent provide \$25,000 to \$49,000 and 8 percent give bonuses of more than \$50,000.[83] Another study conducted by SHRM/SHRM Foundation reported that sign-on bonuses were provided by 21 percent of responding firms for nonexecutive employees and by 30 percent for executives.[84] Firms are getting creative in shaping executive pay to lure top talent, according to a report in the *Washington Post*. This report states that there is anecdotal evidence that changes are already happening like more signing bonuses and outright cash to replace loans.[85]

It is obvious that all firms are not on the sign-on bandwagon. Financial executives, particularly the chief financial officer (CFO), are in high demand. Yet, they may be reminded that *most* job offers don't come with sign-on bonuses or company cars anymore and that they should be happy to receive a really nice paycheck.[86]

8 OBJECTIVE

Describe an applicant tracking system.

Applicant tracking system (ATS):
A system that automates online recruiting and selection processes.

Applicant Tracking System

An **applicant tracking system (ATS)** automates online recruiting and selection processes. Current systems enable human resource and line managers to oversee the entire process, from screening résumés and spotting qualified candidates, to conducting personality and skills tests and handling background checks. In most cases, the goal is not merely to reduce costs but also to speed up the hiring process and find people who fit an organization's success profile.[87] Ease of use is also a major requirement of a good applicant tracking system.[88]

A few years ago, E*TRADE Financial found itself buried under faxes, e-mail, and paper résumés. That slowed the hiring process to a crawl. So the company installed an applicant tracking system. Now when there is an opening, HR and line managers can select the appropriate job code and send a detailed list of job requirements to the applicant tracking system. It is then possible to match résumés to specific criteria and view a list of potential candidates. The system has provided an 80 percent decrease in data entry, reduced the reliance on outside recruiting firms, and helped E*TRADE Financial spot better candidates.[89]

9 OBJECTIVE

Describe how recruitment methods and sources are tailored to each other.

Tailoring Recruitment Methods to Sources

Because each organization is unique, so are the needed types and qualifications of workers to fill positions. Thus, to be successful, a firm must tailor its recruitment sources and methods to its specific needs.

Figure 5-5 shows a matrix that depicts sources and methods of recruitment for an information technology manager. Managers must first identify the *source* (where prospective employees are located) before choosing the *methods* (how to attract them). Suppose, for example, that a large firm has an immediate need for an information technology (IT) manager with a minimum of five years' experience, and no one within the firm has these qualifications. It is likely that other firms, possibly competitors, employ such individuals or the potential candidates may be self-employed. After considering the recruitment source, the recruiter must then choose the method (or methods) of recruitment that offers the best prospects for attracting qualified candidates. Perhaps it would be appropriate to advertise the job in the classified section of the

External Resources \ External Methods	Advertising	Private and public employment agencies	Recruiters	Special events	Internships	Executive search firms	Professional associations	Employee referrals	Unsolicited walk-in applicants	Open houses	Event recruiting	Virtual job fairs	Sign-on bonuses
High schools													
Vocational schools													
Community colleges													
Colleges and universities													
Competitors and other firms	X	X				X	X						
Unemployed													
Self-employed	X	X				X	X						

Figure 5-5 Methods and Sources of Recruitment for an Information Technology Manager

Wall Street Journal. Alternatively, an executive search firm or a private employment agency may serve as viable options. In addition, the recruiter may attend meetings of professional information technology associations. One or more of these methods will likely yield a pool of qualified applicants.

In another scenario, consider a firm's need for 20 entry-level machine operators, whom the firm is willing to train. High schools and vocational schools would probably be good recruitment sources. Methods of recruitment might include newspaper ads, public employment agencies, recruiters visiting vocational schools, and employee referrals.

External environmental factors, including market supply and job requirements, will determine the appropriate recruitment methods. Each organization should maintain employment records and conduct its own research in order to determine which recruitment sources and methods are most suitable under various circumstances.

10 OBJECTIVE

Explain recruitment for diversity.

Recruitment for Diversity

Equal opportunity legislation outlaws discrimination in employment based on race, religion, sex, color, national origin, age, disability, and other factors. Some firms abide by these laws solely to avoid the legal consequences of violating them. Others, however, also recognize the inherent advantages of heterogeneous groups such as greater creativity and the ability to help a firm expand its customer base. Global competition mandates that firms be innovative. Therefore, forward-thinking organizations actively engage in acquiring a workforce that reflects society and helps the company expand into untapped markets. To accomplish this objective, firms may need to use nontraditional recruitment approaches.

Because of past unequal opportunity, women, minorities, and individuals with disabilities may not be present in traditional recruitment sources nor respond to traditional recruitment methods. A firm might ignore these groups altogether using a typical recruitment process unless it takes specific action to attract them. Therefore, any organization that seeks diversity must implement recruitment practices that ensure that women, minorities, and those with disabilities are included in their recruitment planning. Otherwise, organizations will overlook a great deal of valuable and much-needed talent. Firms that are successful in diversity recruitment will find that inclusiveness in the workplace quickly becomes self-perpetuating.

Analysis of Recruitment Procedures

To ensure that its recruitment program is diversity oriented, a firm must analyze its recruitment procedures. In identifying sources of continuing discrimination, a helpful approach is to develop a *record of applicant flow* or, if feasible, an automated applicant tracking system, as previously described. If the firm has a discriminatory history or operates under an affirmative action program, this record may be mandatory. An applicant flow record includes personal and job-related data concerning each applicant. It indicates whether the firm made a job offer and, if not, an explanation of the decision. Such records enable the organization to analyze its recruitment and selection practices and take corrective action when necessary.

Utilization of Minorities, Women, and Individuals with Disabilities

It is imperative that all recruiters receive training in the use of objective, job-related standards. These individuals occupy a unique position in terms of encouraging or discouraging minorities, women, and the disabled to apply for jobs. Using minorities, women and individuals with disabilities in key recruitment activities, such as visiting schools and colleges and participating in career days, can pay real dividends. They also are in an excellent position to participate in recruitment planning and can effectively serve as referral sources. Pictures of minority, women, and disabled employees in help-wanted advertisements and company brochures give credibility to the message, "We are an equal opportunity employer."

Advertising

Business firms, encouraged by a growing recognition of the value of workplace diversity, emphasize diversity in their advertisements and focus on attracting employees from divergent arenas. This approach augments programs such as employee referrals by building internal morale and promoting the company culture.[90]

With few exceptions, jobs must be open to all individuals. Therefore, gender-segregated ads, for example, are not acceptable unless gender is a bona fide occupational qualification (BFOQ). The BFOQ exception provided in Title VII of the Civil Rights Act requires that qualifications be job related. EEOC and the courts interpret this definition narrowly. The burden of proof is on the employer to establish that the requirements are essential for successful performance of the job. Other approaches that could encourage diversity and limit a firm's legal liability include:

- Ensuring that the content of advertisements does not indicate preference for any race, gender, or age, or that these factors are a qualification for the job.
- Utilizing media directed toward minorities, such as appropriate radio stations.
- Emphasizing the intent to recruit without regard to race, gender, or disabled status by placing appropriate statements in job ads. Recall from Figure 5-4 that the statement "We are an Equal Opportunity Employer" was on the ad.

Employment Agencies

An organization should emphasize its nondiscriminatory recruitment practices when utilizing employment agencies. Even when a business works with private agencies, also covered under Title VII, it's a good idea to list jobs at every level with the state employment service. These agencies can provide valuable assistance to organizations seeking to fulfill diversity goals. In addition, firms should contact agencies and consultant firms that specialize in minority and women applicants.

People with Disabilities

More employers will soon hear about the new Social Security Administration program called Ticket to Work. The program encourages firms to recruit and hire people with disabilities by permitting them to earn tax credits. The program provides incentives to hire people who receive Social Security Disability Income (SSDI) or Supplemental Security Income (SSI). It will cut the SSA's costs by reducing the number of claimants in these programs. In 2001, individuals who filed SSDI claims alone received $60 billion in disability benefits. The program also has incentives for key stakeholders. Employers get up to $2,500 per hire in first-year tax credits. SSDI and SSI claimants receive continued medical benefits for up to 8.5 years. They receive a nine-month trial employment period with continuing disability benefits. They will also get expedited reinstatement of disability benefits if they are unable to continue to work. Employment networks that assist people with disabilities in obtaining employment will receive up to $19,000 per hire in commissions. All 50 states will have this program by 2004.[91]

Other Suggested Recruitment Approaches

Staffing managers should make contact with counselors and administrators at high schools, vocational schools, and colleges with large minority and/or female enrollments. Organizations should make counselors and administrators aware that it is actively seeking minorities, women, and disabled individuals for jobs that they have not traditionally held. Also, counselors and administrators should be familiar with the types of jobs available and the training and education needed to perform these jobs. All parties should investigate the possibilities for developing internships and summer employment. Firms should develop contacts with minority, women's, and other community organizations. These organizations include the National Association for the Advancement of Colored People (NAACP), the League of United Latin American Citizens, the National Urban League, the American Association of University Women, the Federation of Business and Professional Women's Talent Bank, the National Council of Negro Women, and the Veterans Administration. The EEOC's regional offices will assist employers in locating appropriate local agencies.

A Global Perspective

Outsourcing Goes Offshore

Swelling revenues, strong profit growth, profitable contracts, and a huge recruitment drive describe the current information technology industry. That is, if we are businesses in India. In this country, software firms are flourishing thanks to booming outsourcing business from some of the leading global firms. Outsourcing has risen, especially to low-cost locations such as India. As a result, the export revenues of India's software services market reached $6.2 billion last year, an increase from under $500 million a decade ago. When Indian firms entered the outsourcing business, it served all sorts of firms in an industry once dominated by companies such as IBM and EDS. Lower labor costs is one key to India's rapid revenue growth. In addition, the time difference also gives India a selling point. The 10-hour time difference between the United States and India offers American firms 24-hour service by switching to Indian workers during the American nights.[92]

The rise of a globally integrated knowledge economy is a blessing for developing nations. Its effect on the skilled American labor force is less clear. It may mean a difficult readjustment for many white-collar employees. The extraordinary hiring splurge in Asia, Eastern Europe, and Latin America comes at a time when American firms are downsizing. In the Silicon Valley, for example, employment in the IT sector is down by 20 percent since early 2001.[93] The demand for IT workers may even get lower. The Information Technology Association of America (ITAA) found in its latest survey that recruiting managers expect to hire fewer than 500,000 tech workers over a 12-month period; down from predicted demand of 1.1 million in 2002.[94]

With digitization, the Internet, and high-speed data networks that encircle the globe, performance of all kinds of knowledge work is possible virtually anywhere. That is why firms such as Intel and Texas Instruments are actively hiring Indian and Chinese engineers, many with graduate degrees, to design chip circuits. In some countries, you get quality work at 50 percent to 60 percent of U.S. labor costs. From a different perspective, globalizations should keep services prices in check just as it did with clothes, appliances, and home tools. In addition, by spurring economic growth in developing nations, larger foreign markets will be available for U.S. goods and services. The real outcome, however, is up in the air. The rise of the global knowledge industry is so recent that the long-term implications are quite unclear.[95]

Summary

1. Explain the importance of Internet recruiting.
Initiating contact with prospective employers by telephone or through the U.S. Postal Service is fast becoming an outmoded technique for finding jobs. The speed and expanded talent pool offered by the Web help make their recruiting processes more efficient and cost-effective. Basically, recruiting on the Web expands individual employment options, and improves the recruitment process for businesses. The age-old task of matching candidates with jobs is being revolutionized.

2. Explain alternatives to recruitment.
Alternatives include outsourcing, contingent workers, employee leasing, and overtime.

3. Explain the external and internal environment of recruitment.
Factors external to the organization can significantly affect the firm's recruitment efforts. The organization's own practices and policies also affect recruitment.

4. Describe the recruitment process.
Recruitment frequently begins when a manager initiates an employee requisition. Next, the firm determines whether qualified employees are available from within (the internal source) or must be recruited externally from sources such as colleges, universities, and other firms. Sources and methods are then identified.

5. Describe internal recruitment methods.
Job posting is a method of internal recruitment that is used to communicate the fact that job openings exist. Job bidding is a system that permits individuals in an organization to apply for a specific job within the organization.

6. Identify external sources of recruitment.
External sources of recruitment include high schools and vocational schools, community colleges, colleges and universities, competitors and other firms, the unemployed, older individuals, military personnel, and self-employed workers.

7. Identify external recruitment methods.
External recruitment methods include advertising, employment agencies, recruiters, internships, executive search firms, professional associations, employee referrals, unsolicited walk-in applicants, open houses, event recruiting, virtual job fairs, and sign-on bonuses.

8. Describe an applicant tracking system.
An applicant tracking system (ATS) automates online recruiting and selection processes. Current systems enable human resource and line managers to oversee the entire process, from screening résumés and spotting qualified candidates, to conducting personality and skills tests and handling background checks.

9. Describe how recruitment methods and sources are tailored to each other.
Recruitment must be tailored to the needs of each firm. In addition, recruitment sources and methods often vary according to the type of position being filled.

10. Explain how to recruit for diversity.
Forward thinking organizations actively engage in acquiring a workforce that reflects society and helps the company expand into untapped markets. To accomplish this objective, firms may need to use nontraditional recruitment approaches.

Key Terms

- **Recruitment, 118**
- **Contingent workers, 121**
- **Professional employer organizations (PEOs), 122**
- **Promotion from within (PFW), 125**
- **Employee requisition, 127**
- **Recruitment sources, 127**
- **Recruitment methods, 127**
- **Job posting, 129**
- **Job bidding, 129**
- **Advertising, 133**
- **Employment agency, 135**

- **Internet recruiter, 136**
- **Job fair, 136**
- **Internship, 137**
- **Executive search firms, 137**
- **Contingency search firms, 138**
- **Retained search firms, 138**
- **Applicant tracking system (ATS), 140**

Questions for Review

1. Why has Internet recruiting become so important?
2. What are the typical alternatives to recruitment that a firm may use?
3. What are the basic components of the recruitment process?
4. What are the various external and internal factors that may affect recruitment?
5. What are the steps involved in the recruitment process?
6. Define *job posting* and *job bidding*.
7. What are the advantages and disadvantages of internal recruitment?
8. Define *sources* and *methods* of recruitment.
9. What are the sources of recruitment that are available?
10. What are the methods of recruitment that are available?
11. What are the sources and methods of recruitment that might be used for the following jobs:
    a. college professor who just received his or her Ph.D.
    b. senior accountant with a CPA
    c. entry-level accountant
    d. skilled automobile mechanic
    e. entry-level machine operator
12. What is an applicant tracking system?
13. How can a firm improve its recruiting efforts to achieve diversity?

A Problem Ad?

Dorothy Bryant, recruiting supervisor for International Manufacturing Company in Salt Lake City, Utah, had been promoted to her position after several years as a group leader in the production department. One of Dorothy's first assignments was to recruit two software design engineers for International. After considering various recruitment alternatives, Dorothy placed the following ad in a local newspaper with a circulation in excess of 1,000,000:

EMPLOYMENT OPPORTUNITY
FOR SOFTWARE DESIGN ENGINEERS

2 positions available for software design engineers desiring career in growth industry.

Prefer recent college graduates with good appearance.

Apply Today! Send your résumé,

in confidence, to: D. A. Bryant

International Manufacturing Co., P.O. Box 1515

Salt Lake City, UT 84115

More than 300 applications arrived in the first week, and Dorothy was elated. When she reviewed the applicants, however, it appeared that few people possessed the desired qualifications for the job.

Questions

1. Dorothy overlooked some of the proper recruiting practices, which resulted in an excessive number of unqualified people applying. What are they?
2. Identify the hiring standards that should be avoided in the ad.

HRM Incident 2

HRM Incident 2: Can the Internet Help Us?

Shane Bordeaux is the HR director for a medium-sized chemical company located on the outskirts of Baton Rouge, Louisiana. Although the company is relatively small, it has a reputation for being quite innovative. The firm employs 15 engineers, primarily graduates from colleges in the general area. It pays its employees well, benefits are far better than most in the Southeast, and there has been little turnover, with only three engineers being hired in the last two years.

For several years the company has been bidding on a major government contract that could thrust it into the forefront of chemical processing technology. A decision on the contract is expected soon. As Shane sits in his office one morning, he receives a call from company president Dave Louder, who tells him to come down to his office. When he arrives, Dave excitedly tells him that it has happened, the contract is theirs! They now have to get everything in gear and begin production. Successful completion of the contract would make them a major player in the industry. Things have to move fast now. Shane is excited until he realizes that the company will need at least 20 new engineers immediately. Shane then says, "I don't believe I can get those engineers on board that fast. The college placement centers at most of the colleges where I recruit don't have a lot of people graduating this semester, and the demand for engineers is real high these days." Dave replies, "Well, we have to have those people fast or the government will yank the contract. Get to it."

That night Shane discusses his dilemma with his friend Natalie Villamizar. He says, "All my recruitment methods are going to take longer than Dave will allow. We advertise in *Chemical Monthly*, but that takes a long time to get published. Our internship program has been successful, but it takes way too much time. We have gotten one worker from an employment agency, but that individual just wanted to get back to the Baton Rouge area. Primarily, I have been recruiting on college campuses in the region." Natalie leans back in her chair and says, "Have you tried recruiting on the Internet? My company has been really successful at recruiting on the Web. Maybe you should give it a shot."

Question

1. Do you agree with Natalie that Shane should consider the Internet for recruiting?

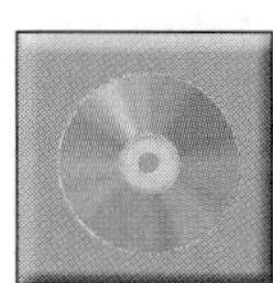

Human Resource Management Skills

Chapter 5: Recruitment Recruitment is the focus of the second portion of the Skills module entitled *Strategic Planning and Recruitment*. Specific sections within the module address: the relevant labor market, internal and external recruitment, the use of replacement charts and succession planning, advantages and disadvantages of both internal and external recruiting, recruitment sources, recruitment advertising, and using yield ratio to assess the value of recruitment sources.

Several recruitment scenarios are presented to give students realistic experience in dealing with the topic.

A test is provided at the end of the module to determine mastery of the material included in the Skills Module. Also, directions are given for assignments that can be used in class or assigned as homework.

Take it to the Net

We invite you to visit the Mondy homepage on the Prentice Hall Web site at

www.prenhall.com/mondy

for updated information, Web-based exercises, and links to other HR-related sites.

Notes

1. "Finders, Keepers," *Nursing Management* 33 (April 2002): 20.
2. E-Recruiting Is Alive, Well and Established," *Internet Wire* (August 20, 2002).
3. Ibid.
4. "The High-Tech Resume," *St. Louis Post-Dispatch* (August 9, 2002): B8.
5. "'Dot-Coma' a Monster Problem: Career Web Site Has Job-Search Issue of Its Own as it Struggles in a

Struggling Job Market," *National Post* (November 15, 2002): FP11.

6. Bernie Cullen, "e-Recruiting Is Driving HR Systems Integration," *Strategic Finance* 83 (July 2001): 22–26.
7. Adapted from articles by Ray Schreyer and John McCarter, "10+ Steps to Effective Internet Recruiting," *HR Focus* (September 1998): S6; and Scott Hays, "Hiring on the Web," *Workforce* (August 1999): 76–84.
8. Victor Godinez, "Job Seekers May Need to Use Low-Tech Tactics," *Dallas Morning News* (March 3, 2002): 9L.
9. "How Two Organizations Are Achieving HR Value," *HR Focus* (January 2003): 7.
10. Michelle Neely Martinez, "Recruiting Here and There," *HRMagazine* 47 (September 2002): 96.
11. Thomas Hoffman, "Big Outsourcing Shift Predicted for IT Jobs," *Computerworld* (January 27, 2003): 12.
12. Pete Engardio, Aaron Bernstein, and Manjeet Kripalani, "Is Your Job Next," *BusinessWeek* (February 3, 2003): 50–51.
13. Charles J. Muhl, "What Is an Employee? The Answer Depends on the Federal Law," *Monthly Labor Review* 125 (January 2002): 3.
14. Peter Allan, "The Contingent Workforce: Challenges and New Directions," *American Business Review* (June 1, 2002): 103.
15. Shari Caudron, "Another God That's Failed," *Across the Board* 39 (May/June 2002): 54–55.
16. Cassandra Hayes and Charlene Solomon, "The Lure of Tempting," *Black Enterprise* 26 (February 1996): 120–122.
17. Carroll Lachnit, "HR Takes Charge of Contingent Staffing," *Workforce* 81 (March 2002): 50.
18. Drew Edwards, "Risk Managers Must Learn ABCs of PEOs," *National Underwriter* (Property & Casualty/Risk & Benefits Management Edition) (April 30, 2001): 18.
19. Andrea C. Bassoff, "Staff Leasing Firm Markets Fewer Hassles with Workers," *Washington Times* (September 20, 1999): D3.
20. Harold F. Krieger, Jr., "Is a 'Professional Employer Organization' in Your Future," *The National Public Accountant* (April/May 2003): 30.
21. Ibid.
22. Jay Finegan, "Look Before You Lease," *Inc.* 19 (February 1997): 106.
23. Daniel Kadlec, "Where Did My Raise Go?" *Time* (May 26, 2003): 44.
24. Bruce Adams, "Creativity Counts When Filling Positions," *Hotel and Motel Management* (January 15, 2001): 47.
25. Engardio, Bernstein, and Kripalani, "Is Your Job Next?"
26. "Outsourcing from the New Silicon Valley," *Wall Street Journal* (January 27, 2000).
27. Mike Johnson, "The Global Search for Talent Gets Tougher," *Financial Executive* 18 (June 2002): 42–43.
28. Ken Dubrowski, "What Employers Can and Cannot Ask," *HR Focus* 72 (June 1995): 3.
29. Donald L. Caruth and Gail D. Handlogten, *Staffing the Contemporary Organization* (Westport, CT: Praeger Publishers, 1997): 90.
30. "The High-Tech Resume," *St. Louis Post-Dispatch* (August 9, 2002): B8.
31. Gillian Flynn, "E-Recruiting Ushers in Legal Dangers," *Workforce* 81 (April 2002): 70–72.
32. Ibid.
33. Ibid.
34. "A Compliance Roadmap," *HR Focus* 80 (April 2003): 1.
35. Jill Jusko, "Secrets to Longevity," *Industry Week* 252 (March 2003): 24.
36. Charlene Marnier Solomon, "HR's Push for Productivity," *Workforce* 81 (August 2002): 28.
37. Lisa Bertagnoli, "Employee Relations," *Crain's Chicago Business* (June 4, 2001): E20-E21.
38. Carolyn Hirschman, "Closing the Deal," *HRMagazine* 47 (April 2002): 70.
39. Michelle Neely Martinez, "Recruiting Here and There," *HRMagazine* 47 (September 2002): 95–96.
40. Some firms have managers go online and create or approve the requisition. The requisition then becomes automatic employee search criteria for posting to company Web services.
41. Jonathan A. Segal, "Hiring Days Are (Almost) Here Again," *HRMagazine* 47 (June 2002): 125.
42. Barbara Davison, "The Importance of Cost Per Hire," *Workforce* 80 (January 2001): 32–34.
43. Charles Fishman, "Moving Toward a Balanced Work Life," *Workforce* 79 (March 2000): 40.
44. "The Top HR Issues of 2000," *HR Focus* 77 (April 2000): 1.
45. Ann Harrington, "Make That Switch: Has Your Career Lost Steam? Or Worse, Derailed?" *Fortune* (February 4, 2002): 159.
46. "How Outsourced Recruiting Saves Time and Money — And Gets Quality Hires," *HR Focus* 79 (September 2002): 6.
47. Sandra Grabczynski, "Nab New Grads by Building Relationships with Colleges," *Workforce* 79 (May 2000): 98.
48. Bill Leonard, "Recruiting from the Competition," *HRMagazine* 46 (February 2001): 78–79.
49. Art Kleiner, George Roth, and Nina Kruschwitz, "Should a Company Have a Noble Purpose?" *Across the Board* 37 (January 2001): 18.
50. Adapted from case by Winn Schwartau, "Cyber Ethics in the Workplace," *Network World* (January 21, 2002): 47.
51. Joe Grimm, "Talent Bank: It's All About Access," *Editor and Publisher: The Fourth Estate* (April 24, 2000): 36–39.
52. "Work Still to Be Done: ADA Has Had a Big Impact Since It Became Law in 1990," *State Journal Register*, Illinois (July 29, 2001): 15.
53. Phaedra Brotherton, "Tapping into an Older Workforce," *Mosaics* 6 (March/April 2000): 4.
54. Miles Z. Epstein and David G. Epstein, "Hiring Veterans: A Cost-Effective Staffing Solution," *HRMagazine* 43 (November 1998): 108.
55. John F. Welch, Jr., with John A. Byrne, *Jack Straight from the Gut* (New York: Warner Books, Inc., 2001): 198–199.
56. Evan J. Douglas, "Self-Employment as a Career Choice: Attitudes, Entrepreneurial Intentions, and Utility Maximization," *Entrepreneurship: Theory and Practice* 28 (Spring 2002): 81.
57. "Incentive Pay Plans: Which Ones Work and Why," *HR Focus* 78 (April 2001): 3.
58. "Recruiting Survey Finds Online Advertising Best Return on Investment," *PR Newswire* (October 22, 2002): 1.
59. Ibid.
60. Bennie L. Garcia, Malcolm G. Meador, Jr., and Brian Kleiner, "How to Hire the Right Person the First Time," *Nonprofit World* 21 (March/April 2003): 9.

61. Marilyn Rosenthal, "America's Job Bank," *Library Journal* (October 1, 2002): 70.
62. Andrea C. Poe, "Face Value," *HRMagazine* 45 (May 2000): 60.
63. Sharon Watson, "Hands Off My Staff!" *Computerworld* (January 22, 2001): 50–51.
64. Ibid.
65. http://www.ti.com/recruit/docs/hiringproc.shtml, February 17, 2003.
66. Hirschman, "Closing the Deal."
67. Fred Katayama, "Recruiting in the 90s," *CNNfn, Digital Jam*, http://cnnfn.com/digitaljam/9701/29/job_pkg/index.htm (May 24 1997).
68. Martha Frase-Blunt, "Job Fair Challenges for HR," *HRMagazine* 47 (April 2002): 62–63.
69. Joan Hughes, "Market Tight, but Jobs Still Available: Virtual Job Fair Aids Search," *Richmond Times-Dispatch* (February 10, 2002): S-3.
70. "Virtual Job Fair Offers Opportunities Online," *Bangor Daily News* (February 5, 2003): 5.
71. Lisa Fickenscher, "Grads Clicking with Job Market," *Crain's New York Business* (August 19–25, 2002): 14.
72. Rebecca Simmons, "Internship Experience Invaluable," *University Wire* (July 19, 1999).
73. Jill M. Singer, "Students Leap into Internships and Land Jobs after College," *USA Today* (February 21, 2000): 06D.
74. Barry Higgins, "One Agency's Winning Formula for Retaining Producers," *National Underwriter* (Life & Health/Financial Services Edition) (March 18, 2002): 4–5.
75. Evelyn Beck, "Faculty Interns: A Bargain for Business, a Bonus for the Classroom," *Workforce* 80 (August 2001): 36.
76. Christine Williamson, "Glare of Celebrity Shining on Top Executive Recruiters," *Pensions & Investments* (May 27, 2002): 4, 111.
77. Stephen Mothersole, "Recruitment Consulting," *Chemistry & Industry* (July 15, 2002): 20.
78. http://www.futurestep.com, February 21, 2003.
79. Bob Marshal, "Getting the Most from Your Relationship with a Contingency Search Firm," *AFP-Exchange* 22 (October 2002): 40.
80. Shawn Zeller, "Lobbying: Headhunter 'Shoot-Out' on K Street," *National Journal* (March 31, 2001): 10.
81. http://www.shrm.org/, February 21, 2003.
82. Kevin Wheeler, "Non-Traditional Recruiting Method," *Electronic Recruiting Daily* (March 29, 2000).
83. "Executive Bonuses Decline, but Sign-On Bonuses Still Popular," *HR Focus* 79 (March 2002): 12.
84. Mary Elizabeth Burke, Evren Esen, and Jessica Collison, "2003 Benefits Survey," *SHRM/SHRM Foundation* (June 2003): 38–39.
85. "In: Signing Bonuses, Restricted Stock. Out: Executive Loans, Stock Options," *CFO.com* (February 3, 2003): 1.
86. Lisa Yoon, "Despite the Bleak Job Market, CFOs Very Much in Demand; Highly Prized Finance Chiefs Can 'Name Their Price'," *CFO.com* (April 8, 2003): 1.
87. Samuel Greengard, "Smarter Screening Takes Technology and HR Savvy," *Workforce* 81 (June 2002): 56–60.
88. Bob Neveu, "Applicant Tracking's Top 10," *Workforce* 81 (October 2002): 92–93.
89. Greengard, "Smarter Screening Takes Technology and HR Savvy."
90. Ruth E. Thaler-Carter, "Diversify Your Recruitment Advertising," *HRMagazine* 46 (June 2001): 92.
91. Peter Mead, "Hiring People with Disabilities," *Workforce* 81 (December 2002): 16.
92. "Business: America's Pain, India's Gain; Outsourcing," *The Economist* (January 11, 2003): 59.
93. Engardio, Bernstein, and Kripalani, "Is Your Job Next?"
94. "Tech Bits: Demand May Slow Even More in IT," *Dallas Morning News* (May 11, 2003): 9J.
95. Engardio, Bernstein, and Kripalani, "Is Your Job Next?"

APPENDIX CHAPTER 5 *Internet Recruiting*

DEFINITIONS

The speed and expanded talent pool offered by the Internet help make the recruiting process more efficient and cost-effective. Basically, recruiting on the Internet expands individual employment options, and improves the recruitment process for businesses. The age-old task of matching candidates with jobs is being revolutionized. Unfortunately, Internet recruiting is changing so fast that it is virtually impossible to keep up to date. New Web sites are constantly being created, sites are merging, sites are expanding, and others are being dissolved.

Internet:
The large system of many connected computers around the world that individuals and businesses use to communicate with each other.

Web (World Wide Web):
The system of connected documents on the Internet, which often contains color pictures, video, and sound and can be searched for information about a particular subject.

The **Internet** is the large system of many connected computers around the world that individuals and businesses use to communicate with each other.[1] The **Web (World Wide Web)** is the system of connected documents on the Internet, which often contains color pictures, video, and sound and can be searched for information about a particular subject.[2] Although these two terms are different in several respects, in this text the terms will be used interchangeably.

THE RECRUITMENT PROCESS AND THE INTERNET

As previously defined, *recruitment* is the process of attracting individuals on a timely basis, in sufficient numbers, with appropriate qualifications, and then encouraging them to apply for jobs with an organization. When the Internet is involved in the recruitment process, the definition itself does not change. However, words within the definition may take on different meanings. For example, *on a timely basis* may mean within a month or two with traditional recruitment methods. With the Internet, *timely* may be within a week, a day, or almost immediately. Now consider the term *in sufficient numbers* and see the power of the Internet. Large numbers of qualified applicants usually can be identified, especially in days of high unemployment. Internet recruiting can effectively identify both active and passive applicants. Dissecting the definition still further, we deal with the term *appropriate qualifications*. With the Internet, there are numerous ways to screen applicants to determine if they have the appropriate qualifications for the job. Finally, *applying for a job with the organization* is easy. Individuals can wake up at midnight, decide to change jobs, and have new résumés out for review before going back to bed. Companies can also place a new job advertisement on their homepages at any time. Both employees and employers are embracing the Internet, and this trend will probably expand dramatically in the future.

LIMITATIONS OF INTERNET RECRUITING

It would be unwise for human resource professionals to rely solely on the Internet to attract candidates. The Internet's true recruiting value is its immediacy and ability to interact digitally with potential employees. Employers can post jobs on either a company Web site or employment Web sites. The paperless platform offers companies a way to target talented professionals. Job-seekers can communicate via e-mail and even conduct online interviews. Although the Internet can be valuable, it does have certain potential limitations that must be taken into account.

First, the Internet is not a selection tool. It does not replace conducting background checks, face-to-face interviews, and other steps to assess attitudes and behavior that are vital to finding qualified employees. Second, HR professionals are frustrated with the Internet's lack of a personal touch. An applicant should not look for a personal response if he or she is not a fit when applying for a job over the Internet. The volume of résumés is often just too large.[3] Third, the number of résumés has grown dramatically, and organizations have to deal with this increase. Fourth, there is more competition for qualified employees from small and medium, as well as global, companies. Smaller companies can reach out to applicants from all parts of the country, even globally. Fifth, spending on Internet recruiting is increasing, but often at the expense of other, more traditional approaches. Finally, confidentiality could be a problem, since all of the applicant's information is on one or more Web sites, which could be violated by hackers.[4]

Intranet:
A system of computers that enables people within an organization to communicate with each other.

INTERNAL RECRUITMENT—USING THE INTRANET

The **intranet** is a system of computers that enables people within an organization to communicate with each other.[5] In the past, many a disgruntled employee has discovered that a vacancy existed in another location long after it was filled. Posted jobs often did not find their way to the bulletin boards in all locations. This approach has changed in many companies across the nation and internationally with the use of the intranet.[6]

The common format approach permits each applicant to be analyzed on an equal basis. Many organizations have already had all of their employees complete a standardized application form. In this case, the applicant merely submits the completed application when applying for a vacant position. Distance is not a factor when using the intranet for internal recruiting. Assuming that several qualified applications exist, the company has the option of using teleconferencing to conduct the initial screening. Or, the screening may actually result in an immediate hiring.

The intranet is a good way to keep everyone up to date, especially in a global age where workers are dispersed. After General Electric revamped its intranet, the number of hits jumped from a couple of thousand to 10 million a week. An online marketplace also offers discounts on GE appliances, Dell computers, and other products. AT&T has an intranet where workers can manage benefits, check their 401(k) plans, and make investment changes, as well as check company news, which is updated daily. Hallmark Cards even posts the cafeteria menu, as well as the employee newsletter and job-training resources, on its intranet. Texas Instruments allows new hires to access the intranet before their first day on the job, thereby helping them to get up to speed quicker. The site also includes a concierge service that will plan vacations and run errands, and provides a way to pick doctors from the health plan. American Century Investments uses its intranet for classified ads and information on competitors.[7]

THE CORPORATE WEB SITE

Individuals desiring jobs with a particular organization discover job opportunities on the corporate Web site. Checking out a Web site is a way to be a smart job shopper. "You want to make sure it's going to be a good culture fit and if it's a company you want to pursue. It gives you a chance to look at the market and keep your anonymity at the same time," says Robin Hunt, director of recruiting at Quantum Resources, a technical staffing company specializing in scientific, engineering, and information technology personnel. "Job searchers should try to draw some conclusions about the company by assessing its Web site. Its presentation is a window into the company's professionalism and, quite possibly, its success, just as a résumé is your window into who you are."[8] A Web site is essential, but creating a site that is easy to use and that produces good results is not easy. It takes time and experimentation to create a really successful site.

GENERAL EMPLOYMENT WEB SITES

Using the Internet for recruitment can make the process more timely and cost-effective, and provide access to a broader pool of job candidates. Those are key drivers behind the proliferation of employment Web sites in the past few years.[9] A lot more exposure for the dollar is one of the advantages of posting help-wanted ads online versus newspaper ads. The rates vary widely for online ads—from free to about $300 for one posting, or $10,000 annually for unlimited postings.[10] Firms utilize employment Web sites by simply typing in key job criteria, skills, and experience and indicating their geographic location. They next click *Search for Candidates* and in seconds have a ranked list of résumés from candidates who match the firm's requirements. The number of sites seems to expand and contract daily. Therefore, only the most widely recognized general employment Web sites—Monster.com, HotJobs.com, and CareerBuilder.com—will be briefly discussed.

Monster.com

The largest employment Web site is Monster.com.[11] The company is organized around three geographic regions (Asia/Pacific, Europe, and North America) and has more than 490 of the *Fortune* 500 companies as clients.[12] Valuable information to job-seekers such as résumé tips, interview tips, salary information, and networking information is available on the site.[13] Monster can be very cost-effective since a 60-day job ad costs $305 and a company can post a job and search Monster's database for $705.[14]

HotJobs.com

HotJobs.com, a subsidiary of Yahoo!, is a recruiting solutions and software company.[15] Approximately 7,000 employers use the Web site which features a database of 7 million résumés. Revenue is generated from the fees charged to employers but job-seekers are not charged. In addition to its HotJobs Career Expo job fairs, it offers recruiting software and a business-to-business desktop application program, AgencyExchange, which connects hiring managers and recruiters.[16] Valuable information to job applicants such as industry news, community information, interviewing tips, résumé-writing tips, salary and benefits information, job searching tips, and education and training opportunities are available on the site.[17]

CareerBuilder.com

Gannett Co., Inc., has teamed with Knight Ridder and Tribune Company as an equal partner of CareerBuilder.com. More than 90 Gannett newspapers are now CareerBuilder.com affiliates and CareerBuilder.com powers the career channel on USATODAY.com. With presence in over 200 local markets, CareerBuilder.com has the recruitment industry covered nationwide.[18] In addition to its online presence on the Web sites of the newspapers and television station, Careerbuilder.com delivers local help-wanted ads to a combined Sunday circulation of 15 million through more than 130 newspapers of Gannett, Knight Ridder, and Tribune Company.[19] Careerbuilder.com offers a confidential personal search agent that will hunt for job opportunities in expressed areas of interest and automatically e-mail them to job-seekers. The site provides online career assessment, coaching for interviews, and tips for salary negotiations.[20]

DIRECTEMPLOYERS.COM

DirectEmployers.com:
A search engine that was developed by a group of corporations that enables job candidates to search member companies' job listings and be taken directly to a member company Web site once a desired position is identified.

DirectEmployers.com is a search engine that was developed by a group of corporations; it enables job candidates to search member companies' job listings and be taken directly to a member company Web site once a desired position is identified. Since its release, DirectEmployers.com has had a major impact on Internet recruiting.[21] Companies such as Unisys, IBM, Cisco, and Intel contributed a total of $5 million to create and operate the site.[22] Businesses can join for $10,000 a year, with unlimited listings (job postings are indexed from corporate Web sites daily); nonprofits pay $5,000.[23]

The concept originated because some corporations had made large investments in the "careers" sections of their Web sites, and wanted to bring traffic there instead of buying ads on job boards. Don Guaglianone, Unisys' vice president for global recruiting, said, "Nothing would please me more [than] to be less reliant on the boards. The company spends $250,000 on online listings. In 1998, a company would have paid a job board $20,000 to $30,000 to list 1,000 jobs. That would cost over $200,000 today."[24] Extra fees were sometimes charged to link candidates directly to corporate Web sites.[25] DirectEmployers.com uses a different approach than most job boards where companies buy ads and the job listings reside on the job board. Candidates can go to the site and if a job comes up that looks interesting, one click sends it straight to the employer's Web site. The average visitor to the site stays just seconds before being taken to a corporate site. There are no jobs to view on the site and no ads to slow things down.[26] DirectEmployers.com has experienced an increase in membership of 500 percent since its launch and reports that the search engine is driving more traffic to its sites than commercial job boards.[27]

NICHE SITES

Niche sites:
Web sites that cater to a specific profession.

Peter Weddle, author of *Jobseeker's Guide to Employment Web Sites*, said, "A year ago, most companies began looking for qualified candidates by going to one of the large general-purpose job boards. Now, they begin at niche job sites that specialize in a particular field."[28] Sites that specialize by industry and level of employment are becoming much more common.[29] **Niche sites** are Web sites that cater to a specific profession; a few of these sites will be discussed next. There appears to be a site for everyone. A few catchy ones include:

- cfo.com (a comprehensive online resource center for senior finance executives)[30]
- CPACareerNet (an online recruiting service that provides CPA firms with assistance in locating qualified employees)[31]
- careerjournal.com (content comes from the editorial resources of the *Wall Street Journal*. Positions featured include senior and general management, sales, marketing, finance, technology, and a range of related fields)[32]
- brassring.com (site for finding IT jobs, tech jobs, Internet jobs, and job fair information)[33]
- dice.com (a leading provider of online recruiting services for technology professionals)[34]

- internships.wetfeet.com (employers who are exclusively looking for interns)[35]
- brilliantpeople.com (an executive search firm)[36]
- hospitalsoup.com (global hospital careers)[37]
- hireintellect.com (caters to mid-level to executive marketing and communications professionals with *Fortune* 1000 companies in metro Atlanta's high-tech, telecommunications, financial services, business-to-business, and consumer industries)[38]
- joyjobs.com (international employment for teachers)[39]
- employment911.com (provides help for finding a job in an emergency)[40]
- techies.com (carries only technology-based job openings)[41]
- techjobbank.com (focuses on the recruiting needs of the technology companies)[42]
- coolworks.com (lists adventure jobs such as park ranger)[43]
- sixfigurejobs.com (provides executives and experienced professionals with access to some of the most exclusive executive jobs, executive recruiters, and career management tools available)[44]
- TVjobs.com (jobs in broadcasting)[45]
- layover.com (jobs in trucking)[46]
- monstertrak.com (job listings and résumé service that target college students and alumni)[47]
- mfgjobs.com (created exclusively for manufacturing and engineering professionals)[48]

A niche is even available for professors who desire to change jobs. Formerly, college and university professors had to go to their library and thumb through the many pages of *The Chronicle of Higher Education* to hunt for a job. Now, sitting in the comfort of their own home they can enter (www.chronicle.com/) which takes them to *The Chronicle of Higher Education* Web site. All the jobs listed with the *Chronicle* are available to view free. Each position announcement has a hot link to a university homepage where additional information can be obtained. The universities pay the fees.

CONTRACT WORKERS' SITES

In Chapter 5, contract workers were mentioned as an alternative to recruitment. Sites are now available to assist this segment of the workforce. Professionals searching for freelance work are increasingly turning to Web sites that let them market themselves globally. Now specialized Web sites let workers advertise their skills, set their price, and pick an employer. Three such sites are listed below:

- Freelance.com is a résumé distribution service created specifically for freelancers, consultants, and temporary workers. Freelancers can gain exposure on their search engine for a price. Instant Web presence and a portfolio can be developed. They will even design a Web site for a business.[49]
- FreeAgent.com lets contractors search in fields such as technical writing, customer support, and real estate. They can also network online with other freelancers and showcase their skills to employers with an online portfolio.[50]
- AllFreelanceWork.com is a central information base for freelancers to find everything that they could need all in one place. Freelancers can search for projects using advanced fields or browse with ease through different categories. Project managers can post jobs with advanced options to ensure that the right candidates respond to their project posting. This service is free.[51]

NACElink:
The result of an alliance between two nonprofit associations—the National Association of Colleges and Employers (NACE) and Direct Employers Association, Inc.—and an initial collaborating group of career centers.

NACELINK

NACElink is the result of an alliance between two nonprofit associations—the National Association of Colleges and Employers (NACE) and DirectEmployers Association, Inc.—and an initial collaborating group of career centers. NACElink was launched in 2002 with 27 schools from across the country involved in the initial development and testing.[52] Job posting, résumé database and interview-scheduling components are integrated in one database system that makes it easier for students and employers to interact. Shirley Marciniak, associate director of employer relations at Purdue University, said, "This means fewer missed opportunities for students and more exposure for employers." The service is free for NACE-member colleges, but a fee is charged to employers. Employers may post a job opening at up to five schools for $75 or advertise the same job opening to all schools in the system for $245. Ted Glatt, manager of university relations and talent sourcing for Lockheed Martin Corp., said it's worth the cost. "NACElink is uniquely designed to complement our on-campus recruiting efforts," he said. Students may access the site through their college's career center Web site. Employers and colleges may sign up for the service directly at www.nacelink.com.[53]

HOURLY WORKERS' JOB SITES

After years of focusing primarily on professionals and their prospective employers, the big general employment job sites are trying to attract blue-collar and service workers. The three major boards are now listing hourly workers' applications. Since 60 percent of the nation's labor force is hourly workers, it provides an attractive new base of activity because more and more blue-collar workers are using the Internet. The hourly job market has usually been filled through newspaper classified ads or staffing agencies.[54]

Traditionally, there have been major differences between the ways hourly and salaried workers look for jobs. Most hourly workers pursue jobs by filling out applications rather than creating and sending out résumés. So sites allow job-seekers to build an application that can be viewed by employers. Recognizing that some hourly workers do not have computer access, they have set up phone-based services to accept applications. Some job boards have bilingual call center operators who can help job applicants through the process.[55]

Careerbuilder.com enables skilled and hourly workers to apply for hourly jobs by indicating their work preferences, education, and experience.[56] Other innovations by Careerbuilder.com include providing Spanish-speaking applicants the ability to gain quick and easy access to more than 25,000 of the top employers nationwide. With the new bilingual job search center, Hispanics define their job search criteria by company, job type, industry, and city, and receive job postings matching these criteria in Spanish.[57]

DESIGNING A WEB SITE FOR JOB-SEEKERS

Job applicants have discovered that establishing their own Web sites can be very useful in their job searches. Recruiters and HR professionals like them because they are an easy way to get more information about a job candidate. Recruiters can study an applicant's background and only initiate a contact if they are really interested. It is really much easier than playing telephone tag. From the applicants' standpoint, they are able to tailor the information presented in a most positive light.

Web sites allow job-seekers to expand their résumés beyond the traditional format. Recruiters can read it or skip it. For instance, a Web site could contain a list of projects the individual managed and details about each one. A Web site is also a good place to post letters of reference and biographical details that might be of interest to employers, but that are not job related, such as volunteer work and a list of recent awards. An effective Web site should have a simple design, consisting of a homepage with an executive summary, home address, phone numbers, and an e-mail address. Links to other pages, such as chronological work history, educational background, career highlights and accomplishments, photo and personal biographical sketch, references and letters of recommendation, are often quite useful. The two most popular Internet browsers, Netscape and Internet Explorer, offer free tutorials.

PASSIVE JOB-SEEKERS

Passive job-seekers: Individuals who are willing to change jobs if the right opportunity comes along.

Businesses planning for the future are looking at recruiting technology to build relationships with talented professionals. Hire.com software is geared to attract **passive job-seekers,** those who are willing to change jobs if the right opportunity comes along. "They are the type of candidates that headhunters would look for if companies had the money to hire headhunters," says Robert Tate, Hire.com's vice president of field marketing. Passive job-seekers want to be in control of the process, so the software lets them be anonymous by simply providing an e-mail address and selecting a password. The software will alert them when a job that matches their interests becomes available. "Most boards require first name, last name, address, e-mail address, and password," Hire CEO Kevin Bethke says. "If you're a passive job-seeker, you don't want to give that much information."[58]

Russell Rueff, senior vice president of HR at Electronic Arts, the world's largest publisher of video games, pursues talent, not in the usual places, but in the privacy of living rooms and bedrooms. "Our best candidates hang out online and read gaming magazines," he says. I think about our next generation of employees when they're 16 years old. I can get to them because our games are in their living rooms and their bedrooms. All I need is their e-mail address." Those addresses flow into an applicant-tracking system from Hire.com, a cornerstone of Electronic Arts' talent-management strategy.[59]

EXTERNAL SOURCES OF RECRUITMENT AND THE INTERNET

In Chapter 5, we discussed external sources of recruitment that included high schools and vocational schools, community colleges, colleges and universities, competitors in the labor market, former employers, the unemployed, persons with disabilities, older individuals, military personnel, and self-employed workers. These recruitment sources also remain viable in the Internet environment.

EXTERNAL RECRUITMENT METHODS AND THE INTERNET

In Chapter 5, the section entitled "External Recruitment Methods" included such topics as advertising, private and public employment agencies, recruiters, job fairs, virtual job fairs, internships, executive search firms, professional associations, walk-in applicants, open houses, event recruiting, and sign-on bonuses. As Internet recruitment is described, some of these general topics will again be discussed and others will be added.

Advertising

Print advertising will probably not be abandoned in the near future. However, go to any of the major job boards or company Web sites and it becomes readily apparent that advertising plays a major role. Employment Web sites and the homepages of most Web sites make people feel like studying the information presented. The classified section of the Sunday newspaper is now also available on the Internet. A positive aspect of this form of advertising is that the total number of ads placed has increased. Trade journals have also benefited from the Internet.

Private Employment Agencies

Employment agencies often have their own Web sites to show prospective employees the array of jobs that are available through their agencies. Rather than bombard the agency representative with phone calls, a searcher can review the site to see what jobs might provide a fit, then contact the agency. Job-seekers are matched with a personal recruiter who can help them sort through job opportunities and give career advice over the phone.

Public Employment Agencies

America's Job Bank is a partnership between the U.S. Department of Labor and the state-operated public employment service. It is the largest online source for national and international employment. It offers job posting for employers and résumé posting and job searching by occupation, keyword, and zip code for job-hunters.[60] For employers, it provides rapid, national exposure for job openings and an easily accessible pool of candidates. America's Job Bank may be reached at www.ajb.dni.us. There is no charge to either employers who list their job vacancies or to job-seekers who utilize the Job Bank to locate employment. Help is available for those who have difficulty in writing. Assistance in preparing a résumé and writing a cover letter is also available.[61]

College Recruiters

The Internet is a dramatic tool for recruiting college students. The job of the college recruiter is changing drastically with the advent of the Internet. Some recruiters are using computers to communicate with college career counselors and interview students through a videoconferencing system without leaving the office.

Online Job Fairs

Most major job boards regularly conduct online job fairs targeting major U.S. and international job markets. The fairs are featured on the boards' homepages as well as on various other pages. Each corporate logo takes a user to a page with information on each company, job openings, and an online response form. A fair may include 25 or more companies. Each company tells a little about itself and lists the jobs available. Each job can be viewed, and if the applicant believes he or she is qualified, an application can be immediately processed.

Internships

Currently, students find out about many internship programs by using the Internet. Numerous job sites focus on assisting students in obtaining internships. For example, internships.wetfeet.com focuses on student internship programs. Employers who are exclusively looking for interns can find students on this site. Students can also search a large database of internships, read internship reviews or create their own real-intern profile, or research companies and careers. Companies advertise their internship programs or individual internship openings to over 250,000 job-seekers each month. They can also search the database of candidate profiles.[62]

Executive Search Firms

The primary difference between work traditionally done by executive search firms before and after the Internet is one of speed. Often searches now take weeks instead of months. Some firms provide customized recruitment solutions to employers—and offer candidates access to exclusive job opportunities around the world. They combine traditional search expertise with the reach and speed of the Internet.

Professional Associations

Professional associations can combine the print and online components better than anyone. The Society for Human Resource Management has an excellent Web site for human resource professionals. At the homepage click "HR Careers." This will take you to a site where a person is identified as a job-seeker or employer. Clicking "Job Seeker" takes you to a board to "Search Jobs" and you can do so by title, date, or location. Searching by title shows all the HR jobs available by job title. Clicking one will provide you with a position description.[63] Most national professional associations operate their career sites in much the same manner.

Unsolicited Walk-In Applicants

If an organization has the reputation of being a good place to work, it may be able to attract qualified prospects even without extensive recruitment efforts. With the Internet, it is now much easier for unsolicited walk-in applicants to apply for a job. A person merely has to pull up a firm's homepage to find out more about a company. For example, to many, Ford Motor Company has the reputation of being a good place to work, and therefore, an applicant may make a deliberate decision to visit Ford's homepage. Immediately, they see "Careers" and click the icon. Then they click "View Today's Jobs" to see the current job openings. They also have the option of "On the Team," "Our Company," "Career Programs," and "How We Hire" to learn more about employment at Ford Motor Company. Applicants are then asked to answer questions to determine if there is a match of interest and positions available. Assuming that a position is available, applicants are asked to fill out their skills questionnaire. The questionnaire lets applicants tell about their personal interests, background, and experiences and helps Ford match the applicant to openings.[64] An applicant has not applied for a position until the questionnaire is completed. Recall the section on Legal Aspects of Internet Recruiting from Chapter 5. Much the same procedure is followed at General Motors' homepage.[65] Topics you have to choose from when you click "Find a Job" include "Apply on Line," "Attend an Event," "GM Career Paths," "Why Join GM," "Student Center," "Life in Michigan," and "Career Maps."[66]

Talent Auctions

Talent auction: The act of a person or persons placing their qualifications on a Web site and having organizations bid on their services.

A **talent auction** is the act of a person or persons placing their qualifications on a Web site and having organizations bid on their services. In early 2000, a group of 16 trailblazing engineers tried to sell their services on eBay.com for a starting bid of more than $3.14 million. They eventually withdrew their offer, but the idea of people auctioning themselves on the Internet was born. It continues to be used today primarily by free agents and consultants. ITAuctionHouse.com uses an auction format, where placement agencies and employers bid on the services of IT professionals. Once a successful match is made, an ITAuctionHouse representative facilitates job negotiations.[67]

POSTING RÉSUMÉS ON THE INTERNET

When writing their résumés, applicants should realize that most companies now use automated résumé systems. These systems assume a certain résumé style. Résumés that deviate from the assumed style are ignored or simply deleted.[68]

These systems require a common format known as ASCII that stands for "American Standard Code for Information Interchange." ASCII text is the simplest form of text, meaning there is no formatting within the document and the text is not application specific. ASCII is the text format widely used when you read and write e-mail. Because of its simplicity, ASCII text enables anyone to construct an online résumé that prospective employers can view over the Internet no matter what kind of computer software is being used.[69]

The e-mail has become a popular method of providing résumés to organizations. In creating an ASCII résumé, type it using your word processing application such as Microsoft Word, and then save it as a text-only document. This should be an option under your "Save as" command. Since your résumé will appear as ASCII text, it will not recognize special formatting commands specific to your word processing program.[70] Therefore, you must watch for these common mistakes:

- Avoid special characters.
- Do not use tabs; use your space bar.
- Do not use the word-wrap feature when composing your résumé; instead, use hard carriage returns to insert line breaks.
- Use the default font and size.
- Do not use boldface and italics.
- Do not use blocks.
- Do not use columns.
- Do not place names or lines on the sides of resumes.[71]

Here are some additional tips to help you to get your e-mail résumé reviewed:

- Résumé submission should not be compressed. Some people cannot or will not take the time to open a ZIP file. The same can be said about saving your résumé as an Adobe Acrobat PDF file or PowerPoint presentation.
- Copy the résumé's text into e-mail. Send a copy to yourself to double-check. Once you are satisfied, send it to the employer.[72]

RÉSUMÉ MANAGEMENT SYSTEMS

Résumé management systems:
Systems that scan résumés into databases, search the databases on command, and rank the résumés according to the number of resulting hits they receive.

Several electronic résumé databases have been developed and they vary widely in size, content, accessibility, and cost. **Résumé management systems** scan résumés into databases, search the databases on command, and rank the résumés according to the number of resulting hits they receive. At times such searches utilize multiple (10–20) criteria. Major corporations and recruitment firms usually use résumé management systems to do a better job of pre-screening résumés arriving in response to Web ads. The system ranks the résumés in order, from most likely to match the company's requirements to least likely to match.

The reliance upon résumé management systems, coupled with the downsizing of human resource departments in many corporations, has resulted in a situation whereby many résumés are never seen by human eyes once they enter the system. Therefore, á job applicant should make his or her résumé as computer/scanner friendly as possible so that its life in a database will be extended and its likelihood of producing *hits* enhanced.

Keywords:
Those words or phrases that are used to search databases for résumés that match.

Keyword résumé:
A resume that contains an adequate description of the job seeker's characteristics and industry-specific experience presented in keyword terms in order to accommodate the electronic/computer search process.

To make the process work, a new résumé style should be used. **Keywords** refer to those words or phrases that are used to search databases for résumés that match. This match is called a *hit* and occurs when one or more résumés are selected as matching the various criteria (keywords) used in the search. Keywords tend to be more of the noun or noun phrase type (Word 2000, UNIX, BioChemist) as opposed to power action verbs often found in traditional résumés (developed, coordinated, empowered, organized). Another way to look at keyword phrases is to think in terms of job duties. Detailing an individual's job duties may require a change in mindset away from traditional résumés writing. The **keyword résumé** is one that contains an adequate description of the job-seeker's characteristics and industry-specific experience presented in keyword terms in order to accommodate the electronic/computer search process. These are the words and phrases that employers and recruiters use to search the databases for *hits*. Failure to provide sufficient hits may limit the usefulness of the resume.[73]

An example of a keyword résumé may be seen in Appendix Figure A5–1. Job-seekers usually need to prepare two versions of their résumés, a keyword résumé and a traditional one (described in Chapter 6). The traditional résumé will continue to be designed to be read by *real people* in "20 seconds or less" and will follow the various formats presented by untold numbers of résumé writers and résumé-writing programs. The keyword résumé, however, should be added to the job-seeker's arsenal, and utilized in any situation where computer scanning or

HENRY SANCHEZ
1508 Westwood Drive
New York, NY 20135
(914) 555-3869

OBJECTIVE:

To obtain an entry-level position in a public accounting firm.

EMPLOYMENT HISTORY:

11/2003–Present, Assistant Administrator at Touch of Class Foods Corporation
**Built Accounts Payable and Accounts Receivable ledgers.
**Originated a responsive invoice program.
**Prepared corporate tax returns and all schedules.
**Oversaw intern program.
**Initiated ISO-9002 Certifications in all areas of plant production.
05/01–11/2003 *Personal Assistant* at Park Board of Trustees
**Research and Development with City Sewer District.
**Assisted with general accounting procedures.
**Assisted with customer-related issues.
**Assisted with the allocation of public funds.

EDUCATION:
**M.B.A., University of New York, 2000, GPA: 3.8
**B.S. in Business Administration, concentration in Individual and Corporate Taxation with an emphasis in Management Information Systems, 2000, GPA: 3.2

COMPUTER SKILLS:
**Microsoft Word, AmiPro, WordPerfect 7.0
**Lotus 123, Microsoft Excel, Quattro Pro, Quicken
**Windows and Windows XP Applications

AFFILIATIONS:
**ISO-9002
**TQM National Association

Figure A5-1 Sample Keyword Résumé

posting online might possibly be involved. The key to success in the future is to prepare both correctly, and then get them to prospective employers.[74]

TALENTOLOGY.COM

Technology used by talentology.com allows employers and job-seekers to search for candidates and jobs by unique skills, as opposed to misleading or unreliable keywords.[75] "So many employers waste their recruitment budgets, and so many job hunters waste their time, filtering through meaningless matches generated by traditional keyword and résumé searches," said Talentology President and CEO Frank Pirri. "Talent is proved in skill, not words. You have to go beyond words on a résumé and consider their content. Our system is the next generation of job search technology." Job-seekers create background profiles using the same terms employers use to post job descriptions. Both access a common language of over 12,000 specific skills, allowing the software to generate exact, percentage-ranked matches. Employers can easily identify the most qualified candidates at the top of the list and then invite them for interviews. "Our system connects the right person with the right opportunity," Pirri said. "It recognizes that looking good on paper is not always good enough." Talentology.com protects the confidentiality of its job-seekers and presents full contact information to an employer only when an interview agreement is made. Employers are not charged any fees for the service until an interview invitation is accepted, to save costs and risks.[76]

Key Terms

- **Internet, 149**
- **Web (World Wide Web), 149**
- **Intranet, 150**
- **DirectEmployers.com, 151**
- **Niche sites, 151**
- **NACElink, 152**
- **Passive job-seekers, 153**
- **Talent auction, 155**
- **Résumé management systems, 156**
- **Keywords, 156**
- **Keyword Résumé, 156**

Notes

1. "Internet," *Cambridge International Dictionaries*, Cambridge University Press (2000).
2. Ibid.
3. Adam Geller, "Resume Limbo," *Tulsa World* (October 20, 2002): E7.
4. More Pros and Cons to Internet Recruiting," *HR Focus* 77 (May 2000): 8–9.
5. *Cambridge International Dictionaries*, Cambridge University Press (2000).
6. "Web Technology Dominates HR Delivery," *HR Focus* 77 (May 2000): 9.
7. Stephanie Armour, "Corporate Intranets Help Bring Employees into the Loop," *USA Today* (March 20, 2000): 03B.
8. Barbara Kreisler, "Electronic Age Has Changed the Job Hunt," *Richmond Times-Dispatch* (October 27, 2002): S-6.
9. Mike Moralis, "Web-Based Recruitment Gaining Power Through Standardization," *Canadian HR Reporter* (May 20, 2002): G9.
10. "High-Tech Hiring," *Nation's Restaurant News* (October 28, 2002): T4.
11. Liz Claman and Brad Goode, "TMP Worldwide — Chairman & CEO Interview," *CNBC/Dow Jones Business Video* (Maryland; February 13, 2003).
12. "TMP Worldwide Inc.," *Hoover's Company Capsules* (February 1, 2003).
13. http://content.monster.com/, August 1, 2003.
14. https://secure.monster.com/index.asp?ECOMAD=emplogin,PAJ2, August 1, 2003.
15. HotJobs.com, Ltd.," *Hoover's Company Capsules* (February 1, 2003).
16. *Hoover's Company Capsules* (February 1, 2003).
17. http://www.hotjobs.com/htdocs/tools/index.html, August 1, 2003
18. http://www.careerbuilder.com/share/AboutUs/Index.htm?zbid=X185E1A6720B8FB2FB4EA1506C8A7CE4D262CAA4EEEAB7E600881AA149210B0F5C, August 1, 2003.
19. Careerbuilder.com Successfully Completes Launch of Gannett Newspapers and Its Television Stations as Career Builder.com Affiliates," *PR Newswire* (December 19, 2002).
20. Ibid.
21. Directemployers Association Reports Tremendous Growth in First Year of Operation," *PR Newswire* (February 13, 2003).
22. James M. Von Bergen, "Group of Companies Dumps Job Listing Sites, Forms Own Job Board," *Philadelphia Inquirer* (February 19, 2002).
23. Ann Harrington, "Can Anyone Build a Better Monster?" *Fortune* (May 13, 2002): 189–192.
24. Von Bergen, "Group of Companies Dumps Job Listing Sites, Forms Own Job Board."
25. Todd Raphael, "A Detour Around the Job Boards," *Workforce* 81(May 2002): 18.
26. Ibid.
27. "Directemployers Association Reports Tremendous Growth in First Year of Operation."
28. T. Shawn Taylor, "With So Many Resumes on the Internet, Many End Up Cyber-Trashed," *Chicago Tribune* (February 14, 2002): 50P.
29. George Capulet, "The Job Site Evolution," *Rough Notes* 146 (March 2003): 173–174.
30. http://www.cfo.com, August 1, 2003.
31. Susan B. Anders, "Website of the Month: CPA CareerNet," *The CPA Journal* 72 (November 2002): 17.
32. http://www.careerjournal.com/aboutus/index.html, August 1, 2003.
33. http://www.brassring.com/EN/ASP/CIM/br_home.asp, August 1, 2003
34. http://about.dice.com/ireye/ir_site.zhtml?ticker=dice&script=2100, August 1, 2003.
35. http://internships.wetfeet.com/, August 1, 2003.
36. http://www.brilliantpeople.com/employers.htm, August 1, 2003.
37. http://www.hospitalsoup.com, August 1, 2003.
38. http://www.hireintellect.com/frameset.html, August 1, 2003.
39. http://www.joyjobs.com, August 1, 2003.
40. http://www.employment911.com/asp/about.asp, August 1, 2003.
41. http://www.techies.com/, August 1, 2003.
42. http://www.techjobbank.com/cfm_techjob_about.cfm?APPEMP=A, August 1, 2003.
43. http://www.coolworks.com, August 1, 2003.
44. http://www.sixfigurejobs.com, August 1, 2003.
45. http://www.TVjobs.com, August 1, 2003.
46. http://www.layover.com, August 1, 2003.
47. http://www.monstertrak.com/, August 1, 2003.
48. Jill Jusko, "Online Network Targets Manufacturing," *Industry Week* 251 (July 2002): 15.
49. http://www.allfreelance.com/, August 1, 2003.
50. http://www.freeagent.com/about/index.asp, August 1, 2003.
51. http://www.allfreelancework.com/, August 1, 2003.
52. http://www.nacelink.com/nl_about.asp, August 1, 2003.
53. Tischelle, George, "NACElink Offers Grads Low-Cost Job-Search Option," *InformationWeek* (July 15, 2002): 24.
54. "Job Web Sites Aim for Hourly Workers," *AP Online* (January 24, 2003).
55. Ibid.
56. "Careerbuilder.com Launches National Marketing Campaign to Promote the Smarter Way to Find a Better Job," *PR Newswire* (December 23, 2002).
57. Ibid.
58. Tischelle, George, "Rousing the Passive Job Seeker," *InformationWeek* (June 3, 2002): 75.
59. Eric Krell, "Recruiting Outlook: Creative HR for 2003," *Workforce* (December 1, 2002): 40.
60. Marilyn Rosenthal, "America's Job Bank," *Library Journal* (October 1, 2002): 70.
61. http://www.ajb.dni.us, August 1, 2003.
62. http://internships.wetfeet.com/, August 1, 2003.
63. http://www.shrm.org/jobs/jobdetail, August 1, 2003.
64. http://www.ford.com, August 1, 2003.
65. http://www.gm.com/, August 1, 2003.

66. http://www.gm.com/company/careers/find_job.html, August 1, 2003.
67. www.itauctionhouse.com/about.asp, August 1, 2003.
68. Ted Daywalt, "Tips on Developing a Technical Resume," *Printed Circuit Design* 19 (September 2002): 26.
69. "ASCII Resumes," www.careermosaic.com, February 28, 2000.
70. "How to Find a Job on the Internet," *Computer Desktop Encyclopedia*, The Computer Language Co. Inc. (October 1, 2002).
71. Daywalt, "Tips on Developing a Technical Resume," 26.
72. Kim Komando, "Tech Tools Help with Job Search," *Times Union (Albany)* (January 1, 2003): D2.
73. Taunee Bensson, "Does Your Resume Vanish into a Black Hole?" www.careers.wsj.com, March 3, 2000.
74. Wayne M. Gonyea, "Tips on Using Keywords for Electronic Resumes," www.careermosaic.com, February 28, 2000.
75. Searching for the Right Talent for the Right Job Just Got Better," *PR Newswire* (March 6, 2003): 1.
76. Talentology.com Creates Online Job Searching Based on Skill, Not Words," *PR Newswire* (August 21, 2002).

CHAPTER OBJECTIVES

After completing this chapter, students should be able to

1. Explain the significance of employee selection.
2. Identify environmental factors that affect the selection process.
3. Describe the general selection process.
4. Explain the importance of the preliminary interview.
5. Describe reviewing applications and résumés.
6. Explain the administration of selection tests including the advantages, potential problems, and characteristics of properly designed selection tests.
7. Explain the types of validation studies.
8. Describe types of employment tests.
9. Describe the concept of genetic testing.
10. Discuss assessment centers as a means of selection.
11. Explain the importance of the employment interview, including interview planning and the content of the interview.
12. Describe the general types of interviewing.
13. Explain the growing influence of the behavioral interview.
14. Describe the various methods of interviewing.
15. Explain the legal implications of interviewing.
16. Explain the use of personal reference checks, background investigations, and polygraph tests.
17. Describe the selection decision, the medical examination, and notification of candidates.

CHAPTER 6

Selection

HRM IN *Action:*
Credential Fraud

Selecting capable employees is one of management's top priorities. In order to make sound selection decisions, managers must be able to evaluate reliable data from candidates. This has become increasingly difficult in recent years and the basic problem is that credential fraud has become more prevalent. Some applicants may exaggerate their skills, education, and experience when given the opportunity. Others are not even who they say they are. Recently, Automatic Data Processing (ADP) conducted a study of 2.6 million background verifications. The study found that 44 percent of employment records showed a difference of information between what the applicant provided and the previous employer reported. Thirteen percent of these information differences contained negative remarks from the past employer regarding the applicant's work habits.[1] Between January 1998 and October 2000, American Background Information Services Inc. (ABI), based in Winchester, Virginia, found undisclosed criminal backgrounds on 12.6 percent of the people it screened. Other experts say that number is typical. "Ten to 20 percent of applicants flat out lie," says Randy Baker, HR manager at Birch Telecomm in Emporia, Kansas. "About 8.3 percent of applicants screened have a criminal history, and 23 percent have misrepresented their employment or education credentials," says Blair Cohen, CEO of InfoMart Inc., an employment screening company based in Atlanta. In some industries, these figures are even higher. Telemarketing applicants have a criminal rate of 30 percent to 40 percent, according to Kit Fremin, owner of Background Check International LLC in Temecula, California.[2]

The best way for organizations to detect fraudulent applications is to conduct background investigations. A guiding statute in this process is the federal Fair Credit Reporting Act (FCRA) which requires, in most instances, that an applicant be notified of and agree to background checks. Between the FCRA and state privacy laws there are many restrictions on how information gathered in background checks may be used. Organizations must be careful, because they could find themselves facing costly litigation.[3]

Credential fraud has the potential for presenting all sorts of difficulties for employers. In addition to the dilemmas related to hiring an unsatisfactory employee, a huge legal problem that has emerged is negligent hiring, discussed later in this chapter. Regardless of the difficulties in conducting background investigations, the process is considered mandatory for many organizations.

We began this chapter with a discussion of credential fraud. This is followed by a discussion of the significance of employee selection and identification of environmental factors that affect the selection process. Next, we describe the general selection process. The next two sections involve the preliminary interview and review of applications and résumés. Then we explain the administration of selection tests including the advantages of tests, their potential problems, and characteristics of properly designed selection tests. Sections describing the types of validation studies and types of employment tests follow this. Then the importance of the employment interview, including interview planning, and the content of the interview are emphasized. Next, the general types of interviewing and the growing influence of the behavioral interview are presented. A discussion of the various methods of interviewing and the legal implications of interviewing are discussed next. The final portion of this chapter is devoted to a discussion of the use of personal reference checks, background investigations, polygraph tests, the selection decision, the medical examination, and notification of candidates.

OBJECTIVE

Explain the significance of employee selection.

Selection: The process of choosing from a group of applicants those individuals best suited for a particular position and organization.

SHRM HR Links

www.shrm.org/hrlinks/default.asp

This SHRM Web site covers various selection issues.

The Significance of Employee Selection

Whereas recruitment encourages individuals to seek employment with a firm, the purpose of the selection process is to identify and employ the best-qualified individuals. **Selection** is the process of choosing from a group of applicants the individual best suited for a particular position and organization. As you would expect, a firm's recruitment success has a significant impact on the quality of the selection decision. When recruitment efforts fail to produce qualified applicants, the organization must hire marginally qualified people. There are many ways to improve productivity, but none is more powerful than making the right hiring decision. Top performers in an organization contribute anywhere from five to 22 times more value to their companies than mid-level or low performers.[4] A firm that selects high-quality employees reaps substantial benefits, which recur every year the employee is on the payroll. On the other hand, poor selection decisions can cause irreparable damage. A bad hire can affect the morale of the entire staff, especially in a position where teamwork is critical.[5] Selecting the wrong person for any job can cost a firm money. And, the stakes are even higher for expatriate assignments. Global projects always require extra care in handling different cultures, politics, and business practices. A selection failure can cost anywhere from two times to five times an employee's annual salary.[6]

Most managers recognize employee selection as one of their most difficult and important business decisions. Hiring people has never been easy. Around 2,000 years ago, administrators in the Han dynasty tried to make a science of the selection process by creating long and detailed job descriptions for civil servants. Since new hires seldom worked out as well as anticipated, archaeological records suggest that the poor results of their efforts frustrated these officials.[7]

Michael J. Lotito, former chair of the SHRM board of directors, declared, "HR has traditionally been seen as the soft side of business, but I submit that attracting and retaining the right people for your organization is the hard side of business because that is the foundation upon which everything is based."[8] Libby Sartain, vice president of human resources for Southwest Airlines, provides another perspective. She states, "We would rather go short and work overtime than hire one bad apple."[9] If a firm hires many *bad apples*, it cannot be successful for long even if it has perfect plans, a sound organizational structure, and finely tuned control systems. Competent people must be available to ensure the attainment of organizational goals. Today, with many firms having access to the same technology, the *people* make the real difference. An organization's distinctive advantage has become increasingly dependent upon its human resources.

Small businesses, especially, cannot afford to make hiring mistakes. While an incompetent person's mistake in a large firm may have insignificant consequences, a similar error in a small company may be devastating. In the smaller, less specialized firm, each person typically accounts for a larger part of the business's activity.

Properly matching people with jobs and the organization is the goal of the selection process. If individuals are overqualified, underqualified, or for any reason do not *fit* either the job or the organization's culture, they will be ineffective and probably leave the firm, voluntarily or otherwise.

OBJECTIVE

Identify environmental factors that affect the selection process.

Environmental Factors Affecting the Selection Process

A standardized screening process followed consistently would greatly simplify the selection process. However, circumstances may require making exceptions. The following sections describe environmental factors that affect the selection process.

Other HR Functions

The selection process affects, and is affected by, virtually every other HR function. For instance, if the selection process provides the firm with only marginally qualified workers, the organization may have to intensify its training efforts. If the compensation package is inferior to those provided by the firm's competition, hiring the best-qualified applicants will be difficult or impossible. The same situation applies if the firm's safety and health record is substandard.

Legal Considerations

Legal matters play a significant role in HR management due to legislation, executive orders, and court decisions. The impact is especially prominent in a firm's selection practices as this is when the individual and the employer first make direct contact. One survey found that about one-fourth of all discrimination claims resulted from the employers' recruitment and selection actions.[10] Therefore, while the basic purpose of selection is to determine candidates' eligibility for employment, it is also essential for organizations to maintain nondiscriminatory practices.

Applications by Immigrants. The need to stem illegal immigration prompted Congress to enact the Immigration Reform and Control Act (IRCA) of 1986, discussed previously in Chapter 3. The IRCA toughened criminal sanctions for employers who hire illegal aliens, denied illegal aliens federally funded welfare benefits, and legitimized some aliens through an amnesty program. To comply with the IRCA, candidates for employment are not required to be U. S. citizens but they must prove they are eligible to work in the United States. Employers must require all new employees to complete and sign a verification form (Form I-9) to certify their eligibility for employment. These individuals can establish their eligibility for employment by presenting a U.S. passport, alien registration card with photograph, or a work permit that establishes the person's identity and employment eligibility. Employers should recognize that faked documents are not uncommon and should protect themselves by conducting a background investigation.

Applications via the Internet. Dramatic increases in firms using the Internet for recruiting has added to management's challenge. For example, EEOC guidelines suggest that companies with more than 100 employees keep records for a minimum of two years.[11] This information enables a compilation of demographic data—including age, race, and gender—based on that applicant pool.[12] The EEOC uses these data to assess a company's hiring practices.

The selection process is also impacted by the 9/11 national disaster. For example, the U.S. Food and Drug Administration recently encouraged restaurants to implement such measures as criminal background checks on employees to protect the nation's food from terrorists.[13] As noted in the global perspective at the end of this chapter, the rules concerning hiring employees born outside the United States have not varied much after 9/11, but the way the Bureau of Citizenship and Immigration Service (formerly the Immigration and Naturalization Service) implements the rules has changed.

Speed of Decision Making

The time available to make the selection decision can also have a major effect on the selection process. Suppose, for instance, that the production manager for a manufacturing firm comes to the human resource manager's office and says, "My only quality control inspectors just had a fight and both resigned. I can't operate until those positions are filled." In this situation, speed is crucial and a few phone calls, two brief interviews, and a prayer may constitute the entire selection procedure. On the other hand, conducting a national search to select a chief executive officer may take months.

In bureaucracies, it is not uncommon for the selection process to take a considerable amount of time. However, as discussed in a later section, if the process drags on too long, the best candidates will be working for another, more efficient employer. As one Atlanta business owner put it, "if you aren't ready to make a judgment and offer a good prospect a job within 24 hours, they are gone. They've gone to the next guy who can make a decision."[14] This extreme urgency obviously does not exist in all situations. Nevertheless, the point is well made.

Organizational Hierarchy

Organizations usually take different approaches to filling positions at varying levels. For instance, consider the differences in hiring a chief executive officer and a data entry clerk. Extensive background checks and multiple interviews would most likely apply for the executive position. On the other hand, an applicant for a clerical position would probably take a word processing test and perhaps have a short employment interview.

Applicant Pool

The number of qualified applicants for a particular job can also affect the selection process. The process can be truly selective only if there are several qualified applicants. Yet, only a few applicants with the required skills may be available. The selection process then becomes a matter of choosing from whomever is at hand. Expansion and contraction of the labor market also exert considerable influence on availability, and thus, the selection process. Tightening of the market was the problem confronting many businesses in the spring of 2000, when the unemployment rate was under 4 percent, the lowest in over three decades. Three years later, that problem faded as the unemployment rate in January of 2004 was 5.6 percent.[15]

Selection ratio:
The number of people hired for a particular job compared to the total number of individuals in the applicant pool.

The number of people hired for a particular job compared to the individuals in the applicant pool is often expressed as a **selection ratio**, or

$$\text{Selection} \frac{\text{Number of open positions}}{\text{Number of available applicants}}$$

A selection ratio of 1.00 indicates that there is only one qualified applicant for an open position. An effective selection process is impossible if this situation exists as applicants who might normally be rejected receive job offers. The lower the ratio falls below 1.00, the more alternatives the manager has in making a selection decision. For example, a selection ratio of 0.10 indicates that there are 10 qualified applicants for an open position.

Type of Organization

The sector of the economy employing individuals—private, governmental, or not-for-profit—can also affect the selection process. A private sector business is heavily profit oriented. Prospective employees who can help achieve profit goals are the preferred candidates. Consideration of the total individual, including job-related personality factors, is involved in the selection of future employees for this sector.

Government civil service systems typically identify qualified applicants through competitive examinations. Often a manager may select only from among the top three applicants for a position. A manager in this sector may not have the prerogative of interviewing other applicants.

Individuals considered for positions in not-for-profit organizations (such as the Boy Scouts and Girl Scouts, YMCA, or YWCA) confront still a different situation. The salary level may not be competitive with those of private and governmental organizations. Therefore, a person who fills one of these positions must be not only qualified but also dedicated to this type of work.

Probationary Period

Many firms use a probationary period that permits them to evaluate an employee's ability based on established performance. This practice may be either a substitute for certain phases of the selection process or a check on the validity of the process. The rationale is that if an individual can successfully perform the job during the probationary period, the process does not require other selection tools. In any event, newly hired employees need monitoring to determine whether the hiring decision was a good one.

Even in unionized firms, the labor/management agreement typically does not protect a new employee until after a certain probationary period. This period is typically from 60 to 90 days. During that time, an employee can be terminated with little or no justification. On the other hand, firing a marginal employee in a union environment may prove to be quite difficult after the probationary period. When a firm is unionized, it becomes especially important for the selection process to identify the most productive workers. Once the probationary period is completed, workers are under the labor/management agreement and the firm must follow its terms in changing the workers' status.

 **OBJECTIVE**

Describe the general selection process.

The Selection Process

Figure 6-1 illustrates a generalized selection process that may vary by organization. It typically begins with the preliminary interview, after which the firm rejects unqualified candidates. Next, applicants complete the firm's application for employment. Then they progress through a series of selection tests, one or more employment interviews, and reference and background checks. The hiring manager offers the successful applicant a job, subject to successful completion of a medical examination.

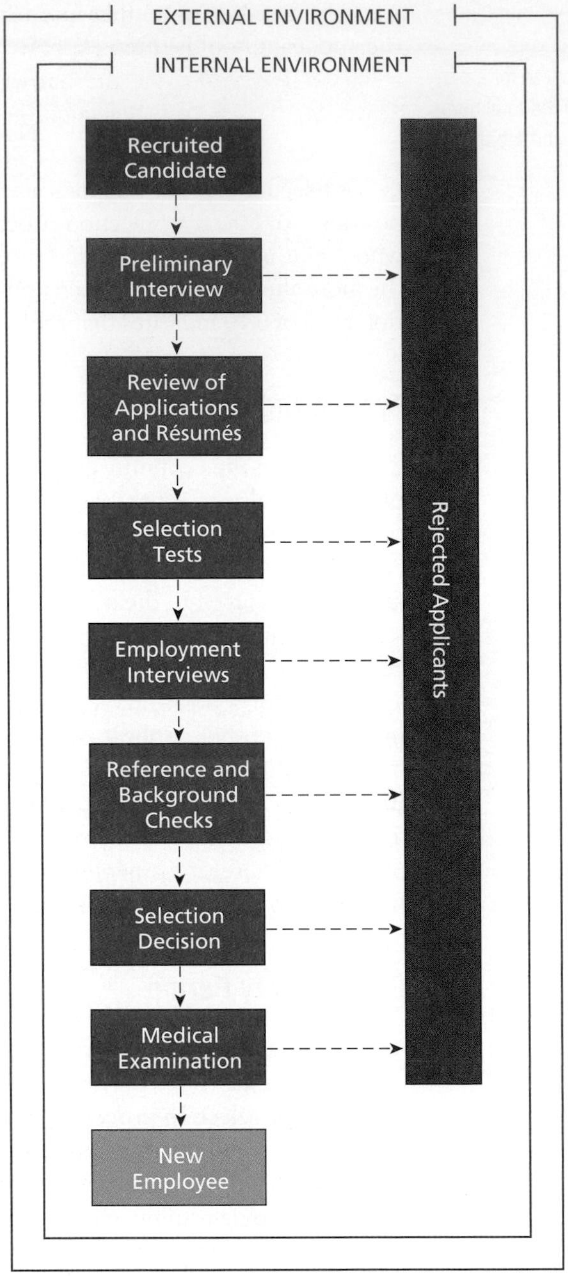

Figure 6-1 The Selection Process

OBJECTIVE

Explain the importance of the preliminary interview.

The Preliminary Interview

The selection process often begins with a preliminary interview. The basic purpose of this initial screening of applicants is to eliminate those who obviously do not meet the position's requirements. At this stage, the interviewer asks a few straightforward questions. For instance, a position may require specific qualifications such as certified public accountant (CPA). If the interview determines that the candidate is not so certified, any further discussion regarding this particular position wastes time for both the firm and the applicant.

In addition to eliminating obviously unqualified job applicants quickly, a preliminary interview may produce other positive benefits for the firm. It is possible the position for which the applicant applied is not the only one available. A skilled interviewer will know about other vacancies in the firm and may be able to steer the prospective employee to another position. For instance, a skilled interviewer may decide that while an applicant is not a good fit for the applications-engineering job, she is an excellent candidate for an internal R&D position. This type of interviewing not only builds goodwill for the firm but also can maximize recruitment and selection effectiveness. In addition to face-to-face preliminary interviews, several other options are available. Three of these alternatives are discussed next.

Telephone Interview

Organizations are always struggling to keep selection costs down. While there is nothing new in using telephone interviews, the potential cost savings warrant their attention. This method obviously lacks the advantages of face-to-face contact. For example, it is not possible to observe nonverbal cues from the candidate that may give hints to aspects of the candidate's interpersonal skills. Also, while the interviewer should not be biased by the candidate's physical appearance, the candidate's voice, particularly any regional accent, may have an even greater effect. Nevertheless, the telephone may be the most economically feasible way to exchange information with applicants in distant locations. In addition, an employer can screen a larger number of candidates using this method.

Videotaped Interview

A videotaped interview is another method that can reduce selection costs in some situations. Executive search firms have been using video interviews for over a decade.[16] Organizations may use consulting firms with many interviewers available throughout the nation to assist with this method. Using a structured interview format designed by the hiring firm, the interviewer can videotape the candidate's responses. To assure standardized treatment of other similarly conducted interviews, the interviewer may not interact with the candidate, but only repeat the question, if necessary. The videotaped interview has definite shortcomings and does not replace personal interviews. However, as with the telephone interview, it does allow a firm to conduct a broader search and get more people involved in the selection process.

Virtual Job Interview

Miller Brownstein, a third-year student at Boston University School of Law, arrived for a scheduled interview only to find that he was facing not another human, but a camera. He proceeded to cope with an electronic eye in a process called the Virtual Interview Portal (VIP) developed by Treeba, Inc., a New York firm. VIP records an interviewer's responses to predetermined questions and then distributes the interview to a number of firms via the Internet. Miller's biggest concern was his inability to "establish rapport with this plastic ball." In addition, he missed the opportunity to adjust his responses based on the interviewer's feedback. While it remains unclear how popular the virtual job interview will become, there is no doubt that more and more firms are using Internet technology in their recruitment and selection efforts.[17]

OBJECTIVE

Describe reviewing applications and résumés.

Review of Applications

Having the applicant complete an application for employment is another early step in the selection process. This may either precede or follow the preliminary interview. The employer then evaluates it to see whether there is an apparent match between the individual and the position. A well-designed and properly used application form can be helpful since essential information is included and presented in a standardized format. Applications may not be required for many management and professional positions. In these cases, a résumé may suffice.

The specific information requested on an application for employment may vary from firm to firm, and even by job type within an organization. An application form typically contains sections for name, address, telephone number, military service, education, and work history. Preprinted statements that are important when the applicant signs the form include certification that everything on the form is true. Employers will likely reject candidates who make false claims for major issues. When not prohibited by state law, the form should also state that the position is *employment at will* and that either the employer or the employee can terminate employment at any time for any reason or no reason. Finally, the form should contain a statement whereby the candidate gives permission to have his or her background checked.

An employment application form must reflect not only the firm's informational needs but also EEO requirements. Conoco provides an example of a well-designed application form. Looking at Figure 6-2, notice the following statement in the employee release and privacy section: "I agree and understand that any employment which may be offered to me will not be for any definite period of time and that such employment is subject to termination by me or by Conoco Inc. at any time, with or without cause." Potentially discriminatory questions inquiring about such factors as gender, race, age, and number of children living at home do not appear on the form.

Employment managers compare the information contained in a completed application for employment to the job description to determine whether a potential match exists between the firm's requirements and the applicant's qualifications. As you might expect, this judgment is often difficult.

Résumés Tips

www.free-resume-tips.com/10tips.html

This Web site provides tips for improving résumé preparation.

Review of Résumés

Historically, managers and HR representatives reviewed résumés manually, a time-consuming process. However, this practice has evolved into a more advanced procedure in many companies, with résumés automatically evaluated in terms of typos, spelling errors, and job-hopping. Some systems allow employers to flag résumés that appear to misrepresent the truth, present misleading information, or are in other ways suspicious. This can be an efficient means for filtering out 10 to 20 percent of candidates. Firms such as Blockbuster Inc., The Home Depot Inc., and Target Corporation rely on this technology to quickly, and efficiently, screen applicants.[18] Figure 6-3 illustrates a traditional résumé. You recall that a description of résumés used for online applications appeared in the appendix to Chapter 5.

6 OBJECTIVE

Explain the administration of selection tests including the advantages, potential problems, and characteristics of properly designed selection tests.

Administration of Selection Tests

Recognizing the shortcomings of other selection tools, an increasing number of firms have added pre-employment tests to their hiring process. These tests rate the personality, abilities, and motivation of potential employees, allowing managers to choose candidates according to how they will fit into the open positions and corporate culture. Tests alone are not enough to make a sufficient evaluation of a candidate because they are not foolproof.[19] Firms need to use them in conjunction with other selection tools including behavioral interviews, discussed in a later section. The public sector uses tests more than the private sector and medium-sized and large companies use them more than small companies. Large organizations are likely to have trained specialists to run their testing programs.

Employers should be aware that tests might be unintentionally discriminatory. When it excludes a protected class at a significant rate, the test is unlawful unless the employer can show the test is job related for the position in question and consistent with business necessity. The topic of adverse impact was discussed in Chapter 3.

Application for Employment

Application No. 125413

Equal Employment Opportunity—It is our policy to provide equal employment opportunity throughout the Company for all qualified persons without regard to race, color, religion, age, sex, national origin, disability, or veteran status.

Instructions
• Please print in black ink or type information.

Name (Last, First, Middle)		Are you over 18 years of age? ☐ Yes ☐ No	Social Security Number
Present Address (Street, City, State, ZIP Code)			Phone Number (Area Code First) ( )
Permanent Address (Street, City, State, ZIP Code)			Phone Number (Area Code First) ( )
Date Available for Employment	Employment Desired ☐ Temporary ☐ Regular, Full-Time	Would you accept temporary employment? ☐ Yes ☐ No	Will you perform shift work? ☐ Yes ☐ No
Position Desired—First Preference		Second Preference	
Geographical Location Preferred		Geographical Location Where You Will Not Consider Employment	
Will you work overtime? ☐ Yes ☐ No		Are you legally authorized to work in the United States on a regular, full-time basis? ☐ Yes ☐ No	
Have you been previously employed by Conoco? ☐ No ☐ Yes If yes, where ______ when ______			
Do you have relatives currently employed by Conoco? ☐ No ☐ Yes If yes, Name ______ Relationship ______ Department ______ Location ______			
If you are presently employed, may we contact your employer for a reference? ☐ Yes ☐ No			

Indicate Source Which Referred You

☐ Campus Placement Office	☐ Walk-in	☐ Private Employment Agency	☐ Published Advertisement
☐ Employee Referral	☐ Write-In	☐ Governmental Employment Agency	☐ Other (Specify)
	☐ Rehire		

Employment Record (List below your employment in reverse chronological order. Include part-time and summner experience)

From Mo./Yr / **To Mo./Yr**	/	/	/	/	/	/	/	/
Employer								
Address								
Supervisor's Name and Telephone No. (Area Cose First)	( )		( )		( )		( )	
Position(s) Held								
Reason for Leaving								

Identify and explain any time lapses in your above employment record.

Figure 6-2 An Application for Employment: Conoco, Inc.
Source: Courtesy of Conoco, Inc.

Advantages of Selection Tests

Research indicates that customized tests are a reliable and accurate means to predict on-the-job performance.[20] And, the cost of employment testing is small in comparison to ultimate hiring costs and a successful program will bolster a firm's bottom line. When one-fourth of new hires leave a firm in the first year, making a decision to test

Education—Circle Highest Grade Completed 1 2 3 4 5 6 7 8 9 10 11 12	Course of Study Major—Minor	Degree Received	Grade Average		Degree Date
			Overall	Major	
High School Attended and Location		Diploma ☐ Yes ☐ No			
Vocational or Technical School Attended		Completed ☐ Yes ☐ No			
College or University					
College or University					
College or University					

Other—1) Include information you believe is important, such as: special training, apprenticeships completed, military experience, other education, or foreign language fluency.

—2) List those machines and/or equipment you are qualified to operate and any other skills you possess.

—3) Titles of these and special research projects.

Completion of this section is optional.

Conoco Inc. is a government contractor subject to Section 503 of the Rehabilitation Act and Section 402 of the Veterans Readjustment Act. As such, we must take affirmative action to employ and advance in employment individuals with disabilities, special disabled veterans, and veterans of the Vietnam era. If you are such an individual and would like to be considered under the affirmative action program, please indicate below.

☐ I am a **special disabled veteran** because **either:** (1) I am entitled to compensation under VA law for disability rated at 30% or more, or for disability rated at 10% or 20% for a serious employment handicap; **or** (2) I was discharged or released from active duty because of a service-connected disability.

☐ I am a **veteran of the Vietnam era** because part or all of my active military service occured between 8/5/64 and 5/7/75 **and either:** (1) I was on active duty for more than 180 days and my discharge or release was not dishonorable; **or** (2) I was discharged or released from active duty because of a service-connected disability.

Submission of this information is voluntary, and disclosure or refusal to provide it will not subject you to adverse treatment. This information shall be used only as allowed by law and shall be kept confidential except that (i) supervisors and managers may be informed about restrictions on work or job duties and necessary accommodations, (ii) first aid or safety personnel may be informed where appropriate in case of an emergency, and (iii) government officials investigating compliance with the law shall be informed.

You may omit references in this section which you feel might reveal age, race, color, sex, national origin, or handicap.

Name and description of scholastic honors received including scholarships.

Name honorary, technical and professional organizations of which you have been a member, or other extracurricular activities in which you have participated, including offices held. (List professional licenses held.)

This form will usually provide the necessary information. It may be supplemented, however, by a letter or personal resume.

PLEASE READ THE FOLLOWING CAREFULLY BEFORE SIGNING.

I authorize any third parties, including former employers, schools, law enforcement authorities, and any persons named above, to give to Conoco Inc. any information they may have regarding me and my background, whether or not such information is contained in written records. I hereby release these third parties from all liability for any damage whatsoever for providing information to Conoco Inc. in connection with this application. I also release Conoco Inc., its agents, employees, and representatives from any liability in connection with their collection and use of information obtained from third parties during the application process. I certify that all information furnished in this application, signed and dated by me this date, is true and complete to the best of my knowledge and belief and that falsification or omission of information requested in this application or in the application process shall be grounds for disqualification from further consideration or for termination.

I understand that if an employment offer is extended, I may be required to undergo a physical examination and/or drug screen test at the expense of Conoco Inc. I further understand that if I do not successfully complete the physical examination or drug screen test, Conoco Inc. may refuse to hire me, and I agree to hold Conoco Inc. harmless for such refusal. I also understand that employment is conditional on my ability to verify my identity and eligibility for employment as required by the Immigration Reform and Control Act of 1986.

I agree and understand that any employment which may be offered to me will not be for any definite period of time and that such employment is subject to termination by me or by Conoco Inc. at any time, with or without cause. I also agree and understand that nothing contained in this application nor any verbal statements made during the application process or during my employment shall be deemed to constitute an employment contract between me and Conoco Inc.

Signature	Date

12-21 (R), 3-92

Figure 6-2 *(continued)*

becomes easier because it costs $8,000 to $12,000 per employee for advertising, recruiting, interviewing, and training expenses.[21] The primary explanation for high turnover is bad hiring decisions.[22] The reason organizations use tests is to identify attitudes and job-related skills that interviews cannot recognize. They are a more efficient way to get at that type of information and may result in better-quality people being hired. This has been true at Cox Communications, a telecommunications company in Rancho Santa Margarita, California. This firm has used tests since 1996 and

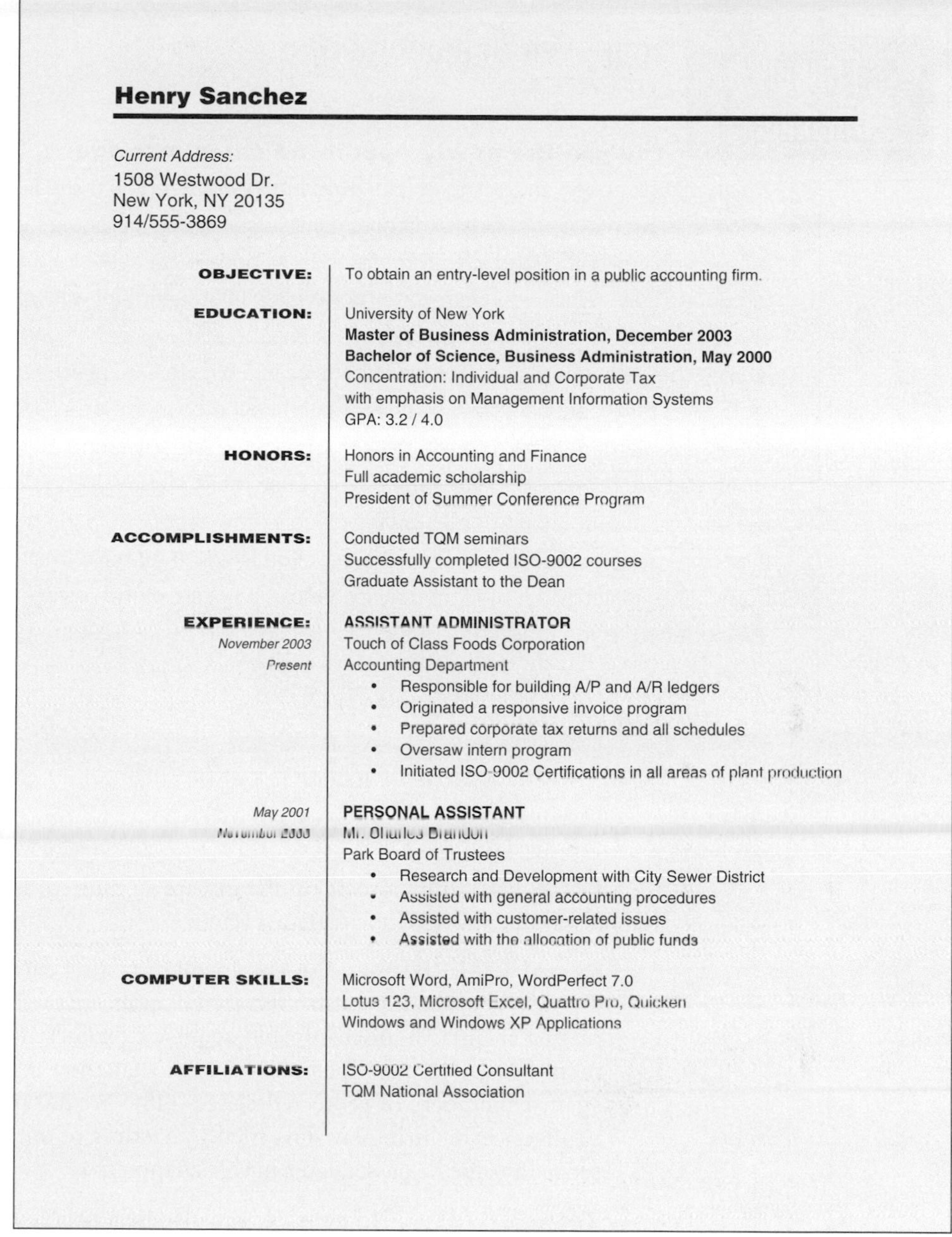

Henry Sanchez

Current Address:
1508 Westwood Dr.
New York, NY 20135
914/555-3869

OBJECTIVE:	To obtain an entry-level position in a public accounting firm.
EDUCATION:	University of New York **Master of Business Administration, December 2003** **Bachelor of Science, Business Administration, May 2000** Concentration: Individual and Corporate Tax with emphasis on Management Information Systems GPA: 3.2 / 4.0
HONORS:	Honors in Accounting and Finance Full academic scholarship President of Summer Conference Program
ACCOMPLISHMENTS:	Conducted TQM seminars Successfully completed ISO-9002 courses Graduate Assistant to the Dean
EXPERIENCE: *November 2003* *Present*	**ASSISTANT ADMINISTRATOR** Touch of Class Foods Corporation Accounting Department • Responsible for building A/P and A/R ledgers • Originated a responsive invoice program • Prepared corporate tax returns and all schedules • Oversaw intern program • Initiated ISO-9002 Certifications in all areas of plant production
May 2001 *November 2003*	**PERSONAL ASSISTANT** Mr. Charles Brandon Park Board of Trustees • Research and Development with City Sewer District • Assisted with general accounting procedures • Assisted with customer-related issues • Assisted with the allocation of public funds
COMPUTER SKILLS:	Microsoft Word, AmiPro, WordPerfect 7.0 Lotus 123, Microsoft Excel, Quattro Pro, Quicken Windows and Windows XP Applications
AFFILIATIONS:	ISO-9002 Certified Consultant TQM National Association

Figure 6-3 Example of Traditional Résumé

they have proven to be an effective part of its screening process. The tests used measure honesty, safety, work values, drug avoidance, customer service skills, and attitude toward supervision.[23]

As with all selection procedures, it is important to identify the essential functions of each job and determine the skills needed to perform it. Selection tests must be job related and must meet the standards outlined in the EEOC's *Uniform Guidelines on Employee Selection Procedures*.

Potential Problems Using Selection Tests

Job performance depends on an individual's ability and motivation to do the work. Selection tests may accurately predict an applicant's ability to perform the job, the *can do*, but they are less successful in indicating the extent to which the individual will be motivated to perform it, the *will do*. The most successful employees have two things in common: they identify with their firm's goals and they are highly motivated. For one reason or another, many employees with high potential never seem to reach it. The

Ethical Dilemma

Employee Selection Criteria?

You are the newly appointed sales manager for a large manufacturing organization that has been struggling of late, even though your region is the firm's most successful one. Your office is located in a very close-knit community where people place a high value on local basketball. In fact, it didn't take you long to realize that to most people, local basketball is even more important than the Super Bowl. While you were watching a game the other night with your biggest customer, who purchases almost 40 percent of your yearly volume, he told you that the star on the team may soon be leaving the community because his father was laid off. He has heard that your region has an opening for a sales representative, and he asks you to hire the boy's father. You tell him that you will be glad to review the man's résumé, but you think that you have already found an extremely qualified person.

As you are reviewing the résumé of your customer's recommended candidate the next day, the person you are replacing comes by the office to say goodbye. In the conversation he mentions that in this town, people do each other favors, and that is how they build trust. He also tells you that if the boy's father is not hired, the firm may lose most, if not all, of the buyer's business. That is quite a shock because you realize that the customer's candidate lacks some qualifications for the position.

What would you do?

factors related to success on the job are so numerous and complex that selection may always be more of an art than a science.

Legal Liabilities. Pre-employment testing carries with it legal liabilities of two types.[24] One is a lawsuit from rejected applicants who claim a test was not job related or that it unfairly discriminated against a protected group violating federal employment laws. Organizations must ensure that their selection tests do not discriminate against members of protected classes. The second potential legal problem relates to negligence-in-hiring lawsuits filed by victims of employee misbehavior or incompetence (a topic discussed later in this chapter).

Test Anxiety. Test anxiety can also be a problem. Applicants often become quite anxious when confronting yet another hurdle that might eliminate them from consideration. The test administrator's reassuring manner and a well-organized testing operation should serve to reduce this threat. Actually, although a great deal of anxiety is detrimental to test performance, a slight degree is helpful.

The problems of hiring unqualified or less qualified candidates and rejecting qualified candidates, along with other potential legal problems, will continue regardless of the procedures followed. Well-developed tests administered by competent professionals help organizations minimize such consequences. Nevertheless, selection tests rarely, if ever, are perfect predictors. For this reason, the selection process should not rely on tests alone but rather use them in conjunction with other tools.

Characteristics of Properly Designed Selection Tests

Properly designed selection tests are standardized, objective, based on sound norms, reliable, and, of utmost importance, valid. We discuss the application of these concepts next.

Standardization

Standardization:
Uniformity of the procedures and conditions related to administering tests.

Standardization is the uniformity of the procedures and conditions related to administering tests. In order to compare the performance of several applicants on the same test, it is necessary for all to take the test under conditions that are as close to identical as possible. For example, the content of instructions provided and the time allowed must be the same, and the physical environment must be similar. If one person takes a test in a room with jackhammers operating just outside and another takes it in a more tranquil environment, differences in test results are likely.

Objectivity

Objectivity:
The condition that is achieved when all individuals scoring a given test obtain the same results.

Objectivity in testing occurs when everyone scoring a test obtains the same results. Multiple-choice and true-false tests are objective. The person taking the test either chooses the correct answer or does not.

Norms

Norm:
A frame of reference for comparing an applicant's performance with that of others.

A **norm** is a frame of reference for comparing an applicant's performance with that of others. Specifically, a norm reflects the distribution of many scores obtained by people similar to the applicant being tested. A score by itself is insignificant. It becomes meaningful only when compared with other applicants' scores.

When a sufficient number of employees are performing the same or similar work, employers can standardize their own tests. Typically, this is not the case, and a national norm for a particular test is used. A prospective employee takes the test, the score obtained is compared to the norm, and the significance of the test score is then determined.

Reliability

Reliability:
The extent to which a selection test provides consistent results.

Reliability is the extent to which a selection test provides consistent results. Reliability data reveal the degree of confidence placed in a test. If a test has low reliability, its validity as a predictor will also be low. However, the existence of reliability alone does not guarantee the test's validity.

Validity

Validity:
The extent to which a test measures what it claims to measure.

The basic requirement for a selection test is that it be valid. **Validity** is the extent to which a test measures what it claims to measure. If a test cannot indicate ability to perform the job, it has no value as a predictor. And, if used, it will result in poor hiring decisions and a potential legal liability for the employer.

Validity, commonly reported as a correlation coefficient, summarizes the relationship between two variables. For example, these variables may be the score on a selection test and some measure of employee performance. A coefficient of 0 shows no relationship, while coefficients of either +1.0 or −1.0 indicate a perfect relationship, one positive and the other negative. Naturally, no test will be 100 percent accurate, yet organizations strive for the highest feasible coefficient. If a job performance test has a high positive correlation coefficient, most prospective employees who score high on the test will probably later prove to be high performers.

Requirement for Job Relatedness

Title VII requires that whatever employment tests measure must be job related. The test must work without having an adverse impact on minorities, females, and individuals with backgrounds or characteristics protected under the law.[25] If using the test results in an adverse impact, the firm must have a compelling reason why it is used; that is, it must validate the test. Employers are not required to validate their selection tests automatically. Generally, validation is required only when the selection process as a whole results in an adverse impact on women or minorities. However, an organization cannot know whether the test is actually measuring desired qualities and abilities without validation.

OBJECTIVE

Explain the types of validation studies.

Types of Validation Studies

The *Uniform Guidelines* established three approaches to validating selection tests: criterion-related validity, content validity, and construct validity.

Criterion-Related Validity

Criterion-related validity: A test validation method that compares the scores on selection tests to some aspect of job performance determined, for example, by performance appraisal.

Criterion-related validity is determined by comparing the scores on selection tests to some aspect of job performance determined, for example, by performance appraisal. Performance measures might include quantity and quality of work, turnover, and absenteeism. A close relationship between the score on the test and job performance suggests that the test is valid. The two basic forms of criterion-related validity are concurrent and predictive validity.

Concurrent validity: A validation method in which test scores and criterion data are obtained at essentially the same time.

Concurrent Validity. **Concurrent validity** is determined when the firm obtains test scores and the criterion data at essentially the same time. For instance, it administers the test to all currently employed telemarketers and compares the results with company records that contain current information about each employee's job performance. If the test is able to identify productive and less productive workers, one could say that it is valid. A potential problem in using this validation procedure results from changes that may have occurred within the work group. For example, firms may have fired the less productive workers, and promoted the more productive employees out of the group.

Predictive validity: A validation method that involves administering a selection test and later obtaining the criterion information.

Predictive Validity. **Predictive validity** involves administering a test and later obtaining the criterion information. For instance, all applicants take the test but the firm uses other selection criteria, not the test results, to make the selection decision. After observing employee performance over time, the company analyzes test results to determine whether they differentiate the successful and less successful employees. Predictive validity is a technically sound procedure. Because of the time and cost involved, however, its use is often not feasible.

Content Validity

Content validity: A test validation method whereby a person performs certain tasks that are actual samples of the kind of work a job requires or completes a paper-and-pencil test that measures relevant job knowledge.

Although statistical concepts are not involved, many practitioners believe that content validity provides a sensible approach to validating a selection test. **Content validity** is a test validation method whereby a person performs certain tasks that are actually required by the job or completes a paper-and-pencil test that measures relevant job knowledge. This form of validation requires thorough job analysis and carefully prepared job descriptions. An example of the use of content validity is giving a data-entering test to an applicant whose primary job would be to enter data. Court decisions have supported the concept of content validity.

Construct validity: A test validation method to determine whether a selection test measures certain traits or qualities that have been identified as important in performing a particular job.

Construct Validity

Construct validity is a test validation method that determines whether a test measures certain constructs, or traits, that job analysis finds to be important in performing a job.

For instance, a job may require a high degree of creativity or reasoning ability. Construct validity may be important for various types of psychological tests such as those involving aptitude, achievement, and interests. However, it is not a primary method for validating selection tests.

 **OBJECTIVE**

Describe types of employment tests.

Types of Employment Tests

Individuals differ in characteristics related to job performance. These differences, which are measurable, relate to cognitive abilities, psychomotor abilities, job knowledge, work samples, vocational interests, and personality. Other possible tests administered include substance abuse testing and genetic testing, a controversial issue that Congress may eliminate as an employment test. Another type of test we discuss that is debatable, at least in the United States, is graphology, or handwriting analysis. Many organizations utilize the Internet for administering some types of employment tests and we present this topic at the end of this section.

Buros Center for Testing (Mental Measurement Yearbook)

www.unl.edu/buros/

This Web site is the Buros Center for Testing which publishes the widely used Mental Measurement Yearbook.

Cognitive Aptitude Tests

Cognitive aptitude tests: Tests that determine general reasoning ability, memory, vocabulary, verbal fluency, and numerical ability.

Cognitive aptitude tests are tests that determine general reasoning ability, memory, vocabulary, verbal fluency, and numerical ability. They may be helpful in identifying job candidates who have extensive knowledge bases. As the content of jobs becomes broader and more fluid, employees must be able to adapt quickly to job changes and rapid technological advances. It is likely that testing for more general traits will be necessary to match the broader range of characteristics required for successful performance of these flexible jobs.

Psychomotor Abilities Tests

Psychomotor abilities tests: Aptitude tests that measure strength, coordination, and dexterity.

Psychomotor abilities tests measure strength, coordination, and dexterity. Miniaturization in assembly operations has accelerated the development of tests to determine these abilities. Much of this work is so delicate that magnifying lenses are necessary, and the psychomotor abilities required to perform the tasks are critical. Standardized tests are not available to cover all these abilities, but those involved in many routine production jobs and some office jobs are measurable.

Job-Knowledge Tests

Job knowledge tests: Tests designed to measure a candidate's knowledge of the duties of the job for which he or she is applying.

Job-knowledge tests measure a candidate's knowledge of the duties of the job for which he or she is applying. Such tests are commercially available but individual firms may also design them specifically for any job, based on data derived from job analysis.

Work-Sample Tests (Simulations)

Work-sample tests: Tests that require an applicant to perform a task or set of tasks representative of the job.

Work-sample tests, or simulations, are tests that require an applicant to perform a task or set of tasks representative of the job. Data-entry tests are an excellent way to evaluate a candidate applying for a clerical position. For positions that require heavy use of spreadsheets, having the applicant sit at a computer and construct a sample spreadsheet, with data the firm provides, will be useful in assessing a required ability.[26] Such tests by their nature are job related. Not surprisingly, the evidence concerning this type of test is that it produces a high predictive validity, reduces adverse impact, and is more acceptable to applicants. A real test of validity, in the opinion of some experts, should be a performance assessment: take individuals to a job and give them the opportunity to perform it.

Vocational Interest Tests

Vocational interest tests:
A method of determining the occupation in which a person has the greatest interest and from which the person is most likely to receive satisfaction.

Vocational interest tests indicate the occupation a person is most interested in and the one likely to provide satisfaction. These tests compare the individual's interests with those of successful employees in a specific job. Although interest tests have application in employee selection, their primary use has been in counseling and vocational guidance.

Personality Tests

Personality tests:
Self-reported measures of traits, temperaments, or dispositions.

Personality tests are self-reported measures of traits, temperaments, or dispositions. Personality tests, unlike ability tests, are not time constrained and do not measure specific problem-solving skills. These questionnaires tap into softer areas such as leadership, teamwork, and personal assertiveness.[27] A properly designed personality profile can measure and match the appropriate personality dimensions to the requirements of the job. For example, research indicates that two important predictors for successful salespeople are extroversion and conscientiousness. The ability to test for these traits can mean a significant increase in selection effectiveness.[28]

Some firms use these tests to classify personality types. With this information, organizations can create diverse teams for creativity or homogeneous teams for compatibility. The use of personality tests as selection tools is controversial since a great deal of research has concluded that their validity is low relative to other predictors. Nevertheless, use of personality tests is at an all-time high, according to the *New York Times*. There are currently 2,500 tests on the market supplied by the $400 million-a-year "personality-assessment" industry.[29] According to a recent survey by SHRM, 40 percent of *Fortune* 100 companies use some form of psychological testing in their employment selection.[30]

Personality assessments shed light on each person's needs, attitudes, motivations, and behavioral tendencies. Consensus is building in the research community that five factors shape our overall personalities and testing firms are trying to use these to measure fit for a job. These dimensions include:[31]

- the relative need for stability
- whether we are solitary or social
- whether we strive more for innovation or efficiency
- the degree to which we stick to our positions or accept others' ideas
- whether we are more linear or flexible in our approach to goals

Personality tests consist of questions that gauge a person's natural comfort level within these categories.

Honesty and integrity are important personality traits to consider in the selection process. Since the polygraph test has been effectively banned in the private sector as a hiring tool, other psychological tests, called pen-and-pencil honesty tests, have been used to detect dishonest candidates. However, it has been suggested that other effective ways to ensure that employees are honest are to thoroughly check references prior to hiring and, afterwards, to use appropriate control systems.[33]

National Center of Addiction and Substance Abuse

www.casacolumbia.org/

This Web site is the homepage for a unique think/action tank that engages all disciplines to study every form of substance abuse as it affects our society.

Substance Abuse Testing

Few issues generate more controversy today than substance abuse testing. Yet, drug and alcohol abuse are definitely workplace issues. According to the federal government, about 71 percent of alcohol and drug abusers have jobs.[34] In addition, substance abuse has increased dramatically since the tragic events of September 11, 2001. According to a study by the National Center of Addiction and Substance Abuse at

Trends & Innovations

The Team Roles Test

PsychTests.com, a leader in Web-based psychological and HR testing, has added the Team Roles Test[32] to its extensive battery of tests. This test assesses individuals' preferences for the roles that people typically play in teams. It helps to identify natural tendencies and pinpoints what makes a person tick (or what ticks people off) in the workplace. Dr. Ilona Jerabek, head of PschTests' research team, states, "Employers generally look to hire strong leaders, but you don't want to end up with four leaders in the same group struggling for power . . . and nobody to follow them. The key to success is balance."

The test has a wide range of applications. HR departments can use it in the selection process to identify suitable candidates. In addition, it helps in placement — matching the right people with the right teams. The test is also valuable as a team-building exercise with existing workgroups or in career development seminars.

The Team Roles Test asks individuals 40 questions designed to identify preferences in realistic work-related situations. The resulting report offers a detailed personalized interpretation, showing most prominent tendencies, pros and cons, practical advice on effective interaction and key elements of effective teams. The assessment further breaks down where the individual fits on several scales: Coordinator, Go Getter, Cheerleader, Questioner, Team Worker, Verifier, Networker, Peacemaker, Thinker, and Brainstormer. An advice section provides guidelines on turning individuals into team players.

The Team Roles Test was developed based on extensive research of various team functioning theories. From the HR manager's viewpoint, the test provides invaluable information that is difficult to gather from a regular interview. Individuals can use the interpretation to discover where their team competencies lie and how to overcome their concerns and limitations, to become stronger team players.

Columbia University, the emotional stress and strain caused by the terrorist attacks of 9/11 combined with the threat of bioterrorism have given rise to greater numbers of Americans seeking treatment for drug and alcohol abuse.[35]

Rationale for Testing. The vast majority of *Fortune* 500 firms and a growing number of small to mid-sized businesses embrace substance abuse testing.[36] These proponents of drug testing programs contend that they are necessary to ensure workplace safety, security, and productivity. The National Institute on Drug Abuse reported that drug-abusing employees inflict losses on their companies with both missed time and frequent accidents. They are more than twice as likely to leave work early or miss days, are two-and-a-half times more likely to be absent for eight days or more and are three times more likely to be late for work. They are also more than three-and-a-half times more likely to be involved in a workplace accident and five times more likely to file a workers' compensation claim.[37] Drug testing may serve as an accurate measure of drug use and a means to deter it. Critics of drug testing argue just as vigorously that drug testing is an unjustifiable intrusion into private lives.

Testing Methods. Pre-employment alcohol testing by means of breath, urine, blood, saliva, or hair samples are possible methods. The method of choice by law enforcement agencies and the transportation industry is breath alcohol analysis. However, most experts regard blood tests as the forensic benchmark against which to compare others. The problem with this approach is that it is invasive and requires trained personnel for administration and analysis. The use of hair samples is unique in that drug traces will remain in the hair and will not likely diminish over time. While urine and blood testing can detect only current drug use, advocates of hair sample analysis claim it can detect drug use from three days to 90 days after drug consumption. This would prohibit an applicant from beating the test by short-term abstinence. From a prospective employee's viewpoint, hair testing may be less embarrassing than a urine test. For example, it is humiliating for a candidate to hear, "We're really happy to have you on board. But, will you take this cup and fill it?"

The "yuck factor" associated with urine testing gives employers reason to welcome a potentially superior method: *the oral fluid option*. Using this method, the person simply places a swab in his or her mouth. When the collection pad is saturated, the individual places the swab in a collection vial, snaps off the handle, seals the container and hands it over for analysis. Oral fluid is a great deterrent because it can be done immediately in the workplace; it does not give an individual an opportunity to adulterate or substitute a urine specimen. There are not sufficient research results available to recommend this method without reservation. However, this test may well offer a superior method for substance abuse testing and is worth further investigation.[38]

Ways to Avoid Tests. Even with all the drug and alcohol testing, there is only about a 2 to 6 percent positive rate among tested applicants in the United States. The fact that many applicants who use *hard* drugs avoid their use for several days prior to the test may account for this low rate. In addition, there are well-publicized and easily available means of eluding positive urine test results. In fact, contaminating test samples has become an underground science, as evidenced by the numerous Internet Web sites advertising methods and products designed to help drug users beat urine tests.[39] One such approach to defeating the test comes from an individual who, for $69 plus postage, sells five ounces of his urine in a small plastic bag, along with 30 inches of plastic tubing and a tiny heat pack designed to keep the fluid at body temperature. By taping these bags to their bodies, individuals are able to substitute this urine during workplace drug testing.[40] Among the many available methods advertised online for beating drug tests is a shampoo for detoxifying hair follicles.

Legal Aspects. Although the controversy remains, along with legal questions, it appears that drug testing is becoming more commonplace, and half of major U.S. firms now test their employees.[41] The law requires some companies, such as those in interstate commerce, to give a drug test.[42] In addition to concerns about privacy, organizations may worry that applicants denied employment after taking drug tests might seek protection as persons with a disability under the Americans with Disabilities Act. The act, however, is actually supportive of testing when carefully performed. Those engaging in the illegal use of drugs are excluded from the act's definition of *qualified individual with a disability*. It is important to note, however, that persons who have successfully completed or are participating in a supervised drug-rehabilitation program and who no longer engage in illegal drug use are not automatically excluded from this definition. Some firms achieve their goal of a drug-free workplace by having their employees sign a pledge to abide by their firm's drug-free policy and agree to be fired if they bring drugs into the workplace or if they are under the influence while on duty. This makes termination much easier and makes the employer less vulnerable to legal challenges.[43]

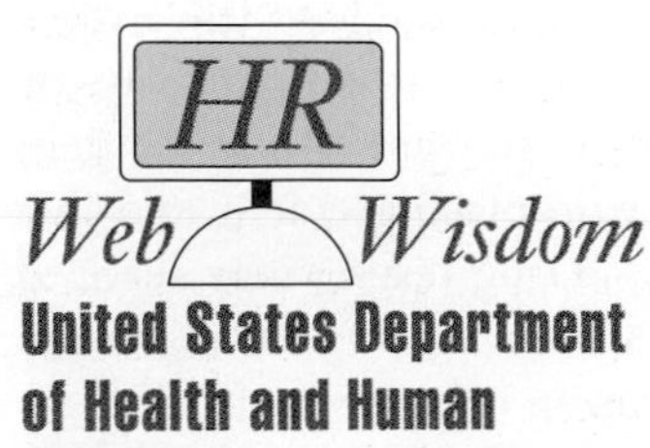

United States Department of Health and Human Services

www.os.dhhs.gov/

This government Web site provides information about how America can be led to better health, safety, and well-being.

Employer's Catch-22. Failure to test for drugs can have a disastrous effect. For instance, *Cake for You* is a small specialty bakery. Its service includes delivering wedding cakes to reception sites. In hiring a delivery driver, *Cake for You* owners were always careful to determine that the potential candidate had a valid driver's license. The owners were quite pleased with their new employee, Mike. He was prompt, neatly attired, and seemed to have a pleasant demeanor. Unfortunately, while making a delivery one morning, Mike was involved in, and in fact caused, a four-vehicle accident that resulted in one fatality. The investigation revealed that Mike was "high" on marijuana. Had the owners of the firm included drug testing as part of their screening process, they might not be facing a huge lawsuit.[44]

Employers appear to be in a no-win situation. *USA Today* reported that employees are filing more lawsuits with claims of erroneous drug test results. In addition, juries are awarding six-figure verdicts, not only for job loss and wages but also for reputation damages. When the Department of Health and Human Services inspected testing labs, nearly 300 results out of about 13 million were questionable. Three hundred out of thirteen million is not a lot, but it could lead to three hundred lawsuits. Because of this legal uncertainty, employers must plan their drug testing strategies with great care.[45]

9 OBJECTIVE

Describe the concept of genetic testing.

Genetic testing:
Testing that can determine whether a person carries the gene mutation for certain diseases, including heart disease, colon cancer, breast cancer, and Huntington's disease.

Genetic Testing

Genetic testing is given to identify predisposition to inherited diseases, including cancer, heart disease, neurological disorders, and congenital diseases.[46] As genetic research progresses, confirmed links between specific gene mutations and diseases are emerging. Scientists have assembled the entire set of genetic instructions for building a human body and world leaders likened this achievement to putting a human being on the moon. This announcement brings both hope and concerns to the forefront in employment testing.

Gene tests may predict a predisposition to having a disease. However, such tests cannot tell whether a person is certain to get the disease or would become ill at age 30 or 90. In addition, everyone has some disposition to genetic disease and a genetic predisposition is not the same as a pre-existing condition. Protective laws recognize that there is a difference between a present medical condition and a genetic tendency toward a certain illness.[47] Nevertheless, a survey conducted by the American Management Association indicated that from 6 to 10 percent of employers were conducting genetic tests.[48]

There are two primary reasons for genetic testing. One is that predictive testing allows employers to reject certain employees and maintain a more productive workforce. Genetic testing offers a way for the firm to foresee likely health-care costs and to avoid hiring at-risk candidates. Another purpose is that it enables therapeutic intervention, thereby allowing carriers to get appropriate therapy.

The major concerns with genetic testing relate to the possible misuse of information. Some perceive the process as being highly invasive and believe it communicates to employees that the firm really does not care about them. Also, once the results of a genetic test are in a medical record, they may be made available to employers and insurers without an individual's knowledge or consent. It is one thing knowing that a genetic predisposition might be passed down. It is another thing to record that information in the person's personnel file.[49]

Guidelines issued by the EEOC interpreted the Americans with Disabilities Act as covering discrimination on the basis of genetic information. In addition, states have begun to act. Hawaii, Utah, and Virginia have recently joined the more than half of the states that have enacted legislation banning employment discrimination against individuals based on genetic characteristics, genetic information, or test results.[50] After years of discussing the issue, a Senate committee approved legislation in May 2003 to bar employers and insurers from discriminating against people based on genetic information. The legislation has bipartisan support and would bar health insurance firms from using genetic information to deny coverage or to set premiums, and would prohibit employers from using such information to hire or fire workers. Neither insurers nor employers could ask for genetic information or require people to take genetic tests.[51] An executive order applicable to every aspect of federal employment, issued in 2000, prohibits discrimination against employees based on genetic information.[52]

Graphoanalysis (Handwriting Analysis)

Many people in the United States view handwriting analysis in the same context as psychic readings or astrology. In Europe, however, many employers use graphoanalysis to help screen and place job applicants. For example, over 80 percent of employers in Israel and Switzerland use graphoanalysis, and in France the percentage of employers using the technique is almost as high.[53]

There are two distinct schools of handwriting analysis: the Gestalt theory, developed in Germany, and the trait method, developed mainly in France, England, and the United States. The latter method examines handwriting to determine defined traits such as how people cross their "tees" or make loops for letters such as "ell." Although no definitive study exists on the extent of its use in the United States, according to some handwriting experts, graphoanalysis is becoming more common. A basic reason for the reluctance of U.S. employers to use this approach appears to be a concern over the ability to validate such tests.[54] And, there is little research demonstrating the effectiveness of graphology in employee selection.[55] This and the worry about possible legal action seem to make many American employers wary of the process.

Know It All, Inc.

www.proveit.com/

This Web site offers job-skills testing as a service to firms that lack the resources to evaluate candidates on their own.

Internet Testing

Organizations are increasingly using the Internet to test various skills required by applicants. Firms may design and have their own tests available online or use an external source. For example, a new type of Web service is available that tests job applicants on their alleged technical abilities. For example, Know It All, Inc., in Philadelphia (www.proveit.com) offers job-skills testing as a service to firms that lack the resources to evaluate candidates on their own. For a small fee, you can confirm job candidates' skills online without ever laying eyes on them. The tests are not merely pass-fail, but measure applicants' skill level as well.

10 OBJECTIVE

Discuss assessment centers as a means of selection.

Assessment center:
A selection technique that requires individuals to perform activities similar to those they might encounter in an actual job.

Assessment Centers

An **assessment center** is a selection technique that requires individuals to perform activities similar to those they might encounter in an actual job. The assessment center is one of the most powerful tools for assessing managerial talent. Research has established the validity of assessment center methods to evaluate individuals' current job performance and also to determine how well they are likely to handle new or expanded assignments.[56] Because assessment centers are expensive to conduct, their use is more common as an internal selection and development device for managerial positions.

In an assessment center, candidates perform a number of exercises that simulate the tasks they will carry out in the job they seek. Among the typical assessment center tests, the applicants may complete *in-basket exercises* and perform in *management games*, *leaderless discussion groups*, *mock interviews*, and other simulations. The traditional in-basket exercise may receive a technological boost by replacing the paper memos with e-mail messages, faxes, or voice mail. Assessment centers measure candidates' skills in prioritizing, delegating, and decision making. The professional assessors who evaluate the candidates' performances usually observe them away from the workplace over a certain period of time, perhaps a single day. The assessors selected are typically experienced managers who may not only evaluate performances, but also participate in the exercises. Numerous organizations use assessment centers, including small firms and such large firms as General Electric Company, JCPenney Company, Ford Motor Company, and AT&T.

An advantage of the assessment center approach is the increased reliability and validity of the information provided. Research has shown that the in-basket exercise, a typical component of assessment centers, is a good predictor of management performance. Its face validity provides an alternative to paper-and-pencil tests.

11 OBJECTIVE

Explain the importance of the employment interview, including interview planning and the content of the interview.

The Employment Interview

Employment interview: A goal-oriented conversation in which an interviewer and an applicant supposedly exchange information.

The **employment interview** is a goal-oriented conversation in which the interviewer and applicant supposedly exchange information. Sometimes, however, interviewers begin the interview by telling candidates what they are looking for, and then are excited to hear candidates parrot back their own words. Other interviewers are delighted to talk through virtually the entire interview, either to take pride in their organization's accomplishments or to express their frustrations over their difficulties. After dominating the meeting for an hour or so, these interviewers feel good about the candidate.[57]

These approaches have not given interviews a good name. Of greater significance, interviews have not been valid predictors of success on the job. For 500 years, Leonardo da Vinci's *Mona Lisa* has confounded viewers who try to read her expression. Like the *Mona Lisa*, every job applicant presents a mysterious façade.[58] Nevertheless, interviews continue to be the primary method companies use to evaluate applicants. As we discuss later in this chapter, some firms have made significant progress in improving the validity of interviews. The employment interview is especially important because the applicants who reach this stage are the survivors. They have endured the preliminary interview and scored satisfactorily on selection tests. At this point, the candidates appear to be qualified, at least on paper. Every seasoned manager knows, however, that appearances can be quite misleading. Additional information is needed to indicate whether the individual is willing to work and can adapt to that particular organization.

Interview Planning

Interview planning is essential to effective employment interviews. A primary consideration should be the speed in which the process occurs. Many studies have demonstrated that the top candidates for nearly any job are hired and off the job market within anywhere from 1 to 10 days. It is imperative that interview schedulers keep this in mind.

The physical location of the interview should be both pleasant and private, providing for a minimum of interruptions. The interviewer should possess a pleasant personality, empathy, and the ability to listen and communicate effectively. He or she should become familiar with the applicant's qualifications by reviewing the data collected from other selection tools. As preparation for the interview, the interviewer should develop a job profile based on the job description/specification. After listing job requirements, it is helpful to have an interview checklist that includes these hints:

- Compare an applicant's application and résumé with job requirements
- Develop questions related to the qualities sought
- Prepare a step-by-step plan to present the position, company, division, and department
- Determine how to ask for examples of past applicant behavior, not what future behavior might be

Content of the Interview

Both the interviewer and the candidate have agendas for the interview. After establishing rapport with the applicant, the interviewer seeks additional job-related information to complement data provided by other selection tools. The interview permits clarification of certain points, the uncovering of additional information, and the elaboration of data needed to make a sound selection decision. The interviewer should provide information about the company, the job, and expectations of the candidate. Other areas typically included in the interview are discussed next.

Occupational Experience. The interviewer will explore the candidate's knowledge, skills, abilities, and willingness to handle responsibility. Although successful performance in one job does not guarantee success in another, it does provide an indication of the person's ability and willingness to work.

Academic Achievement. In the absence of significant work experience, a person's academic record takes on greater importance. Managers should, however, consider grade point average in light of other factors. For example, involvement in work, extracurricular activities, or other responsibilities may have affected an applicant's academic performance.

Interpersonal Skills. An individual may possess important technical skills significant to accomplishing a job. However, if the person cannot work well with others, chances for success are slim. This is especially true in today's world with the increasing use of teams. According to R. Wendell Williams, managing director of the Atlanta-based Emergenetics Consulting Group, the biggest mistake an interviewee can make is thinking that firms hire people only for their technical skills. He says that the personal impact made on the recruiter is equally important.[59]

Personal Qualities. Personal qualities normally observed during the interview include physical appearance, speaking ability, vocabulary, poise, adaptability, and assertiveness. As with all selection criteria, employers should consider these attributes only if they are relevant to job performance.

Organizational Fit. A hiring criterion *not* prominently mentioned in the literature is *organizational fit*. Using *fit* as a criterion raises legal and diversity questions, and perhaps this explains the low profile. Nevertheless, there is evidence that managers use it in making selection decisions and it is not a minor consideration.

Organizational fit:
Management's perception of the degree to which the prospective employee will fit in with the firm's culture or value system.

Organizational fit refers to management's perception of the degree to which the prospective employee will fit in with the firm's culture or value system. Dr. Elisabeth Marx, director of Norman Broadbent International, executive recruitment consultants, is familiar with many instances where a company has failed to match a candidate to its culture. The result is that the working relationship ends with the candidate's dismissal or hasty departure.[60] Russell Yaquinto, who coaches managerial job-seekers for the outplacement firm Right Management Consultants in Dallas, states that "There's very widespread agreement . . . that you can have the credentials, but if you aren't going to fit [the culture], it doesn't matter. Before long, you'll be out of there." An employee who fits not only the skill requirements but also the culture, values, and belief systems of the organization is typically three times more productive and two times less likely to leave the firm.[61]

The Candidate's Role and Expectations

While the interviewer will provide information about the company, it is still important that candidates do their homework, including checking the library and the firm's Web site. Many sites include information tailored to job-seekers. These sites often provide a history of the company and a description of its products and customers.[62] In fact, the candidate should learn as much as possible about the firm. A person applying for a management position, especially, should have a thorough understanding of the firm's business priorities, its strengths and weaknesses, and its chief competitors. Applications should consider how they would address some of the issues facing the company,[63] and they need to be able to detail their accomplishments. You must be honest, but you cannot be vague about anything that is on your résumé.

Recruiters need to remember that interviewees also have objectives for the interview. One might be to determine what the firm is willing to pay as a starting salary. A survey conducted by the Society for Human Resource Management indicated that 8 out of 10 recruiters were willing to negotiate pay and benefits with job applicants. However, only one-third of the job applicants surveyed said they felt comfortable negotiating.[64] Job-seekers have other goals that may include the following:

- To be listened to and understood
- To have ample opportunity to present their qualifications
- To be treated fairly and with respect
- To gather information about the job and the company
- To make an informed decision concerning the desirability of the job

Candidates can learn what interviewing skills they need to improve by undergoing a mock interview or two. Having a colleague or friend to interview them, then critically reviewing their own responses can be beneficial. This mock interview allows candidates to analyze their strengths and interests that they would bring to a job. The process would also help them prioritize the points they want to make in the real interview.[65]

After the final interview, management must determine whether the candidate is suitable for the open position and organization. If the conclusion is positive, the process continues; if there appears to be no match, the candidate is no longer considered.

12 OBJECTIVE

Describe the general types of interviewing.

General Types of Interviews

"Tell me about yourself" was once a question often asked in interviews. However, more probing questions generally followed in typical flowing sessions. Types of interviews are often placed in two broad classifications: structured or unstructured. A discussion of the differences between the two follows.

The Unstructured (Nondirective) Interview

Unstructured interview: A meeting with a job applicant during which the interviewer asks probing, open-ended questions.

An **unstructured interview** is one in which the interviewer asks probing, open-ended questions. This type of interview is comprehensive, and the interviewer encourages the applicant to do much of the talking. The nondirective interview is often more time-consuming than the structured interview and results in obtaining different information from different candidates. This adds to the potential legal woes of organizations using this approach. Compounding the problem is the likelihood of discussing ill-advised, potentially discriminatory information. The applicant who is being encouraged to pour his heart out may volunteer facts that the interviewer does not need or want to know. Unsuccessful applicants subjected to this interviewing approach may later claim in court that the reason for their failure to get the job was the employer's use of this information.

The Structured (Directive or Patterned) Interview

Structured interview: A process in which an interviewer consistently presents the same series of job-related questions to each applicant for a particular job.

The **structured interview** is a series of job-related questions asked of each applicant for a particular job. Although interviews have historically been very poor predictors for making selection decisions, use of structured interviews increases reliability and accuracy by reducing the subjectivity and inconsistency of unstructured interviews.

A structured job interview typically contains four types of questions.

- **Situational questions** are those that pose a typical job situation to determine what the applicant did in a similar situation.
- **Job-knowledge questions** are those that probe the applicant's job-related knowledge; these questions may relate to basic educational skills or complex scientific or managerial skills.
- **Job-sample simulation questions** involve situations in which an applicant may be required to answer questions related to performance of a task.
- **Worker requirements questions** are those that seek to determine the applicant's willingness to conform to the requirements of the job. For example, the interviewer may ask whether the applicant is willing to perform repetitive work or move to another city.

13 OBJECTIVE

Explain the growing influence of the behavioral interview.

Behavioral interview: A structured interview where applicants are asked to relate actual incidents from their past that are relevant to the target job.

Behavioral Interviews

The **behavioral interview** is a structured interview where applicants are asked to relate actual incidents from their past relevant to the target job. They assume that past behavior is the best predictor of future behavior.[66] The behavioral interview has become a primary interviewing tool. The reason for increased use of behavioral interviews is that older methods have proven to be poor predictors of a candidate's success. The premise that past behavior is the best predictor of future behavior avoids having to make judgments about applicants' personalities and precludes hypothetical and self-evaluative questions.

John Madigan, IT human resource vice president at The Hartford Financial Services Group, Inc., explains that a behavioral job interview reveals a pattern of behavior. "We actually ask what you did in specific situations," Madigan says. "Concrete examples will demonstrate a person's preferred way of dealing with those situations and give you a better idea of that person and how they're likely to act on the job."[67] Behavioral interviewers look for three main things: a description of a challenging situation, what the candidate did about it, and measurable results.[68]

Behavioral Questions

In the behavioral interview, the situational behaviors are selected for their relevance to job success. Questions are formed from the behaviors by asking applicants how they performed in the described situation. For example, when probing for professional or technical knowledge, the candidate might be asked, "Describe a situation where your expertise made a significant difference." Or, if seeking to determine the applicant's enthusiasm, the question might be, "Relate a scenario where you were responsible for motivating others."[69] Benchmark answers derived from behaviors of successful employees are prepared for use in rating applicant responses. A candidate's response to a given situation provides the means to develop an insight into his or her job potential. In behavioral interviews, candidates may unwittingly reveal information about their attitudes, intelligence, and truthfulness. Arrogance, lack of cooperation with team members, and anger can all spill out during such an interview. While some candidates may think the interview is all about technical skills, it is as much about them as anything. This aspect of a candidate is important, as evidenced in one study's finding that 97 percent of job failures result from personality clashes rather than technical deficiencies.[70]

Developing a behavior-based interview would likely include these steps:[71]

- Analyze the job to determine the knowledge, skills, abilities (KSAs), and behaviors important for job success.
- Determine which behavioral questions to ask about the particular job to elicit the desired behaviors.
- Develop a structured format tailored for each job.
- Set benchmark responses: examples of *good*, *average*, and *bad* answers to questions.
- Train the interviewers.

Questions asked in behavior description interviewing are legally safe since they are job related. Equally important, since both questions and answers are related to successful job performance, they are more accurate in predicting whether applicants will be successful in the job they are hired to perform. Research indicates that while traditional interviewing has a success rate of about 14 percent, behavioral interviewing has a success rate of around 55 percent.[72]

Evaluating Candidates

A rating scale may be helpful in comparing several candidates. The same individuals who develop the interview questions can determine the appropriate responses for each level of the scale. These people are thoroughly familiar with the job for which the interview was developed. The scale may have only three levels; for example, 5 — Excellent (responses that reflect probable success); 3 — Marginal (probable difficulty in performing the task); and 1 — Poor (probable failure). Management can then obtain a total score for each applicant.[73] A positive feature about behavioral interviewing is its ability to serve as a tiebreaker. This technique can help select the one who is most likely to excel in the job when several candidates appear to possess similar skills, experiences, and qualifications. It answers the one question both the hiring manager and the candidate want to know most: Is this a good *fit*?

Broad Application but Potential Problem

Although once used exclusively for senior executive positions, behavioral interviewing is now a popular technique for lower-level positions. At CIGNA Corporation all candidates hired for positions through the company's corporate staffing department undergo behavioral interviewing. Whether applying for a clerical or management position, each candidate is put through the process.[74]

One difficulty with behavioral interviewing is that some job-seekers have gotten wise to the process. A growing number of candidates, especially those coming from business and law schools, deliberately misrepresent themselves during the interview. The stories some concoct about who they are and what they did in real-life situations are pure fiction.

14 OBJECTIVE

Describe the various methods of interviewing.

Methods of Interviewing

Organizations conduct interviews in several ways. The level of the open position and the appropriate labor market determine the most fitting approach. A discussion of these methods follows.

One-on-One Interview

In a typical employment interview, the applicant meets one-on-one with an interviewer. As the interview may be a highly emotional occasion for the applicant, meeting alone with the interviewer is often less threatening. The environment this method provides may allow an effective exchange of information to take place.

Group Interview

Group interview: A meeting in which several job applicants interact in the presence of one or more company representatives.

In a **group interview,** several applicants interact in the presence of one or more company representatives. This approach, while not mutually exclusive of other interview types, may provide useful insights into the candidates' interpersonal competence as they engage in a group discussion. Another advantage of this technique is that it saves time for busy professionals and executives.

Board Interview

Board interview: A meeting in which several representatives of a company interview a candidate in one or more sessions.

In a **board interview,** several of the firm's representatives interview a candidate in one or more sessions. At Texas Instruments, for example, the potential hire's peers, subordinates, and supervisors interview the prospective employee. James Mitchell, vice president of corporate staff, claims that using multiple interviewers not only leads to better hiring decisions; it also begins the transition process.[75] Amazon.com, IBM, and Motorola use peers to interview and do so successfully. Small firms also find much to praise about this hiring process. The payback is substantial and results in a higher degree of acceptance of a candidate and a higher degree of retention. This approach permits the firm to get a more holistic view of the candidate. It also gives the candidate a chance to learn more about the company from a variety of perspectives. The result of this type interview is a stronger, more cohesive team that shares the company's culture and helps assure organizational fit.[76]

Stress Interview

Stress interview: A form of interview that intentionally creates anxiety to determine how a job applicant will react in certain types of situations.

Most interviewers strive to minimize stress for the candidate. In the **stress interview,** however, the interviewer intentionally creates anxiety. The interviewer deliberately makes the candidate uncomfortable by asking blunt and often discourteous questions. The purpose is to determine the applicant's tolerance for stress that may accompany the job. Knowledge of this factor may be important if the job requires the ability to deal with a high level of stress.

Stress interviews aren't new. The late Admiral Hyman G. Rickover, father of the U.S. Navy's nuclear submarine program, was known to offer interviewees a chair that had one or two legs shorter than the other. The candidates' problems were compounded by the chair's polished seat. The admiral once stated that "they had to maintain their wits about them as they answered questions while sliding off the chair."[77]

Information technology recruiters may use old-fashioned logic problems or ask questions that call for a wild guess to determine how the candidate thinks on his or her feet. Financial service employers also enjoy pitching curveballs, as do marketing companies. How would you answer this question, "How many gallons of white paint are sold in the U.S. every year?" Firms at the cutting edge of technology such as dot.coms, software design, and engineering are more likely to ask these kinds of questions and, presumably, they have job relevance. Web sites, such as Vault.com (www.vault.com), are available for job-seekers to gain tips on how to deal with brainteasers.[78]

Realistic Job Previews

Many applicants have unrealistic expectations about the prospective job and employer. This inaccurate perception may have negative consequences, yet it is often encouraged when interviewers paint false, rosy pictures of the job and company. This practice leads to mismatches of people and positions. What compounds the problem is when candidates exaggerate their own qualifications. To correct this situation from the employer's side, firms should provide a realistic job preview to applicants early in the selection process and, definitely, before a job offer is made.

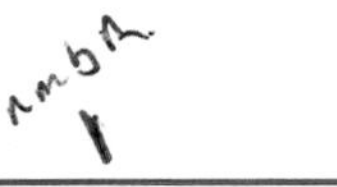

Realistic job preview (RJP): A method of conveying both positive and negative job information to an applicant in an unbiased manner.

A **realistic job preview (RJP)** involves conveying both positive and negative job information to the applicant in an unbiased manner. An RJP conveys information about tasks the person would perform and the behavior required to *fit into* the organization and adhere to company policies and procedures.[79] This approach helps applicants develop a more accurate perception of the job and the firm. Research shows employers who give detailed RJPs get two results: fewer employees accept the job offer and, applicants who do accept the offer are less likely to leave the firm.[80] Given an RJP, some candidates will take themselves out of the selection process and that will minimize the number of unqualified candidates.[81] Another reason to use RJPs is the benefit a firm receives from being an up-front, ethical employer.

15 OBJECTIVE

Explain the legal implications of interviewing.

Legal Implications of Interviewing

Recall from Chapter 3 that the definition of a test in the *Uniform Guidelines* includes "physical, education and work experience requirements from *informal or casual interviews*." Because the interview is a test, if adverse impact is shown, it is subject to the same validity requirements as any other step in the selection process. For unstructured interviews, this constraint presents special difficulties. Historically, the interview has been more vulnerable to charges of discrimination than any other tool used in the selection process. One simple rule governs interviewing: *all questions must be job related.* In addition to being a waste of time, irrelevant or personal questions are dangerous and often improper. Since behavioral interviews necessarily consist of job-related questions, their popularity is understandable.

To elicit needed information in any type of interview, the interviewer must create a climate that encourages the applicant to speak freely. However, the conversation should not become too casual. Whereas engaging in friendly chitchat with candidates might be pleasant, in our litigious society, it may be the most dangerous thing an interviewer can do.

To avoid the appearance of discrimination, employers should ask all applicants for a given position the same questions. It is also critical to record the applicant's responses. If a candidate begins volunteering personal information that is not job related, the interviewer should steer the conversation back on course. It might do well to begin the interview by tactfully stating, "This selection decision will be based strictly on qualifications. Let's not discuss topics such as religion, social activities, national origin, gender, or family situations. We are definitely interested in you, personally. However, these factors are not job related and will not be considered in our decision." Table 6-1 shows potential problems that can threaten the success of employment interviews.

The Americans with Disabilities Act also provides warning for interviewers. Interviewers should inquire about the need for reasonable accommodations in only a few situations. For example, the topic is appropriate if the applicant is in a wheelchair and has an obvious disability that will require accommodation. Also, the applicant may voluntarily disclose a disability or even ask for some reasonable accommodation. Otherwise, employers should refrain from broaching the subject. Instead, interviewers should frame questions in terms of whether applicants can perform the essential functions of the jobs for which they are applying.

Table 6-1 Potential Interviewing Problems

Inappropriate Questions

Although no questions are illegal, many are clearly inappropriate. When they are asked, the responses generated create a legal liability for the employer. The most basic interviewing rule is this: "Ask only job-related questions!"

Premature Judgments

Research suggests that interviewers often make judgments about candidates in the first few minutes of the interview. When this occurs, a great deal of potentially valuable information is not considered.

Interviewer Domination

In successful interviews, relevant information must flow both ways. Therefore, interviewers must learn to be good listeners as well as suppliers of information.

Inconsistent Questions

If interviewers ask all applicants for a given job essentially the same questions and in the same sequence, all the applicants are judged on the same basis. This enables better decisions to be made while decreasing the likelihood of discrimination charges.

Central Tendency

When interviewers rate virtually all candidates as average, they fail to differentiate between strong and weak candidates.

Halo Error

When interviewers permit only one or a few personal characteristics to influence their overall impression of candidates, the best applicant may not be selected.

Contrast Effects

An error in judgment may occur when, for example, an interviewer meets with several poorly qualified applicants and then confronts a mediocre candidate. By comparison, the last applicant may appear to be better qualified than he or she actually is.

Interviewer Bias

Interviewers must understand and acknowledge their own prejudices and learn to deal with them. The only valid bias for an interviewer is to favor the best-qualified candidate for the open position.

Lack of Training

When the cost of making poor selection decisions is considered, the expense of training employees in interviewing skills can be easily justified.

Behavior Sample

Even if an interviewer spent a week with an applicant, the sample of behavior might be too small to judge the candidate's qualifications properly. In addition, the candidate's behavior during an interview is seldom typical or natural.

Nonverbal Communication

Interviewers should make a conscious effort to view themselves as applicants do to avoid sending inappropriate or unintended nonverbal signals.

When the interviewer has obtained the necessary information and answered the applicant's questions, he or she should conclude the interview. At this point, the interviewer should tell the applicant that he or she will be notified of the selection decision shortly. Keeping this promise helps maintain a positive relationship with the applicant.

16 OBJECTIVE

Explain the use of personal reference checks, background investigations, and polygraph tests.

Reference checks: Validations that provide additional insight into the information furnished by the applicant and allow verification of its accuracy.

Personal Reference Checks

Reference checks are validations that provide additional insight into the information furnished by the applicant and allow verification of its accuracy. In fact, applicants are often required to submit the names of several references that can provide additional information about them. The basic flaw with this step in the selection process is that virtually every living person can name three or four individuals willing to make favorable statements about him or her. Even so, there is anecdotal evidence that personal references do not always sugarcoat the information they provide. They may not necessarily be committed to shading the truth for the applicant. Still, it appears that most organizations place more emphasis on professional references included in background investigations.

Background Investigations and Professional Reference Checks

Background investigations involve obtaining data from various sources, including previous employers and business associates. These professional references are a valuable source of information along with credit bureaus, government agencies, and academic institutions. The principal reason for conducting background investigations is to hire better workers. As we shall see, however, there are other critical reasons as well. The intensity of background investigations depends on the nature of the open position's tasks and its relationship to customers or clients. To be legally safe, employers should ask applicants to sign a liability waiver permitting a background investigation. A comprehensive waiver releases former employers, business references, and others from liability. The waiver can also authorize checks of court records and the verification of the applicant's educational history and other credentials. The employer should fully document the results of all reference and background checks.

The high incidence of credential fraud, discussed at the beginning of this chapter, provides a compelling reason for firms to conduct background investigations. We present additional rationale for conducting background investigations in the next section.

Negligent Hiring

Negligent hiring: The liability an employer incurs when it fails to conduct a reasonable investigation of an applicant's background, and then assigns a potentially dangerous person to a position where he or she can inflict harm.

Negligent hiring is the liability an employer incurs when it fails to conduct a reasonable investigation of an applicant's background, and then assigns a potentially dangerous person to a position where he or she can inflict harm. *Reasonable care* varies according to the nature of the job.

At-Risk Employers. The risk of harm to third parties, for example, requires a higher standard of care when hiring a taxi driver as opposed to a bank teller. Employers who operate home-service businesses, day-care centers, and home health-care operations are particularly at risk as are those with employees who drive company vehicles, visit customer locations, handle money, or work with children, the elderly, or the impaired. The primary consideration in negligent hiring is whether the risk of harm from a dangerous employee was reasonably foreseeable.

An Illustration of Negligent Hiring. Let us illustrate the problem: a health-care employer hired a male applicant as an aide in a home health-care program run by a visiting nurses' association. Soon after assignment to the home of a paraplegic, the employee murdered the patient and then robbed him. In investigating the situation, it was found that the individual had lied about where he had worked before; had lied about not having a criminal history; had lied about having a nursing degree; had lied about being licensed. A check on any of these claims would have disqualified the person from employment. In court, the health-care organization attempted to defend itself by claiming that it was not standard practice to conduct in-depth background investigations because they were too expensive. The jury was not impressed and the result was a $26.5 million award.[82]

OSHA's Role. The law requires employers to provide employees a safe place to work and this responsibility extends to providing *safe employees*. The courts have reasoned that a dangerous worker is comparable to a defective machine. Specifically, employers have a responsibility under the general duty clause of the Occupational Safety and Health Act to furnish a workplace free from recognized hazards that are causing or are likely to cause death or serious physical harm.[83]

Double Jeopardy. If an employer fails to conduct a *reasonable* background investigation, it may be legally liable for negligent hiring. Or, if the investigation reveals negative information about the applicant, invasion of privacy or defamation charges may be filed. Once again, an employer is in a potential *Catch-22* situation. Still another potential liability, **negligent retention**, occurs when a company keeps persons on the payroll whose records indicate strong potential for wrongdoing, and fails to take steps to defuse a possible violent situation.[84]

Negligent retention:
When a company keeps persons on the payroll whose records indicate strong potential for wrongdoing and fails to take steps to defuse a possible violent situation.

Due Diligence Required. The employer can be held responsible for the employee's unlawful acts even if the employee's actions are not job related. Negligent hiring cases often involve awards in the hundreds of thousands of dollars and, in addition, they are likely to be upheld on appeal. Therefore, it is imperative that human resource managers exercise due diligence in conducting background investigations of all prospective employees.[85]

Hiring organizations cannot avoid the possibility of legal action. However, following sound selection procedures and keeping written records of the investigations will serve them well and may prove to be money well spent.

Elements to Verify

As previously stated, background investigations primarily look for data from various sources, including professional references. An effective and comprehensive background investigation will include examination and verification of the following elements:[86]

- previous employment
- education
- personal references
- criminal history
- driving record
- civil litigation
- workers' compensation history
- credit history
- Social Security number

Fair Credit Reporting Act

Congress created an obstacle for employers when it amended the federal Fair Credit Reporting Act (FCRA), mentioned at the beginning of this chapter. This 1997 amendment places new obligations on employers who use certain information brought to light through background investigations. Employers' obligations are triggered under the act when they use "consumer" reports that contain information about an individual's personal and credit characteristics, character, general reputation, and lifestyle. The FCRA only covers reports that are prepared by a "consumer reporting agency" such as a credit bureau. In accordance with the FCRA, employers using information from such an agency to make employment decisions must take these actions:[87]

- Obtain prior authorization from the applicant
- Provide a certification of compliance with the act to the consumer reporting agency
- Notify the applicant if it takes any adverse employment action based on the report

Other Legal Aspects

Regardless of the difficulties encountered in background investigations and reference checks, employing organizations have no choice but to engage in them. And, recognizing the importance of investigations in selecting employees, over half the states in the United States have passed laws offering varying degrees of protection to employers who provide good-faith references and who release truthful information about current or former employees. The intent of this legislation is to make it easier for employers to give and receive meaningful information. However, there has been some hesitancy on the part of firms to take advantage of it. Apparently, there is a wait-and-see attitude, and although a protective law does exist, it may take litigation and court rulings before employers fully understand, and have confidence in, the statutes.

Problems in Obtaining Information from Professional References

A related problem in obtaining information from previous employers is their general reluctance to reveal such data. The Privacy Act of 1974, although limited to the public sector, provides a major reason for this hesitancy. Employers and employees in the private sector have become very sensitive to the privacy issue. There are two schools of thought with regard to supplying information about former employees. One is, "Don't tell them anything." The other is, "Honesty is the best policy." In the more conservative approach, the employer typically provides only basic data, such as starting and termination dates and last job title. The *honesty* approach is based on the reality that facts honestly given or opinions honestly held constitute a solid legal defense. When former employers are unwilling to give any information about a job applicant, both the potential employer and the applicant are at a disadvantage. A red flag is quickly raised when a former employer refuses to talk about a one-time employee. For those firms that freely give out information about previous employees, questions about the applicant's integrity and character are appropriate. It is helpful to know why the person left that job. If the response differs from that given by the applicant, it is definitely a red flag.[88]

Negligent Referral

Negligent referral: When a former employer fails to offer a warning about a particularly severe problem with a past employee.

A relatively new concept, negligent referral, has added still another dimension to the investigation process. **Negligent referral** may occur when a former employer fails to offer a warning about a particularly severe problem with a past employee. Although this concept is not yet widely accepted, some courts have recognized a cause of action for negligent references.

Outsourcing Investigations

Small firms may not possess the staff to screen backgrounds of prospective employees thoroughly. Even large organizations may prefer to utilize the specialized services of professional screening firms. Firms can outsource their background-checking duties to a handful of third-party investigators that the Fair Credit Reporting Act regulates. They also require a signed release from the applicant. Some firms charge an average of $40 to $50 per inquiry but their fee may exceed $100 if a complicated search is required.[89]

Regardless of how they are accomplished, background investigations have become increasingly important in making sound selection decisions and avoiding charges of negligent hiring and retention. The investigations may provide information critical to selection decisions since firms can verify virtually every qualification an applicant lists.

Polygraph Tests

For many years, another means used to verify background information has been the polygraph, or lie detector test. One purpose of the polygraph was to confirm or refute the information contained in the application blank. However, the Employee Polygraph Protection Act of 1988 severely limited the use of polygraph tests in the private sector. It made unlawful the use of a polygraph test by any employer engaged in interstate commerce. Even so, the act does not apply to governmental employers, and there are limited exceptions. The act permits use of polygraph tests in the private sector to certain prospective employees of security service firms and pharmaceutical manufacturers, distributors, and dispensers. The act also permits, with certain restrictions, polygraph testing of certain employees reasonably suspected of involvement in a workplace incident, such as theft or embezzlement. Persons who take polygraph tests have a number of specific rights. For example, they have the right to a written notice before testing, the right to refuse or discontinue a test, and the right not to have test results disclosed to unauthorized persons.

The Selection Decision

Describe the selection decision, the medical examination, and notification of candidates.

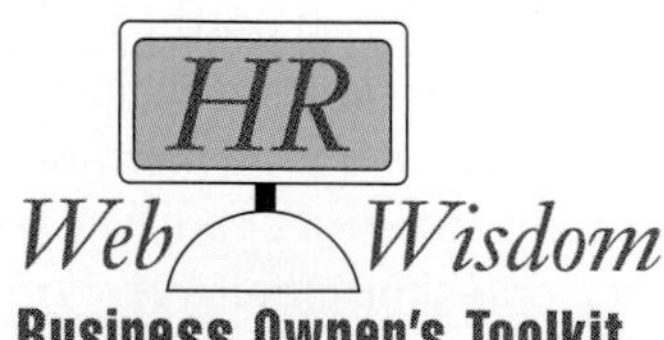

Business Owner's Toolkit

www.toolkit.cch.com

This Web site offers detailed instructions for the small business owner to hire, manage, and retain employees.

An organization obtains and evaluates information about the finalists in a job selection process. At this point, the buck stops with the manager who must take the most critical step of all: the actual hiring decision. The final choice is made from among those still in the running after reference checks, selection tests, background investigations, and interview information have been evaluated. The individual with the best overall qualifications may, or may not, be hired. Usually, the person selected has qualifications that most closely conform to the requirements of the open position and the organization. On the other hand, some firms feel that a candidate's development potential is as important as his ability to fill the current position. Jim Kutz, IT recruiting director at Capital One Financial Corporation, says, "we often look not only at what the person can do now, but what he can do in the next job."[90] If a firm is going to invest thousands of dollars to recruit, select, and train an employee, it is important for the manager to hire the most qualified available candidate according to the hiring firm's criteria. To a point, the more screening tools used to assess a good fit, the greater the chance of making a good selection decision. The odds of a successful hire are 14 percent with an interview and a résumé, but 75 percent if tests show that a candidate's skills and personality are compatible with the job and the organization.[91]

Human resource professionals may be involved in all phases leading up to the final employment decision. However, especially for higher-level positions, the person who normally makes the final selection is the manager who will be responsible for the new employee's performance. In making this decision, the operating manager will review results of the selection methods used. All will not likely be weighted the same. The question then becomes, "Which data are most predictive of job success?" For each firm or group of jobs, the optimum selection method may be different.

Medical Examination

The Americans with Disabilities Act (ADA) does not prohibit pre-employment testing. However, it does determine the permitted tests and at what point they may be administered during the selection process. ADA explicitly states that all exams must be directly relevant to the job requirements and that a firm cannot order a medical exam until the applicant is offered employment. Typically, a job offer is contingent on the applicant's passing of this examination. The basic purpose of the medical examination is to determine whether an applicant is physically capable of performing the work.

Managers must be aware of the legal liabilities related to medical examinations. The *Uniform Guidelines* state that these examinations are for rejecting applicants only when the results show that job performance would be adversely affected. The Rehabilitation Act of 1973 and the Americans with Disabilities Act of 1990 require employers to take affirmative action to hire qualified disabled persons who, with reasonable accommodation, can perform the essential components of a job.

Notification of Candidates

Management should notify both successful and unsuccessful candidates of selection decisions as soon as possible. This action is simply a matter of courtesy and good public relations. Any delay may also result in the firm losing a prime candidate, as top prospects often have other employment options.

If currently employed by another firm, the successful candidate customarily gives between two and four weeks' notice. Even after this notice, the individual may need some personal time to prepare for the new job. This transition time is particularly important if the new job requires a move to another city. Thus, the amount of time before the individual can join the firm is often considerable.

Employers may reject applicants at any time during the selection process. Research has indicated that most people can accept losing if they lose fairly. Problems occur when the selection process appears to be less than objective. It is therefore important for firms to develop and utilize rational selection tools. Increasingly, time constraints prevent firms from spending much time explaining a decision to an unsuccessful candidate. A rejection letter is a more likely method. However, a letter with a personal touch may reduce the stigma of rejection and avoid the applicant's having a negative feeling about the company. An impersonal letter is likely to have the opposite effect. The best an organization can do is to make selection decisions objectively. Hopefully, most unsuccessful individuals can, with time, accept the fact that they were not chosen.

A Global Perspective

Hiring Foreign Workers in a Post-9/11 World

The rules concerning hiring employees born outside the United States have not changed much since 9/11, but the way INS implements the rules has. Employers who want to hire foreign nationals today continue to hire them but there are hurdles to overcome. If a company is considering hiring a person from a country that is of concern to the government, such as Iraq or Libya, greater delays are likely, but the person usually can still be hired. A company wanting to hire a person from Germany or Brazil should not experience any more difficulty than before 9/11.[92]

Certain questions should be asked if a company wants to hire people from other countries. First, can the person and the job qualify for an H-IB visa (the typical category under which a foreign worker may be brought to the United States)? The H-IB is specifically for professional workers and is not meant for manual laborers and individuals who do not have a college education. Essentially, a foreign worker cannot be brought here to drive a taxicab. Second, "What are the credentials of the foreign national?" Credentials must match the job.[93]

A third issue a company needs to consider concerns questions such as "What business is the company involved in? How many employees does it have? How much money does it make? Is it publicly or privately held?"

Paying fair wages is another requirement an employer must meet. Before H- IB approval is given, employers are required to submit to the Labor Department a document that says: "I intend to put someone in this job, at this location, at this salary, and I swear this salary is the highest among the prevailing wages for the community."[94]

There are additional categories under which a foreign national can be brought to the United States. If a company is truly multinational with offices outside the United States, greater opportunity is afforded it in bringing in foreign workers. They can be transferred in as intra-company transferees under an L-visa. They transfer as managers or executives or as people with "specialized knowledge" of the company or its products. The advantage of the L-1 visa is that people can move people more quickly than under the H-1B category and wage restrictions are not a problem.[95]

Fewer U.S. companies can use the H-1B program these days by saying qualified Americans are not available. Still, employers look for ways to cut labor costs. They have found that they can use firms that hire L-1s, which is designed for intra-company transfers by multinational corporations, to get rid of high-paid Americans in favor of cheaper workers from abroad. As a result, many companies are subcontracting thousands of jobs to outsourcing companies such as Tata, Infosys Technologies, and Wipro Technologies, the three largest Indian software servicing companies, which all are using more L-1s. There is a growing backlash to programs such as these because, although legal, they may be violating the spirit of the law.[96]

Summary

1. Explain the significance of employee selection.
Selection is the process of choosing from a group of applicants those individuals best suited for a particular position. There are many ways to improve productivity, but none is more powerful than making the right hiring decision.

2. Identify environmental factors that affect the selection process.
The environmental factors that affect the selection process include legal considerations, speed of decision making, organizational hierarchy, applicant pool, type of organization, and probationary period.

3. Describe the general selection process.
The selection process typically begins with the preliminary interview where obviously unqualified candidates are rejected. Next, applicants complete the firm's application blank, and this is followed by the administration of selection tests and a series of employment interviews with reference and background checks. Once the selection decision has been made, the prospective employee may be given a company medical examination.

4. Explain the importance of the preliminary interview.
The selection process begins with an initial screening of applicants to remove individuals who obviously do not fulfill the position requirements.

5. Describe reviewing applications and résumés.
Having the applicant complete an application for employment is another early step in the selection process. The employer then evaluates it to see whether there is an apparent match between the individual and the position. Historically, managers and HR representatives reviewed résumés manually, a time-consuming process. However, this practice has evolved into a more advanced procedure, with résumés automatically evaluated in terms of typos, spelling errors, and job-hopping.

6. Explain the administration of selection tests including the advantages, potential problems, and characteristics of properly designed selection tests.

Research indicates that customized tests are a reliable and accurate means to predict on-the-job performance. Pre-employment testing carries with it legal liabilities of two types. One is lawsuits from rejected applicants who claim a test was not job related or that it unfairly discriminated against a protected group violating federal employment laws. Organizations must ensure that their selection tests do not discriminate against members of protected classes. The second potential legal problem relates to negligence-in-hiring lawsuits filed by victims of employee misbehavior or incompetence. Test anxiety can also be a problem. Properly designed test characteristics include: standardization, objectivity, norm, reliability, and validity.

7. Explain the types of validation studies.

Criterion-related validity is determined by comparing the scores on selection tests to some aspect of job performance as determined, for example, by performance appraisal. Concurrent validity is where the test scores and the criterion data are obtained at essentially the same time. Predictive validity is administering a test and later obtaining the criterion information.

8. Describe types of employment tests.

Types of employment tests include cognitive aptitude, psychomotor abilities, job-knowledge, work-sample, and vocational interest tests. Few issues generate more controversy today than alcohol and drug testing. Genetic testing can now determine a predisposition to numerous diseases. The Internet is increasingly being used to test various skills required by applicants.

9. Describe the concept of genetic testing.

Genetic testing is given to determine whether a person carries the gene mutation for certain diseases, including heart disease, colon cancer, breast cancer, and Huntington's disease. As genetic research progresses, confirmed links between specific gene mutations and diseases are emerging. This announcement brings both hope and concerns to the forefront in employment testing.

10. Discuss assessment centers as a means of selection.

An assessment center is a selection technique used to identify and select employees for positions in the organization. Candidates are subjected to a number of exercises that simulate tasks they will perform in the job for which they are being considered.

11. Explain the importance of the employment interview, including interview planning and the content of the interview.

Interview planning is essential to effective employment interviews. Both the interviewer and the candidate have agendas for the interview. After establishing rapport with the applicant, the interviewer seeks additional job-related information to complement data provided by other selection tools. The interview permits clarification of certain points, the uncovering of additional information, and the elaboration of data needed to make a sound selection decision. The interviewer should provide information about the company, the job, and expectations of the candidate.

12. Describe the general types of interviewing.

The general types of interviews are the unstructured interview and the structured interview, including the behavioral interview. The interviewer should provide information about the company, the job, and expectations of the candidate.

13. Explain the growing influence of the behavioral interview.

The behavioral interview is a structured interview where applicants are asked to relate actual incidents from their past relevant to the target job. They assume that the past is the best predictor of the future.

14. Describe the various methods of interviewing.

The methods of interviewing include meeting one-on-one with an interviewer, a group interview, the board interview, a stress interview, and the realistic job preview.

15. Explain the legal implications of interviewing.
Because the interview is considered to be a test, it is subject to the same validity requirements as any other step in the selection process, should adverse impact be shown.

16. Explain the use of personal reference checks, background investigations, and polygraph tests.
Personal reference checks may provide additional insight into the information furnished by the applicant and allow verification of its accuracy. Background investigations primarily seek data from various sources, including professional references. One purpose of the polygraph was to confirm or refute the information contained in the application blank. However, the Employee Polygraph Protection Act of 1988 severely limited the use of polygraph tests in the private sector. It made unlawful the use of a polygraph test by any employer engaged in interstate commerce.

17. Describe the selection decision, the medical examination, and notification of candidates.
The selection decision is when the final choice is made from among those still in the running after reference checks, selection tests, background investigations, and interview information are evaluated. The physical is used to screen out individuals who have a contagious disease and to determine if an applicant is physically capable of performing the work. The medical examination information may be used to determine if there are certain physical capabilities that differentiate between successful and less successful employees. The selection process results should be made known to both successful and unsuccessful candidates as soon as possible.

Key Terms

- **Selection, 162**
- **Selection ratio, 164**
- **Standardization, 173**
- **Objectivity, 173**
- **Norm, 173**
- **Reliability, 173**
- **Validity, 173**
- **Criterion-related validity, 174**
- **Concurrent validity, 174**
- **Predictive validity, 174**
- **Content validity, 174**
- **Construct validity, 174**
- **Cognitive aptitude tests, 175**
- **Psychomotor abilities tests, 175**
- **Job-knowledge tests, 175**
- **Work-sample tests, 175**
- **Vocational interest tests, 176**
- **Personality tests, 176**
- **Genetic testing, 179**
- **Assessment center, 180**
- **Employment interview, 181**
- **Organizational fit, 182**
- **Unstructured interview, 183**
- **Structured interview, 183**
- **Behavioral interview, 184**
- **Group interview, 186**
- **Board interview, 186**
- **Stress interview, 186**
- **Realistic job preview (RJP), 187**
- **Reference checks, 189**
- **Negligent hiring, 189**
- **Negligent retention, 190**
- **Negligent referral, 191**

Questions for Review

1. What is the significance of employee selection?
2. What environmental factors could affect the selection process? Discuss each.
3. What basic steps normally are followed in the selection process?
4. What is the general purpose of the preliminary interview?
5. What is the purpose of the application form?
6. What types of questions should be asked on an application form?
7. What would be the selection ratio if there were 15 applicants to choose from and only 1 position to fill? Interpret the meaning of this selection ratio.
8. What are the advantages and potential problems in the use of selection tests?
9. Define *genetic testing*.
10. What is the purpose of an assessment center?
11. What are the basic characteristics of a properly designed selection test?
12. What are the types of validation? Define each.
13. Identify and describe the various types of employment tests.

14. What information should be gained from the interview?
15. What are the general types of interviews?
16. What is a behavioral interview? What types of questions would make up a behavioral interview?
17. What are the various methods of interviewing? Define each.
18. What are the legal implications of interviewing?
19. Why should an employer be concerned about negligent hiring and retention?

HRM Incident 1

A Matter of Priorities

As production manager for Thompson Manufacturing, Jack Stephens has the final authority to approve the hiring of any new supervisors who work for him. The human resource manager performs the initial screening of all prospective supervisors, then sends the most likely candidates to Jack for interviews.

One day recently, Jack received a call from Pete Peterson, the human resource manager: "Jack, I've just spoken to a young man who may be just who you're looking for to fill the final line supervisor position. He has some good work experience and appears to have his head screwed on straight. He's here right now and available if you could possibly see him."

Jack hesitated a moment before answering. "Gee, Pete," he said, "I'm certainly busy today, but I'll try to squeeze him in. Send him on down."

A moment later Allen Guthrie, the applicant, arrived at Jack's office and introduced himself. "Come on in, Allen," said Jack. "I'll be right with you after I make a few phone calls." Fifteen minutes later Jack finished the calls and began talking with Allen. Jack was quite impressed. After a few minutes Jack's door opened and a supervisor yelled, "We have a small problem on line 1 and need your help." Jack stood up and said, "Excuse me a minute, Allen." Ten minutes later Jack returned, and the conversation continued for ten more minutes before a series of phone calls again interrupted the pair.

The same pattern of interruptions continued for the next hour. Finally, Allen looked at his watch and said, "I'm sorry, Mr. Stephens, but I have to pick up my wife."

Sure thing, Allen," Jack said as the phone rang again. "Call me later today."

Questions

1. What specific policies should a company follow to avoid interviews like this one?
2. Explain why Jack, not Pete, should make the selection decision.

HRM Incident 2

But I Didn't Mean To!

David Corbello, the office manager of the *Daily Gazette*, a Midwestern newspaper, was flabbergasted as he spoke with the HR manager, Amanda Dervis. He had just discovered that he was the target of a lawsuit filed by an applicant who had not been selected. "All I did was make friendly inquiries about her children. She seemed quite receptive about talking about them. She was real proud of her family. She even told me about every aspect of the difficult divorce she had just gone through. She seemed to want to talk so I let her. I thought I was merely breaking the ice and setting the tone for an effective dialogue. I thought nothing of it when she told me that she needed a day-care facility when she went to work. A year later she claims to have been the victim of sexual discrimination because she believes that a man would not have been asked questions about his children. There's nothing to this lawsuit, is there, Amanda?"

Question

1. How should Amanda respond to David's question?

Human Resource Management Skills

Chapter 6: Selection

A Skills Module entitled *Selection* is presented to provide additional insight into topics in this chapter. Sections within the module focus on selection of qualified employees in terms of job and organizational fit; initial, substantive, and final stages of evaluation in the selection process and types of techniques used at each stage such as use of application forms at the initial stage, ability and job knowledge tests at the substantive stage, and last interview at the final stage; reliability and types of validity; legal compliance; and interview techniques.

Several selection scenarios are presented to give students realistic experience in dealing with the topic.

A test is provided at the end of the module to determine mastery of the material included in the Skills Module. Also, directions are given for assignments that can be used in class or assigned as homework?

Take it to the Net

We invite you to visit the Mondy homepage on the Prentice Hall Web site at

www.prenhall.com/mondy

for updated information, Web-based exercises, and links to other HR-related sites.

Notes

1. Kate Link, "Security at the Forefront: Focus on Employment Screening," *Women in Business* 54 (May/June 2002): 38.
2. Merry Mayer, "Background Checks in Focus," *HRMagazine* 47 (January 2002): 59–62.
3. Robert McGarvey, "Lies, Damned Lies and Resumes," *Electronic Business* (April 15, 2003): 17.
4. Megan Santosus, "Loyalty, Shmoyalty," *CIO* (April 15, 2002): 40.
5. Sara Fisher Gale, "Three Companies Cut Turnover with Tests," *Workforce* 81 (April 2002): 66.
6. Andrea C. Poe, "Selection Savvy," *HRMagazine* 47 (April 2002): 77.
7. Claudio Fernandez-Araoz, "Hiring without Firing," *Harvard Business Review* 77 (July 1999): 108.
8. Bill Leonard, "Our Horizons Are Limitless," *HRMagazine* 45 (January 2000): 44–49.
9. Katrina Brooker, "Can Anyone Replace Herb?" *Fortune* (April 17, 2000): 192.
10. Ken Dubrowski, "What Employers Can and Cannot Ask," *HR Focus* 72 (June 1995): 3.
11. Donald L. Caruth and Gail D. Handlogten, *Staffing the Contemporary Organization* (Westport, CT: Praeger Publishers, 1997): 90.
12. "The High-Tech Resume," *St. Louis Post-Dispatch* (August 9, 2002): B8.
13. Dina Berta, "Industry Increases Applicant Screening Amid Labor Surplus, Security Concerns," *Nation's Restaurant News* (February 25, 2002): 18.
14. Dina Berta, "Chains Tap Psychological Profiling to Trim HR Turnover," *Nation's Restaurant News* (September 30, 2002): 1.
15. Bureau of Labor Statistics, http://stats.bls.gov/, February 8, 2004.
16. "Virtual Job Interviews Gain Popularity: Who's Applying on Videotape—or Live, via Webcam? Only a Handful of Job Seekers, for Now. But Signs Show That May Change," *The Telegram* (January 5, 2001): A9.
17. Ibid.
18. Igor Kotlyar and Kim Ades, "Don't Overlook Recruiting Tools," *HRMagazine* 47 (May 2002): 98.
19. Gale, "Three Companies Cut Turnover with Tests," 66–69.
20. Michael Mercer, "5 Overlooked Ways to Hire Winners," *Manage* (January 1, 2002): 16.
21. Gilbert Nicholson, "Screen and Glean," *Workforce* 79 (October 2000): 70–72.
22. Gale, " Three Companies Cut Turnover with Tests."
23. Kathryn Tyler, "Put Applicants' Skills to the Test," Supplement, *HRMagazine* 45 (January 2000): 74–75.
24. "Tests and the Law," *Workforce* 79 (October 2000): 73.
25. Gillian Flynn, "A Legal Examination of Testing," *Workforce* 92 (June 2002): 92.
26. Bennie L. Garcia, Malcolm G. Meador, Jr., and Brian Kleiner, "How to Hire the Right Person the First Time," *Nonprofit World* 21 (March/April 2003): 9.
27. James Kelly, "Testing Times," *Chemistry & Industry* (July 16, 2001): 443–444.
28. Kotlyar and Ades, "Don't Overlook Recruiting Tools."
29. Barbara Ehrenreich, "What Are They Probing For?" *Time* (June 4, 2001): 86.
30. Joan Axelrod-Contrada, "Personality Assessments' Value Draws Some Debate," *Boston Globe* (October 20, 2002): 10.
31. Steve Bates, "Personality Counts," *HRMagazine* 47 (February 2002): 30.
32. Thiagarajan Srinivasan, Leh-Cheng Hou, Niko Cain, Amity Perry et al., "Hire the Best, but Hire with Care," *Nonprofit World* 20 (November/December 2002): 9.
33. Janet Forgrieve, "Small Firms Aided in Drug War," *Tampa Tribune* (January 10, 2000): 8.
34. "Synergize' Your Organization with Team Fit Assessment: PsychTests.com Introduces New Team Roles Test," *Internet Wire* (October 1, 2002): 1.
35. Bill Current, "New Solutions for Ensuring a Drug-Free Workplace," *Occupational Health & Safety* 71 (April 2002): 34.
36. Ken Kunsman, "Oral Fluid Testing Arrives," *Occupational Health & Safety* 69 (April 2000): 28–34.
37. William Atkinson, "The Liability of Employee Drug Testing," *Risk Management* 49 (September 2002): 40.
38. Kunsman, "Oral Fluid Testing Arrives."
39. Ibid.
40. Peter Carlson, "Foiling Drug Tests Has Become His Business," *Minneapolis Star Tribune* (September 3, 1999): 11A.
41. Dana Hawkins, "Tests on Trial," *U.S. News & World Report* (August 12, 2002): 46.
42. Lisa Frederiksen Bohannon, "Employment Testing: Be Prepared," *Career World* 29 (January 2001): 12.

43. Lisa Bee, "Beware the EPL Perils of Drug Testing," *National Underwriter* (Property & Casualty/Risk & Benefits Management Edition) (May 20, 2002): 19.
44. Jane H. Philbrick, Barbara D. Bart, and Marcia E. Hass, "Pre-Employment Screening: A Decade of Change," *American Business Review* 17 (June 1999): 75.
45. Atkinson, "The Liability of Employee Drug Testing."
46. Lena Chow, "The New Challenges of Personalized Medicine," *Medical Marketing and Media* 38 (March 2003): 68.
47. Genetic Breakthrough May Open Door to New Workplace Bias Worries," *CCH NetNews*: Human Resources Management (July 24, 2000): 1.File:// C:\Program Files\Qualcomm\EudoraPro\Attach\HRMNNO724.htm
48. Genetic Tests by Employers Should Be Banned," *The Michigan Daily*, http://www.pub.umich.edu/daily/1999/jul/07-06-99/edit/edit2.html, April 30, 2000.
49. Steve Bates, "Science Friction," *HRMagazine* 46 (July 2001): 34.
50. Richard R. Nelson, "State Labor Legislation Enacted in 2002," *Monthly Labor Review* (January 1, 2003): 3.
51. Laura Meckler, "Genetic Discrimination Ban Advances," *AP Online* (May 21, 2003).
52. "Executive Order to Prohibit Discrimination in Federal Employment Based on Genetic Information," *Regulatory Intelligence Data, Industry Group* (February 8, 2000): 1.
53. Bill Leonard, "Reading Employees," *HRMagazine* 44 (April 1999): 67–73.
54. Ibid.
55. Steven L. Thomas and Steve Vaught, "The Write Stuff: What the Evidence Says About Using Handwriting Analysis in Hiring," *Advanced Management Journal* 66 (Autumn 2001): 31–35.
56. Judi Brownell, "Applied Research in Managerial Communication: The Critical Link Between Knowledge and Practice," *Cornell Hotel and Restaurant Administration Quarterly* 44 (April 2003): 39.
57. Michael Zwell and James L. Lubawski, "Hiring the Right Management Team," *Trustee* 53 (February 2000): 24.
58. Martin G. Enterlin, "Are You Asking Applicants the Right Questions?" *Security Management* 46 (October 2002): 134.
59. Bob Weinstein, "Acing Interviews Takes More than Technical Know-How," *Minneapolis Star Tribune* (July 18, 1999): 01J.
60. Al Senter, "Recruiting to Stop the Revolving Door," *Management Today* (February 1999): 80.
61. Bill Carpitella, "Interviewing 101: Listen for Organizational Fit," *Professional Builder* 66 (December 2001): 30.
62. Olivia Crosby, "Employment Interviewing," *Occupational Outlook Quarterly* 44 (Summer 2000): 14.
63. Max Messmer, "Interviewing for a Senior Management Position," *Strategic Finance Magazine* 83 (May 2002): 15.
64. Kim Clark, "Gimme, Gimme, Gimme," *U.S News & World Report* (November 1, 1999): 88.
65. Andrew P. Chastain, "Stand Out! Preparing for Interviewing Success," *Healthcare Financial Management* 56 (May 2002): 96–98.
66. Allen I. Huffcutt, Jeff A. Weekley, and Willi H. Wiesner, "Comparison of Situational and Behavior Description Interview Questions for Higher-Level Positions," *Personnel Psychology* 54 (Autumn 2001): 619.
67. Judith Trotsky, "Oh, Will You Behave?" *Computerworld* (January 8, 2001): 42.
68. Lisa Yoon, "Increasingly, Job Candidates Are Being Asked to Critique Their Own Careers," *CFO.com* (February 27, 2003): 1.
69. "Behavioral Interviewing," Career Services Job Search Preparation, University of Nebraska-Lincoln (April 26, 2003), http://www.unl.edu/careers/prepare/behavioral/ htm.
70. Huffcutt, Weekley, and Wiesner, "Comparison of Situational and Behavior Description Interview Questions for Higher-Level Positions," 619.
71. Alice M. Starcke, "Tailor Interviews to Predict Performance," *HRMagazine* 41 (July 1996): 49.
72. Jay Zack and Mark Van Beusekom, "Making the Right Hire: Behavioral Interviewing," *The Tax Advisor* 27 (September 1996): 570.
73. Arthur H. Bell, "How to Score a Behavior-Based Structured Interview," *Personic, Workforce On Line*, http://www.workforce.com/archive/article/000/48/82.xci?topicname=staffing, April 24, 2000.
74. Ibid.
75. Kitty Winkler and Inez Janger, "You're Hired! Now How Do We Keep You?" *Across the Board* 35 (July/August 1998): 17.
76. Martha Frase-Blunt, "Peering into an Interview," *HRMagazine* 46 (December 2001): 71.
77. Martha Frase-Blunt, "Games Interviewers Play," *HRMagazine* 46 (January 2001): 107–108.
78. Ibid.
79. John P. Wanous, "Tell It Like It Is at Realistic Job Previews," in Kendrith M. Rowland, Manual London, Gerald R. Ferris, and Jay L. Sherman (eds.), *Current Issues in Personnel Management* (Boston: Allyn & Bacon, 1980): 41–50.
80. Mercer, "5 Overlooked Ways to Hire Winners."
81. "Dear Workforce," *Workforce* 82 (February 2003): 56.
82. William Atkinson, "Keeping Violent Employees Out of the Workplace," *Risk Management* 48 (March 2001): 12.
83. Merry Mayer, "Breaking Point," *HRMagazine* 46 (October 2001): 112.
84. Michael Prince, "Violence in the Workplace on the Rise," *Business Insurance* (May 12, 2003): 19.
85. Donald L. Caruth and Gail D. Handlogten, "Common Law Torts: The Latest Employment Lawsuit Nightmare," *Supervision* 63 (November 2002): 3–6.
86. Edward Niam, "Check Before You Hire," *HR Focus* 75 (December 1998): S10.
87. Timothy S. Bland, "Background Checks," *Journal of Property Management* 65 (September/October 2000): 26–31.
88. Martin G. Enterlin, "Are You Asking Applicants the Right Questions?" *Security Management* 46 (October 2002): 134.
89. Jerome R. Stockfisch, "Background Checks Can Be Costly, Incomplete," *Tampa Tribune* (January 11, 2000): 1.
90. Trotsky, "Oh, Will You Behave?"
91. Michele Bitoun Blecher, "Testing Benefits Entrepreneurs: Screening Helps Avoid Costly Bad Hires," *Crain's Chicago Business* (February 12, 2001): SB16.
92. Gillian Flynn, "Hiring Foreign Workers in a Post-9/11 World," *Workforce* 81 (July 2002): 78–79.
93. Ibid.
94. Ibid.
95. Ibid.
96. Brian Grow and Manjeet Kripalani, "A Loophole as Big as a Mainframe: More Companies Are Using L-1 Visas to Bring in Low-Wage Foreign IT Workers—and Replace Americans," *BusinessWeek* (March 10, 2003): 82–83.

PART FOUR

Human Resource Development

CHAPTER OBJECTIVES

After completing this chapter, students should be able to

1. Distinguish between career and job security.
2. Define *training* and *development (T&D)*.
3. Explain the relationship that exists between organization change and T&D.
4. Explain factors influencing T&D.
5. Describe the T&D process and how training and development needs are determined and objectives established.
6. Describe the various T&D methods.
7. Explain the importance of corporate universities and community colleges to training.
8. Describe management development.
9. Define *orientation* and identify its purposes.
10. Identify special training areas.
11. Identify the means by which T&D programs are implemented and evaluated.
12. Describe the training partnerships that exist between business, government, and education.
13. Explain career planning and development.
14. Define *organization development (OD)* and describe various OD techniques.

CHAPTER

Training and Development

HRM IN *Action:*

Job and Career Security

OBJECTIVE

Distinguish between career and job security.

Job security:
Implies security in one job, often with one company.

Career security:
Requires developing marketable skills and expertise that help ensure employment within a range of careers.

The term **job security** implies security in one job, often with one company. Historically, this type of security depended upon an employee doing a good job and keeping his or her nose clean.

Increased competition, largely due to technological advances and a global economy, has changed that model considerably. For many workers, that type of security no longer exists. **Career security** is distinctly different; it requires developing marketable skills and expertise that help ensure employment within a range of careers. Career security results from the ability to perform within a broad range of careers well enough to be marketable in more than one job and to more than one organization.

In an article in *Time* entitled, "What Will Be the 10 Hottest Jobs? . . . and What Jobs Will Disappear?" the primary jobs identified for extinction included stockbrokers, auto dealers, mail carriers, and insurance and real estate agents. The reason given for the predicted demise of these jobs was that the Internet would eliminate the middlemen. Other predictions for ultimate career demise include: telephone linemen (wireless technology will take over), computer data entry personnel (voice recognition technology and scanning devices will eliminate the manual effort), and library researchers.[1] The researcher of yesterday pulled journals and books from the shelves, copied pertinent pages, and turned them over to the investigator. Today, the investigator sits at his or her computer and accesses any library in the world through the Internet. Automation will also affect the types of jobs needed. Grocery stores will not need as many cashiers, because checkout stands will be automated. FedEx and UPS will not need as many workers, because machines will do more sorting. Not as many longshoremen will be needed because machines will determine which packages belong on which trucks.[2]

As jobs disappear and change, workers must strive to constantly add value to their careers. This may appear to be self-serving, but nevertheless, it is a logical and realistic career path.[3] John Humphrey, CEO of executive-training powerhouse Forum Corporation, talks about adding personal value as if it could be stored in a toolbox that workers carry with them each day. According to

Humphrey, "The old {career} ladder was a rigid thing. Now the question is, what skills have you got in your toolbox so that you can carry them anywhere and ply your craft?"[4] An individual's toolbox must be ever expanding and continual personal development is a necessity.[5] In today's environment, many workers view themselves as independent contractors who must constantly improve their skills. The better an employee's qualifications, the greater the opportunities he or she has in the job market.[6] A person must discover what companies need, then develop the necessary skills to meet these needs as defined by the marketplace. Individuals should always be doing something that contributes significant, positive change to the organization. If any vestige of job security exists, this is it. Basically, the primary tie that binds a worker to the company, and vice versa, is mutual success resulting in performance that adds value to the organization.

OBJECTIVE

Define *training* and *development* (T&D).

Human resource development (HRD):
A major HRM function that consists not only of T&D but also individual career planning and development activities and performance appraisal.

Training and development (T&D):
The heart of a continuous effort designed to improve employee competency and organizational performance.

Training:
Activities designed to provide learners with the knowledge and skill needed for their present jobs.

Development:
Learning that goes beyond today's job and has a more long-term focus.

American Society for Training and Development

www.astd.org

This Web site is the homepage for the American Society for Training and Development.

We devoted the first portion of this chapter to the job and career security. Next, we explain the scope of training and development and its relationship to organizational change. Following this, we discuss factors that influence T&D and present the T&D process along with how training needs are determined and objectives established. Then, we look at numerous T&D methods. A discussion of corporate universities and community colleges follows in the next sections. Management development is the next topic. Then orientation and special training areas are described. We next discuss how T&D programs are implemented and evaluated. After that, we cover partnerships created among businesses, government, and education. Career planning and development and organization development are the final topics of this chapter.

Training and Development

Human resource development (HRD) is a major HRM function that consists not only of training and development but also individual career planning and development activities, organization development, and performance appraisal, an activity that emphasizes T&D needs. As we see in this chapter, **training and development (T&D)** is the heart of a continuous effort designed to improve employee competency and organizational performance. Some managers use the terms *training* and *development* interchangeably. However, other sources make the following distinction: **Training** provides learners with the knowledge and skills needed for their present jobs. Showing a worker how to operate a lathe or a supervisor how to schedule daily production are examples of training. On the other hand, **development** involves learning that goes beyond today's job and has a more long-term focus. It prepares employees to keep pace with the organization as it changes and grows. T&D activities have the potential to align a firm's employees with its corporate strategies.

In virtually every market, customers are demanding higher quality, lower costs, and faster cycle times. To meet these requirements, firms must continually improve their overall performance. Rapid advances in technology and improved processes have been important factors in helping businesses meet this challenge. However, the most important competitive advantage for any firm is its workforce—one that must remain competent through continuous T&D efforts. Organizations spend over $50 billion every year on formal T&D programs.[7] To many, this may seem like a tremendous amount of money. However, successful organizations realize that well-structured and significant employee T&D programs correlate strongly with long-term success.[8]

Learning organizations: Firms that recognize the critical importance of continuous performance-related training and development and take appropriate action.

Improved performance, the bottom-line purpose of T&D, is a strategic goal for organizations. Toward this end, a number of forward-thinking firms have become or are striving to become learning organizations. A **learning organization** is a firm that recognizes the critical importance of continuous performance-related T&D and takes appropriate action. Such a firm views training as a strategic investment rather than a budgeted cost. Once undervalued in the corporate world, training programs are now credited with strengthening customer satisfaction, contributing to partnership development, enhancing research and development activities and, finally, reinforcing the bottom line.[9]

Training's potential in influencing productivity, relative to other key factors, was emphasized in a study funded by the U.S. Department of Education with the Bureau of Census. The results were:[10]

- Increasing capital stock by 10 percent increases productivity by 3.2 percent.
- Increasing an individual's work hours by 10 percent increases productivity by 6.0 percent.
- Increasing an individual's educational level by 10 percent increases productivity by 8.6 percent.

It is important to note that *formal* training refers to training activity that is planned, structured, and occurs when people are called away from their workstations to participate in it. It does not include informal on-the-job-training or the increasing numbers of *free agent learners* who seek development on their own. You can trace the growth of free agent learning to a decline in formal career planning and development programs in many firms, perhaps due to an economic crunch. We discuss this topic later in the chapter and provide further elaboration in the appendix to this chapter.

One survey found that a majority of U.S. firms plan to increase their funding for workforce development. What accounts for the increased interest? In its annual coverage of the "100 Best Companies to Work for in America," *Fortune* magazine noted that extensive and ongoing training and development is second only to stock options as a primary means of attracting and retaining talented workers. In a survey of information technology workers, more than 80 percent of respondents said that receiving feedback, having individual development plans, and having access to nontechnical skills training would make them less likely to leave their companies.[11] On nearly every survey, training ranks in the top three benefits that employees want from their employers and they search for firms that will give them the tools to advance in their professions. Top performing professional/technical employees and those under age 30 tend to put developmental opportunities first on their list of wishes.[12] It is clear that T&D is not merely a nice thing to provide. It is a strategic resource; one that firms must tap to energize their organizations in the twenty-first century.

3 OBJECTIVE

Explain the relationship that exists between organization change and T&D.

Organizational Change and Training and Development

The primary challenge of T&D is to anticipate change and to respond proactively to it. Change involves moving from one condition to another, and it will affect individuals, groups, and entire organizations. All organizations experience change of some sort, and the rate at which change takes place is accelerating. The most prominent changes affecting T&D that were predicted and are actually occurring today in business include the following:

- Changes in organization structure caused by mergers, acquisitions, rapid growth, downsizing, and outsourcing

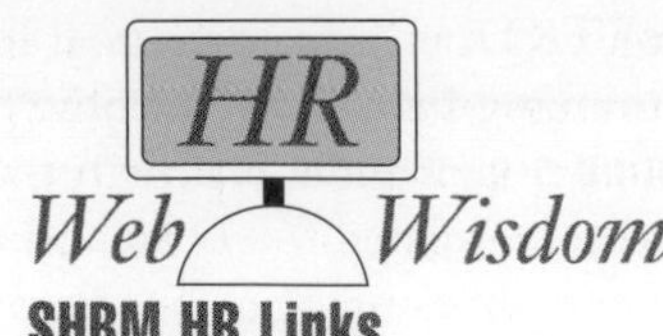

SHRM HR Links

www.shrm.org/hrlinks/default.asp

This SHRM Web site provides training and development information.

- Changes in technology and the need for more highly skilled workers
- Changes in the educational level of employees; some more highly educated, others needing remedial training
- Changes in human resources creating a diverse workforce consisting of many groups
- Competitive pressures necessitating flexible courses and just-in-time and just-what's-needed training
- Increased emphasis on learning organizations and human performance management

Predictions about the future are not always accurate. For example, the prediction that outsourced training would increase has proved to be wrong, at least at this point. As you see in Figure 7-1, outside contractors deliver less than one-third of traditional training programs[13] Nevertheless, managers need to look to the future in order to anticipate changes and to behave proactively.

Change affects every human being. As change agents, managers and staff specialists involved with T&D must understand the difficulties associated with change and the ways to gain acceptance to change.

The impetus for change comes from a belief that the organization and its human resources can be more productive and successful. To implement change successfully, you must proceed systematically. There may be a tendency to feel, "We have always done it this way, so why argue with success?" However, a firm's past success guarantees neither future prosperity nor even survival.

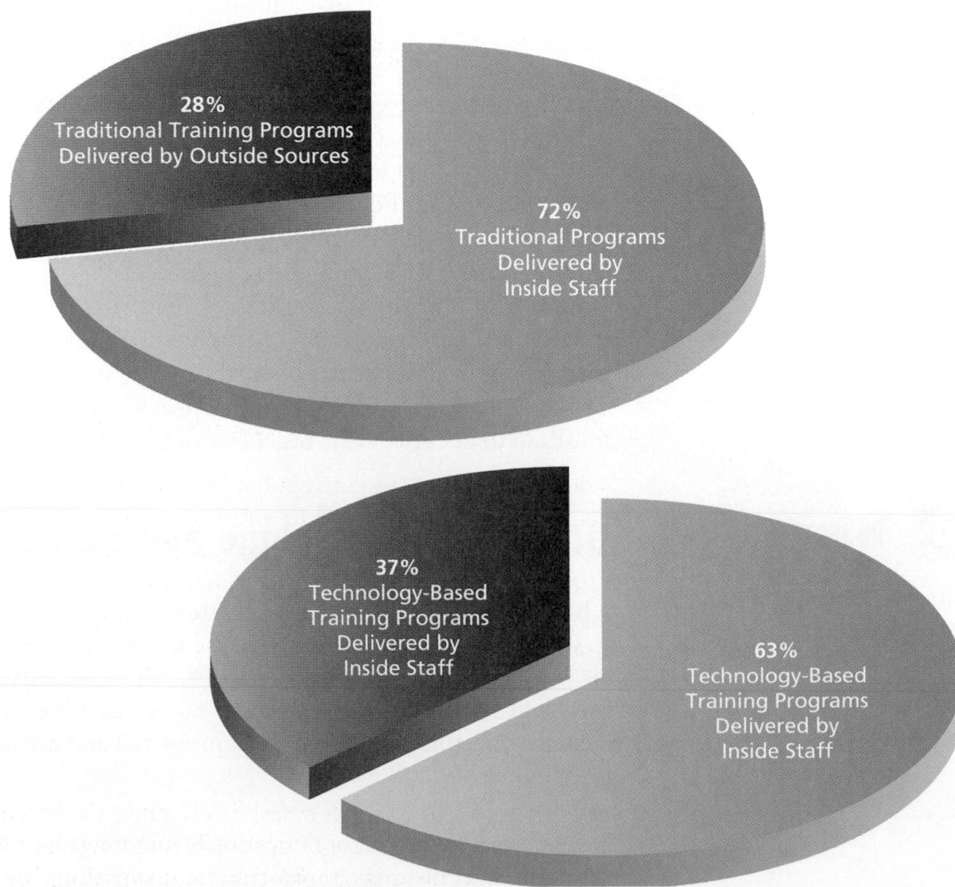

Figure 7-1 Training Delivered by Outside Sources and Inside Staff

Source: Printed with permission from the October 2002 issue of *Training* magazine. Copyright 2002. Bill Communications, Minneapolis, MN. All rights reserved. Not for resale.

Success in overcoming resistance to change is crucial. At times, this may be extremely difficult because it usually requires shifts in attitudes that are not always amenable to change. However, effective implementation of change is possible if management can find a way to reduce and eliminate the resistance to it. Bringing about a change in attitude requires trust and respect between the people attempting to implement the change and the individuals affected by it. This is especially difficult in today's environment with corporate downsizing and scandalous behavior so highly publicized.

Individuals must be aware of the *need* for change and the potential consequences of failing to change. They must have the ability to change and this may require additional training and development.

Being *able* to change is only part of the challenge. A key element in managing the resistance to change is the use of effective, ongoing, and varied communication channels.[14] Employees must also have the *desire* to change. Often, an important factor in this attitudinal transformation is their active involvement in planning the change. This creates a feeling of ownership, and who wants to see their own plans fail?

4 OBJECTIVE

Explain factors influencing T&D.

Factors Influencing Training and Development

Change is obviously one factor that both impacts and is impacted by T&D. Other issues that often determine whether a firm achieves its T&D objectives are discussed next.

Top Management Support

For T&D programs to be successful, leadership support at the top is a requirement. Henry Goldman, managing director of the Goldman-Nelson Group in Huntington Beach, California, can attest to this. His boss, the CEO of Goldman-Nelson, was adamant that the firm's 24 vice presidents understand a new initiative. Goldman asked him to give a short speech at an introductory session so attendees would know that the new program was important to the chief executive. On the day of the program launch, however, the CEO did not show up to give the presentation. The message to the vice presidents was clear; the CEO didn't think the change was important enough to become an active participant. The result: the change never got off the ground.[15] Without top management support, a T&D program will not succeed. The most effective way to achieve success is for executives to take an active part in the training and provide the needed resources.

Commitment from Specialists and Generalists

In addition to top management, all managers, whether they be specialists or generalists, should be committed to and involved in the T&D process. According to one prominent director of corporate management development, "The primary responsibility for training and development lies with line managers, from the president and chairman of the board on down. T&D professionals merely provide the technical expertise."

Technological Advances

Perhaps no factor has influenced T&D more than technology. The computer and the Internet, in particular, are dramatically affecting the conduct of all business functions. As emphasized throughout this chapter, technology has played a huge role in changing

Ethical Dilemma

The Tough Side of Technology

You are the human resource director for a large manufacturing firm that is undergoing major changes. Your firm is in the process of building two technologically advanced plants. When these are completed, the company will close four of its five old plants. It is your job to determine who will stay with the old plant and who will be retrained for the newer plants.

One old plant employee is a 56-year-old production worker who has been with your firm for 10 years. He seems to be a close personal friend of your boss as they are often seen together socially. However, in your opinion, he is not capable of handling the high-tech work required at the new plants, even with additional training. He is not old enough to receive any retirement benefits and there are other qualified workers more senior to him who want to remain at the old plant.

What would you do?

the way knowledge is delivered to employees, and this change is constantly being extended.

Organization Complexity

Flatter organization structures resulting from fewer managerial levels give the appearance of a simpler arrangement of people and tasks. This view, however, is not the case. The tasks of individuals and teams are now both enlarged and enriched. The result is that American workers are spending more time on the job and performing more complex tasks than ever before. Also, the interactions between individuals and groups have become more complicated. The traditional chain of command, which provides a sense of stability at the expense of efficiency, is outdated in many modern organizations.

In recent years, the increasingly rapid changes in technology, products, systems, and methods have had a significant impact on job requirements. Thus, successful employees constantly upgrade their skills and develop an attitude that permits them not only to adapt to change, but also to accept and even seek it. Many organizations have changed dramatically resulting from downsizing, technological innovations, and customer demands for new and better products and services. The result is often that fewer people must accomplish more work at a more complex level. Supervisors and operative employees performing in self-directed teams are taking up much of the slack from dwindling middle-management ranks. All these changes translate into a greater need for T&D.

Learning Styles

The general function of T&D involves knowledge and skill acquisition.[16] Employees at all levels must continually upgrade their expertise in a dramatically changing and increasingly competitive environment.[17]

Although much remains unknown about the learning process, some generalizations stemming from the behavioral sciences have affected the way firms conduct training. Some examples follow:

- Learners progress in an area of learning only as far as they need to, in order to achieve their purposes. Research indicates that unless there is relevance, meaning, and emotion attached to the material taught, the learner will not learn.[18]

- The best time to learn is when the learning can be useful.
- Depending on the type of training, a wise move may be to space out the training sessions.
- Computer technology, the Internet, and intranets have made these approaches economically feasible to a degree never before possible. The ability to deliver knowledge to employees on an as-needed basis, anywhere on the globe, and at a pace consistent with their learning styles, greatly enhances the value of T&D.

Research on student learning styles indicates that most college students have a practical orientation to learning, with a preference for concrete learning activities, rather than a theoretical orientation toward learning that is abstract. Active modes of teaching and learning appear to be more effective than the passive modes of learning most familiar to many instructors and students. Active learning is based on the assumption that students learn best by doing. Active learning situations provide students with the opportunity not only to apply and practice what they have learned, but also to see the results of their practice, determine if they really understood what they did, and gain insight for subsequent application.[19]

Steven Covey, author of *The Seven Habits of Highly Effective People*, suggests that organizations create a culture where every learner becomes a teacher and every teacher becomes a learner. The firm supplies not only individual knowledge but also creates institutional knowledge so that when an employee leaves the organization, another individual still possesses the same knowledge.[20]

Other Human Resource Functions

Successful accomplishment of other human resource functions can also have a crucial impact on T&D. For instance, if recruitment and selection efforts attract only marginally qualified workers, a firm will need extensive T&D programs. A firm's compensation package may also influence T&D efforts. Organizations with competitive pay systems or progressive health and safety programs will find it easier to attract workers who are capable of hitting the ground running, and to retain employees who require less training.

Describe the T&D process and how training and development needs are determined and objectives established.

Just-in-time training: Training provided anytime, anywhere in the world and just when it is needed.

The Training and Development Process

Major adjustments in the external and internal environments necessitate corporate change. You can see the general T&D process that anticipates or responds to change in Figure 7-2. Once the need for change is recognized and the factors that influence T&D are considered, the process of determining T&D needs begins. Essentially, two questions need answers: "What are our training needs?" and "What do we want to accomplish through our T&D efforts?" The objectives might be quite narrow if limited to the supervisory ability of a manager, or they might be broad enough to include improving the management skills of all first-line supervisors.

In exemplary organizations, there is a close link between the firm's strategic mission and the objectives of the T&D program. Review and periodic updating of these objectives is necessary to ensure that they support the changing strategic needs of the organization. After setting the T&D objectives, management can determine the appropriate methods for accomplishing them. Various methods and media are available to implement T&D programs. Naturally, management must continuously evaluate T&D to ensure its value in achieving organizational objectives.

Training Information

www.lir.msu.edu/hotlinks/hr.htm

This Web site provides links to various training information sites.

Global competition has dramatically increased the need for efficiency. One way this impacts T&D is the need for training on a timely basis. **Just-in-time training** is training provided anytime, anywhere in the world and just when it is needed. In addition, there is a need to relate training more closely to organizational goals and specific

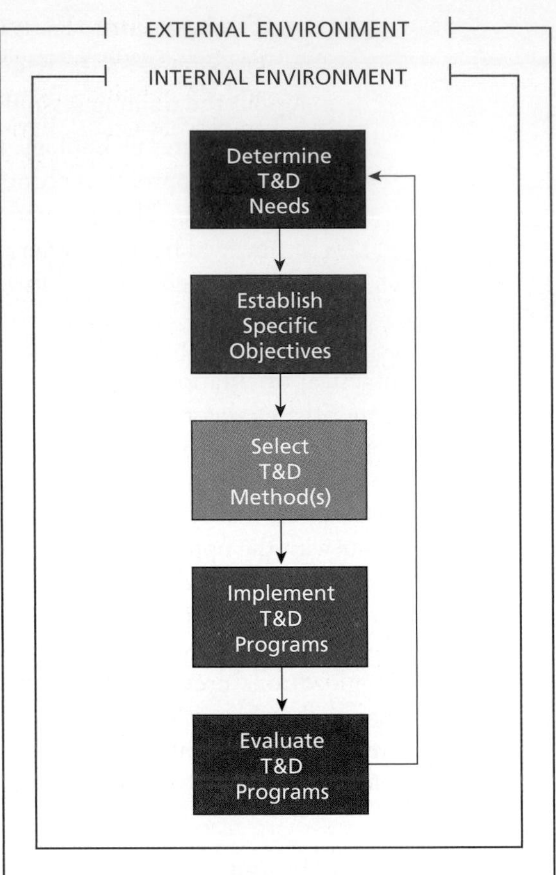

Figure 7-2 The Training and Development (T&D) Process

needs. Recognizing that T&D must be a nonstop process, firms must provide training initiatives that address several critical requirements:

- To guide individual employees in planning and managing their careers
- To help managers coach and mentor employees
- To help managers and employees deal with change

Some say change is the only constant in our lives and is the force that brings about the need for T&D. Determining T&D needs is discussed next.

Determining Training and Development Needs

The first step in the T&D process is to determine specific T&D needs. In today's highly competitive business environment, undertaking programs simply because other firms are doing it is asking for trouble. A systematic approach to addressing bona fide needs must be undertaken.

Training and development needs may be determined by conducting analyses on several levels.

- *Organizational analysis:* From an *overall organizational* perspective, the firm's strategic mission, goals, and corporate plans are studied, along with the results of human resource planning.
- *Task analysis:* The next level of analysis focuses on the *tasks* required to achieve the firm's purposes. Job descriptions are important data sources for this analysis level.

- *Person analysis:* Determining *individual training needs* is the final level. The relevant questions are, "Who needs to be trained?" and "What kind of knowledge, skills and abilities (KSAs) do employees need?" Performance appraisals and interviews or surveys of supervisors and job incumbents are helpful at this level.

Sky Foster, manager for training and associate development for South Carolina–based BMW, states, "We are now training for need, as opposed to rolling out a number of courses. First, it was a check-off list for many of the courses, but now they have more impact and meaning. We specifically ask, 'What knowledge do you want your people to have? What skills do they need? What do they need to do differently from what they're doing today?' We ask more pointed questions and find out exactly what job knowledge and skills the person must have to perform."[21]

Establishing Training and Development Objectives

Training and Development must have clear and concise objectives. Without them, designing meaningful T&D programs would not be possible. Worthwhile evaluation of a program's effectiveness would also be difficult at best. Consider these purposes and objectives for a training program involving employment compliance:

Training Area: Employment Compliance

Purpose. To provide the supervisor with

1. Knowledge and value of consistent human resource practices
2. The intent of EEO legal requirements
3. The skills to apply them

Objectives. To be able to

1. Cite the supervisory areas affected by employment laws on discrimination
2. Identify acceptable and unacceptable actions
3. State how to get help on equal employment opportunity matters
4. Describe why we have discipline and grievance procedures
5. Describe our discipline and grievance procedures, including who is covered

As you see, the *purpose* is established first. The specific *learning objectives* that follow leave little doubt about what the training should accomplish. With these objectives, managers can determine whether training has been effective. For instance, in the example above, a trainee either can or cannot state how to get help on equal employment opportunity matters.

Describe the various T & D methods.

Training and Development Methods

When a person is working in a garden, some tools are more helpful in performing certain tasks than others. The same logic applies when considering various T&D methods. In some cases, it is not feasible to learn while at the same time performing jobs.

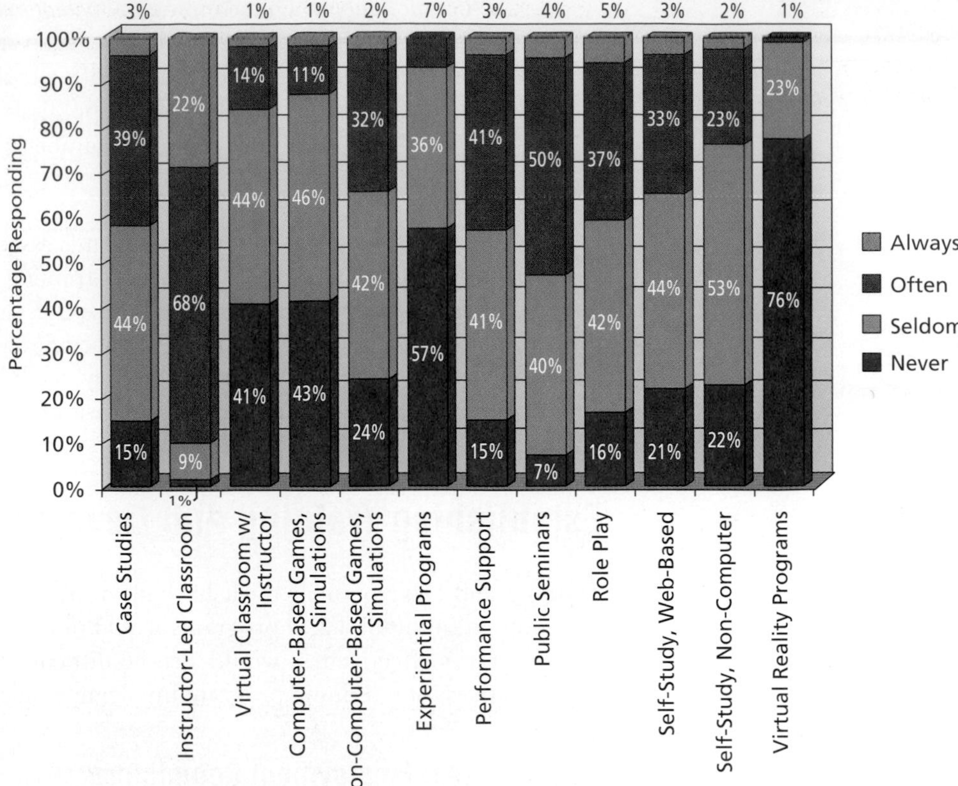

Figure 7-3 Frequency in Which Instructional Methods Are Used
Source: Printed with permission from the October 2002 issue of *Training* magazine. Copyright 2002. Bill Communications, Minneapolis, MN. All rights reserved. Not for resale.

Although an increasing amount of training takes place on the job at the time the employee needs the training, many T&D programs occur away from the work setting. Regardless of whether programs are in-house or are outsourced, firms utilize a number of methods for imparting knowledge and skills to managers and operative employees. We discuss these methods next.

Classroom Programs

Classroom programs continue to be effective for many types of employee training and may incorporate some of the other methods discussed in this section. As you see in Figure 7-3, instructor-led training in the classroom is, by far, the most popular training method.[22]

One advantage of classroom programs is that the instructor may convey a great deal of information in a relatively short time. The effectiveness of classroom programs improves when groups are small enough to permit discussion, and when the instructor is able to capture the imagination of the class and utilize multimedia in an appropriate manner.

Mentoring and Coaching

Mentoring:
An approach to advising, coaching, and nurturing, for creating a practical relationship to enhance individual career, personal, and professional growth and development.

Because the purposes of mentoring and coaching are similar in concept and the terms are often used interchangeably in the literature, we discuss them together. Coaching and mentoring activities, which may occur either formally or informally, are primarily development approaches emphasizing one-to-one learning. **Mentoring** is an approach to advising, coaching, and nurturing, for creating a practical relationship to enhance individual career, personal, and professional growth and development.[23] It focuses on skills to develop protégés to perform to their highest potential, leading to career advancement.[24] Mentors may be anywhere in the organization or even in another

Coaching:
Often considered a responsibility of the immediate boss and provides assistance much the same as a mentor.

firm. **Coaching**, often considered a responsibility of the immediate boss, provides assistance much as a mentor. The coach has greater experience or expertise than the protégé and is in the position to offer wise advice.

Prevalence of Mentoring/Coaching. The mentoring/coaching relationship may be formal or may develop on an informal basis, and studies indicate that almost 85 percent of employees believe they receive formal or informal mentoring. Between 25 and 40 percent of *Fortune* 500 companies provide executive coaches for their employees.[25] AT&T, IBM, and Kodak are among large firms that believe in coaching, but according to an SHRM/SHRM Foundation survey, formal mentoring programs declined from 41 percent in 2001 to 28 percent in 2003.[26] While some companies have become too lean to provide inside coaches, individual managers have independently sought out their own.

Mentoring/Coaching for Women and Minorities. How important is it for a manager to have a mentor? Some believe that having a mentor is essential to *make it to the top*, and the lack of one may explain the difficulty women and minorities have encountered with the glass ceiling. For various reasons, mentors tend to seek out their mirror images. Since women and minorities are not equally represented at the firm's top levels, they are often left without a mentor. Studies also show that women who are mentored, particularly by other women, are more likely to enhance and expand career skills, advance in their careers, receive higher salaries, and enjoy their work more.[27] The main point is that women and minorities need to have advantages provided by mentors to effectively use their talents and realize their potential, not only for their personal benefit but to assist their firms.[28]

Specific Roles. Depending on their organizational relationship, mentors may perform various roles: they provide coaching, sponsor advancement, provide challenging assignments, protect employees from adverse forces, and encourage positive visibility. They also offer personal support, friendship, acceptance, counseling, and role modeling. Mentoring has additional advantages for new hires. A study sponsored by Deloitte & Touche found that Generation Xers were entrepreneurial, hardworking, confident, and committed. However, they were less loyal to their employers than their predecessors. What makes a difference for them? The study found that it was mentoring.[29]

Potential Problems. Although mentoring has many obvious advantages, there are two reasons why the process is not foolproof. One reason is the mentor; the other is the protégé. Some managers do not have the temperament to become a mentor or coach. The role imposes additional work, and some literally have no time. Others just do not want to be bothered. On the other side, some new hires are argumentative or uninterested. Even if both parties are generally willing, there may be a personality conflict. Ultimately, the proper pairing of individuals in a mentoring/protégé relationship is critical to its success.

Reverse Mentoring. Today's coaches are sometimes different from those of the past because of a vastly changed environment that has led to reverse mentoring. There are people in organizations approaching retirement who do not want to retire, and who have tremendous knowledge that should not go to waste. Then, we have young people who know things others do not know and who are anxious to expand their horizons.[30] The existence of these two diverse, but potentially mutually helpful populations, has led to reverse mentoring. **Reverse mentoring** is a process where the older employees learn from the younger ones. General Electric's reverse mentoring program was so impressive that, in early 2000, the program grew to include the top 3,000 managers in the company. According to CEO Welch, reverse mentoring is a great way to turn an organization upside down. GE even recruited a "mentor" for the board; Scott McNealy, youthful CEO of Sun Microsystems.[31]

Reverse mentoring:
A process where the older employees learn from the younger employees.

According to a recent study, 41 percent of respondents use reverse mentoring to spread technical expertise and 26 percent rely on younger staff members to help executives gain a more youthful perspective.[32] Benefits can stem from either group. It seems reasonable that "new economy" managers and "old economy" managers can learn from each other. A classic example of this arrangement is Microsoft's CEO Bill Gates, who regularly consults business guru Warren Buffett for advice.[33]

Case Study

Case study:
A training method in which trainees are expected to study the information provided in the case and make decisions based on it.

The **case study** is a training method in which trainees study the information provided in the case and make decisions based on it. If an actual company is involved, the student would be expected to research the firm to gain a better appreciation of its financial condition and environment. Often, the case study method occurs in the classroom with an instructor who serves as a facilitator.

Videotapes

Behavior modeling:
A training method that utilizes videotapes to illustrate effective interpersonal skills and the ways managers function in various situations.

The use of videotapes continues to be a popular training method. This method may be especially appealing to small businesses that cannot afford more expensive approaches. In addition, videotapes provide the flexibility desired by any firm. Behavior modeling, long a successful training technique provides an illustration of the use of videotapes. **Behavior modeling** utilizes videotapes to illustrate interpersonal skills and shows how managers function in various situations. Behavior modeling has been used to train supervisors in such tasks as conducting performance appraisal reviews, correcting unacceptable performance, delegating work, improving safety habits, handling discrimination complaints, overcoming resistance to change, orienting new employees, and mediating individuals or groups in conflict.

Role Playing

Role playing:
A training method in which participants are required to respond to specific problems they may actually encounter in their jobs.

In **role playing,** participants are required to respond to specific problems they may encounter in their jobs. Rather than hearing an instructor talk about how to handle a problem or discussing it, they learn by doing. Role playing is often used to teach such skills as interviewing, grievance handling, conducting performance appraisal reviews, team problem solving, effective communication, and leadership style analysis.

Modern Apprenticeships

www.realworkrealpay.info/lsc/default

This Web site is the homepage for Modern Apprenticeships.

Apprenticeship Training

Apprenticeship training:
A combination of classroom instruction and on-the-job training.

Apprenticeship training combines classroom instruction with on-the-job training. Such training is common with craft jobs, such as those of plumber, barber, carpenter, machinist, and printer. While in training, the employee earns less than the master craftsperson who is the instructor. Apprenticeship programs last from two to five years, with four years being the average length.[34]

The days of narrow training just for job skills are past for some crafts. In today's workplace, communication and interpersonal relationships are essential. For example, a Pennsylvania apprenticeship program now requires electrician hopefuls to earn an associate's degree in order to graduate. The program requires academic courses right alongside electrical wiring in a mix of traditional vocational-technical training.[35]

Vestibule Training

Vestibule training:
Training that takes place away from the production area on equipment that closely resembles the actual equipment used on the job.

Vestibule training takes place away from the production area on equipment that closely resembles equipment actually used on the job. For example, a group of lathes may be located in a training center where the trainees receive instruction in their use. A primary advantage of vestibule training is that it removes the employee from the pressure of having to produce while learning. The emphasis is focused on learning the skills required by the job.

Simulations

Simulation:
A training approach that utilizes devices or programs replicating tasks away from the job site.

Simulations are training approaches that utilize devices or programs replicating tasks away from the job site. The devices range from simple paper mock-ups of mechanical devices to computerized simulations of total environments. Training and development specialists may use simulated sales counters, automobiles, and airplanes. Although simulator training may be less valuable than on-the-job training for some purposes, it has certain advantages. A prime example is the training of airline pilots in a simulator; simulated crashes do not cost lives or deplete the firm's fleet of jets.

Simulations also serve to train managers. Consider this scenario:

> *"Be in the boardroom in 10 minutes," reads the e-mail from Senior Vice President Alan Young. The CEO is out on his boat, and a storm has knocked out all communications. Worse, there has been a massive fire in the call center in South America. "We could lose billions," Young says. The board has given senior staff emergency powers. You're a top manager who has been called in to help. What do you do?*[36]

This is the final setting in a new computer-based simulation called Virtual Leader. It represents the newest high-tech training ground for managers.

Business Games

Business games:
Simulations, computer-based or non-computer-based, that attempt to duplicate selected factors in a particular business situation, which the participants manipulate.

Business games are *simulations*, computer-based or non-computer-based, that attempt to duplicate selected factors in a particular business situation, which the participants manipulate. Business games involve two or more hypothetical organizations competing in a given product market. The participants receive roles such as president, controller, or marketing vice president. They make decisions affecting price levels, production volumes, and inventory levels. Often, a computer program manipulates their decisions, with the results simulating those of an actual business situation. Participants are able to see how their decisions affect other groups and vice versa. The best thing about this type of learning is that if a poor decision costs the company $1 million, no one gets the axe, yet the business lesson is learned.

In-Basket Training

In-basket training:
A simulation in which the participant is asked to establish priorities for and then handle a number of business papers such as memoranda, reports, and telephone messages, that would typically cross a manager's desk.

In-basket training is a simulation in which the participant is asked to establish priorities for and then handle a number of business papers or e-mail messages such as memoranda, reports, and telephone messages that would typically cross a manager's desk. The messages, presented in no particular order, call for anything from urgent action to routine handling. The participant is required to act on the information contained in these messages. In this method, the trainee assigns a priority to each particular situation before making any decisions. Assessment centers, discussed in Chapter 6, commonly make use of this training method.

Distance Learning and Videoconferencing

For a number of years, many firms in the United States have used videoconferencing and satellite classrooms for training. This approach to training is interactive and appears to offer the flexibility and spontaneity of a traditional classroom. A great deal of training is beginning to take place using this technology, offering the prospect of increasing the number of trainees and at the same time saving companies money. Global firms in particular can benefit from this technology. With far-flung operations, travel expenses are increasing. Potential terrorist attacks also make this approach more appealing. Distance learning, videoconferencing, and similar technology can increase access to training, ensure consistency of instruction, and reduce the cost of delivering T&D programs.

Computer-Based Training

Computer-based training: A teaching method that takes advantage of the speed, memory, and data manipulation capabilities of the computer for greater flexibility of instruction.

Computer-based training takes advantage of the speed, memory, and data manipulation capabilities of the computer for greater flexibility of instruction. Computer-based training offers several advantages over traditional instructor-led training.[37] A basic benefit is that it is self-paced and individualized. The concept can be repeated as often as needed. Help screens can also be included in the program to give additional explanation for those who need it. In a computer lab, participants can be working on different parts of a program, at varying speeds and in different languages. Computer-based training may also utilize multimedia to enhance learning with audio, animation, graphics, and interactive video.

Virtual Reality

Virtual reality: A unique computer-based approach that permits trainees to view objects from a perspective otherwise impractical or impossible.

Virtual reality is a unique computer-based approach that permits trainees to view objects from a perspective otherwise impractical or impossible. For example, it is not feasible to turn a drill press on its side so a trainee can inspect it from the bottom. A computer easily permits this type of manipulation.

One form of computer-based training involves live synchronous learning in a virtual classroom. This form enables students to do anything they could do in a classroom. They can share a whiteboard, get class feedback, view video material, and so forth. This cyberspace classroom is becoming quite popular.[38]

There are several ways to deliver computer training. The most common delivery methods appear in Figure 7-4. Note that a self-paced Web course is currently the most popular delivery method, accounting for 48 percent of computer training. Use of CD-ROM/DVD/Diskette is next in popularity at 41 percent.[39] We discuss Web-based computer training next.

E-Learning (Web-Based Training)

E-learning: An umbrella term describing online instruction.

E-learning is an umbrella term describing online instruction. The versatility of online instruction has important implications for T&D since the demand for an educated and empowered workforce is critical in the new economy. An overwhelming advantage of using Web-based training is that it is available anytime, anywhere in the world,

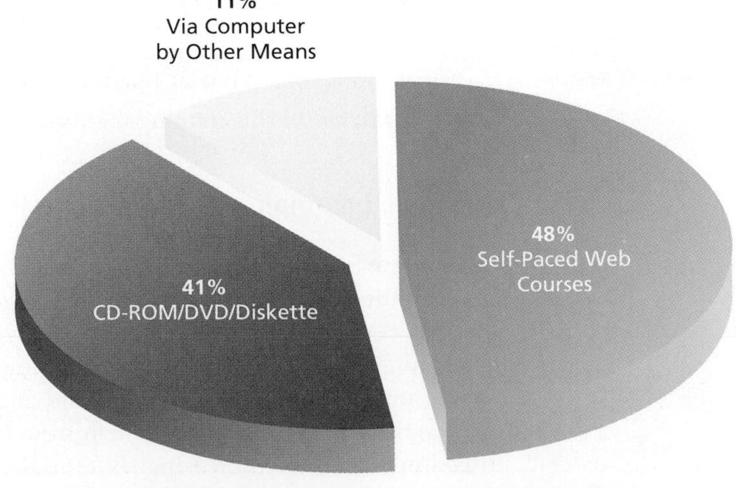

Figure 7-4 How Computer-Delivered Training Breaks Down
Source: Printed with permission from the October 2002 issue of *TRAINING* magazine. Copyright 2002. Bill Communications, Minneapolis, MN. All rights reserved. Not for resale.

and in different languages. Individuals involved in e-learning are no longer constrained by the need to be in a classroom at a specific location and time.[40] Animation, video, and multimedia make presentations vivid and appealing.

In the past two years, about 80 percent of Wachovia Bank's 84,000 employees have taken e-learning courses. Ron Garrow, director of learning strategy and senior VP, says, "We do have key learning centers throughout our footprint, but in this day and time, people need bite-sized chunks of training. They need it when they can get to it."[41]

One way to reduce training costs is for firms to cooperate, as some have done to form LearnShare, a consortium of large, noncompeting manufacturing companies. This group, which includes Owens Corning, General Motors, Motorola, 3M, and three research universities, has combined resources to develop a Web site and acquire the materials for multimedia training. Although the firms are in different types of businesses, a survey indicated that 74 percent of their training needs were the same. For example, diversity training for GM employees should differ little from that needed by Reynolds Metals, Deere & Company, or others in the consortium. As these participants consolidate their resources to take advantage of technology, their consortium can distribute educational materials anywhere on earth almost instantly and with less cost than if each company acted alone.[42]

On-the-Job Training

On-the-job training (OJT): An informal approach to training in which an employee learns job tasks by actually performing them.

The preceding discussions presented T&D methods used primarily away from the workplace. **On-the-job-training (OJT)** is an *informal* approach to training that permits an employee to learn job tasks by actually performing them. It is the most commonly used approach to T&D and in today's fast-paced environment, a firm may have no other choice. The key to this training is to transfer knowledge from a highly skilled and experienced worker to a new employee, while maintaining the productivity of both workers.[43] Individuals may also be more highly motivated to learn because it is clear to them that they are acquiring the knowledge needed to perform their jobs. At

Trends & Innovations

Teaching Through Interactive Satellite Broadcasts and the Web

Rather than fly T&D staff to 7,000 dealerships, General Motors University now uses interactive satellite broadcasts to teach salespeople the best way to highlight features on the new Buick. Six months before rolling out a hot new pickup, GM used the broadcasts to teach mechanics how to repair it; and at one point, 1,400 employees around North America were tuned in. "If we'd had to send everyone to a brick-and-mortar class, we never would have gotten all of it done," says GM learning chief Donnee Ramelli.[44]

Several years ago, Anheuser-Busch implemented what it calls the Wholesaler Integrated Learning (WIL) program to its 700 independently owned distributors and their employees, as well as to the 13 company-owned branch operations and 12 breweries. In this program, employees can access the WIL Web site from any location and take a test that measures their proficiency in areas deemed important for their job description. The test is scored instantly, and the employee sees the gaps between his or her abilities and those required for the position. The system then offers suggestions — classroom training, online courses, books, and on-the-job activities — on how to close those gaps. The plan report is linked to a list of available resources and then to the enrollment system. WIL has grown from reaching 3,500 students to more than 32,000 distributor employees. Currently, more than 20,000 users have completed competency assessments and are working on their assignments.[45]

times, however, the trainee may feel so much pressure to produce that learning is negatively affected. Firms should be selective about who provides on-the-job training. The trainers are often supervisors. However, peer-to-peer communication can provide a very powerful means for training.[46] Regardless of who does the training, that person must have a good work ethic and correctly model the desired behavior.

Job Rotation

Job rotation:
A form of OJT where employees move from one job to another to broaden their experience.

Job rotation is a form of OJT where employees move from one job to another to broaden their experience. Higher-level tasks often require this breadth of knowledge. Rotational training programs help new employees understand a variety of jobs and their interrelationships. Organizations are widely applying entry-level rotational training programs. Streamlined firms have to do more with less so it makes sense to develop employees who can jump in anywhere they are needed. Sherry Zapp's experience illustrates the potential benefits of job rotation:

> *Sherry is a recent graduate of the University of Florida with a double major in finance and management. She attended a university job fair, was interviewed and hired by United Technologies Corporation (UTC). After assignment to a division of Pratt & Whitney, she works on special financial projects. The firm's rotational job program influenced her decision to join UTC. "Coming straight from college, I wasn't exactly sure what to do, not having had a 'real job' before," Zapp says. She continues, "I'm thankful I learned the skill of being able to move on and seek new opportunities without fear."*[47]

Internships

As we mentioned in Chapter 5, an internship program is a recruitment method typically involving students in higher education who divide their time between attending classes and working for an organization. Internships also serve as an effective OJT method, allowing participants to integrate theory learned in the classroom with business practices. As evidence of their current popularity, three out of four students now complete internships before graduation; up from one in 36 in 1980.[48]

OBJECTIVE

Explain the importance of corporate universities and community colleges to training.

Corporate Universities

The corporate training institution differs from many traditional training programs in that its focus is on creating organizational change. It is proactive and strategic rather than reactive and tactical. An estimated 2,000 corporate universities exist in the United States today.[49] This number includes almost half of *Fortune* 500 companies.[50] If this growth rate continues, the roughly 3,700 traditional universities will someday be outnumbered. The best-known corporate universities include those at General Motors, McDonald's, Disney, Motorola, GE, Sears, and Intel. Intel University in Arizona administers programs developed by 73 training groups located worldwide. Intel offers technology courses ranging from using Microsoft Word to training in lithography, one of the stages of computer-chip manufacturing. The university also teaches nontechnical skills such as dealing with conflict and harassment avoidance.[51] In 1997, General Motors founded GM University, which is one of the largest corporate educational programs in the world. The university currently has 15 functional colleges charged with developing curricula tailored to the professional needs and challenges facing GM employees.[52]

Growth in the number of corporate universities may be attributed to their flexibility, which permits students to learn on their own time, and the use of various modes including CD-ROM programs, audio- and videotapes and, of course, the Internet.[53] Also, firms are better able to control the quality of training and to ensure that their employees receive the same messages. The remarkable growth rate of corporate universities clearly illustrates that they have something going for them. However, many public and private colleges and universities are taking similar approaches to training and education. Corporate training programs often partner with colleges and universities or other organizations, such as the American Management Association, to deliver training.

Community Colleges

What do businessmen Ross Perot and Black and Decker Chairman and CEO Nolan Archibald have in common? They are alumni of *community colleges* — publicly funded higher education establishments that provide vocational training and associate degree programs.[54] Some employers, including General Motors, have discovered that community colleges can provide certain types of training better and more cost-effectively than they can.

In 2000, in a report entitled "The Knowledge Net," the American Association of Community Colleges (AACC) argued that community colleges should increase their collaborations with business, industry, and other educational entities as a primary strategy to develop a higher-quality, better-prepared workforce.[55] Apparently, many organizations agree. Rapid technological changes and corporate restructuring have created a new demand by industry for community college training resources. Here are some examples:

- In Phoenix, PepsiCo Inc., has established its own training program with community college help. Its Gatorade factory in suburban Tolleson and a neighboring container manufacturer host an electricity-theory class taught by Maricopa Community College faculty.[56]
- In Cedar Rapids, Iowa, Kirkwood Community College is part of a development consortium known as the Workplace Learning Connection that helps 700 local firms recruit and train workers.[57]
- Connecticut Community Colleges include as clients some of our nation's most prestigious firms: Cigna, Clairol, Eli Lilly, Frito Lay Inc., General Electric, International Paper, Pitney Bowes, Pratt & Whitney, The Travelers, and United Technologies, to name a few.[58]

The federal government has joined industry in an increased interest in community college involvement in educating the national labor force. The Workforce Investment Act (WIA), discussed later in this chapter, dramatically altered the federal system of job training and workforce development. This huge and comprehensive federal law assures the participation of community colleges, as they are a critical factor in the success of this legislation.[59]

8 OBJECTIVE

Describe management development.

Management development: Learning experiences provided by an organization for the purpose of upgrading skills and knowledge required in current and future managerial positions.

Management Development

Management development consists of all learning experiences provided by an organization resulting in an upgrading of skills and knowledge required in current and future managerial positions. While leadership is often depicted as an exciting and glamorous endeavor, there is another side; failure can quickly result in losing one's position. The risks are especially high due to today's rapid changes.[60] This situation magnifies the importance of providing development opportunities for a firm's management group.

A fundamental problem is not the lack of management support or ample financial expenditure. It is the huge disparity between the money spent and the return from that investment, compared to the return possible with effective T&D.[61]

Significance of Development

The number of management candidates is declining. Between 2000 and 2015, there will be 15 percent fewer 35- to 45-year-old employees to prepare for management positions.[62] Yet, a firm's future lies largely in the hands of its managers. This group performs certain functions essential to the organization's survival and prosperity. Managers must make the right choices in most of their decisions; otherwise, the firm will not grow and may even fail. Therefore, it is imperative that managers keep up with the latest developments in their respective fields and, at the same time, manage an ever-changing workforce operating in a dynamic environment. Also note that as managers reach higher levels in the organization, it is not so much their technical skills that they need, but their interpersonal skills and their business knowledge.[63]

Need for Personal Commitment

While development programs provide critical knowledge and skills, the process also requires the individual manager's personal commitment. Development is a choice a person makes, not something an individual can do to someone else. An employee's manager may be able to provide support for development, but he or she can't develop the employee.[64] Taking responsibility for one's own development may be the most important aspect in the process; an approach developed later in this chapter and in its appendix.

Amercian Management Association—KnowledgeNet

www.knowledgenet.com/courselibrary/ama/index.jsp

This Web site provides a means by which the American Management Association's (AMA) courses are identified.

Development Programs: In-House Versus Outsourced

First-line supervisors, middle managers, and executives may all participate in management development programs. These programs are available in-house, by professional organizations, and at colleges and universities. Training and Development specialists often plan and present in-house programs, at times utilizing line managers. Organizations such as the Society for Human Resource Management and the American Management Association conduct conferences and seminars in a number of specialties. Numerous colleges and universities also provide management T&D programs. Colleges and universities may possess expertise not available within business organizations. In these cases, academicians and management practitioners can advantageously present T&D programs jointly. The most frequently mentioned reasons to conduct management training outside the company include these:

- An outside perspective
- New viewpoints
- Exposure to faculty experts and research
- Broader vision

The most frequently mentioned reasons for keeping management training inside the company are the following:

- Training that is more specific to needs
- Lower costs

- Less time
- Consistent, relevant material
- More control of content and faculty
- Development of organizational culture and teamwork

Organizations in the United States focus training efforts on managers and professionals. In fact, more than half their training dollars go for these two types of employees. Training for professionals accounts for 29 percent of the total; training for managers, 27 percent; and sales training, 12 percent.[65]

Executive and Management Development at IBM

IBM conducts formal management development programs for various organizational levels. These programs vary from three-day sessions for recently appointed managers to two-week programs designed for new executives having worldwide responsibilities. Specifically, the firm provides these programs: New Manager Training—U.S. Policy and Practices; New Manager School—IBM Leadership Program; IBM Business Management Institute; and IBM Global Executive Program.

New Manager Training—U.S. Policy and Practices is for newly appointed managers at various locations. This three-day program's purpose is to develop an understanding of IBM's basic management policies, practices, and skills. It focuses on performance management, compensation, diversity, career development, and management of individuals.

New Manager School—IBM Leadership Program is for all individuals appointed to the initial level of management responsibility. The three-and-a-half-day school normally begins within 60 to 90 days after the appointment and takes place at the Central Headquarters Management Development Center in Armonk, New York.

IBM Business Management Institute is an eight-day program held worldwide. It is for individuals newly appointed to responsibility for an organization having significant impact on IBM's success in the marketplace. The program focuses on profitability and customer satisfaction. Case studies and business models focus on actual IBM business problems.

IBM Global Executive Program is for newly named executives with worldwide responsibilities. This two-week program is conducted in New York and La Hulpe, Belgium. The program focuses on building global perspectives, fostering performance and change, and leveraging IBM's capabilities. A significant part of the program involves addressing a strategic business issue, including the presentation of results to the sponsoring senior executive.

OBJECTIVE

Define *orientation* and identify its purposes.

Orientation:
The initial T&D effort for new employees that strives to inform them about the company, the job, and the workgroup.

Orientation

First impressions are often the most lasting. This lesson may apply to new employees' impressions of their employers, and orientation programs give organizations an opportunity to begin the relationship with a good start. **Orientation** is the initial T&D effort for new employees and strives to inform them about the company, the job, and the work group. Dennis Liberson, executive vice president for human resources at Capital One Financial Corporation, says, "We have programs in place to *immediately* show people what the culture is all about and what it's going to take to succeed."[66]

Purposes of Orientation

Orientation formats are unique to each firm. However, some basic purposes include explaining the employment situation (the job, department, and company), company policies and rules, compensation and benefits, corporate culture, team membership, employee development, dealing with change, and socialization.

- *The Employment Situation.* At an early point in time, it is helpful for the new employee to know how his or her job fits into the firm's organizational structure and goals.
- *Company Policies and Rules.* Every job within an organization must be performed within the guidelines and constraints provided by policies and rules. Employees must understand these to ensure a smooth transition to the workplace.
- *Compensation and Benefits.* Employees have a special interest in obtaining information about the reward system. Management normally provides this information during the recruitment and selection process and often reviews it during orientation.
- *Corporate Culture.* The firm's culture reflects, in effect, "how we do things around here." This relates to everything from the way employees dress to the way they talk. Remember our earlier discussion of the importance of *organizational fit* to an employee's success.
- *Team Membership.* A new employee's ability and willingness to work in teams were likely determined before he or she was hired. In orientation, the program may again emphasize the importance of becoming a valued member of the company team.
- *Employee Development.* An individual's employment security is increasingly becoming dependent upon his or her ability to acquire needed knowledge and skills that are constantly changing. Thus, firms should keep employees aware not only of company-sponsored developmental programs but also those available externally.
- *Dealing with Change.* We discussed the significance of change at the beginning of this chapter. Simply put, employees at all levels must learn to deal effectively with change to survive in their jobs. The best way anyone can prepare for change is to continually expand his or her skills.
- *Socialization.* To reduce the anxiety that new employees may experience, the firm should take steps to integrate them into the informal organization. Some organizations have found that employees subjected to socialization programs, including the topics of politics and career management, perform better than those who have not undergone such training.

Responsibility for and Scheduling of Orientation

Although orientation is often the joint responsibility of the training staff and the line supervisor, peers often serve as excellent information agents. There are several reasons for using peers in performing this function. For one thing, they are accessible to newcomers, often more so than the boss. Peers also tend to have a high degree of empathy for new people. In addition, they have the organizational experience and technical expertise to which new employees need access.

Orientation may occupy a new employee's first few days on the job. However, some firms believe that learning is more effective if spread out over time. For example, a company may deliver a program in a system of 20 one-hour sessions over a period of several weeks. Some firms are sensitive to information overload and make information available to employees on an "as needed" basis. For example, a new supervisor may eventually have the responsibility for evaluating his or her subordinates. But, knowledge of how to do this may not be needed for six months. A training segment on performance evaluation may be placed on the Internet or a firm's intranet and be available when the need arises. This approach is consistent with "just-in-time training," discussed earlier.

Orientation at FedEx

Orientation is a common type of formal training in U.S. organizations, and some firms have developed sophisticated approaches. As in other areas, technology has given a big boost to this T&D effort. For example, FedEx uses computer-based training for orienting new employees in a two-hour program that offers detailed information on the corporate culture, benefits, policies, and procedures. It also outlines the company's organizational structure and features a video message from the CEO. Successful orientation speeds up the adaptation process by helping new employees feel comfortable in the organization and by making them more productive on the job.[67]

Additional Benefits of Orientation

Orientation also results in reduced employee turnover and provides other benefits. For example, one survey of 1,400 financial officers resulted in an overwhelming 83 percent of respondents indicating that formal orientation programs are effective in retaining and motivating personnel.[68] Orientation programs may contribute to the success of both employees and organizations.

OBJECTIVE

Identify special training areas.

Special Training Areas

As noted, managers, professionals, and salespersons have historically received the bulk of T&D programs. Of course, many organizations also have extensive programs for supervisors and operative employees. These programs often emphasize specific tasks required to perform given jobs. Other programs may deal with critical areas that surround the job. Included in this category are training involving such areas as diversity, English as a second language, ethics, telecommuting, customer service, conflict resolution, teamwork, empowerment, and remediation.

Diversity

Diversity training: Attempts to develop sensitivity among employees about the unique challenges facing women and minorities and strives to create a more harmonious working environment.

Diversity training attempts to develop sensitivity among employees about the unique challenges facing women and minorities and strives to create a more harmonious working environment. Many firms recognize the significance of a diverse workforce and view diversity training to be essential. Don Showell, senior director of transportation solutions at Ryder Systems, Inc., located in Alpharetta, Georgia, says a key to the success of the company's diversity efforts is that they are based on specific objectives tied to the organization's mission and goals. Respect for diversity becomes a part of the organization's fabric and provides real meaning to, and recognition of, the value of individual differences, whether they are obvious or subtle.[69]

English as a Second Language (ESL)

Training in ESL shows sensitivity to diversity issues and helps firms deal with employees in a way that optimizes personal work relationships.[70] In this spirit, four unrelated Texas restaurants have worked together to create an ESL course that focuses on vocabulary crucial to restaurant settings. It also doubles as a Spanish-language course for English-speakers. Restaurant operators have long known that teaching English to Spanish-speakers can improve customer service and improve an employee's skill and confidence. La Madeleine, Carlson Restaurants Worldwide, Dave & Buster's (based in Dallas), and San Antonio–based Taco Cabana, each with large numbers of Spanish-speaking employees, wanted a uniform, self-taught program based on the vocabulary needed for restaurants. They also wanted something that would allow English-speaking employees to learn Spanish with the same tools. The group used the brain-power of all four companies to create a system that builds an extensive restaurant vocabulary by using flashcards and pictorials. The tools offer words spelled in English and Spanish and spelled phonetically in both languages.[71]

Ethics

In the wake of Enron and other corporate scandals, many firms are emphasizing ethics. By stressing fair play and a respect for law, they intend to develop a corporate culture that rewards ethical behavior. This emphasis has a practical side. Under federal guidelines, companies convicted of crimes are eligible for reduced sentences if they have previously established programs to prevent and detect fraud. Recall from Chapter 2 that the Sarbanes-Oxley Act of 2002 also requires companies to adopt ethics programs.[72]

Olin Corporation, based in Norwalk, Connecticut, decided to move to a *values-based* ethics program. The focus of this program is not to merely obey the rules but to "do what's right." This program reflects two key areas: training and communication. Olin's CEO is actively engaged in the program but hourly people are as well. Audio clips featuring hourly employees describing what Olin's values mean to them have gone over well with other employees.[73]

There are alternatives for firms that decide not to develop their own ethics programs. For example, LRN, the Legal Knowledge Company, based in Los Angeles, offers over 100 interactive courses on everything from money laundering to conflicts of interest. It says it has contracts to provide Internet-based training to about 4 million employees stationed worldwide, including seven-figure deals with Ford Motor Company and Johnson & Johnson, among others.[74]

Telecommuter

Both telecommuters and their supervisors need *telecommuter training*. Telecommuter training should emphasize effective communication strategies that permit managers and employees to define job responsibilities and set goals and job expectations.[75] The primary challenge for the telecommuter is to be able to work without direct supervision; the challenge for the supervisor is to make a shift from *activity-based management* to *results-based management*.[76] This is a difficult transition for the many managers who feel that workers cannot be productive unless they are at their workplace.

Customer Service

Customer service training teaches employees the skills needed to meet and exceed customer expectations. Communication skills, including listening skills, and the recognition of diverse customer needs and requirements receive special emphasis.

Conflict Resolution

Conflict within an organization can be valuable and often aids in growth and change. But, it is critical that the conflict be recognized, managed, and transformed into a positive force for advancing the firm's goals.[77] *Conflict resolution training* focuses on developing the communication skills needed to resolve gridlock in relationships. While a degree of conflict can be constructive when it improves the quality of decisions and stimulates creativity, uncontrolled conflict is eventually destructive.

Teamwork

Teamwork training strives to teach employees how to work in groups that often have considerable authority in making decisions. This type of training is essential because our culture has historically nurtured individual accomplishments, yet organizations are increasingly using teams. We discuss team building as an organizational development intervention later in this chapter.

Empowerment

Empowerment training teaches employees and teams how to make decisions and accept responsibility for results. It often accompanies teamwork training because some firms have delegated considerable authority to teams. For example, work teams may actually hire employees for their group, determine pay increases, and plan work schedules.

Remedial

Remedial training focuses on foundation skills such as basic literacy and mathematics skills. A large percentage of individuals are entering the workforce without the requisite skills to handle the jobs that technology has produced. David Kearns, former CEO of Xerox, believes that the failure of public school education costs industry at least $50 billion a year. In addition to problems within our public school systems, a great deal of learning takes place, or should take place, in the home. Breakdowns in American family units have also contributed to the problem. Regardless of the causes, it is estimated that as many as one-third of new employees require remedial training after high school to become qualified for work.[78]

11 OBJECTIVE

Identify the means by which T&D programs are implemented and evaluated.

Implementing Training and Development Programs

A perfectly conceived training program can fail if management cannot convince the participants of its merits. Participants must believe that the program has value and will help them achieve their personal and professional goals. A long string of successful programs certainly enhances the credibility of T&D.

Implementing traditional T&D programs is often difficult. One reason is that managers are typically action oriented and feel that they are too busy for T&D. According to one management development executive, "Most busy executives are too involved chopping down the proverbial tree to stop for the purpose of sharpening their axes." Another difficulty in program implementation is that qualified trainers must be available. In addition to possessing communication skills, the trainers must know the company's philosophy, its objectives, its formal and informal organization, and the goals of the training program. Training and development requires more creativity than perhaps any other human resource function.

Implementing training programs presents unique problems. Training implies change, which employees may vigorously resist. Participant feedback is vital at this stage because there are often bugs in new programs. It may be difficult to schedule the training around present work requirements. Unless the employee is new to the firm, he or she undoubtedly has specific full-time duties to perform.

Another difficulty in implementing T&D programs is record keeping. It is important to maintain training records including how well employees perform during training and on the job. This information is important in terms of measuring program effectiveness and charting the employees' progress in the company. The problems mentioned have solutions; however, the more effectively and efficiently they are resolved, the better the chances for success.

Evaluating Training and Development

Although corporate America spends billions of dollars a year on employee training, there is no clear consensus within the training community on how to determine its value. What may be missing in programs is a clearly stated business objective for the outcome. It is impossible to evaluate the effectiveness of the activity without clear objectives.[79] And, if you do not collect accurate data and feedback on the effectiveness of your training programs, you just may be wasting money.[80]

Obviously, T&D can enhance its integrity within a firm if it shows tangible benefits to the organization. Thus, the T&D department must document its efforts and demonstrate that it provides a valuable service. Organizations have taken several approaches to evaluate the worth of specific programs. The Kirkpatrick model for training evaluation is widely used in learning environments. The levels in this model are: (1) participants' opinions, (2) extent of learning, (3) behavioral change (transfer of training to the job), and (4) accomplishment of T&D objectives (impact on performance).[81]

Participants' Opinions

Evaluating a T&D program by asking the participants' opinions of it is an approach that provides a response and suggestions for improvements. You cannot always rely on such responses, however. The training may have taken place in an exotic location with time for golfing and other fun activities, and the overall experience may bias some reports. Nevertheless, this approach is good way to obtain feedback and to get it quickly and inexpensively. Perhaps this explains why almost 80 percent of firms in one survey indicated they use this approach.[82]

Extent of Learning

Some organizations administer tests to determine what the participants in a T&D program have learned. The pre-test–post-test control group design is one evaluation procedure that may be used. In this procedure, both groups receive the same test before and after training. The experimental group receives the training but the control group does not. Each group receives randomly assigned trainees. Differences in pre-test and post-test results between the groups are attributed to the training provided. A potential problem with this approach is controlling for variables other than training that might affect the outcome.

Behavioral Change

Tests may accurately indicate what trainees learn, but they give little insight into whether the training leads participants to change their behavior. For example, it is one thing for a manager to learn about motivational techniques but quite another matter for this person to apply the new knowledge. A manager may sit in the front row of a training session dealing with empowerment of subordinates, absorb every bit of the message, understand it totally, and then return the next week to the workplace and continue behaving in the same old autocratic way.

Accomplishment of T&D Objectives

Still another approach to evaluating T&D programs involves determining the extent to which programs have achieved stated objectives and have actually impacted performance. For instance, if the objective of an accident prevention program is to reduce the number and severity of accidents by 15 percent, comparing accident rates before and after training provides a useful measurement of success. For another example, a firm might establish a *return on investment (ROI)* goal. A realistic expectation for ROI is earning what you paid for plus an increase in revenue. In some circumstances, the actual ROI number may be hard to establish because of the difficulty in isolating the effects of training.[83] In fact, the problem is that many programs dealing with broader topics are more difficult to evaluate.

Benchmarking

By some estimates, up to 70 percent of American firms engage in some type of benchmarking. This effort involves monitoring and measuring a firm's internal processes, such as operations, and then comparing the data with information from companies that excel in those areas. Some firms are now expanding benchmarking beyond core business operations and applying the approach to T&D activities.

Because training programs for individual firms are unique, the training measures are necessarily broad. Common benchmarking questions focus on such areas as: training costs, the ratio of training staff to employees, and whether new or more traditional delivery systems are used. Information derived from these questions probably lacks the detail to permit specific improvements of the training curricula. However, a firm may recognize, for example, that another organization is able to deliver a lot of training for relatively little cost. This information could then trigger the firm to follow up with interviews or site visits to determine whether that phenomenon represents a "best practice." As T&D becomes more crucial to organizational success, determining model training practices and learning from them will become increasingly important.

Training and Development Evaluation: Difficult but Necessary

In evaluating T&D programs, managers should strive for proof that they are effective. Although such proof may be difficult to establish, a company must at least estimate the effect on performance to show whether the training achieved its desired purpose. In spite of problems associated with evaluation, managers responsible for T&D must continue to strive for solid evidence of its contributions in achieving organizational goals.

12 OBJECTIVE

Describe the training partnerships that exist between business, government, and education.

Business/Government/Education Training Partnerships

Government funds to support training have been dwindling. However, one federal program that has promise, while eliminating much bureaucracy, is the Workforce Investment Act. Congress created another partnership when it passed the School-to-Work Opportunities Act. The overriding purpose of these and other partnerships is to develop a skilled workforce for tomorrow.

Workforce Investment Act

The Workforce Investment Act (WIA) became law in 1998. This legislation replaced the problem-riddled Job Training Partnership Act (JTPA) and consolidated *more than 70* federal job-training programs. It provides states with the flexibility to develop streamlined systems in partnership with local governments. A primary focus of WIA is

U.S. Department of Labor Employment & Training Administration

www.doleta.gov/

This Web site is the homepage for the U.S. Department of Labor Employment & Training Administration.

to meet the needs of business for skilled workers and to satisfy the training, education, and employment needs of individuals.[84]

One-stop service centers are at the heart of the new system. These centers provide job-seekers with a range of services including career counseling, skill assessments, training, job search assistance, and referrals to programs and services, depending on need. As with the Job Training Partnership Act, the WIA is led by participants from the private sector. For ASTD's summary of the law and direct links to governors' offices, go to www.astd.org/virtual_community/public_policy.

The WIA is up for renewal for the 2004 fiscal year. According to Cynthia Pantazis, director of legislative affairs for ASTD, Congress will be making decisions that should have some far-reaching effects on workforce development issues.[85]

School-to-Work Opportunities Act (STWOA) and Other Partnerships

A retired communications firm executive, John Clendenin, states, "the bottom line in America's fight for long-term competitiveness ultimately will be won or lost not in the halls of Congress, not in the boardrooms around the world, but in America's classrooms." In meeting this challenge, the School to-Work Opportunities Act[86] provides seed money for states to implement school-to-work plans. The National School-to-Work Office, a partnership between the Departments of Education and Labor, administers grants and coordinates communication between the states and local partnerships. Organizations such as the National Employer Leadership Council are helping companies tailor their participation in school-to-work activities.

Most sources report that school-to-work has been a true success story. Preparing students for work through classroom efforts is nothing new. However, the money provided by the STWOA has meant a huge increase in work-based learning experiences for students. In many states, it represents a comprehensive change in education policy.[87]

13 OBJECTIVE

Explain career planning and development.

Career Planning and Development

Career:
A general course that a person chooses to pursue throughout his or her working life.

Career planning:
An ongoing process whereby an individual sets career goals and identifies the means to achieve them.

Organizational career planning:
The planned succession of jobs worked out by a firm to develop its employees.

A **career** is a general course that a person chooses to pursue throughout his or her working life. Today, the career may change several times due to technological changes or the individual's desire to do something different. Recall from Chapter 1 that the average person graduating from college today may face five to seven career changes in his or her working years.[88]

Career planning is an ongoing process whereby an individual sets career goals and identifies the means to achieve them. The foundation of career planning is to know yourself.[89] The major focus of career planning should be on matching personal goals and abilities with opportunities that are realistically available. While individuals are primarily responsible for their careers, some organizations take an active role in the process. **Organizational career planning** is the planned succession of jobs worked out by a firm to develop its employees. Organizational career planning helps ensure that a firm improves its ability to perform by identifying needed capabilities and the type of people needed to perform in an ever-evolving business environment.

Individual and organizational career planning are not separate and distinct. Individuals who cannot realize their career aspirations within the organization, at some time will probably leave the firm. If career opportunities are not available elsewhere, employees may, in effect, "leave" the firm by letting their productivity decline. Thus, organizations should assist employees in career planning so both parties can satisfy their needs.

There was a time when most people remained with one company and career for the majority of their adult years.[90] But, for many workers today, this assumption is not valid.[91] Employers once preached job security, but the message recently heard among numerous firms is that corporate loyalty to employees is dead.[92] To reciprocate, employee loyalty to these organizations has also died. For many, loyalty has shifted to themselves and to their craft or profession. The appendix to this chapter provides additional information about career planning and development.

Training and development activities provide a basic means for adding skills to employees' toolboxes. And, firms vary significantly in the amount of T&D activities they provide. Organizations that are interested in developing their employees provide a healthy budget for T&D and anyone searching for a job would be wise to seek out these employers.

Individuals and groups receive the bulk of T&D effort. However, some firms believe that to achieve needed change, you must move the entire organization in the desired direction. Efforts to achieve this are the focus of *organization development* and we cover this topic next.

14 OBJECTIVE

Define *organization development (OD)* and describe various OD techniques.

Organization Development

Various factors in the firm's corporate culture affect employees' behavior on the job. To bring about desired changes in these factors and behavior, organizations must be transformed into market-driven, innovative, and adaptive systems if they are to survive and prosper in today's highly competitive global environment. Many firms are beginning to face this urgent need by practicing organization development, a human resource development approach that involves the entire system. **Organization development (OD)** is the planned process of improving an organization by developing its structures, systems, and processes to improve effectiveness and achieve desired goals.[93] Organization development is a major means of achieving change in the corporate culture. This type of development is increasingly important as both work and the workforce diversify and change.

Organization development (OD):
The planned process of improving an organization by developing its structures, systems, and processes to improve effectiveness and achieve desired goals.

Organization development applies to an entire system, such as a company or a plant. Although OD does not produce a blueprint for how to do things, it does provide an adaptive strategy for planning and implementing change and strives for a long-term reinforcement of change.

Numerous OD interventions are available to the practitioner. Interventions discussed elsewhere in this book include performance appraisal, compensation systems, career planning and development, and employee wellness. Interventions covered in the following section include survey feedback, a technique often combined with other interventions, quality circles, team building, and sensitivity training.

Survey Feedback

Survey feedback is a process of collecting data from an organizational unit using questionnaires, interviews, and objective data from other sources such as records of productivity, turnover, and absenteeism.[94] It enables management teams to help organizations create working environments that lead to better working relationships, greater productivity, and increased profitability. A developing trend has been to combine survey feedback with other OD interventions including work design, structural change, and intergroup relations.[95] Survey feedback generally involves the following steps:

Survey feedback:
A process of collecting data from an organizational unit through the use of questionnaires, interviews, and objective data from other sources such as records of productivity, turnover, and absenteeism.

- Members of the organization, including top management, are involved in planning the survey.
- All members of the organizational unit participate in the survey.
- The OD consultant usually analyzes the data, tabulates results, suggests approaches to diagnosis, and trains participants in the feedback process.
- Data feedback usually begins at the top level of the organization and flows downward to groups reporting at successively lower levels.

- Feedback meetings provide an opportunity to discuss and interpret data, diagnose problem areas, and develop action plans.[96]

Quality Circles

Quality circles:
Groups of employees who voluntarily meet regularly with their supervisors to discuss problems, investigate causes, recommend solutions, and take corrective action when authorized to do so.

America received the concept of quality circles from Japan several decades ago. This version of employee involvement is still in use today, improving quality, increasing motivation, boosting productivity, and adding to the bottom line. **Quality circles** are groups of employees who voluntarily meet regularly with their supervisors to discuss their problems, investigate causes, recommend solutions, and take corrective action when authorized to do so.[97] The team's recommendations are presented to higher-level management for review, and the approved actions are implemented with employee participation.

In order to implement a successful quality circle program, the firm must set clear goals for the program, gain top management's support, and create a climate conducive to participative management. In addition, a qualified manager is essential for the program and the program's goals must be communicated to all concerned. Individuals participating in the program must receive quality-circle training. Most organizations that implement continuous improvement cultures, or team systems, teach their employees tools to use in reaching decisions and solving problems. The tools include four basic steps: problem definition, data collection to confirm the root cause of the problem, solution generation, and action planning. In addition, the firm designs a tracking system to determine results of the action taken.[98]

The key to the success of quality circles is the sincerity of management in dealing with the teams where the participants view their role as an essential part of company decisions. Even those employees who are not part of the circle generally become enthusiastic. Although they have not personally taken part in the planning, they will accept the decisions because their peers, not just the boss, have helped form them. The work becomes more interesting and the employees more motivated when they recognize that successful task completion requires a mutual effort of management and operative employees.[99]

One thing seems certain: if a firm is to sustain employee interest and enthusiasm for quality-circle activities, the employees must share in the economic gain. Nonfinancial rewards are important, as we will discuss in a later chapter. However, if, over the long run employees are excluded from monetary rewards, they will wonder who really benefits from the programs.[100]

Team Building

Team building:
A conscious effort to develop effective workgroups and cooperative skills throughout the organization.

Team building is a conscious effort to develop effective work groups and cooperative skills throughout the organization.[101] It helps members diagnose group processes and devise solutions to problems.[102] Effective team building can be the most efficient way to boost morale, employee retention, and company profitability. Whether it's a lieutenant leading troops into battle or executives working with their managers, the same principles apply.[103] An important by-product of team building is that it is one of the most effective interventions for improving employee satisfaction and work-related attitudes. Individualism has deep roots in American culture. This trait has been a virtue and will continue to be an asset in our society. Now, however, there are work situations that make it imperative to subordinate individual autonomy in favor of cooperation with a group. It seems apparent that teams are clearly superior in performing many of the tasks required by organizations. The building of effective teams, therefore, has become a business necessity.

Organizations must provide much training effort prior to efficient and effective functioning of work teams. Fortunately, most managers know this. Team building utilizes *self-directed teams*, each composed of a small group of employees responsible for an entire work process or segment. Team members work together to improve their operation or product, to plan and control their work, and to handle day-to-day problems. They may even become involved in broader, company-wide issues, such as vendor quality, safety, and business planning.

Team building may begin as soon as an applicant is hired. At Southwest Airlines, the firm divides new employees into teams and gives them a raw egg in the shell, a handful of straws, and some masking tape. Their task is, in a limited amount of time, to protect that delicate cargo from an eight-foot drop. The exercise prepares teams of employees for creative problem solving in a fast-paced environment.[104]

A few years ago, physical-challenge exercises were the rage in team building. These activities have their place but are not suited for every team-building need. As a result, some new, inventive concepts have emerged, from building towers to cooking up a feast.

The Lake Forest Graduate School of Management has developed an approach it calls Team Banquets. An internationally recognized executive chef helped develop this program, which brought together people with different knowledge, skills, and experience to accomplish a single goal: create a banquet. The exercise is based on the discovery that some of the most effective, efficient teams in the world are in the kitchens of fine restaurants. These settings serve as models of organization, communication, and results-oriented processes. The Team Banquet brings together 25 to 30 employees and challenges them to prepare a gourmet banquet within two hours. Only the raw ingredients and equipment are provided. The assigned roles may put a mail clerk in charge while a group manager serves as an assistant. Each team is assigned a specific portion of the banquet preparation, from entrée to decorations and food presentation. Participants receive safety instructions but not recipes. Teams must rely on their own knowledge and creativity in devising the dishes they serve. The initial response to this approach was skepticism. However, management and participants soon discovered that the exercise provided an excellent analogy to the workplace and provided an outstanding means for developing teamwork.[105]

Take Charge Consults, in Downington, Pennsylvania, and Litow Consulting, in Baltimore, Maryland, designed another cooking exercise, Recipes for Success. Lynn Litow Flayhard, Recipes for Success co-founder and trainer, says, "In the workplace, people use all of their senses and learn from real-life experiences that they are involved in. Yet, so many training programs are passive. Our premise is that people learn actively. We involve all of their senses and they actually practice the techniques we teach as we are teaching them. Cooking allows the perfect vehicle for this interaction."[106]

Sensitivity Training

Sensitivity training: An organization development technique that is designed to help individuals learn how others perceive their behavior (also know as T-group training).

Sensitivity training, or T-group training, is a procedure designed to help individuals learn how others perceive their behavior. It is based on the assumption that a number of individuals meeting in an unstructured situation will develop working relations with each other. From this experience, they will learn much about themselves as perceived by the other group members.[107] It differs from many traditional forms of training, which stress the learning of a predetermined set of concepts. When sensitivity training begins, there is no agenda, no leaders, no authority, and no power positions. Essentially, a vacuum exists until participants begin to talk. Through dialogue, people begin to learn about themselves and others. The trainer's purpose is to serve as a facilitator in this unstructured environment. Participants are encouraged to learn about themselves and others in the group. Some objectives of sensitivity training are to increase the participants' self-awareness and sensitivity to the behavior of others. The training also strives to develop an awareness of the processes that facilitate or inhibit group and intergroup functioning, and to increase the participants' ability to achieve

A Global Perspective

They Might Speak English, But . . .

Even when people are colleagues, all speak English, and all are familiar with the material, their attitudes about training and learning are governed strongly by their cultural backgrounds. For example, planning the start, finish, and break times is often quite different. The Dutch generally believe in making the most of their time but trainers do not count on Germans staying much beyond 3:00 P.M. on Fridays. In continental Europe, the smoking issue is handled much differently than it is in the United States and the United Kingdom. If you have a large number of smokers, they expect regular smoking breaks or they will light up in the middle of a lecture.[108]

In the United Kingdom, a relaxed yet professional style is appropriate, and the odd joke is almost standard. Other nationalities, however, are not used to jokes. They will sit with a semi-smile frozen on their faces as they desperately try to figure out what the trainer is really saying. That is particularly true for Eastern Europeans, most of whom are more comfortable with a formal style. In Scandinavian countries and the United Kingdom, first names are generally used. In other countries, such as Germany, colleagues still address each other formally using Mr. or Ms.[109]

Different nationalities have different attitudes about asking questions and taking part in a group discussion. People from Eastern Europe ask fewer questions than people from Western Europe because asking questions is not the classroom style they grew up with. People from the Far East seldom ask questions because they do not want to ask a question the instructor might not be able to answer. The British, Dutch, and Americans are always ready to ask a question, and they will keep asking it in a different way until it is answered. With some nationalities, calling on a person could insult him or her so much that he or she would not return to class after a break. The most common mistake is to assume that because people understand the shared language they have the same cultural background. That assumption arises most often when the common language is English.[110]

effective interpersonal relationships. T-group training was once a prominent OD intervention. A central problem with sensitivity training, according to some, is that its purpose is to change individuals, not necessarily the environment in which they work. When participants attempt to use what they have learned, they often find their coworkers unwilling to accept it, or worse, what they have learned may not be appropriate for their own work situation.[111]

Summary

1. Distinguish between career and job security.

Job security implies security in one job, often with one company. Career security requires developing marketable skills and expertise that help ensure employment within a range of careers.

2. Define *training* and *development* (T&D).

Training is designed to permit learners to acquire knowledge and skills needed for their present jobs. Development involves learning that goes beyond today's job.

3. Explain the relationship that exists between organization change and T&D.

The basic purpose of T&D is to anticipate change and to respond proactively to it. Change involves moving from one condition to another, and it will affect individuals, groups, and entire organizations.

4. Explain factors influencing T&D.

Increasingly rapid changes in technology, products, systems, and methods have had a significant impact on job requirements making T&D a must. T&D programs must have top management's full support; all managers should be committed to and involved in the T&D process. They must be convinced that there will be a tangible payoff if resources are committed to this effort.

5. Describe the T&D process and how training needs are determined and objectives established.

Once the need for change has been recognized and the factors that influence intervention considered, the process of determining T&D needs begins. After stating the T&D objectives, management can determine the appropriate methods for accomplishing them. Various training methods are available to use. T&D must be continuously evaluated. T&D needs may be determined by conducting analyses on several levels. Clear and concise objectives must be formulated for T&D. Without them, designing meaningful T&D programs would not be possible.

6. Describe the various T&D methods.

Training and development methods include classroom programs, mentoring and coaching, case study, videotapes, role playing, apprenticeship training, vestibule training, simulations, business games, in-basket training, distance learning and videoconferencing, computer-based training, virtual reality and e-learning, on-the-job training, job rotation, and internships.

7. Explain the importance of corporate universities and community colleges to training.

The corporate training institution differs from many traditional training programs in that its focus is on creating organizational change. It is proactive and strategic rather than reactive and tactical. An estimated 2,000 corporate universities exist in the United States today. Some employers have discovered that community colleges can provide certain types of training better and more cost-effectively than they can.

8. Describe management development.

Management development consists of all learning experiences provided by an organization for the purpose of providing and upgrading skills and knowledge required in current and future managerial positions.

9. Define *orientation* and identify its purposes.

Orientation is the guided adjustment of new employees to the company, the job, and the work group. Orientation acquaints employees with the employment situation, company policies, and rules, compensation and benefits, and corporate culture.

10. Identify special training needs.

Special training needs include training involving telecommuting, diversity, customer service, conflict resolution, values, teamwork, empowerment, and remedial training.

11. Identify the means by which T&D programs are implemented and evaluated.

Means by which T&D programs are evaluated include participants' opinions, extent of learning, behavioral change, accomplishment of T&D objectives, and benchmarking.

12. Describe the training partnerships that exist between businesses, government, and education.

Federal programs include the Workforce Investment Act and the School-to-Work Opportunities Act.

13. Explain career planning and development.

A career is a general course that a person chooses to pursue throughout his or her working life. Career planning is an ongoing process whereby an individual sets career goals and identifies the means to achieve them. Firms engaging in organizational career planning may identify paths — a succession of jobs — and activities for individuals as they develop.

14. Define *organization development (OD)* and describe various OD techniques.
Organization development (OD) is the planned process of improving an organization by developing its structures, systems, and processes to improve effectiveness, and achieving desired goals. Interventions include survey feedback, a technique often combined with other interventions, quality circles, team building, and sensitivity training.

Key Terms

- **Job security, 201**
- **Career security, 201**
- **Human resource development (HRD), 202**
- **Training and development (T&D), 202**
- **Training, 202**
- **Development, 202**
- **Learning organization, 203**
- **Just-in-time training, 207**
- **Mentoring, 210**
- **Coaching, 211**
- **Reverse mentoring, 211**
- **Case study, 212**
- **Behavior modeling, 212**
- **Role playing, 212**
- **Apprenticeship training, 212**
- **Vestibule training, 212**
- **Simulations, 213**
- **Business games, 213**
- **In-basket training, 213**
- **Computer-based training, 214**
- **Virtual reality, 214**
- **E-learning, 214**
- **On-the-job training (OJT), 215**
- **Job rotation, 216**
- **Management development, 217**
- **Orientation, 219**
- **Diversity training, 221**
- **Career, 226**
- **Career planning, 226**
- **Organizational career planning, 226**
- **Organization development (OD), 227**
- **Survey feedback, 227**
- **Quality circles, 228**
- **Team building, 228**
- **Sensitivity training, 229**

Questions for Review

1. What is the difference between job security and career security? Which one would you rather have?
2. Define *training* and *development*.
3. What is the relationship that exists between organization change and T&D?
4. What are some factors that influence T&D?
5. What are the steps that exist in the T&D process?
6. What are the various T&D methods? Briefly describe each.
7. Why do organizations use on-the-job training?
8. Why have corporate universities and community colleges become important in training?
9. Define *management development*. Why is it important?
10. Define *orientation* and explain the purposes of orientation.
11. What are some special training needs? Briefly describe each.
12. How are T&D programs evaluated?
13. What type of training partnerships exist between businesses, government, and education?
14. Define each of the following:
    a. career
    b. career planning
    c. organizational career planning
15. Define each of the following:
    a. organization development
    b. survey feedback
    c. quality circles
    d. sensitivity training
    e. team building

HRM Incident 1

Training at Keller-Globe

Lou McGowen was worried as she approached the training director's office. She is the supervisor of six punch press operators at Keller-Globe, a maker of sheetmetal parts for the industrial refrigeration industry. She had just learned that her punch presses would soon be replaced with a continuous-feed system that would double the speed of operations. She was thinking about how the workers might feel about the new system when the training director, Bill Taylor, opened the door and said, "Come on in, Lou. I've been looking forward to seeing you."

After a few pleasantries, Lou told Bill of her concerns. "The operators really know their jobs now. But this continuous-feed system is a whole new ball game. I'm concerned, too, about how the workers will feel about it. The new presses are going to run faster. They may think that their job is going to be harder."

Bill replied, "After talking with the plant engineer and the production manager, I made a tentative training schedule that might make you feel a little better. I think we first have to let the workers know why this change is necessary. You know that both of our competitors changed to this new system last year. After that, we will teach your people to operate the new presses."

"Who's going to do the teaching?" Lou asked. "I haven't even seen the new system."

"Well, Lou," said Bill, "the manufacturer has arranged for you to visit a plant with a similar system. They'll also ship one of the punch presses in early so you and your workers can learn to operate it."

"Will the factory give us any other training help?" Lou asked.

"Yes, I have asked them to send a trainer down as soon as the first press is set up. He will conduct some classroom sessions and then work with your people on the new machine."

After further discussion about details, Lou thanked Bill and headed back to the production department. She was confident that the new presses would be a real benefit to her section and that her workers could easily learn the skills required.

Question

1. Evaluate Keller-Globe's approach to training.

HRM Incident 2

Career Versus Job Security?

J. D. Wallace, a 30-year-old employee with Bechtel Engineering, headquartered in Houston, Texas, describes his assessment of career development. "My present job is to work with an engineering software design program, Plant Design System (PDS) that is used to create a 3-dimensional model of a petro-chem refinery. PDS is the fastest-growing and most demanded skill in the industry. The system has grown into a major design system that clients prefer. It has become very difficult for designers to find new jobs or keep their current jobs if they do not have the ability to run this system. Unfortunately, a lot of the designers have been caught with their pants down. They didn't see the need to get new skills. They believe, 'I've done it this way for 20 years and I have not needed computer skills. Computers will never replace board drafting. This company needs me and they will not be able to replace me because of my many years of experience.'

"On the other hand, some designers realize the importance of learning new technology. These designers can, for the most part, write their own ticket. They have become the highest-paid and most sought-after employees. I believe that it is very important to constantly increase your value to the company. For example, my college degree opened the door for me. Once the door opened, it was up to me to keep learning. I had to continue to train, retrain, and learn new systems. Some of the systems that I have invested time in learning have quickly become obsolete. However, I have not lost anything in the process. Improving skills is never a waste of time. It is amazing how fast the industry can change. Skills that you obtain and thought you would never use, can be the only reason you have a job tomorrow.

"Workers today must do whatever it takes to get the training needed to keep their jobs. Some of the things you could do include going back to school, or changing companies to get the necessary training. Very few companies spend the time and money needed to give workers all the training they need. Everybody must realize that they must stay current or they will be left behind.

In the last year alone the market for designers with PDS training has grown so fast that companies can no longer be assured of having an adequate work pool to draw from. The pay scale has expanded rapidly and is still growing. A good friend of mine has recently quit his present job for a 35 percent pay increase. Another company has lost many of its 10-year-plus employees to huge salary offers. Workers with the needed skills now have a lot of options. They can (for the most part) pick the company they want—by location, benefits, permanent staff, or contract. They currently have a lot of leverage. Workers without those skills have very limited choices because they do not add value to their companies."

Questions

1. Is J. D. concerned more with job security or career security? Discuss.
2. Do you agree with J. D.'s statement that "improving your skills is never a waste of time," considering that he has learned systems which quickly became obsolete? Discuss.

Human Resource Management Skills

Chapter 7: Training and Development

A Skills Module entitled *Employee Training and Development* is presented to provide additional insight into topics in this chapter. Specific sections within the module include the following: training, socialization, development, and orientation; needs assessment based on organizational analysis, task analysis, and person analysis; how to conduct a needs assessment; orientation agenda; employment development including tuition reimbursement, mentoring, and job rotation; socialization; on-the-job training; skills inventories; conditions of practice (learning styles, massed versus space-practice sessions), whole versus part learning, over learning, knowledge of results, and task sequencing; retention of material learned: meaningfulness of material, degree of original learning, and inference; assessment; and behavioral assessment and result-based assessment.

Several training and development scenarios are presented to give students realistic experience in dealing with the topic.

A test is provided at the end of the module to determine mastery of the material included in the Skills Module. Also, directions are given for assignments that can be used in class or assigned as homework.

Take it to the Net

We invite you to visit the Mondy homepage on the Prentice Hall Web site at

www.prenhall.com/mondy

for updated information, Web-based exercises, and links to other HR-related sites.

Notes

1. Julie Rawe, "What Will Be the 10 Hottest Jobs? . . . and What Jobs Will Disappear? *Time* (May 22, 2000): 73.
2. Todd Raphael, "Crystal Gazing and the Future of Work," *Workforce* 81 (September 2002): 112.
3. "Moving Up the Career Ladder," *AFP Exchange* 22 (September/October 2002): 9, 11+.
4. Anne Fisher, "Six Ways to Supercharge Your Career," *Fortune* (January 13, 1997): 46+.
5. Mark Morgan "Career-Building Strategies," *Strategic Finance* 83 (June 2002): 38–43.
6. Barbara DePompa Reimers, "Who Moved My IT Job?" *Computerworld* (December 2, 2002): 49–50.
7. Tammy Galvin, "Industry Report 2002," *Training* 39 (October 2002): 27.
8. T. L. Stanley, "Good Training Programs Don't Just Happen," *Supervision* 83 (June 2002): 8.
9. Eric Krell, "Training Earns Its Keep," *Training* 38 (April 2001): 68.
10. Ricky Smith, "Assessing Your Maintenance Training Needs," *Plant Engineering* 55 (August 2001): 56.
11. Carla Johnson, "Employee, Sculpt Thyself — With a Little Help," *HRMagazine* 48 (May 2001): 60.
12. Bruce Pfau and Ira Kay, "Playing the Training Game and Losing," *HRMagazine* 47 (August 2002): 49.
13. Galvin, "Industry Report 2002," 64
14. Denise Laframboise, Rodney L. Nelson, and Jason Schmaltz, "Managing Resistance to Change in Workplace Accommodation Projects," *Journal of Facilities Management* (February 2003): 306.
15. "Making Change Work — For Real," *HR Focus* 80 (January 2003): S1.
16. Kenneth N. Wexley and Gary P. Latham, *Developing and Training Human Resources in Organizations*, 3rd ed. (Upper Saddle River, N J: Prentice Hall, 2002): 3.
17. Russ Alan Prince, "Agents' Progress Depends on Career-Long Learning," *National Underwriter* (Life & Health/Financial Services Edition) (April 24, 2000): 17.
18. Steve Barkley and Terri Bianco, "Learning Experts Examine Shortfalls in On-Site and On-Line Training," *Supervision* 82 (January 2001): 11.
19. Deborah A. Smith and Regina Glover, "Teaching Job Application and Personnel Selection Skills," *College Teaching* 50 (Summer 2002): 83.
20. Steven R. Covey, "Teaching Organizations," *Executive Excellence* (March 2000): 20.
21. Holly Ann Suzik, "Built from Scratch," *Quality* 38 (October 1999): 32–34.
22. Galvin, "Industry Report 2002," 41.
23. Clara Y. Young and James V. Wright, "Mentoring: The Components for Success," *Journal of Instructional Psychology* 28 (September 2001): 202.
24. Ken Fracaro, "Mentoring: Tool for Career Guidance," *Supervision* 63 (September 2002): 10–12.
25. Andrea C. Poe, "Coaching HR," *HRMagazine* 47 (October 2002): 54.
26. Mary Elizabeth Burke, Evren Esen, and Jessica Collison, "2003 Benefits Survey," *SHRM/SHRM Foundation* (June 2003): 29.
27. Lisa Keating, "Women Mentoring Women: The Rewards of Giving," *Women in Business* 53 (January/February 2002): 28.
28. Jonathan A. Segal, "Mirror-Image Mentoring," *HRMagazine* 45 (March 2000): 157–166.

29. "Money Isn't Everything," *The Journal of Business Strategy* 21 (March/April 2000): 4.
30. Mathew Budman, "Bob Thomas Explains Why You're Never Too Young or Too Old," *Across the Board* 39 (September/October 2002): 13.
31. John F. Welch, Jr., with John A. Byrne, *Jack Straight from the Gut* (New York: Warner Books, Inc., 2001): 347.
32. Samuel Greengard, "Moving Forward with Reverse Mentoring," *Workforce* 81 (March 2002): 15.
33. Brent Schlender, "The Odd Couple," *Fortune* (May 1, 2000): 106–114.
34. Wexley and Latham, *Developing and Training Human Resources in Organizations*, 180–181.
35. Michelle Merlo, "Training Program Prepares Future Electricians," *Electric Perspectives* 27 (May/June 2002): 29.
36. Ulrich Boser, "Gaming the System, One Click at a Time," *U.S. News & World Report* (October 28, 2002): 60.
37. Susan S. Harrington and Bonnie L. Walker, "A Comparison of Computer-Based and Instructor-Led Training for Long-Term Care Staff," *The Journal of Continuing Education in Nursing* 33 (January/February 2002): 39–45.
38. Helen Jezzard, "That Eureka! Moment," *Information World Review* (October 1, 2001): 20.
39. Galvin, "Industry Report 2002," 45.
40. Doyle Young, "Log On to a More Successful Career with E-learning," *Chicago Daily Herald* (December 1, 2002): 4.
41. Kristi Nelson, "Wachovia's Merger Lessons," *Information Week* (May 12, 2003): 71.
42. Michael Blumfield, "Learning to Share," *Training* 34 (April 1997): 38.
43. Paul Rosenberg, "Learning Through On-The-Job Training," *Electrical Construction and Maintenance* 100 (February 2001): 78.
44. Mary Lord, "They're Online and on the Job," *U.S. News & World Report* (October 15, 2001): 72.
45. Kathryn Tyler, "Take E-Learning to the Next Step," *HRMagazine* 47 (February 2002): 57–58.
46. "Time Tested Training," *National Petroleum News* 95 (January 2003): 49.
47. Martha Frase-Blunt, "Ready, Set, Rotate," *HRMagazine* 46 (October 2001): 46.
48. Malcolm Coco, "Internships: A Try Before You Buy Arrangement," *Advanced Management Journal* 65 (Spring 2000): 41.
49. Kristine Ellis, "Corporate U's: High Value or Hot Air," *Training* (September 2002): 60.
50. Michael Schrage, "Sorry, No Keg Parties Here: This University Is on the Desktop," *Fortune* (June 7, 1999): 224.
51. Glen Creno, "More Companies Serving up Training\Corporate 'Colleges' Take Lead from McDonald's Hamburger University," *Arizona Republic* (May 16, 1999): AZ4.
52. Bill Leonard, "GM Drives HR to the Next Level," *HRMagazine* 47 (March 2002): 46.
53. Russell V. Gerbman, "Corporate Universities 101," *HRMagazine* 45 (February 2000): 101–106.
54. Linda Leung, "Community Minded-Curriculum," *Network World* (January 6, 2003): 47.
55. Margaret Terry Orr, "Community Colleges and Their Communities: Collaboration for Workforce Development," *New Directions for Community Colleges* 115 (Fall 2001): 39.
56. Jeff Bailey, "Community Colleges Can Help Small Firms with Staffing — Programs with Two-Year Institutions Aid in Developing Skills in Short Supply," *Wall Street Journal* (February 19, 2002): B2.
57. Ibid.
58. "Partial Client Listing," Business & Industry Services Network, Connecticut Community Colleges (April 29, 2003), http://www.commnet.edu/bisn/clients.html.
59. James Jacobs, "Community Colleges and the Workforce Investment Act: Promises and Problems of the New Vocationalism," *New Directions for Community Colleges* 115 (Fall 2001): 93.
60. Ronald A. Heifetz and Marty Linsky, "A Survival Guide for Leaders," *Business Credit* 105 (March 2003): 44.
61. Jack Zenger, Dave Ulrich, and Norm Smallwood, "The New Leadership Development," *Training & Development* 54 (March 2000): 22.
62. William C. Byham, "Bench Strength: Succession Planning, As We Know It, Is Dead. Long Live Acceleration Pools," *Across the Board* 37 (February 2000): 34.
63. Melissa Solomon, "Tailoring Leadership Strategies," *Computerworld* (July 24, 2000): 51.
64. George Ferguson, "D is for Development," *T+D* 56 (January 2002): 57.
65. "Where Do the Training Dollars Go," *Training* 36 (October 1999): 60.
66. Martin Delahoussaye, "Capital One," *Training* 38 (March 2001): 70.
67. Sabrina Hicks, "Successful Orientation Programs," *Training & Development* 54 (April 2000): 59.
68. Max Messmer, "Orientation Programs Can Be Key to Employee Retention," *Strategic Finance Magazine* 81 (February 2000): 12.
69. Lin Grensing-Pophal, "Reaching for Diversity," *HRMagazine* 47 (May 2002): 55.
70. Andrew Hubbard, "Accommodating Diversity in the Training Environment," *Mortgage Banking* 63 (January 2003): 106.
71. Dina Berta, "Language Smarts: Shared Ideas Form ESL Program," *Nation's Restaurant News* (September 16, 2002): 18.
72. Richard B. Schmitt, "Companies Add Ethics Training: Will It Work?" *Wall Street Journal* (November 4, 2002): B1.
73. Andrew W. Singer, "Olin Corporation's 'Values-Based' Ethics Program," *Ethikos* (May 1, 2001): 7.
74. Schmitt, "Companies Add Ethics Training."
75. Michelle M. Robertson, Wayne S. Maynard, and Jamie R. McDevitt, "Telecommuting: Managing the Safety of Workers in Home Office Environments," *Professional Safety* 48 (April 2003): 30.
76. Lin Grensing-Pophal, "Training Supervisors to Manage Teleworkers," *HRMagazine* 44 (January 1999): 67.
77. Robert S. Adams, "Facing Up to Board Conflict," *Association Management* 55 (April 2003): 56.
78. Martin L. Gross, *The Conspiracy of Ignorance: The Failure of American Public Schools* (New York: HarperCollins, 1999): 6.
79. Zenger, Ulrich, and Smallwood, "The New Leadership Development."
80. Kathryn Tyler, "Evaluating Evaluations," *HRMagazine* 47 (June 2002): 85.

81. Ajay Pangarkar and Teresa Kirkwood, "Systematic Strategies," *CMA Management* 76 (December 2002/January 2003): 36.
82. Tyler, "Evaluating Evaluations."
83. Elysa Wallach, "I Before E," *Journal of Property Management* 67 (September/October 2002): 42–44.
84. Cynthia Pantazis, "The New Workforce Investment Act," *Training & Development* 53 (August 1999): 48–49.
85. Bill Leonard, "Congress' Concerns Over War, Economy Overshadow Health Care, HR Issues," *HRMagazine* 48 (March 2003): 32.
86. Stephanie Overman, "Gearing up for Tomorrow's Workforce," *HR Focus* 76 (February 1999): 1.
87. Sandy Cutshall, "School-to-Work: Has it Worked?" *Techniques* (Association for Career and Technical Education) 76 (January 2001): 18.
88. Russ Westcott, "Has Your Work Life Plateaued?" *Quality Progress* 34 (October 2001): 60.
89. Jerry Kanter, "Planning and Managing Your Career," *Information Strategy* 19 (Winter 2003): 43.
90. Vicky Eckenrode, "Workplace Feels Generation Gap," *Augusta Chronicle* (June 23, 2002): D06.
91. John A. Challenger, "The Changing Workforce: Workplace Rules in the New Millennium," *Vital Speeches of the Day* (September 15, 2001): 721–728.
92. Megan Santosus, "Loyalty, Shmoyalty," *CIO* (April 15, 2002): 40.
93. "What is Organization Development," *Training & Development* 54 (August 2000): 65.
94. Ibid.
95. Thomas G. Cummings and Christopher G. Worley, *Organization Development and Change*, 7th ed. (Cincinnati: South-Western College Publishing, 2001), 133.
96. Cummings and Worley, *Organization Development and Change*,135–136.
97. "Quality Circles Are Alive and Well," *Office Systems* 16 (February 1999): 12.
98. Helene F. Uhlfelder, "It's All about Improving Performance," *Quality Progress* 33 (February 2000): 47.
99. Michael Crom, "Interesting, Engaging Work Motivates Employees," *Gannett News Service* (February 20, 2003).
100. Ron Mitchell, "Quality Circles in the U.S.: Rediscovering Our Roots," *Journal for Quality & Participation* 22 (November/December 1999): 28.
101. Clinton O. Longenecker and Mitchell Neubert, "Barriers and Gateways to Management Cooperation and Teamwork," *Business Horizons* 43 (September/October 2000): 37–44.
102. Cummings and Worley, *Organization Development and Change*, 149.
103. James M. Lennox, "Team-Building for a Better Tomorrow," *Journal of Property Management* 66 (September/October 2001): 10.
104. Kathryn Tyler, "Take New Employee Orientation off the Back Burner," *HRMagazine* 43 (May 1998): 49.
105. Howard Prager, "Cooking up Effective Team Building," *Training & Development* 53 (December 1999): 14–15.
106. Jeff Barbian, "Now We're Cooking," *Training* 38 (February 2001): 26.
107. W. H. Weiss, "Training Methods and Programs," *Supervision* 61 (January 2000): 9–13.
108. Els S. Van Leeuwen, "Quick Donkey Bridge," *T + D* 55 (November 2001): 84–85.
109. Ibid.
110. Ibid.
111. W. H. Weiss, "Training Methods and Programs."

APPENDIX CHAPTER 7 Career Planning and Development

CAREER PLANNING AND DEVELOPMENT DEFINED

As defined in Chapter 7, a *career* is a general course that a person chooses to pursue throughout his or her working life. Historically, a career was a sequence of work-related positions an individual has occupied during a lifetime, although not always with the same company. However, there are a few relatively static jobs that require infrequent training and virtually no development for maintaining acceptable productivity levels.

Career planning is an ongoing process whereby an individual sets career goals and identifies the means to achieve them. Career planning should not concentrate only on advancement opportunities since the present work environment has reduced many of these opportunities. At some point, career planning should focus on achieving successes that do not necessarily entail promotions.

Organizational career planning is the planned succession of jobs worked out by a firm to develop its employees. With organizational career planning, the organization identifies paths and activities for individual employees as they develop. A *career path* is a flexible line of movement through which an employee may move during employment with a company. Following an established career path, the employee can undertake career development with the firm's assistance. From a worker's perspective, following a career path may involve weaving from company to company and from position to position as he or she obtains greater knowledge and experience.

Career development is a formal approach used by the organization to ensure that people with the proper qualifications and experiences are available when needed. Formal career development is important to maintain a motivated and committed workforce.[1] Career development tools, which are specified during career planning and utilized in the career development program, most notably include various types of training and the application of organizational development techniques (discussed in Chapter 7). Career planning and development benefit both the individual and the organization and must therefore be carefully considered by both.

JOB SECURITY VERSUS CAREER SECURITY

There was a time when most people remained with one company and career for the majority of their adult years. By planning for a single career it was easier for them to identify their strengths and weaknesses, their likes and dislikes, what they were good and less good at, and the employment opportunities available. A basic assumption was that change would not occur or would occur slowly. But, for most workers today, this assumption is not valid. The old social contract between employers and employees no longer exists.[2] Downsizing, reorganization, refocusing business strategies, and of course, executive betrayal in such companies as Enron, WorldCom, and Arthur Andersen changed all the old rules. The decision to leave or stay is based not only on an employee's career prospects in the present company but also on how it might prepare him or her to move on elsewhere.[3] Therefore, the way people approached their careers in the past is history.

Career security is the development of marketable skills and expertise that help ensure employment within a range of careers. Career security is different from job security in that *job security* implies security in one job, often with one company. With career security, workers are offered opportunities to improve their skills—and thus their employability in an ever-changing work environment. Under this so-called **employability doctrine**, employees owe the company their commitment while employed and the company owes its workers the opportunity to learn new skills—but that is as far as the commitment goes. Under the employability doctrine, loyalty in either direction is not expected. Even with the employability doctrine, career planning and development are essential to ensure that a qualified internal workforce is available.

Employability doctrine: Employees owe the company their commitment while employed and the company owes its workers the opportunity to learn new skills—but that is as far as the commitment goes.

CAREER PLANNING

As Alice said in *Through the Looking Glass*, "If you don't know where you're going, any road will get you there." Such is the case with career planning.[4] As one HR professional stated, "You need to always have a sense of crisis with your career, a sense of emergency. If you don't have a back-up plan, you get caught off guard."[5] Career planning must now accommodate a number of objectives and enable us to prepare for each on a contingency basis. It will need updating to accommodate changes in our own interests as well as in the work environment. Historically, it was thought that career planning was logical, linear, and indeed planned. That is not the case today, as individuals have experienced or seen downsizing, job creation, and job elimination. Further, just as once blue-collar jobs were exported from the United States, companies are beginning to do the same thing with white-collar jobs. For instance, software engineers have seen their jobs exported to low-priced professionals in India and China.[6] Because of the many changes that are occurring, career planning is essential for survival for individuals and organizations.

As previously discussed, organizational career planning involves the identification of paths and activities for employees as they develop. Career planning at the individual level and organizational career planning are interrelated and interdependent; therefore, success requires parallel planning at both levels.

Individual Career Planning—The Self-Assessment

Through career planning, a person continuously evaluates his or her abilities and interests, considers alternative career opportunities, establishes career goals, and plans practical developmental activities. Individual career planning must begin with self-understanding or self-assessment. Then, the person is in a position to establish realistic goals and determine what to do to achieve these goals.[7] This action also lets the person know whether his or her goals are realistic.

Self-assessment:
The process of learning about oneself.

Self-assessment is the process of learning about oneself. Anything that could affect one's performance in a future job should be considered. Realistic self-assessment may help a person avoid mistakes that could affect his or her entire career progression. Often an individual accepts a job without considering whether it matches his or her interests and abilities. This approach often results in failure. A thorough self-assessment will go a long way toward helping to match an individual's specific qualities and goals with the right job or profession. Deborah Warner, founder of Career Development Partners, said, "Applicants should pay attention to the skills they want to use and the ones they no longer want to use. When an individual has to frequently use skills [he doesn't] enjoy using, that can lead to job dissatisfaction and burnout."[8] For many people, being fired causes them to take stock of themselves for the first time, and to analyze their strengths and weaknesses.[9]

Some useful tools include a strength/weakness balance sheet and a likes and dislikes survey.[10] However, any reasonable approach that assists self-understanding is helpful.

Strength/weakness balance sheet:
A self-evaluation procedure, developed originally by Benjamin Franklin that helps people to become aware of their strengths and weaknesses.

Strength/Weakness Balance Sheet. A self-evaluation procedure, developed originally by Benjamin Franklin, that assists people in becoming aware of their strengths and weaknesses is the **strength/weakness balance sheet**. Employees who understand their strengths can use them to maximum advantage. By recognizing their weaknesses, they are in a better position to overcome them.[11] This statement sums up that attitude; "If you have a weakness, understand it and make it work for you as a strength; if you have a strength, do not abuse it to the point where it becomes a weakness."

To use a strength/weakness balance sheet, the individual lists strengths and weaknesses as he or she perceives them. This is quite important because believing, for example, that a weakness exists even when it does not can equate to a real weakness. Thus, a person who believes that he or she will make a poor first impression when meeting someone will probably make a poor impression. The perception of a weakness often becomes a self-fulfilling prophecy.

The mechanics for preparing the balance sheet are quite simple. To begin, draw a line down the middle of a sheet of paper. Label the left side *Strengths* and the right side *Weaknesses*. Record all perceived strengths and weaknesses. You may find it difficult to write about yourself. Remember, however, that no one else need see the results. The primary consideration is complete honesty.

Table A7-1 shows an example of a strength/weakness balance sheet. Obviously, Wayne (the person who wrote the sheet) did a lot of soul-searching in making these evaluations. Typically, a person's weaknesses will outnumber strengths in the first few iterations. However, as the individual repeats the process, some items that first appeared to be weaknesses may eventually be recognized as strengths and should then be moved from one column to the other. A person should devote sufficient time to the project to obtain a fairly clear understanding of his or her strengths and weaknesses. Typically, the process should take a minimum of one week. The balance sheet will not provide all the answers regarding a person's strengths and weaknesses, but many people have gained a better understanding of themselves by completing it. Analyzing oneself should not be just a one-time event. People change and every few years the process should again be undertaken.[12] You can determine means to react to your findings and, perhaps overcome a weakness after you have conducted the self-assessment.[13]

Table A7-1 Strength/Weakness Balance Sheet

Strengths	Weaknesses
Work well with people.	Get very close to few people.
Like to be given a task and get it done in my own way.	Do not like constant supervision.
Good manager of people.	Don't make friends very easily with individuals classified as my superiors.
Hard worker.	Am extremely high-strung.
Lead by example.	Often say things without realizing consequences.
People respect me as being fair and impartial.	Cannot stand to look busy when there is no work to be done.
Tremendous amount of energy.	Cannot stand to be inactive. Must be on the go constantly.
Function well in an active environment.	Cannot stand to sit at a desk all the time.
Relatively open-minded.	Basically a rebel at heart but have portrayed myself as just the opposite. My conservatism has gotten me jobs that I emotionally did not want.
Feel comfortable in dealing with high-level businesspersons.	Am sometimes nervous in an unfamiliar environment.
Like to play politics (This may be a weakness.)	Make very few true friends.
Get the job done when it is defined.	Not a conformist but appear to be.
Excellent at organizing other people's time. Can get the most out of people who are working for me.	Interest level hits peaks and valleys.
Have an outgoing personality—not shy.	Many people look on me as being unstable. Perhaps I am. Believe not.
Take care of those who take care of me. (This could be a weakness.)	Divorced.
Have a great amount of empathy.	Not a tremendous planner for short range.
Work extremely well through other people.	Long-range planning is better.
	Impatient—want to have things happen fast.
	Do not like details.
	Do not work well in an environment where I am the only party involved.

Source: Wayne Sanders.

Likes and dislikes survey:
A procedure that helps individuals recognize restrictions they place on themselves.

Likes and Dislikes Survey. An individual should also consider likes and dislikes as part of a self-assessment. A **likes and dislikes survey** assists individuals in recognizing restrictions they place on themselves. For instance, some people are not willing to live in certain parts of the country, and such feelings should be noted as a constraint. Some positions require a person to spend a considerable amount of time traveling. Thus, an estimate of the amount of time a person is willing to travel would also be helpful. Recognition of such self-imposed restrictions may reduce future career problems. Another limitation is the type of firm an individual will consider working for.

The size of the firm might also be important. Some like a major organization whose products are well known; others prefer a smaller organization, believing that the opportunities for advancement may be greater or that the environment is better suited to their tastes. All factors that could affect an individual's work performance should be listed in the likes and dislikes survey. An example of this type of survey is shown in Table A7-2.

Table A7-2 Likes and Dislikes Survey

Likes	Dislikes
Like to travel.	Do not want to work for a large firm.
Would like to live in the East.	Will not work in a large city.
Enjoy being my own boss.	Do not like to work behind a desk all day.
Would like to live in a medium-sized city.	Do not like to wear suits all the time.
Enjoy watching football and baseball.	
Enjoy playing racquetball.	

Source: Wayne Sanders.

A self-assessment such as this one helps a person understand his or her basic motives, and sets the stage for pursuing a management career or seeking further technical competence. A person with little desire for management responsibilities should probably not accept a promotion to supervisor or enter management training. People who know themselves can more easily make the decisions necessary for successful career planning. Many people get sidetracked because they choose careers based on haphazard plans or the wishes of others rather than on what they believe to be best for them.

Getting to know oneself is not a singular event. As individuals progress through life, priorities change. Individuals may think that they know themselves quite well at one stage of life and later begin to see themselves quite differently. Therefore, the self-assessment should be viewed as a continuous process. Career-minded individuals must heed the Red Queen's admonition to Alice: "It takes all the running you can do, to keep in the same place."[14] This admonition is so very true in today's work environment.

Using the Web for Assistance in the Self-Assessment

The Internet has valuable information to assist in developing a self-assessment. Some sites are free and some charge a modest fee. The American Career Test (acareertest.com) identifies the top careers that match your interests and career aptitude, unique blend of personality traits, and work-style patterns. It provides a person with relative measures of seven personality traits and four work styles. It will also provide a person with a ranking of the top careers that match a person's personality, work-style profile, and interests (as well as offer insight on how to best position oneself), and track and plan related career options. Costs range from $7.95 for the basic report to $59.95 for the full report.[15] At CareerMaze.com, an assessment of vocational interests and weaknesses, interests, and capabilities for every job-seeker at every level, is provided. The cost is $19.95 to take the approximately 10-minute test.[16] Career-intelligence.com is a career resource site targeted toward women. Career-assessment planning information, exercises, and assessment tools are available in addition to a multitude of other resources.[17]

Two free career-assessment quizzes include:

- The Career Key—www.ncsu.edu/careerkey
- Princeton Review Career Quiz—
www.review.com/career/careerquizhome.cfm

Students may be more inclined to take these, but adults second-guessing their present profession may be interested as well. Created by the makers of the Birkman Method, Princeton Review Career Quiz analyzes your skills and interests and attempts to steer you toward a career. You must register (free) for full results. The Career Key assessment test is based upon the Holland Personality Types. Results are links to the Occupational Outlook site.[18]

Using the Web for Career Planning Assistance

The Web can often be an excellent tool for assisting you in planning your career. Listed below is some advice on how the Web can assist you.

- There is a large amount of free information available on the Web that should prove helpful in a job search.[19] Virtually all of the major job boards provide tips for writing a cover letter and résumés. For example, at HotJobs.com click the "Click Tools" tab and a tremendous amount of valuable information becomes available including industry news, résumé preparation, salary and benefits, job searching, education and training, and tests.[20]
- The Web can be used to develop and maintain a professional network. It is much easier and convenient to keep in touch with other professionals through e-mail. This is important since approximately 7 out of 10 jobs are obtained through networking.[21] Individuals that you have met at conferences or business meetings may provide useful assistance in a job search. A network should be maintained even though you are satisfied with your present job.

- The Web should be used to investigate specific companies before seeking employment or going for an interview. For instance, with WetFeet.com, a job-seeker can research companies, careers, and industries.[22]

ORGANIZATIONAL CAREER PLANNING

As previously defined, the process of establishing career paths and activities for individuals within a firm is referred to as *organizational career planning*. Organizational career planning should begin with a person's job placement and initial orientation. Management then observes the employee's job performance and compares it to job standards. At this stage, strengths and weaknesses will be noted, enabling management to assist the employee in making a tentative career decision. Naturally, this decision can be altered later as the process continues. This tentative career decision is based on a number of factors, including personal needs, abilities and aspirations, and the organization's needs. Management can then schedule development programs that relate to the employee's specific needs.

Remember that career planning is an ongoing process. It takes into consideration the changes that occur in people, in organizations, and in the environment. This type of flexibility is absolutely necessary in today's dynamic organizational environment. Not only do the firm's requirements change, but individuals may also choose to revise their career expectations. For example, they may move sideways, with no change in salary or title, to a more dynamic department; leave the company perhaps for a more rewarding career elsewhere; remain in the same position and try to enhance their skills and explore new horizons; or move down to a job that may carry less weight but promise more growth. These options will be discussed later in the section entitled "Career Paths."

Although the primary responsibility for career planning rests with the individual, organizational career planning must closely parallel individual career planning if a firm is to retain its best and brightest workers. Employees must see that the firm's organizational career planning effort is directed toward furthering their specific career objectives. Companies must, therefore, help their employees obtain their career objectives and, most notably, career security. They must provide them with a diversity of opportunities to learn and do different things. Performing the same or similar task over and over provides little development.

Organizational career planning must begin with a virtual redefinition of the way work is done. Creativity, resourcefulness, flexibility, innovation, and adaptability are becoming much more important than the ability to perform a precisely specified job. Through effective organizational career planning a pool of men and women can be developed who can thrive in any number of organizational structures in the future.

Firms should undertake organizational career planning programs only when the programs contribute to achieving current and future organizational goals. Therefore, the rationale and approach to career planning programs vary among firms. This rationale is more important in today's environment. Career planning programs are expected to achieve one or more of the following objectives:

- *Effective development of available talent.* Individuals are more likely to be committed to development that is part of a specific career plan. This way, they can better understand the purpose of development.
- *Self-appraisal opportunities for employees considering new or nontraditional career paths.* Some excellent workers do not view traditional upward mobility as a career option since firms today have fewer promotion options available. Other workers see themselves in dead-end jobs and seek relief. Rather than lose these workers, a firm can offer career planning to help them identify new and different career paths.
- *Development of career paths that cut across divisions and geographic locations.* The development should not be limited to a narrow spectrum of one part of a company.
- *A demonstration of a tangible commitment to EEO and affirmative action.* Adverse impact can occur at virtually any level in an organization. Firms that are totally committed to reducing adverse impact often cannot find qualified women and minorities to fill vacant positions. One means of

overcoming this problem is an effective career planning and development program.

- *Satisfaction of employees' specific development needs.* Individuals who see their personal development needs being met tend to be more satisfied with their jobs and the organization. They tend to remain with the organization.
- *Improvement of performance.* The job itself is the most important influence on career development. Each job can provide different challenges and experiences.
- *Increased employee loyalty and motivation, leading to decreased turnover.* Individuals who believe that the firm is interested in their career planning are more likely to remain with the organization.
- *A method of determining training and development needs.* If a person desires a certain career path and does not presently have the proper qualifications, this identifies a training and development need.

Successful career planning depends on a firm's ability to satisfy those that it considers most crucial to employee development and the achievement of organizational goals.

CAREER PATHS

Career paths have historically focused on upward mobility within a particular occupation, a choice not nearly as available as in the past. Other career paths include the network, lateral skill, dual career paths, adding value to your career, and even demotion. By selecting an alternative career path, a person may transfer current skills into a new career, one that was only dreamed about in the past.[23] Typically, these career paths are used in combination and may be more popular at various stages of a person's career.

Traditional Career Path

The following is a quote from a recent *Fortune* magazine article:

> *Close your eyes and picture an object that embodies the word* career. *If you joined the workforce, say, 15 or 20 or 25 years ago, you're probably hard-wired, as the techies say to visualize your working life as a predictable series of narrow and distinctly separate rungs that lead straight up (or down)—in other words, a ladder. Ha! Ha, ha, ha! My friend, the ladder has been chopped up into little pieces and dumped in the garbage pile. A team of sanitation engineers disposed of it at dawn, while you were dreaming.*[24]

Although the traditional career path is somewhat dated, understanding it furthers one's comprehension of the various career path alternatives.

Traditional career path: A vertical line of career progression in which an employee progresses vertically upward in the organization from one specific job to the next.

The **traditional career path** is one in which an employee progresses vertically upward in the organization from one specific job to the next. The assumption is that each preceding job is essential preparation for the next higher-level job. Therefore, an employee must move, step-by-step, from one job to the next to gain needed experience and preparation. One of the biggest advantages of the traditional career path is that it is straightforward. The path is clearly laid out, and the employee knows the specific sequence of jobs through which he or she must progress.

Today, the old model of a career in which an employee worked his way up the ladder in a single company is becoming somewhat rare. Some of the factors contributing to this situation include the following:

- A massive reduction in management ranks due to mergers, downsizing, stagnation, growth cycles, and reengineering.
- Extinction of paternalism and job security.
- Erosion of employee loyalty.
- A work environment where new skills must constantly be learned.

The certainties of yesterday's business methods and growth have disappeared in many industries, and neither organizations nor individuals can be assured of ever regaining them. However, the one certainty that still remains is that there will always be top-level managers and individuals who strive to achieve these positions. Unfortunately, it is just more difficult to obtain one of these positions.

Network career path: A method of job progression that contains both a vertical sequence of jobs and a series of horizontal opportunities.

Network Career Path

The **network career path** contains both a vertical sequence of jobs and a series of horizontal opportunities. The network career path recognizes the interchangeability of experience at certain levels and the need to broaden experience at one level before promotion to a higher level. Often, this approach more realistically represents opportunities for employee development in an organization than does the traditional career path. For instance, a person may work as an inventory manager for a few years and then move to a lateral position of shift manager before being considered for a promotion. The vertical and horizontal options lessen the probability of blockage in one job. One major disadvantage of this type of career path is that it is more difficult to explain to employees the specific route their careers may take for a given line of work.

Lateral Skill Path

Lateral skill path: A career path that allows for lateral moves within the firm that are taken to permit an employee to become revitalized and find new challenges.

Traditionally, a career path was viewed as moving upward to higher levels of management in the organization. The previous two career path methods focused on such an approach. The availability of these two options has diminished considerably in recent years, but this does not mean that an individual has to remain in the same job for life. The **lateral skill path** allows for lateral moves within the firm that are taken to permit an employee to become revitalized and find new challenges. Neither pay nor promotion may be involved, but by learning a different job, an employee can increase his or her value to the organization and also become revitalized and reenergized. Firms that want to encourage lateral movement may choose to utilize a skill-based pay system that rewards individuals for the type and number of skills they possess. Another approach, which we discussed in Chapter 4, is job enrichment. This approach rewards (without promotion) an employee by increasing the challenge of the job, giving the job more meaning, and giving the employee a greater sense of accomplishment.

Dual-Career Path

Dual-career path: A career path that recognizes that technical specialists can and should be allowed to contribute their expertise to a company without having to become managers.

The dual-career path was originally developed to deal with the problem of technically trained employees who had no desire to move into management through the normal upward mobility procedure. The **dual-career path** recognizes that technical specialists can and should be allowed to contribute their expertise to a company without having to become managers. A dual-career approach is often established to encourage and motivate professionals in such fields as engineering, sales, marketing, finance, and human resources. Individuals in these fields can increase their specialized knowledge, make contributions to their firms, and be rewarded without entering management. Whether on the management or technical path, compensation would be comparable at each level.

The dual-career path is becoming increasingly popular at some firms. At AlliedSignal Inc. in Morristown, New Jersey, turnover among the top technical performers traditionally has hovered around 25 percent. Technical people were leaving because they felt they had nowhere to go unless they went into management. Since the company created a dual-career system, no top talent has been lost.[25] The dual system is also used in higher education, where individuals can move through the ranks of instructor, assistant professor, associate professor, and professor without having to go into administration.

Demotion

Demotions have long been associated with failure, but limited promotional opportunities in the future and the fast pace of technological change may make demotion a legitimate career option. If the stigma of demotion can be removed, more employees, especially older workers, might choose to make such a move. Working long hours for a limited promotional opportunity loses its appeal to some, especially if the worker can financially afford the demotion. In certain instances, this approach might open up a clogged promotional path and at the same time permit a senior employee to escape unwanted stress without being viewed as a failure.

Free agents: People who take charge of all or part of their careers, by being their own bosses or by working for others in ways that fit their particular needs or wants.

Free Agents (Being Your Own Boss)

Free agents are people who take charge of all or part of their careers by being their own bosses or by working for others in ways that fit their particular needs or wants. Some free agents work full-time; others work part-time. Other free agents work full-time and run a small business in the hope of converting it into their primary work. Free agents come in many shapes and sizes, but what distinguishes them is a commitment to controlling part or all of their careers. They have a variety of talents and are used to dealing with a wide range of audiences and changing their approach on the spot in response to new information or reactions. They also tend to love challenges and spontaneity.[26] Check out the Web sites for free agents in the appendix to Chapter 5.

CAREER DEVELOPMENT

Career development tools: Skills, education, and experiences, as well as behavioral modification and refinement techniques that allow individuals to work better and add value.

As previously mentioned, career development is a formal approach taken by the organization to ensure that people with the proper qualifications and experiences are available when needed. Career development benefits both the organization and the employee because properly developed employees are better prepared to add value both to themselves and to the company. Thus, career development includes exposure to any and all activities that prepare a person for satisfying the present and future needs of the firm. **Career development tools** consist of skills, education, and experiences, as well as behavioral modification and refinement techniques that allow individuals to work better and add value. Specific methods were discussed in Chapter 7 under the heading "Training and Development Methods." These methods can also apply to career development at all levels, even nonmanagerial. Once only managers were thought to need developing, but the current move toward a team-based environment has created the need for a wider range of worker development. Developmental efforts, therefore, are also often quite important for nonmanagerial employees.

Although skills, education, and experiences are very important, the behavior of an organization as a whole has become more important as the workforce diversifies and becomes more interdependent. Therefore, the need for organizational development (discussed in Chapter 7) is often essential. Organizational development is important because it helps develop total unit behaviors. Organizational development efforts include a number of interventions such as survey feedback, quality circles, sensitivity training, and team building.

Many key individuals must work together if an organization is to have an effective career development program. Management must first make a commitment to support the program by making policy decisions and allocating resources to the program. Human resource professionals often provide the necessary information, tools, and guidance. The worker's immediate supervisor is responsible for providing support, advice, and feedback. Through the supervisor, a worker can find out how supportive of career development the organization actually is. Finally, individual employees are ultimately responsible for developing their own careers.[27] In today's environment, workers may be more in tune with what is needed for their career development than is the company. If they do not see the career development efforts of the company matching their specific needs, a change in organizations often is forthcoming.

CAREER PLANNING AND DEVELOPMENT METHODS

There are numerous methods for career planning and development. Some currently utilized methods, most of which are used in various combinations, are discussed next.

Discussions with Knowledgeable Individuals

In a formal discussion, the superior and subordinate may jointly agree on what type of career planning and development activities are best. The resources made available to achieve these objectives may also include developmental programs. In some organizations, human resource professionals are the focal point for providing assistance on the topic. In other instances, psychologists and guidance counselors provide this service. In an academic setting, colleges and universities often provide career planning and development information to students. Students often go to their professors for career advice.

Company Material

Some firms provide material specifically developed to assist their workers in career planning and development. Such material is tailored to the firm's special needs. In addition, job descriptions provide valuable insight for individuals to personally determine if a match exists between their strengths and weaknesses and specific positions.

Performance Appraisal System

The firm's performance appraisal system can also be a valuable tool in career planning and development. Noting and discussing an employee's strengths and weaknesses with his or her supervisor can uncover developmental needs. If overcoming a particular weakness seems difficult or even impossible, an alternate career path may be the solution.

Workshops

Some organizations conduct workshops lasting two or three days for the purpose of helping workers develop careers within the company. Employees define and match their specific career objectives with the needs of the company.[28] At other times, the company may send workers to workshops available in the community or workers may initiate the visit themselves. Consider just two of the developmental activities available for HR professionals:

- *Society for Human Resource Management Seminar Series*—Many HR seminars are available to SHRM members. For instance, the Advanced HR Generalist Certificate Program is a two-and-a-half-day program designed for senior HR professionals to position themselves as a strategic partner by establishing links between HR and the organization's other business units. This program is designed for HR professionals in policy-making positions within their organizations and explores the transformation of HR from an operational to a strategic function.[29]

- *American Management Association Human Resource Seminars*—Human resources seminars offered through the AMA provide the skills, behaviors, and strategies needed to attract and retain a talented and diverse workforce.[30]

Personal Development Plans (PDPs)

Many employees write their own personal development plans. This is a summary of a person's personal development needs and an action plan to achieve them. Workers analyze their strengths and weaknesses, as previously described in this appendix. A PDP could be the nucleus of a wider career plan such as setting out alternative long-term strategies, identifying one's long-term learning needs, and setting out a plan of self-development.[31] It is important that a person not depend on someone else to drive his or her career.[32]

Sabbaticals

Sabbaticals: Temporary leaves of absence from an organization, usually at a reduced amount of pay.

Sabbaticals are temporary leaves of absence from an organization, usually at a reduced amount of pay.[33] Some firms and companies—mostly in the service field—are discovering that periodic sabbaticals or leaves help their best employees. At Fleishman-Hillard, a global public relations firm, employees with four or more years of service can take a six-week sabbatical. Benefits, such as health insurance, continue throughout. The firm pays for two weeks; the employee uses two weeks of vacation and then takes more weeks without pay. Or employees can take up to one year of unpaid leave and can pay their share of health insurance. They retain the benefit of lower rates from being in the company's pool. "We were looking for ways to attract and retain employees," said Agnes Gioconda, Fleishman-Hillard's chief talent officer. "We find that it reduces employee burnout. They need new ideas for their clients. And it gives us cross-training and career development for others who are out (on leave)."[34]

As another example, every employee who has worked at Arrow Electronics, a New York–based distributor of computer products and electronic components, for seven years is eligible for an eight- to ten-week sabbatical. "Employees can use the time off as they wish," says Kathy Bernhard, director of management development. "We tend to run people really hard," she explains. "There's a lot of travel associated with many of these jobs, and it's a high-stress, high-change industry, so it's really just a chance for people to get recharged." Another benefit of the sabbatical program is that of employee development. Employees showing promise and a willingness to learn are assigned to the vacant positions. The opportunity enhances their careers and increases their understanding of the business.[35]

Some companies use sabbaticals to reduce costs in difficult financial times. Accenture, a global consulting firm, offered employees an unusual proposal: workers who agreed to take an 80 percent pay cut would be allowed a six- to twelve-month sabbatical with full benefits. More than 1,400 of the 17,000 eligible workers in the United States accepted the offer.[36] Cisco Systems in San Jose, California, experienced a similar employee response when it created a pilot sabbatical program. Workers who accepted a two-thirds pay cut were offered a chance to volunteer for a year at one of 29 not-for-profit organizations chosen by Cisco. In addition to paying one-third of those employees' salaries, the company would continue to provide full benefits and stock options. Eighty people were ultimately eligible to sign on.[37]

DEVELOPING UNIQUE SEGMENTS OF THE WORKFORCE

Career planning and development is essential for the continual evolution of the labor force and the success of organizations, as well as individuals. Certain groups of employees are unique because of the specific characteristics of the work they do or who they are. In previous editions of this text, our discussion began with Generation X, progressed to the new factory worker, and then to Generation Y and then Generation I. But, a strange event occurred on the way to Generation I. Up popped the baby boomers again as valued members of the workforce, though many had written them off into retirement. Because of certain differences between these groups, each group must be developed in rather unique ways. Although generalizations about a group are risky, the following are offered simply to provide additional insight into what some members of each group may require developmentally.

Baby Boomers

Baby boomers:
People born between just after World War II and 1964.

Only a few years ago the discussion of baby boomers in the same topic of developing a unique segment of the workforce would have been unheard of. **Baby boomers** were born during the period from just after World War II to 1964. Corporate downsizing in the 1980s and 1990s cast aside millions of baby boomers.[38] Companies are now again recruiting these retirees. They are realizing that many older workers have skills and experience that are critically needed. Companies today place high value on experience, corporate memory, and know-how, the traits older individuals are most likely to possess, and these companies have backed that realization by hiring older workers in record numbers.[39] Training replacement workers for an organization is very expensive. Bringing back retirees reduces training costs. Retirees and laid-off former employees can quickly move into production with little or no training. Many companies have started recruiting knowledgeable retirees as an alternative to adding additional staff or hiring unknown outside contractors. In addition, the pool of high-quality young workers is shrinking, and the demand for skilled and experienced workers is increasing. Firms such as Gruman Corporation, Travelers Insurance, NCR, McDonald's, and Days Inn use retirees to augment their staffs.[40]

Generation X Employees

Generation X:
The label affixed to the 40 million American workers born between 1965 and 1976.

Generation X is the label affixed to the 44 million American workers born between 1965 and 1976.[41] Many organizations have a growing cadre of Generation X employees, roughly 27 to 38 years old, who possess lots of energy and promise.[42] They are one of the most widely misunderstood phenomena facing the HR professional today. Generation Xers differ from previous generations in some significant ways including their natural affinity for technology and their entrepreneurial spirit. In fact, four out of five new enterprises are the work of Xers.[43] Job instability and the breakdown of traditional employer–employee relationships in today's era of restructuring brought a realization to Generation Xers that the world of work is different for them than for past generations. For example, more than 85 percent of Gen X women say having a loving family is extremely important, compared with 18 percent who put the priority on earning a great deal of money.[44]

Managers who understand how circumstances have shaped Generation Xers' outlook on career issues can begin to develop a positive relationship with these workers and harness their unique abilities. Developing Generation X employees requires support for their quest to acquire skills and expertise. Generation Xers recognize that their careers cannot be founded securely on a relationship with any one employer. Today, Xers are very skeptical, particularly when it comes to the business world and job security.[45] They think of themselves more as free agents in a mobile workforce and expect to build career security, not job security, by acquiring marketable skills and expertise.[46] They are not afraid of changing jobs quite often.[47] The surest way to gain Xers' loyalty is to help them develop career security. When a company helps them expand their knowledge and skills—in essence, preparing them for the job market—Xers will often want to stay on board to learn those very skills.

The New Factory Workers

Today, life on the factory line requires more brains than brawn[48]—so laborers are taking evaluation examinations to identify skill and educational strengths and weaknesses and adaptability. After being evaluated, new factory workers are heading for development in the form of training, classroom lectures, computer-aided learning, organizational development techniques, and so on. Tens of thousands of factory workers across America are going back to school. These days, in an economy where even factory work increasingly is defined by blips on a computer screen, more schooling is the road to success.

Over the past decade, managers have been equipping factory workers with industrial robots and teaching them to use computer controls to operate technologically advanced manufacturing processes. At the same time, managers are funneling information through the computers, thereby bringing employees into the data loop. Workers are trained to watch inventories, and to know suppliers and customers, as well as be aware of costs and prices. Knowledge that long separated brainworkers from brawnworkers is now available from computers on the factory floor.[49]

The trend toward high-skills manufacturing began with innovative companies such as Corning, Motorola, and Xerox. They replaced rote assembly-line work with an industrial vision that requires skilled and nimble workers to think while they work. Large, old-line companies have learned that investments in people boost productivity, often at less cost than capital investments. Indeed, the old formula of company loyalty, a strong back, and showing up on time no longer guarantees job security or even a decent paycheck. Today, industrial workers will thrive only if they use their wits and keep adding to their skills base by continual development. Closing the skills gap requires carefully considered career development programs to ensure that workers can compete in the factories of the future.

Generation Y as Present and Future Employees

Generation Y: The sons and daughters of boomers; people who were born between 1979 and 1994.

Generation Y comprises approximately 80 million[50] young people born between the late 1970s and early 1990s.[51] They have never wound a watch, dialed a rotary phone, or plunked the keys of a manual typewriter. But without a thought they format disks, download music from the Internet, and set the clock on a videocassette recorder.[52] These individuals are the leading edge of a generation that promises to be the richest, smartest, and savviest ever. These Generation Yers, often referred to as the echo boomers, and nexters,[53] are the coddled, confident offspring of post–World War II baby boomers. Generation Y individuals are a most privileged generation, who came of age during the hottest domestic economy in memory. They want a workplace that is both fun and rewarding. They want jobs that conform to their interests and don't accept the way things have been done in the past. They are the first generation to grow up in the digital world and they know how to use technology to create a life and work environment that supports their lifestyle.[54] Their enthusiasm and experience is seemingly of people much older and they are willing to tackle major challenges and have the technology to back it up. The new workforce will require more team effort and this group is well equipped to work successfully in this environment.[55]

Yers' childhoods have been short-lived, as they have been exposed to some of the worst things in life: schoolyard shootings, drug use, the Clinton sex scandal, and war. This new wave of young Americans has given early notice of its potential, especially when it comes to leadership and success. One of the predictors is the group's penchant for self-employment. The U.S. Labor Department has charted record levels of part-time employment among Yers', many still too young to officially enter the world of work, and the U.S. Small Business Administration has charted a leap in business ownership among the age group's elder statesmen.[56]

Generation I as Future Employees

Generation I: Internet-assimilated children, born after 1994.

First it was Generation X, and then came Generation Y. Bill Gates, the chairman of Microsoft Corporation, recently referred to children born after 1994 as Generation I. Specifically, **Generation I** are Internet-assimilated children, born after 1994. According to Gates, "These kids will be the first generation to grow up with the Internet. The Web will change Generation I's world as much as television transformed our world after World War II. That is why it is so critical to ensure that new teachers understand how to incorporate technology into their instruction and that teachers have the technological training they want and need. We cannot afford to have any teacher locked out of the greatest library on earth— the Internet."[57]

Key Terms

- **Employability doctrine, 237**
- **Self-assessment, 238**
- **Strength/weakness balance sheet, 238**
- **Likes and dislikes survey, 238**
- **Traditional career path, 242**
- **Network career path, 242**
- **Lateral skill path, 243**
- **Dual-career path, 243**
- **Free agents, 243**
- **Career development tools, 243**
- **Sabbaticals, 245**
- **Baby boomers, 246**
- **Generation X, 246**
- **Generation Y, 247**
- **Generation I, 247**

Notes

1. "IPD Publication Urges Employers to Wise Up to Career Development," *Management Services* 44 (April 2000): 4.
2. Joel Schettler, "A New Social Contract," *Training* 39 (April 2002): 62.
3. M. F. Wolff, "Despite Layoffs, It's Still Tough to Find and Keep the Best," *Research Technology Management* 45 (November/December 2002): 4–5.
4. Richard Ream, "Changing Jobs? It's a Changing Market," *Information Today* 17 (February 2000): 18.
5. Kevin Voigt, "The New Face of HR," *Far Eastern Economic Review* (September 5, 2002): 61.
6. Michael Schrage, "We're Under Attack: Online Forum," *Newsweek* (April 29, 2002): 56–58.
7. Rob Yeung, "Business: Managing Your Career—Goal Attack," *Accountancy* 130 (November 2002): 60.
8. Emily Walls Ray, "Tap-Tap-Tap into Internet Job Research: Good Tool, but Remember Basic Steps in Any Search," *Richmond Times-Dispatch* (February 10, 2002): S-5.
9. Charles S. Lauer, "Really Pursue Those 'Other Interests'" *Modern Healthcare* (February 3, 2003): 31.
10. Julie Demers, "Keys to a Successful Career Transition," *CMA Management* 76 (June 2002): 11–12.
11. Barbara Moses, "Career Intelligence: The 12 New Rules for Success," *The Futurist* 33 (August 1999): 28–35.
12. Paul W. H. Bohne, "Achieving Career Goals Through Self-Evaluation," *Healthcare Financial Management* 56 (September 2002): 100–102.
13. Amy Newman, "Trainer, Assess Thyself," *T + D* 56 (July 2002): 53–55.
14. Lewis Carroll, *Through the Looking Glass* (New York: Norton, 1971): 127.
15. http://www.acareertest.com/, August 1, 2003.
16. http://www.careermaze.com/home.asp?licensee=CareerMaze, August 1, 2003.
17. http://www.career-intelligence.com/, August 1, 2003.
18. Kelly Sparks, "The Career Key / Princeton Review Career Quiz," *Library Journal* (May 1, 2002): 30.
19. Mary Ellen Slayter, "How to Navigate the Web to Find the Right Job," *Washington Post* (November 25, 2002): E03.
20. http://hotjobs.yahoo.com/, August 1, 2003.
21. Cassandra Hayes, "Building a Solid Network," *Black Enterprise* 33 (December 2002): 127.
22. http://www.wetfeet.com/asp/home.asp, August 1, 2003.
23. James J. Kirk, Bridget Downey, Steve Duckett, and Connie Woody, "Name Your Career Development Intervention," *Journal of Workplace Learning* 12 (2000): 205–216.
24. Anne Fisher, "Six Ways to Supercharge Your Career," *Fortune* (January 13, 1997): 46+.
25. Barb Cole-Gomolski, "Dual Career Paths Reduce Turnover Practicing," *Computerworld* (February 22, 1999): 24.
26. Barbara Reinhold, "Choosing Free Agency," *T + D* 56 (November 2002): 56–57.
27. Loretta D. Foxman and Walter L. Polsky, "Aid in Employee Career Development," *Personnel Journal* 69 (January 1990): 22.
28. Robert McLuham, "There Are No Dead Ends, Only Crossroads," *Independent on Sunday* (November 22, 1998): 2.
29. http://www.shrm.org/seminars/certificate/advanced.asp#dates, August 1, 2003.
30. http://www.amanet.org/seminars/cmd2/Human.htm, August 1, 2003.
31. Mark Morgan, "Career-Building Strategies," *Strategic Finance* 83 (June 2002): 38–43.
32. Steve Bates, "Facing the Future," *HRMagazine* 47 (July 2002): 26–32.
33. Kirk, Downey, Duckett, and Woody, "Name Your Career Development Intervention," 205–216.
34. Repps Hudson, "Leaves of Absence Can Recharge a Worker or Drain a Career," *St. Louis Post-Dispatch* (February 19, 2002): 1.
35. Joel Schettler, "Successful Sabbaticals," *Training* 39 (June 2002): 26.
36. Pamela Paul, "Time Out," *American Demographics* 24 (June 2002): 34–41.
37. Ibid.
38. T. L. Stanley, "Don't Let the Gray Hair Fool You," *Supervision* 62 (July 2001): 7–10.
39. John A Challenger, "The Changing Workforce: Workplace Rules in the New Millennium," *Vital Speeches of the Day* (September 15, 2001): 721–728.
40. Stanley, "Don't Let the Gray Hair Fool You."
41. Joanne Sujansky, "The Critical Care and Feeding of Generation Y," *Workforce* 81 (May 2002): 15.
42. Steve Bates, "Unique Strategies Urged to Keep 'Emerging Leaders'" *HRMagazine* 47 (September 2002): 14.
43. Jean Chatzky, "Gen Xers Aren't Slackers After All," *Time* (April 8, 2002): 87.
44. Stephanie Armour, "Why Work so Hard? Fed Up, Disillusioned Employees Rethinking Where They Spend Their Time," *Chicago Sun Times* (December 8, 2002): 26.
45. Christopher S. Stewart, "Gen X Rising," *Potentials* 35 (September 2002): 22–31.
46. Amy Zuber, "Across the Great Divide: Managing Differences Between Generations," *Nation's Restaurant News* (June 10, 2002): 68.
47. Chatzky, "Gen Xers Aren't Slackers After All."
48. William Sampson, "Using Brain Over Brawn," *CabinetMaker* 16 (April 2002): 6.
49. George Weimer, "Manufacturing Is a Job for Knowledge Workers," *Material Handling Management* 57 (June 2002): 20.
50. Sujansky, "The Critical Care."
51. Joe Jancsurak, "The Value of 'Y,'" *Appliance Manufacturer* 50 (June 2002): 13.

52. "Is 'Generation Y' a Cinch to Save Xmas?" *Barron's* (November 25, 2002): 11.
53. Denies Markley, "Here Comes Y," *Successful Meetings* 51 (July 2002): 39–40.
54. Ibid.
55. Ibid.
56. Sharon Linstedt, "Generation Yers Turning Out Take Charge Entrepreneurs," *Buffalo News* (May 13, 2002): C-1.
57. Bill Leonard, "After Generations X and Y Comes I," *HRMagazine* 45 (January 2000): 21.

CHAPTER OBJECTIVES

After completing this chapter, students should be able to

1. Describe the 360-degree feedback evaluation method.
2. Define *performance appraisal* and identify the uses of performance appraisal.
3. Discuss the performance appraisal environmental factors.
4. Describe the performance appraisal process.
5. Identify the aspects of a person's performance that an organization should evaluate.
6. Identify who may be responsible for performance appraisal and the performance period.
7. Identify the various performance appraisal methods used.
8. Describe how computer software is used in performance appraisal.
9. List the problems that have been associated with performance appraisal.
10. Explain the characteristics of an effective appraisal system.
11. Describe the legal implications of performance appraisal.
12. Explain how the appraisal interview should be conducted.

CHAPTER 8

Performance Appraisal

HRM IN *Action:*

The 360-Degree Feedback Evaluation

OBJECTIVE

Describe the 360-degree feedback evaluation method.

360-degree feedback evaluation method: An increasingly popular appraisal method that involves evaluation input from multiple levels within the firm and external sources as well.

The **360-degree feedback evaluation** is an increasingly popular appraisal method that involves evaluation input from multiple levels within the firm as well as external sources. In this method, people all around the rated employee may provide ratings, including senior managers, the employee himself or herself, supervisors, subordinates, peers, team members, and internal or external customers. According to HR consulting firm William M. Mercer, 40 percent of companies used 360-degree feedback in 1995 and by 2000, the figure jumped to 65 percent.[1] Businesses using 360-degree feedback include McDonnell-Douglas, AT&T, Allied Signal, Dupont, Honeywell, Boeing, and Intel. These firms use 360-degree feedback to provide evaluations for conventional uses. However, for many other firms, this process is used strictly for employee development and only the managers being rated see the feedback.[2]

Unlike traditional approaches, 360-degree feedback focuses on skills needed across organizational boundaries. Also, by shifting the responsibility for evaluation to more than one person, many of the common appraisal errors can be reduced or eliminated. Thanks to computer networks, the people who provide the ratings can do so quickly and conveniently since many rating instruments are available online. The 360-degree feedback method may provide a more objective measure of a person's performance. Including the perspective of multiple sources results in a broader view of the employee's performance and may minimize biases that result from limited views of behavior. Personal development, which is essential in the workplace, requires good, honest, well-expressed, and specific feedback.

360-Degree Feedback Evaluation

www.cognology.biz/Learningcenter.htm

This Web site provides information regarding the 360-degree feedback method and other appraisal information.

Having multiple raters also makes the process more legally defensible. However, it is important for all parties to know the evaluation criteria, the methods for gathering and summarizing the feedback, and the use to which the feedback will be put. This involvement is critical to ensure stakeholder support of, and commitment to, the feedback process. An appraisal system involving numerous evaluators will naturally take more time and, therefore, be more costly. Nevertheless, the way firms are being organized and managed may require innovative alternatives to traditional top-down appraisals.

When employees work in teams, and their appraisal system focuses entirely on individual results, it is not surprising that they show little interest in their teams. But, this problem can be corrected. If teamwork is essential, make it a criterion for evaluating employees. Rewarding collaboration will encourage teamwork.[3]

After describing the 360-degree feedback evaluation method, we begin this chapter by defining *performance appraisal* and discussing its relationship to performance management. We then explain the uses made of appraisal data and the environmental factors affecting the performance appraisal process. Then we identify the potential aspects of a person's performance to consider for evaluation, the individuals responsible for appraisal, and the appraisal period. Next, we discuss the various performance appraisal methods, the use of computer software in performance appraisal, the problems associated with performance appraisal, and the characteristics of an effective appraisal system. This chapter concludes with discussions of the legal aspects of performance appraisal and the appraisal interview.

2 OBJECTIVE

Define *performance appraisal* and identify the uses of performance appraisal.

Performance Appraisal

Performance appraisal (PA): A formal system of review and evaluation of individual or team task performance.

Performance management: A management system consisting of all organizational processes that determine how well employees, teams, and ultimately, the organization perform.

Performance appraisal (PA) is a formal system of review and evaluation of individual or team task performance. While evaluation of team performance is critical when teams exist in an organization, the focus of PA in most firms remains on the individual employee. Regardless of the emphasis, an effective appraisal system evaluates accomplishments and initiates plans for development, goals, and objectives.

Performance management consists of all organizational processes that determine how well employees, teams, and ultimately, the organization perform. Every HR function contributes to this performance. The process includes HR planning, employee recruitment and selection, T&D, career planning and development, and compensation. Performance appraisal is especially critical to its success. An organization must have some means of assessing the level of individual and team performance in order to make appropriate developmental plans. While performance appraisal is but one component of performance management, it is vital in that it directly reflects the organization's strategic plan.[4]

SHRM HR Links

www.shrm.org/hrlinks/default.asp

This SHRM Web site provides information on employee assessment.

As emphasized before, global competition affects virtually every American business firm. For survival and success, it is imperative that these organizations remain competitive in this environment. Organizations maintain continued competence only through ceaseless development of human resources. Employee performance appraisal is a potential mechanism for this growth. It is vital for managers to realize that performance appraisal must be comprehensive and that it is a continuous process; definitely not merely a periodic event.

Appraiser Discomfort

Conducting performance appraisals is often a frustrating human resource management task. One management guru, Edward Lawler, noted the considerable documentation showing that performance appraisal systems neither motivate individuals nor effectively guide their development. Instead, he maintains, they create conflict between supervisors and subordinates and lead to dysfunctional behaviors.[5] This caveat is important. If a performance appraisal system has a faulty design, or improper administration, the employees will dread receiving appraisals and the managers will despise giving them. In fact, some managers have always loathed the time, paperwork, difficult choices, and discomfort that often accompanies the appraisal process. Going through the procedure cuts into a manager's high-priority workload and the experience can be especially unpleasant when the employee in question has not performed well. According to a British source, one in eight managers would actually prefer to visit the dentist than carry out a performance appraisal.[6] When reviews are not fair, accurate, and timely, they fail to reward star performers, fail to provide encouragement and guidance to borderline workers, and fail to give proper feedback to those whose work is distinctly substandard.[7]

Critics of performance appraisal offer a number of compelling arguments against its use. Anecdotal, empirical, and personal experience demonstrate a multitude of problems with appraisal system practices.[8]

Employee Anxiety

The evaluation process may also create anxiety for the appraised employee. Opportunities for promotion, better work assignments, and increased compensation may hinge on the results. This could cause not only apprehension, but also outright resistance.[9] One opinion is that if you surveyed typical employees, they would tell you performance appraisal is management's way of highlighting all the bad things they did all year.[10]

HR Web Wisdom

Mercer Human Resource Consulting

www.mercerhr.com/

This Web site provides information on a human resource consulting firm.

Rationale for Performance Appraisal

If performance appraisal is often a negative, disliked activity and one that seems to elude mastery, why don't organizations just eliminate it? Actually, some managers might do just that *if* they didn't need to provide feedback, encourage performance improvement, make valid decisions, justify terminations, identify training and development needs, and defend personnel decisions.[11] On top of these considerations, managers must be concerned about legal ramifications.

Performance appraisals provide so many important legal and other benefits that employers should be reluctant to part with them. Linda Peterson, vice president of HR at Kettering University in Flint, Michigan, says, "It isn't perfect, but nothing really is. Just because it is imperfect, we should not resort to throwing out the baby with the bath water."[12] Indeed, performance appraisal serves many purposes and improved results and efficiency are increasingly critical in today's globally competitive marketplace. Therefore, abandoning the only program with *performance* in its name and *employees* as its focus would seem to be an ill-advised overreaction.

Developing an effective performance appraisal system has been and will continue to be a high priority for human resource management. Regardless of the criticism this management process has received, America's best-managed corporations consider performance appraisal to be serious business.[13] Remember that performance appraisal is not an end in itself, but rather the means to impact performance. For example, a National Science Foundation report found that firms that switched from a system that did not measure work to one that measured work and included performance feedback raised productivity an average of 43 percent. When both performance feedback and incentives (discussed in the next chapter) were instituted, productivity rose 63.8 percent on average.[14]

Uses of Performance Appraisal

For many organizations, the primary goal of an appraisal system is to improve individual and organizational performance. There may be other goals, however. A potential problem with PA, and possible cause of much dissatisfaction, is expecting too much from one appraisal plan. For example, a plan that is effective for developing employees may not be the best for determining pay increases. Yet, a properly designed system can help achieve organizational objectives and enhance employee performance. In fact, PA data are potentially valuable for virtually every human resource functional area.

Human Resource Planning

In assessing a firm's human resources, data must be available that describe the promotability and potential of all employees, especially key executives. Management succession planning (discussed in Chapter 4) is a key concern for all firms. A well-designed appraisal system provides a profile of the organization's human resource strengths and weaknesses to support this effort.

Recruitment and Selection

Performance evaluation ratings may be helpful in predicting the performance of job applicants. For example, it may be determined that a firm's successful managers (identified through performance evaluations) exhibit certain behaviors when performing key tasks. These data may then provide benchmarks for evaluating applicant responses obtained through behavioral interviews, which we discussed in Chapter 6. Also, in validating selection tests, employee ratings may be used as the variable against which test scores are compared. In this instance, determination of the selection test's validity would depend on the accuracy of appraisal results.

Training and Development

A performance appraisal should point out an employee's specific needs for training and development (T&D). For instance, if Pat Compton's job requires skill in technical writing and her evaluation reveals a deficiency in this factor, she may need additional training in written communication. If a firm finds that a number of first-line supervisors are having difficulty in administering discipline, training sessions addressing this problem may be appropriate. By identifying deficiencies that adversely affect performance, human resource and line managers are able to develop T&D programs that permit individuals to build on their strengths and minimize their deficiencies. An appraisal system does not guarantee properly trained and developed employees. However, determining T&D needs is more precise when appraisal data are available. One HR representative from a manufacturing firm put it this way: "awareness of any discrepancy between how we see ourselves and how others see us enhances self-awareness." He feels that enhanced self-awareness is a key to maximum performance, and thus a foundation block for employee growth and development.[15]

Career Planning and Development

Career planning and development may be viewed from either an individual or organizational viewpoint. In either case, performance appraisal data are essential in assessing an employee's strengths and weaknesses and in determining the person's potential. Managers may use such information to counsel subordinates and assist them in developing and implementing their career plans.

Compensation Programs

Performance appraisal results provide a basis for rational decisions regarding pay adjustments. Most managers believe that you should reward outstanding job performance tangibly with pay increases. They believe that *the behaviors you reward are the behaviors you get.* Rewarding the behaviors necessary for accomplishing organizational objectives is at the heart of a firm's strategic plan. To encourage good performance, a firm should design and implement a reliable performance appraisal system and then reward the most productive workers and teams accordingly.

Internal Employee Relations

Performance appraisal data are also frequently used for decisions in several areas of internal employee relations, including promotion, demotion, termination, layoff, and transfer. For example, an employee's performance in one job may be useful in determining his or her ability to perform another job on the same level, as is required in the consideration of transfers. When the performance level is unacceptable, demotion or even termination may be appropriate. When employees working under a labor agreement are involved, seniority is typically the basis for layoffs. However, when management has more flexibility, an employee's performance record is generally a more relevant criterion.

Assessment of Employee Potential

Some organizations attempt to assess employee potential as they appraise their job performance. While past behaviors may be the best predictors of future behaviors, an employee's past performance in one job may not accurately indicate future performance in a higher level or different position. The best salesperson in the company may not have what it takes to become a successful district sales manager, where the tasks are distinctly different. Similarly, the best computer programmer may, if promoted, be a disaster as an information technology (IT) manager. Overemphasizing technical skills and ignoring other equally important skills is a common error in promoting employees into management jobs. Recognition of this problem has led some firms to separate the appraisal of performance, which focuses on past behavior, from the assessment of potential, which is future oriented. These firms have established *assessment centers,* discussed in Chapter 6 as a selection method, and we mention them again later in this chapter as an adjunct to appraisal.

3 OBJECTIVE

Discuss the performance appraisal environmental factors.

Performance Appraisal Environmental Factors

Many external and internal environmental factors can influence the appraisal process. For example, legislation requires that appraisal systems be nondiscriminatory. In the case of *Mistretta v Sandia Corporation* (a subsidiary of Western Electric Company, Inc.), a federal district court judge ruled against the company, stating, "There is sufficient circumstantial evidence to indicate that age bias and age based policies appear throughout the performance rating process to the detriment of the protected age group." The *Albermarle Paper v Moody* case supported validation requirements for performance appraisals, as well as for selection tests. Organizations should avoid using any appraisal method that results in a disproportionately negative impact on a protected group.

The labor union is another external factor that might affect a firm's appraisal process. Unions have traditionally stressed seniority as the basis for promotions and pay increases. They may vigorously oppose the use of a management-designed performance appraisal system used for these purposes.

Factors within the internal environment can also affect the performance appraisal process. For instance, a firm's corporate culture can assist or hinder the process.

Today's dynamic organizations, which increasingly utilize teams to perform jobs, recognize overall team results as well as individual contributions. A nontrusting culture does not provide the environment needed to encourage high performance by either individuals or teams. In such an atmosphere, the credibility of an appraisal system will, suffer regardless of its merits.

4 OBJECTIVE

Describe the performance appraisal process.

The Performance Appraisal Process

As shown in Figure 8-1, the starting point for the PA process is identifying performance goals. Next, this ongoing cycle continues with communicating the goals to those concerned and establishing performance criteria. Then decisions are made regarding who will be responsible for the appraisal, the appraisal period, the appraisal method(s) to be used, and the role of computer software, if applicable. During the process, potential problems in appraisal will be anticipated and considered along with the characteristics of effective systems. Management will then provide coaching and other suitable T&D support as the appraisal period continues and the employee's work is observed. Performance is then formally appraised. The final step involves discussing the appraisal with the employee, setting tentative goals, and the cycle repeats.

An appraisal system probably cannot effectively serve every desired purpose so management should select those specific goals it believes to be most important and realistically achievable. For example, some firms may want to stress employee development, whereas other organizations may want to focus on administrative decisions, such as pay adjustments. Too many PA systems fail because management expects too much from one method and does not determine specifically what it wants the system to accomplish.

After the firm establishes specific appraisal goals, workers and teams must understand their expectations in accomplishing their tasks. This understanding is greatly facilitated when employees have had input into setting the goals. At the end of the appraisal period, the appraiser and the employee together review work performance

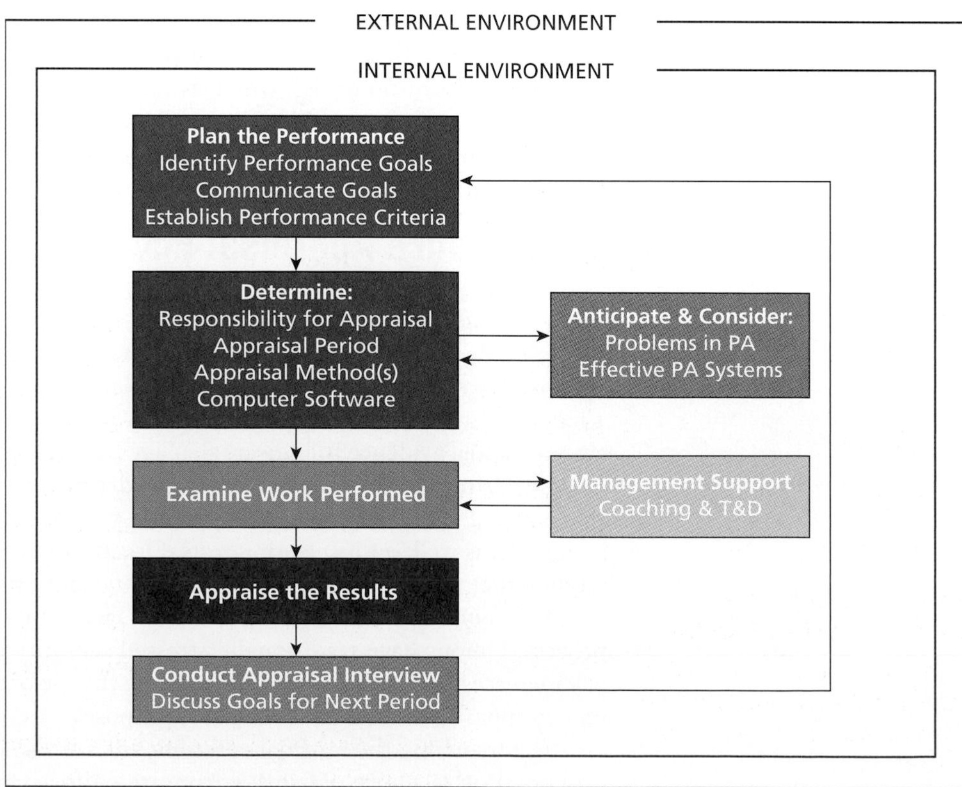

Figure 8-1 The Performance Appraisal Process

and evaluate it against established performance standards. This review helps determine how well employees have met these standards, determines reasons for deficiencies, and develops a plan to correct the problems. The discussion also establishes goals for the next evaluation period.

5 OBJECTIVE

Identify the aspects of a person's performance that an organization should evaluate.

Establish Performance Criteria

What aspect of a person's performance should an organization evaluate? Recent research suggests that even within the same company managers often use entirely different performance criteria.[16] In practice, the most common appraisal criteria are traits, behaviors, competencies, goal achievement, and improvement potential.

Traits

Certain employee traits such as *attitude*, *appearance*, and *initiative* are the basis for some evaluations. However, many of these commonly used qualities are subjective and may be either unrelated to job performance or difficult to define. In such cases, inaccurate evaluations may occur and create legal problems for the organization as well. At the same time, certain traits may relate to job performance and, if this connection is established, using them may be appropriate.

Behaviors

When an individual's task outcome is difficult to determine, organizations may evaluate the person's task-related behavior or competencies. For example, an appropriate behavior to evaluate for a manager might be *leadership style*. For individuals working in teams, *developing others*, *teamwork and cooperation*, or *customer service orientation* might be appropriate. Desired behaviors may be appropriate as evaluation criteria because if they are recognized and rewarded, employees tend to repeat them. If certain behaviors result in desired outcomes, there is merit in using them in the evaluation process.

Competencies

Competencies: Include a broad range of knowledge, skills, traits and behaviors that may be technical in nature, relate to interpersonal skills or be business oriented.

Competencies include a broad range of knowledge, skills, traits and behaviors that may be technical in nature, relate to interpersonal skills or be business oriented. Dick Grote, president of Grote Consulting Corporation in Dallas, recommends the need to include cultural competencies such as ethics and integrity for all jobs. He adds that there are also competencies that are job specific. For example, analytical thinking and achievement orientation might be essential in professional jobs. In leadership jobs, relevant competencies might include developing talent, delegating authority and people management skills. The competencies selected for evaluation purposes should be those that are closely associated with job success.[17]

Grote Consulting Corporation

www.novatrain.com/trainers/dickgrote.html

This Web site provides information on a leading provider of professional training and education.

Research conducted by the University of Michigan Business School and sponsored by SHRM and the Global Consulting Alliance determined that success in HR is dependent on competency and specific skills in the following five key areas:[18]

- *Strategic contribution:* Connecting firms to their markets and quickly aligning employee behaviors with organizational needs
- *Business knowledge:* Knowing how businesses are run and translating this into action
- *Personal credibility:* Demonstrating measurable value; being part of executive team

- *HR delivery:* Providing efficient and effective service to customers in the areas of staffing, performance management, development, and evaluation
- *HR technology:* Using technology and Web-based means to deliver value to customers

For additional information on this research, visit www.shrm.org/competencies.

HR Web Wisdom
Global Consulting Alliance
www.pass-gca.com/
This Web site is for a worldwide network of consulting companies with partners in all five continents.

Goal Achievement

If organizations consider *ends* more important than *means*, goal achievement outcomes become an appropriate factor to evaluate. Firms follow this approach when a goals-oriented process is used. The outcomes established should be within the control of the individual or team and should be those results that lead to the firm's success. At upper levels, the goals might deal with financial aspects of the firm such as profit or cash flow, and market considerations such as market share or position in the market. At lower organizational levels, the outcomes might be meeting the customer's quality requirements and delivering according to the promised schedule.[19]

To assist the process, the manager needs to provide specific examples of how the employee can further his or her development and achieve specific goals. Both parties should reach an agreement as to the employee's goals for the next evaluation period and the assistance and resources the manager needs to provide. This aspect of employee appraisal should be the most positive element in the entire process and help the employee focus on behavior that will produce positive results for all concerned.

Improvement Potential

When organizations evaluate their employees' performance, many of the criteria used focus on the past. From a performance management viewpoint, the problem is that you cannot change the past. Unless a firm takes further steps, the evaluation data become merely historical documents. Therefore, firms should emphasize the future, including the behaviors and outcomes needed to develop the employee, and, in the process, achieve the firm's goals. This involves an assessment of the employee's potential.[20] As previously stated, many firms use assessment centers for this purpose. In any event, including this factor in the evaluation process helps to ensure more effective career planning and development.

We should remember that the evaluation criteria presented here are not mutually exclusive. In fact, many appraisal systems are a hybrid of these approaches.

6 OBJECTIVE

Identify who may be responsible for performance appraisal and the performance period.

Responsibility for Appraisal

In most organizations, the human resource department is responsible for coordinating the design and implementation of performance appraisal programs. However, it is essential that line managers play a key role from beginning to end. Often, these individuals conduct the appraisals, and they must directly participate in the program if it is to succeed. Several possibilities exist as to the person who will actually rate the employee, and these are presented next.

Immediate Supervisor

An employee's immediate supervisor has traditionally been the most common choice for evaluating performance. This continues to be the case, and there are several reasons for this approach. In the first place, the supervisor is usually in an excellent position to observe the employee's job performance. Another reason is that the supervisor has the responsibility for managing a particular unit. When someone else has the task of evaluating subordinates, the supervisor's authority may be undermined. Finally, subordinate training and development is an important element in every manager's job and, as previously mentioned, appraisal programs and employee development are usually closely related.

On the negative side, the immediate supervisor may emphasize certain aspects of employee performance and neglect others. Also, managers have been known to manipulate evaluations to justify pay increases and promotions.

When geography separates subordinates from their supervisors, evaluation becomes increasingly difficult. In other cases, the appraised employee may be more technically knowledgeable than the boss, and this presents another potential problem. One suggestion for overcoming these disadvantages is to bring subordinates into the process more closely. Have them suggest ways to fairly evaluate their performance and then use their suggestions as part of the appraisal criteria.[21]

In most instances, the immediate supervisor will probably continue to be involved in evaluating performance. Organizations will seek alternatives, however, because of the organizational innovations that have occurred and a desire to broaden the perspective of the appraisal.

Subordinates

Historically, our culture has viewed evaluation by subordinates negatively. However, this thinking has changed somewhat. Some firms have concluded that evaluation of managers by subordinates is both feasible and needed. They reason that subordinates are in an excellent position to view their superiors' managerial effectiveness. Advocates of this approach believe that supervisors will become especially conscious of the workgroup's needs and will do a better job of managing. Critics are concerned that the manager will be caught up in a popularity contest or that employees will be fearful of reprisal. If this approach has a chance for success, one thing is clear: the firm must guarantee anonymity of the evaluators. Assuring this might be particularly difficult in a small department and especially if demographic data on the appraisal form could identify raters.

Peers

A major strength of using peers to appraise performance is that they work closely with the evaluated employee and probably have an undistorted perspective on typical performance, especially in team assignments.[22] Organizations are increasingly using teams, including those that are self-directed. The rationale for evaluations conducted by team members includes the following:

- Team members know each others' performance better than anyone and can, therefore, evaluate performance more accurately.
- Peer pressure is a powerful motivator for team members.
- Members who recognize that peers within the team will be evaluating their work show increased commitment and productivity.
- Peer review involves numerous opinions and is not dependent on one individual.

Problems with peer evaluations include the reluctance of some people who work closely together, especially on teams, to criticize each other. On the other hand, if an employee has been at odds with another, he or she might really unload on the "enemy" resulting in an unfair evaluation.[23] Another problem concerns peers who interact infrequently, as is the case with boards of directors, who often lack the information needed to make an accurate assessment. In some cases, team members may have little or no appraisal training. Team members obviously need training in performance appraisal, as does anyone involved in the evaluation process.

Self-Appraisal

If employees understand their objectives and the criteria used for evaluation, they are in a good position to appraise their own performance. Many people know what they do well on the job and what they need to improve. If they have the opportunity, they will criticize their own performance objectively and take action to improve it. Also, because employee development is self-development, employees who appraise their own performance may become more highly motivated. Even if a self-appraisal is not a part of the system, the employee should at least provide a list of his or her most important accomplishments and contributions over the appraisal period. This will prevent the manager from being blind-sided when the employee complains, perhaps justifiably, "You didn't even mention the Bandy contract I landed last December!"

As a complement to other approaches, self-appraisal has great appeal to managers who are primarily concerned with employee participation and development. For compensation purposes, however, its value is considerably less. Some individuals are masters at attributing good performance to their own efforts and poor performance to someone else's.

Customer Appraisal

Customer behavior determines a firm's degree of success. Therefore, some organizations believe it is important to obtain performance input from this critical source. Organizations use this approach because it demonstrates a commitment to the customer, holds employees accountable, and fosters change. Customer-related goals for executives generally are of a broad, strategic nature, while targets for lower-level employees tend to be more specific. For example, an objective might be to improve the rating for accurate delivery or reduce the number of dissatisfied customers by half. It is important to have employees participate in setting their goals and to include only those factors within the employees' control.

The Appraisal Period

Formal performance evaluations are usually prepared at specific intervals. Even more significant, however, is the continuous interaction, primarily informal, including coaching and other developmental activities that continue throughout the appraisal period. Performance feedback once a year is just not good enough. HR should condition managers to understand that managing performance is a continuous process that is built into their job every day.[24]

While there is nothing magical about the period for formal appraisal reviews, in most organizations they occur either annually or semiannually. Often, a subordinate's first appraisal may occur at the end of a probationary period, anywhere from 30 to 90 days after his or her start date.[25]

In high-tech organizations, the speed of change mandates that a performance period be shorter, perhaps three or four months. One source has the opinion that conducting reviews only once or twice a year is like trying to get in shape by working out just once a month; it simply does not work.[26]

It is necessary to link performance communication to the actual work cycle. Discussions of accomplishments can then keep pace with new goals and priorities. In

the current business climate, it may be well for all firms to consider monitoring performance often. Changes occur so fast that employees need to look at objectives and their own roles throughout the year to see if changes are in order. Conducting formal appraisals at predetermined intervals is a good idea if it is not the only time managers and employees discuss performance. If managers are not in the habit of coaching their employees regularly, the formal appraisal can be overwhelming.[27]

Some organizations use the employee's date of hire to determine the rating period. However, in the interest of consistency, it may be advisable to perform evaluations on a calendar basis rather than on anniversaries. If firms do not conduct all appraisals at the same time, it may be impossible to make needed comparisons between employees.

7 OBJECTIVE

Identify the various performance appraisal methods used.

Performance Appraisal Methods

Managers may choose from among a number of appraisal methods. The type of performance appraisal system utilized depends on its purpose. If the major emphasis is on selecting people for promotion, training, and merit pay increases, a traditional method such as rating scales may be appropriate. Collaborative methods, including input from the employees themselves, may prove to be more suitable for helping employees become more effective.

Performance Appraisal—The Complete Online Guide

www.performance-appraisal.com/home.htm

This Web site is for a company that designs, develops, and delivers offline and online (Web-enabled) performance appraisal and corporate evaluation systems, together with associated consulting and training services.

The 360-Degree Feedback Evaluation

Recall that the 360-degree feedback evaluation was discussed in the "HRM in Action" at the beginning of this chapter. According to some managers, the 360-degree feedback method is only appropriate for developmental purposes. Their rationale stems from a concern that when raters believe that they may hurt others by what they say in the evaluation, they will not be honest. This is the view of GE's former CEO Jack Welch who maintained that the 360-degree system in his firm had been "gamed" and that people were saying nice things about one anothers resulting in all good ratings.[28] Another critical view with an opposite twist is that input from peers, who may be competitors for raises and promotions, might intentionally distort the data and sabotage the colleague. Yet, since so many firms use 360-degree feedback evaluation, including virtually every *Fortune* 100 company,[29] it seems that many firms have found ways to avoid the pitfalls.

An in-depth study of 43 global organizations determined six best practices that organizations use to get the most from 360-degree feedback evaluation: [30]

- Use the system primarily for individual development
- Link the process to strategic imperatives
- Exert high administration control over every aspect of the process
- Use senior management as role models
- Use highly trained internal coaches
- Evaluate the return on investment or effectiveness of the process

The biggest risk with 360-degree feedback is confidentiality. Many firms outsource the 360-degree process to make participants feel comfortable that the information they share and receive is completely anonymous. The information is very sensitive and, in the wrong hands, could impact careers.[31]

Rating scales method: A widely used performance appraisal method that rates employees according to defined factors.

Rating Scales

The **rating scales method** is a widely used appraisal approach that rates employees according to defined factors. Using this approach, evaluators record their judgments

Name	Job Title
Supervisor/Manager	Department
Appraisal Period: From	To

Evaluate the performance in each of the following factors on a scale of 1 to 5:
5 = **Outstanding,** consistently exceeds expectations for this factor.
4 = **Above Expectations,** consistently meets and occasionally exceeds expectations.
3 = **Meets Expectations,** consistently meets expectations.
2 = **Below Expectations,** occasionally fails to meet expectations.
1 = **Needs Improvement,** consistently fails to meet expectations.

Part 1—Task Outcomes (Weighted 80% of total score)
List mutually agreed-to performance factors from the job description and goals established from the preview performance review. **Points**

- ________________ ____
- ________________ ____
- ________________ ____
- ________________ ____
- ________________ ____
- Quality of work ____
- Quantity of work ____

Total Points ____
Average Score (Divide total points by number of factors used) ____ Multiplied by **16** = ____
Comments ________________

Part 2—Personal Behaviors (10% of total score)

- Leadership ____
- Interpersonal skills ____
- Developing others ____
- Customer service ____
- Teamwork ____

Total Points ____
Average Score (Divide total points by number of applicable factors) ____ Multiplied by **2** = ____
Comments ________________

Figure 8-2 Rating Scales Method of Performance Appraisal

about performance on a scale. The scale includes several categories, normally five to seven in number, defined by adjectives such as *outstanding*, *meets expectations*, or *needs improvement*. While systems often provide an overall rating, the method generally allows for the use of more than one performance criterion. One reason for the popularity of the rating scales method is its simplicity, which permits quick evaluations of many employees. When you quantify the ratings, the method facilitates comparison of employees' performances.

The factors chosen for evaluation are typically of two types: job-related and personal characteristics. Note that in Figure 8-2, job-related factors include quality and quantity of work, whereas personal factors include such behaviors as interpersonal skills and traits like adaptability. The rater (evaluator) completes the form by indicating the degree of each factor that is most descriptive of the employee and his or her performance. In this illustration, evaluators total and then average the points in each part. They then multiply this average by a factor representing the weight given each section. The final score (total points) for the employee is the total of each section's points.

Part 3—Personal Traits (10% of total score)
- Adaptability ____
- Judgment ____
- Appearance ____
- Attitude ____
- Initiative ____

Total Points ____

Average Score (Divide total points by 5) ____ Multiplied by **2** = ____

Comments ____

Points from Part 1 ____ **+ Part 2** ____ **+ Part 3** ____ **= Total Points** ________

Performance goals for next appraisal period:
- ____
- ____
- ____
- ____
- ____

Self-development activities for this employee

Employee comments

Evaluated By:	Title	Date
Approved	Title	Date
Employee's Signature (Does not necessarily indicate agreement)	Title	Date

Figure 8-2 *(continued)*

Some firms provide space for the rater to comment on the evaluation given for each factor. This practice may be especially encouraged, or even required, when the rater gives an extreme rating, either the highest or lowest. For instance, if an employee is rated *needs improvement* (a 1 on the sample form) on *teamwork*, the rater provides written justification for this low evaluation. The purpose of this requirement is to focus on correcting deficiencies and to discourage arbitrary and hastily made judgments.

In order to receive an *outstanding* rating for a factor such as *quality of work*, a person must consistently go beyond the prescribed work requirements. While the sample form is deficient in this respect, the more precise the definition of factors and degrees, the more accurately the rater can evaluate worker performance. When the various performance levels are described merely as *above expectations* or *below expectations* without further elaboration, what has the employee really learned? These generalities do not provide the guidance needed for improving performance. It is important that each rater interpret the factors and degrees in the same way. Raters acquire this ability through performance appraisal training. Many rating scale forms also provide for consideration of future behavior. Notice that the form shown as Figure 8-2 has space for performance goals for the next period and self-development activities for the next appraisal period.

Critical Incidents

Critical incident method:
A performance appraisal technique that requires a written record of highly favorable and highly unfavorable employee work behavior.

The **critical incident method** requires keeping written records of highly favorable and highly unfavorable work actions. When such an action—a *critical incident*—affects the department's effectiveness significantly, either positively or negatively, the manager writes it down. At the end of the appraisal period, the rater uses these records along with other data to evaluate employee performance. With this method, the appraisal is more likely to cover the entire evaluation period and not focus on the last few weeks or months.

Essay

Essay method:
A performance appraisal method in which the rater writes a brief narrative describing an employee's performance.

In the **essay method,** the rater simply writes a brief narrative describing the employee's performance. This method tends to focus on extreme behavior in the employee's work rather than routine day-to-day performance. Ratings of this type depend heavily on the evaluator's writing ability. Supervisors with excellent writing skills, if so inclined, can make a marginal worker sound like a top performer. Comparing essay evaluations might be difficult because no common criteria exist. However, some managers believe that the essay method is not only the most simple but also an acceptable approach to employee evaluation.

Work Standards

Work standards method:
A performance appraisal method that compares each employee's performance to a predetermined standard or expected level of output.

The **work standards method** compares each employee's performance to a predetermined standard or expected level of output. Standards reflect the normal output of an average worker operating at a normal pace. Firms may apply work standards to virtually all types of jobs, but production jobs generally receive the most attention. Several methods are available to determine work standards, including time study and work sampling. An obvious advantage of using standards as appraisal criteria is objectivity. However, in order for employees to perceive that the standards are objective, they should understand clearly how the standards were set. Management must also explain the rationale for any changes to the standards.

Ranking

Ranking method:
A performance appraisal method in which the rater simply places all employees from a group in rank order of overall performance.

In the **ranking method,** the rater simply places all employees from a group in rank order of overall performance. For example, the best employee in the group is ranked highest, and the poorest is ranked lowest. You follow this procedure until you rank all employees. A difficulty occurs when individuals have performed at comparable levels (as perceived by the evaluator).

Paired comparison is a variation of the ranking method in which the performance of each employee is compared with every other employee in the group. A single criterion, such as overall performance, is often the basis for this comparison. The employee who receives the greatest number of favorable comparisons receives the highest ranking.

Some professionals in the field argue for using a comparative approach, such as ranking, whenever management must make human resource decisions. They believe that employees are promoted or receive the highest pay increases not because they achieve their objectives, but rather because they achieve them better than others in their workgroup. Such decisions go beyond a single individual's performance and, therefore, need consideration on a broader basis.

Forced Distribution

Forced distribution method: A performance appraisal method which requires the rater to assign individuals in a work group to a limited number of categories similar to a normal frequency distribution.

Forced distribution methods require the rater to assign individuals in a workgroup to a limited number of categories similar to a normal frequency distribution. Forced distribution systems have been around for decades and several of *Fortune*'s Most Admired Companies like Microsoft, Cisco Systems, Hewlett-Packard, Sun Microsystems, Conoco, Capital One Financial Corporation, Intel, and General Electric use them today.[32] Because of a slowing economy and an increased focus on pay for performance, many firms have instituted such rankings or gotten tougher with their existing systems. Proponents of forced distribution believe they facilitate budgeting and guard against weak managers who are too timid to get rid of poor performers. They think that forced rankings require managers to be honest with workers about how they are doing.[33]

In GE's system, all top executives are ranked with the best performers placed in the top 20 percent, the next group in the middle 70 percent, and the poorest performing group wind up in the bottom 10 percent. The underperformers are, after being given time to improve their performance, generally let go.[34] If any of the underperformers are able to improve their performance, you might wonder if any in the 70 percent group would get nervous!

Although used by some prestigious firms, the forced distribution system such as GE's appears to be unpopular with many managers. According to one source, it fosters cutthroat competition, paranoia, and general ill will and destroys employee loyalty. A Midwestern banker states that his company "recently began a rank-and-yank system that flies directly in the face of the 'teamwork' that senior management says it wants to encourage. Don't tell me I'm supposed to put the good of the team first and then tell me the bottom 10 percent of us are going to lose our jobs because, team be damned, I'm going to make sure I'm not in that bottom 10 percent."[35]

Critics of forced distribution contend that they compel managers to penalize a good, although not a great, employee who is part of a superstar team. One reason employees are opposed to forced ranking is that they suspect that the rankings are a way for companies to rationalize firings more easily. In any event, according to Lorraine Ahlers-Mack, a New York City employment lawyer, there will be a lot of litigation surrounding this issue.[36] Goodyear Tire & Rubber Company abandoned the forced distribution portion of its performance rating system for salaried employees just as discrimination attorneys were planning to file a class action lawsuit over it. The plan had called for a "10–80–10" feature similar to the one developed by General Electric.[37]

Behaviorally Anchored Rating Scales

Behaviorally anchored rating scale (BARS) method: A performance appraisal method that combines elements of the traditional rating scale and critical incident methods.

The **behaviorally anchored rating scale (BARS)** method combines elements of the traditional rating scales and critical incident methods. In this method, various performance levels are shown along a scale with each described in terms of an employee's specific job behavior. In evaluating a group of employees working as interviewers, for example, suppose the factor chosen for evaluation is *Ability to Absorb and Interpret Policies.* On the *very positive* end of this factor might be "This interviewer could be expected to serve as an information source concerning new and changed policies for others in the organization." On the *very negative* end of this factor might be "Even after repeated explanations, this interviewer would be unable to understand new procedures." There might be several levels in between the very negative and the very positive. Rather than have the raters judge the quality of a subordinate's performance, the rater is able to determine more objectively how frequently the employee performs in each defined level.

BARS differs from rating scales because, instead of using adjectives at each scale point, it uses behavioral anchors related to the criterion being measured. This modification clarifies the meaning of each point on the scale and reduces rater bias and error by anchoring the rating with specific behavioral examples based on job analysis information. Instead of providing a space for entering a rating figure for a category such as *Above Expectations*, the BARS method provides examples of such behavior. This approach facilitates discussion of the rating because it addresses specific behaviors; thus overcoming weaknesses in other evaluation methods. Regardless of apparent advantages of BARS, reports on its effectiveness are mixed. A specific deficiency is that the behaviors used are *activity* oriented rather than *results* oriented. Also, the method may not be economically feasible since each job category requires its own BARS. Yet, among the various appraisal techniques, BARS is perhaps the most highly defensible in court because it is based on actual observable job behaviors.[38]

Results-Based Systems

Results-based system: A performance appraisal method in which the manager and the subordinate jointly agree on objectives for the next appraisal period.

The manager and the subordinate jointly agree on objectives for the next appraisal period in a **results-based system,** in the past a form of *management by objectives*. In such a system, one objective might be, for example, to cut waste by 10 percent. At the end of the appraisal period, an evaluation focuses on how well the employee achieved this objective.

Since organizations exist to achieve goals, a results-based system has obvious value. A distinct advantage of this approach is that it provides a measure of achievement against predetermined objectives. However, since performance outcomes do not indicate *how* to change, the method may be less helpful in employee development. Nevertheless, a results-oriented approach remains a popular technique to evaluate employees, especially managers.[39]

Assessment Centers

The primary use of assessment centers is to identify and select employees for higher-level positions, as discussed in Chapter 7. Their role in employee development is also important. Assessment centers allow candidates to demonstrate job-related dimensions of performance in exercises that replicate the important situations that occur on the job.[40] Some performance appraisals attempt to not only evaluate performance, which essentially focuses on the past, but also determine an individual's potential for advancement, which is future oriented. Recognizing the differences in purposes and the difficulty that a PA system will have in achieving both aims, some firms opt to use an assessment center as an adjunct to their appraisal system.

Finding the *best* performance evaluation system seems to be an unending challenge for most organizations. Some, however, appear to be taking a more strategic approach to the process. Instead of using the familiar "check the box, write a comment" ritual, some organizations are integrating the company's mission statement, vision, and values into their PA systems.[41]

8 OBJECTIVE

Describe how computer software is used in performance appraisal.

Use of Computer Software

Computer software is available for recording the appraisal data. As an example, KnowledgePoint's *Performance Now* provides a standardized, yet thorough, set of templates for the review. The rater begins by adding employees in a tabbed dialog box, selecting a specific category of job such as clerical, management, or manufacturing. *Performance Now* then adds the appropriate performance categories to the review, along with dummy text for each category. The rater edits the text in the built-in word processor. A toolbar button provides context-sensitive advice, including suggestions for how to improve employee performance. This software simplifies reviews and provides not only consistency, but also a professional appearance.[42]

KnowledgePoint

www.Knowledgepoint.com

This Web site is for computer software that is available for recording appraisal data.

A big advantage in utilizing the computer is reduction of paperwork required. Also, managers have the option of customizing most programs. This is necessary to reflect the goals and values of the organization more accurately and to permit fair evaluations.[43]

PerformancePro.net is another example of software that can provide the tools and easy access to make appraisal and employee development easier. Web-based delivery eliminates dreaded paperwork and gives users 24-hour access to performance information. Employers can track employees' progress toward established goals and evaluate progress over established time frames. The ability to check on performance at any point provides early warning indicators where some performance or goal adjustment might be required. Employees have an easy way to keep a manager fully informed and to access a degree of personal performance self-management.[44]

A number of vendors are providing employee evaluation tools. In this market are such firms as KnowledgePoint, PeopleSoft, Halogen Software, and Performaworks Inc. Three critical areas of performance management are often featured: (1) goal-setting, (2) appraisal, and (3) development planning.[45]

9 OBJECTIVE

List the problems that have been associated with performance appraisal.

Problems in Performance Appraisal

As indicated at the beginning of this chapter, performance appraisal has come under a heavy barrage of criticism. The *rating scales method* seems to have been the most vulnerable target. Yet, in all fairness, many of the problems commonly mentioned are not

Trends & Innovations

Performance Appraisal at Seagate Technology

In 2003, employees at Seagate Technology LLC received, for the first time, annual performance reviews that evaluated how close each employee came to achieving his or her professional goals.[46] This new system asks each person in its professional workforce to consider CEO Steve Luczo's top five organizational goals before proposing his or her own goals. The resulting personal targets, all 56,000 of them, are available online to any employee.

What could be a potential data-management nightmare doesn't turn out to be one. Karen Hanlon, Vice President of human resources at Seagate, credits software from Performaworks Inc., for the process. Luczo typed his objectives into the system and in the following weeks, senior executives, managers, and professional staffers also signed in. Each typed in their own goals after viewing the goals set by their higher-ups.

The process is ongoing; each quarter managers work with employees on updating their goals. A section of the site provides coaching on how to develop and align them with the company's objectives. Employees can see all the objectives that lie between their own and those of their CEO that started the chain. Online reminders alert employees of things such as due dates for meeting goals, and workflow functions let managers shift goals from one worker to others who might benefit from the same objectives. At evaluation time, the software calculates a score for each employee based on his or her success at meeting goals and other measured behaviors. That score feeds into an internal compensation system that helps determine bonuses and merit increases. The system also links to Seagate's Oracle HR system, which manages general employee data.

Like Seagate, other firms are striving to do a better job of aligning their employees' efforts with top business objectives. Hanlon says, "To be competitive five years ago was much less challenging than it is today and will probably be more challenging in five years." She adds, "We have to be able to communicate our priorities to employees faster and be able to make changes more rapidly."

inherent in this method but, rather, reflect improper implementation. For example, firms may fail to provide adequate rater training; or they may use appraisal criteria that are too subjective and lack job relatedness. The following section highlights some of the more common problem areas.

Lack of Objectivity

A potential weakness of traditional performance appraisal methods is that they lack objectivity. In the rating scales method, for example, commonly used factors such as attitude, appearance, and personality are difficult to measure. In addition, these factors may have little to do with an employee's job performance. While subjectivity will always exist in appraisal methods, employee appraisal based primarily on personal characteristics may place the evaluator and the company in untenable positions with the employee and equal employment opportunity guidelines. The firm may be hard-pressed to show that these factors are job related.

Bias

Halo error:
An error that occurs when a manager generalizes one positive performance feature or incident to all aspects of employee performance.

A huge challenge that impedes an effective performance evaluation is the bias that we all have. A bias can be either positive or negative. **Halo error** occurs when a manager generalizes one *positive* performance feature or incident to all aspects of employee performance resulting in a higher rating.[47] For example, Rodney Pirkle, accounting supervisor, placed a high value on *neatness*, a factor used in the company's performance appraisal system. As Rodney was evaluating the performance of his senior accounting clerk, Jack Hicks, he noted that Jack was a very neat individual and gave him a high ranking on this factor. Also, consciously or unconsciously, Rodney permitted the high ranking on neatness to carry over to other factors, giving Jack undeserved high ratings on all factors. Of course, if Jack had not been neat, the opposite could have occurred. This phenomenon is known as the "horn effect."[48] Either way, the bias distorts the appraisal and destroys its value.

Rater bias can make the appraisal process more like gambling than an objective observation process. If perceived negatively by employees, they will be skeptical of the evaluation results and even more doubtful of their managers' ability to perform the task.[49]

Leniency/Strictness

Leniency:
Giving an undeserved high performance appraisal rating to an employee.

Giving undeserved high ratings is referred to as **leniency.** This behavior is often motivated by a desire to avoid controversy over the appraisal. It is most prevalent when highly subjective (and difficult to defend) performance criteria are used, and the rater is required to discuss evaluation results with employees. One research study found that when managers know they are evaluating employees for administrative purposes, such as pay increases, they are likely to be more lenient than when evaluating performance to achieve employee development.[50] Leniency, however, may result in failure to recognize correctible deficiencies. The practice may also deplete the merit budget and reduce the reward available for superior employees. In addition, an organization will find it difficult to terminate poor performing employees who continuously receive positive evaluations.

Few people enjoy delivering bad news to employees, but good managers understand that doing so, when deserved, is crucial to an organization's long-term success. Not tolerating unsatisfactory performance can also be a tonic for top performers who relish working in an environment free of noncontributors. A climate that openly tolerates mediocrity demoralizes this group of employees.[51]

Strictness:
Being unduly critical of an employee's work performance.

Being unduly critical of an employee's work performance is referred to as **strictness.** Many firms make it difficult for managers to rate more than a very few of their employees as outstanding. They are relentless in making sure that *evaluation inflation* does not creep into the process. But, what happens when a manager has five superstars yet is told that only three are eligible for the bonus pool? It is one thing to have a system that demotivates average performers, but to demotivate top performers is self-destructive.[52]

Although leniency is usually more prevalent than strictness, some managers, on their own initiative, apply an evaluation more rigorously than the company standard. This behavior may be due to a lack of understanding of various evaluation factors. The worst situation is when a firm has both lenient and strict managers and does nothing to level the inequities. Here, the weak performers get relatively high pay increases and promotions from a lenient boss, while the strict manager shortchanges the stronger employees. This can have a demoralizing effect on the morale and motivation of the top-performing people.

Central Tendency

Central tendency: A common error in performance appraisal that occurs when employees are incorrectly rated near the average or middle of a scale.

Central tendency is a common error that occurs when employees are incorrectly rated near the average or middle of the scale. This practice may be encouraged by some rating scale systems that require the evaluator to justify in writing extremely high or extremely low ratings. With such a system, the rater may avoid possible controversy or criticism by giving only average ratings. However, since these ratings tend to cluster in the "fully satisfactory" range, employees do not often complain about this. Nevertheless, this error does exist and it influences the accuracy of evaluations.[53]

Recent Behavior Bias

Anyone who has observed the behavior of young children several weeks before Christmas can readily identify with the problem of recent behavior bias. Suddenly, the wildest kids in the neighborhood develop angelic personalities in anticipation of the rewards they hope to receive from Old Saint Nick. Individuals in the workforce are not children, but they are human. Virtually every employee knows precisely when a performance review is scheduled. Although his or her actions may not be conscious, an employee's behavior often improves and productivity tends to rise several days or weeks before the scheduled evaluation. It is only natural for a rater to remember recent behavior more clearly than actions from the more distant past. However, formal performance appraisals generally cover a specified time, and an individual's performance over the entire period should be considered. Maintaining records of performance throughout the appraisal period helps avoid this problem.

Personal Bias (Stereotyping)

This pitfall occurs when supervisors allow individual differences such as gender, race, or age to affect the ratings they give. Not only is this problem detrimental to employee morale, but it is blatantly illegal and can result in costly litigation.[54] The effects of cultural bias, or stereotyping, can definitely influence appraisals. We establish mental pictures of what we consider ideal typical workers and employees who do not match this picture may be unfairly judged.[55]

While existing legislation protects employees in protected groups, discrimination continues to be an appraisal problem. Discrimination in appraisal can be based on other factors as well. For example, mild-mannered employees may be appraised more harshly simply because they do not seriously object to the results. This type of behavior is in sharp contrast to the *hell raisers*, who often confirm the adage, "the squeaky wheel gets the grease." In another example, one study concluded that people perceived to be smokers received lower performance evaluations than nonsmokers, the implication being that if they stopped smoking, they would get higher ratings.[56]

Table 8-1 Reasons for Intentionally Inflating or Lowering Ratings

Inflated Ratings

- The belief that accurate ratings would have a damaging effect on the subordinate's motivation and performance
- The desire to improve an employee's eligibility for merit raises
- The desire to avoid airing the department's dirty laundry
- The wish to avoid creating a negative permanent record of poor performance that might hound the employee in the future
- The need to protect good performers whose performance was suffering because of personal problems
- The wish to reward employees displaying great effort even when results are relatively low
- The need to avoid confrontation with certain hard-to-manage employees
- The desire to promote a poor or disliked employee up and out of the department

Lowered Ratings

- To scare better performance out of an employee
- To punish a difficult or rebellious employee
- To encourage a problem employee to quit
- To create a strong record to justify a planned firing
- To minimize the amount of the merit increase a subordinate receives
- To comply with an organization edict that discourages managers from giving high ratings

Source: Clinton Longenecker and Dean Ludwig, "Ethical Dilemmas in Performance Appraisal Revisited," *Journal of Business Ethics* 9 (December 1990): 963. Reprinted by permission of Kluwer Academic Publishers.

Manipulating the Evaluation

In some instances, supervisors control virtually every aspect of the appraisal process and are therefore in a position to manipulate the system. For example, a supervisor may want to give a pay raise to a certain employee. In order to justify this action, the supervisor may give the employee a high performance evaluation. Or, the supervisor may want to get rid of an employee and so may give the individual a low rating. In either instance, the system is distorted and the goals of performance appraisal cannot be achieved. Additionally, in the latter example, if the employee is a member of a protected group, the firm may wind up in court. If the organization cannot adequately support the evaluation, it may suffer significant financial loss.

One study revealed that over 70 percent of responding managers believe that inflated and lowered ratings are given *intentionally*. Table 8-1 shows these managers' explanations for their rationale. The results suggest that the validity of many performance appraisal systems is flawed, although another study indicated that appraisal data are valid 75 percent of the time.[57] Yet, developing invalid appraisal data 25 percent of the time would be nothing to brag about. It seems obvious that evaluator training emphasizing the negative consequences of rater errors would pay for itself many times over.

OBJECTIVE

Explain the characteristics of an effective appraisal system.

Characteristics of an Effective Appraisal System

The basic purpose of a performance appraisal system is to improve performance of individuals, teams, and the entire organization. The system may also serve to assist in the making of administrative decisions concerning pay increases, transfers, or terminations. In addition, the appraisal system must be legally defensible. Although a perfect system does not exist, every system should possess certain characteristics. Organizations should seek an accurate assessment of performance that permits the development of a plan to improve individual and group performance. The system must honestly inform people of how they stand with the organization. The following factors assist in accomplishing these purposes.

Ethical Dilemma

Abdication of Responsibility

You are the new Vice President for Human Resources of a company that has not been performing well, and everyone, including yourself, has a mandate to deliver results. The pressure has never been heavier. Shareholders are angry after 31 months of a "tough" market that has left their stock "under water." Many shareholders desperately need stock performance to pay for their retirement. Working for you is a 52-year-old manager with two kids in college. In previous evaluations, spineless executives told him he was doing fine, when he clearly was not, and his performance is still far below par.

If you are to show others in the company that you are willing to make tough decisions, you feel you must fire this individual. The question is who's going to suffer: the firm and ultimately shareholders whose retirement is in jeopardy or a nice guy who's been lied to for 20 years, through no fault of his?[58]

What would you do?

Job-Related Criteria

Job relatedness is perhaps the most basic criterion in employee performance appraisal. The *Uniform Guidelines* and court decisions are quite clear on this point. More specifically, evaluation criteria should be determined through job analysis. Subjective factors, such as initiative, enthusiasm, loyalty, and cooperation are obviously important; however, unless clearly shown to be job related, they should not be used.

Performance Expectations

Managers and subordinates must agree on performance expectations in advance of the appraisal period. How can employees function effectively if they do not know what they are being measured against? On the other hand, if employees clearly understand the expectations, they can evaluate their own performance and make timely adjustments as they perform their jobs without having to wait for the formal evaluation review. The establishment of highly objective work standards is relatively simple in many areas, such as manufacturing, assembly, and sales. For numerous other types of jobs, however, this task is more difficult. Still, evaluation must take place based on clearly understood performance expectations

Standardization

Firms should use the same evaluation instrument for all employees in the same job category who work for the same supervisor. Supervisors should also conduct appraisals covering similar periods for these employees. Although annual evaluations are most common, many successful firms evaluate their employees more frequently. Regularly scheduled feedback sessions and appraisal interviews for all employees are essential.

Formal documentation of appraisal data serves several purposes including protection against possible legal action. Employees should sign their evaluations. If the employee refuses to sign, the manager should document this behavior. Records should also include a description of employee responsibilities, expected performance results, and the role these data play in making appraisal decisions. While performance appraisal is important for small firms, they are not expected to maintain performance appraisal systems that are as formal as those used by large organizations. Courts have reasoned that objective criteria are not as important in firms with only a few employees because smaller firms' top managers are more intimately acquainted with their employees' work.

Trained Appraisers

The individual or individuals who observe at least a representative sample of job performance *normally* have the responsibility for evaluating employee performance. This person is often the employee's immediate supervisor. However, as previously discussed, other approaches are gaining in popularity.

A common deficiency in appraisal systems is that the evaluators seldom receive training on how to conduct effective evaluations. Unless everyone evaluating performance receives training in the art of giving and receiving feedback, the process can lead to uncertainty and conflict.[59] The training should be an ongoing process in order to ensure accuracy and consistency. The training should cover how to rate employees and how to conduct appraisal interviews. Instructions should be rather detailed and stress the importance of making objective and unbiased ratings. A training module posted on the Internet or company intranet may serve to provide information for managers as needed

Continuous Open Communication

Most employees have a strong need to know how well they are performing. A good appraisal system provides highly desired feedback on a continuing basis. There should be few surprises in the performance review. Managers should handle daily performance problems as they occur and not allow them to pile up for six months or a year and then address them during the performance appraisal interview. When something new surfaces, the manager probably did not do a good enough job communicating with the employee throughout the appraisal period. Even though the interview presents an excellent opportunity for both parties to exchange ideas, it should never serve as a substitute for the day-to-day communication and coaching required by performance management.

Performance Reviews

In addition to the need for continuous communication between managers and their employees, a special time should be set for a formal discussion of an employee's performance. Since improved performance is a common goal of appraisal systems, withholding appraisal results is absurd. Employees are severely handicapped in their developmental efforts if denied access to this information. A performance review allows them to detect any errors or omissions in the appraisal, or an employee may simply disagree with the evaluation and want to challenge it.

Constant employee performance documentation is vitally important for accurate performance appraisals. Although the task can be tedious and boring for managers, maintaining a continuous record of observed and reported incidents is essential in building a useful appraisal. We discuss the appraisal interview in a later section.

Due Process

Ensuring due process is vital. If the company does not have a formal grievance procedure, it should develop one to provide employees an opportunity to appeal appraisal results that they consider inaccurate or unfair. They must have a procedure for pursuing their grievances and having them addressed objectively.

 OBJECTIVE

Describe the legal implications of performance appraisal.

Legal Implications

Employee lawsuits may result from negative evaluations. Employees often win these cases, thanks in part to the employer's own performance appraisal procedures.[60] A review of court cases makes it clear that legally defensible performance appraisal systems should be in place. Perfect systems are not expected, and the law does not preclude supervisory discretion in the process. However, the courts normally require these conditions:

- Either the absence of adverse impact on members of protected classes or validation of the process
- A system that prevents one manager from directing or controlling a subordinate's career
- The appraisal should be reviewed and approved by someone or some group in the organization
- The rater, or raters, must have personal knowledge of the employee's job performance
- The appraisal systems must use predetermined criteria that limit the manager's discretion

Mistakes in appraising performance and decisions based on invalid results can have serious repercussions. For example, discriminatory allocation of money for merit pay increases can result in costly legal action. In settling cases, courts have held employers liable for back pay, court costs, and other costs related to training and promoting certain employees in protected classes. At one time, Amtrak agreed to settle a racial discrimination lawsuit by paying $8 million. Without admitting liability, the firm said it would change its hiring, promotion, and performance appraisal procedures to make them more evenhanded. An employer may also be vulnerable to a negligent retention claim if an employee who continually receives unsatisfactory ratings in safety practices, for example, is kept on the payroll and he or she causes injury to a third party. In these instances, firms might reduce their liability if they provide substandard performers with training designed to overcome the deficiencies.

Performance appraisals definitely have the potential for discrimination. For example, a female employee who was due for promotion sued the firm when her promotion was denied. She claimed she was the victim of unlawful sex discrimination under the Civil Rights Act. Her supervisor had noted in her appraisal that she needed to "take a course in a charm school, walk more femininely, talk more femininely, dress more femininely, wear makeup and wear jewelry."[61] While these remarks are inexcusable, the firm would have been in a much better position to defend itself if the appraisal had read differently, perhaps stating that the employee lacked interpersonal skills rather than implying gender in the remarks.

It is unlikely that any appraisal system will be immune to legal challenge. However, systems that possess the characteristics previously discussed are apparently more legally defensible. At the same time, they can provide a more effective means for achieving performance management goals.

12 OBJECTIVE

Explain how the appraisal interview should be conducted.

The Appraisal Interview

The appraisal interview is the Achilles' heel of the entire evaluation process. In fact, appraisal review sessions often create hostility and can do more harm than good to the employee–manager relationship. To minimize the possibility of hard feelings, the face-to-face meeting and the written review must have performance improvement, not criticism, as their goal. The reviewing manager must utilize all the tact he or she can muster in discussing areas needing improvement. Managers should help employees understand that they are not the only ones *under the gun*. Rating managers should emphasize their own responsibility for the employee's development and commitment for support.

The appraisal interview definitely has the potential for confrontation and undermining the goal of motivating employees. The situation improves considerably when several sources provide input, including perhaps the employee's own self-appraisal. Regardless of the system used, employees will not trust a system they do not understand. Secrecy will invariably breed suspicion and thereby thwart efforts to obtain employee participation.

Scheduling the Interview

Supervisors usually conduct a formal appraisal interview at the end of an employee's appraisal period. Employees usually know when their interview should take place, and their anxiety tends to increase when their supervisor delays the meeting. Interviews with top performers are often pleasant experiences for all concerned. However, supervisors may be reluctant to meet face-to-face with poor performers. They tend to postpone these anxiety-provoking interviews.

Interview Structure

A successful appraisal interview should be structured in a way that allows both the supervisor and the subordinate to view it as a problem-solving rather than a faultfinding session. The manager should consider three basic purposes when planning an appraisal interview:

1. Discussing the employee's performance
2. Assisting the employee in setting goals and personal development plans for the next appraisal period
3. Suggesting means for achieving established goals, including support from the manager and firm

For instance, a worker may receive an average rating on a factor such as *quality of production*. In the interview, both parties should agree to the *specific* improvement needed during the next appraisal period and *specific* actions that each should take.

During performance reviews, managers might ask employees if their current duties and roles are effective in achieving their goals. In addition to reviewing job-related performance, they might also discuss subjective topics, such as career ambitions. For example, in working on a project, perhaps an employee discovered an unrealized aptitude. This awareness could result in a new goal or serve as a springboard to an expanded role in the organization.[62]

The amount of time devoted to an appraisal interview varies considerably with company policy and the position of the evaluated employee. Although costs are a consideration, there is merit in conducting separate interviews for discussing (1) employee performance and development and (2) pay increases. Many managers have learned that as soon as the topic of pay emerges in an interview, it tends to dominate the conversation with performance improvement taking a back seat. For this reason, if pay increases are involved in the appraisal, it might be advisable to defer those discussions for one to several weeks after the appraisal interview.

Use of Praise and Criticism

As suggested at the beginning of this section, conducting an appraisal interview requires tact and patience on the part of the evaluator. Praise is appropriate when warranted, but it can have limited value if not clearly deserved. Criticism, even if warranted, is especially difficult to give. The employee may not perceive it as being *constructive*. It is important that discussions of these sensitive issues focus on the deficiency, not the person. Effective managers minimize threats to the employee's self-esteem whenever possible. When giving criticism, managers should emphasize the positive aspects of performance, criticize actions, not the person, and ask the employee how he or she would change things to improve the situation. Also, the manager should avoid supplying all the answers and try to turn the interview into a win-win situation so that all concerned gain.

Employees' Role

From the employees' side, two weeks or so before the review, they should go through their diary or files and make a note of every project worked on, regardless of whether they were successful or not. The best recourse for employees in preparing for an appraisal review is to prepare a list of creative ways they have solved problems with limited resources. They will look especially good if they can show how their work bolstered the bottom line.[63] This information should be on the appraising manager's desk well before the review. Reminding managers of information they may have missed should help in developing a more objective and accurate appraisal.[64]

Concluding the Interview

Ideally, employees will leave the interview with positive feelings about management, the company, the job, and themselves. If the meeting results in a deflated ego, the prospects for improved performance will be bleak. While you cannot change past behavior, future performance is another matter. The interview should end with specific and mutually agreed upon plans for the employee's development. Managers should assure employees who require additional training that it will be forthcoming and that they will have the full support of their supervisor. When management does its part in employee development, it is up to the individual to perform in an acceptable manner.

Conducting performance appraisal in the United States presents significant challenges to domestic managers. But, the technique offers even greater problems in the global human resources arena, as the following global perspective illustrates.

A Global Perspective

Two Cultures' View of Performance Appraisal

Performance appraisal is an area of human resource management that has special problems when translated into different cultural environments. Chinese managers often have a different idea about what performance is than do Western managers, as Chinese companies tend to focus appraisals on different criteria. Chinese managers appear to define performance in terms of personal characteristics, such as loyalty and obedience, rather than outcome measurement. Chinese performance appraisals place great emphasis upon "moral" characteristics. Western performance appraisal seeks to help achieve organizational objectives, and this is best obtained by concentrating on individual outcomes and behaviors that are related to the attainment of those objectives.[65]

Chinese organizational objectives often differ widely from the objectives of Western firms. Chinese firms have had to fulfill state political objectives such as maximizing employment, and internal HRM practices were oriented to serve these objectives. Many overseas Chinese business practices are grounded in the traditions of Chinese family business, where a primary objective is to maintain family control of the business. Even when the business is incorporated and publicly traded, the family often maintains majority control and maintaining family control is a major organizational objective. The organization may tolerate less than optimal performance because maintaining family control is so important. One implication of this is that performance appraisals would tend to favor workers that supported the family over workers that challenged family authority. These differing objectives will influence the way in which appraisal judgments are made.[66]

There are other well-known characteristics of the Chinese that also have a direct bearing on the practice of performance appraisal. Three such characteristics are face (*mianzi*), fatalism, and the somewhat broad term *Confucianism. Mianzi* is the social status that one has, and a person's *mianzi* will have an effect on that person's ability to influence others. It is particularly important that performance reviews be held in private, since a poor review in public will cause a subordinate to lose *mianzi.* It is for this reason that the Chinese tend to avoid the possibility of confrontation and loss of face that could result from a formal appraisal process. This concern with *mianzi* also makes it difficult to publicly act on performance problems.[67]

Fatalism also has a direct impact on performance appraisal. Research has indicated that Chinese individuals are more likely to blame their own problems on external factors, and since the outcome is due to things outside the individual's control, the poor achievement will not lead to a loss in face. Such a defensive reaction is natural and occurs in all cultures, but appears to be stronger and more formally ritualized in mainland China.[68]

One legacy of Confucianism is an emphasis on morality as a basis for evaluation. Under the Confucian view, the most important characteristic of an individual was the moral basis of his or her character. A quotation from the Confucian classic *Da Xue* (Great Wisdom) says "Cultivate oneself, bring order to the family, rule the country, and bring peace to the world." Thus, peace, harmony, and success all start with cultivating oneself, including the cultivation of one's moral character. In the view of the Chinese, a "moral" worker will also be an effective worker. Therefore, evaluation of performance and achievement carries strong elements of judgments of the employee's moral character.[69]

Summary

1. Describe the 360-degree feedback evaluation method.

The 360-degree feedback evaluation is an increasingly popular appraisal method that involves evaluation input from multiple levels within the firm as well as external sources. In this method, people all around the rated employee may provide ratings, including senior managers, the employee himself or herself, supervisors, subordinates, peers, team members, and internal or external customers.

2. Define *performance appraisal* and identify the uses of performance appraisal.

Performance appraisal (PA) is a system of review and evaluation of an individual's or team's job performance. Performance appraisal data are potentially valuable for use in numerous human resource functional areas including human resource planning, recruitment and selection, training and development, career planning and development, compensation programs, internal employee relations, and assessment of employee potential.

3. Discuss the performance appraisal environmental factors.
Many of the external and internal environmental factors discussed in Chapter 1 can influence the appraisal process. For example, legislation requires that appraisal systems be nondiscriminatory.

4. Describe the performance appraisal process.
The identification of specific goals is the starting point for the PA process and the beginning of a continuous cycle. Then job expectations are established with the help of job analysis. The next step involves examining the actual work performed. Performance is then appraised. The final step involves discussing the appraisal with the employee.

5. Identify the aspects of a person's performance that an organization should evaluate.
The aspects of a person's performance that an organization should evaluate include traits, behaviors, and task outcomes.

6. Identify who may be responsible for performance appraisal and the performance period.
People who are usually responsible for performance appraisal include immediate supervisors, subordinates, peers, groups, the employee, customers; and for the 360-degree feedback evaluation method, perhaps all of the above.

7. Identify the various performance appraisal methods used.
Performance appraisal methods include 360-degree feedback evaluation, rating scales, critical incidents, essay, work standards, ranking, forced distribution behaviorally anchored rating scales, and results-oriented approaches.

8. Describe how computer software is used in performance appraisal.
Computer software is available for recording the appraisal data. A big advantage in utilizing the computer is the reduction of paperwork required. Also, managers have the option of customizing most programs.

9. List the problems that have been associated with performance appraisal.
The problems associated with performance appraisals include the lack of objectivity, halo error, leniency/strictness, central tendency, recent behavior bias, personal bias, and judgmental role of the evaluator.

10. Explain the characteristics of an effective appraisal system.
Characteristics include job-related criteria, performance expectations, standardization, trained appraisers, continuous open communication, performance reviews, and due process.

11. Describe the legal implications of performance appraisal.
It is unlikely that any appraisal system will be totally immune to legal challenge. However, systems that possess certain characteristics are more legally defensible.

12. Explain how the appraisal interview should be conducted.
A successful appraisal interview should be structured in a way that allows both the supervisor and the subordinate to view it as a problem-solving rather than a faultfinding session.

Key Terms

- **360-degree feedback evaluation, 251**
- **Performance appraisal (PA), 252**
- **Performance management, 252**
- **Competencies, 257**
- **Rating scales method, 261**
- **Critical incident method, 264**
- **Essay method, 264**
- **Work standards method, 264**
- **Ranking method, 264**
- **Forced distribution methods, 265**
- **Behaviorally anchored rating scale (BARS), 265**
- **Results-based system, 266**
- **Halo error, 268**
- **Leniency, 268**
- **Strictness, 268**
- **Central tendency, 269**

Questions for Review

1. What is the purpose of the 360-degree feedback evaluation method?
2. Define *performance appraisal* and briefly discuss its basic purposes.
3. What are the environmental factors affecting performance appraisal?
4. What are the steps in the performance appraisal process?
5. What aspects of a person's performance should an organization evaluate?
6. Many different people can conduct performance appraisals. What are the various alternatives?
7. How is computer software used in performance appraisal?
8. Briefly describe each of the following methods of performance appraisal:
   a. Rating scales
   b. Critical incidents
   c. Essay
   d. Work standards
   e. Ranking
   f. Forced distribution
   g. Behaviorally anchored rating scales
   h. Results-based systems
9. What are the various problems associated with performance appraisal? Briefly describe each.
10. What are the characteristics of an effective appraisal system?
11. What are the legal implications of performance appraisal?
12. Explain why the following statement is often true: "The Achilles' heel of the entire evaluation process is the appraisal interview itself."

HRM Incident 1

These Things Are a Pain

"There, at last it's finished," thought Rajiv Chaudhry as he laid aside the last of 12 performance appraisal forms. It had been a busy week for Rajiv, who supervises a road maintenance crew for the Georgia Department of Highways.

In passing through Rajiv's district a few days earlier, the governor had complained to the area superintendent that repairs were needed on several of the highways. Because of this, the superintendent assigned Rajiv's crew an unusually heavy workload. In addition, Rajiv received a call from the personnel office that week telling him that the performance appraisals were late. Rajiv explained his predicament, but the personnel specialist insisted that the forms be completed right away.

Looking over the appraisals again, Rajiv thought about several of the workers. The performance appraisal form had places for marking *quantity of work*, *quality of work*, and *cooperativeness*. For each characteristic, the worker could be graded *outstanding*, *good*, *average*, *below average*, or *unsatisfactory*. As Rajiv's crew had completed all of the extra work assigned for that week, he marked every worker *outstanding* in *quantity of work*. He marked Joe Blum *average* in *cooperativeness* because Joe had questioned one of his decisions that week. Rajiv had decided to patch a pothole in one of the roads, and Joe thought the small section of road surface ought to be broken out and replaced. Rajiv didn't include this in the remarks section of the form, though. As a matter of fact, he wrote no remarks on any of the forms.

Rajiv felt a twinge of guilt as he thought about Roger Short. He knew that Roger had been sloughing off, and the other workers had been carrying him for quite some time. He also knew that Roger would be upset if he found that he had been marked lower than the other workers. Consequently, he marked Roger the same to avoid a confrontation. "Anyway," Rajiv thought, "these things are a pain, and I really shouldn't have to bother with them."

As Rajiv folded up the performance appraisals and put them in the envelope for mailing, he smiled. He was glad he would not have to think about performance appraisals for another six months.

Question

1. What weaknesses do you see in Rajiv's performance appraisals?

HRM Incident 2

Performance Appraisal?

As the production supervisor for Sweeny Electronics, Mike Mahoney was generally well regarded by most of his subordinates. Mike was an easygoing individual who tried to help his employees in any way he could. If a worker needed a small loan until payday, he would dig into his pocket with no questions asked. Should an employee need some time off to attend to a personal problem, Mike would not dock the individual's pay; rather, he would take up the slack himself until the worker returned.

Everything had been going smoothly, at least until the last performance appraisal period. One of Mike's workers, Bill Overstreet, had been experiencing a large number of personal problems for the past year. Bill's wife had been sick much of the time and her medical expenses were high. Bill's son had a speech impediment and the doctors had recommended a special clinic. Bill, who had already borrowed the limit the bank would loan, had become upset and despondent over his general circumstances.

When it was time for Bill's annual performance appraisal, Mike decided he was going to do as much as possible to help him. Although Bill could not be considered more than an average worker, Mike rated him outstanding in virtually every category. Because the firm's compensation system was heavily tied to the performance appraisal, Bill would be eligible for a merit increase of 10 percent in addition to a regular cost-of-living raise.

Mike explained to Bill why he was giving him such high ratings, and Bill acknowledged that his performance had really been no better than average. Bill was very grateful and expressed this to Mike. As Bill left the office, he was excitedly looking forward to telling his friends about what a wonderful boss he had. Seeing Bill smile as he left gave Mike a warm feeling.

Questions

1. From Sweeny Electronics' standpoint, what difficulties might Mike Mahoney's performance appraisal practices create?
2. What can Mike do now to diminish the negative impact of his evaluation of Bill?

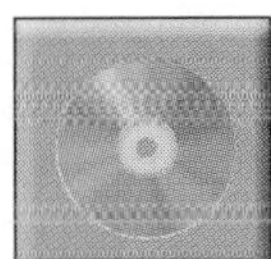

Human Resource Management skills

Chapter 8: Performance Appraisal

A Skills Module entitled *Performance Management* is presented to provide additional insight into topics in this chapter. Specific sections within the module cover the following topics: factors that must be in place for a performance management system to succeed; performance management versus performance appraisal; use of performance appraisal information; types of rating errors; evaluating traits, behaviors, and task outcomes; and types of performance appraisal methods.

Several performance appraisal scenarios are presented to give students realistic experience in dealing with the topic.

A test is provided at the end of the module to determine mastery of the material included in the Skills Module. Also, directions are given for assignments that can be used in class or assigned as homework.?

Take it to the Net

We invite you to visit the Mondy homepage on the Prentice Hall Web site at

www.prenhall.com/mondy

for updated information, Web-based exercises, and links to other HR-related sites.

Notes

1. Bruce Pfau and Ira Kay, "Does 360-Degree Feedback Negatively Affect Company Performance?" *HRMagazine* 47 (June 2002): 56.
2. Leanne Atwater and David Waldman, "Accountability in 360 Degree Feedback; Is It Time to Take the 360-Degree Feedback Method to Its Next Step?" *HRMagazine* 43 (May 1998): 96.
3. Jonathan A. Segal, "86 Your Appraisal Process?" *HRMagazine* 45 (October 2000): 199.

4. Dick Grote, "Public Sector Organizations: Today's Innovative Leaders in Performance Management," *Public Personnel Management* 29 (Spring 2000): 2.
5. Edward E. Lawler III, "Performance Management: The Next Generation," *Compensation & Benefits Review* 26 (May/June 1994): 16.
6. David Butcher, "It Takes Two to Review," *Management Today* (November 2002): 54.
7. Carla Joinson, "Making Sure Employees Measure Up," *HRMagazine* 46 (March 2001): 36.
8. Gary E. Roberts, "Employee Performance Appraisal System Participation: A Technique That Works," *Public Personnel Management* 32 (Spring 2003): 89.
9. Donna L. Maloney, "Meeting Performance Appraisal Head-On," *Public Libraries* 40 (May/June 2001): 178.
10. Skip Waugh, "Delivering Solid Performance Reviews," *Supervision* (August 2002): 16.
11. Dick Grote, "Performance Appraisal," *Executive Excellence* 19 (December 2002): 12.
12. Tony Juncaj, "Do Performance Appraisals Work?" *Quality Progress* (November 2002): 45.
13. Dick Grote, "The Secrets of Performance Appraisal," *Across the Board* 37 (May 2000): 14.
14. Ron Zemke, "The Service Edge," *Incentive* 177 (April 2003): 59.
15. "How Our Readers Make Performance Management Work," *HR Focus* 78 (October 2001): S2.
16. Peter Gwynne, "How Consistent are Performance Review Criteria?" *MIT Sloan Management Review* 43 (Summer 2002): 15.
17. Grote, "The Secrets of Performance Appraisal."
18. Susan Meisinger, "Adding Competencies, Adding Value," HRMagazine 48 (July 2003): 8.
19. Jack Zigon, "Is Your Performance Appraisal System Team-Friendly," *Zigon Performance Group*, http://zigonperf.com/Articles/Team_Friendly.htm, July 3, 2000.
20. Assessment Centers were discussed as a method for selecting employees in Chapter 6. They may also be used as an adjunct to a performance appraisal system in assessing potential.
21. Dick Grote, "Performance Appraisals: Solving Tough Challenges," *HRMagazine* 45 (July 2000): 145–146.
22. George T. Milkovich and Jerry M. Newman, with the assistance of Carolyn Milkovich, *Compensation*, 7th ed. (Boston: McGraw-Hill, 2002): 368.
23. Susan A. Salladay, "Fair Appraisal, or Hatchet Job," *Nursing* (December 1, 2002): 65.
24. Deborah Keary, Dyane Holt, and Ruhal Dooley, "Appraising Performance, 'Hoteling,' Volunteering," *HRMagazine* (May 2003): 41.
25. David K. Lindo, "Can You Answer Their Questions," *Supervision* 64 (January 2003): 20.
26. Ellyn Spragins, "Destructive Criticism," *Fortune Small Business* 12 (December 2002/January 2003): 92.
27. Julia McCarthy, "Performance Evaluation," *Journal of Property Management* 65 (September/October 2000): 22.
28. John F. Welch, Jr., *Jack: Straight from the Gut* (New York: Warner Business Books, 2001): 157–158.
29. Evelyn Rogers, Charles W. Rogers, and William Metley, "Improving the Payoff from 360-Degree Feedback," *Human Resource Planning* 25 (2002): 44.
30. Ibid., 44–54.
31. Paddy Kamen, "The Way That You Use It," *CMA Management* 77 (April 2003): 10.
32. Dick Grote, "Forced Ranking: Behind the Scenes," *Across the Board* (November/December 2002): 40.
33. Mathew Boyle, "Performance Reviews: Perilous Curves Ahead," *Fortune* (May 28, 2001): 187.
34. Welch, Jr., *Jack: Straight from the Gut*.
35. Anne Fisher, "I'm Not Shedding Tears for Dot-Commers Facing Reality," *Fortune* (December 9, 2002): 244.
36. Boyle, "Performance Reviews."
37. Timothy Aeppel, "Goodyear Ends Ratings System Ahead of Lawsuit," *Wall Street Journal* (September 12, 2002): B.8.
38. Joseph J. Martocchio, *Strategic Compensation*, 2nd ed. (Upper Saddle River, NJ: Prentice Hall, 2001): 77.
39. Ibid., 561.
40. Dennis A. Joiner, "Assessment Centers: What's New?" *Public Personnel Management* 31 (Summer 2002): 179.
41. Dick Grote, "Staff Performance Advice for CPAs," *Journal of Accountancy* 188 (July 1999): 51.
42. David Haskin, "Performance Now 3.0," *Computing* 17 (November 1999): 101.
43. Gail Dutton, "Making Reviews More Efficient and Fair," *Workforce* 80 (April 2001): 76.
44. Gary Meyer, "Performance Reviews Made Easy, Paperless," *HRMagazine* 45 (October 2000): 181–184.
45. Kara Parlin, "Strengthen Corporate Foundations with Employee-Evaluation Tools," *Internet World* (February 1, 2003): 16.
46. Mary Hayes, "Goal Oriented," *InformationWeek* (March 10, 2003): 34–42.
47. Bob Losyk, "How to Conduct a Performance Appraisal," *Public Management* 84 (April 2002): 8.
48. Ibid., 9.
49. Gary Gray, "Performance Appraisals Don't Work," *Industrial Management* 44 (March/April 2002): 15.
50. "Research on Performance Appraisals Wins Award," *HR News* 16 (July 1997): 13.
51. Grote, "The Secrets of Performance Appraisal."
52. Michael Schrage, "How the Bell Curve Cheats You," *Fortune* (February 21, 2000): 296.
53. Peter W. Kennedy and Sandy Gorgan Dresser, "Appraising and Paying for Performance: Another Look at an Age-Old Problem," *Employee Benefits Journal* 26 (December 2001): 8–14.
54. D. Allen Miller, "Management," *Commercial Law Bulletin* 18 (January/February 2003): 16.
55. Peter W. Kennedy and Sandy Gorgan Dresser, "Appraising and Paying for Performance: Another Look at an Age-Old Problem," *Employee Benefits Journal* 26 (December 2001): 8–14.
56. G. Ronald Gilbert, Edward L. Hannan, and Kevin B. Lowe, "Is Smoking Stigma Clouding the Objectivity of Employee Performance Appraisal?" *Public Personnel Management* 27 (Fall 1998): 285.
57. Iris Randall, "Performance Appraisal Anxiety," *Black Enterprise* 25 (January 1995): 60.
58. Adapted from story presented in Geoffrey Colvin, "Between Right and Right," *Fortune* (November 11, 2002): 66.
59. Pfau and Kay, "Does 360-Degree Feedback Negatively Affect Company Performance?"

60. Patricia S. Eyres, "Performance Management without Pain—And Without Lawsuits," *Agency Sales* 33 (March 2003): 49.
61. William E. Lissy, "Performance Appraisals Can Be a Weapon for Employees," *Supervision* 58 (March 1997): 17.
62. Liz Hughes, "Motivating Your Employees," *Women in Business* (March 1, 2003): 17.
63. Susan Scherreik, "Your Career: Your Performance Review: Make it Perform," *BusinessWeek* (December 17, 2001): 139.
64. Stephen Kindel, "The No-Beg Bonus," *Esquire* 133 (February 2000): 48.
65. Paul S. Hempel, "Differences Between Chinese and Western Managerial Views of Performance," *Personnel Review* 30 (2001): 203–226.
66. Ibid.
67. Ibid.
68. Ibid.
69. Ibid.

PART FIVE

Compensation and Benefits

CHAPTER OBJECTIVES

After completing this chapter, students should be able to

1. Discuss whether or not top executives are paid too much.
2. Describe the various forms of compensation.
3. Explain the concept of equity in financial compensation.
4. Identify the determinants of individual financial compensation.
5. Describe the organization as a determinant of financial compensation.
6. Describe factors that should be considered when the labor market is a determinant of financial compensation.
7. Explain how the job is a determinant of financial compensation.
8. Describe job pricing.
9. Identify factors related to the employee that are essential in determining financial compensation.
10. Explain compensation for special groups.
11. Explain how executive compensation is determined and the types of executive compensation.

CHAPTER 9

Compensation

HRM IN *Action*: *Are Top Executives Paid Too Much?*

 **OBJECTIVE**

Discuss whether or not top executives are paid too much.

Over the past decade, the rise of executive compensation has truly been rapid. One survey of publicly held corporations found that the full pay package of chief executives jumped 537 percent in the 1990s while the Standard & Poor's 500 rose 297 percent and profits 116 percent over the same period. Workers' pay grew only 32 percent.[1]

Although pay packages declined in 2002, the average CEO received $7.4 million. Alfred Lerner, former CEO of MBNA Corporation, exercised stock options worth $194.9 million, making him the highest paid chief executive. In the number-two spot, Jeffrey C. Barbakow, of Tenet Healthcare Corporation, exercised options for a $111.1 million gain. Even with declines in executive pay over the past two years, CEOs still earn more than 200 times the average worker.[2]

The expanded role of executive search firms, legislation encouraging stock options, and a booming stock market have combined to boost executive pay. More sophisticated executive search firms made it easier for top executives to move to other firms and this job mobility added to an executive's marketability. Consider that in 1980, 1 out of 14 of the 850 largest firms had hired its CEO from outside the firm; by 1996, it was 1 in 3.[3]

Usually, shareholders do not object to high compensation for top executives when their firm is profitable. In fact, they generally feel it is essential to reward them highly to retain them. However, what should the attitude be when things do not go well with the executive's firm? Under CEO Michael Armstrong, AT&T Corporation tumbled $6.8 billion into the red in 2001, down from earnings of $4.1 billion the previous year. In addition, the firm's shares in 2001 slid 28 percent from their January peaks. What kind of bonus or stock options should this executive receive? Despite the bloodbath, AT&T's compensation committee gave Mr. Armstrong a pay package totaling $21 million, including stock options worth $12.2 million.[4] This is a prime example of why many stakeholders now view pay for executives, especially CEOs, with a skeptical eye. While shareholders and rank-and-file employees expressed little opposition to astronomical executive pay during the long-running bull market, the mood certainly changed with the decline in the market and the rash of corporate scandals. A recent Harris

Poll found that 87 percent of the respondents believe that executives had gotten rich at the expense of ordinary workers, and 87 percent felt that top executives receive more than they deserve.[5] The need for rational compensation decisions seems imperative, especially since the collapse of Enron and other firms, in which top executives pocketed enormous sums in allegedly shady deals.

Directors of firms are exhibiting a new degree of conservatism, knowing they will have to justify their compensation decisions. And, perhaps seeing the handwriting on the wall, some executives have given back large amounts of their pay. Even the CEO of a highly successful firm, Richard D. Kinder, co-founder of Kinder Morgan, Inc., works for $1 a year despite the fact that his firm produced a three-year total return to shareholders of 113 percent.[6]

Across corporate America, proxy resolutions aimed at curbing CEO pay are winning unprecedented victories.[7] And abroad, shareholders of GlaxoSmithKline PLC recently voted to reject a proposal that would boost the compensation package of its chief executive officer, J. P. Garnier, the latest sign that outrage over executive pay has spilled over from the United States to Europe.[8]

OBJECTIVE

Describe the various forms of compensation.

Compensation: The total of all rewards provided employees in return for their services.

Direct financial compensation: Pay that a person receives in the form of wages, salary, bonuses, and commissions.

Indirect financial compensation: All financial rewards that are not included in direct compensation.

Nonfinancial compensation: The satisfaction that a person receives from the job itself or from the psychological and/or physical environment in which the job is performed.

SHRM HR Links

www.shrm.org/hrlinks/default.asp

This SHRM Web site provides useful information regarding compensation.

We began this chapter by considering the question of whether top executives are paid too much. Next, we describe the various forms of compensation and explain the concept of equity in financial compensation. Then we discuss determinants of individual financial compensation and describe how the organization influences financial compensation. This is followed by discussions of how both the labor market and the job are factors in determining financial compensation. Then we explore how jobs are priced. Next, factors related to the employee that are essential in determining financial compensation are described. Finally, we consider compensation for special groups, how executive compensation is determined, and the types of executive compensation.

Compensation: An Overview

Compensation administration is one of management's most difficult and challenging human resource areas because it contains many elements and has a far-reaching impact on an organization's strategic goals. **Compensation** is the total of all rewards provided to employees in return for their services. The overall purposes of providing compensation are to attract, retain, and motivate employees. The components of a total compensation program are shown in Figure 9-1. **Direct financial compensation** consists of the pay that a person receives in the form of wages, salaries, commissions and bonuses. **Indirect financial compensation** (benefits) consists of all financial rewards that are not included in direct compensation. As you can see in Figure 9-1, this form of compensation includes a wide variety of rewards normally received indirectly by the employee.

Nonfinancial compensation consists of the satisfaction that a person receives from the job itself or from the psychological and/or physical environment in which the person works. This aspect of nonfinancial compensation involves both psychological and physical factors within the firm's working environment.

It is not possible to provide a perfect pay package. However, to ensure that their reward system is effective and meeting employee needs, a number of firms allow their people to customize their own compensation package as much as is technically, legally,

EXTERNAL ENVIRONMENT			
INTERNAL ENVIRONMENT			
Compensation			
Financial		**Nonfinancial**	
Direct	**Indirect (Benefits)**	**The Job**	**Job Environment**
Wages Salaries Commissions Bonuses	**Legally Required Benefits** Social Security Unemployment Compensation Workers' Compensation Family & Medical Leave	Skill Variety Task Identity Task Significance Autonomy Feedback	Sound Policies Competent Employees Congenial Co-workers Appropriate Status Symbols Working Conditions
	Voluntary Benefits Payment for Time Not Worked Health Care Life Insurance Retirement Plans Employee Stock Option Plans Supplemental Unemployment Benefits Employee Services Premium Pay Unique Benefits		**Workplace Flexibility** Flextime Compressed Workweek Job Sharing Flexible Compensation Telecommunicating Part-Time Work Modified Retirement

Figure 9-1 Components of a Total Compensation Program

financially, and organizationally desirable.[9] We discuss flexible compensation (cafeteria compensation) in the next chapter.

The various rewards described comprise a *total compensation system*. Historically, compensation practitioners have focused primarily on financial compensation and benefits. However, this has changed over time and in 2000, the expanded emphasis was reflected in the name change of this field's professional organization. The American Compensation Association, as noted in Chapter 2, is now WorldatWork, the Professional Association for Compensation, Benefits, and *Total Rewards*.[10] This new model includes the characteristics of nonfinancial compensation.

3 OBJECTIVE

Explain the concept of equity in financial compensation.

Equity:
The perception by workers that they are being treated fairly.

External equity:
Payment of employees at rates comparable to those paid for similar jobs in other firms.

Internal equity:
Payment of employees according to the relative values of their jobs within the same organization.

As indicated in Figure 9-1, the rewards employees receive in a total compensation program stem from numerous factors. To remain competitive, organizations are increasingly rewarding employee performance that influences their key goals. People have different reasons for working, and the most appropriate compensation package depends in large measure on those reasons. When individuals are hard pressed to provide food, shelter, and clothing for their families, money may well be the most important reward. However, some people work long hours each day, receive relatively little pay, and yet love their work because it is interesting or provides an environment that satisfies other needs. To a large degree, adequate compensation is in the mind of the receiver. It is often more than the financial compensation received in the form of a paycheck.

Equity in Financial Compensation

Organizations must attract, motivate, and retain competent employees. Because a firm's financial compensation system plays a huge role in achieving these goals, organizations ought to strive for equity. **Equity**, in the context of financial compensation, means fair pay treatment for employees. As we shall see, firms and individuals view fairness from several perspectives. Ideally, compensation will be evenhanded to all parties concerned and employees will perceive it as such. However, this is a very elusive goal. As you read this section, remember that nonfinancial factors can alter one's perception of equity.

Watson Wyatt

www.watsonwyatt.com

This Web site is for a worldwide consulting firm in the area of compensation and benefits.

External equity exists when a firm's employees receive pay comparable to workers who perform similar *jobs in other firms*. Compensation surveys help organizations determine the extent to which external equity is present. **Internal equity** exists when employees receive pay according to the relative value of their *jobs within the same organization*. Job evaluation is a primary means for determining internal equity. A Watson Wyatt survey of 13,000 U.S. employees found that a majority of respondents were

Employee equity:
A condition that exists when individuals performing similar jobs for the same firm are paid according to factors unique to the employee, such as performance level or seniority.

Team equity:
Equity that is achieved when teams are rewarded based on their group's productivity.

dissatisfied with their perception of both external equity (59 percent) and internal equity (52 percent).[11]

Employee equity exists when individuals performing *similar jobs for the same firm* receive pay according to factors unique to the employee, such as performance level or seniority. **Team equity** is achieved when teams are rewarded based on their *group's productivity*. Performance levels for teams, as well as individuals, may be determined through performance appraisal systems, discussed in Chapter 8.

Inequity in any category can result in morale problems. If employees feel that their compensation is unfair, they may leave the firm. Even greater damage may result for the firm if the employees choose not to leave but stay and restrict their efforts. In either event, the organization's overall performance is damaged. Regarding employee equity, for example, suppose that two accountants in the same firm are performing similar jobs, and one is clearly the better performer. If both workers receive equal pay increases, employee equity does not exist, and the more productive employee is likely to be unhappy. Most workers are concerned with both internal and external pay equity. From an employee relations perspective, internal pay equity may be more important simply because employees have more information about pay matters within their own organizations, and they use this information to form perceptions of equity. On the other hand, an organization must be competitive in the labor market to remain viable. In a competitive environment, and especially for high-tech employees, it becomes clear that the market is of primary importance. IBM's experience makes this point.

OBJECTIVE

Identify the determinants of individual financial compensation.

Wage and Salary Information

www.lir.msu.edu/hotlinks/hr.htm

This Web site provides links to numerous sites related to wage and salary information.

IBM's *old* culture was most apparent in the company's strong emphasis on internal equity over external equity. In any given salary grade, accountants, development engineers, HR professionals, programmers, and manufacturing managers were paid comparably off the same salary structure, regardless of what market data revealed about trends for each job family. IBM established this approach during the years when it virtually dominated its industry. The program was sound in that environment as it was hard to be overly concerned with compensation competitiveness when the firm was larger than its seven largest rivals *combined*. The focus on internal equity made sense. However, times have changed dramatically. This model could not survive in a new generation that lives under constant pressure to win against relentless competition.[12]

Determinants of Individual Financial Compensation

Compensation theory has never been able to provide a completely satisfactory answer to what an individual's service performing a job is worth. While no scientific approach is available, organizations typically use a number of relevant factors to determine individual pay. These determinants appear in Figure 9-2. Historically, the *organization*, the *labor market*, the *job*, and the *employee* all have influenced job pricing and the ultimate determination of an individual's financial compensation. These factors continue to play an important role. However, for more and more business firms, the world has become the marketplace. As global economics increasingly establishes the cost of labor, the global labor market grows in importance as a determinant of financial compensation for individuals. With labor costs accounting for an average exceeding 50 percent of sales,[13] it may be natural for employers to outsource an increasing number of functions to cheaper foreign labor. As an example, if you call for service on your new personal computer, you may well wind up talking with a technical expert in India who may make a third of the salary of a comparable technician in the United States.

OBJECTIVE

Describe the organization as a determinant of financial compensation.

WorldatWork

www.worldatwork.org

This Web site provides information on the Professional Association for Compensation, Benefits, and Total Rewards.

The Organization as a Determinant of Financial Compensation

Managers tend to view financial compensation as both an expense and an asset. It is an expense in the sense that it reflects the cost of labor. In service industries, labor costs

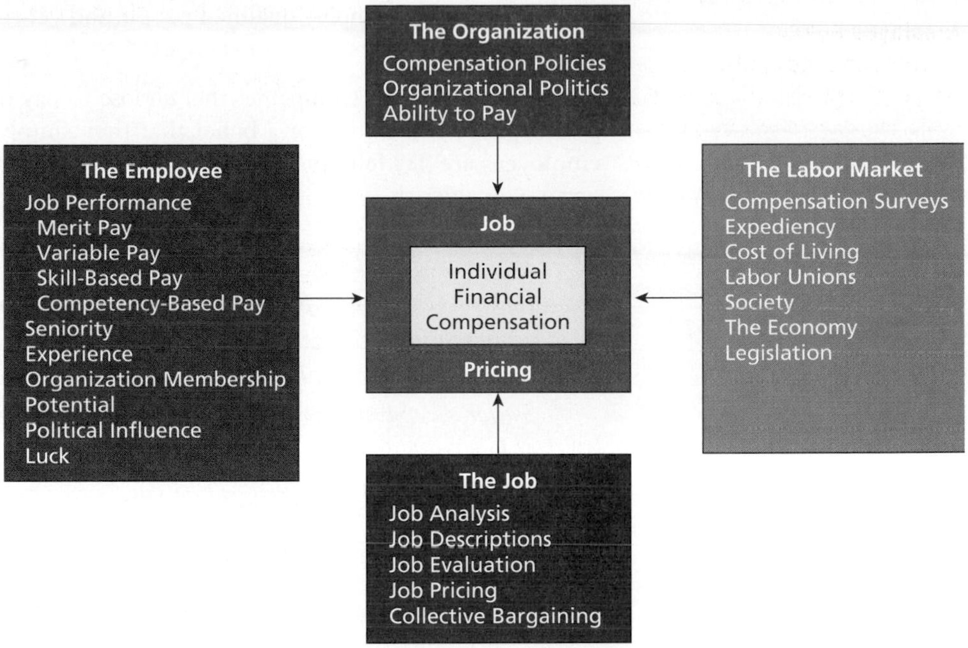

Figure 9-2 Primary Determinants of Individual Financial Compensation

account for more than 50 percent of all expenses. However, financial compensation is clearly an asset when it is instrumental in recruiting and hiring good people, encouraging them to put forth their best efforts and remain in their jobs. A firm that pays well attracts many applicants, enabling management to pick and choose the skills and traits it values. It holds onto these quality hires by equitably sharing the fruits of its financial success, not only among the management team but also with the rank-and-file.[14] Compensation programs have top management's attention because they have the potential to influence employee work attitudes and behavior that leads to improved organizational performance and implementation of the firm's strategic plan.

Compensation Policies

Compensation policy: Policies that provide general guidelines for making compensation decisions.

A **compensation policy** provides general guidelines for making compensation decisions. Employees may perceive their firm's compensation policies as being fair and unbiased and others may have different opinions. For example, one study of compensation policies found that 21 percent of nonexempt workers believed that their employers' policies take advantage of them by requiring work outside the regular workplace and normal work hours. This attitude stems from the extra hours of work made feasible due to employer-required cell phones, pagers, laptops, and other tools of a modern mobile workplace.[15] The result of these perceptions may well have an effect on employees' perception of fairness and result in lower productivity or turnover.

An organization often, formally or informally, establishes compensation policies that determine whether it will be a pay leader, a pay follower, or strive for an average position in the labor market.

Pay leaders: Those organizations that pay higher wages and salaries than competing firms.

Pay Leaders. **Pay leaders** are organizations that pay higher wages and salaries than competing firms. Using this strategy, they feel that they will be able to attract high-quality, productive employees and thus achieve lower per-unit labor costs. Higher-paying firms usually attract more highly qualified applicants than lower-paying companies in the same labor market.

Market (going) rate: The average pay that most employers provide for the same job in a particular area or industry.

The Market Rate. The **market rate,** or **going rate,** is the average pay that most employers provide for a similar job in a particular area or industry. Many organizations have a policy that calls for paying the market rate. In such firms, management believes that it can employ qualified people and yet remain competitive by not having to raise the price of its goods or services.

Pay followers:
Companies that choose to pay below the going rate because of a poor financial condition or a belief that they simply do not require highly capable employees.

Pay Followers. Companies that choose to pay below the market rate because of poor financial condition or a belief that they simply do not require highly capable employees are **pay followers.** When organizations follow this policy, difficulties often occur. Consider the case of Trig Ekeland.

> *Trig managed a large, but financially strapped farming operation in South Dakota. Although no formal policies were established, Trig had a practice of paying the lowest wage possible. One of his farmhands, Charlie Roberts, was paid minimum wage. During a period of three weeks, Charlie wrecked a tractor, severely damaged a combine, and tore out the transmission in a new pickup truck. Charlie's actions prompted Trig to remark, "Charlie is the most expensive darned employee I've ever had."*

As Trig discovered, paying the lowest wage possible did not save money—actually, the practice was quite expensive. In addition to hiring unproductive workers, organizations that are pay followers may have a high turnover rate as their most qualified employees leave to join higher-paying organizations. Equally important, in situations where incompetent or disgruntled employees make contact with customers, they may not provide the kind of customer service management desires. If management does not give its employees first-class treatment, customers may also suffer, and this is not the formula for success in anyone's business.

Organizational Level

The organizational level in which compensation decisions are made can also have an impact on pay. Upper management often makes these decisions to ensure consistency. However, in some cases, there may be advantages to making pay decisions at lower levels where better information may exist regarding employee performance. In addition, extreme pressure to retain top performers may override the desire to maintain consistency in the pay structure. Organizations increasingly make exceptions for just this reason.

Organizational Politics

We have noted that compensation surveys, job analysis, job evaluation, and the employee are all involved in setting base pay. Political considerations may influence these factors in the following ways:

- Managers could make their firm appear to be a wage leader by stacking their compensation survey with organizations that are pay followers.
- A firm's choice of compensable factors for the job evaluation plan could manipulate the value of certain jobs.
- As mentioned in the previous chapter, managers sometimes intentionally distort performance appraisal ratings.

Organizational politics can destroy a sound, objective compensation system. Managers should become aware of this danger and take appropriate action.

Ability to Pay

An organization's assessment of its ability to pay is also an important factor in determining pay levels. Financially successful firms tend to provide higher-than-average compensation. However, an organization's financial strength establishes only the upper limit of what it will pay. To arrive at a specific pay level, management must consider other factors.

6 OBJECTIVE

Describe factors that should be considered when the labor market is a determinant of financial compensation.

The Labor Market as a Determinant of Financial Compensation

Labor market:
The labor market consists of potential employees located within the geographic area from which employees are recruited.

Potential employees located within the geographic area from which employees are recruited comprise the **labor market**. Labor markets for some jobs extend far beyond the location of a firm's operations. An aerospace firm in Seattle, for example, may be concerned about the labor market for engineers in Fort Worth or Orlando, where competitive firms are located. Managerial and professional employees are often recruited from a wide geographic area. In fact, some firms engage in global recruitment for certain skills and top executives. Telecommuting, discussed in the next chapter, makes a global labor market feasible for numerous jobs.

Pay for the same jobs in different labor markets may vary considerably. Secretarial jobs, for example, may carry an average salary of over $30,000 per year in a large, urban community but only $18,000 or less in a smaller town. Compensation managers must be aware of these differences in order to compete successfully for employees. The market rate is an important guide in determining pay. Many employees view it as the standard for judging the fairness of their firm's compensation practices.

Compensation Surveys

Compensation survey:
A means of obtaining data regarding what other firms are paying for specific jobs or job classes within a given labor market.

A **compensation survey** strives to obtain data regarding what other firms are paying for specific jobs or job classes within a given labor market. Virtually all compensation professionals use compensation surveys either directly or indirectly. The surveys may be purchased, outsourced to a consulting firm, or be conducted by the organization itself. Organizations use surveys for two basic reasons: to identify their relative position with respect to the chosen competition in the labor market, and to provide input in developing a budget and compensation structure. Of all the wage criteria, market rates remain the most important standard for determining pay. In a competitive environment, the marketplace determines economic worth, and this is *the* critical factor.

Large organizations routinely conduct compensation surveys that typically provide the low, high, and average salaries for a given position. Sometimes the market rate, or going rate, is defined as the 25th to 75th percentile range of pay for jobs rather than a single, specific pay point. They give a sense of what other companies are paying employees in various jobs.

A primary difficulty in conducting a compensation survey involves determining comparable jobs. Surveys that utilize brief job descriptions are far less helpful than surveys that provide detailed and comprehensive descriptions. As the scope of jobs becomes broader, this difficulty grows. Increasingly, employees receive pay for skills and competencies they bring to the job rather than for performing traditional job descriptions. Therefore, compensation levels must be matched to these broader roles. Although the specific information a company requires depends upon its business needs, for many firms this trend changes the nature of the data needed and makes the task of conducting a compensation survey more complex.

Compensation surveys provide information for establishing both direct and indirect compensation. Before conducting a compensation survey, a firm must make these determinations:

- The geographic area of the survey
- The specific firms to contact
- The jobs to include

The geographic area in the survey is often determined from employment records. Data from this source may indicate maximum distance or time that employees are willing to travel to work. Also, the firms to be contacted in the survey may be product-line competitors or competitors for certain skilled employees. However, only 50 to 75 percent of the firms may be willing to share data.[16] Because obtaining data on all jobs in the organization may not be feasible, compensation surveys often include only benchmark jobs. A **benchmark job** is one well known in the company and industry and one performed by a large number of employees.

Benchmark job:
A well-known job in the company and industry and one performed by a large number of employees.

In addition to surveys, there are other ways to obtain compensation data. Some professional organizations, such as WorldatWork and the Society for Human Resource Management, periodically conduct surveys, as do several industry associations. Consulting firms including Hewett Associates, Towers Perrin, Hay & Associates, and Mercer Human Resource Consulting also conduct surveys. The U.S. Bureau of Labor Statistics conducts the following four surveys that may be valuable:[17]

- National Compensation Survey
- Employee Benefits in Small Private Establishments
- Employee Benefits in Medium and Large Private Establishments
- Employee Benefits in State and Local Governments

The National Compensation Survey, conducted by the Bureau of Labor Statistics, contains pay and benefits information for approximately 700 occupational classifications. It provides information on a national basis for 9 census regions and for 154 metropolitan and nonmetropolitan areas within each of the 50 states. Compensation data are presented by worker traits and by characteristics of the establishment. The survey attempts to respond to common questions from employers such as: What is the average salary for secretaries in my area? How have wage costs changed over the past year? How have benefit costs, and specifically health-care costs changed over the past year? What is the average employer cost for a defined benefit plan as opposed to a defined contribution plan? The goal of the National Compensation Survey is to be able to answer these questions and many more.[18]

Mercer Human Resource Consulting, in conjunction with the Society for Human Resource Management, conducts annual surveys covering nearly 46,000 HR professionals in 109 HR positions ranging from top management to clerical.[19] The survey is normally completed by May of each year.

While standard compensation surveys are generally useful, managers in highly technical and specialized areas occasionally need to utilize nontraditional means to determine what constitutes competitive compensation for scarce talent and niche positions. They need real-time information and must rely on recruiters and hiring managers on the front lines to let them know what's happening in the job market.[20]

Expediency

While compensation surveys assist organizations in developing logical pay structures, there are times when firms ignore the data derived from such efforts. Sometimes the competition for highly skilled employees is so intense in some labor markets that managers occasionally are left to their own devices. For example, Disney has given certain managers the authority to award salary increases on the spot. Managers at FedEx have also been delegated the authority to reward employees with instant raises and bonuses.[21] While the decisions these managers make are likely within certain guidelines provided by the firms' policies, the historical pressure to maintain consistency (internal equity) throughout a firm may be gone for many employers.

Cost of Living

Although not a problem in recent years, the logic for using cost of living as a pay determinant is both simple and sound: when prices rise over time and pay does not, *real pay* is actually lowered. A pay increase must be roughly equivalent to the increased cost of living if a person is to maintain a previous level of real wages. For instance, if someone earns $42,000 during a year in which the average rate of inflation is 4 percent, a $140 per month pay increase will be necessary merely to maintain the purchasing ability of that employee.

People living on fixed incomes (primarily the elderly and the poor) are hit hard by inflation, but they are not alone as most employees also suffer financially. Recognizing this problem, some firms index pay increases to the inflation rate. In fact, in a questionable practice, some organizations sacrifice *merit pay* to provide across-the-board increases designed to offset the results of inflation.

Inflation is not the only factor affecting cost of living; as mentioned, location also comes into play. For example, according to a comparative salary calculator from Westlake Village, California-based Homestore.com Inc., an income of just less than $50,000 in Sioux Falls, South Dakota, would be equivalent to $100,000 in Chicago.[22]

Official measures of inflation such as the Consumer Price Index (CPI) are market oriented, measuring only the decrease in our money's power to purchase products currently available for sale. An interesting alternative way to view cost of living includes nonmarket elements of our existence, such as the rising costs from crime, lawsuits, pollution, and family breakdown.[23] To this list of factors comprising "hidden inflation," after 9/11, we could include the threat of terrorism.

Labor Unions

An excerpt from the Wagner Act, discussed in Chapter 12, prescribes the areas of mandatory collective bargaining between management and unions as "wages, hours, and other terms and conditions of employment." These broad bargaining areas obviously have great potential impact on compensation decisions. When a union uses comparable pay as a standard in making compensation demands, the employer needs accurate labor market data. When a union emphasizes cost of living, it may pressure management into including a cost-of-living allowance. A **cost-of-living allowance (COLA)** is an escalator clause in the labor agreement that automatically increases wages as the U.S. Bureau of Labor Statistics cost-of-living index rises. Cost-of-living allowances in union contracts have been disappearing. In 1976, 61 percent of union workers covered by major collective bargaining contracts had COLA provisions, but by the end of 1995, COLA coverage had fallen to 22 percent. While there is no agreement as to which factors are responsible for this decline, one view attributes the decline to less inflationary uncertainty. Another view emphasizes the erosion of union power.[24]

Cost-of-living allowance (COLA):
An escalator clause in a labor agreement that automatically increases wages as the U.S. Bureau of Labor Statistics' cost-of-living index rises.

Society

Compensation paid to employees often affects pricing of the firm's goods or services. For this reason, consumers may also become interested in compensation decisions. In past times, the government has responded to public opinion and stepped in to encourage businesses to hold down wages and prices.

Businesses in a local labor market are also concerned with the pay practices of new firms locating in their area. For instance, local civic leaders confronted the management of a large electronics firm when it announced plans to locate a branch plant in their small community. Their questions largely concerned the new firm's wage and salary rates. Subtle pressure was applied to keep the company's wages in line with other wages in the community.

The Economy

The economy definitely affects financial compensation decisions. For example, a depressed economy generally increases the labor supply and this serves to lower the market rate. A booming economy, on the other hand, results in greater competition for workers and the price of labor is driven upward. In addition, the cost of living typically rises as the economy expands. Recently, however, the inflation rate has been both low and stable even as the economy has grown. This condition serves to minimize the prevalence of cost-of-living increases.

Legislation

Federal and state laws can also affect the amount of compensation a person receives. Equal employment legislation, including the Civil Rights Act, the Age Discrimination in Employment Act, the Americans with Disabilities Act, and the Family and Medical Leave Act, all prohibit discrimination against specified groups in employment matters, including compensation. The same is true for federal government contractors or subcontractors covered by Executive Order 11246 and the Rehabilitation Act. States and municipal governments also have laws that affect compensation practices. Our focus in the next section, however, is on the federal legislation that provides broad coverage and specifically deals with compensation issues.

Davis-Bacon Act of 1931. The Davis-Bacon Act of 1931 was the first national law to deal with minimum wages. It mandates a prevailing wage for all federally financed or assisted construction projects exceeding $2,000. The Secretary of Labor sets the prevailing wage at the union wage, regardless of what the average wage is in the affected locality.[25]

Walsh-Healy Act of 1936. The Walsh-Healy Act of 1936 requires companies with federal supply contracts exceeding $10,000 to pay prevailing wages. This legislation also requires one-and-a-half times the regular pay rate for hours over eight per day or 40 per week.

Fair Labor Standards Act of 1938, as Amended (FLSA). The most significant law affecting compensation is the Fair Labor Standards Act of 1938 (FLSA). The purpose of the FLSA is to establish minimum labor standards on a national basis and to eliminate low wages and long working hours. The FLSA attempts to eliminate low wages by setting a minimum wage, and to make long hours expensive by requiring a higher pay rate, overtime, for excessive hours.[26] It also requires record keeping, and provides standards for child labor. The Wage and Hour Division of the U.S. Department of Labor (DOL) administers this act. The act currently provides for a minimum wage of not less than $5.15 an hour. It also requires overtime payment at the rate of one-and-one-half times the employee's regular rate after 40 hours of work in a 168-hour period. Although the act covers most organizations and employees, certain classes of employees are specifically exempt from overtime provisions. However, nonexempt employees, many of whom are paid salaries, must receive overtime pay.

Exempt employees: Those categorized as executive, administrative, or professional employees and outside salespersons.

Exempt employees are categorized as executive, administrative, professional employees and outside salespersons. An *executive employee* is essentially a manager (such as a production manager) with broad authority over subordinates. An *administrative employee*, while not a manager, occupies an important staff position in an organization and might have a title such as account executive or market researcher.[27] A *professional employee* performs work requiring advanced knowledge in a field of learning, normally acquired through a prolonged course of specialized instruction. This type of employee might have a title such as company physician, legal counsel, or senior statistician. *Outside salespeople* sell tangible or intangible items away from the employer's place of business. *Nonexempt employees* are those in jobs not conforming to the above definitions.

For medium and large organizations with many white-collar employees, the most common violations of the FLSA involve incorrectly identifying jobs as exempt. Another common violation relates to the failure of employers to include payments such as bonuses and other forms of compensation in calculating the pay rate for overtime purposes. If firms offer employees a bonus for achieving a certain goal, therefore giving up discretion as to whether they receive it, the bonus payment must be included in figuring the regular rate of pay for overtime purposes. Special-occasion bonuses given at the employer's discretion do not need to be included.

Still another problem relates to the FLSA's prohibiting private employers from docking an *exempt* worker's pay for less than a full day's absence. If an employer improperly docks even one exempt employee, and regulators discover this practice, the Labor Department can assume all employees in this exempt category are being treated as nonexempt workers. The firm can then lose the exempt status for all its exempt employees.

Most violations result from ignorance of the law and can be resolved at an early stage of the investigation. If an employer has doubts about any aspect of complying with the FLSA, it may be advisable to check with the Wage-Hour Division. This practice may insulate the employer from violations without raising a red flag. The absolute worst thing an employer can do is to try to conceal a problem.

Business and professional groups, such as SHRM, are urging Congress to update FLSA and revise this legislation written for a bygone era. For example, the law requires that workers in nonexempt jobs be paid time-and-a-half for any hours worked over 40 hours a week. The proposed Working Families Flexibility Act (WFFA) would allow workers to choose pay or compensatory time off for overtime at their discretion. (This option has been available to public employees since1985 as an amendment to the FLSA). Workers would be able to bank a certain number of hours each pay period that could then be taken as paid days off to extend a vacation, care for a sick child, take in an afternoon soccer game, or visit the dentist. The time off could be taken at the worker's discretion except when it would *unduly disrupt the operations of the employer*. This is one sticking point. Sponsors of the bill say there are safeguards built into the bill that prevent abuses including coercion by employers who want employees to take time off during slack periods in lieu of paying out cash during crunch times. Opponents of this concept maintain that Congress should not enact the WFFA without explaining when the use of compensatory time would "unduly disrupt the operations of the employer."[28]

Equal Pay Act of 1963. The Equal Pay Act of 1963 (an amendment to the FLSA) prohibits an employer from paying an employee of one gender less money than an employee of the opposite gender, if both employees do work that is substantially the same. Jobs are considered *substantially* the same when they require equal skill, effort, and responsibility and they are performed under similar working conditions.

The act covers work within the same physical place of business. For example, an employer could pay a female more in San Francisco than a male working in the same position in Slippery Rock even if the jobs were substantially the same. Also, a male working in a position that requires five years' experience may legally be paid more than a female who is in a position that requires only three years' experience. The EPA permits pay distinctions based on the following factors:[29]

- Unequal responsibility
- Dissimilar working conditions
- Differences due to seniority
- Differences resulting from a merit pay system
- Differences based on quantity or quality of production

The EPA also includes a catchall provision that permits pay differentials based on *any* factor other than sex. One issue that the courts have found does *not* warrant differential pay is basing the current pay solely on the employee's earnings at a previous employer.

In 2001, median weekly earnings for women who were full-time workers were 76 percent of their male counterparts.[30] While pay inequities obviously exist and no doubt reflect gender discrimination to some degree, there may be legitimate reasons for part of the problem. Supply-and-demand factors help explain the persistence of pay inequity. Traditionally, many women held occupations many men did not consider, such as schoolteacher, secretary, social worker, nurse, waitress, and other low-paying jobs. However, times are changing. For example, after only three decades as members of the mainstream workforce, one in three wives now earns more than her spouse, up from one in five in 1980. Women with MBAs are doing even better as nearly 60 percent have direct deposits larger than their spouses'. The picture will even get brighter for women since 20 percent more women than men are graduating from college, and more women are joining the managerial ranks every year.[31]

One thing is certain, the Equal Pay Act has teeth and they will get sharper because the U.S. Department of Labor is aggressively enforcing the act and seeking harsher penalties against companies that violate it. For example, in 1999, following a Department of Labor audit, Texaco agreed to pay $3.1 million to female employees who had been consistently paid less than their male counterparts.[32] More recently, the money-management unit of American Express Company agreed to pay $31 million to settle a sex and age discrimination lawsuit filed on behalf of more than 4,000 women who said they were denied equal pay and promotion.The settlement, approved by a federal judge in Washington, D.C., also required American Express Financial Advisors, Inc., to appoint a diversity officer, institute mandatory diversity training for financial advisers and managers and, by 2005, increase its hiring of women to 32 percent of all new financial advisers. The company claims that about 25 percent of the unit's financial advisers are currently women.[33]

Since 1992, the Labor Department has collected an average of $32 million annually from government contractors for violations, or alleged violations, of the act. The number of charges filed with the EEOC has declined since 1992, when 1,294 claims were made, to 1,044 claims in 1999. Even with fewer claims, the monetary awards increased from $2.2 million in 1992 to $2.9 million in 1999.[34]

To prove a violation of the Equal Pay Act, an employee must show that a male and a female worker employed by the same firm are paid different wages for equal work, on the basis of sex. The burden then shifts to the employer, who may rebut any of the allegations or prove that the unequal pay resulted from an exception to the EPA. HR professionals need to keep these points in mind:

- Understand that the EPA is limited strictly to pay differences based on gender.
- Remember that nothing would prevent males from claiming pay inequality (although such instances have been rare).
- Treat *red-circle* rates with care (we discuss these later in this chapter).
- Ensure that supervisory titles accurately reflect job duties and responsibilities.

Explain how the job is a determinant of financial compensation.

The Job as a Determinant of Financial Compensation

The individual employee and market forces are most prominent as wage criteria. However, the job itself continues to be a factor, especially in those firms that have internal pay equity as an important consideration. These organizations pay for the value they attach to certain duties, responsibilities, and other job-related factors such as working conditions. Management techniques utilized for determining a job's relative worth include job analysis, job descriptions, and job evaluation. When present in a firm, unions normally prefer to determine compensation through the process of collective bargaining, a topic covered in Chapter 13.

Job Analysis and Job Descriptions

Before an organization can determine the relative difficulty or value of its jobs, it must first define their content. Normally, it does so by analyzing jobs. Recall from Chapter 4 that job analysis is the systematic process of determining the skills and knowledge required for performing jobs. Remember also that the primary by-product of job analysis is the job description, a written document that describes job duties or functions and responsibilities. Job descriptions reflect essential job functions, those that are fundamental or a business necessity.[35] People work best when they understand their job descriptions; a document that lets them know management's expectations.[36]

Job descriptions serve many different purposes, including data for evaluating jobs. They are essential to all job evaluation methods that depend heavily on their accuracy and clarity for success.

Job Evaluation

Critics claim that job evaluation is inherently political and subject to favoritism, both reinforcing bureaucratic thinking.[37] Nevertheless, organizations have evaluated the worth of jobs for decades and continue to do so in spite of criticism of the method. **Job evaluation** is a process that determines the relative value of one job in relation to another. The basic purpose of job evaluation is to eliminate internal pay inequities that exist because of illogical pay structures. For example, a pay inequity probably exists if the mailroom supervisor earns more money than the chief accountant. For obvious reasons, organizations prefer internal pay equity. However, when a job's pay rate is ultimately determined to conflict with the market rate, the latter is almost sure to take precedence. Job evaluation measures job worth in an administrative rather than an economic sense. The latter can be determined only by the marketplace and revealed through compensation surveys. Nevertheless, many firms continue to use job evaluation for the following purposes:

Job evaluation:
A process that determines the relative value of one job in relation to another.

- To identify the organization's job structure
- To eliminate pay inequities and bring order to the relationships among jobs
- To develop a hierarchy of job value for creating a pay structure

The human resource department is typically responsible for administering job evaluation programs. However, committees often perform actual evaluations. A typical committee might include the chief human resource executive and representatives from other functional areas such as finance, production, information technology, and marketing. If a labor union is present, representation from this group might also be involved if the union is not opposed to the concept of job evaluation. The composition of the committee usually depends on the type and level of the jobs being evaluated. In all instances, it is important for the committee to keep personalities out of the evaluation process and to remember it is evaluating the *job*, not the person(s) performing the job. Some people have a difficult time making this distinction. This is understandable since some job evaluation systems are very similar to some performance appraisal methods. In addition, the duties of a job may, on an informal basis, expand, contract, or change depending on the person holding the job.[38]

Small and medium-sized organizations often lack job evaluation expertise and may elect to use an outside consultant. When employing a qualified consultant, management should require that the consultant not only develop the job evaluation system but also train company employees to administer it properly.

The four traditional job evaluation methods are the *ranking*, *classification*, *factor comparison*, and *point* methods. There are innumerable versions of these methods, and a firm may choose one and modify it to fit its particular purposes. Another option is to purchase a proprietary method such as the Hay Plan. We discuss this system, a variation of the point method, later in this section. The ranking and classification methods are nonquantitative, whereas the factor comparison and point methods are quantitative approaches.

Job evaluation ranking method:
A method in which the raters examine the description of each job being evaluated and arrange the jobs in order according to their value to the company.

Ranking Method. The ranking method is the simplest of the four job evaluation methods. In the **job evaluation ranking method,** the raters examine the description of each job being evaluated and arrange the jobs in order according to their value to the company. The procedure is essentially the same as that discussed in Chapter 8 regarding the ranking method for evaluating employee performance. The only difference is that you evaluate jobs, not people. The first step in this method, as with all the methods, is conducting job analysis and writing job descriptions.

Classification method:
A job evaluation method in which classes or grades are defined to describe a group of jobs.

Classification Method. The **classification method** involves defining a number of classes or grades to describe a group of jobs. In evaluating jobs by this method, the raters compare the job description with the class description. Class descriptions reflect the differences between groups of jobs at various difficulty levels. The class description that most closely agrees with the job description determines the classification for that job. For example, in evaluating the job of word processing clerk, the description might include these duties:

1. Data-enter letters from prepared drafts
2. Address envelopes
3. Deliver completed correspondence to unit supervisor

Assuming that the remainder of the job description includes similar routine work, this job would probably be placed in the lowest job class.

Each class is described in such a way that it captures sufficient work detail, yet is general enough to cause little difficulty in slotting a job description into its appropriate class.[39] Probably the best-known illustration of the classification method is the federal government's 18-class evaluation system.

Factor comparison method:
A job evaluation method in which raters need not keep an entire job in mind as they evaluate it; instead, they make decisions based on separate aspects or factors of the job.

Factor Comparison Method. The factor comparison method is somewhat more involved than the two previously discussed qualitative methods. In the **factor comparison method,** raters need not keep the entire job in mind as they evaluate; instead, they make decisions on separate aspects or factors of the job. A basic underlying assumption is that there are five universal job factors:

- Mental requirements, which reflect mental traits such as intelligence, reasoning, and imagination
- Skills, which pertain to facility in muscular coordination and training in the interpretation of sensory impressions
- Physical requirements, which involve sitting, standing, walking, lifting, and so on
- Responsibilities, which cover areas such as raw materials, money, records, and supervision
- Working conditions, which reflect the environmental influences of noise, illumination, ventilation, hazards, and hours

In this method, the evaluation committee creates a monetary scale, containing each of the five universal factors, and ranks jobs according to their value for each factor. Unlike most other job evaluation methods that produce relative job worth only, the factor comparison method determines the absolute value as well.[40]

Point method: An approach to job evaluation in which numerical values are assigned to specific job components, and the sum of these values provides a quantitative assessment of a job's relative worth.

Point Method. In the **point method,** raters assign numerical values to specific job factors—such as knowledge required—and the sum of these values provides a quantitative assessment of a job's relative worth. Historically, some variation of the point plan has been the most popular option.

Because job factors vary from one group to another, the point method requires each job cluster to have its own customized set of factors. Therefore, a separate plan for each group of similar jobs (job clusters) is appropriate. Production jobs, clerical jobs, and sales jobs are examples of job clusters. Figure 9-3 illustrates the procedure for establishing a point method. After determining the cluster you want to study, analysts (or supervisors in smaller firms) conduct job analyses and write job descriptions if current descriptions are not available. The job evaluation committee will later use these descriptions to make evaluation decisions.

Next, the committee selects and defines the factors for measuring job value. These factors become the standards used for the evaluation of jobs. Individuals who are thoroughly familiar with the content of the jobs under consideration are best qualified to identify the factors. Education, experience, job knowledge, mental effort, physical effort, responsibility, and working conditions are examples of factors. Each should be significant in helping to differentiate jobs. Factors that exist in equal amounts in all jobs within a cluster obviously would not serve this purpose. As an example, in evaluating a company's clerical jobs, the working conditions factor would be of little value in differentiating jobs if all jobs in the cluster had approximately the

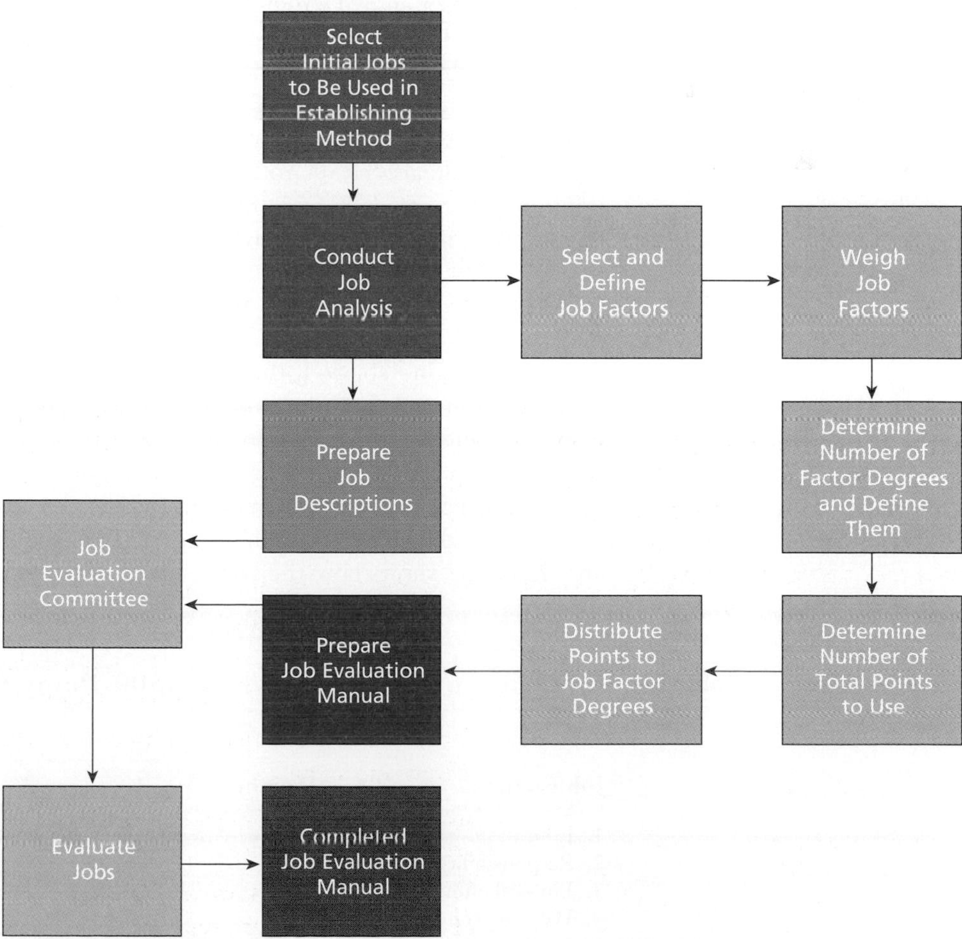

Figure 9-3 Procedure for Establishing the Point Method of Job Evaluation

same working conditions. The number of factors used varies with the job cluster under consideration. It is strictly a subjective judgment.

The committee must establish factor weights according to their relative importance in the jobs considered for evaluation. For example, if experience is quite important for a particular job cluster, you might weight this factor as much as 35 percent. The weight for physical effort (if used at all as a factor in an office cluster) would likely be low—perhaps less than 10 percent.

The next consideration is to determine the number of degrees for each job factor and define each degree. Degrees represent the number of distinct levels associated with a particular factor. The number of degrees needed for each factor depends on job requirements. If jobs in a particular cluster required similar levels of experience, for example, a smaller number of degrees would be appropriate compared to clusters that required a broad range of experience.

The committee then determines the total number of points to use in the plan. The number may vary, but 500 or 1,000 points may work well. The use of a smaller number of points (for example, 50) would not likely permit the proper distinctions among jobs, whereas a larger number (such as 50,000) would be unnecessarily cumbersome. The total number of points in a plan indicates the maximum points that any job could receive.

The next step is to distribute point values to job factor degrees (see Table 9-1, Overview of the Point System). In this illustration, Education and Physical effort each have five degrees; Responsibility has four; and Working Conditions has three. Degree 1 under Education, for example, might indicate the need for a high school education to perform the job. Degree 5 might mean that a master's degree is required. A job given degree 1 for Education would receive 50 points, whereas a job that required a graduate degree would receive 250 points, or the maximum for that factor. You can calculate the maximum points for each factor by multiplying the total points in the system by the assigned weights. For example, the maximum points any job could receive for Education would be 250 (50 percent weight multiplied by 500 points). If the interval between factors is to be a constant number, points for the minimum degree may take the value of the percentage weight assigned to the factor. For instance, the percentage weight for Education is 50 percent, so the minimum number of points would also be 50. You can figure the degree interval by subtracting the minimum number of points from the maximum number and dividing by the number of degrees used minus 1. For example, the interval for factor 1 (Education) is:

$$\text{Interval} = 250 - 50 = 50$$

As you can see in Table 9-1, the interval between each degree for Education is 50.

The approach just mentioned to determine the number of points for each degree is called *arithmetic progression*. An arithmetic progression is simple to understand and explain to employees. In the example, we are assuming that the factors are so defined that the intervals between the degrees are equal. However, if this is not the case, another method, such as a geometric progression, may be more appropriate. Table 9-2 shows how the factor Experience Required might be defined with an

Table 9-1 Overview of the Point System (500-Point System)

		Degree of Factor				
Job Factor	**Weight**	**1**	**2**	**3**	**4**	**5**
1. Education	50%	50	100	150	200	250
2. Responsibility	30%	30	70	110	150	
3. Physical effort	12%	12	24	36	48	60
4. Working conditions	8%	0	24	40		

Table 9-2 Illustration of Arithmetic and Geometric Progression

	Degree of Factor			
Job Factor	1	2	3	4
Experience Required	1 year	3 years	5 years	7 years
	(--------------------Arithmetic Progression--------------------)			
	Degree of Factor			
Job Factor	1	2	3	4
Experience Required	1 year	2 years	4 years	8 years
	(--------------------Geometric Progression--------------------)			

equal spread between degrees (arithmetic progression) and when the spread is on a geometric basis. We have chosen an easy factor for this illustration; the task would require more skill in writing factor degree definitions for a factor such as Knowledge Required.

The next step involves preparing a job evaluation manual. Although there is no standard format, the manual often contains an introductory section, factor and degree definitions, and job descriptions. As a final step, the job evaluation committee then evaluates jobs in each cluster by comparing each job description with the factors in the job evaluation manual.

Point plans require time and effort to design. Historically, a redeeming feature of the method has been that, once developed, the plan was useful over a long time. In today's environment, the shelf life may be considerably less. In any event, as new jobs are created and old jobs substantially changed, job analysis must be conducted and job descriptions rewritten on an ongoing basis. The job evaluation committee evaluates the jobs and updates the manual. Only when job factors change, or for some reason the weights assigned become inappropriate, does the plan become obsolete.

Hay guide chart-profile method (Hay Plan): A refined version of the point method of job evaluation that uses the factors of know-how, problem solving, accountability, and additional compensable elements.

Hay Group

www.hay group.com

This Web site is for the Hay Plan, which is probably the most widely used evaluation system.

The Hay Guide Chart-Profile Method (Hay Plan). The **Hay Guide chart-profile method** is a refined version of the point method. About 5,000 employers worldwide employ the Hay Guide Chart-Profile Method and it is probably the most widely used evaluation system. It utilizes the compensable factors of know-how, problem solving, accountability, and additional compensable elements.[41] Point values are assigned to these factors to determine the final point profile for any job.

Know-how is the total of all knowledge and skills needed for satisfactory job performance. It has three dimensions including the amount of practical, specialized, or scientific knowledge required; the ability to coordinate many functions; and the ability to deal with and motivate people effectively.

Problem solving is the degree of original thinking required by the job for analyzing, evaluating, creating, reasoning, and making conclusions. Problem solving has two dimensions: the thinking environment in which problems are solved (from strict routine to abstractly defined), and the thinking challenge presented by the problems (from repetitive to uncharted). Problem solving is expressed as a percentage of know-how, since people use what they know to think and make decisions.

Accountability is the responsibility for action and accompanying consequences. Accountability has three dimensions including the degree of freedom the job incumbent has to act, the job impact on results, and the extent of the monetary impact of the job. The fourth factor, *additional compensable elements*, addresses exceptional conditions in the job's environment. Because the Hay Plan is a job evaluation method used by employers worldwide, it facilitates job comparison among firms. Thus, the method serves to determine both internal and external equity.

Most job evaluation plans determine the relative value of jobs resulting in a job hierarchy. The next step is to determine the actual price of each job. Job pricing, and the details involved, is the topic of the next section.

 **OBJECTIVE**

Describe job pricing.

Job Pricing

The primary considerations in pricing jobs are the organization's policies, the labor market, and the job itself. Consideration of individual factors is also important. Recall that the process of job evaluation results in a job hierarchy. It might reveal, for example, that the job of senior accountant is more valuable than the job of computer operator, which, in turn, is more valuable than the job of data entry clerk. At this point, you know the *relative* value of these jobs to the company, but not their *absolute* value. **Job pricing** results in placing a dollar value on the job's worth. It takes place after evaluation of the job and the relative value of each job in the organization has been determined. Firms often use pay grades and pay ranges in the job pricing process.

Job pricing:
Placing a dollar value on the worth of a job.

Pay Grades

Pay grade:
The grouping of similar jobs to simplify the job-pricing process.

A **pay grade** is the grouping of similar jobs to simplify pricing jobs. For example, it is much more convenient for organizations to price 15 pay grades than 200 separate jobs. The simplicity of this approach is similar to a college or university's practice of grouping grades of 90 to 100 into an *A* category, grades of 80 to 89 into a *B*, and so on. In following this approach, you also avoid a false implication of preciseness. While job evaluation plans may be systematic, none is scientific.

Plotting jobs on a scatter diagram is often useful to managers in determining the appropriate number of pay grades for a company. Looking at Figure 9-4, notice that each dot on the scatter diagram represents one job. The location of the dot reflects the job's relationship to pay and evaluated points, which reflect its worth. When this procedure is used, a certain point spread determines the width of the pay grade (100 points in this illustration). While each dot represents one job, it may involve dozens of individuals who have *positions* in that one job. The large dot at the lower left represents the job of data entry clerk, evaluated at 75 points. The data entry clerk's hourly rate of

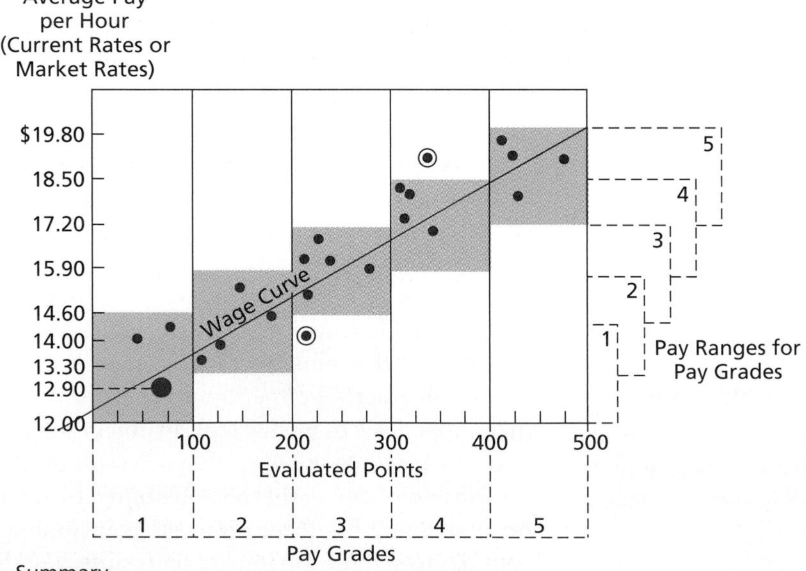

Summary

Evaluated Points	Pay Grade	Minimum	Pay Range Midpoint	Maximum
0–99	1	$12.00	$13.30	$14.60
100–199	2	13.30	14.60	15.90
200–299	3	14.60	15.90	17.20
300–399	4	15.90	17.20	18.50
400–500	5	17.20	18.50	19.80

Figure 9-4 Scatter Diagram of Evaluated Jobs Illustrating the Wage Curve, Pay Grades, and Pay Ranges

Wage curve:
The fitting of plotted points on a curve to create a smooth progression between pay grades (also known as the *pay curve).*

$12.90 represents either the average wage currently paid for the job or its market rate. This decision depends on how management wants to price its jobs.

A **wage curve** (or pay curve) is the fitting of plotted points to create a smooth progression between pay grades. The line drawn minimizes the distance between all dots and the line; a line of best fit may be straight or curved. However, when the point system is used (normally considering only one job cluster), a straight line is often the result, as in Figure 9-4. You can draw this wage line either freehand or by using a statistical method.

Pay Ranges

Pay range:
A minimum and maximum pay rate for a job, with enough variance between the two to allow for a significant pay difference.

After pay grades have been determined, the next decision is whether all individuals performing the same job will receive equal pay or whether you should use pay ranges. A **pay range** includes a minimum and maximum pay rate with enough variance between the two to allow for a significant pay difference. Pay ranges are generally preferred over single pay rates because they allow a firm to compensate employees according to performance and length of service. Pay then serves as a positive incentive. When pay ranges are used, a firm must develop a method to advance individuals through the range.

Points Along the Range. Referring again to Figure 9-4, note that anyone can readily determine the minimum, midpoint, and maximum pay rates per hour for each of the five pay grades. For example, for pay grade 5, the minimum rate is $17.20, the midpoint is $18.50, and the maximum is $19.80. The minimum rate may be the *hiring in* rate that a person receives when joining the firm, although in practice, new employees often receive pay that starts above this level. The maximum pay rate represents the maximum that an employee can receive for that job, regardless of how well he or she performs the job.

The Problem of "Topping Out." A person at the top of a pay grade will have to be promoted to a job in a higher pay grade in order to receive a pay increase unless (1) an across-the-board adjustment is made or (2) the job is reevaluated and placed in a higher pay grade. This situation has caused numerous managers some anguish as they attempt to explain the pay system to an employee who is doing a tremendous job but is at the top of a pay grade. Consider this situation:

> *Everyone in the department realized that Beth Smithers was the best administrative assistant in the company. At times, she appeared to do the job of three people. Bob Marshall, Beth's supervisor, was especially impressed. Recently, he had a discussion with the human resource manager to see what he could do to get a raise for Beth. After Bob described the situation, the human resource manager's only reply was, "Sorry, Bob. Beth is already at the top of her pay grade. There is nothing you can do except have her job upgraded or promote her to another position."*

Situations like Beth's present managers with a perplexing problem. Many would be inclined to make an exception to the system and give Beth a salary increase. However, this action would violate a traditional principle, which holds that every job in the organization has a maximum value, regardless of how well an employee performs the job. The rationale is that making exceptions to the compensation plan would result in widespread pay inequities. Having stated this, we recognize that today, many organizations are challenging traditional concepts as they strive to retain top-performing employees. For example, if Beth Smithers worked for Microsoft or Southwest Airlines, she might get a raise.

Rate Ranges at Higher Levels. The rate ranges established should be large enough to provide an incentive to do a better job. At higher levels, pay differentials may need to be greater to be meaningful. There may be logic in having the rate range become increasingly wide at each consecutive level. Consider, for example, what a $200-per-month salary increase would mean to a file clerk earning $2,000 per month (a 10 percent increase) and to a senior cost accountant earning $5,000 per month (a 4 percent increase). Assuming an inflation rate of 4 percent, the accountant's *real pay* would remain unchanged.

Broadbanding

Broadbanding:
A compensation technique that collapses many pay grades (salary grades) into a few wide bands in order to improve organizational effectiveness.

The pressure on U.S. business firms to do things better, faster, and less expensively has caused management to scrutinize all internal systems. Compensation in particular has received attention because of its ability to affect job behavior. Responding to this need, someone came up with the idea called *broadbanding*. **Broadbanding** is a technique that collapses many pay grades (salary grades) into a few wide bands to improve organizational effectiveness. Organizational downsizing and restructuring of jobs create broader job descriptions, with the result that employees perform more diverse tasks than they did previously. Broadbanding creates the basis for a simpler compensation system that de-emphasizes structure and control and places greater importance on judgment and flexible decision making.

The decreased emphasis on job levels should encourage employees to make cross-functional moves to jobs that are on the same or even a lower level because their pay rate would remain unchanged. Broadbanding also minimizes the problem previously mentioned concerning employees at the top of their pay grade. Moving an employee's job to a higher band would occur only when there was a significant increase in accountability. However, considerable advancement in pay is possible within each band. This is particularly important in firms with flatter organizational structures that offer fewer promotional opportunities. Figure 9-5 illustrates broadbanding as it relates to pay grades and rate ranges.

Broadbanding is not the only means for improving the effectiveness and efficiency of a compensation system and is not appropriate for every organization. However, it has many potential benefits. For example, even massive General Electric has managed to place all its exempt jobs into five bands.[42] Although broadbanding is successful in some organizations, the practice is not without pitfalls. Since each band consists of a broad range of jobs, the market value of these jobs may also vary considerably. Unless carefully monitored, employees in jobs at the lower end of the band could progress to the top of the range and become overpaid.

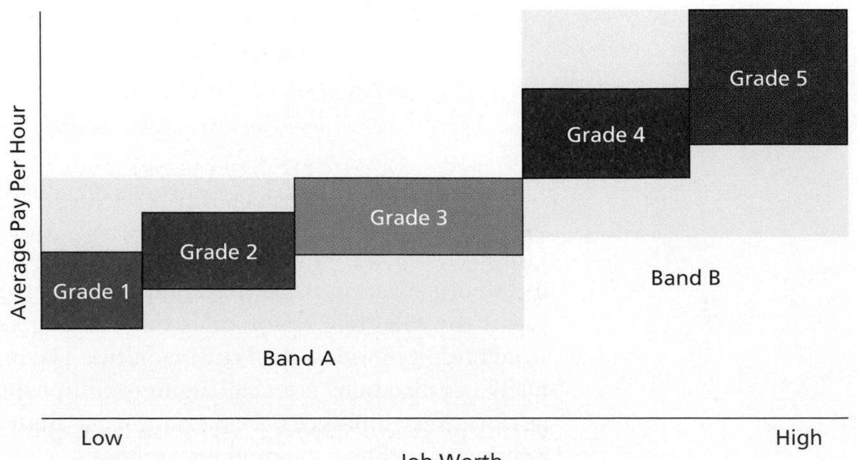

Figure 9-5 Broadbanding and Its Relationship to Traditional Pay Grades and Ranges
Source: Adapted from Joseph J. Martocchio, *Strategic Compensation*, 2nd ed. (Upper Saddle River, NJ: Prentice Hall, 2001): 218.

In a recent year, one survey indicated that 21 percent of large companies had instituted broadbanding programs, up from 6 percent five years earlier and practically zero a few years before that.[43] The rapid growth in the use of broadbanding suggests its potential benefits. For example, bands may add flexibility to the compensation system and require less time making fine distinctions among jobs.[44] Bands may also promote lateral development of employees and direct attention away from vertical promotional opportunities.

While the number of firms in the United States implementing broadbanding continued to increase through 1999, the rate of increase appears to be flattening out.[45] In contrast, a survey in the United Kingdom found that 68 percent of the organizations had pay structures with five or fewer bands. The most common reason given for implementing broadbanding was to provide more flexibility in rewarding people. The next most important reason was to reflect the flattening of organizational structures resulting in fewer levels.[46]

Broadbanding at Georgia-Pacific Corporation

When the compensation group at Atlanta-based Georgia-Pacific realized the firm's system with 27 grades between entry level and vice president had become counterproductive, it started to consider broadbanding. George Murphy, director of corporate compensation, said, "We found that in today's environment, jobs are no longer very segmented. You can't take a cookie-cutter approach that a controller is a controller is a controller."

The firm has plans to move away from the incremental advancement that dominates employees' career planning. Murphy continues, "We're hiring bright people who want to be challenged, but when you have these narrow salary structures and job-evaluation systems, you have difficulty getting people to do what you want them to do—and allowing them to do what they can do. The inherent message in a traditional structure is that we can measure the minute differences in positions, and that the way to move up is to move to the next higher position. A broadbanding structure doesn't deliver that message."[47]

Single-Rate System

Pay ranges are not appropriate for some workplace conditions such as assembly-line operations. For instance, when all jobs within a unit are routine, with little opportunity for employees to vary their productivity, a single-rate system (or fixed-rate system) may be more appropriate. When single rates are used, everyone in the same job receives the same base pay, regardless of productivity. This rate may correspond to the midpoint of a range determined by a compensation survey.

Adjusting Pay Rates

When pay ranges have been determined and jobs assigned to pay grades, it may become obvious that some jobs are overpaid and others underpaid. You normally bring underpaid jobs up to the minimum of the pay range as soon as possible. Referring again to Figure 9-4, you can see that a job evaluated at about 225 points and having a rate of $14.00 per hour is represented by a circled dot immediately below pay grade 3. The job was determined to be difficult enough to fall in pay grade 3 (200-299 points). However, employees working in the job are being paid 60 cents per hour less than the minimum for the pay grade ($14.60 per hour). If one or more female employees should be in this circled job, the employer might soon learn more than desired about the Equal Pay Act. Good management practice would be to correct this inequity as rapidly as possible by placing the job in the proper pay grade and increasing the pay of those in that job.

Overpaid jobs present a different problem. Figure 9-4 illustrates an overpaid job for pay grade 4 (note the circled dot above pay grade 4). Employees in this job earn $19.00 per hour, or 50 cents more than the maximum for the pay grade. This type of overpayment, as well as the kind of underpayment discussed earlier, is called a *red circle rate.*

An ideal solution to the problem of an overpaid job is to promote the employee to a job in a higher pay grade. This is a great idea if the employee is qualified for a higher-rated job and a job opening is available. Another possibility would be to bring the job rate and employee pay into line through a pay cut. While this decision may appear logical, it is generally not a good management practice, as this action would punish employees for a situation they did not create. Somewhere in between these two possible solutions is a third: to freeze the rate until across-the-board pay increases bring the job into line. In an era where this type of increase is declining in popularity, it might take a long time for this to occur.

Pricing jobs is not an easy task. It requires effort that never ends. It is one of those tasks that managers may dislike but must do anyway.

 **OBJECTIVE**

Identify factors related to the employee that are essential in determining financial compensation.

The Employee as a Determinant of Financial Compensation

In addition to the organization, the labor market, and the job, factors related to the employee are also essential in determining pay equity. These factors include performance on the job, seniority, experience, membership in the organization, and potential. Other factors, less controlled by the employee, are political influence and luck.

Performance-Based Pay

A compensation feature generally controllable by employees is their job performance. This performance level is typically determined through performance appraisal. The objective of performance-based pay is to improve productivity. Since a variable pay system is more complex, it could become an administrative headache. However, with current technology, especially available software, and variable pay processes can be powerful tools. This technology has the ability to analyze, track, and pay various types of variable compensation, and it does it more efficiently than unwieldy manual entry systems.[48]

Appraisal data provide the input for such approaches as merit pay, bonuses, and piecework. Appraisals also determine attributes possessed by employees when an organization uses skills or competencies for pay purposes. We discuss each of these approaches to compensation management in the following sections.

Merit pay:
Pay increase given to employees based on their level of performance as indicated in the appraisal. The increase is added to the employee's base pay.

Merit Pay. In theory, **merit pay** is a pay increase given to employees based on their level of performance as indicated in the appraisal. In practice, however, it is often merely a cost-of-living increase in disguise. For example, the average annual merit increases over an 11-year period, adjusted for the Consumer Price Index, have not exceeded 2 percent.

From the employer's viewpoint, a distinct disadvantage to the typical merit pay increase is that it increases the employee's base pay. Therefore, employees receive the added amount each year they are on the payroll regardless of later performance levels. Some firms find it difficult to justify merit pay increases based on a previous employment period but added perpetually to base pay.

Past studies of compensation professionals have determined that merit pay is *marginally successful* in influencing pay satisfaction and performance. Perhaps merit pay should play a more limited role and be used to support alternative reward strategies such as variable pay, gainsharing, team-based pay, and profit sharing, which are discussed later in this chapter.

While many companies continue with merit pay plans, others seek to control fixed costs by using variable pay. Actually, the two approaches are not mutually exclusive; in fact, firms often use them together. Merit pay, which increases base salary, recognizes long-term contributions of employees; variable pay, including bonuses, recognizes current accomplishments.

Bonus (lump-sum payment): A one-time award that is not added to employees' base pay.

Variable Pay (Bonus). The most common type of variable pay for performance is the bonus. The **bonus** is a cost-effective one-time award. There is no carryover into subsequent periods unless employees maintain their performance. Once reserved for high-ranking executives, firms are pushing these forms of pay down through the ranks. The typical large firm spends an average of more than $30 million a year on performance-based compensation. An estimated 5 to 10 percent of *all* workers receive some kind of variable pay, and, among firms with more than 500 employees, about 40 percent receive some form of variable pay.[49]

An effective performance appraisal program is a prerequisite for any pay system tied to performance. Managers commonly contend that performance-based pay is a win-win situation because it boosts production and efficiency and gives employees some control over their earning power. However, labor unions typically call it nothing more than a current version of the *carrot-and-stick philosophy.* According to one compensation expert, "the issue of individual variation of pay is really the antithesis of the union, which says it will treat everybody the same."[50]

Piecework: An incentive pay plan in which employees are paid for each unit produced.

Piecework. **Piecework** is a plan where employees are paid for each unit they produce. Piecework is especially prevalent in the production/operations area. Requirements for the plan include developing output standards for the job and being able to measure the output of a single employee. A piecework plan would not be feasible for many jobs.

A basic question that should precede the introduction of any incentive plan is this: "What effect will it have on productivity and quality?" Although advocates of incentive plans cannot guarantee success, results are often positive.

Skill-Based Pay

Skill-based pay: A system that compensates employees on the basis of job-related skills and the knowledge they possess.

Skill-based pay is a system that compensates employees for their job-related skills and knowledge, not for their job titles. The system assumes that employees who know more are more valuable to the firm and, therefore, they deserve a reward for their efforts in acquiring new skills. The purpose of this approach is to encourage employees to gain additional skills that will increase their value to the organization and improve its competitive position.

Benefits for Individuals and Organizations. When employees obtain additional job-relevant skills, both individuals and the departments they serve benefit. Employees may receive both tangible and intangible rewards: pay increases, job security, greater mobility, and the satisfaction of being more valuable. Acquiring additional skills also allows employees the opportunity to increase their earnings without the necessity of moving permanently to a higher-level job. This factor has additional importance in a highly competitive environment in which promotional opportunities are more limited than in the past. Employees with a broader range of skills provide organizational units with a greater degree of versatility in dealing with absenteeism and turnover.

Appropriate Conditions. Typically, skill pay is most appropriate in settings where the work tends to be routine and less varied, such as skills of assembly or responding to customer service questions. Skill-based pay is also popular with autonomous workgroups or other job enrichment programs. A high commitment to human resource development is necessary to implement such a program successfully. In addition, employees involved in skill-based pay programs must have the desire to grow and increase their knowledge and skills.

Management Challenges. While skill-based pay appears to have advantages for both employer and employee, there are some challenges for management. The firm must provide adequate training opportunities or else the system can become a demotivator. Since research has revealed that it takes an average of only three years for a worker to reach a maximum level in a skill-based pay system, what will keep employees motivated? One answer has been coupling the plan with a pay-for-performance system. An additional challenge associated with skill-based pay is that payroll costs will escalate. It is conceivable that a firm could have, in addition to high training and development costs, a very expensive workforce possessing an excess of skills. In spite of these negative possibilities, a number of firms have achieved lower operating costs and other benefits with their pay-for-skills programs.

Competency-Based Pay

Competency-based pay: A compensation plan that rewards employees for their demonstrated expertise.

Competency-based pay is a compensation plan that rewards employees for their demonstrated expertise. Competencies include skills but also involve other factors such as motives, traits, values, attitudes, and self-concepts.[51] While core competencies may be unique to each company, one service firm identified the following:

- *Team-centered.* Builds productive working relationships at levels within and outside the organization
- *Results-driven.* Is focused on achieving key objectives
- *Client-dedicated.* Works as a partner with internal and external clients
- *Innovative.* Generates and implements new ideas, products, services, and solutions to problems
- *Fast cycle.* Displays a bias for action and decisiveness[52]

Pay for performance focuses on end results; competency-based pay examines how an employee accomplishes the objectives. Although competencies may relate to performance, it appears that they would be more difficult to evaluate than results.

Seniority

Seniority: The length of time that an employee has worked in various capacities with the firm.

Seniority is the length of time an employee has been associated with the company, division, department, or job. While management generally prefers performance as the primary basis for compensation changes, unions tend to favor seniority. They believe the use of seniority provides an objective and fair basis for pay increases. Many union leaders consider performance evaluation systems to be too subjective, permitting management to reward favorite employees arbitrarily. As previously mentioned, labor unions normally prefer collective bargaining for achieving their compensation goals, and seniority will usually be the preferred criterion.

Experience

Regardless of the nature of the task, experience has potential for enhancing a person's ability to perform. However, this possibility materializes only if the experience acquired is positive. Knowledge of the basics is usually a prerequisite for effective use of a person's experience. This is true for a person starting to play golf, learn a foreign language, or manage people in organizations. People who express pride in their many years of managerial experience may be justified in their sentiments, but only if their experience has been beneficial. Those who have been bull-of-the-woods autocrats for a number of years would likely not find their experience highly valued by a *Fortune*

100 firm. Nevertheless, experience is often indispensable for gaining the insights necessary for performing many tasks.

A relatively new aspect of experience relating to organizational value stems from the creation of a new economy. How do you best do things in a dot-com world as opposed to the old economy? Nowadays, it is possible for experience to become somewhat irrelevant. Still, employees receive compensation for their experience and the practice is justified if the experience is positive and relevant to the work

Membership in the Organization

Employees receive some compensation components without regard to the particular job they perform or their level of productivity. They receive them simply because they are members of the organization. For example, an average performer occupying a job in pay grade 1 may receive the same number of vacation days, the same amount of group life insurance, and the same reimbursement for educational expenses as a superior employee working in a job classified in pay grade 10. In fact, the worker in pay grade 1 may get more vacation time if he or she has been with the firm longer. The purpose of rewards based on organizational membership is to maintain a high degree of stability in the workforce and to recognize loyalty.

Potential

Potential is useless if it is never realized. However, organizations do pay some individuals based on their potential. In order to attract talented young people to the firm, for example, the overall compensation program must appeal to those with no experience or any immediate ability to perform difficult tasks. Many young employees are paid well, perhaps not because of their ability to make an immediate contribution, but because they have the *potential* to add value to the firm as a professional, first-line supervisor, manager of compensation, vice president of marketing, or possibly even chief executive officer.

Political Influence

Firms should obviously not permit political influence to be a factor in determining financial compensation. However, to deny its existence would be unrealistic. There is an unfortunate element of truth in the statement, "It's not *what* you know, it's *who* you know." To varying degrees in business, government, and not-for-profit organizations, a person's *pull* or political influence may sway pay and promotion decisions. It may be natural for a manager to favor a friend or relative in granting a pay increase or promotion. Nevertheless, if the person receiving the reward is not deserving of it, the workgroup will soon know about it. The result will probably be devastating to employee morale.

Luck

You have undoubtedly heard the expression, "It helps to be in the right place at the right time." There is more than a little truth in this statement as it relates to compensation. Opportunities are continually presenting themselves in firms. Realistically, there is no way for managers to foresee many of the changes that occur. For instance, who could have known that the purchasing agent, Joe Flynn, an apparently healthy middle-aged man, would suddenly die of a heart attack? Although the company may have been grooming several managers for Joe's position, none may be capable of immediately assuming the increased responsibility. The most experienced person, Tommy Loy, has been with the company only six months. Tommy had been an assistant buyer for a competitor for four years. Because of his experience, Tommy receives the promotion and the increased financial compensation. Tommy Loy was lucky; he was in the right place at the right time.

When asked to explain their most important reasons for success and effectiveness as managers, two chief executives responded candidly. One said, "Success is being at the right place at the right time *and being recognized as having the ability to make timely decisions.* It also depends on having good rapport with people, a good operating background, and the knowledge of how to develop people." The other replied, "My present position was attained by being in the right place at the right time *with a history of getting the job done.*" Both executives recognize the significance of luck combined with the ability to perform. Their experiences lend support to the idea that luck works primarily for the efficient.

10 OBJECTIVE

Explain compensation for special groups.

Compensation for Special Groups

Compensation for several employee groups merits special attention. The groups include teams, the entire organization, professionals, sales employees, and contingency workers. We discuss executive compensation in a separate section.

Team-Based Pay

Since team performance consists of individual efforts, individual employees should be recognized and rewarded for their contributions. However, if a team is to function effectively, firms should provide a reward based on the overall team performance as well. Changing a firm's compensation structure from an individual-based system to one that involves team-based pay can have powerful results. By so doing, a firm can improve efficiency, productivity, and profitability. However, making the switch is not for the faint of heart and does not work for all companies. One survey of *Fortune* 1,000 corporations indicated that in 1990, about 59 percent of companies surveyed were employing a team-based compensation system. The figure had risen to 80 percent by 1999, the last year for which data are available. But, these figures do not mean that team-based compensation is used throughout the firms; it just means they were used somewhere in the organization. Virtually no firm has team-based compensation as a company-wide practice.[53]

In Canada, more than 30 percent of unionized workplaces have variable pay plans in place despite opposition from union leaders. These plans typically reward performance of a team, group, or even the entire company, rather than individuals. In these plans, employees are offered additional compensation if the organization meets profit and performance goals. It is most effective when a clear relationship between performance and the firm's success is recognized. The plans result in increased productivity, a safer work environment, a better understanding of the business by employees, and little risk of employees losing base pay. Properly designed and implemented, incentive plans can lead to higher performance levels.[54]

Advantages and Disadvantages. Team incentives have both advantages and disadvantages. On the positive side, firms find it easier to develop performance standards for groups than for individuals. For one thing, there are fewer standards to determine. Also, the output of a team is more likely to reflect a complete product or service. Another advantage is that employees may be more inclined to assist others and work collaboratively if the organization bases rewards on the team's output.

A potential disadvantage for team incentives relates to exemplary performers. If individuals in this category perceive that they contribute more than other employees in the group, they may become disgruntled and leave.

An Example of Team-Based Pay. Unisys provides an example of team-based pay. This firm has made dramatic changes in the way people work. In the company, there are more than 140 people organized into 10 teams at their Bismarck, North Dakota, office. These teams handle various accounting functions, such as the firm's accounts payable and employees' business travel reimbursements. Each team takes care of an entire process, from opening mail to issuing checks, and seeks solutions internally to any problems it encounters. All employees receive a base wage in addition to payment for the performance of their team.[55]

Company-Wide Plans

In baseball, you do not judge the team based on its ace pitcher or great outfield. The criterion for success is overall team performance, its win-loss record. In business, company-wide plans offer a possible alternative to the incentive plans previously discussed. Organizations normally base company-wide plans on the firm's productivity, cost savings, or profitability. To illustrate the concept of company-wide plans, we first discuss profit sharing and then, a gainsharing plan known as the Scanlon Plan.

Profit sharing:
A compensation plan that results in the distribution of a predetermined percentage of the firm's profits to employees.

Profit Sharing. **Profit sharing** is a compensation plan that results in the distribution of a predetermined percentage of the firm's profits to employees. Many firms use this type of plan to integrate the employees' interests with those of the company. Profit-sharing plans can aid in recruiting, motivating, and retaining employees, which usually enhances productivity.

There are several variations of profit-sharing plans, but three basic kinds of plans are used today: current profit sharing, deferred profit sharing, and combination plans.[56]

- *Current plans* provide payment to employees in cash or stock as soon as profits have been determined.
- *Deferred plans* involve placing company contributions in an irrevocable trust, credited to individual employees' accounts. The funds are normally invested in securities and become available to the employee (or his or her survivors) at retirement, termination, or death.
- *Combination plans* permit employees to receive payment of part of their share of profits on a current basis, while deferring payment of part of their share.

Normally, most full-time employees are included in a company's profit-sharing plan after a specified waiting period. Vesting determines the amount of *profit* an employee owns in his or her account. Firms often determine this sum on a graduated basis. For example, an employee may become 25 percent vested after being in the plan for two years; 50 percent vested after three years; 75 percent vested after four years; and 100 percent vested after five years. This gradual approach to vesting encourages employees to remain with the firm, thereby reducing turnover.

The results of profit sharing include increased efficiency and lower costs. In recent years however, the increased popularity of defined contribution plans (discussed in the next chapter) has slowed the growth of profit-sharing plans. Also, variations in profits may present a special problem. When employees have become accustomed to receiving added compensation from profit sharing, and then there is no profit to share, they may become disgruntled.

A basic problem with a profit-sharing plan stems from the recipients' seldom knowing precisely how they helped generate the profits, beyond just doing their jobs. And, if employees continue to receive a payment, they will come to expect it and depend on it. If they do not know what they have done to deserve it, they may view it as an entitlement program and the intended *ownership* attitude may not materialize.

Gainsharing:
Plans designed to bind employees to the firm's productivity and provide an incentive payment based on improved company performance.

Gainsharing. **Gainsharing** plans, designed to bind employees to the firm's productivity, provide an incentive payment based on improved company performance. It is one of the most popular company-wide plans. The goal of gainsharing is to focus on improving cost-efficiency, reducing costs, improving throughput, and improving profitability. Gainsharing helps align an organization's people strategy with its business strategy.[57] Gainsharing plans (also known as *productivity incentives, team incentives,* and *performance sharing incentives*) generally refer to incentive plans that involve many or all employees in a common effort to achieve a firm's performance objectives.

New Jersey–based NYF, a privately owned distributor of electronic hardware, found that its performance management program released the firm's creativity and allowed it to utilize the knowledge, skills, flexibility, and drive of its employees. The centerpiece of NYF's performance management system is gainsharing, which includes a financial measurement and feedback process, and which monitors company performance and then distributes gains in the form of bonuses when appropriate. Due to the program, employees think like entrepreneurs and make daily decisions affecting company performance. They understand how their decisions affect company performance and are confident management will honor these decisions.[58]

Scanlon plan: A gainsharing plan that provides a financial reward to employees for savings in labor costs that result from their suggestions.

Joseph Scanlon developed the first gainsharing plan during the Great Depression, and it continues to be a successful approach to group incentive, especially in smaller firms. The **Scanlon plan** provides a financial reward to employees for savings in labor costs that result from their suggestions. Employee-management committees evaluate these suggestions. Participants in these plans calculate savings as a ratio of payroll costs to the sales value of what that payroll produces. If the company is able to reduce payroll costs through increased operating efficiency, it shares the savings with its employees.

Scanlon plans are not only financial incentive systems, but also systems for participative management.[59] The Scanlon Plan embodies management–labor cooperation, collaborative problem solving, teamwork, trust, gainsharing, open-book management, and servant leadership. The four basic principles emphasized are the following:[60]

1. *Identity.* To focus on employee involvement, the firm's mission or purpose must be clearly articulated.
2. *Competence.* The plan requires the highest standards of work behavior and a continual commitment to excellence.
3. *Participation.* The plan provides a mechanism for using the ideas of knowledgeable employees and translating these into productivity improvements.
4. *Equity.* Equity is achieved when three primary stakeholders—employees, customers, and investors, share financially in the productivity increases resulting from the program.

Such firms as Herman Miller, Ameritech, Martin Marietta, Donnelly Mirrors, Motorola, and Boston's Beth Israel Hospital are realizing benefits from the Scanlon plan. They have created formal participative means for soliciting suggestions and are sharing the revenue resulting from increases in productivity. Gainsharing studies indicate that firms using these plans increase their productivity from 10 to 12 percent a year.[61]

Compensation for Professionals

The Fair Labor Standards Act defines a professional as an employee whose primary duty consists of work requiring advanced knowledge in a field of science or learning, work as a teacher in an educational institution, or work in a recognized field of artistic endeavor.[62] Examples of exempt professionals often employed in industry include scientists, engineers, and accountants. Their pay, initially, is for the knowledge they bring to the organization. Gradually, however, some of this knowledge becomes obsolete, and their salaries reflect this. At times, this encourages professionals to enter management to make more money. A problem with this move is that many are not suited for a managerial role. To deal with this potential dilemma, some organizations have created a *dual compensation track.* This approach provides a separate pay structure for professionals, which overlaps the managerial pay structure. With this system, high-performing professionals are not required to enter management to obtain greater pay. Some firms face a serious problem when a highly competent and effective professional feels compelled to become a manager for more pay and is unable to perform well in this role.

The unstable nature of professional jobs and their salaries results in a heavy emphasis on market data for job pricing. This has resulted in the use of maturity curves that reflect the relationship between professional compensation and years of experience. Such maturity curves reveal a rapid increase in pay for roughly five to seven years, and then a more gradual rise as technical obsolescence erodes the value of jobs.[63]

Compensation for Sales Employees

Designing compensation programs for sales employees involves unique considerations. For this reason, this task may belong to the sales staff rather than to human resources. Nevertheless, many general compensation practices apply to sales jobs. For example, job content, relative job worth, and job market value are all relevant factors.

The *straight salary* approach is one extreme in sales compensation. In this method, salespersons receive a fixed salary regardless of their sales levels. Organizations use straight salary primarily to emphasize continued product service after the sale. For instance, sales representatives who deal largely with the federal government often receive this form of compensation.

At the other extreme, the person whose pay is totally determined as a percentage of sales is on *straight commission.* If the salesperson makes no sales, the individual working on straight commission receives no pay. On the other hand, highly productive sales representatives can earn a great deal of money under this plan.

Between these extremes is the endless variety of *part-salary, part-commission* combinations. The possibilities increase when a firm adds various types of *bonuses* to the basic compensation package. The emphasis given to either commission or salary depends on several factors, including the organization's philosophy toward service, the nature of the product, and the amount of time required to close a sale.

In addition to salary, commissions, and bonuses, salespersons often receive other forms of compensation that are intended to serve as added incentives. Sales contests that offer products such as DVD players, notebook computers, or expense-paid vacations to exotic locations are common. If any one feature sets sales compensation apart from other programs, it is the emphasis on incentives. You can usually relate sales volume to specific individuals, a situation that encourages payment of incentive compensation. Experience in sales compensation practices over the years has supported the concept of directly relating rewards to performance.

The headache so long associated with calculating various bonuses disappears when software automates the process. Firms apparently feel the cost is worth it to achieve a simplified system of setting up, managing, and tracking incentive compensation plans. Computer software makes it feasible to evaluate sales performance more precisely, such as the ability to measure factors like gross profits per line of billing, profitability per customer, profitability per product, and sales costs as a percentage of gross profit per territory. Technology has made it possible to align the sales reward system with corporate strategy and to reward the behaviors affecting the bottom line.

Compensation for Contingency Workers

Contingency workers who are employed through an employment agency or on an on-call basis often earn less than traditional employees. Contingency workers who are independent contract workers typically earn more. However, both classes of contingency workers receive fewer benefits, if they receive them at all. As discussed in

Chapter 5, flexibility and lower costs for the employer are key reasons for the growth in the use of contingency workers. An inherent compensation problem relates to internal equity. You may have two employees working side-by-side, one a temporary employee (temp) and the other a regular employee, performing same or near identical tasks, and one makes more money than the other. One approach to dealing with this is for the firm to promote the idea of temps comprising a pool of candidates for more permanent positions. Or, the firm might sell the notion that it is offering opportunities for employees to acquire more marketable skills than they would in traditional situations, thereby increasing their career security.[64] These approaches may or may not work.

In most cases, contingents earn less pay and are far less likely to receive health or retirement benefits than their permanent counterparts. This disparity in wages and benefits may lead to demands for legislative protections for the contingents. Some proposals have called for amending the Fair Labor Standards Act and the Family and Medical Leave Act to make contingents eligible for coverage. Since one advantage of using contingents is to reduce labor costs, such actions may discourage employers from hiring them.[65]

Of all compensation areas, executive compensation is especially difficult to determine. The executive's job is quite different from most others in a firm, especially in terms of responsibility. This difference exists particularly in the chief executive officer's job. We discuss the uniqueness of executive compensation next.

11 OBJECTIVE

Explain how executive compensation is determined and the types of executive compensation.

Towers Perrin

www.towers.com/towers

This Web site is for a global human resource consulting and administration firm that helps organizations manage their investments in people, to achieve measurable financial performance improvements.

Executive Compensation

Executive skill largely determines whether a firm will prosper, survive, or fail. A company's program for compensating executives is a critical factor in attracting and retaining the best available talent. Therefore, in spite of the growing criticism of excessive executive pay mentioned at the beginning of this chapter, providing adequate compensation for these managers is vital.

Determining Executive Compensation

Designing an executive compensation package begins with determining the organization's goals, its objectives, and the anticipated time for achieving them. It is advisable to obtain advice on tax and accounting implications for both the executive and the company. The primary components may include employment or severance agreements, incentive compensation, and supplemental retirement plans.[66] The executive package depends on the magnitude of the responsibility, risk, and effort shouldered by the chief executive as a function of the firm's scale.[67] Organizations typically prefer to relate salary growth for the highest-level managers to market rates and overall corporate performance, including the firm's market value. For the next management tier, they tend to integrate overall corporate performance with market rates and internal considerations to come up with appropriate pay. For lower-level managers, market rates, internal pay relationships, and individual performance are critical factors.

In general, the higher the managerial position, the more difficult it is to define because of the diversity. The descriptions focus on anticipated results rather than tasks or how the work is accomplished. Thus, market pricing may be the best general approach to use in determining executive compensation. Even though the market may support a high salary for managers, the amount may still seem extremely large. However, managers at the executive level represent a relatively small percentage of the total workforce, and the overall impact on total labor costs is small.

In using market pricing, organizations utilize compensation survey data to determine pay levels for a representative group of jobs. These data are available from such sources as William M. Mercer, WorldatWork, Towers Perrin, Hay Associates, and Hewitt Associates.

Types of Executive Compensation

Executive compensation often has five basic elements: (1) base salary, (2) short-term (annual) incentives or bonuses, (3) long-term incentives and capital appreciation plans, (4) employee benefits, and (5) perquisites.[68] Because of changes in tax legislation and the economy, the emphasis on each of these elements also changes. For example, the depressed stock market in the early 2000s directed more attention to cash and away from stock options.

Base Salary. Although it may not represent the largest portion of the executive's compensation package, salary is obviously important. It is a factor in determining the executive's standard of living. Salary also provides the basis for other forms of compensation; for example, it may determine the amount of bonuses and certain benefits.

Short-Term Incentives or Bonuses. Payment of bonuses reflects a managerial belief in their incentive value. The popularity of this compensation component has risen rapidly in recent years and today, 90 percent of executives receive bonuses.[69]

Long-Term Incentives and Capital Appreciation. Stock options, in the form of deferred compensation, remain a major component of executive pay.[70] However, in a declining stock market, when the market price of many stocks is well below the exercise price, this form of compensation is not nearly as attractive, at least in the short run.[71]

The stock option is a long-term incentive designed to integrate the interests of management with those of the organization. To ensure this integration, some boards of directors require their top executives to hold some of the firm's stock. While the motivational value of stock ownership seems logical, research on the subject has not been conclusive. One view is that option grants do not succeed in making executives think and act like shareholders. It makes them think and act like option holders, with a shorter-term perspective than shareholders. A recommended alternative is to provide packages that include long-term cash and stock incentives tied to core organizational goals, with the options being more performance based.[72] An "indexed stock option plan" is discussed later in this chapter.

Stock option plan:
An incentive plan in which managers can buy a specified amount of stock in their company in the future at or below the current market price.

Stock Option Plans. There are various types of plans, but the typical **stock option plan** gives the manager the option to buy a specified amount of stock in the future at or below the current market price. This form of compensation is advantageous when stock prices are rising. However, there are potential disadvantages to stock option plans. A manager may feel uncomfortable investing money in the same organization in which he or she is building a career. As with profit sharing, this method of compensation is popular when a firm is successful, but during periods of decline when stock prices fall, the participants may become disenchanted. Nevertheless, there are several bona fide reasons for including stock ownership in executive compensation plans. In addition to potentially aligning employees' interests with those of shareholders, *retention* of top executives is also a factor.

The tax bill of 1993 encouraged firms to provide stock options and this increased the motivation for granting them. The cost of stock options was not required to be expensed against earnings in the income statements, making them extremely popular with employers. The thriving stock market of the 1990s made the executives happy as well, although this joy subsided with the downturn in the economy beginning in 2000.

With many stocks depressed, cash has become relatively more important than stock options. In addition, a number of firms have voluntarily taken steps to reflect earnings more accurately. For example, Coca-Cola Company was among the first to start expensing stock options granted to employees. A number of other giant firms quickly followed suit. Firms that voluntarily expense stock options lose earnings advantage. Therefore, if stock options cost the company, managers will have to take a closer look at their usage and weigh their advantages and disadvantages.[73] Still, an even more important issue to both executives and employers is a concern for security in deferred compensation plans where the balances often represent more than 50 percent of executive retirement incomes.[74]

Indexed stock option plan: A stock option plan that holds executives to a higher standard and requires that increased stock compensation be tied to outperforming peer groups or a market index.

Indexed Stock Option Plans. An **indexed stock option plan** holds executives to a higher standard and requires that increased stock compensation relate to outperforming peer groups or a market index. This would require the company to earn a minimum rate of return for shareholders before providing a return to executives and employees. The true superstars can still have huge earnings if their company's stock outperforms the index. Federal Reserve Chairman Alan Greenspan supports such a plan, but indexed stock options remain unpopular with executives, perhaps for obvious reasons.[75] However, as shareholders become increasingly disenchanted with high levels of executive compensation, as suggested at the beginning of this chapter, this approach may gain in popularity. Ask yourself this question: "If pay for performance is appropriate for lower-level employees, should top executives be exempt from the same practice?"

Perquisites (perks): Any *special benefits* provided by a firm to a small group of key executives and designed to give the executives something extra.

Executive Benefits (Perquisites). Executive benefits are similar to but usually more generous than benefits received by other employees because they relate to managers' higher salaries. However, current legislation (ERISA) does restrict the value of executive benefits to a certain level above that of other workers. **Perquisites (perks)** are any *special benefits* provided by a firm to a small group of key executives and designed to give the executives something extra. In addition to conveying status, these rewards are either not considered as earned income or else the government taxes them at a lower level than ordinary income.[76] An executive's perks may include some of the following:

- A company-provided car
- Accessible, no-cost, parking
- Limousine service; the chauffeur may also serve as a bodyguard
- Kidnapping and ransom protection
- Counseling service, including financial and legal services
- Professional meetings and conferences
- Spouse travel
- Use of company plane and yacht
- Home entertainment allowance
- Special living accommodations away from home
- Club memberships
- Special dining privileges
- Season tickets to entertainment events
- Special relocation allowances
- Use of company credit cards
- Medical expense reimbursement; coverage for all medical costs
- Reimbursement for children's college expenses
- No- and low-interest loans[77]

Golden parachute contract: A perquisite that protects executives in the event that another company acquires their firm or the executive is forced to leave the firm for other reasons.

Golden Parachutes. A **golden parachute contract** is a perquisite that protects executives in the event that another company acquires their firm or the executive is forced to leave the firm for other reasons. Today's severance package for CEOs is typically several times an annual salary and bonus, and accelerated vesting of options.

Trends & Innovations

Supplemental Executive Retirement Plans (SERPs)

A SERP is a version of the traditional defined benefit pension plan in which a firm sets aside a certain percentage of an employee's pay every year to produce a guaranteed payment. They are now offered by about half of all large, publicly traded firms but apply to only the CEO and the next dozen or so executives. Compensation experts predict that companies will increase their use of SERPs to pick up the slack caused by the stock market's downturn. Stock options, a primary executive compensation component, are less attractive in a down market. If such a condition persists, firms will look for other ways to round out executive compensation programs.

SERPs are not subject to the same restrictions that govern tax-qualified retirement schemes, so corporate boards are free to use them to give virtually any amount of money to an executive at any time. This apparent loophole opens the door wide for worsening the problem of excessive executive pay. Abuse of this benefit is not discouraged since one has to dig to find complex details surrounding executive pensions. Typically, these are deeply buried within a firm's Securities and Exchange Commission (SEC) filings.[78]

Because the competition for top executives is severe, in many cases CEOs have to commit a serious crime to be ineligible for severance.

Severance Pay: An Example. An interesting example of severance pay is the experience of Jill Barad as the top executive at Mattel. Her separation contract called for five years' salary and bonuses worth $26.4 million. She also had the option to buy her office furniture for $1; free financial counseling services; forgiveness of a $4.2 million personal loan; forgiveness of a $3 million home loan; and also $3.31 million to cover the taxes she owed on the forgiveness of her home loan. Ms. Barad's total severance pay package totaled about $47 million, not counting options.[79]

Extreme competition for executive talent is the rationale given for such generosity. The liberality of executive perks grew to such proportions during the 1980s that Congress imposed penalties on *excess* payments in the form of a nondeductible excise tax on individuals and a cap on a company's tax deductibility.

HR's Role in Executive Compensation

With corporate scandals fresh on everyone's mind, it is imperative that management reinforce trust in our economic system. Perceptions of executives receiving obscene levels of compensation do not help in this regard. Therefore, top HR executives who know their company's business must play a key role in this endeavor and assure reasonable and ethical behavior. They can perform this duty working with their firm's compensation committee. This group usually consists of several members of the board of directors who meet periodically and recommend executive compensation. HR can make certain that this group has relevant, fair, and accurate information for decision making, in collaboration with consultants and management.[80]

The tragedy of 9/11 has taught us a great deal. One compensation lesson that we have learned is that our plans may abruptly change in undreamed of ways. Retirement income planning, as an example, must factor in contingency planning for unemployment, health challenges, disability, and even premature death.[81]

Ethical Dilemma

Creative Accounting?

You and your best friend Sam work for the same company. You are vice president for human resources and Sam is an accountant. Sam said, "I don't know if I should tell you this, but there's something going on at work you should know about." Sam then told you, in strict confidence, that the company's chief financial officer was planning to take an aggressive stance on sales revenue reporting that, in Sam's view, would stretch the boundaries of acceptable accounting practices. Sam's accounting expertise and responsibilities center on the company's real estate holdings and he does not deal with sales revenue. But he has a pretty good understanding of what's happening in other areas of the company's financial activities, and he was clearly concerned about what the CFO wanted to do.

The CFO's accounting method would increase your firm's earnings outlook and probably help its stock price. "But it could be risky," Sam said. It could "raise questions" about the firm's methods and even its integrity. What's more, Sam said he wasn't sure the CEO clearly understands the CFO's approach. He might just go along with the CFO since they were college buddies and the CEO personally hired him four years ago. The CEO is 48 and has been with the company for five years. He has boosted sales at double-digit rates every year, but his streak may end soon. Sales gains so far this year have been the lowest in more than six years, and there is no help in the immediate horizon. Your chairman, the son of the founder, is 64 and has been with the company for 35 years. He has spent his career keeping his company on a steady growth path, and he considers the company's reputation and integrity a reflection of his own.[82]

What would you do?

A Global Perspective

One Type Pay Plan Does Not Fit All

In most U.S. and Canadian corporations, pay is correlated positively with performance: the better you perform, the more you earn. This can go from a higher raise for better performance all the way to having some or all of an employee's income depend on performance, as is commonly the case for sales representatives. This principle, which makes complete sense to Western managers is not so obvious in several other parts of the world. In former communist countries, for instance, people were used to a system where pay and performance were not related. Under the old system, good employees were paid the same as poor performers. With the collapse of the Iron Curtain, the idea that pay and performance should be related is now making its way into people's minds. Keep in mind, however, that this is not the situation preferred by the majority of people in many of these countries, as demonstrated by the return to power of several communist parties.[83]

In countries where people value a steady income over the possibility of making a high income if they really shine, a pay-for-performance scheme that includes a high variable fraction is often considered threatening. In countries like France and Greece, where the best graduates often choose government positions with secure paychecks for life, it is quite difficult to attract good employees with pay schemes that include high bonuses for achieving specific objectives. In places like Hong Kong, where people value risk and are motivated by personal financial gains, employees who have achieved a significant professional result expect a financial form of recognition (raise, bonus, or commission) within a matter of weeks. They are likely to look for another employer if they have to wait until their next annual performance review. Because of these and other cultural differences, it is difficult to design a global, "one-size-fits-all" pay scheme that attracts the best talent in all countries. In particular, pay-for-performance schemes often need to be adapted to local preferences by increasing or decreasing the variable portion, depending on whether income security or higher risks and returns are preferred.[84]

Summary

1. Discuss whether or not top executives are paid too much.
The rise of executive compensation has truly been meteoric. However, high compensation for top executives was apparently acceptable to shareholders when firms were performing well. One survey of publicly held corporations found that the full pay package of chief executives jumped 537 percent in the 1990s while the Standard & Poor's 500 rose 297 percent and profits 116 percent over the same period. Workers' pay grew only 32 percent.

2. Describe the various forms of compensation.
Compensation is the total of all rewards provided to employees in return for their services. Forms of compensation include direct financial compensation, indirect financial compensation (benefits), and nonfinancial compensation.

3. Explain the concept of equity in individual financial compensation.
Equity is workers' perceptions that they are being treated fairly. Forms of compensation equity include external equity, internal equity, employee equity, and team equity.

4. Identify the determinants of financial compensation.
The organization, the labor market, the job, and the employee all have an impact on job pricing and the ultimate determination of an individual's financial compensation.

5. Describe the organization as a determinant of financial compensation.
Compensation policies, organizational politics, and ability to pay are organizational factors to be considered.

6. Describe factors that should be considered when the labor market is a determinant of financial compensation.
Factors that should be considered include compensation surveys, expediency, cost-of-living increases, labor unions, society, the economy, and certain federal and state legislation.

7. Explain how the job is a determinant of financial compensation.
Management techniques utilized for determining a job's relative worth include job analysis, job descriptions, and job evaluation.

8. Describe job pricing.
Placing a dollar value on the worth of a job is job pricing.

9. Identify factors related to the employee that are essential in determining financial compensation.
The factors include pay for performance, seniority, experience, membership in the organization, potential, political influence, luck, and special employee classes.

10. Explain compensation for special groups.
The groups include teams, the entire organization, professionals, sales employees, and contingency workers.

11. Explain how executive compensation is determined and the types of executive compensation.
In determining executive compensation, firms typically prefer to relate salary growth for the highest-level managers to overall corporate performance. Executive compensation often has five basic elements: (1) base salary, (2) short-term (annual) incentives or bonuses, (3) long-term incentives and capital appreciation plans, (4) executive benefits, and (5) perquisites.

Key Terms

- Compensation, 284
- Direct financial compensation, 284
- Indirect financial compensation, 284
- Nonfinancial compensation, 284
- Equity, 285
- External equity, 285
- Internal equity, 285
- Employee equity, 286
- Team equity, 286
- Compensation policy, 287
- Pay leaders, 287
- Market (going) rate, 287
- Pay followers, 288
- Labor market, 289
- Compensation survey, 289
- Benchmark job, 290
- Cost-of-living allowance (COLA), 291
- Exempt employees, 292
- Job evaluation, 295
- Job evaluation ranking method, 296
- Classification method, 296
- Factor comparison method, 296
- Point method, 297
- Hay Guide chart-profile method, 289
- Job pricing, 300
- Pay grade, 300
- Wage curve, 301
- Pay range, 301
- Broadbanding, 302
- Merit pay, 304
- Bonus, 305
- Piecework, 305
- Skill-based pay, 305
- Competency-based pay, 306
- Seniority, 306
- Profit sharing, 309
- Gainsharing, 309
- Scanlon plan, 310
- Stock option plan, 313
- Indexed stock option plan, 314
- Perquisites (perks), 314
- Golden parachute contract, 314

Questions for Review

1. Define each of the following terms:
   a. compensation
   b. direct financial compensation
   c. indirect financial compensation
   d. nonfinancial compensation
2. What are the differences among external equity, internal equity, employee equity, and team equity?
3. What are the primary determinants of individual financial compensation? Briefly describe each.
4. What organizational factors should be considered as determinants of financial compensation?
5. What factors should be considered when the labor market is a determinant of financial compensation?
6. How has government legislation affected compensation?
7. What factors should be considered when the job is a determinant of financial compensation?
8. Give the primary purpose of job evaluation.
9. Distinguish between the following job evaluation methods: the ranking, classification, factor comparison, and point methods.
10. Describe the Hay Guide chart-profile method of job evaluation.
11. What is the purpose of job pricing? Discuss briefly.
12. State the basic procedure for determining pay grades.
13. What is the purpose of establishing pay ranges?
14. Define broadbanding.
15. Define each of the following:
    a. merit pay
    b. bonus
    c. skill-based pay
    d. competency-based pay
16. Describe the various factors relating to the employee in determining pay and benefits.
17. What are some company-wide team-based pay plans?
18. What are the various types of executive compensation?

HRM Incident 1

You're Doing a Great Job, Though

During a Saturday afternoon golf game with his friend Randy Dean, Harry Neil discovered that his department had hired a recent university graduate as a systems analyst at a starting salary almost as high as Harry's. Although Harry was good-natured, he was bewildered and upset. It had taken him five years to become a senior systems analyst and attain his current salary level at Trimark Data Systems. He had been generally pleased with the company and thoroughly enjoyed his job.

The following Monday morning, Harry confronted Dave Edwards, the human resource director, and asked if what he had heard was true. Dave apologetically admitted that it was and attempted to explain the company's situation "Harry, the market for systems analysts is very tight, and in order for the company to attract qualified prospects, we have to offer a premium starting salary. We desperately needed another analyst, and this was the only way we could get one."

Harry asked Dave if his salary would be adjusted accordingly. Dave answered, "Your salary will be reevaluated at the regular time. You're doing a great job, though, and I'm sure the boss will recommend a raise." Harry thanked Dave for his time, but left the office shaking his head and wondering about his future.

Questions

1. Do you think Dave's explanation was satisfactory? Discuss.
2. What action do you believe the company should have taken with regard to Harry?

HRM Incident 2

The Controversial Job

David Rhine, compensation manager for Farrington Lingerie Company, was generally relaxed and good-natured. Although he was a no-nonsense, competent executive, David was one of the most popular managers in the company. This Friday morning, however, David was not his usual self. As chairperson of the company's job evaluation committee, he had called a late morning meeting at which several jobs were to be considered for reevaluation. The jobs had already been rated and assigned to pay grade 3. But the office manager, Ben Butler, was upset that one was not rated higher. To press the issue, Ben had taken his case to two executives who were also members of the job evaluation committee. The two executives (production manager Bill Nelson and general marketing manager Betty Anderson) then requested that the job ratings be reviewed. Bill and Betty supported Ben's side of the dispute, and David was not looking forward to the confrontation that was almost certain to occur.

The controversial job was that of receptionist. Only one receptionist position existed in the company, and Marianne Sanders held it. Marianne had been with the firm 12 years, longer than any of the committee members. She was extremely efficient, and virtually all the executives in the company, including the president, had noticed and commented on her outstanding work. Bill Nelson and Betty Anderson were particularly pleased with Marianne because of the cordial manner in which she greeted and accommodated Farrington's customers and vendors, who frequently visited the plant. They felt that Marianne projected a positive image of the company.

When the meeting began, David said, "Good morning. I know that you're busy, so let's get the show on the road. We have several jobs to evaluate this morning and I suggest we begin. . . " Before he could finish his sentence, Bill interrupted, "I suggest we start with Marianne." Betty nodded in agreement. When David regained his composure, he quietly but firmly asserted, "Bill, we are not here today to evaluate Marianne. Her supervisor does that at performance appraisal time. We're meeting to evaluate jobs based on job content. In order to do this fairly, with regard to other jobs in the company, we must leave personalities out of our evaluation." David then proceeded to pass out copies of the receptionist job description to Bill and Betty, who were obviously very irritated.

Questions

1. Do you feel that David was justified in insisting that the job, not the person, be evaluated? Discuss.
2. Do you believe that there is a maximum rate of pay for every job in an organization, regardless of how well the job is being performed? Justify your position.
3. Assume that Marianne is earning the maximum of the range for her pay grade. In what ways could she obtain a salary increase?

Human Resource Management Skills

Chapter 9: Compensation

A Skills Module entitled *Total Rewards* is presented to provide additional insight into topics in the chapter. Specific sections within the module that relate to compensation include the following:

direct and indirect compensation; how total reward programs help a company achieve strategic objectives; conducting job evaluations and compensation surveys; linking total rewards to the strategic goals and objectives of the organization; using the point method of job evaluation; establishing pay grades; identifying benchmark jobs; developing a wage curve; adjusting wages; skilled-based pay; individual performance-based rewards and team based rewards.

Several compensation scenarios are presented to give students realistic experience in dealing with the topic.

A test is provided at the end of the module to determine mastery of the material included in the Skills Module. Also, directions are given for assignments that can be used in class or assigned as homework.

Take it to the Net

We invite you to visit the Mondy homepage on the Prentice Hall Web site at

www.prenhall.com/mondy

for updated information, Web-based exercises, and links to other HR-related sites.

Notes

1. "Investors' Wrath: Use It to Clean Up Boardrooms," *Minneapolis Star Tribune* (June 17, 2002): 10A.
2. Louis Lavelle, Frederick F. Jespersen, Spencer Ante, and Jim Kerstetter, "Executive Pay: The Days of the Fantasyland CEO Pay Package Appear to Be in the Past. A 33% Decline in Compensation Has Returned America's Bosses to the Year 1996," *BusinessWeek* (April 21, 2003): 86.
3. Gene Epstein, "Economic Beat: Charm Offensive," *Barron's* (October 14, 2002): 36.
4. Heike Wipperfurth, "CEOs Make Vast Amounts Even as Firms Earn Less," *Crain's New York Business* (June 17–23, 2002): 19.
5. Eric Krell, "Getting a Grip on Executive Compensation," *Workforce* (February 1, 2003): 30.
6. Lavelle, Jespersen, Ante, and Kerstetter, "Executive Pay."
7. Amy Borrus and Michael Arndt, "Executive Pay: Labor Strikes Back—Recent Union-Led Proxy Victories Could Curb Corner-Office Excesses," *BusinessWeek* (May 26, 2003): 46.
8. Gautam Naik, "Glaxo Holders Reject CEO's Compensation Package," *Wall Street Journal* (May 20, 2003): D.8.
9. Michael Schrage, "Cafeteria Benefits? Ha! You Deserve a Richer Banquet," *Fortune* (April 3, 2000): 274.
10. "ACA Name Change to WorldatWork Reflects Changes in the Profession," *WorldatWork: The Professional Association for Compensation, Benefits and Total Rewards.* http://www.worldatwork.org/home/generic/html/namechange.html, July 30, 2000.
11. Eric Krell, "Recruiting Outlook: Creative HR for 2003," *Workforce* 81 (December 1, 2002): 40.
12. Andrew S. Richter, "Compensation Management and Cultural Change at IBM: Paying the People in Black at Big Blue," *Compensation and Benefits Review* 30 (May/June 1998): 51–59.
13. "Now It's Getting Personal," *BusinessWeek* (December 16, 2002): 90.
14. Dennis W. Organ, "What Pay Can and Can't Do," *Business Horizons* 43 (September/October 2000): 1.
15. "Poll Shows More Americans Taking Their Work Home: 21 Percent of 'Cell-Phone Nation' Workers Believe They Are Being Exploited by Their Employers," *US Newswire* (June 24, 2002): 4.
16. Donald G. McDermott, "Case Studies: Gathering Information for the New Age of Compensation," *Compensation & Benefits Review* 29 (March/April 1997): 57–63.
17. Joseph J. Martocchio, *Strategic Compensation* (Upper Saddle River, NJ: Prentice Hall, 2001): 174–175.
18. William Wiatrowski, "A Formidable New Compensation Tool: Bureau of Labor Statistics' New National Compensation Survey," *Compensation & Benefits Review* 30 (September/October 1998): 29.
19. Joe Vocino, "Annual Pay and Compensation," *T + D* 57 (January 2003): 44.
20. Elizabeth Gardner, "Pay Day! The Compensation Climate," *Internet World* (July 1, 2001): 26.
21. Devin Leonard, "They're Coming to Take You Away," *Fortune* (May 29, 2000): 106.
22. Eric Sharman, "The Simpler Life," *Computerworld* (March 12, 2001): 68.
23. James Devine, "The Cost of Living and Hidden Inflation," *Challenge* 44 (March/April 2001): 73–84.
24. James F. Ragan, Jr., "Un-COLA: Why Have Cost of Living Clauses Disappeared from Union Contracts and Will They Return?" *Southern Economic Journal* 67 (October 2000): 304.
25. Walter Williams, "Congress' Insidious Discrimination," *Augusta Constitution* (March 14, 2003): A05.
26. Jeffrey C. Freedman, "The Fair Labor Standards Act Today: A Primer," *Compensation & Benefits Review* 34 (January/February 2002): 49.
27. "Dealing with the FLSA's Gray Areas," *HR Focus* 79 (January 2002): 10–11.
28. Shawn D. Vance, "Trying to Give Private Sector Employees a Break: Congress's Efforts to Amend the Fair Labor Standards Act," *Hofstra Labor & Employment Law Journal* 19 (Spring 2002): 311–49.

29. Timothy S. Bland, "Equal Pay Enforcement Heats Up," *HRMagazine* 44 (July 1999): 140–145.
30. "Highlights of Women's Earnings in 2001," U.S. Department of Labor, Bureau of Labor Statistics (May 2002): 1.
31. Michelle Conlin, "Look Who's Bringing Home More Bacon," *BusinessWeek* (January 27, 2003): 85.
32. Dan Seligman, "Equal Pay Revisited," *Forbes* (January 22, 2001): 80.
33. Jerry Markon and Jill Carroll, "Financial Firm Agrees to Settle Bias Lawsuit," *Wall Street Journal* (February 21, 2002): A3.
34. Andrew Cicmanec and Brian H. Kleiner, "A Statistical Look at Judicial Decisions Concerning Employment Law," *Managerial Law* 44 (2002): 3–8.
35. "Job Analysis Can Help Determine Which Functions Are Essential," *Library Personnel News* 13 (Fall/Winter 2000): 14.
36. Liz Hubler, "9 to 5: Taking Charge in a New Leadership Role," *Women in Business* 53 (September 1, 2001): 32.
37. Robert L. Heneman, "Job and Work Evaluation: A Literature Review," *Public Personnel Management* 32 (Spring 2003): 47.
38. Christopher Banks, "How to Recognize, Avoid Errors in the Job Evaluation Rating Process," *Canadian HR Reporter* (February 24, 2003): 17.
39. George T. Milkovich and Jerry M. Newman, with the assistance of Carolyn Milkovich, *Compensation*, 7th ed. (Boston: McGraw-Hill, 2002): 127.
40. For basic steps in the factor comparison method, see Richard I. Henderson, *Compensation Management in a Knowledge-Based World*, 8th ed. (Upper Saddle River, NJ: Prentice Hall, 2000): 231–232.
41. Milkovich and Newman, *Compensation*, 35.
42. Steven E. Gross, *Compensation for Teams* (New York: American Management Association) 1995: 66.
43. Mathew Budman, "Mixed Results," *Across the Board* 35 (June 1998): 23.
44. Milkovich and Newman, *Compensation*, 266.
45. Edwin W. Arnold and Clyde J. Scott, "Does Broad Banding Improve Pay System Effectiveness?" *Southern Business Review* 27 (Spring 2002): 1–8.
46. Michael Armstrong, "Feel the Width," *People Management* 6 (February 3, 2000): 34.
47. Budman, "Mixed Results."
48. Drew Robb, "Automation Gives Variable Compensation a Boost," *HRMagazine* 47 (August 2002): 73–74.
49. Daniel Eisenberg, "Paying to Keep Your Job," *Time* (October 15, 2001): 80.
50. Sandy Shore (Associated Press), "Companies Find Merit in Merit Pay; Proponents Call It a Win-Win Situation that Boosts Efficiency and Gives Workers Control," *Denver Rocky Mountain News* (October 11, 1998): 10.
51. Gross, *Compensation for Teams*, 47.
52. Steven E. Gross, "When Jobs Become Team Roles, What Do You Pay For?" *Compensation & Benefits Review* 29 (January/February 1997): 48–51.
53. Charlotte Garvey, "Steer Teams with the Right Pay," *HRMagazine* 47 (May 2002): 70.
54. "Variable Pay: A Bonus for Unionized Workers," *The Worklife Report, Ottawa* 14 (2002): 3.
55. Gross, "When Jobs Become Team Roles, What Do You Pay For?"
56. Joseph J. Martocchio, *Strategic Compensation* (Upper Saddle River, NJ: Prentice Hall, 2001): 107.
57. William Atkinson, "Incentive Pay Programs That Work in Textiles," *Textile World* 151 (February 2001): 55–57.
58. Darren Remmen, "Performance Pays Off," *Strategic Finance* 84 (March 2003): 27.
59. Richard J. Long, "Gainsharing and Power: Lessons from Six Scanlon Plans," *Industrial & Labor Relations Review* 53 (April 2000): 533.
60. Chris Lee, "So Long, 20th Century," *Training* 36 (December 1999): 30–36.
61. Carrie Mason-Draffen, "Companies Find New Ways to Pay/Worker's Performance Tied to Stock Options, Bonuses, Raises," *Newsday* (January 5, 1997): F08.
62. Jerald A. Jacobs, "Exempt Classifications under the Fair Labor Standards Act," *Association Management* 54 (May 2002): 17–18.
63. Milkovich and Newman, *Compensation*, 505.
64. Ibid., 509–510.
65. Peter Allan, "The Contingent Workforce: Challenges and New Directions," *American Business Review* (June 1, 2002): 103.
66. Ross Bevan, "Designing Executive Compensation Programs," *Community Banker* 10 (June 2001): 56.
67. James J. Cordeiro and Rajaram Veliyath, "Beyond Pay for Performance: A Panel Study of the Determinants of CEO Compensation," *American Business Review* (January 1, 2003): 56.
68. Milkovich and Newman, *Compensation*, 498.
69. Ibid., 500.
70. Sonja Lepkowski, "Compensatory Stock Options," *The CPA Journal* 70 (September 2000): 56.
71. Don Delves, "Stock Options: Overused and Underwater," *Workforce* (January, 1, 2003): 50.
72. Ibid.
73. Elayne Robertson Demby, "Weighing Your Options," *HRMagazine* 47 (November 2002): 43, 45.
74. Robert J. Birdsell and David L. Wolfe, "Securing Benefits in an Insecure Time," *Employee Benefits Journal* 27 (September 2002): 9.
75. Jennifer Reingold, "An Options Plan Your CEO Hates," *BusinessWeek* (February 28, 2000): 82.
76. Since the late 1970s, the IRS has required firms to place a value on more perks and has recognized them as imputed income.
77. Henderson, *Compensation Management in a Knowledge-Based World*, 510–511.
78. Janice Revell, "CEO Pensions: The Latest Way to Hide Millions," *Fortune* (April 28, 2003): 69.
79. Suzanne Koudsi, "Why CEOs Are Paid So Much to Beat It," *Fortune* (May 29, 2000): 34.
80. Steve Bates, "Piecing Together Executive Compensation," *HRMagazine* 47 (May 2002): 60–62.
81. Steve Parrish, "It's Time to Improve Nonqualified Executive Bonus Plans," *National Underwriter* (Life & Health/Financial Services Edition) (September 23, 2002): 5–8.
82. Brenda Franklin, David Gebler, Barry Mason, and Jeff Ewing, "Spinning the Numbers," *HRMagazine* 47 (November 2002): 64–69.
83. Lionel Laroche, "Hiring Abroad," *CMA Management* 76 (March 2002): 57–58.
84. Ibid.

CHAPTER OBJECTIVES

After completing this chapter, students should be able to

1. Describe how benefits are communicated and administered on the Web.
2. Define *benefits* as indirect financial compensation.
3. Describe mandated (legally required) benefits.
4. Describe the basic categories of voluntary benefits.
5. Explain legislation concerning benefits.
6. Describe the range of employee benefits.
7. Explain factors involved in nonfinancial compensation.
8. Explain the job as a total compensation factor.
9. Describe the job environment as a total compensation factor.
10. Explain factors that are involved in workplace flexibility.
11. Describe the concepts of severance pay, comparable worth, pay secrecy, and pay compression.

CHAPTER 10

Benefits and Other Compensation Issues

HRM IN *Action:*

Communicating and Administering Benefits on the Web

 OBJECTIVE

Describe how benefits are communicated and administered on the Web.

Employee benefits typically comprise approximately one-third of a firm's financial compensation. Yet, in 2003, there was an overall decrease in the number of organizations offering benefits. This is probably due to employers' trying to reduce costs. Still, it is obvious that benefits continue to play an important role in a company's efforts to attract and retain top employees.

Employees want to know about the benefits that their employer provides, and employers should let employees know how much they cost. Benefits communication to employees and its administration are interrelated in a business environment that spent $1.7 trillion on benefits worldwide as reported in a study conducted by McKinsey & Company. Of this staggering sum, it was estimated that organizations spent approximately $140 billion on paper-based transactions and communications.[1] HR has a definite challenge in controlling this significant overhead expense.

Online tools are available to allow benefits managers to streamline and simplify their administrative work and communicate their benefits packages to employees. Automated enrollment, claims processing, and detailed activity reports are standard practice using Web sites that permit benefits managers and employees to conduct transactions. These innovations are particularly helpful at a time when firms must reduce staffs and cut costs.[2]

To permit employees and their families full-time access to the firm's Web site, employers are putting their benefits portals on the Internet rather than the company intranet. The Internet also makes it possible to build effective sites with greater capabilities and wider reach. For example, having the ability to visit Web sites of benefits vendors, employees can change their 401(k) contributions and allocations, fill prescriptions, and find a doctor all with the click of a mouse.[3]

The Internet has the potential to enhance employees' satisfaction with their benefits. More than one-third of all respondents to a recent MetLife survey and almost two-thirds of large employers say they want to improve the way they use the Internet to help their employees get the most out of their benefits programs. MetLife's research revealed that employees want a system that provides these advantages:[4]

- Availability in the office and at home
- Easy access to clear, brief benefits information
- Supporting material that helps users make decisions
- "Smart" functionality that recognizes users from information already provided
- Ease of use, requiring as few clicks as possible

Employees have some specific ideas about what they want and, knowing this, a benefits provider can design an effective system.

The Employee Retirement Income Security Act provides still another reason for communicating information about a firm's benefits program. This act requires organizations with a pension or profit-sharing plan to provide employees with specific data at specified times. The act further mandates that the information be presented in an understandable manner. With the advent of the Internet and individual intranets, many firms will have little difficulty in achieving the desired communication with employees about anything, including their benefits. A vast majority of organizations go far beyond what is legally required in benefits. In fact, even when the economy is not in high gear, there seems to be no end to the types of benefits some firms offer.

We began this chapter by describing how benefits are communicated and administered on the Web. Benefits as indirect financial compensation are described next. A discussion of mandated and voluntary benefits follows. Next, legislation concerning benefits is presented. Sections on the range of employee benefits and factors involved in nonfinancial compensation are then described. Topics related to the job and the job environment as total compensation factors are then presented. This chapter concludes with factors that are involved in workplace flexibility and concepts of severance pay, comparable worth, pay secrecy, and pay compression.

OBJECTIVE

Define *benefits* as indirect financial compensation.

Benefits:
All financial rewards that employees generally receive indirectly.

Benefits (Indirect Financial Compensation)

Most organizations recognize that they have a responsibility to their employees to provide insurance and other programs for their health, safety, security, and general welfare (see Figure 10-1). These programs, called **benefits**, include all financial rewards that employees generally receive indirectly. Benefits account for about 30 percent of a firm's financial compensation costs with the fastest growing benefit being health care, for which costs rose 10.2 percent in 2002.[5] Benefits generally cost the firm money, but employees usually receive them indirectly. For example, an organization may spend several thousand dollars a year as a contribution to the health insurance premiums for each nonexempt employee. The employee does not receive this money but does obtain the benefit of health insurance coverage. This type of compensation has two distinct advantages: (1) it is generally nontaxable to the employee, and (2) the cost of some benefits may be much less for large groups of employees than for individuals.

As a rule, employees receive benefits because of their membership in the organization. Benefits are typically unrelated to employee productivity; therefore, while they may be valuable in recruiting and retaining employees, they do not generally serve as

EXTERNAL ENVIRONMENT

INTERNAL ENVIRONMENT

Compensation

Financial		Nonfinancial	
Direct	**Indirect (Benefits)**	**The Job**	**Job Environment**
Wages	**Legally Required Benefits**	Skill Variety	Sound Policies
Salaries	Social Security	Task Identity	Competent Employees
Commissions	Unemployment Compensation	Task Significance	Congenial Co-workers
Bonuses	Workers' Compensation	Autonomy	Appropriate Status Symbols
	Family & Medical Leave	Feedback	Working Conditions
	Voluntary Benefits		**Workplace Flexibility**
	Payment for Time Not Worked		Flextime
	Health Care		Compressed Workweek
	Life Insurance		Job Sharing
	Retirement Plans		Flexible Compensation
	Employee Stock Option Plans		Telecommunicating
	Supplemental Unemployment Benefits		Part-time Work
	Employee Services		Modified Retirement
	Premium Pay		
	Unique Benefits		

Figure 10-1 Benefits in a Total Compensation Program

motivation for improved performance. Legislation mandates some benefits, and employers voluntarily provide others.

The cost of benefits is high, and it is growing rapidly. Recently, employers spent an average of $3,539 for each full-time employee for *mandated* benefits. The average cost for voluntary, or *discretionary* benefits was $8,840 per employee.[6] The magnitude of this expenditure no doubt accounts for the less frequent use of the term *fringe benefits*. In fact, the benefits that employees receive today are significantly different from those of just a few years ago. As benefit dollars compete with financial compensation, some employers move away from paternalistic benefits programs. They may shift more responsibilities to employees as with 401(k) retirement plans, discussed later. However, in a competitive labor market, many firms, especially those in high-tech industries, are careful to provide desired benefits to attract and retain employees with critical skills.

Describe mandated (legally required) benefits.

Mandated (Legally Required) Benefits

Employers provide most benefits voluntarily, but the law requires others. These required benefits currently account for about 10 percent of total compensation costs. They include Social Security, workers' compensation, unemployment insurance, and

Ethical Dilemma

A Poor Bid

You are vice president of human resources for a large construction company, and your company is bidding on an estimated $2.5 million public housing project. A local electrical subcontractor submitted a bid that you realize is 20 percent too low because labor costs have been incorrectly calculated. It is obvious to you that compensation benefits amounting to over 30 percent of labor costs have not been included. In fact, the bid was some $30,000 below those of the other four subcontractors. But, accepting it will improve your chance of winning the contract for the big housing project.

What would you do?

U.S. Department of Labor Employee Benefits Security Administration

www.dol.gov/ebsa

This government Web site provides information on employee benefits developed by the Department of Labor.

family and medical leave. The future comparative importance of these benefits will depend on how the United States deals with rising health-care costs and with long-term custodial care for elderly citizens.

Social Security

The Social Security Act of 1935 created a system of retirement benefits. The act established a federal payroll tax to fund unemployment and retirement benefits. It also established the Social Security Administration. Employers are required to share equally with employees the cost of old age, survivors', and disability insurance. Employers are required to pay the full cost of unemployment insurance.

Subsequent amendments to the act added other forms of protection, such as disability insurance, survivors' benefits, and, more recently, Medicare. Medicare spending per beneficiary has doubled in real terms in the past two decades and as baby boomers become eligible, the costs will really escalate. Increased costs to date have resulted from greater use of post-acute care services such as skilled nursing, home health care, and rehabilitation facilities. Adding to the financial concerns, there is fear that in the poorly monitored home health-care industry, there may be outright fraud.[7]

Disability insurance protects employees against loss of earnings resulting from total incapacity. Survivors' benefits are provided to certain members of an employee's family when he or she dies. These benefits are paid to the widow or widower and unmarried children. Unmarried children may be eligible for survivors' benefits until they are 18 years old. In some cases, students retain eligibility until they are 19. Medicare provides hospital and medical insurance protection for individuals 65 years of age and older and for those who have become disabled.

While employees must pay a portion of the cost of Social Security coverage, the employer makes an equal contribution and considers this cost to be a benefit. The 2003 tax rate was 6.2 percent for the Social Security portion and 1.45 percent for Medicare. The total tax rate of 7.65 percent applied to a maximum taxable wage of $87,000. The rate for Medicare, 1.45 percent, applied to all earnings. Today, approximately 95 percent of the workers in this country pay into and may draw Social Security benefits.

Beginning with employees who reached age 62 in 2000, the retirement age increases gradually until 2009, when it reaches age 66. After stabilizing at this age for a time, it will again increase in 2027, when it reaches age 67. These changes will not affect Medicare, with full eligibility under this program holding at age 65.

The Social Security program currently is running a surplus but the retirement of the 77 million–member baby boom generation is looming. Unless Congress makes changes by 2038, the program will have used up its surplus and will no longer be able to pay full benefits. To prepare for this emergency, many members of Congress support the creation of individually controlled, voluntary personal retirement accounts to augment basic Social Security benefits, a system sometimes called *partial privatization*. One version is to divert about 2 percentage points of the 6.2 percent Social Security payroll tax into a personal savings account that employees could invest in the stock market. Proponents of the plan argue that returns on stock investments have averaged 6 to 7 percent a year for many decades (after adjusting for inflation). Such accounts would provide a better rate of return over a 40- to 45-year career than the Social Security trust fund, which is projected to average a real return of about half that. Critics of this approach say it is full of risks. Poor investment choices by individuals or unforeseen market conditions could leave retirees with meager accounts.[8]

Today, 46 million retired and disabled workers, their dependents, and their survivors receive cash benefits from the Social Security system. Medicare provides an additional 40 million people with health insurance. Because any changes to these programs would have a great impact on the lives of all Americans, a careful examination of any proposed reform is critical.[9]

Unemployment Compensation

Unemployment insurance provides workers whose jobs have been terminated through no fault of their own monetary payments for up to 26 weeks[10] or until they find a new job. The intent of unemployment payments is to provide an unemployed worker time to find a new job equivalent to the one lost without suffering financial distress. Without this benefit, workers might have to take jobs for which they are overqualified or end up on welfare. Unemployment compensation also serves to sustain consumer spending during periods of economic adjustment. In the United States, unemployment insurance is based on both federal and state statutes and, while the federal government provides guidelines, the programs are administered by the states and therefore benefits vary by state. A payroll tax paid solely by employers funds the unemployment compensation program.

Workers' Compensation

Workers' compensation benefits provide a degree of financial protection for employees who incur expenses resulting from job-related accidents or illnesses. As with unemployment compensation, the various states administer individual programs, which are subject to federal regulations. Employers pay the entire cost of workers' compensation insurance, and their past experience with job-related accidents and illnesses largely determines their premium expense. These circumstances should provide further encouragement to employers to be proactive with health and safety programs, topics discussed in Chapter 11.

Family and Medical Leave Act of 1993 (FMLA)

The Family and Medical Leave Act applies to private employers with 50 or more employees and to all governmental employers regardless of number. The FMLA provides employees up to 12 weeks a year of unpaid leave in specified situations.[11]FMLA rights apply only to employees who have worked for the employer for at least 12 months and who have at least 1,250 hours of service during the 12 months immediately preceding the start of the leave. The FMLA guarantees that health insurance coverage is maintained during the leave and also that the employee has the right to return to the same or an equivalent position after a leave. The leave can be taken intermittently under certain circumstances. Defining these circumstances often presents a challenge to employers. It may be difficult to determine whether an absence is FMLA related, which therefore complicates management's ability to monitor and discipline employees for attendance matters.[12]

The FMLA prohibits employers from taking any adverse or discriminatory action against employees who exercise their rights under the FMLA. Employers cannot use absence on FMLA leave as a negative factor in any employment action, including performance appraisals, promotions, or bonuses unrelated to individual production. It is important for firms and individual managers to realize that they could be legally responsible for FMLA violations. For example, a federal court in Ohio once held an HR manager personally liable for an employee's damages under the FMLA.[13]

The Department of Labor issued a report that suggests the cost and inconvenience of the FMLA have been insignificant. However, a study by Business and Legal Reports, Inc., revealed significant problems associated with complying with the law. Nearly half the employers responding to the survey reported incurring additional administrative expenses resulting from complying with the FMLA. A few firms even indicated the need to hire additional personnel to meet the increased administrative load. In addition, FMLA reportedly makes maintaining attendance standards more difficult for employers. One-fourth of the respondents to the survey reported increased absenteeism as a serious problem; for example, employees with poor attendance habits have learned that the FMLA can shield them from discipline. According to these sources, this behavior frustrates and demoralizes the rest of the workforce.[14]

While some members of Congress feel that expansion of the FMLA is needed to protect more workers, employers have preferred to cut back on its scope. Business groups feel that Department of Labor regulations and court decisions have pushed the law well beyond its original simple formula and appear to be encouraging workers, increasingly, to invoke FMLA in marginal disputes. A recent Supreme Court decision (*Ragsdale v Wolverine World Wide, Inc.*) was encouraging to employers. It showed that the court can, and will, strike down FMLA regulations when the court believes the DOL has exceeded its statutory authority.[15]

4 OBJECTIVE

Describe the basic categories of voluntary benefits.

Discretionary (Voluntary) Benefits

While the law requires some benefits, organizations voluntarily provide numerous other benefits. These benefits usually result from unilateral management decisions in some firms and from union–management negotiations in others.

Payment for Time Not Worked

In providing payment for time not worked, employers recognize that employees need time away from the job for many purposes. Included in this category are paid vacations, payment for holidays not worked, sick pay, and payment for jury duty, National Guard or other military reserve duty, voting time, and bereavement time. It is also common for organizations to provide payments to assist employees in performing civic duties. Some payments for time not worked are provided for time off routinely taken during work hours. Common benefits in this area include rest periods, coffee breaks, lunch periods, cleanup time, and travel time.

Paid Vacations. Payment for time not worked serves important compensation goals. For instance, paid vacations provide workers with an opportunity to rest, become rejuvenated, and more productive. They may also encourage employees to remain with the firm. Paid vacation time typically increases with seniority. For example, employees with six months' service might receive one week of vacation; employees with one year of service, two weeks; ten years' service, three weeks; and fifteen years' service, four weeks.

Vacation time may also vary with organizational rank. For instance, an executive, regardless of time with the firm, may be given a month of vacation. With an annual salary of $120,000, this manager would receive a benefit worth approximately $10,000 each year while not working. A junior accountant earning $36,000 a year might receive two weeks of vacation time worth about $1,500.

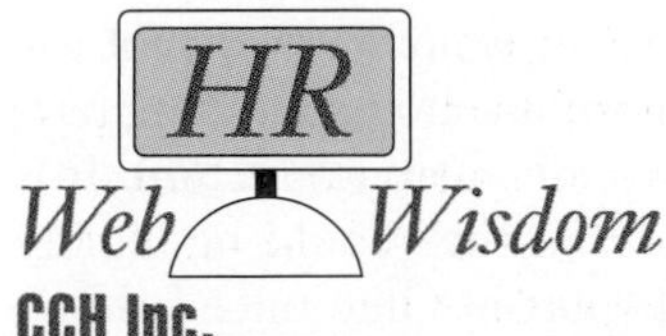

CCH Inc.

www.cch.com

This Web site is for a leading provider of tax and business law information and software.

Sick Pay. Each year many firms allocate to each employee a certain number of days of sick leave, they may use when ill. Employees who are too sick to report to work continue to receive their pay up to the maximum number of days accumulated. As with vacation pay, the number of *sick leave* days often depends on seniority.

Some managers are very critical of sick leave programs. At times, individuals have abused the system by calling in sick when all they really wanted was additional paid vacation. According to a study conducted by CCH Inc., of Chicago, more than three-quarters of the time when workers call in *sick*, they are not. There may be several explanations for this phenomenon. First, Americans log more hours at work than workers in any other industrialized nation in the world. In addition, many employees are working in an environment with reduced staffs due to downsizing or are dealing with any disadvantages associated with the use of temporary employees. Some employees may feel they deserve more pay than they are receiving and therefore seek equity in other ways. One way may be to take a sick day off.[16]

Paid time off (PTO):
A means of dealing with the problem of unscheduled absences by providing a certain number of days each year that employees can use for any purpose they deem necessary.

One approach in dealing with the problem of unscheduled absences is to provide more flexibility. In lieu of sick leave, vacation time, and a personal day or two, a growing number of companies are providing **paid time off (PTO)**, a certain number of days each year that employees can use for any purpose they deem necessary. According to surveys, up to 27 percent of American firms now have such plans. Maureen Brookband, benefits vice president at Marriott, which has such a plan, says that employees tell her, "It's very nice, there's no guilt. You don't have to use a sick day when you aren't really sick."[17] Some critics of the plan feel there is still a need for sick leave. And, as one expert pointed out, a prominent reason for taking sick days is stress, and this factor is not really dealt with. We examine the impact of stress in the next chapter.

Sabbaticals. A benefit once reserved for tenured professors, semi-paid leaves of absence were offered by 15 percent of the 450 large firms surveyed by Mercer Human Resource Consulting in 2000. This number was up from 11 percent the previous year. Driving forces for these benefits were an ailing economy and a desire to mitigate the number of layoffs.[18] Another factor is burnout, discussed in the next chapter.

Health Care

HR Web Wisdom

Americans Benefits Council

www.abcstaff.org

This Web site is for an advocate of employer-sponsored benefit programs.

Health benefits are an important part of an employee's indirect financial compensation. Private-sector employers now spend over $262 billion annually to provide health insurance coverage for their employees.[19] Specific areas include various forms of health, dental, and vision care.

Benefits for health care represent the most expensive item in the area of indirect financial compensation. A number of factors have combined to create this situation:

- An aging population
- A growing demand for medical care
- Increasingly expensive medical technology
- Inefficient administrative processes

It is important for firms to hold the line on their health-care costs. To accomplish this objective, more than half of the employers who responded to a 2002 survey said they expect to raise employee contributions. More than 70 percent said they are considering reducing benefits or boosting co-payments.[20] Health-care costs are growing at eight times the rate of general inflation. The driving force is prescription drugs whose prices are projected to rise at an average annual rate of 11 percent through 2010.[21]

A concern for the future of health plans is the shift underway in the balance of power among the major players in the employer-sponsored health-care arena. These are the insurers, employers, physicians, hospitals, and pharmaceutical companies. The major hospital chains have increased their market power greatly by consolidating regionally. As developers of miracle drugs, the pharmaceutical firms continue to have considerable influence. Health plans, by comparison, are in a far weaker position. When health plans and hospital chains begin their negotiations over how much the insurer will pay, the outcome is more likely to favor the hospitals.[22]

What do you think is the most expensive component of a Chrysler vehicle? It is not steel; it is not plastic; it is health care. Between 1986 and 1999, DaimlerChrysler's health-care costs doubled to $1.4 billion.[23] General Motors also has a considerable problem: providing pension and health-care benefits for its 460,000 U.S. retirees. These costs soaked up almost $900 for every vehicle sold in 2002 and could rise to $1,300 by 2005.[24]

Managed-care systems have been the general response to medical costs that are inching into double digits again and increasing at a rate three times higher than general inflation.[25] These networks are comprised of doctors and hospitals that agree to accept negotiated prices for treating patients. Employees receive financial incentives to use the facilities within the network. Today, most insured American employees participate in some kind of managed-care plan, and the growth of these plans continues.

In addition to *self-insurance* (in which firms provide benefits directly from their own assets) and *traditional commercial insurers* (which supply indemnity insurance covering bills from any health-care provider), employers may utilize one of several managed-care options.

Health maintenance organizations (HMOs): Insurance programs provided by companies that cover all services for a fixed fee, but control is exercised over which doctors and health facilities may be used.

Preferred provider organizations (PPOs): A flexible managed-care system in which incentives are provided to members to use services within the system; out-of-network providers may be utilized at greater cost.

Point-of-service (POS): A managed care option that requires a primary care physician and referrals to see specialists, as with HMOs, but permits out-of-network health-care access.

Exclusive provider organization (EPOs): A managed care option that offers a smaller preferred provider network and usually provides little, if any, benefits when an out-of-network provider is used.

Capitation: The reimbursement method typically used by primary care physicians where providers negotiate a rate for health care for a covered life over a period of time.

Defined contribution health-care system: A system where companies give each employee a set amount of money annually with which to purchase health-care coverage.

Health Organizations. **Health maintenance organizations (HMOs)** cover all services for a fixed fee but control is exercised over which doctors and health facilities a member may use. A **Preferred provider organization (PPO)** is a flexible managed-care system in which incentives are provided to members to use services within the system; out-of-network providers may be utilized at greater cost. An SHRM benefits survey indicated that 81 percent of the respondents use PPOs and 65 percent have HMOs.[26] Recent HMO data indicate that HMO enrollment continues to decline.[27] **Point-of-service (POS)** requires a primary care physician and referrals to see specialists, as with HMOs, but permits out-of-network health-care access.[28] **Exclusive provider organizations (EPOs)** offer a smaller PPO provider network and usually provide little, if any, benefits when an out-of-network provider is used. Only 9 percent of respondents to a recent survey indicated their firm used an EPO; for firms with over 500 employees, this figure increased to 16 percent.[29] Each of these forms of managed-care systems appears to be losing its uniqueness. For example, HMOs are developing products that are more flexible and many offer POS and PPOs. Large, independent PPO companies are providing programs that resemble HMOs. Regardless of the precise form, managed-care systems strive to control health-care costs.

Capitation. **Capitation**, typically the reimbursement method used by primary care physicians, is an approach to health care where providers negotiate a rate for health care for a covered life over a period of time. It remains prevalent in managed care despite the fact that its adoption has slowed in recent years.[30] In fact, many physician organizations are reevaluating their participation in risk-based contracts.[31] Capitation presumes that doctors have an incentive to keep patients healthy and avoid costly procedures when they receive pay for each patient rather than for each service. This approach, long the domain of HMOs, also is present in other managed-care systems. Capitation appears to control costs, reduce paperwork, and requires providers to work within a budget. It also shifts some of the financial risk to the doctors. If providers' costs exceed the cost of providing care, doctors suffer a loss. Some critics fear that since this system shifts the incentive for physicians away from providing care toward limiting care, it results in cost cutting at the expense of health-care quality.[32]

Defined Contribution Health-Care System. In a **defined contribution health care system,** companies give each employee a set amount of money annually with which to purchase health-care coverage. In this health-care system, employees could shop around, probably using online services, for plans that meet their individual needs. The Internet contains a wealth of health information, and individuals frequently access it for this purpose. Health-care content sites are one of the top three in terms of Internet popularity.

The defined contribution system is based on the belief that consumers are in the best position to know what kind of health care they need and how much they want to spend for it. In this plan, employees could choose to buy less expensive plans and put the difference into a *medical savings account.* Or, they could add personal funds to the employers' contribution and purchase more deluxe coverage. While on the surface there are advantages to this type of plan, one primary difficulty is that the amount of money contributed by the employer would be fully taxed under current law.

HR Web Wisdom
SimplyHealth.com
www.simplyhealth.com

This Web site is an online company that promotes defined contribution plans with all health-care decisions in the hands of employees.

Defined health-care contribution plans now account for about 2 percent of all health-care coverage in the United States. However, this approach may grow in the coming years as employers, such as IBM, turn to alternatives to slow the pace of health-care cost increases.[33] The need to do this is clear when you consider that in 2001, employer-sponsored health insurance premiums increased 11 percent. Projected rates of increase for the following five years are even higher.[34] On the other side of the coin, defined contribution plans may cost workers more, especially workers who are sick. According to one source, it is not a very good deal for an employee with a chronic condition.[35]

Among other firms, Xerox is experimenting with an approach similar to the defined contribution system in which employees receive an allowance to choose from an array of plans selected by the company. On the bet that businesses will make the move to defined contribution plans with all health-care decisions in the hands of employees, many online companies are being formed. SimplyHealth.com is one of these online vendors. This firm allows individuals and groups to evaluate and purchase health plans. Eventually, the site may allow individual purchasers to be united together into risk groups, making it possible for them to receive more favorable risk ratings.[36]

Medical savings accounts: A system that allows employees to set aside pretax money (taken out through payroll deductions throughout the year) to pay for medical bills in the coming year that aren't covered by their regular health insurance, including costs like deductibles and co-payments.

Medical Savings Accounts. **Medical savings accounts** allow employees to set aside pretax money (taken out through payroll deductions throughout the year) to pay for medical bills in the coming year that aren't covered by their regular health insurance, including costs like deductibles and co-payments. Although about seven million people use them, participation in programs is limited because of the fear of losing some of the money and the tough decision of how much money to put aside. If there is money left over at the end of the year, most firms keep it.[37] The IRS sets the rules on how the money can be spent but, generally, the key to getting coverage of a medical expense is to get a physician to sign off that something is medically necessary. The IRS has a pamphlet — Publication 502 — that deals with covered expenses.[38]

Major Medical Benefits. Many plans provide for *major medical benefits* to cover extraordinary expenses that result from long-term or serious health problems. The use of *deductibles* is a common feature of medical benefits. For example, the employee may have to pay the first $500 of medical bills before the insurance takes over payment. In order to control health-care costs, a number of firms have increased the amount of deductibles and/or reduced the scope of insurance coverage.

Utilization review: A process that scrutinizes medical diagnoses, hospitalization, surgery, and other medical treatment and care prescribed by doctors.

Utilization Review. Health insurance premiums alone amount to a sizable portion of an employer's total payroll. In a further attempt to curb medical costs, many firms use some type of utilization review service. **Utilization review** is a process that scrutinizes medical diagnoses, hospitalization, surgery, and other medical treatment and care prescribed by doctors. Utilization review may also weed out unnecessary or conflicting ongoing prescriptions. The reviewer, often a registered nurse, explores alternatives to the treatment provided, such as outpatient treatment or admission on the day of surgery. The objective of this process is, of course, to hold down costs. On the negative side, prior authorizations are administratively cumbersome and costly for managed-care organizations. These disadvantages caused United HealthCare to abandon prior authorization requirements for hospitalization in 1999.[39]

Dental and Vision Care. Dental and vision care are popular benefits in the health-care area. The *SHRM/SHRM Foundation 2003 Benefits Survey* indicated that 93 percent of the respondents' firms provide dental insurance and 64 percent furnish vision insurance.[40] Employers typically pay the entire costs for both types of plans except for a deductible, which may amount to $50 or more per year.

Dental plans may cover, for example, 70 to 100 percent of the cost of preventive procedures (including semiannual examinations) and 50 to 80 percent of restorative procedures (including crowns, bridgework, etc.). Some plans also include orthodontic care. Vision-care plans may cover all or part of the cost of eye examinations and glasses. Other company programs that provide health benefits for employees include employee assistance programs (EAPs), wellness programs, and physical fitness programs. We discuss the health aspects of these programs in the next chapter.

Other Medical Coverage. In addition to doctor office visits, health insurance typically includes hospital room and board costs, service charges, and surgical fees. The employer may pay these benefits partially, or totally. *Prescription programs* are also frequently provided benefits; offered by 93 percent of respondents to a recent survey.[41] Both houses of Congress are currently considering legislation that would have a dramatic impact in this area.

Long-Term Care (LTC) Insurance. The increasing costs of 24-hour home health care for elderly relatives has given rise to LTC programs. LTC insurance picks up most or all of the expenses for skilled and custodial care for people in their own homes, in adult day-care centers, in assisted-living facilities, and in nursing homes. It typically covers medically prescribed diagnostic, preventive, therapeutic, and rehabilitative services for patients who are chronically ill or who have severe mental impairment, such as Alzheimer's disease. Employers' role in LTC typically involves establishing and maintaining a payroll deduction program. Employees pay all the costs in most employer-sponsored group policies. Employers that contribute to premiums generally offer a basic plan that employees can enrich by paying more.[42]

Life Insurance

Benefits Plus

www.benefitslink.com

This Web site provides information on various benefit issues.

Group life insurance is a benefit provided by virtually all firms to protect the employee's family in the event of his or her death.[43] Although the cost of group life insurance is relatively low, some plans call for the employee to pay part of the premium. Coverage may be a flat amount (for instance, $50,000) or based on the employee's annual earnings. For example, workers earning $40,000 per year may have $80,000 — twice their annual earnings — worth of group life coverage.

Retirement Plans

Retirement is currently a hot topic because the aging baby boomer generation is nearing retirement. Employers are in the middle of this challenge since they are one of our society's primary providers of retirement income. When stock prices decline, pension plan assets are reduced and firms are required to make contributions to their pension funds in order to address funding shortfalls and to comply with federal laws that protect worker pensions.[44]

Defined benefit plan: A retirement plan that provides the participant with a fixed benefit upon retirement.

Defined Benefit Plans. Retirement plans are generally either defined benefit plans or defined contribution plans. A **defined benefit plan** is a formal retirement plan that provides the participant with a fixed benefit upon retirement. While benefit formulas vary, they are typically based on the participant's final years' average salary and years of service.[45] Plans considered generous provide pensions equivalent to 50 to 80 percent of an employee's final earnings. While use of this type of retirement plan has declined in recent years, a series of federal tax law changes have made this type plan more attractive for many business owners.[46] Forty-two percent of firms responding to a recent survey indicated that a defined benefit retirement plan was in use. The same survey reported that 75 percent of the companies utilized a defined contribution plan, discussed next.[47]

Defined contribution plan: A retirement plan that requires specific contributions by an employer to a retirement or savings fund established for the employee.

Defined Contribution Plans. A **defined contribution plan** is a retirement plan that requires specific contributions by an employer to a retirement or savings fund established for the employee. While employees will know in advance how much their retirement income will be under a defined benefit plan, the amount of retirement income from a defined contribution plan will depend upon the investment success of the pension fund.

401(k) plan:
A defined contribution plan in which employees may defer income up to a maximum amount allowed.

A **401(k) plan** is a defined contribution plan in which employees may defer income up to a maximum amount allowed. Some employers match employee contributions 50 cents for each dollar deferred. While employers typically pay the expenses for their defined benefit pension plans, there is a wide variety of payment arrangements for 401(k) plans. Some plan sponsors pay for everything, including investment fees and costs. Others pay for virtually nothing with the result that nearly all fees are paid out of the plan's assets. In the middle ground are those plans where the sponsor and participants share the expenses.[48]

As 401(k) plans become the primary retirement income design, sponsoring firms are making them more flexible by permitting employees to make more frequent transfers between investment accounts. They are also providing more investment choices for employees. In addition, more firms are starting to provide financial planning for all their employees, not just their top executives. Lauded for their portability, simplicity, flexibility, and low cost to employers, 401(k) accounts held $1.7 trillion, or 19 percent, of all pension assets in 2000. The explosion of 401(k) retirement plans has required about 42 million employees to become *investment managers*, shifting the burden of retirement planning from employers to employees.[49] Employees then often look to their employers for help. Federal law requires employers to give guidance on these plans but forbids their recommending specific investments. Of course, this is just what employees want and need. The employers' role is to get financial planners from firms such as Fidelity and Charles Schwab to provide this advice. Firms must also obtain means for defenses in potential lawsuits if workers lose money.This protection is critically important because poor investment decisions could force individuals to delay retirement or require those already retired to rejoin the workforce.

Discussions about how to reform 401(k) plans relate to a simple point: many Americans aren't saving enough for retirement.[50] This problem becomes a critical issue as Americans are living longer and as confidence in Social Security wanes. Confidence in business also suffered a blow with the collapse of some huge organizations. For example, many Enron employees and retirees lost 70 to 90 percent of their retirement assets after the company restated profits.[51] It is not surprising that, since Enron, companies are taking a second look at the practice of using employer stock to match employees' contributions to 401(k) accounts.[52] Also, despite the popularity of defined contribution plans, several potential problems have emerged that are leading employers to rethink their approach to pension planning. The recent economic downturn and the revelations of wrongdoing at several major companies have highlighted the risk involved with retirement savings. Buck Consultants, a human resources consulting firm, reflected concerns about the economy in a new survey, which revealed that just 73 percent of workers participated in their company's 401(k) retirement savings plans; that's down from a 77 percent participation rate in 1999, the last time this survey was conducted. The drop is disturbing because falling share prices mean many workers need to save more money, not less, to meet their retirement needs. If the trend continues, workers will either have to work longer, live on less in retirement, or significantly boost their savings in their later years to catch up.[53]

Cash balance plan:
A plan with elements of both defined benefit plans and defined contribution plans.

Cash Balance Plans. In designing an appropriate retirement system, some sources suggest ignoring the terms *defined benefit* and *defined contribution*. Instead, they maintain that the focus should be on a plan that meets specific objectives. In other words, for some organizations, a hybrid fund may be the desired approach to retirement plans. A **cash balance plan** is such a plan, with elements of both defined benefit and defined contribution plans. It resembles a defined contribution plan in that it uses an account balance to communicate the benefit amount. However, it is closer to being a defined benefit plan because the employer normally bears the responsibility for and the risks of managing the assets. Also, in contrast to defined contribution plans, the Pension Benefit Guaranty Corporation usually insures cash balance plans.[54] Normally, the employer contributes to each participant's account annually, and investment earnings are at a set amount. If the fund's investment earnings exceed this set amount, the plan sponsor benefits from the performance. If the trust fund does not perform well, the plan sponsor funds the shortfall.

A survey by the U.S. General Accounting Office indicated that 19 percent of *Fortune* 1000 firms sponsored cash balance plans at the end of the last decade. Under different names, Switzerland and the United Kingdom have had these plans for many years and Australia recently introduced them.[55]

Disability Protection. Workers' compensation protects employees from job-related accidents and illnesses. Some firms, however, provide additional protection that is more comprehensive. A firm's sick leave policy may provide full salary for short-term health problems; when these benefits expire, a short-term disability plan may become operative and provide pay equivalent to 50 to 100 percent of pretax pay.[56] Short-term disability plans may cover periods of up to six months.

When the short-term plan runs out, a firm's long-term plan may become active; such a plan may provide 50 to 70 percent of an employee's pretax pay. Long-term disability provides a monthly benefit to employees who due to illness or injury are unable to work for an extended period. Payments of long-term disability benefits usually begin after three to six months of disability and continue until retirement or for a specified number of months.[57]

Employee Stock Option Plans (ESOPs)

Employee stock option plan (ESOP):
A plan in which a firm contributes stock shares to a trust.

An **employee stock option plan** is a plan in which a firm contributes stock shares to a trust. The trust then allocates the stock to participating employee accounts according to employee earnings. Many of the benefits of profit-sharing plans are similar to those cited for ESOPs. Specifically, ESOP advocates have promoted employee ownership plans as a means to align the interests of workers and their companies to stimulate productivity. This practice, long reserved for executives, often includes employees working at lower levels in the firm.

While the potential benefits of ESOPs are attractive, some employees want the ability to sell their shares prior to retirement, which ESOPs do not allow. Many people simply do not want to take the chance that the stock is going to be less valuable when they retire. Periods of wild rides in the stock market also dampen worker enthusiasm for ESOPs.[58] Although the potential advantages of ESOPs are impressive, the other side of the coin is the danger of having *all your eggs in one basket.* The Enron experience makes this point only too well. Yet, a recent survey revealed that 44 percent of responding firms with 500 or more employees offer stock options.[59]

Profit sharing, when the distribution of funds is deferred until retirement, is another form of defined contribution plan. We discuss this topic later in this chapter.

Supplemental Unemployment Benefits (SUB)

Supplemental unemployment benefits first appeared in auto industry labor agreements in 1955. They provide additional income for employees receiving unemployment insurance benefits. These plans have spread to many industries and are usually financed by the company. They tend to benefit newer employees since seniority normally determines layoffs. For this reason, employees with considerable seniority are often not enthusiastic about these benefits.

Employee Services

Organizations offer a variety of benefits that can be termed *employee services.* These benefits encompass a number of areas including relocation benefits, child care, educational assistance, food services/subsidized cafeterias, financial services, and legal services.

Relocation benefits: Company-paid shipment of household goods and temporary living expenses, covering all or a portion of the real estate costs associated with buying a new home and selling the previously occupied home.

Relocation. **Relocation benefits** include shipment of household goods and temporary living expenses, covering all or a portion of the real estate costs associated with buying a new home and selling the previously occupied home. Fifty-eight percent of firms with over 500 employees provide temporary relocation benefits according to an SHRM/SHRM Foundation benefits survey. Fifty-five percent of respondents in this category provide location visit assistance, and 30 percent provide spousal relocation assistance.[60]

While employees once viewed a transfer as a step up, they are now taking a closer look at not only the economic impact of the move, but also what it does to quality of life. This concern has broadened the scope of relocation services to include providing information about crime statistics, childrens' sports teams, tutors, churches, and doctors. Relocation can be as stressful for employees as a death in the family, divorce, or loss of a job. Not only are job-related factors considered, but also the disruption of the familiar patterns of daily life, such as commuting, cultural and recreational opportunities, and school and church affiliations. An Atlas Van Lines survey found family ties were the main reason for rejecting a move for about 75 percent of respondents. The spouse's employment was the second most prominent reason given by about 55 percent of the respondents.[61]

As with any other benefit, employers need consistency to control the rumor mill. This requires a published policy so that when employees accept a move or transfer, they know exactly what they are going to get and can make informed decisions.[62]

Child Care. Another benefit offered by some firms is subsidized *child care.* Nineteen percent of respondents to a 2003 survey, with 500 or more employees, indicated that they provide either on-site child-care centers or offer company-supported child-care centers. Twenty-nine percent of all respondents permit employees to bring their children to work in emergency situations.[63] These benefits are effective recruitment aids and help reduce absenteeism. Two facts emphasize the need for such programs: (1) about 70 percent of working parents missed at least one day within a year because of child-related problems, and (2) U.S. businesses lose $3 billion a year because of child-care-related absences.[64]

Educational Assistance. According to a recent benefits survey, 72 percent of firms provide undergraduate educational assistance and 69 percent provide graduate educational assistance.[65]Such high participation makes sense as employees need additional education to keep pace in a rapidly changing world. In addition, tax rules allow the employer a tax deduction for the expense and it is a tax-free benefit for the employee.[66]

Food Services/Subsidized Cafeterias. There is generally no such thing as a free lunch. However, firms that supply *food services or subsidized cafeterias* provide an exception to this rule. What they hope to gain in return is increased productivity, less wasted time, enhanced employee morale, and, in some instances, a healthier workforce. Most firms that offer free or subsidized lunches feel that they get a high payback in terms of employee relations. Northwestern Mutual is one such company. Free lunches are available in their cafeterias, where the menus list calories instead of prices.[67] Keeping the lunch hour to a minimum is an obvious advantage, but employees also appreciate the opportunity to meet and mix with people they work with. Making one entree a *heart-healthy* choice and listing the calories, fat, cholesterol, and sodium content in food is also appealing to a large number of employees.

Financial Services. Some firms offer various types of financial services. One *financial benefit* that is growing in popularity permits employees to purchase different types of insurance policies through payroll deduction. Using this approach, the employer can offer a benefit at almost no cost and employees can save money by receiving a deeply discounted rate. Firms can offer discounts to employers because the plans usually eliminate the middlemen. Administrative costs are also drastically reduced. For example, the insurance company sends one statement to the business and receives one premium check. Otherwise, this business might involve dozens or even hundreds of individual transactions. It is also possible for employers to offer employees discounted

Trends & Innovations

Unique Benefits

Regardless of economic conditions, it seems that organizations are continually competing for top caliber employees. While benefits may not serve as strong motivators of performance, they are obviously important in attracting and retaining these desired individuals. Among numerous unique benefits offered by American firms are the following:[69]

- Goldman Sachs: Employees get 52 hours of paid volunteer time each year.
- Alcon Laboratories: A rich benefit package includes defibrillators placed everywhere to prevent heart attack deaths.
- Fannie Mae: Employees receive a "healthy-living day off" and a day of "home-purchase leave." Also available is a 100 percent forgivable home loan that is worth up to $33,000 in some markets.
- Starbucks: Even part-timers get health insurance, stock options and, available soon, tuition reimbursement. They even get a free pound of coffee weekly.
- AFLAC: The firm's 32-acre campus has a YMCA fitness center, acute-care clinic, 14 training classrooms, walking trails, child care, and a duck pond. Twelve weeks of paid maternity/paternity leave are available for eligible staff.
- Colgate-Palmolive: New parents get a three-week paid leave on top of regular disability. On-site banking, travel agent, and film processing make errands easier and intramural sports leagues contribute to the fun.
- Eli Lilly: On-site mammograms and gynecological exams (for spouses too) are available, as are colonoscopies for employees, retirees, and spouses. New mothers get 68 weeks of job-protected leave and eligible employees may receive $10,000 adoption assistance.
- Freddie Mac: Included are lactation rooms where women can privately breast-feed or pump milk. The firm also allows new mothers a free consultation with a lactation expert, gives new parents beepers, and has highchairs, coloring books, and crayons in the cafeteria.[70]

International Foundation of Employee Benefit Plans

www.ifebp.org

This Web site provides current news regarding employee benefit plans.

Premium pay: Compensation paid to employees for working long periods of time or working under dangerous or undesirable conditions.

Hazard pay: Additional pay provided to employees who work under extremely dangerous conditions.

policies on automobile or homeowner's insurance. In fact, a company may offer many other benefits through payroll deduction plans.

Legal Services. A recent survey found that the number of Americans covered by some type of legal services plan has increased by almost 20 percent since 2000. An estimated three million employees are currently enrolled in plans sponsored by employers and funded through employee payroll deductions.[68]

Premium Pay

Premium pay is compensation paid to employees for working long periods of time or working under dangerous or undesirable conditions. As we mentioned in Chapter 9, payment for overtime is legally required for nonexempt employees who work more than 40 hours in a given week. However, some firms voluntarily pay overtime for hours worked beyond eight in a given day and pay double time, or even more, for work on Sundays and holidays.

Hazard Pay. Additional pay provided to employees who work under extremely dangerous conditions is called **hazard pay.** A window washer for skyscrapers in New York City might receive extra compensation because of precarious working conditions. Military pilots collect extra money in the form of flight pay because of the risks involved in the job.

Shift differential:
Additional money paid to reward employees for the inconvenience of working less desirable hours.

Shift Differentials. Employees receive a **shift differential** for the inconvenience of working less desirable hours. This type of pay may be provided as additional cents per hour. For example, employees who work the second shift (*swing shift*), from 4:00 P.M. until midnight, might receive $0.75 per hour above the base rate for that job. The third shift (*graveyard shift*) often warrants an even greater differential; for example, an extra $0.90 per hour may be paid for the same job. Shift differentials are sometimes based on a percentage of the employee's base rate.

Benefits for Part-Time Employees

Part-time employees currently comprise 13.6 percent of the workforce, or about 19 million people. Recent studies indicate that employers are offering this group more benefits than ever.[71] Growth in the number of part-timers is due to the aging of the workforce and to an increased desire by more employees to balance their lives between work and home.

According to two studies conducted by Hewitt and RewardsPlus, a majority of employers provide some benefits to their part-time workers. Both studies found that more than 80 percent of employers provide vacation, holiday, and sick leave benefits and that more than 70 percent offer some form of health-care benefits. At Sears, for example, any employee working over 1,000 hours per year is entitled to a full range of benefits, including medical insurance and tuition reimbursement. Employees who work less than 1,000 hours retain some benefits.[72]

Most employers who provide benefits to their part-time employees prorate them. Smaller firms often lack the resources to provide a wide selection of benefits even to their full-time employees.

5 OBJECTIVE

Explain legislation concerning benefits.

Health Care Legislation

Four pieces of federal legislation related to health care are discussed in the next sections.

Consolidated Omnibus Budget Reconciliation Act of 1985 (COBRA)

With the high cost of medical care, an individual without health-care insurance is vulnerable. The Consolidated Omnibus Budget Reconciliation Act of 1985 (COBRA) was enacted to give employees the opportunity to temporarily continue their coverage if they would otherwise lose it because of termination, layoff, or other change in employment status. The act applies to employers with 20 or more employees. Under COBRA, individuals may keep their coverage, as well as coverage for their spouses and dependents, for up to 18 months after their employment ceases. Certain qualifying events can extend this coverage for up to 36 months. The individual, however, must pay for this health insurance and it is expensive.

Health Insurance Portability and Accountability Act of 1996 (HIPAA)

The Health Insurance Portability and Accountability Act provides new protections for approximately 25 million Americans who move from one job to another, who are self-employed, or who have preexisting medical conditions. The prime objective of this legislation is to make health insurance portable and continuous for employees, and to eliminate the ability of insurance companies to reject coverage for individuals because of a pre-existing condition.[73]

As an element of HIPAA, a regulation designed to protect the privacy of personal health information became effective in April of 2003. As a result, health-care providers and insurance carriers will probably react to the new rules by severely restricting the flow of health-care information to employers. This will make it more difficult to manage group health plans. Some experts believe that firms will need to hire extra employees to handle the paperwork requirements. A more serious outcome is the possibility that some employers might reduce or drop employer-provided health benefits; especially affected are cafeteria and flexible-spending-type plans.[74] Additional information on this regulation is available on the U.S. Department of Health and Human Services Web site: http://www.hhs.gov/ocr/hipaa.

Employee Retirement Income Security Act of 1974 (ERISA)

The Employee Retirement Income Security Act of 1974 strengthens existing and future retirement programs. Mismanagement of retirement funds was the primary spur for this legislation. Many employees were entering retirement only to find that the retirement income they had counted on was not available. The act's intent was to ensure that when employees retire, they receive deserved pensions. The purpose of the act is described here:

> *It is hereby declared to be the policy of this Act to protect . . . the interests of participants in employee benefit plans and their beneficiaries . . . by establishing standards of conduct, responsibility and obligations for fiduciaries of employee benefit plans, and by providing for appropriate remedies, sanctions, and ready access to the federal courts.*[75]

Note that the word *protect* is used here because the act does not force employers to create employee benefit plans. It does set standards in the areas of participation, vesting of benefits, and funding for existing and new plans. Numerous existing retirement plans have been altered in order to conform to this legislation.

Older Workers Benefit Protection Act (OWBPA)

The Older Workers Benefit Protection Act is a 1990 amendment to the Age Discrimination in Employment Act and extends its coverage to all employee benefits. Employers must offer benefits to older workers that are equal to or greater than the benefits given to younger workers, with one exception. The act does not require employers to provide equal or greater benefits to older workers when the cost to do so is greater than for younger workers.[76]

Describe the range of employee benefits.

Range of Employee Benefits

A corporation in tune with the needs of its workers will provide a broad range of employee benefits, as you see in Figure 10-2. Companies have addressed numerous needs over the years as they attempted to develop programs that attracted candidates for employment and encouraged them to remain with the employer. Organizations continue to follow this approach in order to remain competitive in the labor market. However, some firms have recently reduced a number of these benefits in certain areas. For example, the number of organizations offering mental-health coverage dropped from 84 percent to 76 percent over five years; on-site vaccinations, from 66 percent to 61 percent in two years, and retiree health-care benefits, from 39 percent to 31 percent in three years. Education assistance, offered at 79 percent of the responding companies in 2002, was down from 88 percent in 1998, and career counseling is available from 29 percent of responding firms, down from 32 percent the previous year.[77]

An ailing economy that began in 2000 has probably been responsible for many reductions in company benefits. If this has been a trend, a healthy business climate should go a long way in reversing it.

Personal Benefits:
Medical Plans: Two options as well as various HMOs are available.
Dental Plans: Two options as well as various Dental Maintenance Alternatives (DMAs) and the MetLife Preferred Dentist Program (PDP) are available.

Work and Personal Life Balancing:
Vacation: 1 to 4 years service—10 days per year
5 to 9 years service (or age 50–59)—15 days
10 to 19 years service or age 60 and over—20 days
20 years or more—25 days
Holidays: 12 days per year (6 observed nationally; other 6 vary with at least one personal choice).
Life Planning Account: $250 of taxable financial assistance each year, with certain conditions.
Flexible Work Schedules, Telecommuting, and Workweek Balancing: (with local management approval).

Capital Accumulation, Stock Purchase, and Retirement:
401(K) Plan: Employees may contribute up to 12 percent of eligible compensation, which is matched 50 percent on the first 6 percent.
Stock Purchase Plan: Employees may contribute up to 10 percent of eligible compensation each pay period for the purchase of company stock (pay 85 percent of average market price per share on date of purchase).
Retirement Plan: Competitive, company-paid retirement benefit plan with vesting after 5 years of continuous service.

Income and Asset Protection: Some of the plans offered include:
Sickness and Accident Income Plans
Long-Term Disability Plan
Group Life Insurance
Travel Accident Insurance
Long-Term Care Insurance

Skills Development:
Tuition Refund: If aligned with business needs and approved.
Educational Leaves of Absence: Under appropriate circumstance and approved by management.

Additional Employee Programs:
Site Offerings: Many sites offer programs including
Fitness Centers
Educational Courses
Award Programs
Career Planning Centers
Clubs: These clubs organize recreational leagues, company-sponsored trips, and a variety of classes and programs.

Figure 10-2 An Example of a Corporation's Benefit Program

OBJECTIVE

Explain factors involved in nonfinancial compensation.

Nonfinancial Compensation

Historically, compensation departments in organizations have not dealt with nonfinancial factors. However, as indicated in the previous chapter, the new model of WorldatWork indicates that this is changing. One thing is clear: nonfinancial compensation can be a very powerful factor in the compensation equation. Consider this situation:

> *The workplace atmosphere is highly invigorating. Roy, Ann, Jack, Sandra, Britt, and Patsy are excited as they try to keep up with double-digit growth in sales orders. They do whatever it takes to get the job done, wearing multiple hats that would be difficult to cover in a job description. Their jobs have no salary grades, and no one ever formally reviews their performance. This doesn't worry them, however, because they enjoy the camaraderie and teamwork at their firm. They have complete trust in the firm's highly visible management, and they have total confidence their leaders will do what's right for them and the company. Believe it or not, it is a real-life scene from a real-life company.*[78]

As discussed earlier, money, whether provided directly or indirectly, is far from being the sole factor in a firm's reward system. The components of nonfinancial compensation consist of the job, and the job's total environment. A number of work arrangements are included in this environment. These arrangements create a more flexible workplace resulting in a more desirable work life for employees.

8 OBJECTIVE

Explain the job as a total compensation factor.

The Job as a Total Compensation Factor

Some jobs can be so stimulating that the incumbent is anxious to get to work each day. At the evening meal, details of what happened on the job may be shared with family or friends. Given the prospect of getting a generous raise by leaving this job, this worker may quickly say "No" to the opportunity. Unwillingness to change jobs for additional financial compensation suggests that the job itself is indeed an important reward.

On the other hand, a job may be so boring or distasteful that an individual dreads going to work. This condition is sad considering the time a person devotes to his or her job. Most of us spend a large part of our lives working. When work is a drag, life may not be very pleasant and, as we discuss in Chapter 11, if a boring job creates excessive and prolonged stress, the person involved may eventually become emotionally or physically ill.

Job Characteristics Theory

Job characteristics theory: Employees experience intrinsic compensation when their jobs rate high on five core job dimensions: skill variety, task identity, task significance, autonomy, and feedback.

The job itself is a central issue in many theories of motivation. It is also a vital component in a total compensation program. Job characteristics theory goes a long way in explaining the importance of the job itself in determining compensation. According to **job characteristics theory,** employees experience intrinsic compensation when their jobs rate high on five core job dimensions: skill variety, task identity, task significance, autonomy, and feedback. These characteristics create the potential for increased performance, lower absenteeism and turnover, and higher employee satisfaction.[79]

Skill variety: The extent to which work requires a number of different activities for successful completion.

Skill Variety. **Skill variety** is the extent to which work requires a number of different activities for successful completion. This factor is similar to the concept of job enlargement previously discussed in Chapter 4. Some workers enjoy variety in their jobs, and if so, it serves as compensation. One only has to visualize work on an assembly line, where an individual is more like a machine, to realize the importance of skill variety. Expanding the number of job activities is quite important to some workers. When this is the case, skill variety becomes a form of compensation.

Task identity: The extent to which the job includes an identifiable unit of work that is carried out from start to finish.

Task Identity. **Task identity** is the extent to which the job includes an identifiable unit of work performed from start to finish. As a product rolls off the assembly line, the worker might say, "I made that widget." Some individuals enjoy the added responsibility provided by a project that permits involvement to its completion. For example, an author reviewing her recently published book and recognizing the sentences and paragraphs she wrote as her own, provides an example of task identity. No one else can claim responsibility, or take the blame, for the content of the book. Task identity is an element of job enrichment, also discussed in Chapter 4.

Task significance: The impact that the job has on other people.

Task Significance. The impact that the job has on other people constitutes **task significance**, another component of job enrichment. When performance of a person's job influences the life of others, the employee often realizes a real sense of achievement. Jim Stahl, director of wellness for a regional university, designed hundreds of exercise and diet regimens for clients over several decades. When these clients later achieved their personal goals such as weight loss or a reduction in cholesterol level, they were grateful and Jim knew he had performed important work. His success in changing lifestyles for the better emphasized that his job was truly significant.

Autonomy:
The extent of individual freedom and discretion employees have in performing their jobs.

Autonomy. **Autonomy** is the extent of individual freedom and discretion employees have in performing their jobs. Jobs that provide autonomy often lead employees to feel responsible for outcomes of work. Most workers do not want someone standing over their shoulders all day long just waiting for them to make the slightest error. These individuals know what needs to be done and, within reason, want the freedom to get the job done their way. Autonomy is at the very heart of self-directed work teams. Some of these groups have the authority to make decisions such as whom to hire and promote, work scheduling, and methods to follow. This freedom of action creates a sense of responsibility that is probably unachievable in any other manner.

Feedback:
The amounts of information employees receive about how well they have performed the job.

Feedback. **Feedback** is the information employees receive about how well they have performed the job. For some, it is exhilarating to hear the boss or a respected co-worker say, "You did an excellent job." In fact, most people have a strong need to know how they are doing in their jobs. Top salespersons, for example, want and obtain rapid feedback from securing a sale. When they make a sale, one way they get tangible feedback is in the form of a commission check.

These five tasks are vitally important in considering compensation regarding *the Job*. It is without question a significant component of compensation. The job is important whether performed by regular employees, temps, part-timers, consultants, contract workers, or teams. As long as employees exist in organizations, a major management challenge will be to match job requirements with employee abilities and aspirations. Without question, as the scope of many jobs expands and they become more complex, this challenge will also increase in difficulty.

Cyberwork

Cyberwork:
A possibility of a never-ending workday created through the use of technology.

Technology has created an assortment of possibilities that will be rewarding for some individuals, but not for others. Development of the Internet has had significant implications for the job. For example, cyberspace engineers are intent on giving users anywhere, anytime access to the Internet. The wireless industry, whose market has already surpassed that of personal computers, has created the potential for **cyberwork,** a possibility of a never-ending workday created through the use of technology. Cell phones and the Internet have stretched work at both ends. What will employees scattered across the globe do when their managers need information from them at an inconvenient hour—wait until 8:00 A.M. their time? Obviously, this would be an option. Individuals could turn off their smart phones, notebooks, or pocket devices to prevent such inconvenient intrusions. However, many career-minded people who want to advance will not make this decision, simply because they are competing with others for promotions and bonuses; these individuals will choose to be available when needed.[80] Some employees will jump at the chance to be maximally involved, while others will place greater value on their privacy and off-duty time.

9 OBJECTIVE

Describe the job environment as a total compensation factor.

The Job Environment as a Total Compensation Factor

Performing a challenging, responsible job in a pigsty would not be rewarding to most people. The *physical environment* of the job must also be satisfactory. In addition, the *psychological climate* must be positive. Employees can draw satisfaction from their work through several nonfinancial factors. Reasonable policies, competent supervisors, congenial co-workers, appropriate status symbols, and pleasant physical working conditions are all important features. Another factor of increasing importance is the flexibility employees have in their work situations. We present these factors in the following sections.

Sound Policies

Human resource policies and practices reflecting management's concern for its employees can serve as positive rewards. If a firm's policies show consideration rather than disrespect, fear, doubt, or lack of confidence, the result can be rewarding to both the employees and the organization. Policies that are arbitrary and too restrictive turn people off.

To assist in meeting the challenges of attracting and retaining the right employees in tight labor markets, some firms have articulated the goal of *having fun* in their mission or value statements. A survey by William M. Mercer Inc., shows:[81]

- Eight percent of employers surveyed include the goal of incorporating humor into the work environment.
- Among firms without a formal statement, 29 percent say fun is encouraged as part of the work culture.
- Sixty-two percent of the surveyed firms believe encouraging fun or humor in communications or management style benefits employees and the firm as a whole. Of these, 55 percent say fun and humor reduce workplace stress.

Competent Employees

Successful organizations emphasize continuous development and assure employment of competent managers and nonmanagers. Competitive environments and the requirement for teamwork will not permit otherwise. "Bad apples," as described by Libby Sartain, vice president of human resources for Southwest Airlines, can disrupt any organization.

Congenial Co-Workers

Although a few individuals in this world may be quite self-sufficient and prefer to be left alone, they will become lonely indeed in the team-oriented organizations that exist today. The American culture has historically embraced individualism, yet most people possess, in varying degrees, a desire for acceptance by their workgroup. It is very important that management develop and maintain congenial workgroups. A workgroup's need for creativity may require individuals with diverse backgrounds. However, to be effective, they must be compatible in terms of sharing common values and goals.

Appropriate Status Symbols

Status symbols:
Organizational rewards that take many forms such as office size and location, desk size and quality, private secretaries, floor covering, and title.

Status symbols are organizational rewards that take many forms such as office size and location, desk size and quality, private secretaries, floor covering, and job title. Some firms make liberal use of these types of rewards; others tend to minimize them. This latter approach reflects a concern about the adverse effect they may have on creating and maintaining a team spirit among members at various levels in the firm. This is true within many workplaces where the corner office and private washroom have given way to more democratic arrangements. For example, Andy Grove, former CEO of Intel Corporation, occupied a cubicle inside the company's headquarters because he did not care for the *mahogany row* syndrome.[82]

Working Conditions

The definition of *working conditions* has broadened considerably during the past decade. At one time, an air-conditioned and reasonably safe and healthy workplace was satisfactory. Today, many organizations consider numerous additional factors as important. A flexible workplace featuring such practices as flextime and telecommuting definitely enhances the nonfinancial compensation package. These topics appear in the following section.

10 OBJECTIVE

Explain factors that are involved in workplace flexibility.

Workplace Flexibility

For stressed employees seeking to balance work and personal lives, time is nearly as important as money; more important for some. That's why more employees are requesting flexible benefits, including telecommuting from home, flextime, and a compressed workweek.[83] Flexible work arrangements do more than just help new mothers return to full-time work. They comprise an aspect of nonfinancial compensation that allows families to manage a stressful work/home-juggling act. If Congress amends the Fair Labor Standards Act, as discussed in the previous chapter, workplace flexibility will receive an additional boost. As the proposed legislative amendment now stands, the formula calls for an hour and a half of *comp time* for each hour of overtime worked and an employee could accrue up to 160 comp hours.[84]

When labor markets are tight, the competition for highly skilled workers becomes intense. In such an environment, it is important, if not crucial, for survival for firms to find and sustain a balance between quality of life for employees and organizational goals. The Americans with Disabilities Act may also encourage some forms of flexibility. The act requires reasonable accommodation and prompts this question: if an employee could perform the essential functions of the job away from the work site, as is possible for some jobs by telecommuting, would denying the employee this flexibility be acceptable?[85]

For employers, workplace flexibility can be a key strategic factor in attracting and retaining the most talented employees. And, there is a strong statistical correlation between employee satisfaction and increased company profits, according to a nationwide survey of U.S. workers released by the Gallup Organization and Carlson Marketing Group. This survey indicates that nearly seven out of ten employees say nonmonetary forms of recognition provide the best motivation.[86] This prevalent attitude certainly explains the expanded interests of WorldatWork: the Professional Association for Compensation, Benefits, and *Total Rewards*.

Benefits claimed for a flexible workplace include increased productivity, improved recruitment, and retention of employees, and enhanced company image. We discuss some of the key programs that provide flexibility in the following sections. These include flextime, a compressed workweek, job sharing, flexible compensation, telecommuting, part-time work, and modified retirement.

Flextime

Flextime:
The practice of permitting employees to choose, with certain limitations, their own working hours.

Flextime is the practice of permitting employees to choose their own working hours, within certain limitations. For many *old economy* managers who think they must see their employees every minute to make sure they are working, this may be difficult. However, 55 percent of the firms responding to the 2003 SHRM/SHRM Benefits Survey indicated they use flextime.[87] If you wonder why this is such an important benefit, consider the recent Harvard study that asked employees to list their most important job components. Number one on the list was, "having a work schedule that allows me to spend time with my family."[88]

In a flextime system, employees work the same number of hours per day as they would on a standard schedule. However, they work these hours within what is called a *bandwidth*, which is the maximum length of the workday (see Figure 10-3). *Core time* is that part of the day when all employees must be present. *Flexible time* is the period

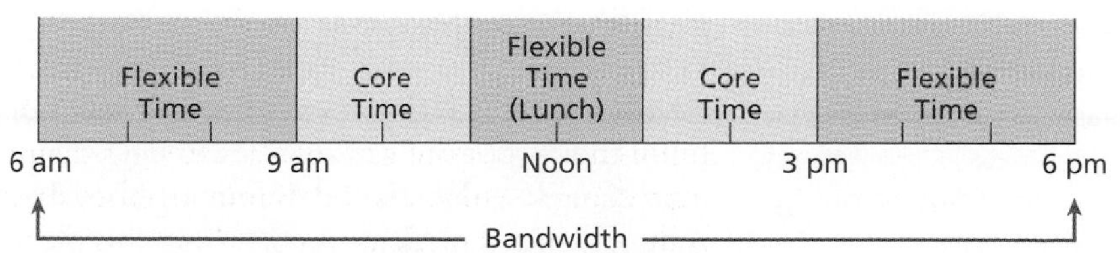

Figure 10-3 Illustration of Flextime

within which employees may vary their schedules. A typical schedule permits employees to begin work between 6:00 A.M. and 9:00 A.M. and to complete their workday between 3:00 P.M. and 6:00 P.M.

After conducting numerous focus groups and interviews with managers, Baxter International, a global medical products and services firm, confirmed the need to support workers' attempts to balance work and home. This intensive investigation resulted in a formalized process to help employees develop solutions for themselves by tinkering with their work arrangements. The program was embraced to the point that nearly 20 percent of Baxter's employees take advantage of some form of alternative work schedule. This does not include the many managers who vary their work hours informally on an as-needed basis. Griffin Lewis, vice president of logistics, says that the program pays off in boosted morale, more effective recruiting, better stress management, and increased productivity.[89]

Because flexible hours are highly valued in today's society, a flexible work schedule gives employers an edge in recruiting new employees and retaining highly qualified employees. In addition, flexible work arrangements actually boost the bottom line, according to a study from HR consultancy Watson Wyatt Worldwide. The reasons for this increased productivity include the following:[90]

- Short-term absences are reduced because of greater control over schedules
- Tardiness is reduced since the workday begins when the employee arrives
- Morning coffee breaks are reduced due to staggered hours
- Employees are more likely to work during their most productive hours: mornings for early birds, evenings for night owls
- Workers are more focused on doing the job as opposed to spending time in the office
- Businesses can offer more flexible service to customers
- Supervisors are forced to communicate more effectively since employees are not always in the office

In addition, Watson Wyatt's Human Capital Index, released in 2002, revealed that a "collegial and flexible workplace" was associated with a 9 percent increase in the overall market value of a firm.[91] With a flexible work schedule, employees are better able to fit family, community, and social commitments into their schedules and they appreciate that. Also, flextime allows employees to expand their opportunities. For example, it may be easier to continue their education than with a traditional work schedule.

The public also seems to reap benefits from flextime. Transportation services, recreational facilities, medical clinics, and other services can be better utilized by reducing competition for service at conventional peak times. Yet, flextime is not suitable for all types of organizations. For example, its use may be severely limited in assembly-line operations and companies utilizing multiple shifts.

In spite of limitations and potential hurdles, flextime is feasible in many situations, benefiting the employee, the employer, and the public. Clearly, flextime and other similar plans are compatible with the desire of employees, especially younger ones, to have greater control over their work situations.

Compressed Workweek

Compressed workweek: Any arrangement of work hours that permits employees to fulfill their work obligation in fewer days than the typical five-day workweek.

The **compressed workweek** is an arrangement of work hours that permits employees to fulfill their work obligation in fewer days than the typical five-day workweek. A common compressed workweek is four 10-hour days. According to a recent survey, 31 percent of responding firms report using this plan.[92]

Working under this arrangement, employees have reported greater job satisfaction. In addition, the compressed workweek offers the potential for better use of leisure time for family life, personal business, and recreation. Employers in some instances have cited advantages such as increased productivity and reduced turnover and absenteeism. Other firms, however, have encountered work scheduling and employee fatigue. In some cases, these problems have resulted in lower product quality and reduced customer service.

Job Sharing

Job sharing: The filling of a job by two part-time people who split the duties of one full-time job in some agreed-on manner and are paid according to their contributions.

Job sharing is an approach to work that is attractive to people who want to work fewer than 40 hours per week. It can also assist with child-care responsibilities.[93] In **job sharing**, two part-time people split the duties of one job in some agreed-on manner and are paid according to their contributions. A survey by SHRM/SHRM Foundation revealed that 22 percent of the respondents offered job sharing. Thirty-three percent of firms with more than 500 employees offered this benefit.[94] Sharing jobs has potential benefits that include the broader range of skills the partners bring to the job. For job sharing to work, however, the partners must be compatible, have good communication skills, and have a bond of trust with their manager.

An Executive Example

Job-sharing normally occurs below executive ranks. However, this is not always the case. Is it hard to believe but Sandra Cavanah and Kathleen Layendecker share the job of vice president of affiliate development and marketing for an Internet media company.[95] The scenario becomes believable when you examine their résumés, which include, for Sandra, a Harvard MBA and for Kathleen, a degree from Yale's School of Management. While their young children are their first priority, these women also wanted to participate in today's exciting business world.

Initially skeptical about a high-level job share, their employer later stated, "I was wrong, I thought a job share would only work in a project-oriented setting. But, any job can function as a job share. It all depends on how well the two individuals work together."

While each job sharer spends just three days in the office, those days are long, sometimes stretching to 12 hours. And, they meet informally twice a week for one to three hours. From this experience, it appears that while a successful job share is difficult to pull off, especially at this level, it can be done. It requires professional soul mates, trusted individuals possessing about the same skills and work ethic. And, as you may have guessed, the job sharers must be extremely well organized.

Flexible Compensation (Cafeteria Compensation)

Flexible compensation plan: A plan that permits employees to make yearly elections to largely determine their compensation package by choosing between taxable cash and numerous benefits.

Flexible compensation plans permit employees to make yearly elections to largely determine their compensation package by choosing between taxable cash and numerous benefits.[96] For example, they have considerable latitude in determining how much they will take in the form of salary, life insurance, pension contributions, and other benefits. Cafeteria plans permit flexibility in allowing each employee to determine the compensation components that best satisfy his or her particular needs.

Twenty years ago or so firms offered a uniform package that generally reflected a *typical* employee. Today, the workforce has become considerably more heterogeneous, and this prototype is no longer representative. To accommodate such diversity, flexible compensation plans appear to provide a satisfactory solution. Recent studies suggest that flexible compensation programs are becoming increasingly popular among employers. Firms are discovering that providing a one-size-fits-all approach is a definite liability in vying for talent. As a result, organizations are taking a renewed interest in more flexible compensation arrangements.[97]

Table 10-1 Compensation Vehicles Utilized in a Cafeteria Compensation Approach

Accidental death, dismemberment insurance	Health maintenance organization fees
Birthdays (vacation)	Home health care
Bonus eligibility	Hospital-surgical-medical insurance
Business and professional membership	Incentive growth fund
Cash profit sharing	Interest-free loans
Club memberships	Long-term disability benefit
Commissions	Matching educational donations
Company medical assistance	Nurseries
Company-provided automobile	Nursing home care
Company-provided housing	Outside medical services
Company-provided or -subsidized travel	Personal accident insurance
Day-care centers	Price discount plan
Deferred bonus	Recreation facilities
Deferred compensation plan	Resort facilities
Dental and eye care insurance	Sabbatical leaves
Discount on company products	Salary continuation
Education costs	Savings plan
Educational activities (time off)	Scholarships for dependents
Free checking account	Severance pay
Free or subsidized lunches	Sickness and accident insurance
Group automobile insurance	Stock appreciation rights
Group homeowners' insurance	Stock bonus plan
Group life insurance	Stock purchase plan

The rationale behind cafeteria plans is that employees have individual needs and preferences. A 60-year-old man would not need maternity benefits in an insurance plan. At the same time, a 25-year-old woman who regularly jogs three miles each day might not place a high value on a parking space near the firm's entrance. Some of the possible compensation vehicles utilized in a cafeteria approach are shown in Table 10-1.

Obviously, organizations cannot permit employees to select all their financial compensation vehicles. For one thing, firms must provide the benefits required by law. In addition, it is probably wise to require that each employee have core benefits, especially in areas such as retirement and medical insurance. Some guidelines would likely be helpful for most employees in the long run. However, the freedom to select highly desired benefits would seem to maximize the value of an individual's compensation. Employees' involvement in designing their own compensation plans would also effectively communicate to them the cost of their benefits.

The existing information regarding employee satisfaction with flexible compensation plans is limited. However, the hope for employers is that it will improve satisfaction with pay and the job and improve understanding of the benefits provided.

The downside to flexible compensation plans is that they are costly. Development and administrative costs for flexible compensation plans exceed those for traditional plans. For example, a firm with 10,000 employees might incur developmental costs of about $500,000.[98] Even though flexible compensation programs add to the organization's administrative burden, some firms apparently find that the advantages outweigh shortcomings.

HR Web Wisdom

International Telework Association and Council

www.workingfromanywhere.org

This Web site is a nonprofit organization dedicated to advancing the growth and success of work independent of location.

Telecommuting:
A work arrangement whereby employees, called *teleworkers* or *telecommuters*, are able to remain at home (or otherwise away from the office) and perform their work using computers and other electronic devices that connect them with their offices.

Telecommuting

Telecommuting is a work arrangement whereby employees, called *teleworkers* or *telecommuters*, are able to remain at home (or otherwise away from the office) and perform their work using computers and other electronic devices that connect them with their offices. Modern communications and information technologies permit people to work just about anywhere. The Department of Labor estimates that between 13 and

19 million full- and part-time employees currently work from sites outside their employers' places of business.[99] The International Telework Association and Council put the number of *teleworkers* at 23.6 million in 2000.[100] In a survey of 551 organizations, 37 percent of the responding firms reported offering telecommuting on a part-time basis and 23 percent offer it for full-time work.[101] Ford Motor Company and Delta Air Lines are currently providing employees with personal computers for home use, and this practice may become common.[102]

When Jill Frankel learned that she had to have bed rest for the last couple of months of her pregnancy, she was afraid that her boss, who didn't have children, would not understand the circumstances. But, as she says, "he was awesome." Jill, the HR analyst at the University of California, Davis, telecommuted from her home. UC Davis has a reputation in the University of California system for having a progressive workplace with many work/life benefits.[103]

Telecommuters generally are information workers. They accomplish jobs that require, for example, analysis, research, writing, budgeting, data entry, or computer programming. Teleworkers also include illustrators, loan executives, architects, attorneys, and desktop publishers. Employees accomplish both training and job duties without losing either efficiency or quality by using the Internet. Advantages of telecommuting accrue to the company, the employee, and the community. You can see these advantages in Figure 10-4.

Another advantage of telecommuting is that it eliminates the need for office space. As one manager put it, "The expense of an employee is not just the person, it's also the fact that I pay $90,000 a year for the office that person sits in." Also, commuting distances are not a factor for teleworkers. Therefore, firms may hire the best available employees located virtually anywhere in the world for many jobs. The ability to utilize disabled workers and workers with small children further broadens the labor market.

While telecommuting has many advantages, it also has some potential pitfalls. For example, it may weaken the ties between employees and their firms. In one survey, telecommuters reported feeling a time crunch and believed that the best assignments went to regular employees who were able to collaborate with colleagues face-to-face.[104]

While telecommuting does not involve additional pay, some employees view it as a benefit because of the advantages of working at home. Therefore, firms must keep diversity goals in mind. Organizations should try to avoid the perception that telecommuting is a form of special treatment. This could easily arise when telecommuters in a workgroup are mostly of one race, gender, or ethnicity.

Firms considering telecommuting will need to think about changes in other policy areas as well. Questions such as the following should be addressed:

- Will compensation and benefits be affected? If so, how?
- Who will be responsible for workers injured at home?

For the Company	For the Employee	For the Community
Aids recruitment and retention	Provides work/life flexibility	Decreases traffic congestion
Broadens labor market (e.g., worker location not a factor; caters to employees with disabilities)	Reduces transportation and clothing costs	Conserves energy and reduces pollution
Reduces sick time and absenteeism	Reduces stress of travel	Relieves public transportation of "rush hour" problems
Improves job satisfaction and productivity	Caters to most productive hours for both "early birds" and "night owls"	Reduces peak-time congestion for many service organizations (e.g., retail and health care)
Saves costs for office space and utilities		

Figure 10-4 Advantages of Telecommuting

- What about the responsibility for purchasing and providing insurance coverage for equipment?
- How will taxes be affected by telecommuting?
- Will overtime be allowed?
- Will security be provided for the telecommuter's work? How?
- Will the firm have safety requirements for the home? Will OSHA be involved?

These kinds of questions seem to suggest that telecommuting poses insurmountable problems. Yet, there are sufficient examples of successful telecommuting to suggest that it can work effectively in certain environments.

Part-Time Work

As mentioned earlier in this chapter, use of part-time workers on a regular basis is common in the United States. Part-time work is particularly evident in the retail industry. Many of these employees are students or parents with young children who need the flexibility provided by part-time work. The U.S. Department of Labor estimates that 38 percent of the retail workforce is comprised of part-time workers and about 84 percent are voluntary.[105]

Part-time employment adds many highly qualified individuals to the labor market by permitting employees to address both job and personal needs. For many reasons, some people neither want nor need full-time employment. Unfortunately, some parties have historically regarded part-time employees as second-class workers. It is necessary to change this perception if part-time programs are to be successful.

Modified Retirement

Modified retirement: An option that permits older employees to work fewer than their regular hours for a certain period of time preceding retirement.

Modified retirement is an option that permits older employees to work fewer than their regular hours for a certain period preceding retirement. This option allows an employee to avoid an abrupt change in lifestyle and move gracefully into retirement. It also affords employers the opportunity to capitalize on needed experience and skills at a relatively low cost.

To prosper with a diverse workforce, organizations need to develop workplace flexibility. Apparently, some firms resist this shift. For example, the view that *presence equals productivity* remains part of many corporate cultures. Flexible options seem to work best in environments characterized by freedom, trust, responsibility, and respect. It is encouraging that some organizations are altering traditional approaches to jobs and work, not only to cut costs, but also to ease conflicts between work and family responsibilities and to attract and retain qualified people. If organizations achieve these goals, it seems reasonable that they will become more productive and more competitive globally.

An Exemplary Work/Life Program

Software giant SAS Institute Inc. has a culture that gives it a powerful competitive edge. The environment and benefits provided for employees are outstanding. To begin, the company's main campus offers day care as inexpensively as $250 per month, free access to a 36,000-square-foot gym, a putting green, sky-lit meditation rooms, and the services of a full-time in-house eldercare consultant. The café also has a pianist at noon and baby seats so children in day care can lunch with their parents. Also available is free juice and soda for employees. There are subsidized cafeterias, casual dress every day, profit sharing (which has been 15 percent every year for 23 years), domestic partner benefits, unlimited sick days, free health insurance, an on-site medical clinic staffed by doctors and nurse practitioners, and free laundering of sweaty gym clothes overnight. There are soccer fields, baseball diamonds, co-ed workout areas, separate workout areas for men and women, and pool tables. Every white-collar employee has a private office and flexible work schedule with a standard 35-hour workweek. All employees have three weeks' paid vacation plus the week off from Christmas to New Year's Day. After 10 years with the firm, employees get an additional week of paid vacation. As if this is not enough, SAS expects to add financial planning services to the lineup, and there is a process for adding still more benefits, including a test for whether they should approve a suggested benefit.

What does all this amount to? SAS has a turnover rate that is never more than 5 percent a year compared to the industry average of over 20 percent. *Harvard Business Review* figured that SAS's low turnover saves the company $75 million a year. SAS has been in the top 10 of *Fortune's* "100 Best Companies to Work For" three years running.[106]

11 OBJECTIVE

Describe the concepts of severance pay, comparable worth, pay secrecy, and pay compression.

Other Compensation Issues

Several issues related to compensation deserve mention. These issues include severance pay, comparable worth, pay secrecy, and pay compression. We examine these topics next.

Severance Pay

Severance pay: Compensation designed to assist laid-off employees as they search for new employment.

Severance pay is compensation designed to assist laid-off employees as they search for new employment. This factor is especially prominent during periods of downsizing. Presently, although some firms are trimming the amount of severance pay offered, they typically offer one to two weeks of severance pay for every year of service, up to some predetermined maximum. The employee's organizational level generally determines the amount of severance pay. For example, nonmanagers may get eight or nine weeks of pay even if their length of service is greater than eight or nine years. Middle managers may receive 12 to 16 weeks.

In spite of headlines describing executives leaving corporations with multimillion-dollar payouts, most companies send departing CEOs out the door with far less. For example, less than 22 percent of respondents to a survey by Right Management Consultants of Philadelphia say they pay a high-level departing executive more than one month's worth of severance per year worked. Over 24 percent said they offer no more than one week's worth per year worked.[107] We discussed golden parachutes, a form of severance pay for executives, in Chapter 9.

Comparable Worth

Comparable worth: A determination of the values of dissimilar jobs (such as company nurse and welder) by comparing them under some form of job evaluation, and the assignment of pay rates according to their evaluated worth.

The comparable worth, or pay equity, theory extends the concept of the Equal Pay Act. While the act requires equal pay for equal work, comparable worth advocates prefer a broader interpretation of requiring equal pay for comparable worth, even if market rates vary and job duties are considerably different. **Comparable worth** requires the value for dissimilar jobs, such as company nurse and welder, to be compared under some form of job evaluation and pay rates for both jobs to be assigned according to their evaluated worth. Although the Supreme Court has ruled that the law does not require comparable worth, a number of state and local governments, along with some jurisdictions in Canada, have passed legislation that mandates this version of pay fairness.

The concept of comparable worth has been around for about 40 years. However, although Congress has rejected every effort for decades, its proponents are now packaging it as "pay equity."[108] Comparable worth advocates argue that the gap between male and female pay is the result of gender bias. Historically, they claim, employers set wages in various occupations based on mistaken stereotypes about women that have stuck over time, leaving the 60 percent of women who work in female-dominated occupations at a disadvantage.[109] Former Congressional Budget Office Director June O'Neill rebuts this notion because, she says, "it conveys the message that women cannot compete in nontraditional jobs and can only be helped through the patronage of a job evaluation."[110]

In the business world, comparable worth would create numerous difficulties. To implement such a system, it would require a reliable way to determine when completely different jobs have a comparable value. Experts cannot agree on any system that would intelligently do this. Remember that in the point system of job evaluation, separate job clusters were considered necessary because of the difficulty relating dissimilar jobs in the *same company.* Comparable worth advocates envision comparing dissimilar jobs not only between job clusters in one firm but jobs *between industries.*

In addition, the concept of comparable worth is antithetical to our nation's free-market economic system. In this system, the market allocates scarce resources according to supply and demand. To implement comparable worth, a bureaucratic government would artificially establish pay levels for jobs it deems *comparable.* If the wages for scarce male-dominated jobs were artificially set below the level that the market would demand, labor shortages would result.

The nation hardly faces an epidemic of pay discrimination. In the past five fiscal years, allegations of Equal Pay Act violations accounted for less than 1.5 percent of charges filled with the EEOC. Moreover, the EEOC, which administers the act, found reasonable cause for determining discrimination in less than 4 out of 100 charges filed.[111]

The goal of nondiscriminatory pay practices is one that every organization should seek to achieve for ethical and legal reasons. Whether comparable worth is an appropriate solution remains to be seen. If the past is any indication, the debate will continue as long as there is a disparity between the compensation of men and women.

Pay Secrecy

Some organizations tend to keep their pay rates secret for various reasons. If a firm's compensation plan is illogical, secrecy may indeed be appropriate because only a well-designed system can stand careful scrutiny. An open system would almost certainly require managers to explain the rationale for pay decisions to subordinates. Secrecy, however, can have some negative side effects including a distortion of the actual rewards people receive. Secrecy also spawns a low-trust environment in which people have trouble understanding the relationship between pay and performance. In such an environment, an otherwise sound program loses its effectiveness.[112]

Pay Compression

Pay compression:
A situation that is created when the pay differential between one or more pay levels becomes too small.

Pay compression is created when the pay differential between one or more pay levels becomes too small. This situation most likely occurs when labor market pay levels increase more rapidly than current employees' pay raises. Pay compression may also take place when firms make pay adjustments at the lower end of the job hierarchy without commensurate adjustments at the top. The explanation for this action may be the firm's need to meet market prices in retaining or hiring people with scarce skills and an inability to make needed adjustments elsewhere in the pay structure. Pay compression is a serious problem in many areas of our economy including nursing, engineering, and higher education. Unfortunately, no easy solution is available if a firm lacks the resources to maintain internal equity or believes that external equity should be of primary concern.

A Global Perspective

Benefits of an Expanded Global Network of Physicians and Care Facilities

Expatriate employees and their families on international assignment have instant access to a service that features an expanded global network of physicians and care facilities accessible by Internet and available in-person around the world. CIGNA International, a division of CIGNA Corporation, and world-leading global medical management and security assistance provider International SOS, combine "online" and "on-call" capabilities with an easy-to-access Web database of physician-screened global health-care resources. These services provide greater peace of mind for employers and their employees working outside their home countries. The new service expands the CIGNA's International Expatriate Benefits organization to nearly 5,500 physicians and hospital facilities outside the United States. "Companies invest millions of dollars sending their best employees abroad. The last thing they want is for employees and families to be anxious about accessing quality health care," says Andrew Mellen, senior vice president, CIGNA International Expatriate Benefits. "Expatriates and their sponsor companies want quality health care that's dependable, accessible and easy to use. That's what this alliance between CIGNA and SOS delivers."[113]

"International SOS's vision and philosophy is to provide expatriates access to world-class standards of medical service and care around the globe," says Arnaud Vaissie, president, chief executive officer, and co-founder of International SOS. "We already handle daily interactions with thousands of physicians and hospitals around the world. By working with CIGNA to make these services available online, we're helping employees feel more at home while they're away from home. It will also help sponsoring companies achieve greater success when placing people in vital international assignments."[114]

"The alliance of CIGNA and International SOS creates an effective way to satisfy these concerns regardless of where people are living around the world," added Dr. Joseph W. Mathey, director, medical affairs, Corning Incorporated, a multinational company with expatriate employees operating around the globe. "The inclusion of online country health briefings coupled with a globally credentialed provider network, supported by physician care–managers will set a new standard unparalleled by other international health-care delivery systems." With the increasing globalization of business, the need for adequate health care and benefits services for international traveling employees continues to expand. "The needs of expatriates are poorly understood by employers generally," says Dr. Stephen Pereira, consultant psychiatrist at London's Priory Healthcare Keats House and The Priory Hospital Hayes Grove. "The stress of relocation for individuals or families can be considerable. This can manifest itself from practical everyday issues to the occupational, domestic, social, educational, and personal areas of one's life. This ultimately affects efficiency and productivity. Any endeavor to deliver quality health care in a convenient and accessible manner would be a huge step forward in helping minimize stress for expatriates and their families."[115]

Summary

1. Describe how benefits are communicated and administered on the Web. Online tools are available to allow benefit managers to streamline and simplify their administrative work and communicate their benefits package to employees. Automated enrollment, claims processing, and detailed activity reports are standard practice using Web sites that permit benefit managers and employees to conduct transactions. These innovations are particularly helpful at a time when firms must reduce staffs and cut costs.

2. Define *benefits* as indirect financial compensation.

Benefits include all financial rewards that generally are not paid directly to the employee.

3. Describe mandated (legally required) benefits.

Legally required benefits include Social Security retirement benefits, disability insurance, and survivors' benefits; Medicare; workers' compensation benefits; and unpaid leave, mandated by the Family and Medical Leave Act.

4. Describe the basic categories of voluntary benefits.

Voluntary benefits include payment for time not worked, health benefits, security benefits, employee services, premium pay, and benefits for part-time employees.

5. Explain legislation concerning benefits.

The Consolidated Omnibus Budget Reconciliation Act of 1985 (COBRA) was enacted to give employees the opportunity to temporarily continue their coverage if they would otherwise lose it because of termination, layoff, or other change in employment status. The Health Insurance Portability and Accountability Act of 1996 provides new protections for approximately 25 million Americans who move from one job to another, who are self-employed, or who have pre-existing medical conditions. The Employee Retirement Income Security Act of 1974 (ERISA) was passed to strengthen existing and future retirement programs. The Older Workers Benefit Protection Act (OWBPA) is a 1990 amendment to the Age Discrimination in Employment Act and extends its coverage to all employee benefits.

6. Describe the range of employee benefits.

A corporation in tune with the needs of its workers will provide a broad range of employee benefits. Companies have addressed numerous needs over the years as they have attempted to develop programs that attracted candidates for employment and motivated them to perform as employees.

7. Explain factors involved in nonfinancial compensation.

The components of nonfinancial compensation consist of the job, and the job's total environment.

8. Explain the job as a total compensation factor.

The job itself is a central issue in many theories of motivation. It is also a vital component in a total compensation program. Job characteristics theory goes a long way in explaining the importance of the job itself in determining compensation. According to job characteristics theory, employees experience intrinsic compensation when their jobs rate high on five core job dimensions: skill variety, task identity, task significance, autonomy, and feedback.

9. Describe the job environment as a total compensation factor.

The *physical environment* and the *psychological climate* are important factors. Employees can draw satisfaction from their work through several nonfinancial factors. Reasonable policies, competent supervisors, congenial co-workers, appropriate status symbols, and pleasant physical working conditions are all important features. Another factor of increasing importance is the flexibility employees have in their work situations.

10. Explain factors that are involved in workplace flexibility.

Workplace flexibility factors such as flextime, the compressed workweek, job sharing, flexible compensation plans, telecommuting, part-time work, and modified retirement are components of nonfinancial compensation.

11. Describe the concepts of severance pay, comparable worth, pay secrecy, and pay compression.

Compensation designed to assist laid-off employees as they search for new employment is referred to as severance pay. Comparable worth requires the value for dissimilar jobs, such as company nurse and welder, to be compared under some form of job evaluation, and pay rates for both jobs to be assigned according to their evaluated worth. With pay secrecy, organizations tend to keep their pay rates secret for various reasons. Pay compression most likely occurs when labor market pay levels increase more rapidly than current employees' pay raises.

Key Terms

- **Benefits, 324**
- **Paid time off (PTO), 329**
- **Health maintenance organizations (HMOs), 330**
- **Preferred provider organization (PPO), 330**
- **Point-of-service (POS), 330**
- **Exclusive provider organizations (EPOs), 330**
- **Capitation, 330**
- **Defined contribution health-care system, 330**
- **Medical savings accounts, 331**
- **Utilization review, 331**
- **Defined benefit plan, 332**
- **Defined contribution plan, 332**
- **401(k) plan, 333**
- **Cash balance plan, 333**
- **Employee stock option plans (ESOPs), 334**
- **Relocation benefits, 335**
- **Premium pay, 336**
- **Hazard pay, 336**
- **Shift differential, 337**
- **Job characteristics theory, 340**
- **Skill variety, 340**
- **Task identity, 340**
- **Task significance, 340**
- **Autonomy, 341**
- **Feedback, 341**
- **Cyberwork, 341**
- **Status symbols, 342**
- **Flextime, 343**
- **Compressed workweek, 344**
- **Job sharing, 345**
- **Flexible compensation plans, 345**
- **Telecommuting, 346**
- **Modified retirement, 348**
- **Severance pay, 349**
- **Comparable worth, 349**
- **Pay compression, 350**

Questions for Review

1. Define *benefits*.
2. What are the legally required benefits? Briefly describe each.
3. What are the basic categories of voluntary benefits? Describe each.
4. What items are included in the voluntary benefit of payment for time not worked?
5. Define each of the following:
   a. Health maintenance organizations (HMO)
   b. Preferred provider organization (PPO)
   c. Point-of-service (POS)
   d. Exclusive provider organizations (EPOs)
   c. Capitation
   f. Defined Contribution Health-Care System
   g. Medical savings accounts
   h. Utilization review
6. There are numerous forms of retirement plans. Describe each of the following:
   a. Defined benefit plan
   b. Defined contribution plan
   c. 401(k) plan
   d. Cash balance plan
7. What is an employee stock option plan?
8. Distinguish among premium pay, hazard pay, and shift differential pay.
9. Define each of the following benefit laws:
   a. Consolidated Omnibus Budget Reconciliation Act of 1985 (COBRA)
   b. Health Insurance Portability and Accountability Act of 1996
   c. Employee Retirement Income Security Act of 1974 (ERISA)
   d. Older Workers Benefit Protection Act (OWBPA)
10. What factors are related to the job as a total compensation factor?
11. What compensation factors are related to the job environment?
12. Define each the following workplace flexibility factors:
    a. flextime
    b. compressed workweek
    c. job sharing
    d. flexible compensation plans
    e. telecommuting
    f. modified retirement

13. Define each of the following:
    a. severance pay
    b. comparable worth
    c. pay compression

A Double Edged Sword

The decline in oil prices during early 2003 adversely affected many industries. Profits were down for all major oil companies and many of their suppliers. The producers of drilling fluids, for example, received few new orders, and many existing orders were canceled or scaled back. As a supplier of drilling fluids, Beta Chemical Company's sales plummeted. Beta, located in Lafayette, Louisiana, supplies companies such as Texaco, Shell, and Pennzoil, as well as independent oil drillers, often called *wildcatters*.

Beta had implemented a comprehensive profit-sharing plan after several years of rapidly increasing sales and profits. The decision was based largely on an attitude survey of the employees at Beta, which showed that they strongly preferred profit sharing over other benefits.

In the late 1990s, the compensation plan at Beta provided for base wages about 20 percent below wage levels for similar jobs in Lafayette. But half of company profits were paid out each quarter as a fixed percentage of employee wages. Distributed profits averaged more than 50 percent of base wages. This caused average total compensation at Beta to be 20 percent above that of the area. Because of the high pay, Beta remained a popular employer, able to take its pick from a long waiting list of applicants.

Benefits were kept to a minimum at Beta. There was no retirement plan and a very limited medical plan designed to cover catastrophic illnesses only. Employees considered this a good bargain, though, in light of the above-average compensation.

Profits were down markedly in 2002, and the profit-sharing bonus was less than half the historical average. Earnings declined further for the first two quarters of 2003. By midyear, it was clear the company would be in the red for the entire second half. A board meeting was called in late August to discuss the profit-sharing program. One director made it known that he felt the company should drop profit sharing. The human resource director, Vince Harwood, was asked to sit in at the board meeting and to make a presentation suggesting what the company should do about compensation.

Questions

1. Evaluate the compensation plan at Beta.
2. If you were Mr. Harwood, what would you recommend for the short term? For the long term?

HRM Incident 2

A Benefits Package Designed for Whom?

Wayne McGraw greeted Robert Peters, his next interviewee, warmly. Robert had an excellent academic record and appeared to be just the kind of person Wayne's company, Beco Electric, was seeking. Wayne is the university recruiter for Beco and had already interviewed six graduating seniors at Centenary College.

Based on the application form, Robert appeared to be the most promising candidate to be interviewed that day. He was 22 years old and had a 3.6 grade point average with a 4.0 in his major field, industrial management. Not only was Robert the vice president of the Student Government Association, but he was also activities chairman for Kappa Alpha Psi, a social fraternity. The reference letters in Robert's file revealed that he was both very active socially and a rather intense and serious student. One of the letters, from Robert's employer during the previous summer, expressed satisfaction with Robert's work habits.

Wayne knew that discussion of pay could be an important part of the recruiting interview. But he did not know which aspects of Beco's compensation and benefits program would appeal most to Robert. The company has an excellent profit-sharing plan, although 80 percent of profit distributions are deferred and included in each employee's retirement account. Health benefits are also good. The company's medical and dental plan pays a significant portion of costs. A company lunchroom provides meals at about 70 percent of outside prices, although few managers take advantage of this. Employees get one week of paid vacation after the first year and two weeks after two years with the company. In addition, there are 12 paid holidays each year. Finally, the company encourages advanced education, paying for tuition and books in full, and, under certain circumstances, allowing time off to attend classes during the day.

Questions

1. What aspects of Beco's compensation and benefits program are likely to appeal to Robert? Explain.
2. In today's work environment, what additional benefits might be more attractive to Robert? Explain.

Human Resource Management Skills

Chapter 10: Benefits and Other Compensation Issues

A Skills Module entitled *Total Rewards* is presented to provide additional insight into topics in this chapter. Specific sections within the module that relate to benefits and other compensation issues cover the following topics: Fair Labor Standards Act of 1938 (FLSA); Equal Pay Act (EPA) and Civil Rights Act of 1964; Employee Retirement Income Security Act (ERISA) and Internal Revenue Code; voluntary and mandatory benefits; defined contribution plan; cafeteria plan including medical insurance and dental plans, accidental death, retirement, insurance, paid time off, and stock-based programs; executive perks; and golden parachutes, severance packages, and golden handcuffs.

Several benefits scenarios are presented to give students realistic experience in dealing with the topic.

A test is provided at the end of the module to determine mastery of the material included in the Skills Module. Also, directions are given for assignments that can be used in class or assigned as homework.

We invite you to visit the Mondy homepage on the Prentice Hall Web site at

www.prenhall.com/mondy

for updated information, Web-based exercises, and links to other HR-related sites.

Notes

1. Robert D. Perussina, "Employee Self-Service Enables Employees to Leverage Benefits and Become Self-Sufficient," *Employee Benefits Journal* 25 (June 2000): 15.
2. Michael Prince, "Web Transactions a Boon to Reduced Benefits Staffs," *Business Insurance* (November 4, 2002): 10.
3. Joanne Wojcik, "Portals Easing Access for Plan Participants," *Business Insurance* (June 24, 2002): T3, T8.
4. James V. Gemus, "Clicking into Benefits," *Best's Review* 102 (November 2001): 128–129.
5. James C. Cooper and Kathleen Madigan, "Sobering Stats that Evaded the Radar," *BusinessWeek* (February 17, 2003): 25.
6. Joseph J. Martocchio, *Strategic Compensation*, 2nd ed. (Upper Saddle River, NJ: Prentice Hall, 2001): 223, 241.
7. Gene Koretz, "Medical Costs of the 'Old Old,'" *BusinessWeek* (January 31, 2000): 34.
8. Spencer Rich, "Social Security: The Devil's in the Details," *National Journal* (July 14, 2001): 15.
9. Loretta Sanchez, "The Privatization Question," *Hispanic Business* 24 (October 2002): 22.
10. Congress has the ability to extend this period, and in the past has done so.
11. Mary-Kathryn Zachary, "Supreme Court Leaves FMLA Law Unclear," *Supervision* 63 (August 2002): 23.
12. Maria Greco Danaher, "Intermittent Leave Under the FMLA," *Workforce Online* (May 2000), http://www.workforce.com/feature/00/04/81.
13. Stephanie M. Cerasano, "Managers Beware: You Can Be Personally Liable for FMLA Violations," *Arizona Employment Law Letter* 6 (October 1999): 1.
14. Ronald J. Andrykovitch and Jeffrey A. VanDoren, "Legal Update: Family and Medical Leave Act's Real Impact," *Getting Results . . . For the Hands-On Manager* (January 1, 1997): 7.
15. Timothy S. Bland, "The Supreme Court Reins in the FMLA (Slightly)," *HRMagazine* 47 (July 2002): 45–48.
16. Elizabeth Chang, "Flexibility Can Cure Problems with Sick Pay," *St. Louis Post-Dispatch* (May 11, 2000): C7.
17. Ibid.
18. Pamela Paul, "Time Out," *American Demographics* 24 (June 2002): 34–41.
19. "BLS Confirms Double-Digit Health Cost Increases," *Employee Benefit Plan Review* 56 (June 2002): 9.
20. Martha Frase-Blunt, "Time to Redo Your Benefits?" *HRMagazine* 47 (December 2002): Anonymous 73.
21. Ellen McGirt, "Insurance: Less Costs More," *Money* 31 (November 2002): 146.

22. Peter Porrino, "Catch a Falling Star," *Best's Review* 103 (October 2002): 104.
23. Susan J. Wells, "Avoiding the Health Care Squeeze," *HRMagazine* 45 (April 2000): 46–52.
24. Janice Revell, "GM's Slow Leak," *Fortune* (October 28, 2002): 105–106.
25. Shari Caudron, "Employee, Cover Thyself," *Workforce* 79 (April 2000): 34–42.
26. Mary Elizabeth Burke, Evren Esen, and Jessica Collison, "2003 Benefits Survey," *SHRM/SHRM Foundation* (June 2003): 22.
27. Study Shows HMO Enrollment Continues to Drop," *Health Care Strategic Management* 21 (May 2003): 6.
28. Kenneth Aaron, "Health Plan Offers New Services," *Times Union* (October 2, 2001): E1.
29. Burke, Esen, and Collison, "2003 Benefits Survey," 18.
30. Meredith B. Rosenthal, Richard G. Frank, Joan L. Buchanan, and Arnold M. Epstein, "Transmission of Financial Incentives to Physician by Intermediary Organizations in California," *Health Affairs* (July 1, 2002): 197.
31. Elizabeth Simpkin and Karen Janousek, "What Are We Without Risk? The Physician Organization at a Crossroads," *Journal of Health Care Finance* 29 (Spring 2003): 1.
32. Rosenthal, Frank, Buchanan, and Epstein, "Transmission of Financial Incentives," 197.
33. Howard Gleckman, "Old, Ill, and Uninsured," *BusinessWeek* (April 7, 2003): 79.
34. Kathryn Tyler, "Meet Your New Health Plan Option," *HRMagazine* 47 (December 2002): 64.
35. Carolyn Hirschman, "More Choices, Less Cost?" *HRMagazine* 47 (January 2002): 38.
36. Caudron, "Employee, Cover Thyself," 34.
37. President Bush supports making the plans more permissive, arguing that people should be able to carry over $500 of their money from one year to the next.
38. Ron Leiber, "Getting Uncle Sam to Cover Your Massage — Rush to Use Up Medical Savings Accounts Prompts Creative Reading of Rules; a Tax Break for Dieters," *Wall Street Journal* (November 5, 2002): D1.
39. Stephan L. Burton, Lauren Randel, Karen Titlow, and Ezekiel J. Emanuel, "The Ethics of Pharmaceutical Benefit Management," *Health Affairs* (September 1, 2001): 150.
40. Burke, Esen, and Collison, "2003 Benefits Survey," 22.
41. Ibid., 22.
42. Carolyn Hirschman, "Long-Term Care Insurance Comes of Age," *HRMagazine* 47 (July 2000): 65.
43. According to the "2003 Benefits Survey" conducted by SHRM/SHRM Foundation, 97 percent of the responding firms reported providing life insurance.
44. Economic Trends," *Workplace Visions, SHRM Research* (2003): 4.
45. George B. Kozol, "Defined-Benefit Plans Emerge As a Better Choice for Held Businesses," *Journal of Financial Service Professionals* 57 (March 2003): 41.
46. Ibid.
47. Burke, Esen, Collison, "2003 Benefits Survey," 38.
48. Charlotte Garvey, "Is Your 401(k) Squeezed by Costs?" *HRMagazine* 47 February 2002): 46.
49. Carolyn Hirschman, "Growing Pains," *HRMagazine* 47 (June 2002): 32.
50. Ibid.
51. Charlotte Garvey, "Company Stock in 401(k) Plans: Say 'When'," *HRMagazine* 47 (March 2002): 61.
52. Elayne Robertson Demby, " Changing the Recipe of 401(k) Plans," *HRMagazine* 47 (September 2002): 59.
53. Ruth Simon, "Bailing Out of the Retirement Plan — Employee Participation in 401(k)s Hits Lowest Level in More Than a Decade," *Wall Street Journal* (March 11, 2003): D.1.
54. Economic Trends," 6.
55. John A. Turner, "Are Cash Balance Plans Defined Benefit or Defined Contribution Plans?" *Benefits Quarterly* 19 (Second Quarter 2003): 71.
56. Martocchio, *Strategic Compensation*, 245.
57. Ibid.
58. Michael Arndt and Aaron Bernstein, "From Milestone to Millstone?" *BusinessWeek* (March 20, 2000): 120, 122.
59. Burke, Esen, and Collison, "2003 Benefits Survey," 33.
60. Ibid., 11.
61. Howard R. Mitchell III, "When a Company Moves: How to Help Employees Adjust," *HRMagazine* 44 (January 1999): 61.
62. Lin Grensing-Pophal, "Rules for (Hitting) the Road," *HRMagazine* 47 (May 2002): 81.
63. Burke, Esen, and Collison, "2003 Benefits Survey," 2.
64. Hillary Chura, "Careers/Fresh Starts; Companies Lend Parents a Hand," *Los Angeles Times*, Home Edition (January 27, 1997): D2.
65. Burke, Esen, and Collison, "2003 Benefits Survey," 38.
66. Mark E. Battersby, "Improving Yourself with Tax Deductions," *Office Solutions* 18 (April 2001): 48–49.
67. Robert Levering and Milton Moskowitz, "100 Best Companies to Work For," *Fortune* (January 20, 2003): 140.
68. Charlotte Garvey, "Access to the Law," *HRMagazine* 47 (September 2002): 83.
69. Levering and Moskowitz, "100 Best Companies to Work For," 136–140.
70. Melissa Solomon, "Betting on Benefits," *Computerworld* (June 18, 2001): 34.
71. Bill Leonard, "Recipes for Part-Time Benefits," *HRMagazine* 45 (April 2000): 56–62.
72. UPS Strike Puts Focus on Part-Time Workers," *Chain Store Age* 73 (October 1997): 88.
73. Donna B. Gilleskie and Bryon F. Lutz, "The Impact of Employer-Provided Health Insurance on Dynamic Employment Transitions," *The Journal of Human Resources* 37 (Winter 2002): 129.
74. Bill Leonard, "Access Denied," *HRMagazine* 47 (October 2002): 38–41.
75. *U.S. Statutes at Large* 88, Part I, 93rd Congress, 2nd Session, 1974: 833.
76. Martocchio, *Strategic Compensation*, 63.
77. Latest Benefits Benchmarks," *HR Focus* 79 (June 2002): 1.
78. Adapted from Craig J. Cantoni, "Learn to Manage Pay and Performance Like an Entrepreneur," *Compensation & Benefits Review* 29 (January/February 1997): 52–58.
79. Martocchio, *Strategic Compensation*, 4.
80. The Wireless Internet," *BusinessWeek* (May 29, 2000): 136–144.
81. Employers Stress Workplace Fun," *National Underwriter (Property & Casualty/Risk & Benefits Management)* (May 17, 1999): 25.
82. Shari Caudron, "The New Status Symbols," *Industry Week* (June 21, 1999): 24.
83. Karla Taylor, "How Far Can You Flex," *Association Management* 53 (September 2001): 56.

84. Barry Shanoff, "Senate Aims at More Flexible Workplace," *Waste Age* 32 (July 2001): 10.
85. Kimberlianne Podlas, "Reasonable Accommodation or Special Privilege? Flex-time, Telecommuting, and the ADA," *Business Horizons* 44 (September/October 2001): 61–65.
86. Recognition Plus Performance Measurement Equals Happy Workers," *HR Focus* 76 (April 1999): 5.
87. Burke, Esen, and Collison, "2003 Benefits Survey," 4.
88. Joel Schettler, "A New Social Contract," *Training* 39 (April 2002): 62.
89. Shelly Reese, "Working Around the Clock," *Business & Health* 18 (April 2000): 71–90; Edward Prewitt, "Flextime and Telecommuting," *CIO* (April 15, 2002): 130.
90. Brian Gill, "Flextime Benefits Employees and Employers," *American Printer* 220 (February 1998): 70.
91. Schettler, "A New Social Contract."
92. Burke, Esen, and Collison, "2003 Benefits Survey," 2.
93. Chris Sheridan, "Government Initiative Promotes a Balanced Home and Work Strategy," *Planning* (April 11, 2003): 22.
94. Burke, Esen, and Collison, "2003 Benefits Survey," 4.
95. Patricia Nakache, "One VP, Two Brains," *Fortune* (December 20, 1999): 327–328.
96. Dennis R. Lassila, "Cafeteria Plans Need to Harmonize with FMLA Mandates," *Practical Tax Strategies* 70 (March 2003): 164.
97. Edward Elliott and Claudine Kapel, "Serving Up Flexible Compensation," *Canadian HR Reporter* (February 12, 2001): 15.
98. Martocchio, *Strategic Compensation*, 241.
99. Gus Manochehri and Theresa Pinkerton, "Managing Telecommuters: Opportunities and Challenges," *American Business Review* (January 1, 2003): 9.
100. Michelle M. Robertson, Wayne S. Maynard, and Jamie R. McDevitt, "Telecommuting: Managing the Safety of Workers in Home Office Environments," *Professional Safety* 48 (April 2003): 30.
101. "Latest Benefits Benchmarks," *HR Focus* 79 (June 2002): 1, 11.
102. Leigh Rivenbark, " Employees Want More Opportunities to Telecommute, Report Reveals," *HR News* 19 (April 2000): 14.
103. Andrea C. Poe, "Family-Friendly University," *HRMagazine* 47 (May 2002): 91.
104. Prewitt, "Flextime and Telecommuting," 130.
105. "UPS Strike Puts Focus on Part-Time Workers," *Chain Store Age* 73 (October 1997): 88.
106. Charles Fishman, "Moving Toward a Balanced Work Life," *Workforce* 79 (March 2000): 39–40.
107. Steve Bates, "Most CEOs Get Modest Severance Packages," *HRMagazine* 48 (May 2003): 10.
108. Diana Furchtgoff-Roth, "Comparable Worth Is Back," *The American Spectator* 33 (September 2000): 38.
109. Amy Gluckman, "Comparable Worth," *Dollars & Sense* (September 1, 2002): 42.
110. Furchtgoff-Roth, "Comparable Worth Is Back."
111. Evan Gahr, "Pay Equity Iniquity," *The American Spectator* 32 (August 1999): 56–57.
112. Edward E. Lawler, "The New Pay: A Strategic Approach," *Compensation & Benefits Review* 27 (July/August 1995): 14–22.
113. Wayne Adams, "CIGNA Teams with International SOS to Launch World's First Online Physician-Led Health Care Network for Employees on Global Assignments, Improves Expatriates' Access to Quality Health Care Around the World; Helps Companies Maximize Their Multimillion-Dollar Investments in Expatriate Assignments," *Internet Wire* (February 14, 2002).
114. Ibid.
115. Ibid.

PART SIX

Safety and Health

CHAPTER OBJECTIVES

After completing this chapter, students should be able to

1. Describe some safety and security strategies for a post–September 11 world.
2. Describe the nature and role of safety and health.
3. Explain the role of the Occupational Safety and Health Act.
4. Describe OSHA's changing role.
5. Describe the economic impact of safety and explain the focus of safety programs in business operations.
6. Explain the problem of identity theft.
7. Describe the consequences of repetitive stress injuries.
8. Explain the purpose of ergonomics.
9. Explain the effects of workplace and domestic violence on businesses.
10. Describe the nature of stress and burnout.
11. Explain sources of stress and means of coping with it.
12. Describe the purposes of wellness programs.
13. Describe the importance of physical fitness programs and substance abuse programs.
14. Describe employee assistance programs.
15. Describe the impact of smoking in the workplace.
16. Explain the possible impact of AIDS in the workplace.

CHAPTER 11

A Safe and Healthy Work Environment

HRM IN *Action:*

Safety and Security Strategies for a Post–September 11 World

 **OBJECTIVE**

Describe some safety and security strategies for a post–September 11 world.

The United States and the world have changed a great deal since September 11, 2001. Safety and security in the workplace has perhaps changed the most. According to an SHRM survey, 52 percent of responding firms have increased security and 26 percent have increased screening of employees prior to hiring.[1] With increased awareness of terrorism and the creation of the U.S. Department of Homeland Security, everyone hopes that emergency procedures will never be needed. However, it is obviously necessary for organizations to be prepared in order to assure a safe and secure workplace. This preparation should include:

- Selection of people responsible for implementing evacuation plans
- Training of key personnel
- Securing of top management support and employee buy-in
- A communication system for alerting employees
- A plan informing employees of what actions to take, as well as safe evacuation plans for all employees, including those with disabilities
- A description of work-site details; its capabilities and systems; for example, means for sealing the building for protection against aerosols[2]

The Department of Homeland Security is preparing to spend $37.7 billion on safety.[3] The shift of attention away from traditional safety and security issues toward terrorism has some sources concerned. Some industry leaders believe that we should strengthen our everyday safety and emergency responses rather than shift toward concentrated anti-terrorism measures. The feeling is that the chance of a widespread terrorist attack on any given location across the country is slight. They maintain that the risk for a fire, natural disaster, or an incidence of workplace violence continues to be much greater.[4]

Still, with the World Trade Center and Pentagon tragedies on everyone's mind, and the knowledge of the destruction terrorists are capable of committing, it is unlikely that our government or industry will lessen their vigilance. President Bush has said that the war against terrorism will be a long one, and that is why we must stay prepared. As an aid in this preparation, the Occupational Health and Safety Administration has prepared guidelines for planning against terrorists attacks on its Web site: http://www.osha.gov/SLTC/biologicalagents/bioterrorism.html.

OBJECTIVE

Describe the nature and role of safety and health.

Safety:
The protection of employees from injuries caused by work-related accidents.

Health:
An employee's freedom from physical or emotional illness.

We began this chapter by describing some safety and security strategies for a post–September 11 world. Next, we describe the nature and role of safety and health and explain the role of the Occupational Safety and Health Act and the agency it created, the Occupational Safety and Health Administration (OSHA). We then describe OSHA's changing role and describe the economic impact of safety and the focus of safety programs in business operations. Next, the problem of identity theft is explained. Then we discuss the consequences of repetitive stress injuries and the purpose of ergonomics. An explanation of the effect of workplace and domestic violence on businesses follows. The nature of stress and burnout is then described as are the sources and means of coping with stress. Then the purposes of wellness programs, the importance of physical fitness programs and substance abuse programs, and the rationale for employee assistance programs will be discussed. This chapter ends with a discussion of the impact of smoking in the workplace and the possible effect of AIDS in the workplace.

The Nature and Role of Safety and Health

In our discussion, **safety** involves protecting employees from injuries caused by work-related accidents. **Health** refers to employees' freedom from physical or emotional illness. Problems in these areas seriously affect the productivity and quality of work life. They can dramatically lower a firm's effectiveness and employee morale. In fact, job-related injuries and illnesses are more common than most people realize. They cost the nation even more than AIDS or Alzheimer's disease. Many citizens grossly underestimate job-related injuries as a contributor to health-care costs in the United States.

Although line managers are primarily responsible for maintaining a safe and healthy work environment, human resource professionals provide staff expertise to help them deal with these issues. In addition, the human resource manager is frequently responsible for coordinating and monitoring safety and health programs.

Explain the role of the Occupational Safety and Health Act.

Workplace Safety and Health

www.lir.msu.edu/hotlinks/safety.htm

This Web site provides numerous links related to workplace safety and health.

Occupational Safety and Health Act

The most important federal legislation in the safety and health area is the Occupational Safety and Health Act of 1970. The purpose of this act is to assure a safe and healthful workplace for every American worker. There is little doubt that the act's intent is justified. Organizations must strive for these goals if they are to reach their full productive potential.

The act's enforcement by the Occupational Safety and Health Administration (OSHA) dramatically altered management's role in the area of safety and health. Financial penalties serve as pointed reminders to the industry of the benefits of maintaining safe and healthy working conditions. Significant costs for workers' compensation insurance, the expense of training new workers, and the fact that risky jobs command higher pay also keep safety and health issues on managers' minds.

In implementing the act, OSHA administrator John Henshaw says he is authorizing stricter enforcement measures for manufacturers and other employers that repeatedly violate health and safety standards. This new policy will increase oversight of firms that have received "high gravity" citations, which may include charges of willful violations and a failure to correct previously noted hazards. This policy will put more teeth in enforcement practices but it will not change the emphasis on improving compliance assistance and reducing reliance on OSHA fines. OSHA has formed agreements with a number of companies, including Dow Chemical, to promote increased safety education and outreach.[5]

OSHA has alerted over 14,000 employers across the country that their injury and illness rates are higher than average and encouraged them to take steps to reduce hazards and protect their workers. OSHA then offers assistance that will help reduce these rates. The agency suggests, among other things, the hiring of outside safety and health consultants and using free safety and health consultation services provided by OSHA through the states. The 14,200 sites mentioned are listed alphabetically, by state, on OSHA's Web site at http://www.osha.gov/as/opa/foia/hot(under)9.html.[6] This list includes 1,692 construction firms, which is 11.9 percent of the total.[7]

SHRM HR Links

www.shrm.org/hrlinks/Links.asp?Category=110

This SHRM Web site deals with topics regarding safety, health, and wellness.

According to the U.S. Bureau of Labor Statistics, manufacturing workers have the highest number of work-related illnesses and injuries even though manufacturing employment continues to decline in the United States. OSHA estimates that about one-third of worker compensation claims, between $15 and 18 billion, goes to pay medical costs and lost wages. However, this is just the tip of the iceberg since a lost-time accident may also require rescheduling production and workers, and may even require firms to recruit, select, and train a replacement worker while the injured employee recuperates.[8]

Even with assistance from 21 states and 2 territories that operate OSHA-approved state plans covering the private sector, the average employer will not likely see an OSHA inspector unless an employee instigates an inspection. When OSHA inspectors come to a site, the employer has the option of denying the inspector access to the work site. In such cases, OSHA would be required to get a warrant to proceed with the inspection. If the employer refuses access to view certain documents, OSHA must obtain an administrative subpoena. Table 11-1 shows the most common categories of violations responsible for OSHA citations. The first and fifth ranked categories, as you can see, emphasize the need for education in providing a safe workplace.

About 70 percent of OSHA inspections have resulted from employee complaints. Under the Occupational Safety and Health Act, an employee can legally refuse to work when the following conditions exist:

- The employee reasonably fears death, disease, or serious physical harm
- The harm is imminent

Table 11-1 **Top Categories Responsible for OSHA Citations**

Rank	Area of Concern	Violations
1	No written hazard communication program	2,496
2	Lack of machine guarding	1,446
3	Lack of written lockout/tagout programs and procedures*	1,191
4	Failure to label hazardous containers	1,179
5	Not providing employees with training about occupational hazards	982

*Lockout/tagout refers to electrical repairs, during which switches for power must be shut off, locked, or tagged so power cannot be turned on while an electrical system is being repaired.

Source: Kent Beall, "Safety's Payback," *Industrial Distribution* 91 (July 2002): S6.

- There is too little time to file an OSHA complaint and get the problem corrected
- The worker has notified the employer about the condition and requested correction of the problem, but the employer has not taken action

OBJECTIVE

Describe OSHA's changing role.

OSHA's Changing Role

Since its inception, OSHA has revised its mission. The current thrust is to give employers a choice between partnership and traditional enforcement, to inject common sense into regulation and enforcement, and to eliminate red tape. The overall purpose, of course, is to reduce injuries, illnesses, and fatalities. To help small businesses, OSHA is expanding its assistance, reducing penalties, and putting more of its informational materials in electronic formats, including CD-ROMs and Internet sites. OSHA's director has emphasized that punishment will not result for these firms for violations if they seek OSHA's assistance in correcting problems.

General perceptions of OSHA have not always been positive. However, it appears that OSHA has overcome most of the past criticisms. A recent Gallup survey of nearly 2,500 workers found customers very satisfied or satisfied with their dealings with the agency. More than 87 percent of workers and employers rated OSHA staff professionalism, competence, and knowledge as satisfactory.[9] Janice Ochenkowski, vice president of External Affairs for the Risk & Insurance Management Society, Inc., said, "We're very pleased with the direction that OSHA is taking . . . it's great that OSHA continues to strive to work with American businesses to make workplaces safer."[10] Older HR types can remember a time when few people representing industry would have made such a statement.

OBJECTIVE

Describe the economic impact of safety and explain the focus of safety programs in business operations.

Safety: The Economic Impact

Job-related deaths and injuries of all types extract a high toll not only in terms of human misery, but also in economic loss. The significant financial costs are often passed along to the consumer in the form of higher prices. Thus, job-related deaths and injuries affect everyone, directly or indirectly. Safety risks can be significant for employers. In addition to workers' compensation costs, OSHA can levy major fines. For example, an amputation at an auto parts manufacturer in Ohio resulted in OSHA fines totaling $176,250 for numerous violations of machine guarding, lockout/tagout procedures, and lack of a safety program.[11] Indirect costs related to turnover and lost productivity add to the expense.

The National Safety Council estimated the total costs of work injuries in 2000 to be over $131 billion (see Table 11-2).[12] The overall on-the-job injury and illness rate dropped 3 percent in 2000, continuing a downward trend. Manufacturing workers experienced the highest injury and illness rate at 9 cases per 100 workers in 2000. Other rates for large industrial sectors were 7.1 per 100 for agriculture, forestry, and fishing; 4.7 per 100 for mining; 8.3 per 100 for construction; 6.9 per 100 for transportation; and 5.9 per 100 for wholesale and retail trade. More details about Bureau of Labor Statistics injury and illness data are available at www.bls.gov.[13]

Companies have come a long way in recognizing the importance and cost benefits of safety. Workplaces are safer, thanks to efforts of employers, insurance companies, unions, and state and federal agencies. Safety professionals strive for lower workers' compensation costs as do insurance companies, who work to keep both their clients' and their own costs down. All parties recognize the value and benefits of a safe workplace.[14]

Some people may be surprised to discover that motor vehicle accidents are the number one cause of death on the job. Since 1980, while workplace deaths declined by

Table 11-2 Work Injury Costs

The true cost to the nation, to employers, and to individuals of work-related deaths and injuries is much greater than the cost of worker's compensation insurance alone. The figures presented below show the National Safety Council's estimates of the total costs of occupational deaths and injuries. Cost estimating procedures were revised for the 1993 edition of *Accident Facts*. In general, cost estimates are not comparable from year to year. As additional or more precise data become available, they are used from that year forward. Previously estimated figures are not revised.

Total Cost in 2000 .... $131.2 billion
Includes wage and productivity losses of $67.6 billion, medical costs of $24.2 billion, and administrative expenses of $22.3 billion. Includes employer costs of $11.5 billion such as the money value of time lost by workers other than those with disabling injuries, who are directly or indirectly involved in injuries, and the cost of time required to investigate injuries, write up injury reports, etc. Also includes damage to motor vehicles in work injuries of $2.2 billion and fire losses of $ 3.4 billion.

Cost per Worker $960
This figure indicates the value of goods or services each worker must produce to offset the cost of work injuries. It is *not* the average cost of a work injury.

Cost per Death $980,000

Cost per Disabling injury $28,000
These figures include estimates of wage losses, medical expenses, administrative expenses, and employer costs, and exclude property damage costs except to motor vehicles.

Source: Injury Facts (Chicago. IL: National Safety Council, 2001): 49.

almost half, car crashes accounted for 25 percent of the total. Homicides accounted for 14 percent and machinery accidents 13 percent.[15]

OSHA

www.osha.gov

This Web site is the homepage for the Occupational Safety and Health Administration.

The Focus of Safety Programs

Faulty management safety policies and decisions, personal factors, and environmental factors are the basic causes of accidents. If defective, these factors result in unsafe working conditions and/or unsafe employee actions. Direct causes of accidents stem from unplanned releases of energy and/or hazardous material. Regardless of the cause, the result is an accident (see Figure 11-1). Every employer needs to have a comprehensive safety program in place regardless of the degree of danger involved.[16] Safety programs may accomplish their purposes in two primary ways: one focusing on *unsafe employee actions* and the other on *unsafe working conditions*.

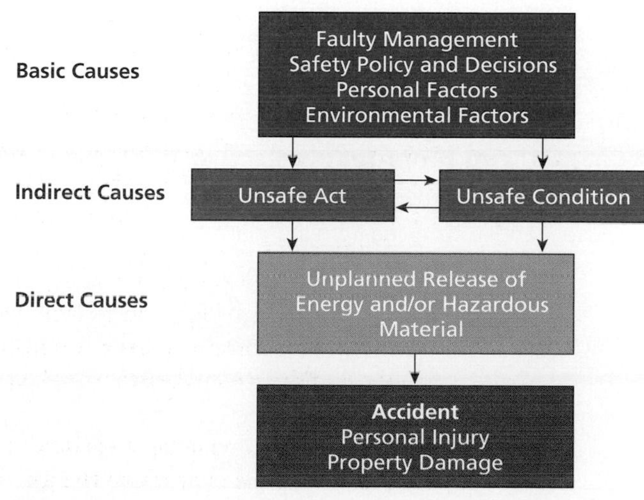

Figure 11-1 Accident Causes
Source: Occupational Safety and Health Administration.

Unsafe Employee Actions

Training and orientation of new employees emphasizing safety is especially important. The early months of employment are often critical because work injuries decrease with length of service. The first approach in a safety program is to create a psychological environment and employee attitudes that promote safety. When workers consciously or subconsciously think about safety, accidents decline. This attitude must permeate the firm's operations, and a strong company policy emphasizing safety and health is crucial. For example, a major chemical firm's policy states: "It is the policy of the company that every employee be assigned to a safe and healthful place to work. We strongly desire accident prevention in all phases of our operations. Toward this end, the full cooperation of all employees will be required." As the policy infers, no individual employee has the task of making the workplace safe. While there is danger that everyone's responsibility will become no one's responsibility, a truly safe environment takes the effort of everyone from top management to the lowest-level employee. While every individual in a firm should be encouraged to come up with solutions to potential safety problems, the firm's managers must take the lead. Management's unique role is clear since OSHA places primary responsibility for employee safety on the employer.

Unsafe Working Conditions

The second approach to safety program design is to develop and maintain a safe physical working environment. Here, altering the environment becomes the focus for preventing accidents. Even if Joe, a machine operator, has been awake all night with a sick child and can barely keep his eyes open, the safety devices on his machine will help protect him. Management should create a physical environment in which accidents cannot occur. It is in this area that OSHA has had its greatest influence.

Developing Safety Programs

Workplace accident prevention requires safety program planning. Plans may be relatively simple, as for a small retail store, or more complex and highly sophisticated, as for a large automobile assembly plant. Regardless of the organization's size, the support of top management is essential if safety programs are to be effective. Top executives in a firm must be aware of the tremendous human suffering and economic losses that can result from accidents.

Table 11-3 shows some of the reasons for top management's support of a safety program. This information suggests that the lost productivity of a single injured

Ethical Dilemma

Illegal Dumping

You have just become aware that the company that disposes of your plant waste is not following Environmental Protection Agency guidelines. The firm is dumping toxic waste at night in a closed landfill six miles from the plant. To make matters worse, your brother-in-law operates the waste disposal company. You have already warned him once, and you have just learned that he is still illegally dumping. You confront him, telling him that you are going to use the hotline to report him if he illegally dumps waste one more time, but he threatens to implicate you if you blow the whistle.

What would you do?

Table 11-3 Reasons for Management Support of a Safety Program

- **Personal loss.** The physical pain and mental anguish associated with injuries are always unpleasant and may even be traumatic for an injured worker. Of still greater concern is the possibility of permanent disability or even death.
- **Financial loss to injured employees.** Most employees are covered by company insurance plans or personal accident insurance. However, an injury may result in financial losses not covered by insurance.
- **Lost productivity.** When an employee is injured, there will be a loss of productivity for the firm. In addition to obvious losses, there are often hidden costs. For example, a substitute worker may need additional training to replace the injured employee. Even when another worker is available to move into the injured employee's position, efficiency may suffer.
- **Higher insurance premiums.** Workers' compensation insurance premiums are based on the employer's history of insurance claims. The potential for savings related to employee safety provides a degree of incentive to establish formal programs.
- **Possibility of fines and imprisonment.** Since the enactment of the Occupational Safety and Health Act, a willful and repeated violation of its provisions may result in serious penalties for the employer.
- **Social responsibility.** Many executives feel responsible for the safety and health of their employees. A number of firms had excellent safety programs years before OSHA existed. They understand that a safe work environment is not only in the best interests of the firm; providing one is the right thing to do.

worker is not the only factor to consider. Every phase of human resource management is involved. For instance, the firm may have difficulty in recruitment if it gains a reputation for being an unsafe place to work. Employee relations erode if workers believe that management does not care enough about them to provide a safe workplace. Firms will see an increase in compensation costs when they must pay a premium to attract qualified applicants and retain valued employees. Maintaining a stable workforce may become very difficult if employees perceive their workplace as hazardous.

Job Hazard Analysis. The main goal of safety and health professionals is to prevent job-related injuries and illnesses. Firms achieve this goal in several ways: by educating workers in the hazards associated with their work, installing engineering controls, defining safe work procedures, and prescribing appropriate personal protective equipment. **Job hazard analysis (JHA)** is a multistep process designed to study and analyze a task or job and then break down that task into steps that provide a means of eliminating associated hazards. JHA can have a major impact on safety performance. It results in a detailed written procedure for safely completing many tasks within a plant. A successful JHA program features several key components: management support, supervisor and employee training, written program, and management oversight.[17] OSHA publication 3071 (2002 Revised), *Job Safety Hazard Analysis*, is a good primer on performing a JHA.

Job hazard analysis (JHA): A multi-step process designed to study and analyze a task or job and then break down that task into steps that provide a means of eliminating associated hazards.

Superfund Amendments Reauthorization Act, Title III (SARA). SARA requires businesses to communicate more openly about the hazards associated with the materials they use and produce and the wastes they generate. Although SARA has been around for several years, many firms do not yet have a satisfactory program for it in place. The hazard communication standard often leads the list of OSHA violations, as you may recall from Table 11-1. Dealing with this standard appears to be relatively simple and inexpensive, except when organizations ignore its provisions.

Employee Involvement. One way to strengthen a safety program is to include employee input, which provides workers with a sense of accomplishment. To prevent accidents, each worker must make a personal commitment to safe work practices. A team concept, where employees watch out for each other as a moral obligation, is a worthy goal. Supervisors can show support for the safety program by conscientiously enforcing safety rules and by closely conforming to the rules themselves. Participation in such teams helps form positive attitudes, and employees develop a sense of ownership of the program. Involved employees may become concerned with not only safety issues but also ways to improve productivity.

The Safety Engineer. In many companies, one staff member coordinates the overall safety program. Such titles as *safety engineer* and *safety director* are common. One of the safety engineer's primary tasks is to provide safety training for company employees. This involves educating line managers about the merits of safety, and recognizing and eliminating unsafe situations. Although the safety engineer operates essentially in an advisory capacity, a well-informed and assertive person in this capacity may exercise considerable influence in the organization. Some major corporations also have *risk management departments* that anticipate losses associated with safety factors and prepare legal defenses in the event of lawsuits.

Accident Investigation

Accidents can happen even in the most safety-conscious firms. Whether or not an accident results in an injury, an organization should carefully evaluate each occurrence to determine its cause and to ensure that it does not recur. The safety engineer and the line supervisor jointly investigate accidents. One of the responsibilities of any supervisor is to prevent accidents. To do so, the supervisor must learn, through active participation in the safety program, why accidents occur, how they occur, where they occur, and who is involved. Supervisors gain a great deal of knowledge about accident prevention by helping to prepare accident reports. The OSHA Form 300 contains space for a description of the establishment, name, city, and state, followed by a one-line space for an entry for each recordable injury and illness.

Evaluation of Safety Programs

Perhaps the best indicator of a successful safety program is a reduction in the *frequency* and *severity* of injuries and illnesses. Therefore, statistics including the number of injuries and illnesses (frequency rate) and the amount of work time lost (severity rate) are often used in program evaluation. In addition to program evaluation criteria, an effective reporting system helps to ensure that accidents are reported and receive attention. With the initiation of a new safety program, the number of accidents may decline significantly. However, some supervisors may fail to report certain accidents to make the statistics for their units look better. Proper evaluation of a safety program depends on the accurate reporting and recording of data.

To be of value, organizations must use the conclusions derived from an evaluation to improve the safety program. Gathering data and permitting this information to collect dust on the safety director's desk will not solve problems or prevent accidents. Accident investigators must transmit evaluation results upward to top management and downward to line managers in order to generate improvements. Most employers will also mail or electronically transmit records of occupational injuries and illnesses directly to OSHA.

Rationale for Safety and Health Trends

There is solid rationale for organizations' increased attention to safety. In addition to legal requirements, the reasons for this concern include the following business issues:

- *Profitability.* Employees can only produce while they are on the job. In addition to payouts related to medical costs, other factors such as lost production and increased recruiting and training requirements add to a firm's expense when an employee is injured or becomes ill.

- *Employee and Public Relations.* A good safety record may provide companies with a competitive edge. Firms with superior safety records have an effective vehicle for recruiting and retaining good employees.
- *Reduced Liability.* An effective safety program can reduce corporate and executive liability for charges when employees are injured.
- *Marketing.* A positive safety record can help firms win contracts.
- *Productivity.* An effective safety program may boost morale and productivity while simultaneously reducing rising costs.

OBJECTIVE

Explain the problem of identity theft.

A New Security Threat: Identity Theft

Trouble began at Ligand Pharmaceuticals, Inc., in San Diego, when an employee stumbled across a box in a storage closet. Inside she found the personnel records of 38 former employees of a firm that Ligand had acquired a few years earlier. Using the information from these files, including names, addresses, Social Security numbers, birth dates, and other information, the employee and her partners in crime fraudulently rented three apartments, operated 20 cellular telephone accounts and established more than 25 credit card accounts. Then they proceeded to buy $100,000 in goods.[18]

Identity theft is one of the nation's fastest-growing white-collar crimes. In one state alone, New York, almost 12,700 cases were reported in 2002, an increase of 80 percent from the previous year. The crime has become so widespread that consumer protection agencies and the financial industry have created a standard checklist of steps victims can take to clear their name. The Federal Trade Commission has helpful information on its Internet site at www.ftc.gov.[19]

Identity thefts, such as the one experienced by Ligand's, could stem from many sources. However, it is of special concern to HR since that is the department that is normally responsible for personnel records containing sensitive data. In addition to injuring victims psychologically, identity theft is also expensive. Nationwide, consumers lost over $34 million last year to identity theft and other scams.[20] The FTC estimates that it costs the average victim $1,000 in long-distance phone calls, notary charges, mailing costs, and lost wages to get his or her financial life back in order after the identity theft occurs. Organizations could alleviate the problem by treating personal data, especially Social Security numbers, as classified rather than treating them casually.[21] Repetitive stress injury, another significant problem in industry, is discussed next.

OBJECTIVE

Describe the consequences of repetitive stress injuries.

Carpal tunnel syndrome: A common repetitive stress injury that results from pressure on the median nerve in the wrist due to repetitive flexing and extension of the wrist.

Repetitive Stress Injuries (RSIs)

The U.S. Bureau of Labor Statistics (BLS) reports that repetitive stress injuries account for 25 percent of cases involving days away from work and that disorders associated with repeated trauma are responsible for nearly 60 percent of all work-related illness.[22] **Carpal tunnel syndrome (CTS),** a common RSI, results from pressure on the median nerve in the wrist due to repetitive flexing and extension of the wrist. People developing this RSI may experience pain, numbness, or tingling in the hands or wrist, a weak grip, the tendency to drop objects, sensitivity to cold, and in later stages, muscle deterioration, especially in the thumb.

The BLS also reported that there were almost 28,000 cases of carpal tunnel syndrome reported as early as 1999 and that CTS is currently the leading cause of lost workdays, with half of all sufferers missing 30 or more days of work per year. CTS sufferers spend an average of 27 days off work, compared to 20 days for amputees and 17 days for fracture victims.[23] People who use their hands and wrists repeatedly in the same way tend to develop carpal tunnel syndrome. Illustrators, carpenters, assembly-line workers, and people whose jobs involve work on personal computers are the ones most commonly affected. Also related to the large number of workers' compensation claims is the increased recognition that such injuries are compensable.

CTS Controversy

A recent study showing that computer users are not at increased risk of developing carpal tunnel syndrome has caused controversy among some CTS experts. The American Academy of Neurology led a study conducted by the Mayo Clinic that evaluated the link between keyboard operating and CTS. They found that there is *no* evidence that spending even seven hours a day keyboarding will lead to CTS.[24] Critics of the study challenge its design and some state that the results did not show that using a computer does not increase the risk of CTS; they show that repetitive stress injury conditions are avoidable with the introduction of correct working practices.[25] However, if the Mayo Clinic study is valid, there have been an incredible number of misdiagnosed cases of CTS.

Non-Work-Related Factors

Some studies suggest that more than half of CTS cases are non-work-related. Several factors may give an employee a predisposition to CTS, including gender and age, since about 70 percent of CTS cases involve middle-aged women. An Australian College of Surgeons conference in 2001 stated that the highest frequency of CTS is among women of menopausal age who are obese, diabetic, and smokers.[26] In light of the latest research on CTS, employers may examine CTS claims more closely, including doctors' diagnoses of CTS.

Preventive Measures

Recent research findings have not changed the fact that repetitive stress injuries do occur. The good news is that carpal tunnel syndrome is preventable, or at least the severity can be reduced. Managers can provide ergonomic furniture, especially chairs, and ensure that computer monitors are positioned at eye level and keyboards at elbow level. Employees can also cooperate by reporting early symptoms of RSIs and by taking the following actions:[27]

- Rest the hand and wrist in a neutral position
- Do not perform the exact activities that caused the syndrome
- Take nonsteroidal anti-inflammatory drugs
- Avoid any physical therapy aimed at exercising the hand muscle-tendon units until after symptoms have disappeared

Other suggested actions include: keep wrists straight, take exercise breaks, alternate tasks, shift positions periodically, adjust chair height, work with feet flat on the floor, and be conscious of posture. Many of these actions suggest the need for ergonomics, the next topic.

OBJECTIVE

Explain the purpose of ergonomics.

Ergonomics

Ergonomics:
The study of human interaction with tasks, equipment, tools, and the physical environment.

A specific approach to dealing with health problems such as repetitive stress injuries and enhancing performance is ergonomics. **Ergonomics** is the study of human interaction with tasks, equipment, tools, and the physical environment. Through ergonomics, the goal is to fit the machine and work environment to the person, rather than require the person to make the adjustment. Ergonomics includes all attempts to structure work conditions so that they maximize energy conservation, promote good posture, and allow workers to function without pain or impairment. Failure to address ergonomics issues results in fatigue, poor performance, and repetitive stress injuries.

Congress and OSHA

Congress rescinded OSHA's controversial ergonomics standards in 2001 in accordance with the Congressional Review Act. In April 2002, OSHA responded to this act by releasing a public notice that it would develop new guidelines addressing ergonomics hazards. The ergonomics guidelines, however, will not be mandatory and cannot carry the force of law. The guidelines simply interpret agency policy at a given point in time.[28] Until ergonomics standards are set forth in legislation, it appears that OSHA will lack authority to enforce ergonomics standards at companies. This will suit some parties who favor volunteer enforcement of standards but will not satisfy others, including the AFL-CIO, which has pushed for aggressive regulations. On the other side, James W. Stanley, vice president of safety and health for AK Steel Corporation and former regional OSHA compliance officer, feels that no great problem exists. He notes that his firm, for example, has an OSHA-recordable rate of less than two musculoskeletal disorders (MSDs) for every 100 workers. "That's hardly an epidemic," he stated.[29] It seems apparent that there is a clear lack of consensus on the need for a new rule.

Meanwhile, OSHA continues to work closely with stakeholders to develop industry- and task-specific guidelines to protect workers from ergonomics-related injuries and illnesses.[30] OSHA recently announced plans to form a National Advisory Committee on Ergonomics. The 15-member committee is part of OSHA's strategy for reducing ergonomics-related injuries and illnesses in the workplace. The committee will be composed of people with experience or expertise with ergonomics issues.[31]

For many firms, a problem exists that needs to be fixed. The question is whether they need federal legislation or whether the private sector is up to the task. California has been a leader in ergonomics regulation and has a standard that became effective in 1999. If many other states follow this lead, some experts believe that the burden caused by uneven and inconsistent standards in the states will eventually lead to federal regulation.[32]

Ergonomics Payoff

It is clear that there is an economic payoff in using ergonomics. For example, when Compaq introduced its health and safety standards in the early 1990s, injury rates decreased 175 percent although its workforce tripled to 68,000. Firms like Allied Signal have discovered that an ergonomic working environment not only helps employees, but also makes good business sense. Reports show that the company saves about $2 million per year in worker compensation costs.[33] Other companies also discovered that improving the work environment boosts morale, lowers injury rates, and yields a positive return on investment (ROI). Employee input in the design and implementation of safety and health programs may well increase the chances for success of such programs.[34]

Another threat to the safety and security of people on the job is workplace violence. We discuss the various ramifications of this phenomenon in the next section.

OBJECTIVE

Explain the effects of workplace and domestic violence on businesses.

Workplace Violence

According to the U.S. Department of Justice nearly one million employees become victims of violent crime at work each year.[35] The Workplace Violence Research Institute places the number at two million and estimates that the cost of violent incidents exceeds $36 billion annually. Because workplace violence is a growing threat,

Workplace Violence Research Institute

noworkviolence.com

This Web site is the homepage for a company that designs and implements workplace violence prevention programs for private and public organizations.

some employers are seeking insurance coverage for the financial impact of workplace violence incidents, a threat previously viewed as a self-insured risk.[36] Another disturbing fact is that employers are increasingly being sued for negligent hiring as a result of violence at work.[37]

Homicide, according to the National Institute of Occupational Safety and Health (NIOSH) is the second-leading cause of death in the workplace. Murder is the number-one workplace killer of women and the third-leading cause of death for men, after motor vehicle accidents and machine-related fatalities. Firearms are involved in the majority of workplace homicides.[38] More than 700 workplace homicides occurred in 1998. Of the 428 workplace homicides in which the association between the victim and perpetrator could be determined, 67 percent were robbers, 15 percent were co-workers or former co-workers, 8 percent were customers or clients, 7 percent were acquaintances, and 4 percent were relatives.[39] Regardless of who commits the crime, consider the horror of random workplace violence:

> *Michael McDermott was a 42-year-old software programmer at Edgewater Technology in Wakefield, Massachusetts. He chose the day after Christmas 2000 for workforce catastrophe. After chatting with other employees until 11 a.m., he strolled through the high-tech firm's lobby with an AK-47 assault rifle, a shotgun, and a semiautomatic handgun. Bypassing the receptionist, he entered the Human Resources office, shot and killed three people; he then headed to accounting, where three employees had barricaded the door. Barging through, he shot and killed two accountants; the third escaped, hidden under her desk. What triggered McDermott's ire? The accounting department had garnished his wages to pay overdue taxes to the IRS.*[40]

Homicide, as terrible as it is, accounts for only a small percentage of the overall incidence of workplace violence. During the decade of the 1990s, yearly averages of workplace violence included 1.48 million simple assaults (verbal threats and arguments), 395,500 aggravated assaults, 50,000 sexual assaults, and 1,000 murders. In addition to the $36 billion annual costs of violence, there is no way to estimate the physical and psychological damage to other employees, who are only onlookers to the violent behavior.

A survey of 1,000 U.S. adults found that more than 25 percent of those polled believe their employers are not prepared to deal with workplace violence. Since one in ten employees has personally experienced violence, the issue facing most large employers is not *if* they will ever deal with an act of workplace violence, but *when*.[41]

While employers must take steps to reduce the potential for employee homicides, they must also take action against more pervasive problems that can inflict havoc day in and out. These include bullying, verbal threats, harassment, intimidation, pushing, shoving, slapping, kicking, and fistfights. The vast majority of these types of assaults and other forms of aggression do not show up in the statistics, as they go unreported.[42]

Vulnerable Employees

Employees at gas stations and liquor stores, taxi drivers, and police officers working night shifts face the greatest danger from violence. Ninety percent of the time, armed criminals threaten these workers, not disgruntled co-workers.[43] Taxi and delivery drivers are 60 times more likely than other workers to be murdered while on the job. NIOSH identified the following factors that put drivers at risk:

- working with the public
- working with cash

- working alone
- working at night
- working in high-crime areas[44]

While these factors increase risk, no workplace is immune from violence. Hospital managers overwhelmingly say the biggest threat that emergency room workers face is patient violence. According to John Gavras, president, Dallas-Ft.Worth Hospital Council, most hospitals now have security guards stationed in their emergency rooms, particularly at times such as Saturday nights, when violence seems to escalate.[45] According to the Bureau of Justice National Crime Victimization Survey, 69,500 nurses were assaulted at work from 1992 to 1998.[46]

Vulnerable Organizations

It is clear that certain businesses are more susceptible to workplace violence. The characteristics of a high-risk workplace, according to the National Safe Workplace Institute, include the following:

- Chronic labor/management disputes
- Frequent grievances filed by employees
- A large number of workers' compensation injury claims, especially for psychological injury
- Understaffing and excessive demands for overtime in an authoritarian management style[47]

There are numerous reasons for violent acts committed by employees or former employees. Among the most common are personality conflicts, marital or family problems, drug or alcohol abuse, and firings or layoffs.

Legal Consequences of Workplace Violence

In addition to the horror of workplace violence, there is also the ever-present threat of legal action. Civil lawsuits claiming *negligent hiring* or *negligent retention* account for more than half of the estimated $36 billion a year costs to businesses. Just having a standard workplace violence policy supports a firm's position should it wind up in court.[48] Other legal consequences of workplace violence include discrimination lawsuits, workers' compensation claims, third-party claims for damages, invasion of privacy actions, and OSHA violation charges.[49] Under OSHA's general duty clause, employers are required to "furnish, to each employee, employment and place of employment that is free from recognizable hazards that are causing, or likely to cause, death or serious harm to the employee."[50]

Individual and Organizational Characteristics to Monitor

Some firms that have had extensive experience with workplace violence are trying an alternative approach. Instead of trying to screen out violent people, they are attempting to detect employees who commit minor aggressive acts and exhibit certain behaviors. These individuals often go on to engage in more serious behaviors. Once identified, these people are required to meet with trained members of the human resources staff for counseling as long as needed. This approach may require more commitment on the part of the firm, but the alternative cost of violence may make this expenditure reasonable in the long run.

Robert Martin, vice president of Gavin de Becker Inc., a company involved with violence prevention, says, "In every case of workplace violence I've seen, there have always been pre-incident indicators." Although every case is different, Martin states that usually a series of exchanges or posturing takes place before the incident.[51] Some warning signs for employers are behaviors such as the following:

- Screaming
- Explosive outbursts over minor disagreements
- Making off-color remarks
- Crying
- Decreased energy or focus
- Deteriorating work performance and personal appearance
- Becoming reclusive

A study of 395 human resource managers and security managers conducted by the University of Southern California's Center for Crisis Management found a link between violence and an uncertain economy or a prolonged recession. Workplace violence was attributed to such organizational deficiencies as inadequate training programs to handle stress, substance abuse, insufficient background-screening checks of employees, poor communications, and general organizational instability.[52]

Preventive Actions

There is no way an employer can completely avoid risk when it comes to violence. Incidences of some unbalanced person coming in and shooting people happen randomly and organizations can do little to anticipate or prevent them. However, firms should consider the following actions both to minimize violent acts and to avoid lawsuits:

- Implement policies that ban weapons on company property, including parking lots
- Under suspicious circumstances, require employees to submit to searches for weapons or examinations to determine their mental fitness for work
- Have a policy stating that the organization will not tolerate any incidents of violence or even threats of violence
- Have a policy that encourages employees to report all suspicious or violent activity to management
- Develop relationships with mental health experts who will be available when emergencies arise
- Equip receptionists with panic buttons to enable them to alert security officers instantly
- Train managers and receptionists to recognize the warning signs of violence and techniques to diffuse violent situations

In spite of the human and financial costs of violence in the workplace, employers generally have not adequately trained supervisors in how to deal with potentially violent individuals.[53] This is unfortunate since research shows that providing workplace violence training to all employees, not just supervisors, may make a difference. For example, in a recent survey, 21.9 percent of firms that provide this training reduced employee-on-employee violence compared with 15.7 percent of firms that did not provide the training.[54]

Can the selection process predict applicants who will be prone to violence? The answer is "No." On the other hand, the profiles of individuals *not* prone to violence tend to have certain things in common. The most important markers for these people include:[55]

- No substance abuse (one of the highest correlating factors)
- Being outwardly focused; having outside interests and friendships rather than being mainly self-involved
- A good work history

In order to confirm these characteristics, the firm must conduct a thorough background investigation. To assist in devising plans for dealing with workplace violence, OSHA has prepared prevention guidelines. These are on the agency's Web site at http://osha.gov/SLTC/workplaceviolence/index.html.[56]

Domestic violence occurs away from the workplace. Nevertheless, this type of violence often spills into the business world and therefore becomes a workplace issue; it is discussed next.

Domestic Violence

Spillover from domestic violence is a threat to both women and their companies. A woman abused at home has a 70 percent chance of being harassed at work. The real workplace exposure begins when she finally leaves her abuser.[57] The Office of Criminal Justice calculates that three to four million women are battered each year. The U.S. Surgeon General's office reports that domestic violence is the most widespread cause of injury for women between 15 and 44 years of age. While women in traditional relationships are the most common victims by far, children and men are also affected. The most tragic aspects of domestic violence affect the home, but the workplace also suffers in terms of lost productivity, increased health-care costs, absenteeism, and sometimes even workplace violence. Studies show domestic violence costs employers $3 to $5 billion annually in higher turnover, lower productivity, and health and safety expenses.[58] Also, employees miss an estimated 175,000 days of work each year because of domestic violence, according to the Family Violence Prevention Fund, a national nonprofit group.[59]

According to the Department of Justice, the incidence of domestic violence decreased in recent years. There are several possible factors explaining this decline, including increased availability of legal services to women, improvement in women's economic status and educational attainment, and demographic trends. The population is aging, and older women are significantly less likely to be victims of domestic violence.[60]

While this trend provides a degree of optimism, it is obvious that this type of behavior remains at an unacceptable level. Business organizations have a huge stake in the problem of violence. The courts apparently agree as they have ruled that employers owe a duty of care for their employees, customers, and business associates to take reasonable steps to prevent violence on their premises. Although domestic violence clearly seems to be a workplace issue, not all agree. One poll of 100 senior executives by Roper ASW, a New York research firm, revealed that while 91 percent believe that domestic violence has an impact on the personal and work lives of their employees, only 12 percent feel that companies should address the problem.[61] There is obvious reluctance on the part of many executives to get involved in their employees' private lives.

One culprit, related to everything from violence to mental and physical health problems, is stress. We discuss this topic in the following section.

Describe the nature of stress and burnout.

Stress:
The body's nonspecific reaction to any demand made on it.

The Nature of Stress

Stress is the body's nonspecific reaction to any demand made on it. It affects people in different ways and is therefore a highly individual condition. Certain events may be quite stressful to one person but not to another. Moreover, the effect of stress is not

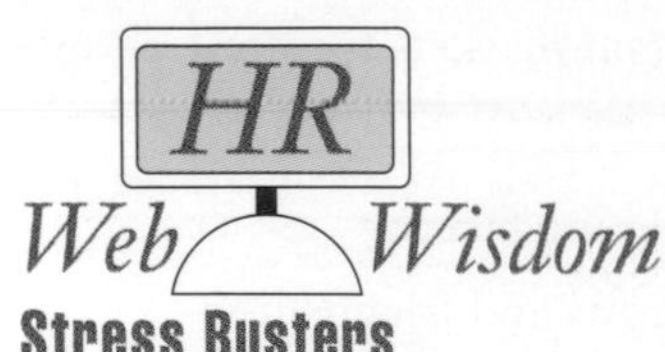

Stress Busters

www.stressrelease.com

This Web site offers thoughts for reducing work stress as well as stress-building concepts.

always negative. For example, mild stress actually improves productivity, and it can be helpful in developing creative ideas.

Stress in the workplace is nothing new. However, a number of studies have shown that in the twenty first century, it is skyrocketing. Several factors account for this rise including increased workloads, terrorism, corporate scandals, and a poor economy.[62] While much of the world has reduced the number of hours worked each year per person over the past decade, Americans have done just the opposite, adding 58 hours to their yearly total. The Japanese, by contrast, have cut more than 191 hours. Still, U.S. workers do not even take what few holidays they get, giving back an average of 1.8 days or almost $19.5 billion total, in unused vacation time to employers each year. If people work longer hours, they often do not have time to refresh.[63]

Potential Consequences of Stress

Although everyone lives under a certain amount of stress, if it is severe enough and persists long enough, it can be harmful. In fact, stress can be as disruptive to an individual as any accident. It can result in poor attendance, excessive use of alcohol or other drugs, poor job performance, or even overall poor health. There is increasing evidence indicating that severe, prolonged stress is related to the diseases that are the leading causes of death, including cardiovascular disease, depression, immune system disorders, alcoholism, and drug addiction; plus the everyday headaches, back spasms, overeating, and other annoying ailments the body has developed in response.[64] The American Institute of Stress estimates that stress and the problems it can cause cost American business more than $300 billion a year.[65] To further illustrate the problem, according to the American Institute on Stress, 78 percent of Americans describe their jobs as stressful. Seventy-five to 90 percent of visits to doctors are for stress-related ailments.[66] Stress tops the list of changeable health risks that contribute to health-care costs, ahead of other top risks including current and past tobacco use, obesity, lack of exercise, high blood-glucose levels, depression, and high blood pressure. According to one study, employees who report being under constant stress, with no coping mechanisms, are responsible for 7.9 percent of total health-care costs. Next on the list are former smokers (5.6 percent) and those considered obese (4.1 percent).[67]

Stressful Jobs

As mentioned, stress affects individuals differently but the type of work individuals perform also plays a role. The National Institute for Occupational Safety and Health has studied stress as it relates to work. This organization's research indicates that some jobs are generally perceived as being more stressful than other jobs. The 12 most stressful jobs are listed in Table 11-4. The common factor among these jobs is lack of employee control over work. Workers in such jobs may feel that they are trapped, treated more like machines than people. Workers who have more control over their jobs, such as college professors and master craftspersons, hold some of the less stressful jobs.

The fact that certain jobs are identified as more stressful than others has important managerial implications. Managers are responsible for recognizing significantly deviant behavior and referring employees to health professionals for diagnosis and treatment. Telling signs include irritability, forgetfulness, social isolation, and sudden changes in appearance such as untidy clothing and weight change. Under excessive stress, a person's dominant trait may become even more obvious. For example, if the individual is a private person, he or she withdraws from colleagues; if the person is upbeat, he or she becomes hyperactive.[68] People can generally handle stress successfully, but when they cannot, burnout may occur. This phenomenon is discussed next.

Table 11-4 Stressful Jobs

The 12 Jobs with the Most Stress

1. Laborer	7. Manager/administrator
2. Secretary	8. Waitress/waiter
3. Inspector	9. Machine operator
4. Clinical lab technician	10. Farm owner
5. Office manager	11. Miner
6. Supervisor	12. Painter

Other High-Stress Jobs (in Alphabetical Order)

Bank teller	Nurse's aide
Clergy member	Plumber
Computer programmer	Police officer
Dental assistant	Practical nurse
Electrician	Public relations worker
Firefighter	Railroad switchperson
Guard	Registered nurse
Hairdresser	Sales manager
Health aide	Sales representative
Health technician	Social worker
Machinist	Structural-metal worker
Meat cutter	Teacher's aide
Mechanic	Telephone operator
Musician	Warehouse worker

Source: From a ranking of 130 occupations by the federal government's National Institute for Occupational Safety and Health.

Burnout

Burnout:
An incapacitating condition in which individuals lose a sense of the basic purpose and fulfillment of their work.

Burnout, while rarely fatal, is an incapacitating condition in which individuals lose a sense of the basic purpose and fulfillment of their work. While some stress is healthy, when the ability to cope with it begins to fail, burnout may be on the horizon. People *burn out* when they lose interest in what they are doing, when their passion for their work leaves and they do not want to get out of bed in the morning. When stress relief tactics fail to work, that is the time to seek professional help.[69]

Burnout Costs

Burnout's price tag is high; it results in reduced productivity, higher turnover, and generally lousy performance.[70] People often become physically and psychologically weakened from trying to combat it. Although some employees try to hide their problems, shifts in their behavior may indicate dissatisfaction. They may start procrastinating or go to the opposite extreme of taking on too many assignments. They may lose things and become increasingly disorganized. Good-natured individuals may turn irritable. They may become cynical, disagreeable, pompous, or even paranoid.

Individuals Most Susceptible to Burnout

Burnout is often associated with a midlife or mid-career crisis, but it can happen at different times to different people. When this occurs, they may lose their motivation to perform. Burnout is the most common factor leading to the decision to "check out" temporarily.[71] Dr. Scott Stacy, clinical program director of the Professional Renewal Center, estimates that the average executive will come dangerously close to burning out two or three times in his career.

Individuals in the helping professions, such as teachers and counselors, seem to be susceptible to burnout because of their jobs, whereas others may be vulnerable because of their upbringing, expectations, or personalities. Burnout is frequently associated with people whose jobs require working closely with others under stressful and tension-filled conditions. However, any employee may experience burnout, and no one is exempt.

The dangerous part of burnout is that it is contagious. A highly cynical and pessimistic burnout victim can quickly transform an entire group into burnouts. Therefore, dealing with the problem quickly is very important. Once it has begun, it is difficult to stop. Ideally, burnout is dealt with before it occurs. To do this, managers must be aware of potential sources of stress. These sources exist both within and outside the organization.

OBJECTIVE

Explain sources of stress and means of coping with it.

Sources of Stress

Regardless of its origin, stress possesses devastating potential. While work-related factors are controllable to varying degrees, others may not be. Three broad areas from which stress may originate include the organization, personal factors, and the general environment. These factors are discussed next.

Organizational Factors

Many aspects associated with a person's employment can be potentially stressful. These include the firm's culture, the individual's job, and general working conditions.

Corporate Culture. Corporate culture has a lot to do with stress. The CEO's leadership style often sets the tone. An autocratic CEO who permits little input from subordinates may create a stressful environment. At the other extreme, a weak CEO may encourage subordinates to compete for power, resulting in internal conflicts. Policies that emanate from the top of the organization may also have a negative effect when it comes to stress. Policies and rules that discourage flexibility in the workplace may create situations that put employees in personal binds. For example, important personal business may be impossible to conduct because of an unyielding work schedule. Also, competition encouraged by the organization's reward system for promotion, pay increases, and status may add to the problem. Even in the healthiest corporate culture, stressful relationships among employees can occur.

The Job Itself. A number of factors related to the jobs people perform may produce excessive stress. As previously stated, some jobs are generally perceived as being more stressful than others due to the nature of the tasks involved and the degree of responsibility and control the job permits. Managerial work may itself be a source of stress. Responsibility for people, conducting performance appraisals, coordinating and communicating layoffs, and conducting outplacement counseling can create a great deal of stress for some people. Other sources of stress related to the job include role ambiguity, role conflict, workload variance, and working conditions.

Role ambiguity:
A condition that exists when employees do not understand the content of their job.

Role ambiguity exists when employees don't understand the content of their jobs. Employees may feel stress when they fail to perform certain duties as expected by their supervisor, or when they attempt to perform tasks that are a part of someone else's job. Role ambiguity is a condition that can easily lead to conflict with one's boss or co-workers and inevitably to stress.

Role conflict:
A condition that occurs when an individual is placed in the position of having to pursue opposing goals.

Role conflict exists when an individual is in the position of having to pursue opposing goals. For example, a manager may be under pressure to increase production while at the same time be responsible for decreasing the size of the workforce. Attaining both goals may be virtually impossible, and stress is likely to result.

Workload variance: Involves dealing with both job overload and job underload.

Job overload: A condition that exists when employees are given more work than they can reasonably handle.

Job underload: Occurs when employees are given menial, boring tasks to perform.

Workload variance involves dealing with both job overload and job underload. When employees have more work than they can reasonably handle, they become victims of **job overload**. A critical aspect of this problem is that the best performers in the firm are often the ones most affected. These individuals have proven that they can perform more, so they often receive more to do. At its extreme, work overload may result in burnout.

Job underload may occur when employees have menial, boring tasks to perform. Individuals who constantly seek challenge in their jobs may experience stress in this situation.

Working Conditions. Working conditions, including the physical characteristics of the workplace and the machines and tools used, can also create stress. Overcrowding, excessive noise, poor lighting, poorly maintained workstations, and faulty equipment can all adversely affect employee morale and increase stress. Working conditions that do not provide workplace flexibility, as discussed in the previous chapter, may also produce excessive stress.

Personal Factors

Stress factors outside the job and job environment also may affect job performance. Although these are often beyond the control of management, managers should recognize that they do exist and may have implications for job performance. Factors in this category include the family and financial problems.

The Family. Although a frequent source of happiness and security, the family can also be a significant stressor. Approximately one half of all marriages end in divorce, which in itself is generally quite stressful. When divorce leads to single parenthood, the difficulties may be compounded. Contrary to conventional wisdom, women feel no more anxiety on the job because they are mothers than do men because they are fathers. However, concern about their children can cause either parent to suffer stress-related health problems. When trouble exists both at home and at work, a double dose of stress exists. On the positive side, a healthy home life provides a protective buffer against work-related stressors such as an overbearing boss.

An increasingly common circumstance involving a change in traditional roles is the dual-career family, discussed in Chapter 3, in which both husband and wife have jobs and family responsibilities. What happens when one partner is completely content with a job, and the other is offered a desired promotion requiring relocation to a distant city? At best, these circumstances are beset with difficulties.

Financial Problems. Problems with finances may place an unbearable strain on the employee. For some, these problems are persistent and never quite resolved. Unpaid bills and bill collectors can create great tension and play a role in divorce or poor work performance. Financial problems are not limited to individuals who are low-wage earners; people at any economic level can wind up with heavy debt due to many factors, including poor personal financial management.

The General Environment

Stress is a part of everyone's everyday life; its potential lurks not only in the workplace and the home, but also in our general environment. Economic uncertainties, war or the threat of war, the threat of terrorism, long commutes in rush hour traffic, unrelenting rain, oppressive heat or chilling cold all can create stress. Excessive noise can also create extreme stress in some people. While stress is seemingly everywhere, there are ways to deal with it. Some suggestions that may be helpful in dealing with stress are discussed in the following sections.

Managing Stress

Only dead people are totally without stress and experts emphasize that some stress is healthy. In fact, moderate stress is the key to survival. Yet, excessive, prolonged stress must be dealt with, and both the individual and organizations have a responsibility to take appropriate measures.

Individual Coping Approaches

There are a number of ways that individuals may control excessive stress. The Canadian Mental Health Association recommends the following approaches:

- Recognize your symptoms of stress
- Look at your lifestyle and see what can be changed
- Use relaxation techniques
- Exercise
- Manage your time well
- Aim for a diet with a balance of fruits, vegetables, whole grains, and foods high in protein, but low in fat
- Get enough rest and sleep
- Talk with others: friends, professional counselors, and support groups
- Help others
- Engage in volunteer work
- Get away for a while
- Ease up on criticism of others
- Don't be too competitive
- Make the first move to be friendly
- Have some fun[72]

Employees can also learn to cope with stressful situations more effectively by following these suggestions:[73]

- Assess your priorities; delay nonessential tasks and focus on those more urgent
- When possible, delegate tasks to others
- Recognize those things over which you have control and those you do not
- Seek help; it is often available for the asking
- Talk with a mentor; often a fresh perspective is needed
- Resolve conflicts; don't let them fester
- Reward your own achievements by, for example, taking time out for a walk or lunch with colleagues
- Strive for work/life balance. All work and no play is not a prescription for either happiness or health
- Individuals can utilize several specific techniques to deal with stress. These methods include hypnosis, biofeedback, and transcendental meditation

Hypnosis:
An altered state of consciousness that is artificially induced and characterized by increased receptiveness to suggestions.

Biofeedback:
A method of learning to control involuntary bodily processes, such as blood pressure or heart rate.

Transcendental meditation (TM):
A stress-reduction technique in which an individual, comfortably seated, mentally repeats a secret word or phrase (mantra) provided by a trained instructor.

Hypnosis. **Hypnosis** is an altered state of consciousness artificially induced and characterized by increased receptiveness to suggestions. Therefore, a person in a hypnotic state may respond to the hypnotist's suggestion to relax. Hypnosis can help many people cope with stress. The serenity achieved through dissipation of anxieties and fears can restore an individual's confidence. A principal benefit of hypnotherapy is that peace of mind continues after the person awakens from a hypnotic state. This tranquility continues to grow, especially when the person has been trained in self-hypnosis.

Biofeedback. **Biofeedback** is a method used to control involuntary bodily processes, such as blood pressure or heart rate. For example, using equipment to provide a visual display of blood pressure, individuals may learn to lower their systolic blood pressure levels.

Transcendental Meditation. **Transcendental meditation (TM)** is a stress-reduction technique in which an individual, comfortably seated, repeats silently a secret word or phrase (mantra) provided by a trained instructor. Repeating the mantra helps prevent distracting thoughts. Transcendental meditation has successfully produced physiologic changes such as decreased oxygen consumption, decreased carbon dioxide elimination, and a decreased breathing rate. This technique results in a decreased metabolic rate and a restful state.

Organizational Coping Approaches

A number of programs and techniques may effectively prevent or relieve excessive stress. General organizational programs, while not specifically designed to cope with stress, may nevertheless play a role. Table 11-5 lists the programs and techniques discussed in this book and the chapter in which each is located. Their effective implementation will achieve the following results:

- A corporate culture emerges that holds anxiety and tension to an acceptable level.

Table 11-5 Organizational Programs and Techniques Helpful in Coping With Stress

General Organizational Programs	Addressed in Chapter
Corporate Culture (effective communication, motivation, and leadership styles)	2
Job Analysis	4
Training and Development	7
Organization Development	7
Career Planning and Development	7
Performance Appraisal	8
Compensation and Benefits	9, 10
Specific Techniques	
Hypnosis	11
Transcendental Meditation	11
Biofeedback	11
Specific Organizational Programs	
Wellness Programs	11
Physical Fitness	11
Alcohol and Drug Abuse	11
Employee Assistance Programs	11

- When firms seek and value employee inputs, employees have greater control over their work and communication is improved.
- Defined roles — insofar as today's environment permits — provides security yet gives encouragement to risk takers and to those who want to assume greater responsibility.
- Individuals receive the training and development they need for performing current and future tasks. Both personal and organizational goals receive attention.
- Individuals are trained to work as effective team members and to develop an awareness of how they and their work relate to others.
- Employees participate in making decisions that affect them. They know what is going on in the firm, what their particular roles are, and how well they are performing their jobs.
- Employees' financial and nonfinancial needs are met through an equitable reward system.

Programs specifically designed to deal with stress and related problems include wellness, physical fitness, substance abuse, and employee assistance programs. These are addressed in the following sections.

12 OBJECTIVE

Describe the purposes of wellness programs.

Wellness Programs

The traditional view that health is dependent on medical care and is simply the absence of disease is changing. Today, it is clear that optimal well-being is often achieved through environmental safety, organizational changes, and healthy lifestyles. Infectious diseases, over which a person has little control, are not the problem they once were. For example, from 1900 to 1970, the death rate from major infectious diseases dropped dramatically. However, the death rate from major chronic diseases, such as heart disease, cancer, and stroke, has significantly increased. Today, heart disease and stroke are the top two killers worldwide. Chronic obstructive pulmonary disease and lung cancer are also growing threats to life. Healthy lifestyle measures such as not smoking, eating healthy foods, and exercising more may help prevent these diseases.[74]

Needs Assessment

Firms should conduct a needs assessment before implementing a wellness program in order to address appropriate employee health needs. After outcome goals are established, these data are needed for each employee:

- Medical records such as blood pressure checks, height-to-weight ratios, and cholesterol levels
- Absenteeism rates
- Health risk appraisals, including employee health habits and family histories

In addition, an assessment of the facility should be made, focusing on the health and safety of the work environment. To protect employee privacy, the company should analyze composite data only. And, while these data will indicate possible areas of health needs, it is also important to measure employee interests. This information can be obtained using surveys, focus groups, e-mails, or meetings.[75]

Lifestyle Changes and Wellness

Chronic lifestyle diseases are much more prevalent today than ever before. The good news is that people have a great deal of control over many of them. These are diseases related to smoking, excessive stress, lack of exercise, obesity, and alcohol and drug abuse. Increased recognition of this has prompted employers to become actively involved with their employees' health and establish wellness programs. A 2003 benefits survey conducted by SHRM/SHRM Foundation showed that 57 percent of responding firms have wellness programs.[76] Physical fitness continues to be an important component of most major programs. However, there has been a shift toward a more holistic approach to improving health. Wellness programs often expand their focus to include other health issues such as diet, stress, substance abuse, employee assistance programs, and smoking cessation.

Trends & Innovations

Applied Wellness at Applied Materials

In 1988, Applied Materials, the largest supplier of products and services to the semiconductor industry, formed an umbrella organization called Applied Wellness.[77] This unit had a mission to enhance employee and company health, well-being, and productivity to support Applied Materials' worldwide profitability and competitive advantage.

A health appraisal is at the heart of the Applied Wellness program. This consists of periodic on site screenings of an employee's cholesterol level, body composition, blood pressure, and glucose level. Employees are strongly encouraged to complete the health appraisal, including a computerized, confidential health assessment, before utilizing the firm's wellness offerings.

In its Santa Clara headquarters and in the Austin manufacturing plant, the company offers convenient fitness centers that employees can access around the clock. In other locations, fitness services include anything from on-site wellness facilities and gym subsidies to subsidized home fitness equipment and recreational leagues.

Education is another key element in the program. Employees interested in nutrition and weight control have the option of lunchtime classes, weight-control program subsidies, and healthy selections in the cafeteria. Those struggling to control their stress levels can take skill-development classes, contact the employee assistance program, or receive an on-site massage. Myriad other programs are available for special populations, including prenatal education programs, parenting seminars, shift-work education classes, and smoking-cessation programs.

The cost of these programs is either free or a small fee to employees. Applied Materials' expense, however, is more than most smaller firms could dream of spending. But, altruism isn't the only motivation for providing such elaborate programs. Applied Materials is in an extremely competitive and stressful environment; employees may work 10-hour-plus days. All employees must be focused on employee productivity and Applied Wellness is alert toward that end. David Hunnicutt, president, Wellness Councils of America, stated, "the company [Applied Materials] is leveraging the latest health and productivity approaches by attempting to link health and well-being with job design and job function."

Union Pacific Railroad's Health Track targets 10 risk factors: asthma, blood pressure, cholesterol, depression, diabetes, fatigue, inactivity, excess weight, smoking, and stress. As to whether Health Track works, consider these data: UP calculated from a pilot program that, overall, every dollar put into Health Track would yield $3.24. Especially noteworthy were blood pressure interventions yielding benefits worth $4.29 and cholesterol interventions returning $5.25 for every dollar invested.[78]

As you just read, wellness programs often include physical fitness as a key component. Since they also appear frequently in organizations with a somewhat different scope, we discuss them in a separate section.

13 OBJECTIVE

Describe the importance of physical fitness programs and substance abuse programs.

Physical Fitness Programs

According to an SHRM/SHRM Foundation study, 31 percent of responding firms have either fitness centers or provide subsidies for fitness center memberships.[79] In addition, thousands of U.S. business firms have exercise programs designed to help keep their workers physically fit. To understand the interest in such programs, consider the results of physical inactivity. They can include obesity, hypertension, heart disease, diabetes, anxiety, depression, and certain types of cancer. It is estimated that physical inactivity costs employers between $200 and $400 per employee per year in health-care costs.[80]

From management's viewpoint, this effort makes a lot of sense. Loss of productivity resulting from coronary heart disease alone costs U.S. businesses billions of dollars annually. Company-sponsored fitness programs often reduce absenteeism, accidents, and sick pay. There is increasing evidence that if employees stick to company fitness programs, they will experience better health, and the firm will have lower costs. A study at Steelcase, an office equipment manufacturer, found that participants in a corporate fitness program had 55 percent lower medical claims costs over a six-year period than did nonparticipants.[81]

Cardiovascular Training Plus Diet

Kenneth Cooper, "Father of Aerobics" and director of the Cooper Aerobics Center in Dallas, has advice for those with or without access to fitness centers. To begin, he feels that moderate exercise is king. "If you're running more than 15 miles a week," he says, "you're doing it for a reason other than fitness." The basic recommendation is 30 minutes of exercise four to five days a week. Studies show that walking two miles in 30 minutes, three times weekly, has the potential of reducing deaths from coronaries or stroke by 58 percent. His studies also show that cardiovascular training is not enough. He now advocates a heart-healthy diet and vitamin supplements like antioxidants. He feels that eliminating tobacco products and habit-forming drugs, controlling alcohol, keeping stress levels down, and getting periodic health exams will round out everyone's fitness picture. For more information about Dr. Cooper's program, check out his website at www.cooperaerobics.com.[82]

A Stretching Program

Lincoln Plating Company, a large, Nebraska-based metal finishing company, implemented a mandatory stretching program before each of the firm's three shifts. For about 15 minutes, employees focus successively on the neck, shoulders, elbows, wrists, arms, hands, fingers, waist, and legs. The company developed a poster that illustrates proper technique for each move and line coordinators lead the exercise, which the company nurse monitors. Without question, the program has been cost-effective. Over a period of five years, Lincoln has saved $800,000; $600,000 from workers' compensation and $200,000 from associated medical claims.[83]

As previously suggested, health depends largely on the lifestyle choices made. Employees will have to do their part if they want to share in the better days ahead. That means getting the best medical care available, but it also requires taking care of yourself by avoiding tobacco and excessive alcohol, eating a good diet, exercising regularly, controlling weight, and managing stress. The formula is simple, but new medical research shows how effective it can be.[84]

Substance Abuse Programs

Substance abuse has increased considerably since the disastrous events of September 2001. According to a study by the National Center of Addiction and Substance Abuse at Columbia University, the emotional stress caused by the terrorist attacks, combined with the threat of bioterrorism, have given rise to greater numbers of Americans seeking treatment for drug and alcohol abuse. The study reported that admissions for treatment increased 10 to 12 percent nationwide.[85] Government studies reveal that 70 percent of illicit drug users aged 18 to 49 work full-time. In addition, the studies show that more than 60 percent of adults know people who have gone to work under the influence of drugs or alcohol. Drug-using employees are 3.5 times more likely to be involved in a workplace accident and five times more likely to file a workers' compensation claim.[86]

Alcohol Abuse

Alcoholism:
A medical disease characterized by uncontrolled and compulsive drinking that interferes with normal living patterns.

Alcoholism is a medical disease characterized by uncontrolled and compulsive drinking that interferes with normal living patterns. Stress plays an important role in a person becoming an alcoholic. However, alcoholism tends to run in families in which a chemical imbalance in the brain's neurotransmitters is a hereditary trait. Sons of alcoholics are four times more likely to become alcoholics themselves, even if they are raised in foster homes by nonalcoholic parents.[87] It is a significant problem that affects people at every level of society, and it can both result from and cause excessive stress. As a person starts to drink excessively, the drinking itself produces greater stress. A vicious cycle is created as this increased stress is dealt with by more drinking. Early signs of alcohol abuse are especially difficult to identify. Often the symptoms are nothing more than an increasing number of absences from work. Although our society attaches a stigma to alcoholism, in 1956, the American Medical Association described it as a treatable disease.

Use of Illicit Drugs

Drug users are increasingly gravitating to the workplace, which is an ideal place to sell drugs. Since 95 percent of *Fortune* 500 companies conduct pre-employment drug screening, 60 percent of employed drug users work for smaller businesses, many of which do not use drug testing. Many young drug users, whose lifestyle includes an unprecedented level of comfort with drug use, will be moving into the workforce, adding a new dimension to the problem.[88]

In certain industries, such as transportation, drug use on the job is especially hazardous and potentially devastating to the firm. Think of the damage a 40-ton truck could do careening out of control. Under ideal conditions, a fully loaded truck in daylight on a dry road can't stop in less than 300 feet, or the length of a football field.

All illegal drugs have some adverse effects. Although some claim that marijuana is harmless, Robert Block, a professor at the University of Iowa, says that if people use marijuana regularly, the drug can damage and destroy cells in the brain. People may have difficulty learning things. Pot also contains cancer-causing chemicals and when a smoker inhales marijuana, it can lead to lung cancer. But, lung cancer is not the only danger. Researchers at UCLA reported that smoking marijuana may increase the risk of developing head and neck cancers. Many people think marijuana is harmless, but it is not.[89]

Misuse of Prescription Drugs

Prescription drugs can also be as addictive, impairing, and destructive as common street drugs. According to drug enforcement agencies, at least 25 to 30 percent of drug abuse in the workplace involves prescription drugs. And, standard drug screens do not always detect these drugs. Currently, Vicodin, a painkiller, is the drug of choice, but other abused drugs include Demerol, Darvon, Tylenol with codeine, anti-anxiety drugs such as Xanax and Valium, and stimulants such as Ritalin.[90]

Chemically dependent employees exhibit behaviors that distinguish them from drug-free workers. In one study, employees who had a positive drug test but were hired anyway missed 50 percent more time from work than other employees. They also had a 47 percent higher chance of being fired. According to the National Institute on Drug Abuse (NIDA), one Utah power company found that drug-positive employees were five times more likely than other employees to cause an on-the-job accident. Substance abuse involving either alcohol or drugs increases employee theft, lowers morale, and reduces productivity.[91]

The National Council on Alcoholism and Drug Dependence (NCADD) reports that 40 percent of workplace fatalities and 47 percent of workplace injuries are related to alcohol consumption. Further, the council reports that about half of those who test positive for drugs in the workplace report using drugs on a daily basis. Absenteeism among illegal drug users is up to 16 times greater than among other workers, and illegal drug users use three times as many sick day benefits as other workers.[92]

Drug-Free Legislation and Workplace Programs

The Drug-Free Workplace Act of 1988 requires firms with large government contracts or grants to make a good faith effort to maintain a *drug-free workplace*. Because substance abuse is so expensive, all firms should have the same objective. Drug testing as a component in an organization's selection process is one means of achieving this goal. However, since a large percentage of substance abusers are employed, this is obviously not the solution to the problem. For one thing, managers must learn to recognize impaired or intoxicated employees and those who may be addicted. Table 11-6 lists signs that *suggest* an employee may be a substance abuser. Remember that none of the signs alone proves impairment. Also, it is necessary to observe behavior over a long period of time.

Many firms have tackled the drug abuse problem head-on by establishing a drug-free workplace program. Such an approach might include the following:[93]

- A clear, consistent zero tolerance policy
- Education and training for workers and supervisors
- A drug-testing program

Table 11-6 Signs of Possible Substance Abuse

- Excessive absenteeism
- Radical mood swings
- Decline in personal appearance
- Smell of alcohol or other physical evidence of substance abuse
- Accident proneness and multiple workers' compensation claims
- Lack of coordination
- Psychomotor agitation or retardation. Alcohol, marijuana, and opioids can all cause fatigue. Cocaine, amphetamines, and hallucinogens can cause anxiety.
- Thought disturbances. Cocaine, alcohol, PCP, amphetamines, and inhalants often cause grandiosity or a subject sense of profound thought.
- Other indicators. Cocaine, PCP, and inhalants can all cause aggressive or violent behavior. Alcohol and other sedatives reduce inhibition. Marijuana increases appetite, whereas stimulants decrease it. Both types of drugs cause excessive thirst.

Sources: "Are You Prepared?" *Safety Management* (January 2003): 7; Deanna Kelemen, "How to Recognize Substance Abuse in the Workplace," *Supervision* 56 (September 1995): 4.

- An employee assistance program to help employees with substance abuse problems

At Texas Instruments, the policy is simple and straightforward: "There will be no use of any illegal drug. There will be no illicit use of a legal drug." The difficult part is not formulating the policy, but rather implementing it. Also, remember that the Americans with Disabilities Act protects an employee in a substance abuse rehabilitation program.

14 OBJECTIVE

Describe employee assistance programs.

Employee assistance program (EAP):
A comprehensive approach that many organizations have taken to deal with burnout, alcohol and drug abuse, and other emotional disturbances.

Employee Assistance Programs (EAPs)

An **employee assistance program (EAP)** is a comprehensive approach that many organizations have taken to deal with numerous problem areas such as burnout, alcohol and drug abuse, and other emotional disturbances. Whether managed in-house or outsourced, EAPs have traditionally focused first on mental health, including substance abuse counseling. Many have expanded to include financial and legal advice, referrals for day care and eldercare and a host of other services including assistance with marital or family difficulties, job performance problems, stress, and grief. Most recently, an Albany, New York–based book publisher applied the concept of an outsourced EAP to a different sort of problem, the physical fitness of its workforce.[94]

In an EAP, most or all of the costs (up to a predetermined amount) are borne by the employer. The EAP concept includes a response to personal psychological problems that interfere with both an employee's well-being and overall productivity. The purpose of assistance programs is to provide emotionally troubled employees with the same consideration and assistance given employees with physical illnesses. Just having an EAP sends a message that the employer cares and this can provide considerable encouragement for employees.[95]

Online EAPs

Since 1999, Florida Power and Light employees have used their computers as outlets for handling emotional turmoil. The firm pays for its 10,600 employees to log on to the Web site MasteringStress.com to use software dealing with bouts of depression, anger, and other emotional turmoil.[96] According to one EAP study, which used Ceridian's LifeWorks Online, 92 percent of the participants found the online system helpful or extremely helpful. Forty-eight percent of the participants chose to go online instead of calling a service or setting up a face-to-face appointment because they could obtain immediate access to help and information. Another 10 percent said their problem was embarrassing and the online service offered anonymity.[97]

Growth of EAPs and the Benefits

The Drug Free Workplace Act of 1988 requires federal employees and employees of firms under government contract to have access to employee assistance program services. As you would imagine, EAPs grew rapidly in number following that act. However, many firms have determined that there are other advantages to be derived from EAPs and have implemented them voluntarily. In 1958, fewer than 50 American firms offered employee assistance counseling. In 2003, a study by SHRM/SHRM Foundation indicated that 64 percent of responding firms had an employee assistance program.[98] Returns on investment in EAPs will vary, but one executive estimates that a mature, well-run program will return a minimum of three dollars for every dollar spent on it. This level of return will not happen, however, unless the employer is committed to promoting the program, educating employees and managers about its purpose, and eliminating any stigma for seeking help. Advantages claimed for EAPs include lower absenteeism, decreases in workers' compensation claims, and fewer accidents.

Some research suggests that about 30 percent of all medical conditions are due to underlying mental or nervous causes, such as stress or depression. When organizations provide EAP services, they will, on average, see about a 10 percent reduction in medical claims, a 15 percent reduction in workers' compensation claims, and an 8 to 10 percent reduction in turnover.[99]

Encouraging Employee Participation

A primary concern is getting employees to use the program. Some employees perceive that there is a stigma attached to *needing help*. Supervisors must receive training designed to provide specialized interpersonal skills for recognizing troubled employees and encouraging them to utilize the firm's employee assistance program. Addicted employees are often experts at denial and deception, and they can fool even experienced counselors.

Two additional health issues of concern to management include smoking and AIDS. These topics are featured in the next sections of this chapter.

OBJECTIVE

Describe the impact of smoking in the workplace.

Smoking in the Workplace

An important health issue facing employers today is environmental tobacco smoke (ETS). Although some smokers and advocates remain adamant that passive cigarette smoke is not harmful, the preponderance of evidence says otherwise.

Effects of Secondhand Smoke

A research committee of the World Health Organization (WHO) reported that secondhand smoke can increase the risk of cancer by as much as 20 to 30 percent. Passive smokers are breathing in the same carcinogens as active smokers and this affects their health. Tobacco is already associated with 90 percent of the lung cancer deaths every year and both active and passive smokers are at increased risk for stomach, liver, cervix, and kidney cancer as well.[100] The Environmental Protection Agency has also determined that ETS is a class A carcinogen, a category reserved for the most dangerous cancer-causing agents in humans. Secondhand smoke kills an estimated 35,000 to 65,000 nonsmoking Americans each year, mostly by causing heart attacks and lung cancer. In fetuses, it increases the risk of low birth weight, and it is responsible for up to 300,000 cases of childhood bronchitis and pneumonia, according to a new government report. It is also linked to childhood asthma and sudden infant death syndrome.[101] In fact, smoking is the leading cause of preventable death, resulting in more deaths than the combined toll from AIDS, cocaine, heroin, alcohol, fire, automobile accidents, homicide, and suicide. These data will likely strengthen efforts to ban smoking. OSHA has proposed banning smoking or limiting it to separately ventilated areas in six million U.S. businesses. Many business and public buildings nationwide are already smoke-free.

Benefits of Smoke-Free Areas

Scientists at the University of California in San Francisco studied 28 offices in the United States, Australia, Canada, and Germany that were either smoke-free, or where smoking was tightly restricted. The study found that nonsmoking workplaces not only protected nonsmokers from passive smoke, but encouraged smokers to quit or reduce their consumption, reducing the total cigarette consumption by 29 percent per employee.[102]

Numerous studies have concluded that workplace smoking is not only hazardous to employees' health, but is also detrimental to the firm's financial health. Employers have begun to develop ways to eliminate smoking in the workplace because the costs associated with tobacco use are staggering. According to public health reports, expenditures in the United States directly related to smoking total $72 billion per year. Costs not related to health but caused by tobacco use include property losses from fires caused by cigarettes or cigars, work productivity losses, and the costs of extra cleaning and maintenance required because of tobacco smoke, smokeless tobacco, and tobacco-related litter. These costs amount to over $44 billion annually.[103] A Gallup survey indicated that a vast majority of Americans, 94 percent, favored some type of restriction on workplace smoking.[104]

Smoking cessation programs are usually cost-effective. That is, they achieve greater-than-average gains in health for each dollar invested. Five hundred thousand dollars spent on smoking-cessation counseling is likely to save more years of life for many people than $500,000 spent on open-heart surgery. It is, therefore, more cost-effective on a per-dollar basis.[105]

Regardless of the twist a firm's smoking policy takes, the company will have to maintain fresh indoor air for its employees. The alternative will be a backlash from nonsmokers and lawsuits from survivors of those who may one day die from secondhand smoke.

16 OBJECTIVE

Explain the possible impact of AIDS in the workplace.

AIDS in the Workplace

AIDS (acquired immune deficiency syndrome): A disease that undermines the body's immune system, leaving the person susceptible to a wide range of fatal diseases.

AIDS (Acquired immune deficiency syndrome) is a disease that undermines the body's immune system, leaving the person susceptible to a wide range of fatal diseases. It is caused by the human immunodeficiency virus (HIV). Over 3 million people in the world died from AIDS in 2002. Currently 42 million people world-wide live with the disease. If AIDS grows at its current pace without a vaccine, scientists predict that nearly 70 million people will die by 2020.[106]

HIV is spread from person to person through direct contamination of the bloodstream with body fluids containing the virus. Such fluids include blood, semen, vaginal fluid, and breast milk. The virus is usually transmitted through sexual intercourse and the sharing of contaminated intravenous needles. Infected women can pass HIV to their babies during pregnancy or during nursing. HIV cannot penetrate intact bodily surfaces, such as skin, and quickly perishes outside the human body. Therefore, casual physical contact or sneezing does not spread the virus. It has been detected in tears and saliva, but it exists there in such low concentrations that transmission from these body fluids is extremely rare.[107]

AIDS is definitely a workplace issue and one that impacts productivity. The majority of large U.S. firms already employ a substantial number of people who have AIDS or are infected with HIV. It was estimated that by the end of the twentieth century, AIDS had cost American business about $55 billion in lost productivity, higher health and disability insurance premiums, and additional expenditures for hiring and training new employees.[108]

Employees fearful of associating with those infected with the virus create an atmosphere not conducive to efficiency. A challenge to management is to educate all employees about the disease, and how to deal with it, and to teach that it is not transmitted through casual contact. Outside of the health-care arena, workplace exposure to blood is rare. Therefore, there is no rational reason for employees to fear working with someone who has AIDS or has been exposed to the virus. Unfortunately, the vast majority of employers have not provided workplace AIDS education for their employees, and few companies have AIDS policies, according to the Center for Disease Control.

Management cannot automatically assume that the infected individual will have anything other than a normal life span in the workplace. This situation is different from the assumption of only a few years ago, when an individual with AIDS was presumed to have a short work life. In 1995, a new class of drugs was introduced which provided more power to combat HIV. Called protease inhibitors (PIs), these drugs stop the action of an enzyme needed by the virus. When a PI is used in combination with other drugs, the combination effectively halts production of the virus in the body. While not a cure, the new drug therapy has been effective in allowing infected individuals to live longer and better manage their infections.[109]

For the infected employee, the Americans with Disabilities Act requires that reasonable accommodations be made. They may include, for example, equipment changes, workstation modifications, adjustments to work schedules, or assistance in accessing the facility.

A Global Perspective

The Stress of an International Assignment

International assignments can be an overwhelming source of stress for business travelers and their families. As a means of reducing stress, companies are offering online services in the areas of career services, cross-cultural training, and employee assistance programs (EAPs). Both long- and short-term assignments bring with them challenges that are associated with working away from the home office. Placing a worker in an environment of working and living within a foreign culture can create stress and impact productivity.[110]

When problems arise, expatriates may be reluctant or unable to cross the time zones to seek help from the corporate office. They may feel that it is too complex a process and that asking questions may reflect poorly on their ability to do the job. Or support services can be hard to access. Through the use of online services, businesses can offer troubled expatriates assistance 24 hours a day, seven days a week. Technology is a time-saving and cost-effective solution for the stress experienced by employees on assignment or doing business travel.[111]

According to a recent survey, 68 percent of companies do not guarantee expatriates a job upon their return. As a result, respondents ranked career management as being one of the most critical and stressful challenges for international assignees. Therefore, technology should be used to provide ongoing contact and support. Outsourced online career services could give expatriates and their spouses the opportunity to upgrade skills. Mentoring programs might be established prior to departure so that the expatriate feels supported by the home office.[112]

Cross-cultural training is needed to facilitate a successful adaptation process, including such things as ethics, etiquette, and conflict resolution. The inability to adapt is one of the most common factors in assignment failure. So while cross-cultural training should occur prior to the business assignment, the assignee needs to have access to cross-cultural training material on a just-in-time basis before entering potentially high-stress situations. For example, an American might have a question on the proper etiquette before a negotiation or attending dinner with a client. Family concerns rank as the most common factors in assignment failure. The accompanying spouse's inability to find adequate employment, the struggles with culture and language barriers that affect the whole family, and child-care and eldercare issues for those on the assignment are immense sources of stress. An international employee assistance program can provide access to counseling and referrals, but EAP and work life resources that are available online around the clock can provide rapid access to considerable information that allow a person to de-stress. An online EAP and work life program can offer timely, self-serve solutions to many of the troubles that plague the business traveler. Programs such as these allow the employee to be proactive so that stress and its impact can be minimized and even avoided, and the employee's time can be spent more productively.[113]

Summary

1. Describe some safety and security strategies for a post–September 11 world.

The United States and the world have changed a great deal since September 11, 2001. Safety and security in the workplace have perhaps changed the most. With increased awareness of terrorism and the creation of the U.S. Department of Homeland Security, everyone hopes that emergency procedures will never be needed. However, it is obviously necessary for organizations to be prepared in order to assure a safe and secure workplace.

2. Describe the nature and role of safety and health.

Safety involves protecting employees from injuries due to work-related accidents. Health refers to the employees' freedom from physical or emotional illness.

3. Explain the role of the Occupational Safety and Health Act.

The role of this act is to assure a safe and healthful workplace for every American worker.

4. Describe OSHA's changing role.

Since its inception, OSHA has revised its mission. The current thrust is to give employers a choice between partnership and traditional enforcement, to inject common sense into regulation and enforcement, and to eliminate red tape. The overall purpose, of course, is to reduce injuries, illnesses, and fatality rates.

5. Describe the economic impact of safety and explain the focus of safety programs in business operations.

Job-related deaths and injuries affect everyone, directly or indirectly. Safety programs may be designed to accomplish their purposes in two primary ways. The first approach is to create a psychological environment and attitudes that promote safety. The second approach to safety program design is to develop and maintain a safe physical working environment.

6. Explain the problem of identity theft.

Identity theft is one of the nation's fastest-growing white-collar crimes.

7. Describe the consequences of repetitive stress injuries.

The U.S. Bureau of Labor Statistics (BLS) reports that repetitive stress injuries account for 25 percent of cases involving days away from work and that disorders associated with repeated trauma account for nearly 60 percent of all work-related illness.

8. Explain the purpose of ergonomics.

Ergonomics is the study of human interaction with tasks, equipment, tools, and the physical environment. Through ergonomics, the goal is to fit the machine and work environment to the person, rather than require the person to make the adjustment.

9. Explain the effect of workplace and domestic violence on businesses.

The fastest-growing form of homicide is murder in the workplace. Homicide is the leading cause of on-the-job death for women and the number-two cause of death for men. Spillover from domestic violence is an unexpected threat to both women and their companies.

10. Describe the nature of stress and burnout.

Stress is the body's nonspecific reaction to any demand made on it. Burnout, while rarely fatal, is an incapacitating condition where individuals lose a sense of the basic purpose and fulfillment of their work.

11. Explain sources of stress and means of coping with stress.

Three general areas from which stress may emanate include the organization (including the firm's culture), the jobs people perform, and working conditions. Personal factors focus on the family and financial problems. Finally, the general environment also contains elements that may produce stress. Stress may be coped with through individual or organizational means.

12. Describe the purposes of wellness programs.

The traditional view is changing. No longer is health considered to be dependent on medical care and simply the absence of disease. Today, the prevailing opinion is that optimal health can generally be achieved through environmental safety, organizational changes, and changed lifestyles.

13. Describe the importance of physical fitness programs and substance abuse programs.

Many U.S. business firms have exercise programs designed to help keep their workers physically fit. These programs often reduce absenteeism, accidents, and sick pay. Substance abuse has increased considerably since the disastrous events of September 2001. Drug-using employees are 3.5 times more likely to be involved in a workplace accident and five times more likely to file a workers' compensation claim.

14. Describe employee assistance programs.

An employee assistance program (EAP) is a comprehensive approach that many organizations develop to deal with marital or family problems; job performance problems; stress, emotional, or mental health issues; financial troubles; alcohol and drug abuse; and grief.

15. Describe the impact of smoking in the workplace.

Workplace smoking is not only hazardous to employees' health, but is also detrimental to the firm's financial health.

16. Explain the possible impact of AIDS in the workplace.

AIDS is a disease that undermines the body's immune system, leaving the person susceptible to a wide range of fatal diseases.

Key Terms

- **Safety, 360**
- **Health, 360**
- **Job hazard analysis (JHA), 365**
- **Carpal tunnel syndrome (CTS), 367**
- **Ergonomics, 368**
- **Stress, 373**
- **Burnout, 375**
- **Role ambiguity, 376**
- **Role conflict, 376**
- **Workload variance, 377**
- **Job overload, 377**
- **Job underload, 377**
- **Hypnosis, 379**
- **Biofeedback, 379**
- **Transcendental meditation (TM), 379**
- **Alcoholism, 383**
- **Employee assistance program (EAP), 385**
- **AIDS (acquired immune deficiency syndrome), 387**

Questions for Review

1. Define *safety* and *health*.
2. What is the purpose of the Occupational Safety and Health Act?
3. What is the current thrust of OSHA?
4. What are the primary ways in which safety programs are designed? Discuss.
5. What is the purpose of job hazard analysis?
6. What is the purpose of the Superfund Amendments Reauthorization Act, Title III (SARA)?
7. In addition to the legal factor, for what other reasons should organizations be involved in safety programs?
8. What is identity theft?
9. Why are companies concerned with repetitive stress injuries? What is carpal tunnel syndrome? Why is there a CTS controversy?
10. Define *ergonomics*. What is the purpose of ergonomics?
11. What effect does workplace and domestic violence have on an organization?
12. Why should a firm attempt to identify stressful jobs?
13. Why should a firm be concerned with employee burnout?

14. What are the major sources of stress?
15. What are means of managing stress?
16. What are the purposes of wellness programs?
17. Why might physical fitness programs be established in organizations?
18. What is the purpose of substance abuse programs in organizations?
19. Explain why employee assistance programs are being established.
20. What concerns should a manager have regarding smoking in the workplace?
21. What is AIDS? How should companies react to AIDS in the workplace?

A Question of Safety

Margie Boudreaux, safety engineer for Sather Manufacturing, was walking through the plant when she spotted a situation that immediately caught her attention. Some employees had backed out of a room where several chemicals were used in a critical manufacturing process. Margie inspected the room but could not determine that anything was wrong or even different from any other day. She was puzzled as to why the workers were reluctant to resume their tasks. As it turned out, the employees were not only hesitant to return to work; they were adamant in maintaining that conditions in the room were unhealthy. Margie and the group's supervisor discussed the situation and wondered whether they should order the people to resume work since the department was already behind schedule.

Question

1. How should Margie and the group supervisor respond to this situation?

HRM Incident 2

A Commitment to Safety?

Wanda Zackery was extremely excited a year ago when she joined Landon Electronics as its first safety engineer. She had graduated from Florida State University with a degree in electrical engineering and had a strong desire to enter business. Wanda had selected her job at Landon Electronics over several other offers. She believed that it would provide her with a broad range of experiences that she could not receive in a strictly engineering job. Also, when the company president, Mark Lincoln, interviewed her, he promised her that the firm's resources would be at her disposal to correct any safety-related problems.

Her first few months at Landon were hectic but exciting. She immediately identified numerous safety problems. One of the most dangerous involved a failure to install safety guards on all exposed equipment. Wanda carefully prepared her proposal, including expected costs, to make needed minimum changes. She estimated that it would take approximately $50,000 to complete the necessary conversions. Wanda then presented the entire package to Mr. Lincoln. She explained the need for the changes to him, and Mr. Lincoln cordially received her presentation. He said that he would like to think it over and get back to her.

But that was six months ago! Every time Wanda attempted to get some action on her proposal, Mr. Lincoln was friendly but still wanted some more time to consider it. In the meantime, Wanda had become increasingly anxious. Recently, a worker had barely avoided a serious injury. Some workers had also become concerned. She heard through the grapevine that someone had telephoned the regional office of OSHA.

Her suspicions were confirmed the very next week when an OSHA inspector appeared at the plant. No previous visits had ever been made to the company. Although Mr. Lincoln was not overjoyed, he permitted the inspector access to the company. Later he might have wished that he had not been so cooperative. Before the inspector left, he wrote violations for each piece of equipment that did not have the necessary safety guards. The fines would total $5,000 if the problems were not corrected right away. The inspector cautioned that repeat violations could cost $50,000 and possible imprisonment.

As the inspector was leaving, Wanda received a phone call. "Wanda, this is Mark. Get up to my office right now. We need to get your project under way."

Questions

1. Discuss Mr. Lincoln's level of commitment to occupational safety.
2. Is there a necessary trade-off between Landon's need for low expenses and the workers' need for safe working conditions? Explain.

Notes

1. "Safety Strategies for a Post-September 11 World," *HR Focus* 79 (October 2002): 3.
2. Ibid, 3–4.
3. Richard Linnett, "Marketing of Safety Enters Mainstream," *Advertising Age* (September 23, 2002): 1.
4. Robin Suttell, "Strategic Security," *Buildings* 96 (August 2002): 38.
5. Neil Franz, "OSHA Pledges Crackdown on Repeat Offenders," *Chemical Week* (March 19, 2003): 14.
6. "OSHA Identifies Workplaces with Highest Injury and Illness Rates; Construction Industry Included in the Injury and Illness Survey," *US Newswire* (February 24, 2003): 1.
7. "OSHA Lists Injury-Prone Firms," *ENR* (March 17, 2003): 13.
8. Kent Beall, "Safety's Payback," *Industrial Distribution* 91 (July 2002): S6.
9. "Customers Give OSHA High Marks," *Job Safety and Health Quarterly* 13 (Winter 2002): 16.
10. Mark A. Hofmann, "OSHA Launches 5-Year Plan," *Business Insurance* (May 19, 2003): 3.
11. Beall, "Safety's Payback."
12. "Job Related Injury Costs," *Injury Facts* (Chicago, IL: National Safety Council, 2001): 49.
13. "Workplace Safety on the Rise," *Job Safety and Health Quarterly* 13 (Winter 2000): 17.
14. Phillip C. Headley, "Keeping Safety a Priority," *Waste Age* 33 (October 2002): 82.
15. "Workplace Fatalities in the U.S.," *Washington Post* (April 27, 2001): 1.
16. Al Tuttle, "Get with the Program," *Industrial Distribution* 91 (October 2002): 55.
17. George Swartz, "Job Hazard Analysis," *Professional Safety* (November 2002): 27–33.
18. Susan J. Wells, "Stolen Identity," *HRMagazine* 47 (December 2002): 31.
19. Chet Bridger, "I.D. Theft Is on the Rise: How to Defeat Vultures Who Would Steal Your Name," *Buffalo News* (March 25, 2003): D7.
20. Kathy M. Kristof, "California Leads Nation in Number of Fraud Complaints; FTC Says the Overall U.S. Figure Rose 73% Last Year, with Identity Theft Responsible for Most of the Growth," *Los Angeles Times* (January 23, 2003): Business, Part C, 1.
21. Ibid.
22. Amanda Levin, "Ergonomic Software Used to Reduce RSI," *National Underwriter* (March 13, 2000): 15.
23. William Atkinson, "Carpal Tunnel Syndrome: A New Look," *Risk Management* 49 (July 2002): 18.
24. Atkinson, "Carpal Tunnel Syndrome," 18–24.
25. Marilynn Larkin, "Carpal Tunnel Syndrome Study Stirs Controversy," *The Lancet* (June 16, 2001): 1953.
26. Atkinson, "Carpal Tunnel Syndrome."
27. Joy M. Ebben, "It's Not Just with Keyboards," *Occupational Health and Safety* (April 1, 2001): 65.
28. Adele L. Abrams, "OSHA & Ergonomics," *Professional Safety* 47 (September 2002): 50.
29. "Steel Industry Condemns Ergonomics Proposal," *CCH NetNews: Employment Safety and Workers' Compensation* (May 8, 2000): 3.
30. "Ergonomics Update," *Job Safety and Health Quarterly* 13 (Summer 2002): 14.
31. Sam Gazdziak, "Improving Workplace Safety by Improving Ergonomics," *Wood & Wood Products* 107 (June 2002): 81.
32. Diane Cadrain, "Workplace Safety's Ergonomic Twist," *HRMagazine* 47 (October 2002): 44–45.
33. John G. Falcioni, "Finding the Right Fit," *Mechanical Engineering* 125 (April 2003): 4.
34. Robert J. Grossman, "Make Ergonomics Go," *HRMagazine* 45 (April 2000): 38–41.
35. Diane Cadrain, ". . . And Stay Out," *HRMagazine* 47 (August 2002): 83.
36. "AIG's American International Companies Introduce Workplace Violence Insurance; Retains Citigate Global Intelligence & Security for Crisis Response Service," *Business Wire* (November 14, 2002): 1A.
37. Jack N. Kondrasuk, Herff L. Moore, and Hua Wang, "Negligent Hiring: The Emerging Contributor to Workplace Violence in the Public Sector," *Public Personnel Management* 30 (Summer 2001): 185.
38. Laurence Miller, "How Safe Is Your Job? The Threat of Workplace Violence," *USA Today* (March 2002): 52.
39. Gary Stussie, "The Real Terror at Work," *Risk Management* 49 (May 2002): 30–33.
40. Mariene Piturro, "Workplace Violence," *Strategic Finance Magazine* 82 (May 2001): 35.
41. "Employees Concerned About Workplace Violence," *Occupational Hazards* 63 (September 2001): 27.
42. William Atkinson, "The Everyday Face of Violence in the Workplace," *Risk Management* 47 (February 2000): 12.
43. Kevin Dobbs, "The Lucrative Menace of Workplace Violence," *Training* 37 (March 2000): 54–62.
44. "Risk Factors and Protective Measures for Taxi and Livery Drivers," U.S. Department of Labor, Occupational Safety and Health Administration (May 2000), http://www.osha.gov/OSHAFacts/taxi-livery-drivers.pdf.
45. Victor Godinez, "ER Workers Say Patient Violence Is a Real Danger," *Dallas Morning News* (December 8, 2002): 1L.
46. Sheila Brown Arbury, "Health-Care Workers at Risk," *Job Safety and Health Quarterly* 13 (Winter 2002): 30.
47. James E. Crockett, "Minimizing the Risk of Workplace Violence," *Business Insurance* 33 (July 1999): 35.
48. Dobbs, "The Lucrative Menace of Workplace Violence."
49. Crockett, "Minimizing the Risk of Workplace Violence."
50. Atkinson, "The Everyday Face of Violence in the Workplace," 14.
51. Carla Joinson, "Controlling Hostility," *HRMagazine* 43 (August 1998): 66.

52. "Workplace Violence Linked to WC Claims, EAP Usage," *National Underwriters*, (Property & Casualty Risk & Benefits Management Edition) (January 8, 1996): 15.
53. Dave Lenckus, "College Shooting Underscores Risks; Training Urged to Avert Violence," *Business Insurance* (November 4, 2002): 3.
54. "The Most Effective Tool Against Workplace Violence," *HR Focus* 80 (February 2003): 11.
55. Atkinson, "Keeping Violent Employees out of the Workplace."
56. Stussie, "The Real Terror at Work," 30.
57. Stephanie Schroeder, "The High Cost of Workplace Violence," *Risk Management* 46 (July 1999): 54.
58. Stephanie Armour, "Domestic Abuse Shows Up at Work," *Money* (October 16, 2002): 1B.
59. Jilian Mincer, "Going to Work on Domestic Violence," *San Diego Union-Tribune* (June 3, 2002): E-9.
60. Amy Farmer and Jill Tiefenthaler, "Explaining the Recent Decline in Domestic Violence," *Contemporary Economic Policy* 21 (April 2003): 158.
61. Diane E. Lewis, "Out in the Field/Employers, Firms Advocate for Battered Employees," *Boston Globe* (November 3, 2002): G2.
62. Cora Daniels, "The Last Taboo," *Fortune* (October 28, 2002): 136.
63. Diane Brady, "Rethinking the Rat Race: Technology Is Making 'All Work and No Play' a Real Possibility. How Will We Strike the Proper Balance of Work and Life?" *BusinessWeek* (August 26, 2002): 143.
64. Daniels, "The Last Taboo," 138.
65. Ibid.
66. Jane Stahl, "Stress Busters," *Successful Meetings* 48 (November 1999): 67.
67. "Healthier Employees Save You Money," *HR Focus* 78 (August 2001): 3.
68. Daniels, "The Last Taboo."
69. Lin Grensing-Pophal, "HR, Heal Thyself," *HRMagazine* 44 (March 1999): 83–88.
70. Frank Hayes, "Avoid Burnout," *Computerworld* (March 24, 2003): 58.
71. Pamela Paul, "Time Out," *American Demographics* 24 (June 2002): 34.
72. John Yuen and Maryjane Martin, "Creative Ways for Managing Work-Place Tension," *Communication World* (August 18, 1998): 18.
73. Max Messmer, "Avoiding Stress and Burnout," *Strategic Finance Magazine* 83 (January 2002): 15–16.
74. "Longevity Facts," *The Johns Hopkins Medical Letter: Health After 50* 9 (September 1997): 1.
75. Michelle Neely Martinez, "Using Data to Create Wellness Programs that Work," *HRMagazine* 44 (November 1999): 110–113.
76. Mary Elizabeth Burke, Evren Esen, and Jessica Collison, "2003 Benefits Survey," *SHRM/SHRM Foundation* (June 2003): 17.
77. Shelly Reese, "Applied Wellness," *Business & Health* 19 (November/December 2001): 45–46.
78. Chad Abresch, Craig Johnson, and Bo Abresch, "Union Pacific—On the Right Track," *Business & Health* 18 (November/December 2000): 59–60.
79. Burke, Esen, and Collison, "2003 Benefits Survey," 18.
80. William Atkinson, "Wellness Programs: Fit Employees Are Inexpensive Employees," *Textile World* 151 (February 2001): 68.
81. Michael Barrier, "How Exercise Can Pay Off," *Nation's Business* 85 (February 1997): 41.
82. Jodi Schneider, "More Fit in Less Time," *U.S. News & World Report* (May 13, 2002): 50–51.
83. Chad Abresch, "A Stretch Goal for Safety," *Business & Health* 19 (April 2001): 46.
84. "Medical Memo: New Studies Offer Good News on Longevity and Disability," *Harvard Men's Health Watch* 7 (June 2003): 5.
85. Bill Current, "New Solutions for Ensuring a Drug-Free Workplace," *Occupational Health & Safety* 71 (April 2002): 34.
86. Todd Nighswonger, "Just Say Yes to Preventing Substance Abuse," *Occupational Hazards* 62 (April 2000): 39.
87. Eric Newhouse, "Alcoholism: Its Origins, Consequences and Costs," *Nieman Reports* 57 (Spring 2003): 28.
88. Jane Easter Bahls, "Drugs in the Workplace," *HRMagazine* 43 (February 1998): 84–85.
89. "Know the Dangers of Marijuana," *Current Health* (April 1, 2001): 6.
90. Bahls, "Drugs in the Workplace."
91. Deanna Kelemen, "How to Recognize Substance Abuse in the Workplace," *Supervision* 56 (September 1995): 3.
92. William Atkinson, "EAPs: Investments, Not Costs," *Textile World* 151 (May 2001): 42.
93. Bahls, "Drugs in the Workplace," 85.
94. Corley Roberts, "Developing a Fitness Employee Assistance Program," *Business & Health* 19 (October 2001): 22.
95. Kevin M. Quinley, "EAPs: A Benefit That Can Trim Your Disability and Absenteeism Costs," *Compensation & Benefits Report* 17 (February 2003): 6.
96. Ron Shinkman, "Utility Workers Plug into Online Therapy," *Modern Healthcare* (October 18, 1999): 46.
97. "Online EAP and Work/Life: An Attractive Option for Employees," *HR Focus* 79 (December 2002): 9.
98. Burke, Esen, and Collison, "2003 Benefits Survey," 22.
99. Atkinson, "EAPs: Investments, Not Costs," 44.
100. "Passive Smoking Increases Cancer Risk, According to WHO," *Chemistry & Industry* (July 1, 2002): 4.
101. "Living by the Numbers: How to Gauge Your Risks," *University of California, Berkeley Wellness Letter: The Newsletter of Nutrition, Fitness, and Self-Care* 16 (June 2000): 4.
102. "Workplace Smoking Ban Would Help Kick Habit," *Occupational Health* 54 (September 2002): 7.
103. Lin Grensing-Pophal, "Smokin' in the Workplace," *HRMagazine* 44 (May 1999): 60–62.
104. Ibid.
105. Bill Gillette, "Promoting Wellness Programs Results in a Healthier Bottom Line," *Managed Healthcare Executive* (February 11, 2001): 45–46.
106. "Health, United States, 2002: HIV/AIDS Surveillance Report," U.S. Department of Health and Human Services.
107. "AIDS (Acquired Immunodeficiency Syndrome)," *Britannica Intermediate Encyclopedia* (December 9, 2002): 1.
108. Alan N. Miller, "Preparing Future Managers to Deal with AIDS/HIV in the Workplace," *Journal of Education for Business* 75 (May/June 2000): 258.
109. "AIDS (Acquired Immunodeficiency Syndrome)."
110. Louise O'Grady, "Using Technology to De-Stress on International Assignment," *Canadian HR Reporter* (September 24, 2001): 8, 12.
111. Ibid.
112. Ibid.
113. Ibid.

PART SEVEN

Employee and Labor Relations

CHAPTER OBJECTIVES

After completing this chapter, students should be able to

1. Describe the partnering of labor and management that is evolving in some sectors.
2. Describe the labor movement prior to 1930.
3. Identify the major labor legislation that was passed after 1930.
4. Explain unionization in the public sector.
5. Describe the broad objectives that characterize the labor movement as a whole.
6. Describe union growth strategies.
7. Explain the reasons why employees join unions.
8. Describe the basic structure of the union.
9. Identify the steps involved in establishing the collective bargaining relationship.
10. Explain union strategies in obtaining bargaining unit recognition.
11. Explain union decertification.
12. Describe the state of unions today.

The Evolution of Labor Unions

CHAPTER

12

HRM IN *Action:*

Partnering of Labor and Management

OBJECTIVE

Describe the partnering of labor and management that is evolving in some sectors.

Admittedly, the idea of partnering labor and management may appear strange, but it is occurring today. Consider the following situation: "We had to make nearly two pounds of product for every one pound we could sell to one of our largest customers," laments Frank Stevens, site general manager, International Specialty Products (ISP) Corporation, Calvert City, Kentucky. He was describing the 58 percent first-pass quality level of their product, bioadhesives. If something could not be done to improve this unacceptable quality the company would be out of business and the union members would be out of a job. Management and the union worked together to solve the problem. The results were remarkable. As Stevens put it, "last year that unit had the highest first-pass yield for any of our products on site at 99.5 percent . . . once we made the appropriate changes."[1]

A working partnership agreement now exists, completely separate from the union contract, that provides specific guidelines for the kind of cooperative relationship they now share. This agreement was created and driven by the union itself. Union leadership recognized that for its members to prosper, it had to become a business partner with management. It responded by creating the partnering agreement, implementation program, and a week-long school to teach it at the local level. The program was developed in concert with a number of manufacturing-management consultants as well as former U.S. Secretary of Labor Ray Marshall. The agreement formalizes a culture of "working together" in terms of strategy, business planning, and the daily operation of a plant's vital functions.[2] "Everybody has the same goal now, to kick the competition's rear," says Edward Seeley, materials handler. "And everybody knows who the competition is. Before, it never occurred to most union employees, like myself, that there even was any competition. Our competition was with the company itself. Now everybody is looking at the overall picture, working to make the plant run more efficiently and stay competitive in the marketplace."[3]

At the GM Powertrain Tonawanda Engine Plant in the town of Tonawanda, New York, unions are working with management in trying to secure a new engine line. At Bethlehem Steel, they are involved in trying to keep the steel maker alive. And at a training center in New York City, they are developing careers in construction. "People have got this stereotype of organized labor as an obstacle," said Kevin Donovan, the Buffalo area director of the United Auto Workers. "We're trying to create jobs with benefits." Union leaders are also playing a key part in area plants run by GM, Delphi Harrison, Ford Motor Co., and American Axle and Manufacturing, according to Donovan.[4]

We're partners in those facilities," he said. "The local unions and the local management are working together to cut their costs and be competitive and secure new business." Donovan also serves as chairman of the AFL-CIO Economic Development Group. It might not seem like a traditional role for labor, but the group says its members have just as large a stake in the success of the local economy as anyone else. In a region where the unions' share of the workforce was an estimated 32 percent in 2001, it is probably not surprising that they are taking an active interest.[5] Even the ironworkers' union has launched a new labor-management trust in which the union will cooperate more closely than ever in a partnering relationship with contractors to boost market share that is being eroded by nonunion employers.[6]

SHRM HR Links

www.shrm.org/hrlinks/Links.asp?Category=68

This Web site provides general labor and employee relations information.

We began this chapter by describing the partnering of labor and management that is evolving in some sectors. Next, we describe the labor movement prior to 1930 and then identify the major labor legislation that was passed after 1930. We then explain unionization in the public sector. Next, we describe the broad objectives that characterize the labor movement as a whole and union growth strategies. Then we explain the reasons why employees join unions. The basic structure of the union is described, followed by a discussion of the steps involved in establishing the collective bargaining relationship. Union strategies in obtaining bargaining unit recognition are then presented. Means for removing a union are discussed in the section on union decertification, and finally, we describe the state of unions today.

OBJECTIVE

Describe the labor movement prior to 1930.

The Labor Movement Before 1930

Unions are not a recent development in American history. The earliest unions originated toward the end of the eighteenth century, about the time of the American Revolution. Although these early associations had few of the characteristics of present-day labor unions, they did bring workers in craft or guild-related occupations together to consider problems of mutual concern. These early unions were local in nature and usually existed for only a short time.[7]

Development of the labor movement has been neither simple nor straightforward. Instead, unionism has experienced as much failure as success. Employer opposition, the impact of the business cycle, the growth of American industry, court rulings, and legislation have exerted their influence in varying degrees at different times. As a result, the history of the labor movement has somewhat resembled the swinging of a pendulum. At times, the pendulum has moved in favor of labor and, at other times, it has swung toward the advantage of management.

Conspiracy:
The act of two or more persons who band together to influence the rights of others or of society (such as by refusing to work or demanding higher wages).

Prior to the 1930s, the trend definitely favored management. The courts strongly supported employers in their attempts to thwart the organized labor movement. This was first evidenced by the use of criminal and civil conspiracy doctrines derived from English common law. A **conspiracy**, generally defined, is the act of two or more persons banding together to prejudice the rights of others or society (e.g., by refusing to work or demanding higher wages). An important feature of the conspiracy doctrine is that an action by one person, though legal, may become illegal when carried out by a group. In 1806, the year in which the conspiracy doctrine was first applied to labor unions, the courts began to influence the field of labor relations.[8] From 1806 to 1842, 17 cases charging labor unions with conspiracies went to trial. These cases resulted in the demise of several unions and certainly discouraged other union activities. The conspiracy doctrine was softened considerably by the decision in the landmark case *Commonwealth v Hunt* in 1842. In that case, Chief Justice Shaw of the Supreme Judicial Court of Massachusetts contended that labor organizations were legal. Thus, in order for a union to be convicted under the conspiracy doctrine, it had to be shown that the union's objectives were unlawful or the means employed to gain a legal end were unlawful. To this day, the courts continue to exert a profound influence on both the direction and character of labor relations.

Injunction:
A prohibiting legal procedure used by employers to prevent certain union activities, such as strikes and unionization attempts.

Yellow-dog contract:
A written agreement between an employee and a company made at the time of employment that prohibits a worker from joining a union or engaging in union activities.

Other tactics used by employers to stifle union growth were injunctions and yellow-dog contracts. An **injunction** is a prohibiting legal procedure used by employers to prevent certain union activities, such as strikes and unionization attempts. A **yellow-dog contract** was a written agreement between the employee and the company made at the time of employment that prohibits a worker from joining a union or engaging in union activities. Each of these defensive tactics, used by management and supported by the courts, severely limited union growth.

In the latter half of the nineteenth century, the American industrial system started to grow and prosper. Factory production began to displace handicraft forms of manufacturing. The Civil War gave the factory system a great boost. Goods were demanded in quantities that only mass production methods could supply. The railroads developed new networks of routes spanning the continent and knitting the country into an economic whole. Employment was high, and unions sought to organize workers in both new and expanding enterprises. Most unions during this time were small and rather weak, and many did not survive the economic recession of the 1870s. Union membership rose to 300,000 by 1872 and then dropped to 50,000 by 1878.[9] This period also marked the rise of radical labor activity and increased industrial strife as unions struggled for recognition and survival.[10]

Out of the turbulence of the 1870s emerged the most substantial labor organization that had yet appeared in the United States. The Noble Order of the Knights of Labor was founded in 1869 as a secret society of the Philadelphia garment workers. After its secrecy was abandoned and workers in other areas were invited to join, it grew rapidly, reaching a membership of more than 700,000 by the mid-1880s. Internal conflict among the Knights' leadership in 1881 gave rise to the nucleus of a new organization that would soon replace it on the labor scene.[11] That organization was the American Federation of Labor (AFL).

Devoted to what is referred to as either *pure and simple unionism* or *business unionism*, Samuel Gompers of the Cigarmakers Union led some 25 labor groups representing skilled trades to found the AFL in 1886. Gompers was elected the first president of the AFL, a position he held until his death in 1924 (except for one year, 1894–1895, when he adamantly opposed tangible support for the Pullman group strikers). He is probably the single most important individual in American trade union history. The AFL began with a membership of some 138,000 and doubled that number during the next 12 years.

In 1890, Congress passed the Sherman Anti-Trust Act, which marked the entrance of the federal government into the statutory regulation of labor organizations. Although the primary stimulus for this act came from public concern over business's monopoly power, court interpretations soon applied its provisions to organized labor. Later, in 1914, Congress passed the Clayton Act (an amendment to the Sherman Act), which, according to Samuel Gompers, was the Magna Carta of Labor. The intent of this act was to remove labor from the purview of the Sherman Act. Again, judicial interpretation nullified that intent and left labor even more exposed to lawsuits.[12] Nonetheless, as a result of industrial activity related to World War I, the AFL grew to almost five million members by 1920.[13]

During the 1920s, labor faced legal restrictions on union activity and unfavorable court decisions. The one exception to such repressive policies was the passage and approval of the Railway Labor Act of 1926. Passage of this legislation marked the first time that the government declared without qualification the right of private employees to join unions and bargain collectively through representatives of their own choosing without interference from their employers. It also set up special machinery for the settlement of labor disputes. Although the act covered only employees in the railroad industry (a later amendment extended coverage to the airline industry), it foreshadowed the extension of similar rights to other classes of employees in the 1930s. Recently, there have been attempts to amend the law to require baseball-style arbitration, which the unions say would strip them of their ability to strike. Under the proposed reform, an arbitration panel would pick between contracts submitted by each side, and there would be no compromising. However, there continues to be debate in this area.[14,15]

3 OBJECTIVE

Identify the major labor legislation that was passed after 1930.

Labor Law

www.lir.msu.edu/hotlinks/laborhistory.htm

This Web site provides links to numerous sites related to labor history.

The Labor Movement After 1930

The 1930s found the United States in the midst of the worst depression in its history. The unemployment rate rose as high as 25 percent.[16] The sentiment of the country began to favor organized labor, as many people blamed business for the agony that accompanied the Great Depression. The pendulum began to swing away from management and toward labor. This swing was assisted by several acts and actions that supported the cause of unionism.

Anti-Injunction Act (Norris-LaGuardia Act)—1932

The Great Depression caused a substantial change in the public's thinking about the role of unions in society. Congress reflected this thinking in 1932 with the passage of the Norris-LaGuardia Act. It affirms that U.S. public policy sanctions collective bargaining and approves the formation and effective operation of labor unions. While this act did not outlaw the use of injunctions, it severely restricted the federal courts' authority to issue them in labor disputes. It also made yellow-dog contracts unenforceable in the federal courts.[17]

National Labor Relations Board

www.nlrb.gov

This government Web site provides information regarding the National Labor Relations Board.

National Labor Relations Act (Wagner Act)—1935

In 1933, Congress made an abortive attempt to stimulate economic recovery by passing the National Industry Recovery Act (NIRA). Declared unconstitutional by the U.S. Supreme Court in 1935, the NIRA did provide the nucleus for legislation that followed it. Section 7a of the NIRA proclaimed the right of workers to organize and bargain collectively. Congress did not, however, provide procedures to enforce these rights.

Undeterred by the Supreme Court decision and strongly supported by organized labor, Congress speedily enacted a comprehensive labor law, the National Labor Relations Act (Wagner Act). This act, approved by President Roosevelt on July 5, 1935, is one of the most significant labor–management relations statutes ever enacted. Drawing heavily on the experience of the Railway Labor Act of 1926 and Section 7a of the NIRA, the act declared legislative support, on a broad scale, for the right of employees to organize and engage in collective bargaining. The spirit of the Wagner Act is stated in Section 7, which defines the substantive rights of employees:

> *Employees shall have the right to self-organization, to form, join, or assist labor organizations, to bargain collectively through representatives of their*

> *own choosing, and to engage in other concerted activities, for the purpose of collective bargaining or other mutual aid or protection.*

The rights defined in Section 7 were protected against employer interference by Section 8, which detailed and prohibited five management practices deemed to be unfair to labor:

1. Interfering with or restraining or coercing employees in the exercise of their right to self-organization
2. Dominating or interfering in the affairs of a union
3. Discriminating in regard to hire or tenure or any condition of employment for the purpose of encouraging or discouraging union membership
4. Discriminating against or discharging an employee who has filed charges or given testimony under the act
5. Refusing to bargain with chosen representatives of employees

The National Labor Relations Act created the National Labor Relations Board (NLRB) to administer and enforce the provisions of the act. The NLRB was given two principal functions: (1) to establish procedures for holding bargaining-unit elections and to monitor the election procedures, and (2) to investigate complaints and prevent unlawful acts involving unfair labor practices. Much of the NLRB's work is delegated to 33 regional offices throughout the country.

Following passage of the Wagner Act, union membership increased from approximately 3 million to 15 million between 1935 and 1947.[18] The increase was most conspicuous in industries utilizing mass production methods. New unions in these industries were organized on an industrial basis rather than a craft basis, and members were primarily unskilled or semiskilled workers. An internal struggle developed within the AFL over the question of whether unions should be organized to include all workers in an industry or strictly on a craft or occupational basis. In 1935, ten AFL-affiliated unions and the officers of two other AFL unions formed a new group. Called the Committee for Industrial Organization, its purpose was to promote the organization of workers in mass production and unorganized industries. The controversy grew to the point that in 1938 the AFL expelled all but one of the Committee for Industrial Organization unions. In November 1938, the expelled unions held their first convention in Pittsburgh, and reorganized as a federation of unions under the name of Congress of Industrial Organizations (CIO). The new federation included the nine unions expelled from the AFL and thirty-two other groups established to recruit workers in various industries. John L. Lewis, president of the United Mine Workers, was elected the first president of the CIO.

The rivalry generated by the two large federations stimulated union-organizing efforts in both groups. With the ensuing growth, the labor movement gained considerable influence in the United States. However, many individuals and groups began to feel that the Wagner Act favored labor too much. This shift in public sentiment was in part related to a rash of costly strikes following World War II. Whether justified or not, much of the blame for these disruptions fell on the unions.

Labor-Management Relations Act (Taft-Hartley Act)—1947

In 1947, with public pressure mounting, Congress overrode President Truman's veto and passed the Labor-Management Relations Act (Taft-Hartley Act). The Taft-Hartley Act extensively revised the National Labor Relations Act and became Title I of that law. A new period began in the evolution of public policy regarding labor. The pendulum had begun to swing toward a more balanced position between labor and management.

Some of the important changes introduced by the Taft-Hartley Act included the following:

1. Modifying Section 7 to include the right of employees to refrain from union activity as well as engage in it
2. Prohibiting the closed shop (the arrangement requiring that all workers be union members at the time they are hired) and narrowing the freedom of the parties to authorize the union shop (the situation in which the employer may hire anyone he or she chooses, but all new workers must join the union after a stipulated period of time)
3. Broadening the employer's right of free speech
4. Providing that employers need not recognize or bargain with unions formed by supervisory employees
5. Giving employees the right to initiate decertification petitions
6. Providing for government intervention in *national emergency strikes*

Another significant change extended the concept of unfair labor practices to unions. Labor organizations were to refrain from the following:

1. Restraining or coercing employees in the exercise of their guaranteed collective bargaining rights
2. Causing an employer to discriminate in any way against an employee in order to encourage or discourage union membership
3. Refusing to bargain in good faith with an employer regarding wages, hours, and other terms and conditions of employment
4. Engaging in certain types of strikes and boycotts
5. Requiring employees covered by union-shop contracts to pay initiation fees or dues in an amount which the Board finds excessive or discriminatory under all circumstances
6. *Featherbedding*, or requiring that an employer pay for services not performed

Right-to-work laws: Laws that prohibit management and unions from entering into agreements requiring union membership as a condition of employment.

One of the most controversial elements of the Taft-Hartley Act is its Section 14b, which permits states to enact right-to-work legislation. **Right-to-work laws** are laws that prohibit management and unions from entering into agreements requiring union membership as a condition of employment. These laws are state statutes or constitutional provisions that ban the practice of requiring union membership or financial support as a condition of employment. They establish the legal right of employees to decide for themselves whether or not to join or financially support a union.[19] Twenty-two states, located primarily in the South and West, have adopted such laws, which are a continuing source of irritation between labor and management.[20] Oklahoma became the most recent right-to-work state.[21] The National Right to Work Committee, based in Springfield, Virginia, provides much of the impetus behind the right-to-work movement.

For about 10 years after the passage of the Taft-Hartley Act, union membership expanded at about the same rate as nonagricultural employment. But all was not well within the organized labor movement. Since the creation of the CIO, the two federations had engaged in a bitter and costly rivalry. Both the CIO and the AFL recognized the increasing need for cooperation and reunification. In 1955, following two years of intensive negotiations between the two organizations, a merger agreement was ratified, the AFL-CIO became a reality, and George Meany was elected president. In the years following the merger, the labor movement faced some of its greatest challenges.

Labor-Management Reporting and Disclosure Act (Landrum-Griffin Act)—1959

Corruption had plagued organized labor since the early 1900s. Periodic revelations of graft, violence, extortion, racketeering, and other improper activities aroused public indignation and invited governmental investigation. Even though the number of unions involved was small, every disclosure undermined the public image of organized labor as a whole.[22] Corruption had been noted in the construction trades and Laborers, Hotel and Restaurant, Carpenters, Painters, East Coast Longshoremen, and Boilermakers unions.

Scrutiny of union activities is a focal point in today's labor environment, but it began to intensify immediately after World War II. Ultimately, inappropriate union activities led to the creation in 1957 of the Senate Select Committee on Improper Activities in the Labor or Management Field, headed by Senator McClellan of Arkansas. Between 1957 and 1959, the McClellan Committee held a series of nationally televised public hearings that shocked and alarmed the entire country. As evidence of improper activities mounted—primarily against the Teamsters and Longshoremen/Maritime unions—the AFL-CIO took action. In 1957, the AFL-CIO expelled three unions (representing approximately 1.6 million members) for their practices. One of them, the Teamsters, was the largest union in the country.

In 1959, largely as a result of the recommendations of the McClellan Committee, Congress enacted the Labor-Management Reporting and Disclosure Act (Landrum-Griffin Act). This act marked a significant turning point in the involvement of the federal government in internal union affairs. The Landrum-Griffin Act spelled out a *Bill of Rights for Members of Labor Organizations* designed to protect certain rights of individuals in their relationships with unions. The act requires extensive reporting on numerous internal union activities and contains severe penalties for violations. Employers are also required to file reports when they engage in activities or make expenditures that might undermine the collective bargaining process or interfere with protected employee rights. In addition, the act amended the Taft-Hartley Act by adding additional restrictions on picketing and secondary boycotts.[23]

In 1974, Congress extended coverage of the Taft-Hartley Act to private, not-for-profit hospitals. This amendment brought within the jurisdiction of the National Labor Relations Board some two million employees. Proprietary (profit-making) health-care organizations were already under NLRB jurisdiction. The amendment does not cover government-operated hospitals; it applies only to the private sector.

Corruption among union officials continues in certain areas. In December 2002, the FBI raided the homes of officials from the Washington Teachers Union, an affiliate of the American Federation of Teachers. The FBI hauled off fur coats, alligator shoes, and even a Tiffany silver service, all of which investigators say were bought with as much as $5 million stolen from member dues. The union-owned insurance company (Ullico) currently faces federal probes into an insider stock deal that rewarded top labor leaders with payouts resulting from an investment in now-failed Global Crossing.[24]

Homeland Security Act of 2002

In November 2002 the Homeland Security Act (Public Law 107-296) was passed which established the new cabinet-level agency. The new agency is responsible for border security, emergency preparedness, biological warfare, intelligence analysis, and protection of the president. Under the new setup, the Bush administration is able to waive Civil Service collective-bargaining rights if direct negotiations with unions fail to yield agreement and the federal mediation service is unable to resolve the dispute. The Homeland Security Act also creates a new senior-level position of chief human capital officer. The department is responsible for taking a present workforce of 170,000 in 22 established federal government agencies, and organizing them under one roof.[25]

4 OBJECTIVE

Explain unionization in the public sector.

The Public Sector

In 1962, President Kennedy signed an executive order allowing federal employees to unionize. Congress put the right to unionize into law as part of the 1978 Civil Service Reform Act. Today, 78 unions represent 1.1 million of the 1.8 million civilian workers in the federal government. The unions range from the tiny 13-member Sport Air Traffic Controllers Organization to the American Federation of Government Employees, which represents 600,000 employees, or one in three federal workers. In addition, four major unions represent most of the 800,000 workers at the Postal Service, which operates under different labor-management rules than the rest of government and sees little or no intervention from the White House.[26] The greater public-sector penetration of unions in recent years indicates that the process of unionization in the public sector differs from that in the private labor market.

Government (public-sector) employees are generally considered a class apart from private-sector workers. This is reflected in their exclusion from coverage of general labor legislation.[27] However, unlike their counterparts in private industry, government employees have demonstrated persistence in organizing in order to gain an effective voice in the terms and conditions of their employment. Unionism is healthy in the public sector and has remained so ever since John F. Kennedy's decision to allow federal workers to organize. For many years the federal government had no well-defined policy on labor–management relations regarding its own employees. In order to address this situation, President Kennedy issued Executive Order 10988. Section 1(a) of the order stated:

> *Employees of the federal government shall have, and shall be protected in the exercise of, the right, freely and without fear of penalty or reprisal, to form, join and assist any employee organization or to refrain from any such activity.*

For the first time in the history of the federal civil service, a uniform, comprehensive policy of cooperation between employee organizations and management in the executive branch of government was established. Employees were permitted to organize and negotiate human resource policies and practices and matters affecting working conditions that were within the administrative discretion of the agency officials concerned. However, Public Law 84-330, passed in 1955, made it a felony for federal employees to strike against the U.S. government.[28]

The U.S. Postal Service is not subject to Title VII of the Civil Service Reform Act of 1978. It was given independent government agency status by the Postal Reorganization Act of 1970. Postal employees were given collective bargaining rights comparable to those governing private industry. National Labor Relations Board rules and regulations controlling representation issues and elections are applicable to the postal service. The NLRB also enforces unfair labor practice provisions. However, the right to strike is prohibited, and union-shop arrangements are not permitted.

The American Federation of Government Employees (AFGE) is the largest federal employee union representing federal government workers nationwide and overseas. Agencies with the highest concentration of union membership include the Department of Defense, the Department of Veterans Affairs, the Social Security Administration, and the Department of Justice.[29] The National Air Traffic

Controllers Association was founded to ensure safety and longevity of air traffic controller positions around the nation. NATCA has grown to represent over 15,000 air traffic controllers throughout the United States, Puerto Rico, and Guam, along with 2,508 other bargaining unit members that range from engineers and architects to nurses and health-care professionals to members of the accounting community.[30]

Although AFL-CIO officials are pleased with these gains in membership among civil servants, serious problems loom. President George W. Bush has not made it any easier for government unions. Thus far in his first term he has done the following:

- Denied collective bargaining rights to the 62,000 employees who secure the nation's air system as employees of the Transportation Security Administration. Many previously belonged to unions
- Reduced union power at the agency level by eliminating partnership councils. President Clinton created the councils by executive order in 1993, requiring federal executives to involve unions in management decisions outside normal bargaining procedures
- Appointed officials, such as Deputy Administrator Ruben King-Shaw at the Centers for Medicare and Medicaid Services, who view union rights more narrowly than their predecessors in the Clinton administration
- Revoked union rights for thousands of employees at the Justice Department, including those in U.S. attorney's offices. Bush's blanket order denying union rights to the employees came as a group of lawyers in the Miami U.S. Attorney's Office were organizing a bargaining unit
- Threatened to deny collective bargaining rights to the 170,000 federal employees who will be transferred into the new Homeland Security Department. About 40,000 of those employees now belong to unions[31]

In 2003, the Bush administration said it will deny 56,000 federal airport security screeners the right to negotiate for better working conditions and higher pay. "Mandatory collective bargaining is not compatible with the flexibility required to wage the war against terrorism," James Loy, head of the Transportation Security Administration, said in an order issued by the administration. The American Federation of Government Employees called the action illegal and said it plans to file.[32]

There is no uniform pattern to state and local labor relations. Some states have no policy at all, whereas a haphazard mixture of statutes, resolutions, ordinances, and civil service procedures exists in others. However, the passage of public-employer legislation by state and local governments accelerated noticeably after the issuance of EO 10988 in 1962.[33]

Employee Associations

In the past, employee associations were concerned primarily with the professional aspects of employment and avoided any semblance of unionism. In recent years, this approach has changed as public- and private-sector unions have actively organized both professional and government employees. Many employee associations now enthusiastically pursue collective bargaining relationships. The National Education Association (NEA) is the largest public-sector union in the United States, with 2.7 million members, and has affiliates in every state, as well as in more than 13,000 local communities across the United States.[34] The American Federation of State, County and Municipal Employees has over 1.3 million members in public service and health care.[35]

 OBJECTIVE

Describe the broad objectives that characterize the labor movement as a whole.

Union Objectives

The labor movement has a long history in the United States. Although each union is a unique organization seeking its own objectives, several broad objectives characterize the labor movement as a whole:

1. To secure and, if possible, improve the living standards and economic status of its members
2. To enhance and, if possible, guarantee individual security against threats and contingencies that might result from market fluctuations, technological change, or management decisions
3. To influence power relations in the social system in ways that favor and do not threaten union gains and goals
4. To advance the welfare of all who work for a living, whether union members or not[36]
5. To create mechanisms to guard against the use of arbitrary and capricious policies and practices in the workplace

The underlying philosophy of the labor movement is that of organizational democracy and an atmosphere of social dignity for working men and women. To accomplish these objectives, most unions recognize that they must strive for continued growth and power. Although growth and power are related, we will discuss them separately to identify the impact of both factors on unionization.

Growth

To maximize its effectiveness, a union must strive for continual growth. Members pay dues, which are vital to promoting and achieving union objectives. Obviously, the more members the union has, the more dues they pay to support the union and the labor movement. Thus, an overall goal of most unions is continued growth. However, the percentage of union members in the private workforce is declining. Since much of a union's ability to accomplish its objectives is derived from strength in numbers, union leaders are concerned with this trend. For this reason, unions continue to explore new sources of potential members. Unions are now directing much of their attention to organizing the service industries, professional employees, and government employees. Specifics related to growth issues are addressed later in the union strategies section of this chapter.

Power

We define *power* here as the amount of external control that an organization is able to exert. A union's power is influenced to a large extent by the size of its membership and the possibility of future growth. However, we also have to consider other factors when assessing the future power base of unions. The importance of the jobs held by union members significantly affects union power. For instance, an entire plant may have to be shut down if unionized machinists performing critical jobs decide to strike. Thus, a few strategically located union members may exert a disproportionate amount of power. The type of firm that is unionized can also determine a union's power. Unionization of truckers, steelworkers, or dock workers can affect the entire country and, subsequently, enhance the union's power base. This is precisely what the longshoremen did in the West Coast strike of 2002, which affected commerce from San

Francisco to Maine. Through control of key industries, a union's power may extend to firms that are not unionized.

By achieving power, a union is capable of exerting its force in the political arena. The political arm of the AFL-CIO is the Committee on Political Education (COPE). Founded in 1955, its purpose is to support politicians who are friendly to the cause of organized labor. The union recommends and assists candidates who will best serve its interests. Union members also encourage their friends to support those candidates. The union's political influence increases as the size of the voting membership grows. With *friends* in government, the union is in a stronger position to maneuver against management.

Reduced union strength contributes to weaker unions at the bargaining table, and therefore, labor leaders will continually strive to increase their political clout. This slowdown in union gains, coupled with declining union membership as a percentage of the workforce, has caused unions to compensate by attempting to increase their political activity. Even though unions have taken their political knocks over the past decade, they remain a fairly potent force. Of the $90 million that labor unions contributed to candidates in 2000, 94 percent, or $85 million, went to Democratic candidates. Union members were among Al Gore's most active supporters during the 2000 presidential campaign and during the Florida recount. Public-sector unions, including the American Federation of Government Employees, the National Treasury Employees Union, and the American Federation of State, County and Municipal Employees, were generous to the Democrats in 2000, giving them $11 million. They gave only $1 million to Republicans.[37]

6 OBJECTIVE

Describe union growth strategies.

Union Growth Strategies

Management may have inadvertently assisted the growth of unions. The recent revelations concerning companies such as Enron, WorldCom, and Arthur Andersen in which many workers lost much of their savings, not to mention their jobs, has given labor a focal point for organizing. A recent survey done by the AFL-CIO found that for the first time in nearly 20 years, more nonunion workers (50 percent) say they would vote to form a union than those who would not (43 percent). Another poll done by a lawyers' group, the Employment Law Alliance, found that 58 percent of workers support more union organizing to protect employees. In addition, over 80 percent of all workers feel they should have an organization to discuss and resolve their concerns with employers.[38] "People are angry that they're losing their savings to a corrupt corporate system they thought they could trust," charges AFL-CIO President John Sweeney. The change in sentiment offers a renewed opportunity for unions, which have seen their ranks shrink for decades.[39] Organized labor's new strategies for a stronger movement involve practices such as greater political involvement, union salting, flooding the community with organizers, corporate labor campaigns, building organizing funds, forming coalitions, the AFL-CIO cyberunion, and befriending laid-off workers. The partnering of labor and management mentioned in the HRM in Action at the beginning of this chapter is another strategy that labor has used, as is the concept of pulling the union through, discussed in the next Trends and Innovations.

Political Involvement

Political involvement now means more than simply endorsing candidates at all levels of politics, and then attempting to deliver the union membership's vote. Unions are giving money to candidates who pledge to help pass pro-labor legislation. The AFL-CIO and its constituent unions spent approximately $500 million in cash and in-kind electoral support of union-friendly politicians in the 2000 elections for president and Congress.[41] The AFL-CIO's Sweeney made political action a top priority and has

Trends & Innovations

Pulling the Union Through

One recent union tactic that has worked effectively is to put pressure on the end user of a company's product in order to have a successful organizing attempt. UAW President Ronald A. Gettelfinger authorized a strike against four Johnson Controls Inc. (JCI) factories that make interior parts for some of the country's best-selling vehicles. The quick two-day strike cost workers little lost income, but it hurt General Motors Corporation and Chrysler Group by shutting down production of their popular Chevy Trail Blazer and Jeep Liberty sport utility vehicles. Worried about lost sales in a profitable segment and desiring to preserve good relations with the UAW, GM and Chrysler played an active behind-the-scenes role by pressuring JCI to settle the dispute. The result was a major UAW victory. Not only did raises increase up to $6 an hour but the strikers won a promise from Johnson Control not to interfere with UAW efforts to organize some 8,000 workers at the 26 other JCI factories that supply the Big Three. The union plans to replicate its strategy at other auto-parts makers.[40]

pumped millions of dollars into political activities that include the training of political organizers and politicians in labor issues. According to some, John J. Sweeney has converted the AFL-CIO into perhaps the Democratic Party's most effective weapon on Election Day.[42] At its recent meeting, the AFL-CIO labor federation's executive council announced a new political action effort to win support from workers year-round instead of only before elections. AFL-CIO President John Sweeney said, "It is the top priority of the labor political program in 2003 and 2004 to take the country forward again by removing our out-of-touch leaders."[43]

Union Salting

Union salting: The process of training union organizers to apply for jobs at a company and, once hired, work to unionize employees.

Union salting is the process of training union organizers to apply for jobs at a company and, once hired, work to unionize employees.[44] Although salting is primarily used by blue-collar labor unions within the construction and building industries, it is a strategy labor unions are also using in other sectors, such as the hotel and restaurant industries.[45] The U.S. Supreme Court has ruled that employers cannot discriminate against *union salts* (*NLRB v Town & Electric Inc.*). Therefore, a company cannot terminate these employees solely because they also work for a union.[46] The practice is on the rise and being supported by AFL-CIO President John Sweeney. "We will be training at least a thousand organizers a year, pouring $20 million into organizing programs, and organizing from the Sunbelt to the Rust Belt and from the health-care industry to the high-tech field," said Sweeney.[47]

Flooding Communities with Organizers

Flooding the community: The process of the union inundating communities with organizers to target a particular business.

Flooding the community is the process of the union inundating communities with organizers to target a particular business. With their flooding campaigns, unions typically choose companies in which nonunionized employees have asked for help in organizing. Generally, organizers have been recruited and trained by the national union. They are typically young, ambitious, college-educated people with a passion for the American labor movement. Organizers meet with employees in small groups and even visit them at home. They know every nuance of a company's operations and target weak managers' departments as a way to appeal to dissatisfied employees who may be willing to organize.

Department of Labor

www.dol.gov

This Department of Labor Web site provides information regarding the labor movement in the 21st century.

Corporate labor campaigns: Labor maneuvers that do not coincide with a strike or organizing campaign to pressure an employer for better wages, benefits, and the like.

Political Awareness Campaigns

Corporate labor campaigns involve labor maneuvers that do not coincide with a strike or organizing campaign to pressure an employer for better wages, benefits, and the like. Increasingly, these campaigns are used as an alternative to strikes because more employers are willing to replace their striking employees. Employers have less recourse against labor campaigns that involve joining political and community groups that support union goals or picketing homes of a company's board of directors. They are also defenseless in dealing with the union's initiating proxy challenges to actions negative to labor, writing letters to the editor of the local newspapers, and filing charges with administrative agencies such as OSHA,[48] the Department of Labor, and the NLRB. These types of public awareness campaigns, which are not tied directly to labor gains, are often effective methods of developing union leverage. Also, fighting such campaigns is time-consuming and costly for companies.[49]

Building Organizing Funds

To encourage workers to come together, the AFL-CIO asked its affiliates to increase organizing funds. The federation also increased funding to its Organizing Institute, which trains organizers, and even launched an advertising campaign to create wider public support for unions.[50] National unions are also creating organizing funds. For example, the United Steelworkers of America (USWA) will create a $40 million fund for organizing. According to George Becker, USWA's president, "Our greatest challenge is organizing. Our ability to organize and grow the union bears directly on our effectiveness at the bargaining table and in the political arena."[51]

An interesting development is the use of a "market recovery fund," a tool increasingly used by U.S. construction unions in their battle with nonunion contractors. The funds use members' dues to subsidize a unionized contractor bidding for work against nonunion competitors, which typically offer lower wage rates. Union contractors hire union plumbers, union electricians, and union artisans from many other crafts. The funds make up the difference in labor costs between a union and nonunion contractor. For instance, if a union shop paid $1 more an hour, the market recovery fund would make up the $1 difference. Union workers would get paid the same, and the contractor would be on an even footing with his or her nonunion competition. Nonunion firms are eligible for market recovery money only if they sign collective bargaining agreements.[52]

AFL-CIO—Cyberunion

The AFL-CIO is now offering members Internet access in an effort to create a Web-based community, and give itself more political clout. The service, called Workingfamilies.com, provides union members with low-cost access as well as full financing for low-cost computers. Workingfamilies.com offers premium Internet service for $14.95 a month.[53] According to John Sweeney, "With Workingfamilies.com, we're helping bridge the growing gap between the technological 'haves' and 'have-nots,' and we're also giving working families new ways to connect with one another and to make their voices heard. This is a twenty-first-century communications tool that will help co-workers share information, help our unions mobilize our members, and hold policy makers more accountable to working families."[54]

Befriending Laid-Off Workers

The AFL-CIO hopes the castoffs from Enron, WorldCom, and others will become advocates for organizing. Some already have. Essentially, a union of laid-off workers was organized. John Challenger, head of the national recruiting firm Challenger,

Ethical Dilemma

A Strategic Move

You are the plant manager for a medium-sized manufacturing company that has been experiencing growing employee tensions and there has been a lot of talk among workers about forming a union. You have even seen what appear to be authorization cards being passed out around the plant. Sandy Marshall, one of the workers in your plant, has been seen talking to many of the workers, obviously about forming a union. Sandy is very influential with the workers throughout the plant and appears to be a natural leader. You believe that if Sandy continues to promote the union, she will have a major impact among the workers in organizing the union. You have a supervisory position that has just come open. It pays a lot more than Sandy makes. You think, "If I make her a supervisor, she won't be able to use her influence to help get the union started." However, there is another worker in your department who is more qualified and has been with the firm several years longer than Sandy, although he is less influential with other workers throughout the plant.

What would you do?

Gray & Christmas, said telecom workers who manage to keep their jobs may be more receptive to unions in the future. "When you have an environment like you do in this industry, the fear and stress breaks down relationships between management and workers," Challenger said. "It's an environment ripe for conflict."[55]

OBJECTIVE

Explain the reasons why employees join unions.

Why Employees Join Unions

Individuals join unions for many different reasons, which tend to change over time, and may involve job, personal, social, or political considerations. It would be impossible to discuss them all, but the following are some of the major reasons: dissatisfaction with management, compensation, job security, management's attitude, the need for a social outlet, the opportunity for leadership, forced unionization, and peer pressure.

Dissatisfaction with Management

Every job holds the potential for real dissatisfactions. Each individual has a boiling point that can trigger him or her to consider a union as a solution to real or perceived problems. Unions look for arbitrary or unfair management decisions and then emphasize the advantages of union membership as a means of solving these problems. "Ninety percent of it is not a money issue," said Ron Hreha, president of Local 339 in Port Huron, Michigan. "Issues like seniority, favoritism, grievance procedures, and other quality of work life issues often loom as more important than wages."[56] Some of the other common reasons for employee dissatisfaction are described in the following paragraphs.

Compensation. Employees want their compensation to be fair and equitable. Wages are important to them because they provide both the necessities and pleasures of life. If employees are dissatisfied with their wages, they may look to a union for assistance in improving their standard of living. According to Bureau of Labor Statistics, union members earned 17.5 percent more than those who are not members, an average of $17.85 per hour for union members compared to $15.19 for nonmembers.[57] However, the difference between the average union wage and nonunion wage is strongly influenced by occupation and geography. The ability of unions to make satisfactory gains in income has been severely hampered in the past few years.

An important psychological aspect of compensation involves the amount of pay an individual receives in relation to that of other workers performing similar work. If an employee perceives that management has shown favoritism by paying someone else more to perform the same or a lower-level job, the employee will likely become dissatisfied. Union members know precisely the basis of their pay and how it compares with others'. In the past, union members have accepted pay inequities if seniority was the criterion used.

Job Security. Historically, young employees have been less concerned with job security than older workers. The young employee seemed to think, "If I lose this job, I can always get another." But as young employees have witnessed management consistently terminating older workers to make room for younger, more aggressive employees, they may have begun to think about job security. If the firm does not provide its employees with a sense of job security, workers may turn to a union. Generally speaking, employees are more concerned than ever about job security because of a decline in employment in such key industries as automobiles, rubber, and steel. Unfortunately for the union, many believe that cooperative employers rather than unions can provide job security.

Attitude of Management. People like to feel that they are important. They do not like to be considered a commodity that can be bought and sold. Thus, employees do not like to be subjected to arbitrary and capricious actions by management.[58] In some firms, management is insensitive to the needs of its employees. In such situations, employees may perceive that they have little or no influence in job-related matters. Workers who feel that they are not really part of an organization are prime targets for unionization.

Management's attitude may be reflected in such small actions as how bulletin board notices are written. Memos addressed "To All Employees" instead of "To *Our* Employees" may indicate that managers are indifferent to employee needs. Such attitudes likely stem from top management, but they are noticed initially by employees in the actions of first-line supervisors. Workers may notice that supervisors are judging people entirely on what they can do, how much they can do, and when they can do it. Employees may begin to feel they are being treated more as machines than people. Supervisors may fail to give reasons for unusual assignments and may expect employees to dedicate their lives to the firm without providing adequate rewards. The prevailing philosophy may be: "If you don't like it here, leave." A management philosophy such as this, which does not consider the needs of employees as individuals, makes the firm ripe for unionization. Management must keep in mind that unions would never have gained a foothold if management had not abused its power. Companies that are pro-employees are not likely to unionize.[59]

A Social Outlet

By nature, many people have strong social needs. They generally enjoy being around others who have similar interests and desires. Some employees join a union for no other reason than to take advantage of union-sponsored recreational and social activities that members and their families find fulfilling. Some unions now offer day-care centers and other services that appeal to working men and women and increase their sense of solidarity with other union members. People who develop close personal relationships, whether in a unionized or union-free organization, will likely stand together in difficult times.

Opportunity for Leadership

Some individuals aspire to leadership roles, but it is not always easy for an operative employee to progress into management. However, employees with leadership aspirations can often satisfy those aspirations through union membership. As with the firm, the union also has a hierarchy of leadership, and individual members have the opportunity to work their way up through its various levels. Employers often notice employees who are leaders in the union, and it is not uncommon for them to promote such employees into managerial ranks as supervisors.

Forced Unionization

Requiring an individual to join a union prior to employment is generally illegal. However, in the 28 states without right-to-work laws, it is legal for an employer to agree with the union that a new employee must join the union after a certain period of time (generally 30 days) or be terminated. This is referred to as a *union-shop agreement*.

Peer Pressure

Some individuals will join a union simply because they are urged to do so by other members of the workgroup. Friends and associates may constantly remind an employee that he or she is not a member of the union. In extreme cases, union members have threatened nonmembers with physical violence and sometimes have carried out these threats.

8 OBJECTIVE

Describe the basic structure of the union.

Union Structure

The labor movement has developed a multilevel organizational structure. This complex of organizations ranges from local unions to the principal federation, the AFL-CIO. Each level has its own officers and ways of managing its affairs. Many national unions have intermediate levels between the national and the local levels. In this section, however, we describe only the three basic elements of union organization: the local union, the national union, and the federation, or AFL-CIO.

The Local Union

Local union:
The basic element in the structure of the U.S. labor movement.

The basic element in the structure of the American labor movement is the **local union** (or simply, the *local*). To the individual union member, it is the most important level in the structure of organized labor. Through the local, the individual deals with the employer on a day-to-day basis. A local union may fill a social role in the lives of its members, sponsoring dances, festivals, and other functions. It may be the focal point of the political organization and activity of its members.[60]

Craft union:
A bargaining unit, such as the Carpenters and Joiners union, which is typically composed of members of a particular trade or skill in a specific locality.

Industrial union:
A bargaining unit that generally consists of all the workers in a particular plant or group of plants.

There are two basic kinds of local unions: craft and industrial. A **craft union,** such as the Carpenters and Joiners union, is typically composed of members of a particular trade or skill in a specific locality. Members usually acquire their job skills through an apprenticeship-training program. An **industrial union** generally consists of all the workers in a particular plant or group of plants. The type of work they do and the level of skill they possess are not a condition for membership in the union. An example of an industrial union is the United Auto Workers.[61]

The local union's functions are many and varied. Administering the collective bargaining agreement and representing workers in handling grievances are two very important activities. Other functions include keeping the membership informed about labor issues, promoting increased membership, maintaining effective contact with the national union, and, when appropriate, negotiating with management at the local level.

The National Union

National union:
An organization composed of local unions, which it charters.

The most powerful level in the union structure is the national union. As we stated previously, most locals are affiliated with national unions. A **national union** is composed of local unions, which it charters. As such, it is the parent organization to local unions.

The local union—not the individual worker—holds membership in the national union. Each local union provides financial support to the national union based on its membership size. The International Brotherhood of Teamsters is the largest in the United States. With about 1.4 million members, the Teamsters represents 16 trade groups, including truckers, UPS workers, warehouse employees, cab drivers, airline workers, construction crews, and other workers. The Teamsters has about 570 local chapters in the United States and Canada.[62]

The national union is governed by a national constitution and a national convention of local unions, which usually meets every two to five years. Elected officers, aided by an administrative staff, conduct the day-to-day operations of the national union. The national union is active in organizing workers within its jurisdiction, engaging in collective bargaining at the national level, and assisting its locals in their negotiations. In addition, the national union may provide numerous educational and research services for its locals, dispense strike funds, publish the union newspaper, provide legal counsel, and actively lobby at national and state levels.

The AFL-CIO

HR Web Wisdom

AFL-CIO

www.aflcio.org

This Web site provides current news about union activities, political candidate positions, and health and safety laws.

The American Federation of Labor and Congress of Industrial Organizations (AFL-CIO) is the central trade union federation in the United States. It is a voluntary federation of 66 national and international labor unions representing more than 13 million members.[63] It represents the interests of labor and its member national unions at the highest level. The federation does not engage in collective bargaining; however, it provides the means by which member unions can cooperate to pursue common objectives and attempt to resolve internal problems faced by organized labor. The federation is financed by its member national unions and is governed by a national convention, which meets every two years.

As shown in Figure 12-1, the structure of the AFL-CIO is complex. The federation is active in all states and Puerto Rico. In addition, national unions can affiliate with one or more of the trade and industrial departments. These departments seek to promote the interests of specific groups of workers who are in different unions but have common interests. The federation's major activities include the following:

1. Improving the image of organized labor
2. Extensive lobbying on behalf of labor interests
3. Politically educating constituencies and others through COPE
4. Resolving disputes between national unions
5. Policing internal affairs of member unions

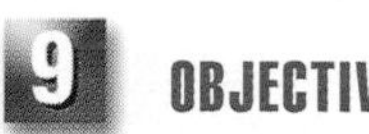

9 OBJECTIVE

Identify the steps involved in establishing the collective bargaining relationship.

Collective bargaining: The performance of the mutual obligation of the employer and the representative of the employees to meet at reasonable times and confer in good faith with respect to wages, hours, and other terms and conditions of employment; or the negotiation of an agreement, or any question arising thereunder; and the execution of a written contract incorporating any agreement reached if requested by either party. Such obligation does not compel either party to agree to a proposal or require the making of a concession.

The AFL-CIO is a loosely knit organization of national unions that has little formal power or control.[64] The member national unions remain completely autonomous and decide their own policies and programs. Not all national unions are members of the federation.

Establishing the Collective Bargaining Relationship: Union Certification

Before a union can negotiate a contract, it must first be certified. The primary law governing the relationship of companies and unions is the National Labor Relations Act, as amended. Collective bargaining is one of the key parts of the act. Section 8(d) of the act defines **collective bargaining** as:

> *The performance of the mutual obligation of the employer and the representative of the employees to meet at reasonable times and confer in good*

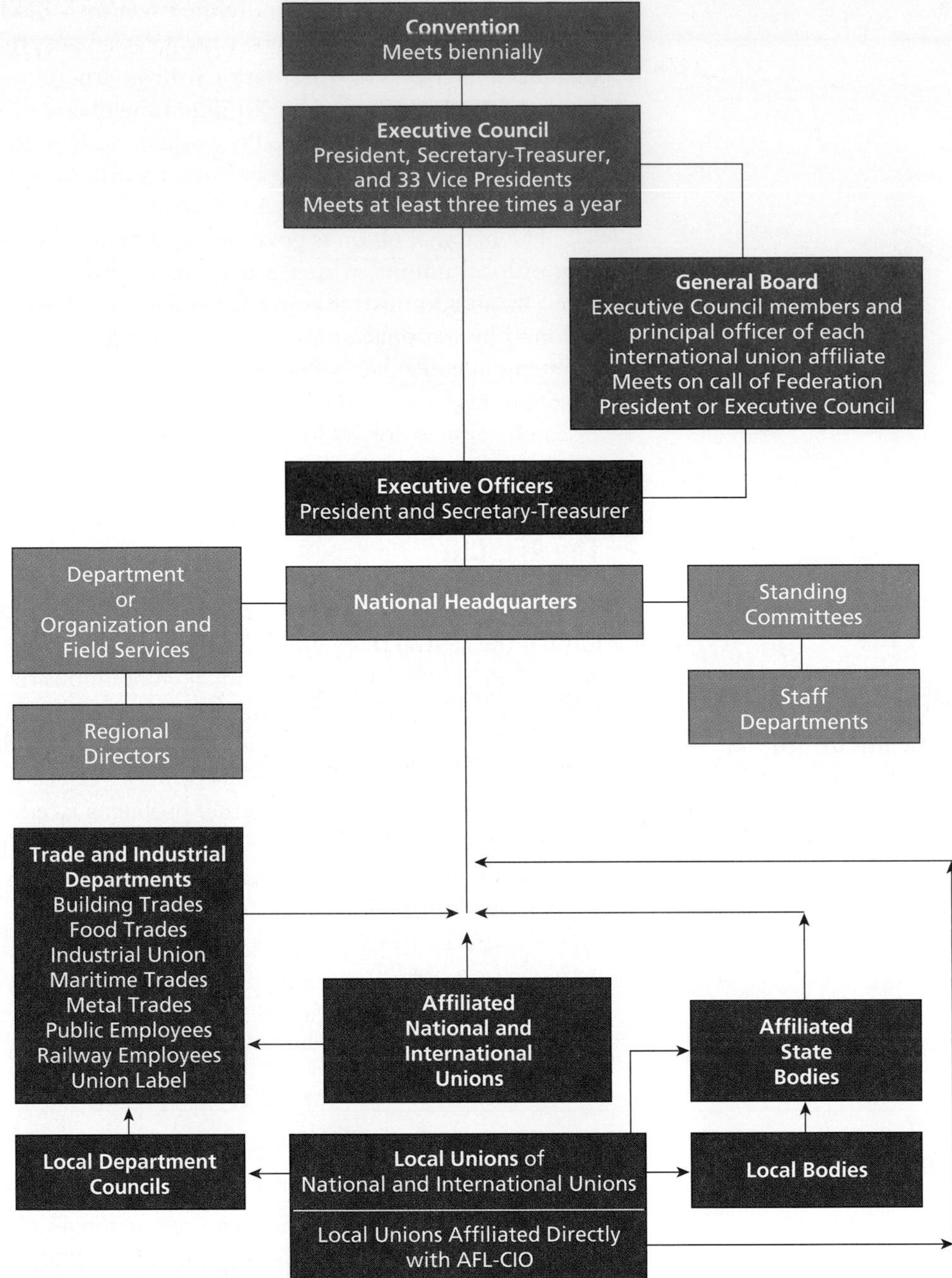

Figure 12-1 The Strucute of the AFL-CIO
Source: Bureau of Labor Statistics, *Directory of National Unions and Employee Associations.*

faith with respect to wages, hours, and other terms and conditions of employment, or the negotiation of an agreement, or any question arising there under, and the execution of a written contract incorporating any agreement reached if requested by either party, but such obligation does not compel either party to agree to a proposal or require the making of a concession.

Bargaining unit: A group of employees, not necessarily union members, recognized by an employer or certified by an administrative agency as appropriate for representation by a labor organization for purposes of collective bargaining.

The act further provides that the designated representative of the employees shall be the exclusive representative for all the employees in the unit for purposes of collective bargaining. A **bargaining unit** consists of a group of employees, not necessarily union members, recognized by an employer or certified by an administrative agency as appropriate for representation by a labor organization for purposes of collective bargaining. A unit may cover the employees in one plant of an employer, or it may cover employees in two or more plants of the same employer. Although the act requires the representative to be selected by the employees, it does not require any

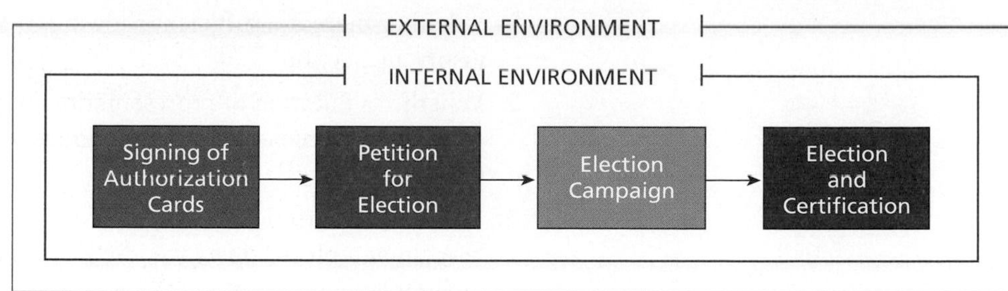

Figure 12-2 The Steps That Lead to Forming a Bargaining Unit

particular procedure to be used so long as the choice clearly reflects the desire of the majority of the employees in the bargaining unit. The employee representative is normally chosen in a secret ballot election conducted by the NLRB. When a union desires to become the bargaining representative for a group of employees, several steps leading to certification have to be taken (see Figure 12-2).

Signing of Authorization Cards

A prerequisite to forming a recognized bargaining unit is to determine whether there is sufficient interest on the part of employees to justify the unit. Evidence of this interest is expressed when at least 30 percent of the employees in a workgroup sign an authorization card. The **authorization card** is a document indicating that an employee wants to be represented by a labor organization in collective bargaining. Most union organizers will not proceed unless at least 50 percent of the workers in the group sign cards. An authorization card used by the International Association of Machinists and Aerospace Workers is shown in Figure 12-3.

Authorization card: A document indicating that an employee wants to be represented by a labor organization in collective bargaining.

Petition for Election

After the authorization cards have been signed, a petition for an election may be made to the appropriate regional office of the *NLRB*. When the petition is filed, the NLRB will conduct an investigation. The purpose of the investigation is to determine, among other things, the following:

1. Whether the Board has jurisdiction to conduct an election

YES, I WANT THE IAM

I, the undersigned, an employee of

(Company) ______________________________,

hereby authorize the International Association of Machinists and Aerospace Workers (IAM) to act as my collective bargaining agent with the company for wages, hours, and working conditions.

NAME (print) ____________ DATE ____________

ADDRESS (print) ____________

CITY ____________ STATE ____________ ZIP ____________

DEPT. ____________ SHIFT ____________ PHONE ____________

Classification ____________

SIGN HERE ✗ ____________

NOTE: THIS AUTHORIZATION IS TO BE SIGNED AND DATED IN EMPLOYEE'S OWN HANDWRITING. YOUR RIGHT TO SIGN THIS CARD IS PROTECTED BY FEDERAL LAW.

Figure 12-3 An Authorization Card
Source: The International Association of Machinists and Aerospace Workers

2. Whether there is a sufficient showing of employee interest to justify an election
3. Whether a question of representation exists (for example, the employee representative has demanded recognition, which has been denied by the employer)
4. Whether the election will include appropriate employees in the bargaining unit (for instance, the Board is prohibited from including plant guards in the same unit with the other employees)
5. Whether the representative named in the petition is qualified (for example, a supervisor or any other management representative may not be an employee representative)
6. Whether there are any barriers to an election in the form of existing contracts or prior elections held within the past 12 months[65]

If these conditions have been met, the NLRB will ordinarily direct that an election be held within 30 days. Election details are left largely to the agency's regional director. Management is prohibited from making unusual concessions or promises that would encourage workers to vote against union recognition.

Election Campaign

When an election has been ordered, both union and management usually promote their causes actively. Unions will continue to encourage workers to join the union, and management may begin a campaign to tell workers the benefits of remaining union-free. The supervisor's role during the campaign is crucial. Supervisors need to conduct themselves in a manner that avoids violating the law and committing unfair labor practices. Specifically, they should be aware of what can and cannot be done in the pre-election campaign period. In many cases, it is not so much what the supervisor says as how it is said.[66] Throughout the campaign, supervisors should keep upper management informed about employee attitudes.

Theoretically, both union and management are permitted to tell their stories without interference from the other side. At times, the campaign becomes quite intense. Election results will be declared invalid if the campaign was marked by conduct that the NLRB considers to have interfered with the employees' freedom of choice. Examples of such conduct include the following:

- An employer or a union threatens loss of jobs or benefits to influence employees' votes or union activities
- An employer or a union misstates important facts in the election campaign when the other party does not have a chance to reply
- Either an employer or a union incites racial or religious prejudice by inflammatory campaign appeals
- An employer fires employees to discourage or encourage their union activities or a union causes an employer to take such an action
- An employer or a union makes campaign speeches to assembled groups of employees on company time within 24 hours of an election

Election and Certification

The NLRB monitors the secret-ballot election on the date set. Its representatives are responsible for making sure that only eligible employees vote and for counting the votes. Following a valid election, the board will issue a certification of the results to the participants. If a union has been chosen by a majority of the employees voting in the bargaining unit, it will receive a certificate showing that it is now the official bargaining representative of the employees in the unit. However, the right to represent employees does not mean the right to dictate terms to management that would adversely affect the organization. The bargaining process does not require either party to make concessions; it only compels them to bargain in good faith.

10 OBJECTIVE

Explain union strategies in obtaining bargaining unit recognition.

Union Strategies in Obtaining Bargaining Unit Recognition

Unions may use various strategies to obtain recognition by management. Unions generally try to make the first move because this places management in the position of having to react to union maneuvers. The search for groups of employees to organize involves a continuous effort by union leaders. To begin a drive, unions often look for areas of dissatisfaction. Union organizers are aware that an overall positive attitude toward management among employees generally indicates that organizing employees will be extremely difficult.

Some situations indicate that employees are ripe for organizing:

- A history of management's unjustified and arbitrary treatment of employees
- Compensation below the industry average
- Management's lack of concern for employee welfare

A union does not normally look at isolated conditions of employee unrest. Rather, it attempts to locate general patterns of employee dissatisfaction. Whatever the case, the union will probably not make a major attempt at organizing unless it believes that it has a good chance of success.

The union may take numerous approaches to getting authorization cards signed. One effective technique is to first identify workers who are not only dissatisfied but also influential in the firm's informal organization. These individuals can assist in developing an effective organizing campaign. Information is obtained through the grapevine regarding who was hired, who was fired, and management mistakes in general. Such information is beneficial to union organizers as they approach company employees. Statements such as this are common: "I hear Bill Adams was fired today. I also understand that he is well liked. No way that would have happened if you had a union."

Ultimately, the union must abandon its secret activities. Sooner or later management will discover the organizing attempt. At this point, union organizers may station themselves and other supporters at company entrances and pass out *throwsheets* or campaign literature proclaiming the benefits of joining the union and emphasizing management weaknesses. They will talk to anyone who will listen in their attempt to identify union sympathizers. Employees who sign an authorization card are then encouraged to convince their friends to sign also. The effort often mushrooms, yielding a sufficient number of signed authorization cards before management has time to react.

Union efforts continue even after the NLRB has approved the election petition. Every attempt is made by the organizers to involve as many workers from the firm as possible. The outside organizers would prefer to take a back seat and let company employees convince their peers to join the union. Peer pressure typically has a much greater effect on convincing a person to join a union than does outside influence. Whenever possible, unions utilize peer pressure to encourage and expand unionization.

 OBJECTIVE

Explain union decertification.

Union Decertification: Reestablishing the Individual Bargaining Relationship

Decertification: Election by a group of employees to withdraw a union's right to act as their exclusive bargaining representative; the reverse of the process that employees must follow to be recognized as an official bargaining unit.

Until 1947, once a union was certified, it was certified forever. However, the Taft-Hartley Act made it possible for employees to decertify a union. This action results in a union losing its right to act as the exclusive bargaining representative of a group of employees. **Decertification** is essentially the reverse of the process that employees must follow to be recognized as an official bargaining unit. The outcome of decertification elections is of increasing concern to unions. Employees have used decertification petitions with increasing frequency and success. In 1965, only 200 decertification elections were held, 64 percent of which the unions lost. Between 1987 and 1991, an average of 636 decertification elections were held each year, resulting in an average union loss rate of 72 percent. Recently, 485 decertification elections were held and the union was ousted in 69 percent of those elections.[67]

Decertification Procedure

The rules established by the NLRB spell out the conditions for filing a decertification petition. At least 30 percent of the bargaining unit members must petition for an election. As might be expected, this task by itself may be difficult because union supporters are likely to oppose the move strongly. Few employees know about decertification and fewer still know how to start the process.[68] Also, although the petitioners' names are supposed to remain confidential, many union members are fearful that their signatures on the petition will be discovered. Timing of the NLRB's receipt of the decertification petition is also critical. The petition must be submitted between 60 and 90 days prior to the expiration of the current contract. When all these conditions have been met, the NLRB regional director will schedule a decertification election by secret ballot.

The NLRB carefully monitors the events leading up to the election. Current employees must initiate the request for the election. If the NLRB determines that management initiated the action, it will not certify the election. After a petition has been accepted, however, management can support the decertification election attempt. If a majority of the votes cast is against the union, the employees will be free from the union. Strong union supporters are all likely to vote. Thus, if a substantial number of employees are indifferent to the union and choose not to vote, decertification may not occur.

Management and Decertification

When management senses employee discontent with the union, it often does not know how to react. Many times, management decides to do nothing, reasoning that it is best not to get involved or that doing so may even be illegal. But if it does want to get involved, management can use a variety of legal tactics. If management really wants the union decertified, it must learn how to be active rather than passive. However, care must be taken to ensure that management's actions do not prompt an unfair labor practice complaint.[69]

Meetings with union members to discuss the benefits of becoming union-free have proven beneficial. In fact, such discussions are often cited as being the most effective campaign tactic. These meetings may be with individual employees, small groups, or even entire units. Management explains the benefits and answers employees' questions.

Management may also provide workers with legal assistance in preparing for decertification. Because the workers probably have never been through a decertification election, this type of assistance may prove invaluable. For example, the NLRB may not permit an election if the paperwork has not been properly completed. Management must always remember that it cannot initiate the decertification action; that is the workers' responsibility.

The most effective means of accomplishing decertification is to improve the corporate culture so workers no longer feel the need to have a union. This cannot be done overnight, as mutual trust and confidence must be developed between workers and the employer. If decertification is to succeed, management must eliminate the problems that initially led to unionization. Although many executives believe that pay and benefits are the primary reasons for union membership, other factors are probably more important. For example, failure to treat employees as individuals is often the primary reason for unionization. The real problems often stem from practices such as failing to listen to employees' opinions, dealing with workers unfairly and dishonestly, and treating employees as numbers and not as people. Employers who desire to remain or become union-free can employ certain strategies and tactics that benefit both employers and employees.

OBJECTIVE

Describe the state of unions today.

Unions Today

Overall, the fall of *Big Labor* since the 1970s has been dramatic. As shown in Figure 12-4, private-sector union membership has fallen from 39 percent of all workers in 1958 to about 9 percent today, the lowest percentage since 1901. It worsened in 2002 when the number of workers who belonged to a national labor union fell to 16.1 million compared to 16.4 million in 2001.[70] The only bright spot for unions was the public sector, where union membership rose 2.3 percent to about 7.4 million workers. Recently, 37.5 percent of all public employees were union members.[71] However, that increase was not nearly enough to offset the 4.8 percent drop in the number of union workers in the private sector, especially in manufacturing, where organized labor rolls fell nearly 8 percent to 2.5 million workers. The United Steelworkers of America's membership was a major loser as dozens of steel makers filed for Chapter 11 bankruptcy protection. Likewise, organized labor in the capital-goods sector saw membership fall, as businesses cut capital-investment spending, prompting manufacturers to make layoffs.[72] In the United States, where unemployment is about 6 percent and all workers are facing cuts in healthcare and pension benefits, labor leaders have not had much success in winning public or political backing.[73] Also, any growth that unions experience will not likely be in manufacturing but in the service sector where wages and benefits are typically lower.[74]

Ever since President Reagan's dismissal of the striking air traffic controllers, labor clout has seriously diminished. Reasons vary, but today, peoples' preference to bargain for themselves and ignore the interests of the collective members of the workforce is becoming more common. Some workers do not like paying union dues, some do not like pay-equalization rules, and some believe that unionized firms might be less competitive and could go out of business (not a problem for public-sector workers).[75]

Figure 12-4 Percentage of the Private Workforce That is Unionized
Source: U.S. Department of Labor.

September 11, 2001, has also had a major negative effect on some unions. For example, the Hotel Employees and Restaurant Employees International Union (HERE) used to be the fastest-growing segment of the AFL-CIO, with some 300,000 members across the United States and Canada. Since 9/11 as many as half of its dues-paying members face job troubles.[76] John Wilhelm, president of Hotel Employees and Restaurant Employees International, and one of the highest-paid leaders, asked that his 2001 salary of $273,100 be cut 20 percent after his union suffered from the problems in the travel industry.[77]

A Global Perspective

The ICFTU Says Union Organizing Can Be Dangerous

According to the International Confederation of Free Trade Unions, thousands of trade unionists were arrested, jailed, tortured, fired, or intimidated, and 223 were murdered or disappeared, across the world in 2001. The ICFTU survey, which draws on data from 132 countries, concluded that over 4,000 trade unionists were arrested, 1,000 injured, and 10,000 fired. Violations were particularly severe in many export-processing zones. Guy Ryder, secretary general of the ICFTU said, "In places like Belarus, Zimbabwe and China, we find that undemocratic governments target trade unions first when their legitimacy is challenged." This umbrella body represents 157 million workers in 225 affiliated organizations in 148 countries.[78]

The report "documents" a long list of abuses, including many in textile and apparel plants in Asia, Africa, Latin America, and also in developed nations like the United States. Juan Somavia, director general of the International Labor Organization, said the report showed that while labor advocates have worked for decades to improve the treatment of workers, "the situation in many countries today shows that the struggle continues." The study alleged that management of JAR Kenya, a clothing maker in Nairobi, embarked on "a hostile attack on the Tailors and Textile Workers Union." It said active union members were "constantly harassed and intimidated. Some were locked up in the factory cell and handed over to the police on fabricated charges." The report added that some were fired solely for joining the union. The survey pointed out that trade union rights are severely violated in many Far Eastern countries. It said police have attacked workers protesting in state-owned textile plants in China. "Any attempt to form a free trade union can be rewarded with huge prison sentences and even life imprisonment," it reported. The ICFTU survey also documented harsh anti-union policies by management of garment and footwear factories in Indonesia and Pakistan, and fierce anti-union tactics in export-promotion zones in the Philippines, Sri Lanka, and other countries.[79]

With regard to the Americas, the report shows hostility toward trade unions is a recurrent problem in many Central and South American countries. In Guatemala, it said, freedom of association "is virtually nonexistent" and added that employers in textile factories or the big multinationals refuse to recognize trade unions. No Guatemalan textile or apparel plants are currently unionized. In the case of the United States, the report estimated that "80 percent of employers engage consultants to assist in anti-union campaigning." ICFTU analysts alleged in the report that "some of the most extreme exploitation" takes place in territories controlled by the United States such as the Northern Mariana Islands. The report argued the conditions there amount to a system of servitude: "Local authorities permit foreign-owned companies to recruit thousands of foreign workers, mainly young women from Thailand, China, the Philippines and Bangladesh." The report contended workers in that region must sign contracts that stipulate they must refrain from asking for wage increases, from seeking other work, or from joining a union. If they violate the contract, they face deportation, the report added.[80]

Summary

1. Describe the partnering of labor and management that is evolving in some sectors.

The agreement formalizes a culture of "working together" in terms of strategy, business planning, and the daily operation of a plant's vital functions.

2. Describe the labor movement prior to 1930.

Prior to the 1930s, the trend definitely favored management. The courts strongly supported employers in their attempts to thwart the organized labor movement.

3. Identify the major labor legislation that was passed after 1930.

Major legislation included the Anti-Injunction Act of 1932, the National Labor Relations Act, the Labor-Management Relations Act, and the Labor-Management Reporting and Disclosure Act. The Homeland Security Act was recently passed.

4. Explain unionization in the public sector.

Employees are permitted to organize and negotiate human resource policies and practices and matters affecting working conditions within the administrative discretion of the agency officials concerned. However, it is a felony for federal employees to strike against the U.S. government.

5. Describe the broad objectives that characterize the labor movement as a whole.

The underlying philosophy of the labor movement is that of organizational democracy and an atmosphere of social dignity for working men and women. To accomplish these objectives, most unions recognize that they must strive for continued growth and power.

6. Describe union growth strategies.

Organized labor's new strategies for a stronger movement include greater political involvement, union salting, flooding the community with organizers, corporate labor campaigns, building organizing funds, organizing students, activism and focus, forming coalitions, and the AFL-CIO cyberunion.

7. Explain the reasons why employees join unions.

Employees join unions due to dissatisfaction with management, need for a social outlet, need for avenues of leadership, forced unionization, and social pressure from peers.

8. Describe the basic structure of the union.

The basic element in the structure of the American labor movement is the local union. The national union is the most powerful level, and the American Federation of Labor and Congress of Industrial Organizations (AFL-CIO) is the central trade union federation in the United States.

9. Identify the steps involved in establishing the collective bargaining relationship.

The steps involved include signing authorization cards, petitioning for election, campaigning, winning the election, and being certified.

10. Explain union strategies in obtaining bargaining unit recognition.

Unions generally try to make the first move because this places management in the position of having to react to union maneuvers. The search for groups of employees to organize involves a continuous effort by union leaders. To begin a drive, unions often look for areas of dissatisfaction.

11. Explain union decertification.

Decertification is essentially the reverse of the process that employees must follow to be recognized as an official bargaining unit.

12. Describe the state of unions today.

Overall, the fall of *Big Labor* has been dramatic since the 1970s.

Key Terms

- **Conspiracy, 396**
- **Injunction, 397**
- **Yellow-dog contract, 397**
- **Right-to-work laws, 400**
- **Union salting, 406**
- **Flooding the community, 406**
- **Corporate labor campaigns, 407**
- **Local union, 410**
- **Craft union, 410**
- **Industrial union, 410**
- **National union, 410**
- **Collective bargaining, 411**
- **Bargaining unit, 412**
- **Authorization card, 413**
- **Decertification, 416**

Questions for Review

1. Describe the development of the labor movement in the United States before 1930.
2. What major labor legislation was passed after 1930?
3. What unfair labor practices by management were prohibited by the Wagner Act?
4. What union actions does the Taft-Hartley Act prohibit?
5. What are the broad objectives that characterize the labor movement as a whole?
6. What growth strategies are unions currently using?
7. In what way does unionization of the public sector differ from unionization of the private sector?
8. What are the primary reasons for employees joining labor unions?
9. Define the following terms:
   a. local union
   b. craft union
   c. industrial union
   d. national union
10. What steps must a union take in attempting to form a bargaining unit? Briefly describe each step.
11. What are ways unions might go about gaining bargaining unit recognition?
12. Define decertification. What are the steps in decertification?

HRM Incident 1

Open the Door

Barney Cline, the new human resource manager for Ampex Utilities, was just getting settled in his new office. He had recently moved from another firm to take this new job. Barney had been selected over several in-house candidates and numerous other applicants because of his record of getting things done. He had a good reputation for working through people to get the job accomplished.

Barney's phone rang. The person on the other end of the line asked, "Mr. Cline, could I set up an appointment to talk with you?" "Certainly," Barney said, "when do you want to get together?" "How about after work? It might be bad if certain people saw me speaking to anyone in management," said the caller.

Barney was a bit puzzled, but he set up an appointment for 5:30 P.M., when nearly everyone would be gone. At the designated time, there was a knock on his door; it was Mark Johnson, a senior maintenance worker who had been with the firm for more than 10 years.

After the initial welcome, Mark began by saying, "Mr. Cline, several of the workers asked me to talk to you. Rumor has it that you're a fair person. The company says it has an open-door policy, but we're afraid to use it. Roy Edwards, one of the best maintenance workers in our section, tried it several months ago. They hassled him so much that he quit last week. We just don't know what to do to get any problems solved. There has been talk of organizing a union. We really don't want that, but something has to give."

Barney thanked Mark for his honesty and promised not to reveal the conversation. In the weeks following the conversation with Mark, Barney was able to verify that the situation existed just as Mark had described. There was considerable mistrust between managers and the operative employees.

Questions

1. What are the basic causes of the problems confronting Ampex Utilities?
2. How should Barney attempt to resolve these problems?

HRM Incident 2

You Are Out Of What?

Marcus Ned eagerly drove his new company pickup onto the construction site. His employer, Kelso Construction Company, had just assigned him to supervise a crew of 16 equipment operators, oilers, and mechanics. This was the first unionized crew Marcus had supervised, and he was unaware of the labor agreement in effect that carefully defined and limited the role of supervisors. As he approached his work area, he noticed one of the cherry pickers (a type of mobile crane with an extendable boom) standing idle with the operator beside it. Marcus pulled up beside the operator and asked, "What's going on here?"

"Out of gas," the operator said.

"Well, go and get some," Marcus said.

The operator reached to get his thermos jug out of the toolbox on the side of the crane and said, "The oiler's on break right now. He'll be back in a few minutes."

Marcus remembered that he had a five-gallon can of gasoline in the back of his pickup. So he quickly got the gasoline, climbed on the cherry picker, and started to pour it into the gas tank. As he did so, he heard the other machines shutting down in unison. He looked around and saw all the other operators climbing down from their equipment and standing to watch him pour the gasoline. A moment later, he saw the union steward approaching.

Questions

1. Why did all the operators shut down their machines?
2. If you were Marcus, what would you do now?

We invite you to visit the Mondy homepage on the Prentice Hall Web site at

www.prenhall.com/mondy

for updated information, Web-based exercises, and links to other HR-related sites.

Notes

1. Tim Stevens, "Perfect Partners," *Industry Week* 251 (October 2002): 59–61.
2. Ibid.
3. Ibid.
4. Ibid.
5. Matt Glynn, "In a New Age, Unions Are Taking on Nontraditional Roles," *Buffalo News* (January 26, 2003): P24.
6. Sherie Winston, "Ironworkers and Contractors Try to Regain Lost Market Share," *ENR* (March 17, 2003): 18.
7. *Brief History of the American Labor Movement*, Bulletin 1000 (Washington, DC: U.S. Department of Labor Statistics, 1970): 1.
8. Benjamin J. Taylor and Fred Witney, *Labor Relations Law*, 5th ed. (Englewood Cliffs, NJ: Prentice Hall, 1987): 12–13.
9. *Brief History of the American Labor Movement*, 9.
10. Foster Rhea Dulles, *Labor in America*, 3rd ed. (New York: Crowell, 1966): 114–125.
11. Ibid., 126–149.
12. E. Edward Herman, Alfred Kuhn, and Ronald L. Seeber, *Collective Bargaining and Labor Relations* (Englewood Cliffs, NJ: Prentice Hall, 1987): 32–34.
13. *Brief History of the American Labor Movement*, 27.
14. Eric Torbenson, "Coalition Seeks Stop to AMR's Efforts to Change Railway Labor Act," *Dallas Morning News* (January 22, 2003): 1.
15. "The Airline Wage Escalator," *Wall Street Journal* (April 18, 2003): A8.
16. *Historical Statistics of the United States, Colonial Times to 1970*, bicentennial ed., part I (Washington, DC: U.S. Bureau of the Census, 1975): 126.
17. Taylor and Witney, *Labor Relations Law*, 78–81.
18. *Brief History of the American Labor Movement*, 65.
19. Robert P. Hunter, "Executive Summary of the Effect of Right-to-Work Laws on Economic Development," *Government Union Review and Public Policy Digest* 20 (2002): 27–30.
20. Ibid.

21. Charles W. Baird, "Unions on the Run," *Government Union Review and Public Policy Digest* 20 (2002): 21–24.
22. Dulles, *Labor in America*, 382–383.
23. *Brief History of the American Labor Movement*, 58–61.
24. "Sandbagging Secretary Chao," *Wall Street Journal* (Mar 3, 2003): A16.
25. Douglas P. Shuit, "New Agency, Huge HR Changes," *Workforce* 82 (January 2003): 15.
26. Brian Friel, "Labor Pains," *Government Executive* 34 (October 2002): 20–26.
27. Examples include the Social Security Act, the Fair Labor Standards Act, and the National Labor Relations Act, as amended.
28. Section 305 of the Labor Management Relations Act of 1947 also makes it unlawful for government employees to participate in any strike.
29. http://www.afge.org/Index.cfm?Page=AboutAFGE, March 10, 2003.
30. http://www.natca.org/about/default.msp, March 10, 2003.
31. Brian Friel, "Labor Pains," 20–26.
32. Ricardo Alonso-Zaldivar, "White House Steps Up Labor Fight, Denies Screeners Right to Organize: Union Calls the Move Illegal and Vows to File Suit on Behalf of 56,000 Airport Workers," *Los Angeles* (January 10, 2003): A16.
33. Herman, Kuhn, and Seeber, *Collective Bargaining and Labor Relations*, 407.
34. http://www.nea.org/aboutnea.html, February 14, 2003.
35. http://www.afscme.org/about/index.html, February 14, 2003.
36. Edwin F. Beal and James P. Begin, *The Practice of Collective Bargaining*, 5th ed. (Homewood, IL: Richard D. Irwin, 1982): 91.
37. Brian Friel, "Labor Pains," *Government Executive* 34 (October 2002): 20–26.
38. T. L. Stanley "Excuse Me, But Are Those Pickets Outside Your Door?" *Supervision* 63 (February 2002): 9–12.
39. Aaron Bernstein, "Will CEO Pain Lead to Labor Gains?" *Business Week* 3799 (September 16, 2002): 6.
40. Joann Muller, "Has the UAW Found a Better Road?" *Business Week* 3791 (July 15, 2002): 108.
41. Charles W. Baird, "Unions on the Run," *Government Union Review and Public Policy Digest* 20 (2002): 21–24.
42. Thomas B. Edsall, "For AFL-CIO and White House, The Great Divide Is Deepening," *Washington Post* (September 2, 2002): A10.
43. "AFL-CIO Focusing on 2004 Elections," *The Washington Times* (February 26, 2003): 1.
44. Kelly Cryderman, "'Salting' to Top List of Labour Code Issues: Committee Will Look at Union Certification and Picketing," *Edmonton Journal* (June 10, 2002): A6.
45. Cory R. Fine, "Covert Union Organizing: Beware the Trojan Horse," *Workforce* 77 (May 1998): 44.
46. Lyncheski and McDermott, "Union Employ New Growth Strategies."
47. Fine, "Covert Union Organizing: Beware the Trojan Horse."
48. Bill Schmitt, "Union Safety Initiative Survives a Big Test," *Chemical Week* 164 (July 3-July 10, 2002): 59.
49. Galvin, "Rising Global Job Market Has Dimmed the Nation's Stake in Labor Strikes/Changing Times Have Unions Organizing to Rejuvenate the Ranks in Solidarity."
50. Sharon Leonard, "Unions Could Be Staging a Comeback," *HRMagazine* 44 (December 1999): 207.
51. "USWA Will Form $40 million Organizing Fund," *Iron Age New Steel* 14 (September 1998): 40.
52. Mike Hughlett, "Unions Use Fund in Bidding Battle Against Non-Union Contractors," *Saint Paul Pioneer Press* (Apr 7, 2002): 1.
53. http://home.workfam.com/, February 13, 2003.
54. Cynthia G. Wagner, "Cyberunions: Organized Labor Goes Online," *The Futurist* 34 (January/February 2000): 7.
55. Kathy Brister, "AFL-CIO Befriends WorldCom Jobless Labor Federation: Has Eye on Future," *The Atlanta Journal and Constitution* (November 13, 2002): D1.
56. John Gallagher, "Workers Consider Much More than Wages When Deciding to Join Union," *Detroit Free Press* (December 27, 2002): 1.
57. David Y. Denholm, "Does Unionism Mean Higher Earnings or Higher Taxes?" *Government Union Review* 20 (2002): 17–32.
58. Ibid.
59. Dave Berns, "Las Vegas Casino Is Not Unionized But Is Not Anti-Union, Executives Say," *Las Vegas Review-Journal* (June 29, 2002).
60. Michael R. Carrell and Christina Heavrin, *Labor Relations and Collective Bargaining*, 5th ed. (Upper Saddle River, NJ: Prentice Hall, 1998): 95.
61. "The National Union International Union, United Automobile, Aerospace and Agricultural Implement Workers of America," *Britannica Intermediate Encyclopedia* (December 09, 2002).
62. "International Brotherhood of Teamsters," *Hoover's Company Capsules* 40458 (February 1, 2003).
63. "AFL-CIO," *Hoover's Company Capsules* (January 15, 2003): 40565.
64. Miller, "Labor on the Rebound?"
65. *A Guide to Basic Law and Procedures Under the National Labor Relations Act* (Washington, DC: U.S. Government Printing Office, October 1978): 11–13.
66. Art Bethke, R. Wayne Mondy, and Shane R. Premeaux, "Decertification: The Role of the First-Line Supervisor," *Supervisory Management* 31 (February 1986): 21–23.
67. Catherine Meeker, "Union Decertification Under the National Labor Relations Act," *The University of Chicago Law Review* 66 (Summer 1999): 999.
68. Ibid.
69. Satish P. Deshpande and Jacob Joseph, "Decertification Elections in Health Care: Some Recent Evidence," *The Health Care Manager* 22 (April-June 2003): 108–112.
70. "Union Membership Declined by 300,000 Last Year," *ENR* 250 (March 3, 2003): 7.
71. David Y. Denholm, "Does Unionism Mean Higher Earnings or Higher Taxes?" *Government Union Review* 20 (2002): 17–32.
72. Carlos Tejada, "Decline in Union Membership in 2002 Was Biggest Since 1995," *Wall Street Journal* (February 26, 2003): A10.
73. Carlos Tejada, "U.S. Economic Woes Favor Management—Labor Leaders, Unlike Counterparts Abroad, Have Difficulty Winning Public Backing," *Wall Street Journal* (December 17, 2002): A2.
74. Tami J. Friedman, "The Workers Aren't Nontraditional—But the Strategy Should Be," *Dollars & Sense* (September 1, 2002): 8.

75. Dan Seligman, "Driving the AFL-CIO Crazy," *Forbes Magazine* 164 (November 1, 1999): 102–108.
76. Carlos Tejada, "A Special News Report About Life on the Job—and Trends Taking Shape There," *Wall Street Journal* (October 2, 2001): A1.
77. Ibid.
78. John Zarocostas, "Organizing in the Third World a Dangerous Job, Study Finds," *International Confederation of Free Trade Unions Reports* (June 25, 2002): 8.
79. Ibid.
80. Ibid.

CHAPTER OBJECTIVES

After completing this chapter, students should be able to

1. Discuss whether or not an adversarial relationship exists between unions and management.
2. Explain labor–management relations and individual bargaining.
3. Describe labor–management relations and collective bargaining.
4. Explain the psychological aspects of collective bargaining.
5. Describe the factors involved in preparing for negotiations.
6. Explain typical bargaining issues.
7. Describe the process of negotiating the agreement.
8. Identify ways to overcome breakdowns in negotiations.
9. Describe what is involved in ratifying the agreement.
10. Explain factors involved in administering the agreement.
11. Describe collective bargaining in the public sector.

CHAPTER 13

Collective Bargaining

HRM IN *Action:*

Does an Adversarial Relationship Exist?

 **OBJECTIVE**

Discuss whether or not an adversarial relationship exists between unions and management.

Today, many believe that to counteract management tactics, organized labor has been using an old-style, adversarial collective bargaining relationship. As evidence, they cite strikes in 1998 at Northwest Airlines, General Motors Corp., and Bell Atlantic. In 1999, the pilots at American Airlines staged a 10-day sickout that forced the airline to cancel more than 6,600 flights. Some believe that this new adversarial relationship has emerged because union leaders need a tougher position at the bargaining table to get higher visibility for organizing purposes. A tougher stance and highly visible strikes help the labor organizing movement.[1]

Whether this adversarial relationship can sustain itself is still unknown, but events have certainly changed since late 1999. Northwest Airlines laid off about 10,000 workers in the aftermath of the September 11 terrorist attacks.[2] American Airlines called for $1.8 billion in concessions from unions as the struggling carrier turned to labor for crucial help in its fight to stem the increasing flow of red ink.[3] Bell Atlantic Corporation purchased GTE Corporation two years ago to form Verizon. Company-wide, Verizon reduced its workforce by more than 23,000 in the year ending in June to 241,000 employees.[4]

Four years ago, Boeing was making 620 airplanes a year to fill orders in a booming economy. When the International Association of Machinists union demanded a new labor pact, management felt it had little choice but to hand over a rich package with 10 percent bonuses, 25 percent pension hikes, and strong job security language. The situation has certainly changed today. The old contract that covered 25,000 IAM workers expired in September 2002, but demands for planes were weak, and management acted like it would not mind shutting down its factories for a while to let orders catch up with production. The company was playing hardball with the union. On August 27, 2002, it placed a final offer of a 2 percent pay hike and none of the job guarantees against overseas outsourcing that union members demanded.[5] The union ultimately accepted the contract offer.[6]

Business and labor must find a new way of dealing with each another. Now may be the time for labor and management to develop a whole new attitude and turn adversarial relationships into productive partnerships. The old adversarial relationships have produced distrust. The game of bargaining one-upsmanship erodes productivity in these days of increased foreign competition. What is needed is an entire change in the process and attitude as management sits with labor to resolve problems.[7] This partnering of management and labor is what is needed to bring about change in the adversarial relationship now existing (recall our discussion from Chapter 12).

The first part of this chapter was devoted to discussing whether or not an adversarial relationship exists between union and management. Next, we discuss labor–management relations involving both individual and collective bargaining. We then describe the psychological aspects of collective bargaining and preparing for negotiations. Next, we address bargaining issues, negotiating the agreement, and breakdowns in negotiations. Then we describe what is involved in ratifying and administering the agreement. Collective bargaining in the public sector is the final section in this chapter.

2 OBJECTIVE

Explain labor–management relations and individual bargaining.

SHRM HR Links

www.shrm.org/hrlinks/default.asp

This SHRM Web site provides information on various labor issues.

Individual Bargaining

We previously stated that approximately 9 percent of the private workforce is unionized.[8] Therefore, over 90 percent of the private workforce bases its labor–management relations on individual bargaining.[9] We also mentioned in Chapter 12 that one of the goals of a union is to gain power, which is largely dependent on the size of union membership. In individual negotiations, however, the worker is alone in negotiating with company representatives. Even so, negotiations can still be on a power basis, depending on the value of the individual to the company. An employee who continuously adds value to him or herself is in a position of power, especially if a demand for a particular skill is high and supply is low. Should an individual desire a raise or other tangible evidence of value, negotiations will likely receive positive results if the company values the worker. Otherwise, the worker can join another company. Seniority means little in this environment. Negotiations are ineffective unless the worker has a positive value component. This was true for the nursing profession even during the depressed economy of early 2003. An individual negotiator usually falls under the concept of employment at will. Employment at will is discussed in greater detail in Chapter 14.

One might think that an individual employee would be extremely vulnerable when dealing with individual negotiations. As our society becomes more legalistic, more and more individual rights are protected. Think back to Chapter 3, which detailed the many laws and court decisions that exist to protect individual rights. In the past, many of these protections were based on union representation. Individual negotiators now possess many of these rights.

Most workers in the U.S. economy are not unionized. However, if a firm desires to remain union-free, management must maintain an environment that discourages unionizing attempts. The old saying that *management gets what it deserves* is never truer than when a union successfully organizes a group of employees. When unionization occurs, collective bargaining follows.

3 OBJECTIVE

Describe labor–management relations and collective bargaining.

Collective Bargaining

The collective bargaining process is fundamental to union–management relations in the United States. Most union–management agreements in the United States are for a three-year period. Thus, on average, one-third of collective bargaining agreements occur each year.

Forms of Bargaining Structures and Union–Management Relationships

The bargaining structure can affect the conduct of collective bargaining. The four major structures are one company dealing with a single union, several companies dealing with a single union, several unions dealing with a single company, and several companies dealing with several unions.

Most contract bargaining is carried out under the first type of structure. The process can become quite complicated when several companies and unions are involved in the same negotiations. However, even when there is only one industry involved and one group of workers with similar skills, collective bargaining can be very difficult.

The type of union–management relationship that exists can have a major impact on the collective bargaining process. When a group of workers decide they want union representation, changes occur in the organization. Sloane and Witney list six types of union–management relations that may exist in an organization:

1. *Conflict.* Each challenges the other's actions and motivation; cooperation is nonexistent, and uncompromising attitudes and union militancy are present.
2. *Armed truce.* Each views the other as antagonistic but tries to avoid head-on conflict; bargaining obligations and contract provisions are strictly interpreted.
3. *Power bargaining.* Management accepts the union; each side tries to gain advantage from the other.
4. *Accommodation.* Each tolerates the other in a *live and let live* atmosphere and attempts to reduce conflict without eliminating it.
5. *Cooperation.* Each side accepts the other, and both work together to resolve human resource and production problems as they occur. Although the National Labor Relations Act of 1935 prohibits management domination of unions, cooperation is allowed if prescribed in the collective bargaining agreement.
6. *Collusion.* Both *cooperate* to the point of adversely affecting the legitimate interests of employees, other businesses in the industry, and the consuming public; this involves conniving to control markets, supplies, and prices illegally and/or unethically.[10]

The nature and quality of union–management relations vary over time.[11] Today, many employers appear unwilling to accept unions.[12] This attitude has created an adversarial relationship with labor. Basically, during the past years, U.S. industry has conducted one of its most successful anti-union wars ever, and many managers appear eager to continue their assault on labor. According to the National Labor Relations Board, companies are increasingly using every weapon, legal or not, to thwart attempts to organize their workers. Some of the tactics that unions have accused management of using include harassing and firing pro-union workers, as well as management coercion that intimidates workers. According to National Association of Manufacturers Vice President Patrick J. Cleary, managers are merely "exercising their First Amendment rights to give [workers] facts about unions" when they campaign against unions. Others believe that there is a disturbing trend of management coercion that inhibits workers.[13]

The Collective Bargaining Process

Regardless of the current state of labor–management relations, the general aspects of the collective bargaining process are the same and are illustrated in Figure 13-1.

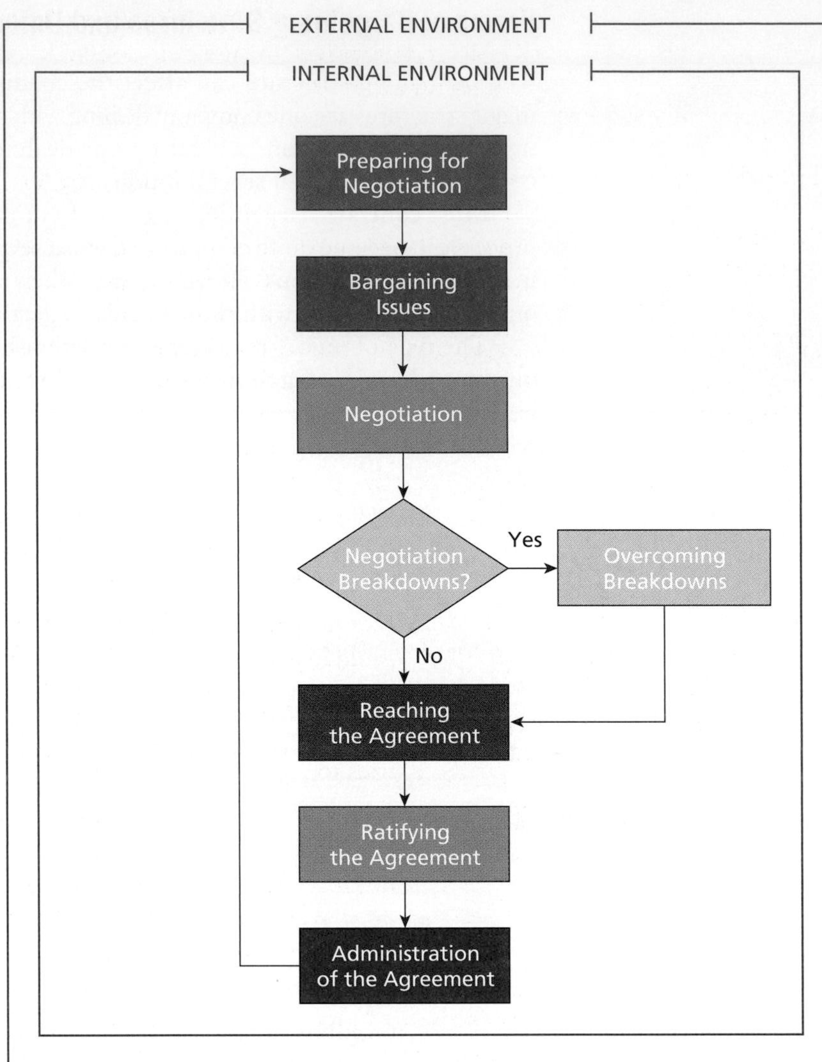

Figure 13-1 The Collective Bargaining Process

Depending on the type of relationship encountered, the collective bargaining process may be relatively simple, or it may be a long, tense struggle for both parties. Regardless of the complexity of the bargaining issues, the ability to reach agreement is the key to any successful negotiation.

As you can see, both external and internal environmental factors can influence the process. Remember the environment that Boeing employees experienced four years ago versus the environment that existed when the workers were forced to take Boeing's final offer of 2 percent. What other kinds of questions regarding collective bargaining arose after 9/11? How have collective bargaining partners balanced their legal rights and obligations with their moral obligations arising out of the 9/11 tragedy, and how will they do so in the future?[14] Labor and management are still coming to grips with questions such as these.

The first step in the collective bargaining process is preparing for negotiations. This step is often extensive and ongoing for both union and management. After the issues to be negotiated have been determined, the two sides confer to reach a mutually acceptable contract. Although breakdowns in negotiations can occur, both labor and management have at their disposal tools and arguments that can be used to convince the other side to accept their views. Eventually, however, management and the union usually reach an agreement that defines the rules of the game for the duration of the contract. The next step is for the union membership to ratify the agreement. Note the feedback loop from "Administration of the Agreement" to "Preparing for

Negotiation" in Figure 13-1. Collective bargaining is a continuous and dynamic process, and preparing for the next round of negotiations often begins the moment a contract is ratified.

OBJECTIVE

Explain the psychological aspects of collective bargaining.

Labor and Industrial Relations

www.lir.msu.edu/hotlinks/ir.htm

This Web site provides links to numerous sites related to labor and industrial relations.

Psychological Aspects of Collective Bargaining

Prior to collective bargaining, both management and union teams have to prepare positions and accomplish certain tasks. Vitally important for those involved are the psychological aspects of collective bargaining. Psychologically, the collective bargaining process is often difficult because it is an adversarial situation and must be approached as such.[15] It is a situation that is fundamental to law, politics, business, and government, because out of the clash of ideas, points of view, and interests come agreement, consensus, and justice.

In effect, those involved in the collective bargaining process will be matching wits with the competition, will experience victory as well as defeat, and will still usually resolve problems, resulting in a contract. The role of those who meet at the bargaining table essentially involves the management of aggression in a manner that allows them to hammer out a collective bargaining agreement. The personalities of those involved have a major impact on the negotiation process. The attitudes of those who will be negotiating have a direct effect on what can be accomplished and how quickly a mutually agreed-on contract can be finalized. Finally, the longer, more involved, and intense the bargaining sessions are, the greater will be the psychological strain on all concerned. As psychological pressures intensify, the gap between labor and management can easily widen, further compounding the problem of achieving mutual accommodation.

Scare tactics intensify the psychological pressures of collective bargaining. Labor may threaten to strike; management may threaten a lockout. Most likely, neither side wants either a strike or a lockout, but it is hoped that the psychological impact of the threat will bring the other side back to the bargaining table. The Boeing bargaining team probably knew that the threat of a strike was useless this time because Boeing would likely relish a strike since demand for planes was down.[16]

OBJECTIVE

Describe the factors involved in preparing for negotiations.

Preparing for Negotiations

Because of the complex issues facing labor and management today, the negotiating teams must carefully prepare for the bargaining sessions. Prior to meeting at the bargaining table, the negotiators should thoroughly know the culture, climate, history, present economic state, and wage and benefits structure of both the organization and similar organizations. Because the length of a typical labor agreement is three years, negotiators should develop a contract that is successful both now and in the future. This consideration should prevail for both management and labor, although it rarely does. During the term of an agreement, the two sides usually discover contract provisions that need to be added, deleted, or modified. These items become proposals to be addressed in the next round of negotiations.

Mandatory bargaining issues: Bargaining issues that fall within the definition of wages, hours, and other terms and conditions of employment; refusal to bargain in these areas is grounds for an unfair labor practice charge.

Permissive bargaining issues: Issues that may be raised but neither side may insist that they be bargained over.

Bargaining issues can be divided into three categories: mandatory, permissive, and prohibited. **Mandatory bargaining issues** fall within the definition of wages, hours, and other terms and conditions of employment (see Table 13-1). These issues generally have an immediate and direct effect on workers' jobs. A refusal to bargain in these areas is grounds for an unfair labor practice charge. In many industries, collective bargaining toward new wage, rules, and benefits agreements typically drags on for a long time.[17] One of the biggest issues in 2003 was the rising health costs and who was going to pay for them.[18]

Permissive bargaining issues may be raised, but neither side may insist that they be bargained over. For example, the union may want to bargain over health benefits

Table 13-1 Mandatory Bargaining Issues

Wages	Plant closedown and relocation
Hours	Change in operations resulting in reclassifying workers from incentive to straight time, or a cut in the workforce, or installation of cost-saving machinery
Discharge	Price of meals provided by company
Arbitration	Group insurance—health, accident, life
Paid holidays	Promotions
Paid vacations	Seniority
Duration of agreement	Layoffs
Grievance procedure	Transfers
Layoff plan	Work assignments and transfers
Reinstatement of economic strikers	No-strike clause
Change of payment from hourly base to salary base	Piece rates
Union security and checkoff of dues	Stock purchase plan
Work rules	Workloads
Merit wage increase	Change of employee status to independent contractors
Work schedule	Motor carrier-union agreement providing that carriers use own equipment before leasing outside equipment
Lunch periods	Overtime pay
Rest periods	Agency shop
Pension plan	Sick leave
Retirement age	Employer's insistence on clause giving an arbitrator the right to enforce an award
Bonus payments	Management rights clause
Cancellation of seniority upon relocation of plant	Plant closing
Discounts on company products	Job posting procedures
Shift differentials	Plant reopening
Contract clause providing for supervisors keeping seniority in unit	Employee physical examination
Procedures for income tax withholding	Arrangement for negotiation
Severance pay	Change in insurance carrier and benefits
Nondiscriminatory hiring hall	Profit-sharing plan
Plant rules	Company houses
Safety	Subcontracting
Prohibition against supervisor doing unit work	Production ceiling imposed by union
Superseniority for union stewards	
Partial plant closing	
Hunting on employer's forest reserve where previously granted	

Source: Reed Richardson, "Positive Collective Bargaining," Chapter 7.5 of ASPA *Handbook of Personnel and Industrial Relations,* 7–121. Copyright 1979 by The Bureau of National Affairs, Inc., Washington, DC. Reprinted by permission.

for retired workers or union participation in establishing company-pricing policies, but management may choose not to bargain over either issue.[19] A permissive bargaining issue would be the AFL-CIO emphasizing work-family issues, particularly child care, in bargaining. According to the head of the AFL-CIO's Department of Working Women, "Despite the fact that over half the women with young children work outside the home, as a country, we still cling to the 'every woman for herself attitude' and dare to call it a solution to the country's child care crisis." This is a critical issue because fewer than 10 percent of Americans feel that the country's child-care system meets the essential child-care criteria.[20]

Prohibited bargaining issues: Issues that are statutorily outlawed.

Prohibited bargaining issues, such as the issue of the closed shop, are statutorily outlawed. The Taft-Hartley Act made the closed shop illegal. However, the act was modified 12 years later by the Landrum-Griffin Act to permit a closed shop in the construction industry. This is the only exception allowed.

The union must continuously gather information regarding membership needs to isolate areas of dissatisfaction. The union steward is normally in the best position to collect such data. Because they are usually elected by their peers, stewards should be well informed regarding union members' attitudes. The union steward constantly fun-

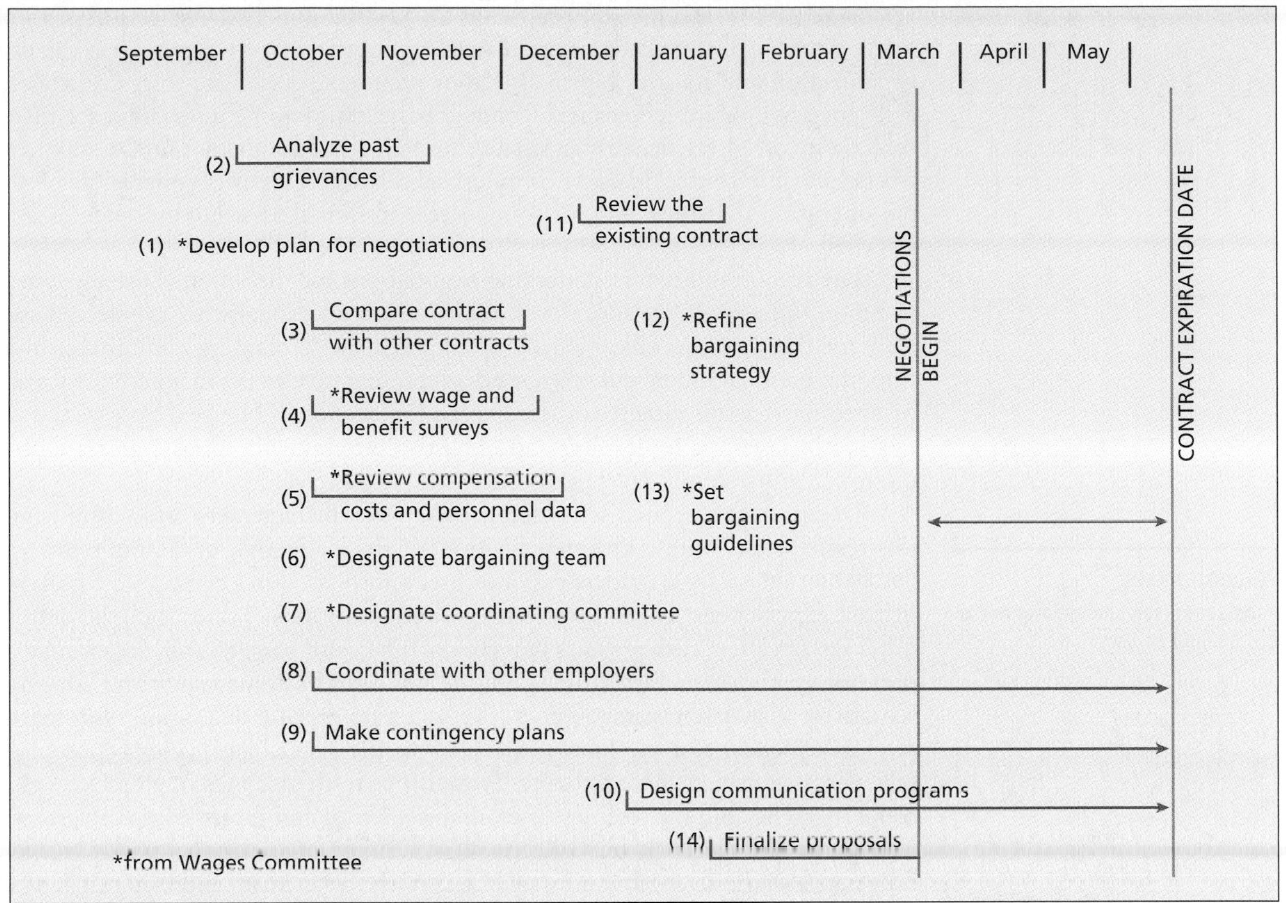

Figure 13-2 An Example of Company Preparations for Negotiations
Source: Adapted from Ronald L. Miller. "Preparations for Negotiations," *Personnel Journal* 57:38. Copyright January 1978. Reprinted with permission.

nels information up through the union's chain of command, where the data are compiled and analyzed. Union leadership attempts to uncover any areas of dissatisfaction because the general union membership must approve any agreement before it becomes final. Because they are elected, union leaders will lose their positions if the demands they make of management do not represent the desires of the general membership.

Management also spends long hours preparing for negotiations. The many interrelated tasks that management must accomplish are presented in Figure 13-2. In this example, the firm allows approximately six months to prepare for negotiations. All aspects of the current contracts are considered, including flaws that should be corrected. When preparing for negotiations, management should listen carefully to first-line managers. These individuals administer the labor agreement on a day-to-day basis and must live with errors made in negotiating the contract. An alert line manager is also able to inform upper management of the demands unions may plan to make during negotiations.

Management also attempts periodically to obtain information regarding employee attitudes. Surveys are often administered to workers to determine their feelings toward their jobs and job environment. Union and management representatives like to know as much as possible about employee attitudes when they sit down at the bargaining table.

Another part of preparation for negotiations involves identifying various positions that both union and management will take as the negotiations progress. Each usually takes an initially extreme position, representing the conditions union or management would prefer. The two sides will likely determine absolute limits to their offers or demands before a breakdown in negotiations occurs. They also usually prepare fallback positions based on combinations of issues. Preparations should be detailed because clear minds often do not prevail during the heat of negotiations.

A major consideration in preparing for negotiations is the selection of the bargaining teams. The makeup of the management team usually depends on the type of organization and its size. Normally, labor relations specialists, with the advice and assistance of operating managers, conduct bargaining. Sometimes, top executives are directly involved, particularly in smaller firms. Larger companies utilize staff specialists (a human resource manager or industrial relations executive), managers of principal operating divisions, and, in some cases, an outside consultant, such as a labor attorney.

The responsibility for conducting negotiations for the union is usually entrusted to union officers. At the local level, rank-and-file members who are elected specifically for this purpose will normally supplement the bargaining committee. In addition, the national union will often send a representative to act in an advisory capacity or even participate directly in the bargaining sessions. The real task of the union negotiating team is to develop and obtain solutions to the problems raised by the union's membership.

Perception set:
A fixed tendency to interpret information in a certain way.

Traditional perceptual set differences between management and union negotiating teams contribute additional friction to the collective bargaining process. A **perception set** is a fixed tendency to interpret information in a certain way. Differences in past experiences, educational background, emotions, values, beliefs, and many other factors affect each person's perception. The word *management*, for example, may provoke an entirely different image in the minds of both managers and labor representatives. Management negotiators may have a perception that union representatives are less educated and less knowledgeable. On the other hand, labor representatives may perceive management as being less sensitive to the feelings of employees than to property rights and the realities of economic survival and future company growth. As part of their preparation for collective bargaining, negotiators on both sides should fully appraise the strengths and weaknesses of the other team and bring this information to bear during negotiations.

Finally, it is imperative that both groups appreciate the environment in which companies in the industry must operate. While there are environmental differences between industries, some basic similarities do exist. There have been rapid technological changes and ever-increasing competitive global pressures. Union membership has fallen and management does not hesitate to transfer lower-skilled and/or labor-intensive jobs overseas. More and more, the jobs remaining in the United States require specific skills, adaptability, and flexibility; traits that many traditional core union members historically lacked. Also, worker involvement is a reality and not an option for many corporations.

6 OBJECTIVE

Explain typical bargaining issues.

Bargaining Issues

The document that emerges from the collective bargaining process is known as a *labor agreement* or *contract*. It regulates the relationship between employer and employees for a specified period of time. Collective bargaining basically determines the relationship between labor and management. It is still an essential but difficult task because each agreement is unique, and there is no standard or universal model. Despite much dissimilarity, certain topics are included in virtually all labor agreements. These include recognition, management rights, union security, compensation and benefits, a grievance procedure, employee security, and job-related factors.

Recognition

This section usually appears at the beginning of the labor agreement. Its purpose is to identify the union that is recognized as the bargaining representative and to describe the bargaining unit, that is, the employees for whom the union speaks. A typical recognition section might read as follows:

The XYZ Company recognizes the ABC Union as the sole and exclusive representative of the bargaining unit employees for the purpose of collective bargaining with regard to wages, hours, and other conditions of employment.

Management Rights

A section that is often but not always written into the labor agreement spells out the rights of management. If no such section is included, management may reason that it retains control of all topics not described as bargainable in the contract. The precise content of the management rights section will vary by industry, company, and union. When included, management rights generally involve three areas:

1. Freedom to select the business objectives of the company
2. Freedom to determine the uses to which the material assets of the enterprise will be devoted
3. Power to discipline for cause

In a brochure the company publishes for all its first-line managers, AT&T describes management's rights when dealing with the union, including the following:

You should remember that management has all such rights except those restricted by law or by contract with the union. You either make these decisions or carry them out through contact with your people. Some examples of these decisions and actions are:

- *To determine what work is to be done and where, when, and how it is to be done.*
- *To determine the number of employees who will do the work.*
- *To supervise and instruct employees in doing the work.*
- *To correct employees whose work performance or personal conduct fails to meet reasonable standards. This includes administering discipline.*
- *To recommend hiring, dismissing, upgrading, or downgrading of employees.*
- *To recommend employees for promotion to management.*[21]

Union Security

Union security is typically one of the first items negotiated in a collective bargaining agreement. The objective of union security provisions is to ensure that the union continues to exist and perform its functions. A strong union security provision makes it easier for the union to enroll and retain members. We describe some basic forms of union security clauses in the following paragraphs.

Closed shop:
An arrangement making union membership a prerequisite for employment.

Closed Shop. A **closed shop** is an arrangement making union membership a prerequisite for employment. Remember that, except for the construction industry, the closed shop is illegal.

Union shop:
A requirement that all employees become members of the union after a specified period of employment (the legal minimum is 30 days) or after a union shop provision has been negotiated.

Union Shop. As we mentioned in Chapter 12, a **union shop** arrangement requires that all employees become members of the union after a specified period of employment (the legal minimum is 30 days) or after a union shop provision has been negotiated. Employees must remain members of the union as a condition of employment.[22] The union shop is generally legal in the United States, except in states that have right-to-work laws.

Maintenance of Membership. Employees who are members of the union at the time the labor agreement is signed or who later voluntarily join must continue their memberships until the termination of the agreement, as a condition of employment. This form of recognition is also prohibited in most states that have right-to-work laws.

Agency shop:
Does not require employees to join the union; a labor agreement provision requiring, as a condition of employment, that each nonunion member of a bargaining unit pay the union the equivalent of membership dues as a service charge in return for the union acting as the bargaining agent.

Agency Shop. An **agency shop** provision does not require employees to join the union; however, the labor agreement requires that, as a condition of employment, each nonunion member of the bargaining unit pay the union the equivalent of membership dues as a kind of tax, or service charge, in return for the union acting as the bargaining agent.[23] Remember that the National Labor Relations Act requires the union to bargain for all members of the bargaining unit, including nonunion employees. The agency shop is outlawed in most states that have right-to-work laws. Also, there could be judicial and legislative problems with permitting agency shops to exist in the public sector.[24]

Open shop:
Employment that has equal terms for union members and nonmembers alike.

Open Shop. An open shop describes the absence of union security, rather than its presence. The **open shop**, strictly defined, is employment that has equal terms for union members and nonmembers alike. Under this arrangement, no employee is required to join or contribute to the union financially.[25]

Checkoff of dues:
An agreement by which a company agrees to withhold union dues from members' paychecks and to forward the money directly to the union.

Dues Checkoff. Another type of security that unions attempt to achieve is the checkoff of dues. A checkoff agreement may be used in addition to any of the previously mentioned shop agreements. Under the **checkoff of dues** provision, the company agrees to withhold union dues from members' paychecks and to forward the money directly to the union. Because of provisions in the Taft-Hartley Act, each union member must voluntarily sign a statement authorizing this deduction. Dues checkoff is important to the union because it eliminates much of the expense, time, and hassle of collecting dues from each member every pay period or once a month.

Compensation and Benefits

This section typically constitutes a large portion of most labor agreements. Virtually any item that can affect compensation and benefits may be included in labor agreements. Some of the items frequently covered include the following:

Wage Rate Schedule. The base rates to be paid each year of the contract for each job are included in this section. At times, unions are able to obtain a cost-of-living allowance (COLA), or escalator clause, in the contract in order to protect the purchasing power of employees' earnings (discussed in Chapter 9).

Overtime and Premium Pay. Another section of the agreement may cover hours of work, overtime pay, hazard pay, and premium pay, such as shift differentials (discussed previously in Chapter 10).

Jury Pay. For some firms, jury pay amounts to the employee's entire salary when he or she is serving jury duty. Others pay the difference between the amount employees receive from the court and the compensation that would have been earned. The procedure covering jury pay is typically stated in the contract.

Layoff or Severance Pay. The amount that employees in various jobs and/or seniority levels will be paid if they are laid off or terminated is a frequently included item.

Holidays. The holidays to be recognized and the amount of pay that a worker will receive if he or she has to work on a holiday are specified. In addition, the pay procedure for times when a holiday falls on a worker's normal day off is provided.

Vacation. This section spells out the amount of vacation that a person may take, based on seniority. Any restrictions as to when the vacation may be taken are also stated.

Family Care. This is a benefit that has been included in recent collective bargaining agreements, with child care expected to be a hot bargaining issue in the near future.

Grievance Procedure

A portion of most labor agreements is devoted to a grievance procedure. It contains the means whereby employees can voice dissatisfaction with and appeal specific management actions. Also included in this section are procedures for disciplinary action by management and the termination procedure that must be followed.

Employee Security

Seniority:
The length of time that an employee has worked in various capacities with the firm.

This section of the labor agreement establishes the procedures that cover job security for individual employees. Seniority is a key topic related to employee security. **Seniority** is the length of time that an employee has worked in various capacities with the firm. Seniority may be determined company-wide, by division, by department, or by job. Agreement on seniority is important because the person with the most seniority, as defined in the labor agreement, is typically the last to be laid off and the first to be recalled. The seniority system also provides a basis for promotion decisions. When qualifications are met, employees with the greatest seniority will likely be considered first for promotion to higher-level jobs.

Job-Related Factors

Many of the rules governing employee actions on the job are also included. Some of the more important factors are company work rules, work standards, and rules related to safety.[26] The World Trade Center massacre has given unions an opportunity to use collective bargaining to address safety and security issues that have been placed on hold for a number of years.[27] This section varies, depending on the nature of the industry and the product manufactured. Work rules are vitally important to both employers and employees, with companies tending to favor less restrictive work rules.

OBJECTIVE

Describe the process of negotiating the agreement.

Negotiating the Agreement

There is no way to ensure speedy and mutually acceptable results from negotiations. At best, the parties can attempt to create an atmosphere that will lend itself to steady progress and productive results. For example, the two negotiating teams usually meet at an agreed-on neutral site, such as a hotel. When a favorable relationship can be established early, eleventh-hour (or last minute) bargaining can often be avoided. It is equally important for union and management negotiators to strive to develop and maintain clear and open lines of communication. Collective bargaining is a problem-solving activity; consequently, good communication is essential to its success. Negotiations should be conducted in the privacy of the conference room, not in the news media. Often in the media the unions belittle management and naturally management strikes back. The media love it because it sells. The results are harmful, often to both sides.[28] If the negotiators feel that publicity is necessary, joint releases to the media may avoid unnecessary conflict.

The negotiating phase of collective bargaining begins with each side presenting its initial demands. Because a collective bargaining settlement can be expensive for a firm, the cost of various proposals should be estimated as accurately as possible. Some changes can be quite expensive, and others cost little or nothing, but the cost of the various proposals being considered must always be carefully deliberated. The term *negotiating* suggests a certain amount of give-and-take, the purpose of which is to

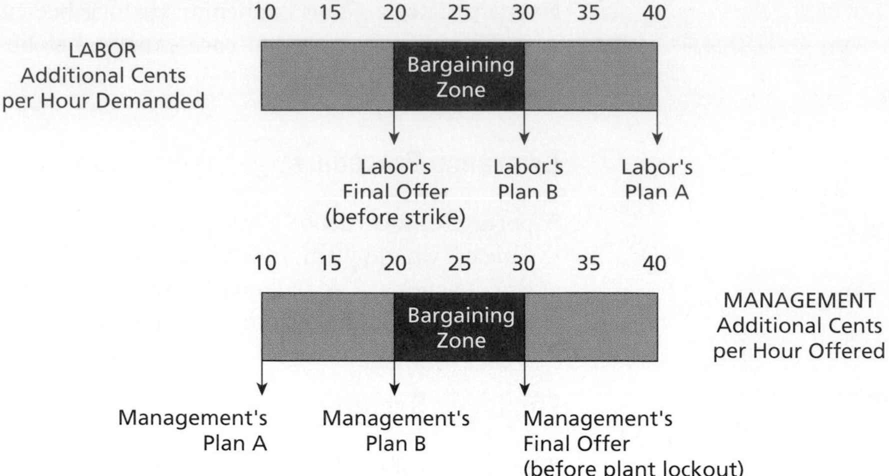

Figure 13-3 An Example of Negotiating a Wage Increase

lower the other side's expectations. For example, the union might bargain to upgrade its members' economic and working conditions and the company might negotiate to maintain or enhance profitability.

One of the most costly components of any collective bargaining agreement is a wage increase provision. An example of the negotiation of a wage increase is shown in Figure 13-3. In this example, labor initially demands a 40-cents-per-hour increase. Management counters with an offer of only 10 cents per hour. Both labor and management—as expected—reject each other's demand. Plan B calls for labor to lower its demand to a 30-cents-per-hour increase. Management counters with an offer of 20 cents. The positions in plan B are feasible to both sides, as both groups are in the bargaining zone. Wages within the bargaining zone are those that management and labor can both accept—in this case, an increase of between 20 cents and 30 cents per hour. The exact amount will be determined by the power of the bargaining unit and the skills of the negotiators.

The realities of negotiations are not for the weak of heart and at times are similar to a high-stakes poker game. A certain amount of bluffing and raising the ante takes place in many negotiations. The ultimate bluff for the union is when a negotiator says, "If our demands are not met, we are prepared to strike." Management's version of this bluff would be to threaten a lockout. We will discuss each of these tactics later as means of overcoming breakdowns in negotiations. The party with the greater leverage can expect to extract the most concessions. Remember that Boeing did not mind a strike because of a large backlog of inventory.

Even though one party in the negotiating process may appear to possess the greater power, negotiators often take care to keep the other side from losing face. They recognize that the balance of power may switch rapidly. This is what happened for the workers at Boeing. In the previous contract they were able to demand and get a rich package with 10 percent bonuses, 25 percent pension hikes, and strong job security language. In the present package, a final offer of 2 percent was demanded by management and accepted by the union. By the time the next round of negotiations occurs, the pendulum may be swinging back in favor of the other side. Even when management appears to have the upper hand, it may make minor concessions that will allow the labor leader to claim gains for the union. Management may demand that workers pay for grease rags that are lost (assuming that the loss of these rags has become excessive). In order to obtain labor's agreement to this demand, management may agree to provide new uniforms for the workers if the cost of these uniforms would be less than the cost of lost rags. Thus, labor leaders, although forced to concede to management's demand, could show the workers that they have obtained a concession from management.

Each side usually does not expect to obtain all the demands presented in its first proposal. However, management must remember that a concession may be difficult to

Ethical Dilemma

Whoops!

You are the vice president of industrial relations for a company involved in negotiations for a new contract with the union. You are under pressure to get the best deal possible for the company. Negotiations are heated and often almost seem to come to blows before calmer heads prevail. The union initially demanded a $3.00-an-hour increase. You don't think that the union really expects to get that much of an increase and you believe that if you negotiate a $1.25-per-hour increase you will have done your job. A secretary in the union office, who has applied for a position with your firm, called you and asked for a private meeting. In your conversation, she tells you, in confidence, that the union will be willing to lower their demands to a 50-cents-an-hour increase before calling a strike. You believe that this individual has a definite motive in providing this information and that it is reliable. If you use the information and are able to get the union to accept a 50-cents-per-hour increase, you will be a hero. If you don't use the information, it will cost your company millions over a three-year contract period. If you use the information, no one, except you and the informant, will ever know. It is highly unlikely that your source would ever reveal the truth.

What would you do?

Beachhead demands: Demands that the union does not expect management to meet when they are first made.

reverse in future negotiations. For instance, if management agreed to provide dental benefits, withdrawing these benefits in the next round of negotiations would be difficult. Labor, on the other hand, can lose a demand and continue to bring it up in the future. Demands for benefits that the union does not expect to receive when they are first made are known as **beachhead demands.**

 **OBJECTIVE**

Identify ways to overcome breakdowns in negotiations.

Breakdowns in Negotiations

At times negotiations break down, even though both labor and management may sincerely want to arrive at an equitable contract settlement. Several means of removing roadblocks may be used in order to get negotiations moving again. Breakdowns in negotiations can be overcome through third-party intervention, union strategies, and management strategies.

Third-Party Intervention

Often an outside person can intervene to provide assistance when an agreement cannot be reached and the two sides reach an impasse. The reasons behind each party's position may be quite rational, or the breakdown may be related to emotional disputes that tend to become distorted during the heat of negotiations. Regardless of the cause, something must be done to continue the negotiations. The two basic types of third-party intervention are mediation and arbitration.

Mediation: A process in which a neutral third party enters and attempts to resolve a labor dispute when a bargaining impasse has occurred.

Mediation. In **mediation**, a process in which a neutral third party enters and attempts to resolve a labor dispute when a bargaining impasse has occured.[29] A mediator basically acts like a facilitator. The objective of mediation is to persuade the parties to resume negotiations and reach a settlement. A mediator has no power to force a settlement but can help in the search for solutions, make recommendations, and work to open blocked channels of communication. Successful mediation depends to a substantial degree on the tact, diplomacy, patience, and perseverance of the mediator.[30] The mediator's fresh insights are used to get discussions going again.

Mediation skills are becoming more important in labor relations and other management areas. Mediation is voluntary at every step of the process. The mediator serves as an informal coach, helping to ensure that the discussions are fair and effective.

Federal Mediation and Conciliation Service (FMCS)

www.fmcs.gov/internet/

This Web site is the homepage for the Federal Mediation and Conciliation Service.

Arbitration: A process in which a dispute is submitted to an impartial third party for a binding decision.

Rights arbitration: Arbitration involving disputes over the interpretation and application of the various provisions of an existing contract.

Interest arbitration: Arbitration that involves disputes over the terms of proposed collective bargaining agreements.

Arbitration. In **arbitration**, a dispute is submitted to an impartial third party for a binding decision; an arbitrator basically acts as a judge and jury.[31] There are two principal types of union–management disputes: rights disputes and interests disputes. Those that involve disputes over the interpretation and application of the various provisions of an existing contract are submitted to **rights arbitration.** This type of arbitration is used in settling grievances and is common in the United States. The other type of arbitration, **interest arbitration,** involves disputes over the terms of proposed collective bargaining agreements. In the private sector, the use of interest arbitration as an alternative procedure for impasse resolution is not a common practice. Unions and employers rarely agree to submit the basic terms of a contract (such as wages, hours, and working conditions) to a neutral party for disposition. They prefer to rely on collective bargaining and the threat of economic pressure (such as strikes and lockouts), to decide these issues. American Airlines is proposing interest arbitration such as that used by professional baseball owners and players.[32]

In the public sector, most governmental jurisdictions prohibit their employees from striking. As a result, interest arbitration is used to a greater extent than in the private sector, although there is no uniform application of this method. A procedure used in the public sector is *final-offer arbitration*, which has two basic forms: package selection and issue-by-issue selection. In package selection, the arbitrator must select one party's entire offer on all issues in dispute. In issue-by-issue selection, the arbitrator examines each issue separately and chooses the final offer of one side or the other on each issue. Final-offer arbitration is often used to determine the salary of a professional baseball player. Both players and management present a dollar figure to an arbitrator. The arbitrator chooses one figure or the other.

The principal organization involved in mediation efforts, other than some state and local agencies, is the Federal Mediation and Conciliation Service (FMCS).[33] In 1947, the Taft-Hartley Act established the FMCS as an independent agency. Either one or both parties involved in negotiations can seek the assistance of the FMCS, or the agency can offer its help if it feels that the situation warrants it. Federal law requires that the party wishing to change a contract must give notice of this intention to the other party 60 days prior to the expiration of a contract. If no agreement has been reached 30 days prior to the expiration date, the FMCS must be notified.

American Arbitration Association

www.adr.org

This Web site is the homepage for the American Arbitration Association.

In arbitration, the disputants are free to select any person as their arbitrator, so long as they agree on the selection. Most commonly, however, the two sides make a request for an arbitrator to either the American Arbitration Association (AAA) or the FMCS. The AAA is a nonprofit organization with offices in many cities.[34] Both the AAA and the FMCS maintain lists of arbitrators. Only people who can show, through references, experience in labor–management relations and acceptance by both labor and management as neutral parties are selected for inclusion on these lists.[35]

Union Strategies for Overcoming Negotiation Breakdowns

There are times when a union believes that it must exert extreme pressure to get management to agree to its bargaining demands. Strikes, boycotts, and activism are the primary means that the union may use to overcome breakdowns in negotiations.

Strike: An action by union members who refuse to work in order to exert pressure on management in negotiations.

Strikes. When union members refuse to work in order to exert pressure on management in negotiations, their action is referred to as a **strike.** A strike halts production, resulting in lost customers and revenue, which the union hopes will force management to submit to its terms. In reality, the United States has always had the lowest percentage of days lost due to strikes of all industrialized nations. There are fewer

Strikes

thebird.org/strikes

This Web site provides current information regarding specific strikes.

strikes today than at any time since such statistics were gathered. Strikes involving 1,000 or more workers have declined sharply since 1970. In 1970 there were 381 strikes involving 1,000 or more workers; in 1975, 235; in 1980, 187; in 1985, 54; in 1990, 44; in 1996, 37 and, since 1997, the nation has had fewer strikes than in any of the past 50 years.[36]

The timing of a strike is important in determining its effectiveness. An excellent time is when business is thriving and the demand for the firm's goods or services is expanding. However, the union might be hard pressed to obtain major concessions from a strike if the firm's sales are down and it has built up a large inventory. In this instance, the company would not be severely damaged.

Contrary to many opinions, unions prefer to use the strike only as a last resort. During a strike workers have little income coming in. The strike fund may only pay for items such as food, utilities, and motor fuel.[37] In recent years, many union members have been even more reluctant to strike because of the fear of being replaced. When a union goes on an economic strike and the company hires replacements, the company does not have to lay off these individuals at the end of the strike. Mel-O-Cream Donuts International Inc., hired permanent replacement workers nearly a month into the first strike against the Springfield company.[38]

A union's treasury is often depleted by payment of strike benefits to its members. In addition, members suffer because they are not receiving their normal pay. Striking workers during one General Motors strike got paid about $150 a week strike pay instead of the roughly $1,000 a week that they might be taking home with all of their overtime.[39] Although strike benefits help, union members certainly cannot maintain a normal standard of living from these minimal amounts. Sometimes during negotiations (especially at the beginning), the union may want to strengthen its negotiating position by taking a strike vote. Members often give overwhelming approval to a strike. This vote does not necessarily mean that there will be a strike, only that the union leaders now have the authority to call one if negotiations reach an impasse. This was the case at Dominick Stores, a grocery store chain in Chicago, when union officials rejected an offer and a strike vote was approved by 80 percent of the union workers.[40] At UC Davis Medical Center in Sacramento and four other University of California teaching hospitals, the state's largest nurses union announced that they would give UC 10 days' notice before any walkout. Ninety-five percent of nurses had voted to authorize a strike.[41] The Teamsters recently abruptly broke off talks with National Master Freight and called for a strike authorization vote.[42] A favorable strike vote can add a sense of urgency to efforts to reach an agreement.

Successful passage of a strike vote has additional implications for union members. Virtually every national union's constitution contains a clause requiring the members to support and participate in a strike if one is called. If a union member fails to comply with this requirement, he or she can be fined. Therefore, union members place themselves in jeopardy if they cross a picket line without the consent of the union. Fines may be as high as 100 percent of wages for as long as union pickets remain outside the company. However, the Supreme Court has ruled that an employee on strike may resign from the union during a strike and avoid being punished by the union. In today's economy, union members are using more subtle measures, such as sickouts and work slowdowns, to successfully avoid the impact of a strike while still bringing pressure on the company to meet union demands.

Boycott:
Refusal by union members to use or buy their firm's products.

Boycotts. The boycott is another of labor's weapons to get management to agree to its demands. A **boycott** involves an agreement by union members to refuse to use or buy the firm's products. A boycott exerts economic pressure on management, and the effect often lasts much longer than that of a strike. Once shoppers change buying habits, their behavior will likely continue long after the boycott has ended. At times, significant pressures can be exerted on a business when union members, their families, and their friends refuse to purchase the firm's products. This approach is especially effective when the products are sold at retail outlets and are easily identifiable by

Trends & Innovations

Unusual Tactics

Press editorial employees, who have been working without a contract since November 30, 2002, have used a variety of protest tools from a byline strike to informational picketing — to show their anger over the lack of progress in talks with the Newspaper Guild.[45] A **byline strike** is where newspaper writers withhold their names from stories. Writers at the *Washington Post* staged their second byline strike in 2002 in a five-day job action.[46] **Informational picketing** is the use of union members to display place cards and hand out leaflets, usually outside their place of business, depicting information the union wants the general public to see. Recently, air traffic controllers from across the country did informational picketing at 100 of the busiest airports in the United States.[47] Informational picketing is not the same as when workers are on strike.

Byline strike: Newspaper writers withhold their names from stories.

Informational picketing: The use of union members to display place cards and hand out leaflets usually outside their place of business depicting information the union wants the general public to see.

Secondary boycott: A union's attempt to encourage third parties (such as suppliers and customers) to stop doing business with a firm.

Lockout: A management decision to keep employees out of the workplace and to operate with management personnel and/or temporary replacements.

brand name. For instance, the boycott against Adolph Coors Company was effective because the name of the product, Coor's beer, was directly associated with the company.[43] Ultimately, the AFL-CIO signed an agreement with Coors that ended a labor boycott of the company.[44]

The practice of a union attempting to encourage third parties (such as suppliers and customers) to stop doing business with the company is known as a **secondary boycott.** The Taft-Hartley Act declared this type of boycott to be illegal.

Management's Strategies for Overcoming Negotiation Breakdowns

Management may also use various strategies to encourage unions to come back to the bargaining table. One form of action that is somewhat analogous to a strike is called a **lockout.** In a lockout, management keeps employees out of the workplace and may run the operation with management personnel and/or temporary replacements. Unable to work, the employees do not get paid. Although the lockout is used rather infrequently, the fear of a lockout may bring labor back to the bargaining table. A lockout is particularly effective when management is dealing with a weak union, when the union treasury is depleted, or when the business has excessive inventories. The lockout is also used to inform the union that management is serious regarding certain bargaining issues. Of recent, Dow is training its salaried employees to operate the plants in the "unlikely" event of a work disruption associated with contract negotiations.[48]

Another course of action that a company can take if the union goes on strike is to operate the firm by placing management and nonunion workers in the striking workers' jobs. Hiring replacements on either a temporary or a permanent basis is legal when the employees are engaged in an economic strike, that is, one that is part of a collective bargaining dispute. However, a company that takes this course of action risks inviting violence and creating bitterness among its employees, which may adversely affect the firm's performance long after the strike ends.

In late 2002, salaried and nonunion workers at Kennecott Utah Copper Corporation plan to keep the company's Utah copper operations going in the event union members decide to strike, and managers expect they will still be able to achieve planned 2002 output.[49] The type of industry involved has considerable effect on the impact of this maneuver. If the firm is not labor intensive and if maintenance demands are not high, such as at a petroleum refinery or a chemical plant, this practice may be quite effective. When appropriate, management may attempt to show how using nonunion employees can actually increase production. At times, management personnel will actually live in the plant and have food and other necessities delivered to them.

 OBJECTIVE

Describe what is involved in ratifying the agreement.

Ratifying the Agreement

Most collective bargaining leads to an agreement without a breakdown in negotiations or disruptive actions. Typically, agreement is reached before the current contract expires. After the negotiators have reached a tentative agreement on all contract terms, they prepare a written agreement covering those terms, complete with the effective and termination dates. The approval process for management is often easier than for labor. The president or CEO has usually been briefed regularly on the progress of negotiations. Any difficulty that might have stood in the way of obtaining approval has probably already been resolved with top management by the negotiators.

However, the approval process is more complex for the union. Until a majority of members voting in a ratification election approve it, the proposed agreement is not final. At times, union members reject the proposal and a new round of negotiations must begin. Many of these rejections might not occur if union negotiators are better informed of the desires of the membership.

10 OBJECTIVE

Explain factors involved in administering the agreement.

Administration of the Agreement

Negotiating, as it relates to the total collective bargaining process, may be likened to the tip of an iceberg. It is the visible phase, the part that makes the news. The larger and perhaps more important part of collective bargaining is administration of the agreement, which the public seldom sees. The agreement establishes the union–management relationship for the duration of the contract. Usually, neither party can change the contract's language until the expiration date, except by mutual consent. However, the main problem encountered in contract administration is uniform interpretation and application of the contract's terms. Administering the contract is a day-to-day activity. Ideally, the aim of both management and the union is to make the agreement work to the benefit of all concerned. Often, this is not an easy task.

Management is primarily responsible for explaining and implementing the agreement. This process should begin with meetings or training sessions not only to point out significant features but also to provide a clause-by-clause analysis of the contract. First-line supervisors, in particular, need to know their responsibilities and what to do when disagreements arise. Additionally, supervisors and middle managers should be encouraged to notify top management of any contract modifications or new provisions required for the next round of negotiations.

The human resource manager or industrial relations manager plays a key role in the day-to-day administration of the contract. He or she gives advice on matters of discipline, works to resolve grievances, and helps first-line supervisors establish good working relationships within the terms of the agreement. When a firm becomes unionized, the human resource manager's function tends to change rather significantly, and may even be divided into separate human resource and industrial relations departments. In such situations, the vice president of human resources may perform all human resource management tasks with the exception of industrial relations. The vice president of industrial relations would likely deal with all union-related matters. As one vice president of industrial relations stated:

> *My first challenge is, wherever possible, to keep the company union-free and the control of its operations in the hands of corporate management at all levels. Where unions represent our employees, the problem becomes one of negotiating collective bargaining agreements which our company can live with, administering these labor agreements with the company's interests paramount (consistent with good employee relations), and trying to solve all grievances arising under the labor agreement short of their going to arbitration, without giving away the store.*

11 OBJECTIVE

Describe collective bargaining in the public sector.

Collective Bargaining in the Public Sector

Executive Order 10988, mentioned in Chapter 12, established the basic framework for collective bargaining in federal government agencies. Subsequent EOs revised and improved this framework and brought about a new era of labor relations in the public sector.[50] In fact, the federal government codified the provisions of those orders and transferred them to Title VII of the Civil Service Reform Act of 1978. This act regulates most of the labor–management relations in the federal service. It establishes the Federal Labor Relations Authority (FLRA), which is modeled on the National Labor Relations Board. The intent of the FLRA is to bring the public-sector model in line with that of the private-sector. Requirements and mechanisms for recognition and elections, dealing with impasses, and handling grievances are covered in the act. Collective bargaining for federal unions has traditionally been quite different from private-sector bargaining because wages were off the table. Title V of the U.S. Code, the law that dictates personnel rules for federal employees, did not allow bargaining over wage issues, except for the U.S. Postal Service.

Higher wages are, however, a problem for the public sector. Private-sector employers usually try to avoid paying higher than competitive wages because they cannot easily pass the resulting cost increases on to their customers. Government-sector employers, on the other hand, are essentially a monopoly. Taxpayers do not have alternative vendors to which to turn. Moreover, taxpayers cannot refuse to pay the taxes the government agencies charge them. Thus government-sector employers can, much more easily than private-sector employers, pass forward any cost increases that result from paying higher wages, and therefore management may not resist union demands at the collective bargaining table as much as private-sector employers do.[51]

There is no uniform pattern to state and local bargaining rights. Forty-one states and the District of Columbia have collective bargaining statutes covering all or some categories of public employees. Also, 38 states have some form of legislation that obligates state agencies and local governments to permit their public employees to join unions and to recognize bona fide labor organizations. However, the diversity of state labor laws makes it difficult to generalize about the legal aspects of collective bargaining at the state and local levels.

A Global Perspective

Total Job Security?

In the United States, union security is spelled out in each firm's labor management agreement. In Germany, there is a national job protection law that is a centerpiece of its postwar economy. However, Germany may be warming up to the idea of being able to fire workers. There are now hopes that the country is moving toward solving its stubborn unemployment problem. For years, economists have said Germany must make its labor market more flexible to compete in the global economy. But unions have resisted suggestions of even minor changes, rejecting the adoption of hire-and-fire methods. Now, with the economy stagnant and high joblessness, a consensus is building that more drastic measures should be taken to get the economy moving again. The head of Germany's massive service workers' union, Verdi, caused a stir when he said changes to job-protection rules should not be ruled out, if that encourages companies to create new jobs. Similar comments followed from other sources, Chancellor Gerhard Schroeder's Social Democratic Party, and the opposition Christian Democrats.[52]

Mr. Schroeder's economics and labor minister, Wolfgang Clement, is working on a proposal that would give small companies more leeway to fire employees, an idea unthinkable just a few years ago. "We can't solve the problems of today with the formulas of yesterday," said Hans-Juergen Uhl, a Social Democratic member of Parliament who is also a worker representative on the supervisory board of Volkswagen AG. In the past, Mr. Uhl opposed lowering job protections. In the 1990s, he helped negotiate a deal in which Volkswagen cut back to a four-day workweek but agreed to forgo any layoffs. Globalization, cross-border trade, and international competition, however, are forcing changes on German labor. "It's different today. We can't always say no," Mr. Uhl said.[53]

Before eliminating jobs, companies usually have to justify their plans in talks with employee representatives, and then give workers months of notice and substantial severance packages. Job cuts are often so time-consuming and costly that companies find other ways to save money. But they also avoid hiring in Germany by expanding operations abroad or using more machinery to automate production. During the past 10 years, for example, DaimlerChrysler AG's Mercedes division has doubled the number of cars it produces but its workforce has remained steady at about 100,000.[54]

The discussion on job protections is part of a broader debate about Germany's "social market economy," a system of consensus between business and labor that is often credited with the country's rapid growth after World War II. Many business leaders now openly call for overhauling the system, and they are beginning to win backing from institutions that normally side with labor unions. Even a senior Catholic Church official said unions have been "unbelievably rigid" and should ease wage demands to help create jobs for others.[55]

Summary

1. Discuss whether or not an adversarial relationship exists between unions and management.
Likely so, but business and labor must find a new way of dealing with each other. It may now be the time for labor and management to develop a whole new attitude and turn adversarial relationships into productive partnerships. The old adversarial relationships have produced distrust. The partnering of management and labor is what is needed to bring about change in the relationship now existing.

2. Explain labor–management relations and individual bargaining.
In individual negotiations, the worker is negotiating with the company representative.

3. Describe labor–management relations and collective bargaining.
Regardless of the current state of labor–management relations, the general aspects of the collective bargaining process are the same. Even though collective bargaining is widely practiced, there is no precise format for what to do or how to do it.

4. Explain the psychological aspects of collective bargaining.
Psychologically, the collective bargaining process is often difficult for both labor and management because an adversarial situation may exist.

5. Describe the factors involved in preparing for negotiations.
Because of the complex issues facing labor and management today, the negotiating teams must carefully prepare for the bargaining sessions. Prior to meeting at the bargaining table, the negotiators should thoroughly know the culture, climate, history, present economic state, and wage and benefits structure of both the organization and similar organizations.

6. Explain typical bargaining issues.
Mandatory bargaining issues are those issues that fall within the definition of wages, hours, and other terms and conditions of employment. Permissive bargaining issues are those issues that may be raised, but neither side may insist that they be bargained over.

7. Describe the process of negotiating the agreement.
There is no way to ensure speedy and mutually acceptable results from negotiations. At best, the parties can attempt to create an atmosphere that will lend itself to steady progress and productive results.

8. Identify ways to overcome breakdowns in negotiations.
Breakdowns in negotiations can be overcome through third-party intervention, union tactics, and management recourse.

9. Describe what is involved in ratifying the agreement.
The president of the organization can make the decision for the firm. However, until a majority of union members voting in a ratification election approve it, the proposed agreement is not final.

10. Explain factors involved in administering the agreement.
Ideally, the aim of both management and the union is to make the agreement work to the mutual benefit of all concerned. Management is primarily responsible for explaining and implementing the agreement. The human resource manager or industrial relations manager plays a key role in the day-to-day administration of the contract.

11. Describe collective bargaining in the public sector.
Collective bargaining for workers in the public sector has traditionally been quite different from private-sector bargaining because wages were off the table.

Key Terms

- **Mandatory bargaining issues, 429**
- **Permissive bargaining issues, 429**
- **Prohibited bargaining issues, 430**
- **Perception set, 432**
- **Closed shop, 433**
- **Union shop, 433**
- **Agency shop, 434**
- **Open shop, 434**
- **Checkoff of dues, 434**
- **Seniority, 435**
- **Beachhead demands, 437**
- **Mediation, 437**
- **Arbitration, 438**
- **Rights arbitration, 438**
- **Interest arbitration, 438**
- **Strike, 438**
- **Boycott, 439**
- **Secondary boycott, 440**
- **Byline strike, 440**
- **Informational picketing, 440**
- **Lockout, 440**

Questions for Review

1. Does an adversarial relationship exist between union and management? Discuss.
2. What is the negotiation process for a worker in a nonunion environment?
3. What are the basic steps involved in the collective bargaining process?
4. With regard to collective bargaining, interpret the statement, "The realities of negotiations are not for the weak of heart and at times are similar to a high-stakes poker game."
5. Distinguish among mandatory, permissive, and prohibited bargaining issues.
6. What are the topics included in virtually all labor agreements?
7. Define each of the following:
   a. Closed shop
   b. Union shop
   c. Agency shop
   d. Maintenance of membership
   e. Checkoff of dues
8. What are the primary means by which breakdowns in negotiations may be overcome? Briefly describe each.
9. What is involved for both management and labor in ratifying the agreement?
10. What is involved in the administration of a labor agreement?
11. How is the collective bargaining process different for federal employees?

Break Down the Barrier

Yesterday, Bill Brown was offered a job as an operator trainee with GEM Manufacturing. He had recently graduated from Milford High School in a small town in the Midwest. Since Bill had no college aspirations, upon graduation he moved to Chicago to look for a job.

Bill's immediate supervisor spent only a short time with Bill before turning him over to Gaylord Rader, an experienced operator, for training. After they had talked for a short time, Gaylord asked, "Have you given any thought to joining our union? You'll like all of our members."

Bill had not considered this. Moreover, he had never associated with union members and his parents had never been members either. At Milford High, his teachers had never really talked about unions. The fact that this union operated as an open shop meant nothing to him. Bill replied, "I don't know. Maybe. Maybe not."

The day progressed much the same way, with several people asking Bill the same question. They were all friendly, but there seemed to be a barrier that separated Bill from the other workers. One worker looked Bill right in the eyes and said, "You're going to join, aren't you?" Bill still did not know, but he was beginning to lean in that direction.

After the buzzer rang to end the shift, Bill went to the washroom. Just as he entered, David Clements, the union steward, also walked in. After they exchanged greetings, David said, "I hear that you're not sure about joining our union. You, and everyone else, reap the benefits of the work we've done in the past. It doesn't seem fair for you to be rewarded for what others have done. Tell you what, why don't you join us down at the union hall tonight for our beer bust? We'll discuss it more then."

Bill nodded yes and finished cleaning up. "That might be fun," he thought.

Questions

1. Why does Bill have the option of joining or not joining the union?
2. How are the other workers likely to react toward Bill if he chooses not to join? Discuss

HRM Incident 2

How About a Strike Vote?

Christina Wilkes, the chief union negotiator, was meeting with management on a new contract. The union team had been preparing for this encounter for a long time. Christina felt that she was on top of the situation. Her only worry was whether the union members would support a strike vote if one were called. Because of the recession, there was high unemployment in the area. The members' attitude was: "We are generally pleased, but get what you can for us." She believed, however, that skillful negotiating could keep the union team from being placed in a position where the threat of a strike would be needed.

In the first session, Christina's team presented its demands to management. Pay was the main issue, and a 30 percent increase spread over three years was demanded. Management countered with an offer of a 10 percent raise over three years. After some discussion, both sides agreed to reevaluate their positions and meet again in two days.

Christina met with her negotiating team in private, and it was the consensus that they would decrease the salary demand slightly. They felt that the least they could accept was a 25 percent increase.

At the next meeting, Christina presented the revised demands to management. They were not well received. Sam Waterson, the director of industrial relations, began by saying: "Our final offer is a 15 percent increase over three years. Business has been down, and we have a large backlog of inventory. If you feel that it is in your best interest to strike, go ahead."

Christina was confident that there was no way that a strike vote could be obtained. Management accurately read the mood of the workers, and Christina quickly asked for additional time to consider the new information.

Questions

1. How important is the threat of a strike to successful union negotiations?
2. What do you recommend that Christina do when she next confronts management?

Take it to the Net

We invite you to visit the Mondy homepage on the Prentice Hall Web site at

www.prenhall.com/mondy

for updated information, Web-based exercises, and links to other HR-related sites.

Notes

1. Stephenie Overman, "Unions: New Activism or Old Adversarial Approach?" *HR Focus* 76 (May 1999): 7–8.
2. Richard Thompson, "Former Technician Sues Northwest Airlines, Unions over Layoffs," *The Commercial Appeal* (April 12, 2002): 1.
3. Edward H. Phillips, "AMR Seeks Massive Cuts in Labor Costs," *Aviation Week & Space Technology* (February 10, 2003): 48–49.
4. Kenneth Aaron, "Verizon to Trim 200 Jobs in Northern Region," *Times Union* (Albany) (October 4, 2002): E1.
5. Stanley Holmes, "Why Boeing May Welcome a Walkout: With Plane Orders Down a Shutdown Could Spell Relief," *BusinessWeek* (September 9, 2002): 56.
6. John Gillie, "SPEEA Weighs Boeing Contract ; 'Best and Final Offer': Deal May Go to Membership Vote," *News Tribune* (Tacoma) (November 12, 2002): D01.
7. Stephen J. Cabot, "United We Stand," *Executive Excellence* 18 (October 2001): 9.
8. Gary T. Pakulski, "As Ohio Workers Look for Security, Unions Could Become Stronger," *The Blade* (June 9, 2002): 1.
9. Hoyt N. Wheeler, "Viewpoint: Collective Bargaining Is a Fundamental Human Right," *Industrial Relations* (July 2000): 535.
10. Arthur A. Sloan and Fred Witney, *Labor Relations*, 4th ed. (Englewood Cliffs, NJ: Prentice Hall, 1981): 28–35.
11. Anne Grant and Judith Clarkson, "Developing Co-Operative Union-Management Relationships: A Partnership Approach to Conflict, *Canadian HR Reporter* (May 7, 2001): 10.
12. Joe Strupp, "Union-Tribune Local Airs Boycott Ad," *New York* (December 18, 1999): 9; Joe LawsThomas and Li-Ping Tang, "Japanese Transplants and Union Membership: The Case of Nissan Motor Manufacturing Corporation," *S.A.M. Advanced Management Journal* 64 (Spring 1999): 16–25; "Contractor Actions Were Not Antiunion Motivated," *ENR* (May 3, 1999): 24; Aaron Bernstein, "All's Not Fair in Labor Wars," *BusinessWeek* (July 19, 1999): 43; Aaron Bernstein and Peter Galuszka, "How LTV's Grand Scheme Hit the Smelter," *BusinessWeek* (September 27, 1999): 103.
13. Bernstein, "All's Not Fair in Labor Wars," 43.
14. L. Robert Batterman and John F. Fullerton III, "Collective Bargaining After September 11: What About Job Security and Workplace Security?" *Cornell Hotel and Restaurant Administration Quarterly* 43 (October 2002): 93–108.
15. Frank N. Wilner, "Interest-Based Bargaining," *Traffic World* (November 1, 1999): 13–14.
16. Holmes, "Why Boeing May Welcome a Walkout."
17. Frank N. Wilner, "Relative Peace," *Railway Age* (May 2000): 47–48.
18. David Stires, "The Breaking Point: Worker Health Costs Will Rise a Staggering 24% This Year: Companies Can No Longer Afford to Pick Up the Bill. The Battle Is Here," *Fortune* March 3, 2003 104.
19. Sue Burzawa, "Health Benefits Issues for Collectively-bargained Plans," *Employee Benefit Plan Review* (May 2000): 12–13.
20. Larry Reynolds, "Washington Update: A Crisis in Childcare?" *HR Focus* 74 (May 1997): 2.
21. "Management/Employee/Union Relations" (Dallas, TX: Southwestern Bell Telephone Company): 3.
22. The CIO's Drive for the Checkoff, Closed Shops, and Straight Seniority," *Iron Age New Steel* (April 1999): 11–15.
23. Aron Gregg, "The Constitutionality of Requiring Annual Renewal of Union Fee Objections in an Agency Shop," *Texas Law Review* (April 2000): 1159–1180.
24. Kathleen Masters and James K. McCollum, "Agency Shop for Baltimore County: No More Free Lunch?" *Journal of Collective Negotiations in the Public Sector* (1999): 153–164.
25. Sherie Winston, "Labor: When Contractors Are Organized," *ENR* (December 20, 1999): 30–32.
26. Terence K. Huwe and Janice Kimball, "Collective Bargaining for Health and Safety: A Handbook for Unions," *Industrial Relations* (July 2000): 547–551.
27. Ernest Allen Cohen, "Collective Bargaining Regarding Safety and Security Issues," *Cornell Hotel and Restaurant Administration Quarterly* 43 (October 2002): 109–118.
28. Stephen J. Cabot, "United We Stand," *Executive Excellence* 18 (October 2001): 9.
29. Philip Zimmerman, "A Practical Guide to Mediation," *The CPA Journal* 73 (January 2003): 66.
30. Llona Geiger, "The Value of Professional Mediation," *Association Management* 54 (November 2002): 87.
31. Martin J. Oppenheimer and John F. Fullerton III, "The Role of the Union in the Arbitration of Statutory Employment Claims," *Dispute Resolution Journal* (May-July 2000): 70–78.
32. Eric Torbenson, "Coalition Seeks Stop to AMR's Efforts to Change Railway Labor Act," *Dallas Morning News* (January 22, 2003): 1.
33. http://www.fmcs.gov/internet/, March 10, 2003.
34. http://www.adr.org/index2.1.jsp, March 10, 2003.
35. Donald Austin Woolf, "Arbitration in One Easy Lesson: A Review of Criteria Used in Arbitration Awards," *Personnel* 55 (September/October 1978): 76; Bill Leonard, "Groups Adopt New Arbitration Procedural Rules," *HRMagazine* 41 (July 1996): 8.
36. National Labor Relations Board and Kevin Galvin, "Rising Global Job Market Has Dimmed the Nation's Stake in Labor Strikes/Changing Times Have Unions Organizing to Rejuvenate the Ranks in Solidarity," *Minneapolis Star Tribune* (July 31, 1998): 03D.

37. Repps Hudson, "Spectrulite Steelworkers Rally over Wage Cuts, Health Benefits," *St. Louis Post-Dispatch* (January 18, 2003): 4.
38. Tim Landis, "Mel-O-Cream Permanently Replacing 48 Strikers: Union Tells NLRB of Unfair Practices," *State Journal Register* (Illinois) (August 2, 2002): 17.
39. Don Gonyea and Daniel Zwerdling, "GM Strike Far from Over," *Weekend All Things Considered*, NPR (July 12, 1998): 1.
40. Patrick Waldron, "Union OKs Strike on Dominick's Store: No New Offer Will Be Made," *Chicago Daily Herald* (November 11, 2002): 1.
41. Lisa Rapaport, "California's Largest Nurses Union Votes to Authorize Strike," *Sacramento Bee* (May 10, 2002): 1.
42. John D. Schulz, "Talks Break Off," *Traffic World* (January 27, 2003): 27–28.
43. Sandra Atchison and Aaron Bernstein, "A Silver Bullet for the Union Drive at Coors?" *BusinessWeek* (July 11, 1988): 61.
44. Heather Draper, "Coors Facing New Boycott: Workers at Brewer's Supplier Locked out After Pact Expired," *Rocky Mountain News* (September 24, 2002): 6B.
45. Joe Strupp, "AP, Guild Have Contract Issues," *Editor & Publisher* (January 20, 2003): 4.
46. Todd Shields, "Bye-Bye, Bylines," *Editor & Publisher* (October 7, 2002): 5.
47. Ken Garland, "Air Controllers Worry About Putting System in Private Sector: Informational Pickets in Knoxville, Airports Across U.S.," *Knoxville News/Sentinel* (December 21, 2002): E6.
48. Gary Taylor, "Dow Prepares for a Potential Strike at Freeport," *Chemical Market Reporter* (January 27, 2003): 3.
49. "Kennecott Plans to Keep Producing if Strike Hits," *Platt's Metals Week* (September 30, 2002): 5.
50. They are Executive Order 11491 (effective January 1, 1970); EO 11616 (effective November 1971); EO 11636 (effective December 1971); and EO 11828 (effective May 1975).
51. Charles W. Baird, "Government Sector Unionism," *Government Union Review and Public Policy Digest* 20 (2002): 25–28.
52. Neal E. Boudette, "Searching for Solutions, Germany May Tackle Taboo—Economic Woes Lead Some to Say Beloved Job Law Is Ripe for Rethinking," *Wall Street Journal* (February 28, 2003): A7.
53. Ibid.
54. Ibid.
55. Ibid.

CHAPTER OBJECTIVES

After completing this chapter, students should be able to

1. Discuss the case for and against downsizing.
2. Define *internal employee relations*.
3. Explain discipline and disciplinary action.
4. Explain how grievance handling is typically conducted under a collective bargaining agreement.
5. Explain how grievance handling is typically conducted in union-free firms.
6. Define *alternative dispute resolution*.
7. Describe how termination conditions may differ with regard to nonmanagerial/nonprofessional employees, executives, managers, and professionals.
8. Explain the concept of employment at will.
9. Describe demotion as an alternative to termination.
10. Explain layoffs in today's environment.
11. Describe transfers, promotions, resignations, and retirements as factors involved in internal employee relations.
12. Explain what is involved in evaluating the human resource management functions.

CHAPTER 14

Internal Employee Relations

HRM IN *Action:*

To Downsize or Not

 **OBJECTIVE**

Discuss the case for and against downsizing.

Downsizing:
A reduction in the number of people employed by a firm (also known as *restructuring*, and *rightsizing*); essentially the reverse of a company growing, and suggests a one-time change in the organization and the number of people employed.

Downsizing, also known as *restructuring* and *rightsizing*, is essentially the reverse of a company growing and suggests a one-time change in the organization and the number of people employed. Typically, both the organizational structure and the number of people in the organization shrink. In some cases downsizing has been successful. Such would be a case if a company was selling off unprofitable assets and the reason for reducing payroll was to improve profitability.[1] However, downsizing does not always turn a company around. The reason is that downsizing often does not solve the fundamental causes of problems. Some organizations have not developed an appropriate strategy for recovery from downsizing; instead, they focus on reducing costs, which is merely attacking a symptom of the problem. Management in these firms gives little thought to who would do the work after the firm has been downsized.[2]

The results of downsizing for the remaining workers are numerous. First, there is the cost associated with low morale of those that remain.[3] These workers become very risk-adverse and worry about their own futures. They do not want to stick their necks out and take risks, which is exactly what the company needs in order to generate new products, new markets, new customers. Workers often become preoccupied with their own personal finances and the security of their families. It is difficult to think about the best way to satisfy a client when your last day of employment is unknown.[4]

Second, often layers are pulled out of a firm, making advancement in the organization more difficult. Thus, more and more individuals are finding themselves plateaued in the same job until they retire. Many well-educated people who entered the workforce and moved rapidly up the corporate ladder in the 1990s have plateaued. The fast movement upward has stalled and even moved downward. At times, individuals who were frantically sought-after in the 1990s have been found bussing tables.[5]

Third, workers begin seeking better opportunities because they believe that they may be the next in line. Often the best workers find other jobs, leaving the business staffed by those unable to find better or more secure jobs elsewhere.[6] This is exactly the opposite of the type of employee the company needs. Workers are needed who can move easily through the uncertainty of being acquired, of layoffs, or the stress of new technology.[7]

Fourth, employee trust is often significantly reduced. For workers who remain after downsizing, the trust level is often low, especially among younger workers.[8] These workers believe that it might happen to them the next time. A common pattern of thought is that "I must take care of myself, because the company will not." Employees who would never have considered changing jobs prior to downsizing may soon start thinking about this option, especially if their present company does not provide them with the necessary development to keep up with industry trends.

Fifth, institutional memory (how the organization comes across to customers in all their dealings)[9] or corporate culture is lost. The fewer seasoned people the company has to pass these on, the less they will be able to maintain the soul of the organization.[10]

Sixth, remaining workers are being required to do more. Companies often take the same amount of work and give it to fewer workers, which produces stress in the long term.[11] Hamilton Beazley, chairman of the Strategic Leadership Group, coined the term "ghost work" to describe the additional workload taken on by surviving employees. "It's as if they're suddenly asked to start speaking Greek," says Beazley. "It can be totally demoralizing and can cripple the individual as well as the organization."[12]

Finally, when demand for the products or services returns, the company often realizes that it has cut too deep. It then begins looking for ways to get the job done. Frequently, the company brings back former workers as independent contractors, which costs the company significantly more than if they had stayed on the payroll.[13] In the past, there was always hope that once the company went through the downsizing process and corrected the problems workers would be rehired. This may not be the case in the future.

In this chapter, we first discussed the case for and against downsizing. Next, we describe internal employee relations. Then we discuss discipline and disciplinary action. We then describe grievance handling under a collective bargaining agreement and for union-free organizations. This is followed by a discussion of alternative dispute resolution and how termination differs for various groups of workers. Employment at will and demotion as an alternative to termination will then be described. Next, layoffs in today's environment, transfers, promotion, resignation, and retirement are discussed. The last portion of this chapter is devoted to evaluating the human resource management functions.

2 OBJECTIVE

Define *internal employee relations.*

Internal employee relations: Those human resource management activities associated with the movement of employees within the organization.

Internal Employee Relations Defined

The status of most workers is not permanently fixed in an organization. Employees constantly move upward, laterally, downward, and out of the organization. To ensure that workers with the proper skills and experience are available at all levels, constant and concerted efforts are required to maintain good internal employee relations. **Internal employee relations** comprise the human resource management activities associated with the movement of employees within the organization. These activities include promotion, transfer, demotion, resignation, discharge, layoff, and retirement. Discipline and disciplinary action are also crucial aspects of internal employee relations.

Some people believe that equal employment opportunity legislation primarily affects individuals entering the company for the first time. Nothing could be further from the truth. The legal environment described in Chapter 3 applies to every aspect of internal employee relations.[14] The thrust of equal employment opportunity legislation is that all workers should receive equal treatment, and internal employee relations must reflect this principle. For instance, are blacks being laid off at a higher rate than whites?[15] Are women not receiving promotional opportunities? The same kinds of questions may be asked about demotions and layoffs.

3 OBJECTIVE

Explain discipline and disciplinary action.

Discipline: The state of employee self-control and orderly conduct; indicates the extent of genuine teamwork within an organization.

Disciplinary action: The invoking of a penalty against an employee who fails to meet established standards.

Discipline and Disciplinary Action

Discipline is the state of employee self-control and orderly conduct and indicates the extent of genuine teamwork within an organization. A necessary but often trying aspect of internal employee relations is the application of disciplinary action.[16] **Disciplinary action** invokes a penalty against an employee who fails to meet established standards. Effective disciplinary action addresses the employee's wrongful behavior, not the employee as a person. Incorrectly administered disciplinary action is destructive to both the employee and the organization. Thus, disciplinary action should not be applied haphazardly.

Disciplinary action is not usually management's initial response to a problem. Normally, there are more positive ways of convincing employees to adhere to company policies that are necessary to accomplish organizational goals.[17] However, managers often must administer disciplinary action when company rules are violated. Disciplinary policies afford the organization the greatest opportunity to accomplish organizational goals, thereby benefiting both employees and the corporation. Written policies should be available regarding disciplinary action so that everyone knows the company philosophy regarding it.[18]

The Disciplinary Action Process

The disciplinary action process is dynamic and ongoing. Because one person's actions can affect others in a work group, the proper application of disciplinary action fosters acceptable behavior by other group members. Conversely, unjustified or improperly administered disciplinary action can have a detrimental effect on other group members.

The disciplinary action process is shown in Figure 14-1. The external environment affects every area of human resource management, including disciplinary policies and actions. Changes in the external environment, such as technological innovations, may render a rule inappropriate and may necessitate new rules. Laws and government regulations that affect company policies and rules are also constantly changing. For instance, the Occupational Safety and Health Act caused many firms to establish safety rules.

Unions are another external factor. Specific punishment for rule violations is subject to negotiation and inclusion in the labor–management agreement. For example, the union may negotiate for three written warnings for tardiness before a worker is suspended instead of the two warnings a present contract might require.

Changes in the internal environment of the firm can also alter the disciplinary action process. Through organizational development, the firm may change its culture. As a result of this shift, first-line supervisors may handle disciplinary action more positively. Organization policies can also have an impact on the disciplinary action process. For instance, a policy of treating employees as mature human beings would significantly affect the process.

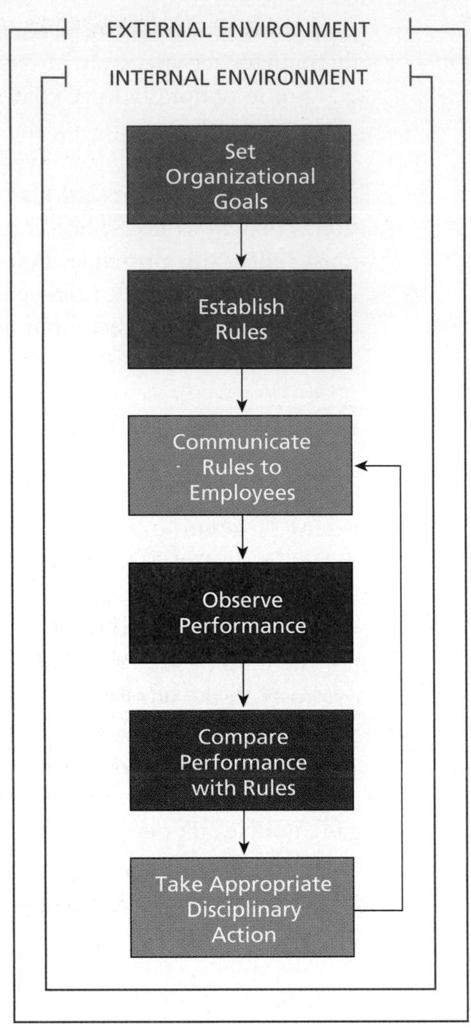

Figure 14-1 The Disciplinary Action Process

The disciplinary action process deals largely with infractions of rules. Rules are specific guides to behavior on the job. The do's and don'ts associated with accomplishing tasks may be highly inflexible. For example, a company rule may forbid employees to use the Internet for personal use at work.

After management has established rules, it must communicate these rules to employees. All must know the standards to be a disciplined person.[19] Individuals cannot obey a rule if they do not know it exists. As long as employee behavior does not vary from acceptable practices, there is no need for disciplinary action, but when an employee's behavior violates a rule, corrective action may be necessary. Taking disciplinary action against someone often creates an uncomfortable psychological climate. However, managers can still sleep well the night after taking disciplinary action if the rules have been clearly articulated to everyone.[20] The purpose of disciplinary action is to alter behavior that can have a negative impact on achievement of organizational objectives, not to chastise the violator. The word "discipline" comes from *disciple*, and when translated from Latin, it means, "to teach." Thus, the intent of disciplinary action should be to ensure that the recipient sees disciplinary action as a learning process rather than as something that merely inflicts pain.[21]

Note that the process shown in Figure 14-1 includes feedback from the point of taking appropriate disciplinary action to communicating rules to employees. When appropriate disciplinary action is taken, employees should realize that certain behaviors are unacceptable and should not be repeated. However, if appropriate disciplinary action is not taken, employees may view the behavior as acceptable and repeat it.

Approaches to Disciplinary Action

Several concepts regarding the administration of disciplinary action have been developed. Three of the most important concepts are the hot stove rule, progressive disciplinary action, and disciplinary action without punishment. Because of its increased use in business today, disciplinary action without punishment is highlighted as a Trends & Innovations feature.

The Hot Stove Rule. One approach to administering disciplinary action is referred to as the *hot stove rule*. According to this approach, disciplinary action should have the following consequences, which are analogous to touching a hot stove:

1. *Burns immediately.* If disciplinary action is to be taken, it must occur immediately so that the individual will understand the reason for it.
2. *Provides warning.* It is also extremely important to provide advance warning that punishment will follow unacceptable behavior. As individuals move closer to a hot stove, its heat warns them that they will be burned if they touch it; therefore, they have the opportunity to avoid the burn if they so choose.
3. *Gives consistent punishment.* Disciplinary action should also be consistent in that everyone who performs the same act will be punished accordingly. As with a hot stove, each person who touches it with the same degree of pressure and for the same period of time is burned to the same extent.
4. *Burns impersonally.* Disciplinary action should be impersonal. The hot stove burns anyone who touches it, without favoritism.[22]

If the circumstances surrounding all disciplinary action situations were the same, there would be no problem with this approach. However, situations are often quite different, and many variables may be present in each individual disciplinary action case. For instance, does the organization penalize a loyal, 20-year employee the same way as an individual who has been with the firm less than six weeks? A supervisor often finds that he or she cannot be completely consistent and impersonal in taking disciplinary action. Because situations do vary, progressive disciplinary action may be more realistic and more beneficial to both the employee and the organization.

Progressive disciplinary action:
An approach to disciplinary action designed to ensure that the minimum penalty appropriate to the offense is imposed.

Progressive Disciplinary Action. **Progressive disciplinary action** is intended to ensure that the minimum penalty appropriate to the offense is imposed. The progressive discipline model was developed in the 1930s in response to the National Labor Relations Act (NLRA) of 1935. The NLRA required that discipline and discharge be based on "just cause."[23] The goal of progressive discipline is to formally communicate problem issues to employees in a direct and timely manner so that they can improve their performance. Its use involves answering a series of questions about the severity of the offense.[24] The manager must ask these questions, in sequence, to determine the proper disciplinary action, as illustrated in Figure 14-2. After the manager has determined that disciplinary action is appropriate, the proper question is, "Does this violation warrant more than an oral warning?"[25] If the improper behavior is minor and has not previously occurred, perhaps only an oral warning will be sufficient. Also, an individual may receive several oral warnings before a *yes* answer applies. The manager follows the same procedure for each level of offense in the progressive disciplinary process. The manager does not consider termination until each lower-level question is answered *yes*. However, major violations, such as assaulting a supervisor or another worker, may justify immediate termination of the employee.

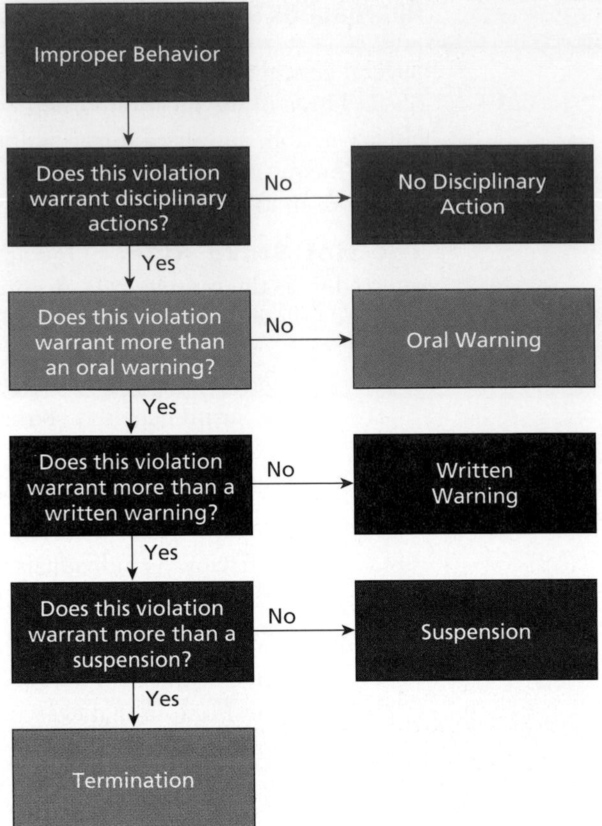

Figure 14-2 The Progressive Disciplinary Approach

To assist managers in recognizing the proper level of disciplinary action, some firms have formalized the procedure. One approach is to establish progressive disciplinary action guidelines, as shown in Table 14-1. In this example, a worker who is absent without authorization will receive an oral warning the first time it happens and a written warning the second time; the third time, the employee will be terminated. Fighting on the job is an offense that normally results in immediate termination. However, specific guidelines for various offenses should be developed to meet the needs of the organization. For example, smoking in an unauthorized area may be grounds for immediate dismissal in an explosives factory. On the other hand, the same violation may be less serious in a plant producing concrete products. Basically, the penalty should be appropriate to the severity of the violation, and no greater.

Table 14-1 Suggested Guidelines for Disciplinary Action

Offenses Requiring First, an Oral Warning; Second, a Written Warning; and Third, Termination
Negligence in the performance of duties
Unauthorized absence from job
Inefficiency in the performance of job
Offenses Requiring a Written Warning and Then Termination
Sleeping on the job
Failure to report to work one or two days in a row without notification
Negligent use of property
Offenses Requiring Immediate Discharge
Theft
Fighting on the job
Falsifying time cards
Failure to report to work three days in a row without notification

Trends & Innovations

Disciplinary Action Without Punishment

The process of giving a worker time off with pay to think about whether he or she wants to follow the rules and continue working for the company is called **disciplinary action without punishment.** The approach is to throw out formal punitive disciplinary policies for dilemmas such as chronic tardiness or a bad attitude in favor of affirming procedures that make employees want to take personal responsibility for their actions and be models for the corporate mission and vision.[28] When an employee violates a rule, the manager issues an oral reminder. Repetition brings a written reminder, and the third violation results in the worker having to take one, two, or three days off (with pay) to think about the situation. During the first two steps, the manager tries to encourage the employee to solve the problem. If the third step is taken, upon the worker's return, the worker and the supervisor meet to agree that the employee will not violate a rule again or the employee will leave the firm. When disciplinary action without punishment is used, it is especially important that all rules be explicitly stated in writing. At the time of orientation, new workers should be told that repeated violations of different rules will be viewed in the same way as several violations of the same rule. This approach keeps workers from taking undue advantage of the process.

Today, numerous organizations have abandoned warnings, reprimands, probations, demotions, unpaid disciplinary suspensions, and all other punitive responses to discipline problems in favor of disciplinary action without punishment. Consider the following examples:

- The Texas Department of Mental Health saw turnover drop from 48.5 to 31.3 to 18.5 percent in the two years following implementation. The system has now been in place for over two decades. In this time, employee turnover has consistently remained at a manageable 20 percent or less per year.
- A Vermont General Electric plant, one of many GE facilities that have adopted discipline without punishment, reported written warnings/reminders dropping from 39 to 23 to 12 in a two-year period.
- GTE's Telephone Operations reduced all grievances by 63 percent and disciplinary grievances by 86 percent in the year after management installed the approach.
- Tampa Electric Co. reduced sick-leave hours per employee from 66.7 in the year before implementation to 31.2 eight years later.[29]

Disciplinary action without punishment: A process in which a worker is given time off with pay to think about whether he or she wants to follow the rules and continue working for the company.

Problems in the Administration of Disciplinary Action

As might be expected, administering disciplinary actions is not a pleasant task, but it should come from the responsible manager.[26] Although the manager is in the best position to take disciplinary action, many would rather avoid it.[27] The reasons managers want to avoid disciplinary action include the following issues.

1. *Lack of training.* The manager may not have the knowledge and skill necessary to handle disciplinary problems.
2. *Fear.* The manager may be concerned that top management will not support a disciplinary action.
3. *Being the only one.* The manager may think, "No one else is disciplining employees, so why should I?"
4. *Guilt.* The manager may think, "How can I discipline someone if I've done the same thing?"

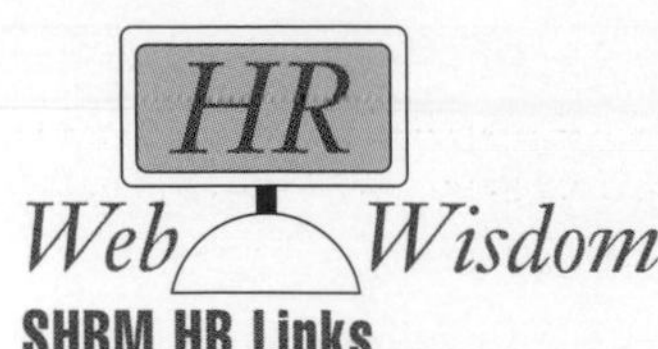

SHRM HR Links

www.shrm.org/hrlinks/Links.asp?Category=71

This Web site provides valuable information regarding arbitration and mediation.

5. *Loss of friendship.* The manager may believe that disciplinary action will damage a friendship with an employee or the employee's associates.
6. *Time loss.* The manager may begrudge the valuable time that is required to administer and explain disciplinary action.
7. *Loss of temper.* The manager may be afraid of losing his or her temper when talking to an employee about a rule violation.
8. *Rationalization.* The manager may think, "The employee knows it was the wrong thing to do, so why do we need to talk about it?"[30]

These reasons apply to all forms of disciplinary action, from an oral warning to termination. Managers often avoid disciplinary action, even when it is in the company's best interest.[31] Such reluctance often stems from breakdowns in other areas of the human resource management function. For instance, if a manager has consistently rated an employee high on annual performance appraisals, the supervisor's rationale for terminating a worker for poor performance would be weak. It is embarrassing to decide to fire a worker and then be asked why you rated this individual so highly on the previous evaluation. It could be that the employee's productivity has actually dropped substantially. It could also be that the employee's productivity has always been low, yet the supervisor may have trouble justifying to upper-level management that the person should be terminated. Rather than run the risk of a decision being overturned, the supervisor retains the ineffective worker.[32]

Finally, some managers believe that even attempting to terminate women and minorities is useless. However, the statutes and subsequent court decisions associated with women and minorities in the workplace were not intended to protect nonproductive workers. Anyone whose performance is below standard can, and should, be terminated after the supervisor has made reasonable attempts to salvage the employee. Occasionally, there will be suits involving members of protected groups. One of the best ways for a company to protect itself against suits claiming discrimination or harassment is to ensure that it has proper, written policies barring unfair treatment of its staff, and a system for ensuring that the policies are followed. Disciplinary actions should be fully documented, and managers should be trained in how to avoid bias claims.[33]

A supervisor may be perfectly justified in administering disciplinary action, but there is usually a proper time and place for doing so. For example, taking disciplinary action against a worker in the presence of others may embarrass the individual and actually defeat the purpose of the action. Even when they are wrong, employees resent disciplinary action administered in public. By disciplining employees in private, supervisors prevent them from losing face with their peers.

In addition, many supervisors may be too lenient early in the disciplinary action process and too strict later. This lack of consistency does not give the worker a clear understanding of the penalty associated with the inappropriate action. A supervisor will often endure an unacceptable situation for an extended period of time. Then, when the supervisor finally does take action, he or she is apt to overreact and come down excessively hard. However, consistency does not necessarily mean that the same penalty must be applied to two different workers for the same offense. For instance, employers would be consistent if they always considered the worker's past record and length of service. For a serious violation, a long-term employee might receive only a suspension, while a worker with only a few months' service might be terminated for the same act. This type of action could reasonably be viewed as being consistent.

To assist management in administering discipline properly, a "Code on Discipline Procedure" has been prepared by the Advisory, Conciliation and Arbitration Service. The purpose of the code is to give practical guidance on how to formulate disciplinary rules and procedures and use them effectively. The code recommends the actions

Table 14-2 Recommended Disciplinary Procedures

- All employees should be given a copy of the employers' rules on disciplinary procedures. The procedures should specify which employees they cover and what disciplinary actions may be taken, and should allow matters to be dealt with quickly.
- Employees should be told of complaints against them and given an opportunity to state their case. They should have the right to be accompanied by a trade union representative or fellow employee of their choice.
- Disciplinary action should not be taken until the case has been fully investigated. Immediate superiors should not have the power to dismiss without reference to senior management, and, except for gross misconduct, no employee should be dismissed for a first breach of discipline.
- Employees should be given an explanation for any penalty imposed, and they should have a right of appeal, with specified procedures to be followed.
- When disciplinary action other than summary dismissal is needed, supervisors should give a formal oral warning in the case of minor offenses or a written warning in more serious cases.

Source: "Code on Discipline Procedure," *Industrial Management* 7 (August 1977): 7. Used with permission.

shown in Table 14-2. As you can see, it stresses communication of rules, telling the employee of the complaint, conducting a full investigation, and giving the employee an opportunity to tell his or her side of the story.

In 1975, the U.S. Supreme Court held that unionized employees have the right to have a co-worker or union representative attend an investigatory meeting with company management when it might subject the employee to disciplinary action. Nonunion workers were not affected by the decision. However, recently the National Labor Relations Board applied the reasoning of the so-called Weingarten decision to the nonunion setting and held that employees in a nonunion setting have the same right.[34] According to this ruling, workers are entitled to have a co-worker present at an investigatory interview that the employee reasonably believes might result in disciplinary action.[35]

Ethical Dilemma

To Fire or Not To Fire

You are a first-line supervisor for Kwik Corporation, a medium-sized manufacturer of automotive parts. Workers in your company and also your department are quite close and you view them as family. The work in your department can be quite dangerous. It is especially important that all workers wear their safety glasses, because in the past there have been some serious injuries. The company has a written policy that states that any employee who does not follow the stated policy will receive a written reprimand on the first offense, and will be terminated on the second violation. You have had to terminate several workers in the past because of similar violations. The other day, Allen Smith, one of your best and most influential employees, violated the safety glasses rule and you gave him a reprimand. You hated to do that because he is by far your best worker and he often helps you if you have a problem with the other workers. He has also been with the company for a long time. You would really be lost without him. You walk up to Allen's workstation and observe him not wearing his safety glasses again. He knows that he has been caught and quickly puts his glasses on and says in a pleading voice, "Please don't fire me. I promise it will never happen again. I have just had a lot on my mind lately."

What would you do?

 OBJECTIVE

Explain how grievance handling is typically conducted under a collective bargaining agreement.

Grievance procedure: A formal, systematic process that permits employees to express complaints without jeopardizing their jobs.

Grievance: An employee's dissatisfaction or feeling of personal injustice relating to his or her employment.

Grievance Handling Under a Collective Bargaining Agreement

If a union represents employees in an organization, workers who believe that they have been disciplined or dealt with unjustly can appeal through the grievance and arbitration procedures of the collective bargaining agreement. The grievance system encourages and facilitates the settlement of disputes between labor and management. A **grievance procedure** is a formal, systematic process that permits employees to express complaints without jeopardizing their jobs. It also assists management in seeking out the underlying causes of and solutions to grievances.

The Grievance Procedure

Virtually all labor agreements include some form of grievance procedure. A **grievance** can be broadly defined as an employee's dissatisfaction or feeling of personal injustice relating to his or her employment. A grievance under a collective bargaining agreement is normally well defined. It is usually restricted to violations of the terms and conditions of the agreement. There are other conditions that may give rise to a grievance, including the following:

- A violation of law
- A violation of the intent of the parties as stipulated during contract negotiations
- A violation of company rules
- A change in working conditions or past company practices
- A violation of health and/or safety standards

Grievance procedures have many common features. However, variations may reflect differences in organizational or decision-making structures or the size of a plant or company. Some general principles based on widespread practice can serve as useful guidelines for effective grievance administration:

- Grievances should be adjusted promptly
- Procedures and forms used for airing grievances must be easy to utilize and well understood by employees and their supervisors
- Direct and timely avenues of appeal from rulings of line supervision must exist

The multiple-step grievance procedure shown in Figure 14-3 is the most common type. In the first step, the employee usually presents the grievance orally and informally to the immediate supervisor in the presence of the union steward. This step offers the greatest potential for improved labor relations, and a large majority of grievances are settled here. The procedure ends if the grievance can be resolved at this initial step. If the grievance remains unresolved, the next step involves a meeting between the plant manager or human resource manager and higher union officials, such as the grievance committee or the business agent or manager. Prior to this meeting, the grievance is written out, dated, and signed by the employee and the union steward. The written grievance states the events, as the employee perceives them, cites the contract provision that allegedly has been violated, and indicates the settlement desired. If the grievance is not settled at this meeting, it is appealed to the third step, which typically involves the firm's top labor representative (such as the vice president of industrial relations) and high-level union officials. At times, depending on the severity of the grievance, the president may represent

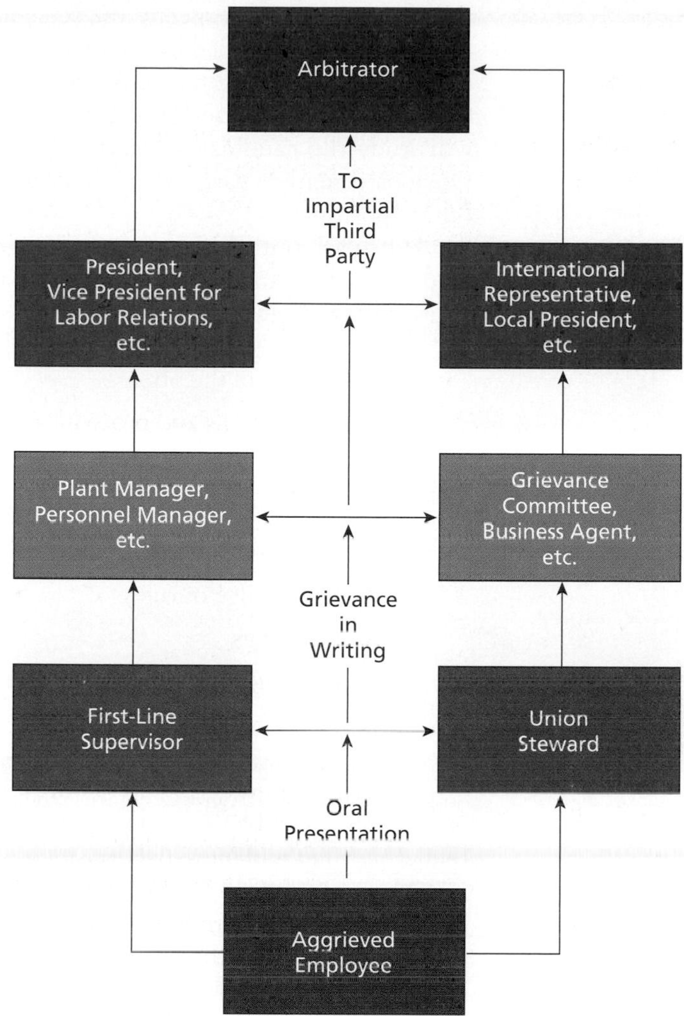

Figure 14-3 A Multiple-Step Grievance Procedure
Source: Robert W. Eckles et al., *Essentials of Management for First-Line Supervision* (New York: John Wiley & Sons, 1974): 529. Reprinted by permission of John Wiley & Sons, Inc.

the firm. A grievance that remains unresolved at the conclusion of the third step may go to arbitration, if provided for in the agreement and the union decides to persevere.

Labor relations problems can escalate when a supervisor is not equipped to handle grievances at the first step. Since the union steward, the aggrieved party, and the supervisor usually handle the first step informally, the supervisor must be fully prepared. The supervisor should obtain as many facts as possible before the meeting, because the union steward is likely to have done his or her homework.

The supervisor needs to recognize that the grievance may not reflect the real problem. For instance, the employee might be angry with the company for modifying its pay policies, even though the union agreed to the change. In order to voice discontent, the worker might file a grievance for an unrelated minor violation of the contract.

HR Web Wisdom

American Arbitration Association

www.adr.org

This Web site provides a vast source of information concerning arbitration rules and procedures, including international arbitration rules, as well as individual state statutes.

Arbitration

Arbitration is a grievance procedure that has successfully and peacefully resolved many labor–management problems. Arbitration is the final step in most grievance procedures. In arbitration, the parties submit their dispute to an impartial third party for resolution. Most agreements restrict the arbitrator's decision to application and interpretation of the agreement and make the decision final and binding on the parties. If the union decides in favor of arbitration, it notifies management. At this point, the union and the company select an arbitrator.

Most agreements specify the selection method, although the choice is usually made from a list supplied by the Federal Mediation and Conciliation Service (FMCS) or the American Arbitration Association (AAA), both of which were discussed in Chapter 13. When considering potential arbitrators, both management and labor will study the candidates' previous decisions in an attempt to detect any biases. Obviously, neither party wants to select an arbitrator who might tend to favor the other's position.

When arbitration is used to settle a grievance, a variety of factors may be considered to evaluate the fairness of the management actions that caused the grievance. These factors include the following:

- Nature of the offense
- Due process and procedural correctness
- Double jeopardy
- Past record of grievant
- Length of service with the company
- Knowledge of rules
- Warnings
- Lax enforcement of rules
- Discriminatory treatment

The large number of interacting variables in each case makes the arbitration process difficult. The arbitrator must possess exceptional patience and judgment in rendering a fair and impartial decision.

After the arbitrator has been selected and has agreed to serve, a time and place for a hearing will be determined. The issue to be resolved will be presented to the arbitrator in a document that summarizes the question(s) to be decided. It will also point out any contract restrictions that prohibit the arbitrator from making an award that would change the terms of the contract.

At the hearing, each side presents its case. Arbitration is an adversarial proceeding, so a case may be lost because of poor preparation and presentation. The arbitrator may conduct the hearing much like a courtroom proceeding. Witnesses, cross-examination, transcripts, and legal counsel may all be used. The parties may also submit or be asked by the arbitrator to submit formal written statements. After the hearing, the arbitrator studies the material submitted and testimony given and is expected to reach a decision within 30 to 60 days. The decision is usually accompanied by a written opinion giving reasons for the decision.

The courts will generally enforce an arbitrator's decision unless (1) the arbitrator's decision is shown to be unreasonable or capricious in that it did not address the issues; (2) the arbitrator exceeded his or her authority; or (3) the award or decision violated a federal or state law. In a recent arbitrator's case that ultimately went to the Supreme Court, the arbitrator's decision appeared to run counter to public policy prohibiting workers who had tested positive for drugs from operating heavy machinery or being permitted to return to work. However, the Supreme Court wrote, "We recognize that reasonable people can differ as to whether reinstatement or discharge is the more appropriate remedy here. But both employer and union have agreed to entrust this remedial decision to an arbitrator."[36]

Proof That Disciplinary Action Was Needed

Any disciplinary action administered may ultimately be taken to arbitration, when such a remedy is specified in the labor agreement. Employers have learned that they must prepare records that will constitute proof of disciplinary action and the reasons for it.[37] Although the formats of written warnings may vary, all should include the following information:

1. Statement of facts concerning the offense
2. Identification of the rule that was violated
3. Statement of what resulted or could have resulted because of the violation
4. Identification of any previous similar violations by the same individual
5. Statement of possible future consequences should the violation occur again
6. Signature and date

An example of a written warning is shown in Figure 14-4. In this instance, the worker has already received an oral reprimand. The individual is also warned that continued tardiness could lead to termination. It is important to document oral reprimands because they may be the first step in disciplinary action leading ultimately to arbitration.[38]

5 OBJECTIVE

Explain how grievance handling is typically conducted in union-free firms.

Grievance Handling in Union-Free Organizations

In the past, few union-free firms had formalized grievance procedures. Today, this is not the case as more and more nonunion firms have established formal grievance procedures and encouraged their use. Although the step-by-step procedure for handling union grievances is a common practice, the means of resolving complaints in

Date: August 1, 2003
To: Alvin Grabert
From: Denny Clark
Subject: Written Warning

We are quite concerned because today you were thirty minutes late to work and offered no justification for this. According to our records, a similar offense occurred on July 25, 2003. At that time, you were informed that failure to report to work on time is unacceptable. I am, therefore, notifying you in writing that you must report to work on time. It will be necessary to terminate your employment if this happens again.

Please sign this form to indicate that you have read and understand this warning. Signing is not an indication of agreement.

____
Name

____
Date

Figure 14-4 An Example of a Written Warning

nonunion firms vary. Generally, a well-designed grievance procedure ensures that the worker has ample opportunity to make complaints without fear of reprisal.[39] If the system is to work, employees must be well informed about the program and convinced that management wants them to use it. Some employees are hesitant to formalize their complaints and must be constantly urged to avail themselves of the process. The fact that a manager says, "Our workers must be happy because I have received no complaints," does not necessarily mean that employees have no grievances. In a closed, threatening corporate culture, workers may be reluctant to voice their dissatisfaction to management.

Typically, an employee initiates a complaint with his or her immediate supervisor. However, if the complaint involves the supervisor, the individual is permitted to bypass the immediate supervisor and proceed to the employee-relations specialist or the manager at the next higher level. The grievance ultimately may be taken to the organization's top executive for a final decision. Brown & Root, a Houston-based engineering, construction, and maintenance company, has a unique dispute resolution program. Whenever workers feel they need to resolve a dispute, the program allows them to choose one or all four options including an open-door policy, a conference, mediation, or arbitration. "We wanted to give our employees several ports of entry to lodge a complaint if they wanted to," says Ralph Morales, manager of employee relations and administrator of the program.[40]

OBJECTIVE

Define *alternative dispute resolution.*

Alternative Dispute Resolution

As the number of employment-related lawsuits increases, companies have looked for ways to protect themselves against the costs and uncertainties of the judicial system. **Alternative dispute resolution (ADR)** is a procedure whereby the employee and the company agree ahead of time that any problems will be addressed by an agreed-upon means. Some of these include arbitration, mediation, or mini-trials. The idea behind ADR is to resolve conflicts between employer and employee through means less costly and contentious than litigation.[41] A successful program can save a company thousands of dollars in legal costs and hundreds of hours in managers' time. Just as important, perhaps, it can protect a company from the demoralizing tension and bitterness that employee grievances can spread through a workforce.[42] Compared to litigation, ADR processes are less adversarial, faster and more efficient, relatively lower in cost, and private.[43]

Dispute Resolution, Arbitration, and Mediation

www.lir.msu.edu/hotlinks/arbitration.htm

This Web site provides links to numerous sites related to dispute resolution, arbitration, and mediation.

Alternative dispute resolution (ADR):
A procedure whereby the employee and the company agree ahead of time that any problems will be addressed by an agreed upon means.

Cases run the gamut from racial, gender, and age discrimination to unfair firings. Although ADR programs vary from employer to employer, many include informal methods that encourage workers to discuss their problem with their supervisor, a department head, or a panel of peers. The two best-known ADR methods are mediation and arbitration. Mediation is the preferred method for most people. When parties agree to mediate, they are able to reach a settlement in 96 percent of the cases.[44] In 1998, an executive order was signed which required federal agencies to (1) promote greater use of mediation, arbitration, early neutral evaluation, agency ombudspersons, and other alternative dispute resolution techniques, and (2) promote greater use of negotiated rulemaking.[45] Mediation in alternative dispute resolution cases has been credited with reducing the EEOC backlog of cases by 50 percent.[46]

The U.S. Supreme Court has issued two decisions pertaining to alternative dispute arbitration agreements. In 2001, the top court rendered an opinion in *Circuit City v Adams* that greatly enhanced an employer's ability to enforce compulsory arbitration agreements. The Court held that the arbitration agreement was valid and enforceable. The Court's decision made clear that ADR applied to the vast majority of employees and was available to employers seeking to enforce compulsory arbitration agreements. However, in 2002, the same Supreme Court, in *EEOC v Waffle House Inc.*, appeared to diminish the enforceability of arbitration agreements. The Court said the EEOC itself may seek all available remedies for job discrimination, regardless of an arbitration agreement signed by the employee. In *Waffle House*, the employee signed an agreement to arbitrate all employment disputes. After he was discharged, he filed a charge of discrimination with the EEOC without proceeding to arbitration. After finding probable cause that discrimination occurred, the EEOC itself filed a lawsuit against Waffle House seeking injunctive relief to stop its past and present unlawful employment practices, as well as relief for employees, such as back pay, reinstatement, and compensatory and punitive damages. The Supreme Court found the EEOC had authority to exercise its full enforcement powers, including damages specific to the individual employee, because the employee, not the EEOC, had agreed to arbitrate. The key here is that the EEOC filed the suit, not the employee. Because the EEOC was not a party to the arbitration agreement between the employee and employer, the EEOC was not limited in what it could do.[47] However, because the EEOC files suit in less than 1 percent of all charges, the implications of *Waffle House* will likely be limited.[48] Thus employers can require employees to arbitrate claims under Title VII of the Civil Rights Act.[49] According to Paul Siegel, a partner in the Woodbury, N.Y., office of the New York–based law firm of Jackson Lewis L.L.P., "The pace of developing arbitration agreement programs does not seem to have been diminished by *Waffle House* and certainly seems to have grown following *Circuit City*."[50]

7 OBJECTIVE

Describe how termination conditions may differ with regard to nonmanagerial/nonprofessional employees, executives, managers, and professionals.

Termination

Termination is the most severe penalty that an organization can impose on an employee; therefore, it should be the most carefully considered form of disciplinary action. The experience of being terminated is traumatic for employees regardless of their position in the organization. They can experience feelings of failure, fear, disappointment, and anger.[51] It is also a difficult time for the person making the termination decision.[52] Knowing that termination may affect not only the employee but an entire family increases the trauma. Not knowing how the terminated employee will react also may create considerable anxiety for the manager who must do the firing. Recall from Chapter 11 that an individual who is terminated may respond with violence in the workplace.

Research has suggested that Friday afternoon is probably the best time to fire an employee, because it gives the employee the weekend to cool off; and ideally it should be done on payday, so the employee can collect the last paycheck. Further, firing a worker at the end of the day leaves little chance for discussion among the remaining staff that may interrupt the workplace. Certainly, managers should try to plan the termination and not make it based on emotions.[53] Regardless of the similarities in the termination of employees at various levels, distinct differences exist with regard to nonmanagerial/nonprofessional employees, executives, managers, and professionals.

Termination of Nonmanagerial/Nonprofessional Employees

Individuals in this category are neither managers nor professionally trained individuals, such as engineers or accountants. They generally include such employees as steelworkers, truck drivers, salesclerks, and waiters. If the firm is unionized, the termination procedure is typically well defined in the labor–management agreement. For example, drinking on the job might be identified as a reason for immediate termination. Absences, on the other hand, may require three written warnings by the supervisor before termination action can be taken.

When the firm is union-free, these workers can generally be terminated more easily. A history of unjustified terminations within a firm, however, may provide an opportunity for unionization. In most union-free organizations, violations justifying termination are included in the firm's employee handbook. At times, especially in smaller organizations, the termination process is informal, with the first-line supervisor telling workers what actions warrant termination. Regardless of the size of the organization, management should inform employees of the actions that warrant termination.

Termination of Executives

Unlike individuals in most organization positions, CEOs do not have to worry about their positions being eliminated. Their main concern is pleasing the board of directors because hiring and firing the CEO is a board's main responsibility.[54] According to a study of 476 companies in 50 industries and 25 countries, nearly half of all current CEOs have held their jobs for less than three years. In the past five years, nearly two-thirds of all companies have installed a new CEO.[55]

Executives usually have no formal appeal procedure. The reasons for termination may not be as clear as those for lower-level employees. Some of the reasons include the following issues:

1. *Economic downturns.* At times, business conditions may force a reduction in the number of executives.
2. *Reorganization/downsizing.* In order to improve efficiency or as a result of merging with another company, a firm may reorganize or downsize, resulting in the elimination of some executive positions.
3. *Philosophical differences.* A difference in philosophy of conducting business may develop between an executive and other key company officials. In order to maintain consistency in management philosophy, the executive may be replaced.
4. *Decline in productivity.* The executive may have been capable of performing satisfactorily in the past but, for various reasons, can no longer perform the job as required.

This list does not include factors related to illegal activities or actions taken that are not in the best interests of the firm. Under those circumstances, the firm has no moral obligation to the terminated executive. Consider such criminal actions of Enron and WorldCom executives. Executives must now face a hostile board of directors that once was solidly in their corner. "Lousy performance won't be tolerated," says Barbara Franklin, who sits on five corporate boards. "Now we're trying to get ahead of the curve and make changes before you have an absolute crisis."[56]

An organization may derive positive benefits from terminating executives, but such actions also present a potentially hazardous situation for the company. Terminating a senior executive is an expensive proposition, often in ways more costly than just the separation package. The impact on the organization should be measured in relationships, productivity, strategic integrity, and investor confidence, as well as dollars. Many corporations are concerned about developing a negative public image that reflects insensitivity to the needs of their employees. They fear that such a reputation would impede their efforts to recruit high-quality managers. Also, terminated executives have, at times, made public statements detrimental to the reputation of their former employer.

Termination of Middle and Lower-Level Managers and Professionals

Typically, the most vulnerable and perhaps the most neglected group of employees with regard to termination has been middle and lower-level managers and professionals, who are generally not union members and thus not protected by a labor–management agreement. Employees in these jobs also may lack the political clout that a terminated executive has. Termination may have been based on something as simple as the attitude or feelings of an immediate superior on a given day.

 **OBJECTIVE**

Explain the concept of employment at will.

Employment at will: An unwritten contract created when an employee agrees to work for an employer but no agreement exists as to how long the parties expect the employment to last.

Employment at Will

In approximately two of every three U.S. jobs, the worker's continued employment depends almost entirely on the continued goodwill of his or her employer.[57] Individuals falling into this category are known as *at-will employees*. **Employment at will** is an unwritten contract created when an employee agrees to work for an employer but no agreement exists as to how long the parties expect the employment to last.[58] Generally, much of the U.S. legal system presumes that the jobs of such employees may be terminated at the will of the employer and that these employees have a similar right to leave their jobs at any time.[59] Historically, because of a century-old common-law precedent in the United States, employment of indefinite duration could, in general, be terminated at the whim of either party.

Although the concept of employment at will had eroded somewhat in recent years, a recent California Supreme Court decision may have reversed the trend. Previously, in the landmark 1988 ruling in *Foley v Interactive Data Corporation*, employees who meet certain criteria, including longevity, promotions, raises, and favorable reviews, can show an "implied-in-fact" contract, to be dismissed only for good cause.[60] In the case of *Guz v Bechtel National, Inc.*, the *Foley* criteria established years earlier do not, in and of themselves, "constitute a contractual guarantee of future employment security," the justices said. Since Bechtel's own written personnel documents "imposed no restrictions upon the company's prerogatives to eliminate jobs or work units, for any or no reason," Guz had no implied-contract case to take to a jury.[61]

Time will tell regarding the employment at will concept. However, at least 20 states from Maine to Hawaii limit discharges in particular circumstances.[62] Some courts have decided that terminations of at-will employees are unlawful if they are contrary to general notions of acceptable *public policy* or if they are done in *bad faith*. Judges, legislators, and employees are increasingly willing to challenge rigid notions of unlimited employer discretion.

Employers can do certain things to help protect them against litigation for wrongful discharge based on a breach of implied employment contract. Statements in such documents as employment applications[63] and policy manuals that suggest job security or permanent employment should be avoided if employers want to minimize charges of wrongful discharge.[64] A person should not be employed without a signed acknowledgment of the at-will disclaimer (Recall the Conoco Inc., application shown in Chapter 6). In addition, the policy manual should have it clearly stated in bold, larger than normal print, so it is very clear to the employee that this is an at-will relationship.[65] Other guidelines that may assist organizations in avoiding wrongful termination suits include clearly defining the worker's duties, providing good feedback on a regular basis, and conducting realistic performance appraisals on a regular basis.

 **OBJECTIVE**

Describe demotion as an alternative to termination.

Demotion: The process of moving a worker to a lower level of duties and responsibilities, which typically involves a reduction in pay.

Demotion as an Alternative to Termination

Termination frequently is the solution when a person is not able to perform his or her job satisfactorily. At times, however, demotions are used as an alternative to discharge, especially when a long-term employee is involved. The worker may have performed satisfactorily for many years, but his or her productivity may then begin to decline for a variety of reasons. Perhaps the worker is just not physically capable of performing the job any longer or no longer willing to work the long hours that the job requires.

Demotion is the process of moving a worker to a lower level of duties and responsibilities, which typically involves a reduction in pay. As firms downsize and reduce the number of layers in the organizational structure, positions that may have been held by highly qualified employees may be eliminated. Rather than lose a valued employee, firms will, at times, offer this employee a lower-level position, often at the same salary.

Emotions may run high when an individual is demoted. The demoted person may suffer loss of respect from peers and feel betrayed, embarrassed, angry, and disappointed.[66] The employee's productivity may also decrease further. For these reasons, demotion should be used very cautiously. If demotion is chosen over termination, efforts must be made to preserve the self-esteem of the individual. The person may be asked how he or she would like to handle the demotion announcement. A positive image of the worker's value to the company should be projected.

The handling of demotions in a unionized organization is usually spelled out clearly in the labor–management agreement. Should a decision be made to demote a worker for unsatisfactory performance, the union should be notified of this intent and given the specific reasons for the demotion. Often the demotion will be challenged and carried through the formal grievance procedure. Documentation is necessary for the demotion to be upheld. Even with the problems associated with demotion for cause, it is often easier to demote than to terminate an employee. In addition, demotion is often less devastating to the employee. For the organization, however, the opposite may be true if the demotion creates lingering ill will and an embittered employee.

10 OBJECTIVE

Explain layoffs in today's environment.

Layoffs in Today's Environment

The business news of today seldom is without a report of additional layoffs. Close to two million jobs in the United States were lost in 2001 and there were 255,000 additional job cuts in the first quarter of 2002.[67] Even McDonald's Corporation, a fast-food icon, plans to eliminate 600 corporate jobs, close about 175 restaurants, and cease or restructure operations in seven unidentified countries in the Middle East and Latin America.[68] Through layoffs, retirement packages, and spin-offs, Lucent has reduced its workforce from a high of about 150,000 to a current total of about 40,000.[69] More than 1,300 mass layoffs (defined as more than 50 employees at once) occurred in the United States in third-quarter 2002, according to Labor Department statistics.[70] The 1.466 million jobs cut in 2002 was the second largest annual total on record.[71] In the past, downsizing was weighed heavily toward blue-collar workers. Recently, cutbacks are skewed toward white-collar workers[72] and often they are the young professionals.[73] According to John A. Challenger, of Challenger, Gray & Christmas, a Chicago-based outplacement firm, "We may not see a revival in hiring of the rank-and-file worker." Instead, companies "will rely more and more on a just-in-time workforce of contract and contingent workers."[74] In addition, significant productivity increases have enabled firms to produce more with fewer employees.

A trend that is expected to continue is the increase in the number of layoffs and the accompanying age discrimination lawsuits.[75] If a disproportionate number of employees subject to layoff fall into one racial, age, or other protected category, then the layoff decisions should be reconsidered. To prevent a layoff from triggering a lawsuit the criteria for who gets eliminated should be nondiscriminatory. If the layoffs are based on performance, it is important to make sure the laid-off workers have lower performance appraisals than do the retained workers. A two-step process should be followed. One group of managers should perform the employee evaluations and another group should select which employees are to be terminated. Potential lawsuits can often be avoided through this process.[76]

Another problem is that when companies go through major layoffs, they often try to eliminate people at higher pay levels. The employees who generally hold those positions are aged 40 or older. So if these older workers get laid off disproportionately to younger workers, they may make a disparate impact claim.[77] The impact of layoffs of senior executives may be especially traumatic since the individual often has been with the firm for many years.[78]

Layoff/Recall Procedures

Even in this rapidly changing environment, recalls are necessary at times. Whether the firm is union-free or unionized, carefully constructed layoff/recall procedures should be developed. Workers should understand when they are hired how the system will work in the event of a layoff. When the firm is unionized, the layoff procedures are usually stated clearly in the labor–management agreement. Seniority usually is the basis for layoffs, with the least senior employees laid off first. The agreement may also have a clearly spelled-out *bumping procedure*. When senior-level positions are eliminated, the people occupying them have the right to bump workers from lower-level positions, assuming that they have the proper qualifications for the lower-level job. When bumping occurs, the composition of the workforce is altered. Procedures for recalling laid-off employees are also usually spelled out in labor–management agreements. Again, seniority is typically the basis for worker recall, with the most senior employees being recalled first.

Union-free firms should establish layoff procedures prior to facing layoff decisions. In union-free firms, productivity of the employee is typically a key consideration. When productivity is the primary factor, management must be careful to ensure that productivity, not favoritism, is the actual basis for the layoff decision. Workers may have an accurate perception of their own productivity level and that of their fellow employees. Therefore, it is important to define accurately both seniority and productivity considerations well in advance of any layoffs.

Outplacement

Some organizations have established a systematic means of assisting laid-off employees in locating jobs. The use of outplacement began at the executive level, but it has also been used at other organizational levels. In **outplacement**, laid-off employees are given assistance in finding employment elsewhere. Through outplacement, the firm tries to soften the impact of displacement.[79] Some of the services provided by group outplacement include the following.

Outplacement:
A company procedure that assists a laid-off employee in finding employment elsewhere.

CareerSoar

www.careersoar.com/

This Web site provides career transition services and customized business solutions to meet the needs of individuals and organizations.

- A financial section that covers pension options, Social Security benefits, expenses for interviews, and wage/salary negotiations
- Career guidance, perhaps using aptitude/interest and personality profile tests and software
- Instruction in self-appraisal techniques, which help in the recognition of the skills, knowledge, experience, and other qualities recruiters may require
- Tutoring in personal promotional techniques, research, and gaining an entry to potential employers
- Help with understanding the techniques that lead to successful interviews
- Development of personal action plans and continuing support[80]

Outplacement may not be used now as much as in the past. When the concept was first introduced, it dealt with specific individuals, usually executives. When it was introduced to address the needs of larger groups, it was still perceived to be in response to a one-time event. As previously mentioned in Chapter 1, the average person graduating from college today may face five to seven career changes (career, not employers) in his or her working years. The outplacement system was designed to guide people from job to similar job, not for the environment that workers face today. Since the advent of Internet recruiting, work search, résumé writing, and company research are available without the need of an outplacement firm.[81]

 OBJECTIVE

Describe transfers, promotions, resignations, and retirements as factors involved in internal employee relations.

Transfers, Promotions, Resignations, and Retirements

A major portion of internal employee relations relates to transfers, promotions, resignations, and retirement.

Transfers

Transfer: The lateral movement of a worker within an organization.

The lateral movement of a worker within an organization is called a **transfer.** A transfer may be initiated by the firm or by an employee. The process does not and should not imply that a person is being either promoted or demoted. Transfers serve several purposes. First, firms often find it necessary to reorganize. Offices and departments are created and abolished in response to the company's needs. In filling positions created by reorganization, the company may have to move employees without promoting them. Relocations for transfers are much more common than for promotions.[82] A similar situation may exist when an office or department is closed. Rather than terminate valued employees, management may transfer them to other areas within the organization. These transfers may entail moving an employee to another desk in the same office or to a location halfway around the world.

A second reason for transfers is to make positions available in the primary promotion channels. Firms are typically organized into a hierarchical structure resembling a pyramid. Each succeeding promotion is more difficult to obtain because fewer positions exist. At times, very productive but unpromotable workers may clog promotion channels. Other qualified workers in the organization may find their opportunities for promotion blocked. When this happens, a firm's most capable future managers may seek employment elsewhere. To keep promotion channels open, the firm may decide to transfer employees who are unpromotable but productive at their organizational level.

Another reason for transfers is to satisfy employees' personal desires. The reasons for wanting a transfer are numerous. An individual may need to accompany a transferred spouse to a new location or work closer to home to care for aging parents, or the worker may dislike the long commute to and from work. Factors such as these may be of sufficient importance that employees may resign if a requested transfer is not approved. Rather than risk losing a valued employee, the firm may agree to the transfer.

Transfers may also be an effective means of dealing with personality clashes. Some people just cannot get along with one another. Because each of the individuals may be a valued employee, transfer may be an appropriate solution to the problem. But managers must be cautious regarding the *grass is always greener on the other side of the fence* syndrome. When some workers encounter a temporary setback, they immediately ask for a transfer before they even attempt to work through the problem.

Finally, because of a limited number of management levels, it is becoming necessary for managers to have a wide variety of experiences before achieving a promotion. Individuals who desire upward mobility often explore possible lateral moves so that they can learn new skills.

If the worker initiates the transfer request, it should be analyzed in terms of the best interests of both the firm and the individual. Disruptions may occur when the worker is transferred. For example, a qualified worker might not be available to step into the position being vacated. Management should establish clear policies regarding transfers. Such policies let workers know in advance when a transfer request is likely to be approved and what its ramifications will be. For instance, if the transfer is for personal reasons, some firms do not pay moving costs. Whether the organization will or will not pay these expenses should be clearly spelled out.

Promotions

Promotion: The movement of a person to a higher-level position in an organization.

A **promotion** is the movement of a person to a higher-level position in the organization. The term *promotion* is one of the most emotionally charged words in the field of human resource management. An individual who receives a promotion normally receives additional financial rewards and the ego boost associated with achievement and accomplishment. Most employees feel good about being promoted. But for every individual who gains a promotion, there are probably others who were not selected. If these individuals wanted the promotion badly enough or their favorite candidate was overlooked, they may slack off or even resign. If the consensus of employees directly involved is that the wrong person was promoted, considerable resentment may result.

Resignations

Even when an organization is totally committed to making its environment a good place to work, workers will still resign. Some employees cannot see promotional opportunities, or at least not enough, and will therefore move on. A certain amount of turnover is healthy for an organization and is often necessary to afford employees the opportunity to fulfill career objectives. When turnover becomes excessive, however, the firm must do something to slow it. The most qualified employees are often the ones who resign because they are more mobile.[83] On the other hand, marginally qualified workers never seem to leave. If excessive numbers of a firm's highly qualified and competent workers are leaving, a way must be found to reverse the trend.

The Exit Interview: Analyzing Voluntary Resignations. Even during times of economic slowdown, unwanted employee turnover is one of the biggest and most costly business problems companies face, and companies are constantly striving to determine why outstanding producers quit to take another job elsewhere.[84] When a firm wants to determine the real reasons that individuals decide to leave, it can use the exit interview and/or the postexit questionnaire. An **exit interview** is a means of revealing the real reasons employees leave their jobs, providing the organization with information on how to correct the causes of discontent, and reducing employee turnover.[85] The most common reason individuals give for taking a job with another company is more money. This explanation, however, may not reveal other weaknesses in the organization.[86] Only after determining the "real" reason for leaving can a firm develop a strategy to overcome the problem.[87]

Exit interview:
A means of revealing the real reasons employees leave their jobs, providing the organization with information on how to correct the causes of discontent, and reducing employee turnover.

Retention Management

www.nobscot.com

This Web site is for an online exit interview company.

Often a third party such as a person in the HR department will conduct the exit interview. A third party may be used because many former employees will not air their problems to their former bosses. The typical exit interview follows the following format:

- Establishing rapport
- Stating the purpose of the interview
- Exploring the employee's attitudes regarding the old job
- Exploring the worker's reasons for leaving
- Comparing old and new jobs
- Recording the changes recommended by the employee
- Concluding the interview[88]

Over a period of time, properly conducted exit interviews can provide considerable insight into why employees are leaving. Patterns are often identified that uncover weaknesses in the firm's human resource management system. Knowledge of the problem permits corrective action to be taken. Also, the exit interview helps to identify training and development needs, to create strategic planning objectives, and to identify those areas in which changes need to be made.

When a *postexit questionnaire* is used, it is sent to former employees several weeks after they leave the organization. Usually, they have already started work at their new companies. The questionnaire is structured to draw out the real reason the employee left. Ample blank space is provided so that a former employee can express his or her feelings about and perceptions of the job and the organization. A strength of this approach is that the individuals are no longer with the firm and may respond more freely to the questions. A weakness is that the interviewer is not present to interpret and probe for the real reasons the person left.

Attitude Surveys: A Means of Retaining Quality Employees. Exit and postexit interviews can provide valuable information for improving human resource management practices. The problem is, however, that these approaches are reactions to events that are detrimental to the organization. The very people you want to save may be the ones being interviewed or completing questionnaires.

Attitude survey:
A survey that seeks input from employees to determine their feelings about topics such as the work they perform, their supervisor, their work environment, flexibility in the workplace, opportunities for advancement, training and development opportunities, and the firm's compensation system.

An alternative, proactive approach is administering attitude surveys (survey feedback was described in Chapter 7). **Attitude surveys** seek input from employees to determine their feelings about topics such as the work they perform, their supervisor, their work environment, flexibility in the workplace, opportunities for advancement, training and development opportunities, and the firm's compensation system. Since some employees will want their responses to be confidential, every effort should be made to guarantee their anonymity. To achieve this, it may be necessary to have the survey administered by a third party. Regardless of how the process is handled, it is clear that attitude surveys have the potential to improve management practices. For this reason, they are widely used throughout industry today.[89]

Employees should be advised of the purpose of the survey. The mere act of giving a survey communicates to employees that management is concerned about their problems, wants to know what they are, and wants to solve them if possible. Analyzing survey results of various subgroups and comparing them with the firm's total population may indicate areas that should be investigated and problems that need to be solved. For instance, the survey results of the production night shift might be compared to the production day shift. Should problems show up, management must be willing to make needed changes. If the survey does not result in some improvements, the process may be a real turn-off for employees and future surveys may not yield helpful data.

Advance Notice of Resignation. Most firms would like to have at least two-weeks' notice of resignation from departing workers.[90] However, a month's notice may be desired from professional and managerial employees who are leaving. When the firm desires notice, the policy should be clearly communicated to all employees. If they want departing employees to give advance notice, companies have certain obligations. For instance, suppose that a worker who gives notice is terminated immediately. Word of this action will spread rapidly to other employees. Later, should they decide to resign, they will likely not give any advance notice.

In addition, treating departing employees as if they were second-class citizens should be avoided.[91] However, permitting a worker to remain on the job once a resignation has been submitted may create some problems. If bad feelings exist between the employee and the supervisor or the company, the departing worker may be a disruptive force. On a selective basis, the firm may wish to pay some employees for the notice time and ask them to leave immediately.[92]

Retirements

Many long-term employees leave an organization by retiring. Retirement plans may be based on attaining a certain age, working a certain number of years with the firm, or both. Upon retirement, former employees usually receive compensation either from a defined benefits plan or a defined contributions plan, both of which were discussed in Chapter 10.

Sometimes employees will be offered early retirement before reaching the organization's normal length-of-service requirement. Historically, early retirement was often viewed as an attractive solution when reductions had to be made. Early retirement plans, which gained popularity in the 1980s, appealed to older workers facing layoffs. They also gave companies an alternative to the negative press involving layoffs. Last year, companies such as Procter & Gamble Co., Tribune Co., and Lucent Technologies Inc., offered early retirement to thousands of workers.[93] The U.S. Postal Service is seeking approval to offer early retirement to about 58,000 workers.[94] Hewlett-Packard plans to eliminate 10,000 jobs and about 4,000 of the cuts are expected to come from their voluntary early retirement program, which is quite generous.[95]

From an organization's viewpoint, early employee retirement also has a negative side and companies are becoming reluctant to use them. "I'm seeing fewer early retirement windows," says Bernadette Kenny, of the outplacement firm Lee Hecht Harrison. From a practical standpoint, with poor economic conditions, many companies cannot afford early retirement packages.[96] Another reason for the decline is that today's workers are more likely to have defined contribution plans, such as 401(k)s. Some workers are too young to use the account and others are afraid to use it because the amount may be too small as they approach older age. Likely one of the major reasons for companies to accept layoffs as opposed to retirement packages is that they are cheaper and layoffs do not draw the publicity they did in the past. Further, often the best employees leave when early retirements are provided.[97]

12 OBJECTIVE

Explain what is involved in evaluating the human resource management functions.

Evaluating the Human Resource Management Function

A recent Society for Human Resource Management (SHRM) survey found that most organizations want a way to measure the cost for new hires. However, only about half actually track those expenditures. The survey found that 83 percent think such a formula is of high or extremely high importance. However, 45 percent still do not track hiring and recruiting costs.[98]

"More people are convinced that the way a company manages its employees makes a difference to the bottom line," says Stephen Gates, principal researcher in The Conference Board's Capabilities Management and Human Resources Strategies Research Unit. "But people are perhaps the most challenging of all assets to measure and manage. They contribute to the value of a company through what they can produce with their competence, relationship ability, and values."[99] The success of any organization depends not only on the formulation and execution of superb plans but also on the continuous evaluation of progress toward the accomplishment of specified objectives. For an organization as a whole, evaluation may be performed in terms of profitability ratios, sales increases, market penetration, and a host of other factors.

How should an organization go about evaluating its human resource management function? An HR self-audit of the functional areas is a good place to start.[100] In this audit, the goal is to determine how well a function is being managed for value added. Are there particular measures or indicators that reveal how well this function is meeting its responsibilities and supporting the organization's efforts to reach its objectives? The two basic methods that may be used to evaluate human resource management activities are checklists and quantitative measures.

The checklist approach poses a number of questions that can be answered either *yes* or *no*. This method is concerned with determining whether important activities have been recognized and, if so, whether they are being performed. Essentially, the checklist is an evaluation of what should be done and the extent to which it is being done. Some typical human resource checklist questions are shown in Table 14-3. The more *yes* answers there are, the better the evaluation; *no* answers indicate areas or activities where follow-up or additional work is needed to increase HRM's effectiveness. Organizations deciding to use this evaluation approach will undoubtedly come up with many other questions to ask. The checklist method is purely an internal evaluation device and might be considered a first step in the audit.

Table 14-3 Typical Human Resource Checklist Questions

- Are all legally mandated reports submitted to requiring agencies on time?
- Have formalized procedures and methods been developed for conducting job analysis?
- Are forecasts for human resource requirements made at least annually?
- Is the recruiting process effectively integrated with human resource planning?
- Does the application form conform to applicable legal and affirmative action standards?
- Are all employees appraised at least annually?
- Are skills inventories maintained on all employees?
- Are career opportunities communicated clearly to all employees?

The other method for evaluating the performance of human resource activities is a quantitative one. It relies on the accumulation of various types of numerical data and the calculation of certain ratios from them. Numerical data are useful primarily as an indicator of activity levels and trends. Ratios show results that are important in themselves but that also reveal (when maintained over a period of time) trends that may be even more important. Possible human resource areas to track include recruitment, turnover, absenteeism, salary levels, temporary help, overtime, unemployment, insurance, and workers' compensation. For instance, what is the cost of recruiting a particular skill? Is one recruitment method superior to another? Employment agencies are commonly used, but they are expensive, so could other methods be more cost-effective?[101] Some examples of quantitative measures for human resource management are listed in Table 14-4.

A detailed example of a quantitative analysis is provided next. To help compute a more precise figure so that companies can create benchmarks and properly assign resources for retention and recruitment, the consulting firm of Kepner-Tregoe, Inc., developed a formula for computing turnover cost. The Turnover Cost Formula involves the following measures:[102]

- Select a department or job function that has high turnover

Table 14-4 Examples of Quantitative Human Resource Management Measures

- Women and minorities selection ratio
- Women and minorities promotion ratio
- Women and minorities termination ratio
- Minority and women hiring percentage
- Minority and women workforce percentage
- Requirements forecast compared to actual human resource needs
- Availability forecast compared to actual availability of human resources
- Average recruiting cost per applicant
- Average recruiting cost per employee hired
- Percentage of positions filled internally
- Average testing cost per applicant
- Percentage of required appraisals actually completed
- Percentage of employees rated in highest performance category
- Percentage of appraisals appealed
- Turnover percentage
- New-hire retention percentage
- Percentage of new hires lost

A Global Perspective

Getting Information to Support Disciplinary Action

Multinational companies face significant challenges when they try to encourage whistle-blowing across a wide variety of cultures. There are a number of cultural factors that discourage international employees from reporting misconduct. In parts of East Asia, members of the corporation are a family; if you view them as family members, it is wrong to report them. In Japan, lifetime employment and a strict seniority system can discourage workers from questioning management decisions, dictating, instead, that employees show unbounded loyalty to their co-workers. In Korea, a subordinate's loyalty to a superior is even greater than his or her loyalty to the company. In China, attempts to introduce corporate hotlines can remind employees of the horrors of the Cultural Revolution when citizens were encouraged to report "illegal activities" to authorities, which included children reporting against parents, students against teachers, and neighbors against neighbors. In Germany, encouraging anonymous or confidential reporting can bring to mind Gestapo tactics from World War II. The aversion to whistle-blowing has been heightened by recent revelations of the far-reaching informant networks of the Stasi in former East Germany.[103]

Numerous time zones and languages also prevent international employees from using corporate whistle-blowing resources. International 800 numbers and international collect calls either do not work or are unknown in many countries. In some locations, even gaining access to a telephone can be difficult. Guy Dehn, Director of the U.K.-based Public Concern at Work, confirmed in a recent interview, "If you're in a village in Northern Indonesia, where are you going to get the telephone to call the Alert Line? At a public telephone with others listening?"[104]

Information tends to leak out through informal networks in Hong Kong, Taiwan, and China, and the whistle-blower's future becomes difficult. In addition to the real threat of losing a job, whistle-blowers can also be subject to legal sanctions and loss of personal reputation. Whistle-blowers in Russia subject themselves to possible persecution (legal or criminal) from company managers or owners. Finally, in certain parts of the world, there have been reports that employees have been murdered in countries from Russia to Guatemala for exposing corruption.[105]

- Use an actual number or estimate the number of people who left during the past 12 months; write that number on line 4
- The average cost of turnover is 25% of an employee's annual salary (line 1) plus the cost of the benefits (line 2). Typical benefits amount to about 30% of wages (the total cost of a complete benefits package on top of payroll). The total cost per employee (line 3) is the total of line 1 and line 2.

1. Annual wage: __________ × .25 = __________
2. Annual benefits: __________ × .30 = __________
3. Total turnover cost per employee (line 1 + 2) = __________
4. Total number of employees who left = __________
5. Total cost of turnover (line 3 × line 4): __________

Today, it is important for human resources to receive the same degree of cost evaluation as operations.

Summary

1. Discuss the case for and against downsizing.

In some cases downsizing has been successful. Such would be the case if a company was selling off unprofitable assets and the reason for cutting people was related to profitability. However, downsizing does not always turn a company around. The reason is that downsizing often does not solve the fundamental causes of problems. Some organizations have not developed an appropriate strategy for recovery from downsizing; instead, they focus on reducing costs, which is merely attacking a symptom of the problem.

2. Define *internal employee relations.*

Internal employee relations consist of the human resource management activities associated with the movement of employees within the firm after they have become organizational members. It includes the actions of promotion, transfer, demotion, resignation, discharge, layoff, and retirement. Discipline and disciplinary action are also included.

3. Explain discipline and disciplinary action.

Discipline is the state of employee self-control and orderly conduct present within an organization. It indicates the extent of genuine teamwork that exists. Disciplinary action occurs when a penalty is invoked against an employee who fails to meet established standards.

4. Explain how grievance handling is typically conducted under a collective bargaining agreement.

The multiple-step grievance procedure is the most common type. In the first step, the employee usually presents the grievance orally and informally to the immediate supervisor in the presence of the union steward. If the grievance remains unresolved, the next step involves a meeting between the plant manager or human resource manager and higher union officials, such as the grievance committee or the business agent or manager. If the grievance is not settled at this meeting, it is appealed to the third step, which typically involves the firm's top labor representative (such as the vice president of industrial relations) and high-level union officials. A grievance that remains unresolved at the conclusion of the third step may go to arbitration, if provided for in the agreement and the union decides to persevere.

5. Explain how grievance handling is typically conducted in union-free firms.

The means of resolving complaints in union-free firms vary. A well-designed union-free grievance procedure ensures that the worker has ample opportunity to make complaints without fear of reprisal.

6. Define *alternative dispute resolution.*

Alternative dispute resolution (ADR) is a procedure whereby the employee and the company agree that any problems will be addressed by an agreed-upon means ahead of time.

7. Describe how termination conditions may differ with regard to nonmanagerial/nonprofessional employees, executives, managers, and professionals.

The conditions for termination differ considerably with regard to nonmanagerial/nonprofessional employees, executives, managers, and professionals.

8. Explain the concept of employment at will.

Employment at will is an unwritten contract that is created when an employee agrees to work for an employer but there is no agreement as to how long the parties expect the employment to last.

9. Describe demotion as an alternative to termination.

At times demotions are used as an alternative to discharge, especially when a long-term employee is involved. Demotion is the process of moving a worker to a lower level of duties and responsibilities, which typically involves a reduction in pay. If demotion is chosen over termination, efforts must be made to preserve the self-esteem of the individual.

10. Explain layoffs in today's environment.
The business news of today seldom is without a report of additional layoffs.

11. Describe transfers, promotions, resignations, and retirements as factors involved in internal employee relations.
The lateral movement of a worker within an organization is called a transfer. A promotion is the movement of a person to a higher-level position in the organization. Even when an organization is totally committed to making its environment a good place to work, workers will still resign. One of the last phases of internal employee relations is retirement.

12. Explain what is involved in evaluating the human resource management functions.
It is important for human resources to receive the same degree of cost evaluation as does operations.

Key Terms

- **Downsizing, 449**
- **Internal employee relations, 450**
- **Discipline, 451**
- **Disciplinary action, 451**
- **Progressive disciplinary action, 453**
- **Disciplinary action without punishment, 456**
- **Grievance procedure, 458**
- **Grievance, 458**
- **Alternative dispute resolution (ADR), 462**
- **Employment at will, 465**
- **Demotion, 465**
- **Outplacement, 467**
- **Transfer, 468**
- **Promotion, 468**
- **Exit interview, 469**
- **Attitude survey, 470**

Questions for Review

1. Define *downsizing*.
2. Define *internal employee relations*.
3. What is the difference between discipline and disciplinary action?
4. Describe the following approaches to disciplinary action:
   a. hot stove rule
   b. progressive disciplinary action
   c. disciplinary action without punishment
5. In progressive disciplinary action, what steps are involved before employee termination?
6. What are the steps that should typically be followed in handling a grievance under a collective bargaining agreement?
7. When arbitration is used to settle a grievance, what factors may be used to evaluate the fairness of management's actions that caused the grievance?
8. How would grievances typically be handled in a union-free firm? Describe briefly.
9. Define *alternative dispute resolution (ADR)*. What is the purpose of ADR?
10. How does termination often differ with regard to nonmanagerial/nonprofessional employees, executives, managers, and professionals?
11. What is meant by the phrase *employment at will*?
12. Briefly describe the techniques available to determine the real reasons that an individual decides to leave the organization.
13. Distinguish between demotions, transfers, and promotions.
14. Why is it important to evaluate the human resource management function?
15. How should an organization go about evaluating its human resource management function?

HRM Incident 1

Should He Be Fired?

Tony Berdit is the Washington D.C.–area supervisor for Quik-Stop, a chain of convenience stores. He has full responsibility for managing the seven Quik-Stop stores in Washington. Each store operates with only one person on duty at a time. Although several of the stores stay open all night, every night, the Center Street store is open all night Monday through Thursday but only from 6:00 A.M. to 10:00 P.M. Friday through Sunday. Because the store is open fewer hours during the weekend, money from sales is kept in the store safe until Monday. Therefore, the time it takes to complete a money count on Monday is greater than normal. The company has a policy that when the safe is being emptied, the manager has to be with the employee on duty, and the employee has to place each $1,000 in a brown bag, mark the bag, and leave the bag on the floor next to the safe until the manager verifies the amount in each bag.

Bill Catron worked the Sunday night shift at the Center Street store and was trying to save his manager time by counting the money prior to his arrival. The store got very busy, and, while bagging a customer's groceries, Bill mistook one of the moneybags for a bag containing three sandwiches and put the moneybag in with the groceries. Twenty minutes later, Tony arrived, and both men began to search for the money. While they were searching, a customer came back with the bag of money. Quik-Stop has a general policy that anyone violating the money-counting procedure could be fired immediately. However, the ultimate decision was left up to the supervisor and his or her immediate boss.

Bill was very upset. "I really need this job," Bill exclaimed. "With the new baby and all the medical expenses we've had, I sure can't stand to be out of a job."

"You knew about the policy, Bill," said Tony.

"Yes, I did, Tony," said Bill, "and I really don't have any excuse. If you don't fire me, though, I promise you that I'll be the best store manager you've got."

While Bill waited on a customer, Tony called his boss at the home office. With the boss's approval, Tony decided not to fire Bill.

Question

1. Do you agree with Tony's decision? Discuss.

Is It Covered in the Contract?

Calvin Scott, the production supervisor for American Manufacturing, was mad at the world when he arrived at work. The automobile mechanic had not repaired his car on time the day before, and he had been forced to take a taxi to work this morning. Because no one was safe around Calvin today, it was not the time for Phillip Martin, a member of Local 264, to report for work late. Without hesitation, Calvin exploded, "You know our company cannot tolerate this type of behavior. I do not want to see you around here anymore. You are fired!" Just as quickly, Phillip replied, "You're way off base. Our contract calls for three warnings for tardiness before you can even suspend me. That's a long way from being fired. My steward will hear about this."

Question

1. How could this incident have been avoided? Discuss.

Human Resource Management Skills

Chapter 14: Internal Employee Relations

A Skills Module entitled *Employee Relations* is presented to provide additional insight into topics in this chapter. Specific sections within the module address the following topics: why employees should be treated fairly; meaning of employment at will and exceptions to employment at will; steps in progressive discipline; positive discipline; suspending employees with or without pay; and alternative dispute resolution, mediation, and arbitration.

Several internal employee relation scenarios are presented to give students realistic experience in dealing with the topic.

A test is provided at the end of the module to determine mastery of the material included in the Skills Module. Also, directions are given for assignments that can be used in class or assigned as homework.

We invite you to visit the Mondy homepage on the Prentice Hall Web site at

www.prenhall.com/mondy

for updated information, Web-based exercises, and links to other HR-related sites.

Notes

1. Melissa Master, "Wayne Cascio is Down on Downsizing," *Across the Board* 39 (November/December 2002): 13–14.
2. Sherry Kuczynski, "Help! I Shrunk the Company!" *HRMagazine* 44 (June 1999): 40–45.
3. "How to Improve Morale Without Breaking the Bank," *HR Focus* 79 (December 2002): 4–6.
4. Jason Jennings, "Five Ugly Truths About Layoffs," *Incentive* 177 (February 2003): 51.
5. Matthew Boyle, "Thirty Nothing," *Fortune* (February 18, 2002): 143–146.
6. Ibid.
7. "Preparing Yourself for Change," *HR Focus* 80 (January 2003): S3.
8. John Di Frances, "Ten Reasons Why Your Company Shouldn't Downsize," *Successful Meetings* 51 (August 2002): 49–51.
9. Ibid.
10. Ibid.
11. Master, "Wayne Cascio is Down on Downsizing."
12. Lisa Takeuchi Cullen, "Where Did Everyone Go?" *Time* (November 18, 2002): 64–66.
13. Di Frances, "Ten Reasons."
14. Janine S. Pouliot, "Workers Are Not the Usual Suspects," *Nation's Business* 86 (February 1998): 48(1).
15. Michael Price, "Anti-discrimination Training Useful to Prevent Bias Claims," *Business Insurance* (January 27, 2003): 12.
16. Cynthia J. Guffey and Marilyn M. Helms, "Effective Employee Discipline: A Case of the Internal Revenue Service," *Public Personnel Management* 30 (Spring 2001): 111–127.
17. Jane F. Miller, "Motivating People," *Executive Excellence* 19 (December 2002): 15.
18. Jeremy Kahn, "Avoiding Judgment Day," *FSB : Fortune Small Business* 12 (April 2002): 77–82.
19. Lorna Harris, "High Standards Allow Employer to Fire Threatening Employee," *Canadian HR Reporter* (October 22, 2001): 8, 10.
20. Charles Cresson Wood, "Integrated Approach Information Security," *Security* 37 (February 2000): 43–44.
21. Ed Lisoski, "Discipline Is for Children," *Supervision* 60 (May 1999): 3–5.
22. Herff L. Moore and Helen L. Moore, "Discipline + Help = Motivation," *Credit Union Management* 21 (August 1998): 33.
23. Guffey and Helms, "Effective Employee Discipline."
24. Stephen Barth, "Pros and Cons of Progressive Discipline," *Lodging Hospitality* (March 15, 2002): 10.
25. Lauren M. Bernardi, "Progressive Discipline: Effective Management Tool or Legal Trap?" *Canadian Manager* 21 (January 1996): 9.
26. Lisa Leland, "Chat, Don't Chasten," *American Printer* 222 (February 1999): 94.
27. Dick Grote, "Discipline Without Punishment," *Across the Board* 38 (September/October 2001): 52–57.
28. George D. Shuman, "How Should Discipline Be Delivered?" *Security Management* 46 (June 2002): 157.
29. Gary A. Bielous, "Five Worst Disciplinary Mistakes (and How to Avoid Them)," *Supervision* (August 1998): 11–13.
30. Wallace Wohlking, "Effective Discipline in Employee Relations," *Personnel Journal* 54 (September 1975): 489.
31. Ed Lisoski, "Nine Common Mistakes Made When Disciplining Employees," *Supervision* 59 (October 1998): 12–14.
32. Kristen Gerencher, "Enterprise Careers: Tackling Terminations," *InfoWorld* (March 1, 1999): 77–78.
33. Kahn, "Avoiding Judgment Day," 77–82.
34. D. Diane Hatch and James E. Hall, "Weingarten Rights for Non-Union Workers," *Workforce* 81 (March 2002): 72.
35. James F. Morgan, James M. Owens, and Glenn M. Gomes, "Union Rules in Nonunion Settings: The NLRB and Workplace Investigations," *S.A.M. Advanced Management Journal* 67 (Winter 2002): 22.
36. "Arbitrator's Decision Upheld," *Business Insurance* (December 4, 2000): 2.
37. Paul Falcone, "A Legal Dichotomy?" *HR Magazine* 44 (May 1999): 110–120.
38. "Avoiding Legal Pitfalls in the Disciplinary Process," *Association Management* 51 (March 1999): 81.
39. Mable H. Smith, "Grievance Procedures Resolve Conflict," *Nursing Management* 33 (April 2002): 13.
40. Jennifer Laabs, "Remedies for HR's Legal Headache," *Personnel Journal* 73 (December 1994): 69.

41. David Sherwyn, "Arbitration of Employment-Discrimination Lawsuits: Legalities, Practicalities, and Realities," *Cornell Hotel and Restaurant Administration Quarterly* 43 (December 2002): 62.
42. Michael Barrier, "A Working Alternative for Settling Disputes," *Nation's Business* (July 1, 1998): 43–46.
43. Cynthia E. Cohen and Murray E. Cohen, "Relative Satisfaction with ADR: Some Empirical Evidence," *Dispute Resolution Journal* 57 (November 2002-January 2003): 36–41.
44. Michael Barrier, "The Mediation Disconnect," *HRMagazine* 48 (May 2003): 54–58.
45. "Memorandum on Agency Use of Alternate Means of Dispute Resolution and Negotiated Rulemaking" (Transcript), *Weekly Compilation of Presidential Documents* (May 4, 1998): 749(2).
46. Mark J. Keppler, "The EEOC's Alternative Dispute Resolution Program: A More Civil Approach to Civil Rights Disputes," *Review of Business* (Winter 2003): 38–42.
47. Gillian Flynn, "Mandatory Arbitration Takes a Hit—but Lives," *Workforce* (May 2002): 70–71.
48. Nancy J. Arencibia, "Is Arbitration Right for Your Company?" *Financial Executive* 18 (December 2002): 46–47.
49. "9th Circuit Says Title VII Claims Are Arbitrable," *Dispute Resolution Journal* 57 (November 2002-January 2003): 5.
50. Mark A. Hofmann, "Arbitration Still Seen as Good Option," *Business Insurance* (January 27, 2003): 10.
51. "Firing: Letting People Go with Dignity Is Good for Business," *HR Focus* 77 (January 2000): 10.
52. Kristen Gerensher, "Tackling Terminations," *InfoWorld* 21 (March 1999): 77–78.
53. Chuck Jones, "When Is the Best Time to Fire an Employee?" *Advisor Today* 97 (December 2002): 78.
54. Bill Roberts, "Shown the Door," *Electronic Business* 29 (January 2003): 44–48.
55. "Goodbye, CEO," *Workforce* 79 (May 2000): 26.
56. Keith Naughton, "The CEO Party Is Over," *Newsweek* (December 30, 2002): 55.
57. Mary-Kathryn Zachary, "Protection for the Ethical Employee—Part I, Common Law Wrongful Discharge Claims," *Supervision* 63 (May 2002): 23–26.
58. Gregg M. Bishop, "Discipline and Safety," *Occupational Health & Safety* 68 (May 1999): 16–20.
59. Falcone, "A Legal Dichotomy?"
60. Matthew Heller, "A Return to At-Will Employment," *Workforce* 80 (May 2001): 42–46.
61. Ibid.
62. Ibid.
63. "Engineer Was Hired and Fired 'At Will'," *ENR* (April 22, 2002): 22.
64. Mable H. Smith, "Protect Your Facility and Staff with Effective Discipline and Termination," *Nursing Management* 33 (July 2002): 15–16.
65. Gillian Flynn, "How Do You Treat the At-Will Employment Relationship?" *Workforce* 79 (June 2000): 178–179.
66. Mark H. McCormack, "Boss Sends You a Message with Demotion," *Arizona Republic* (October 1, 1998): 4.
67. Barbara Davison, "The Difference Between Rightsizing and Wrongsizing," *The Journal of Business Strategy* 23 (July/August 2002): 31–35.
68. Amy Zuber, "McD to Shed 600 Jobs, Shutter Units," *Nation's Restaurant News* (November 18, 2002): 1, 3.
69. Jon Gertner, "The Lost World," *Money* 32 (March 2003): 96–102.
70. Julia Chang, "Life After Layoffs," *Sales & Marketing Management* 155 (January 2003): 10.
71. "Down-Sizers Take Another Breather," *Home Textiles Today* (January 7, 2003): 17.
72. Di Frances, "Ten Reasons."
73. Peter Coy, Michelle Conlin, and Emily Thornton, "A Lost Generation? Young and Mid-Career Job Seekers Are Bearing the Brunt of U.S. Layoffs," *BusinessWeek* (November 4, 2002): 44–46.
74. Terence F. Shea, "Listless Economy Is Squeezing from the Bottom," *HRMagazine* 47 (November 2002): 32.
75. "Layoffs, Lawsuits, & Leave: Issues in '03," *HR Focus* 80 (March 2003): 2.
76. Michael Price "Anti-discrimination Training Useful to Prevent Bias Claims," *Business Insurance* (January 27, 2003): 12.
77. Gillian Flynn, "The Maturing of the ADEA," *Workforce* 81 (October 2002): 86–87.
78. Charles S. Lauer, "Really Pursue Those 'Other Interests'," *Modern Healthcare* (February 3, 2003): 31.
79. Bob Delaney, "Keeping Up with Outplacement," *Canadian HR Reporter* (June 17, 2002): 15, 19.
80. Tony Simper, "Outplacement—A Justifiable Expense," *Insurance Brokers' Monthly and Insurance Advisor* 50 (June 2000): 31.
81. Delaney, "Keeping Up with Outplacement."
82. "Lateral Moves Outweigh Promotions for Transferees," *HR Focus* 76 (October 1999): 16.
83. Marilyn Moats Kennedy, "What Managers Can Find Out from Exit Interviews," *Physician Executive* 22 (October 1996): 45.
84. Craig R. Taylor, "Focus on Talent," *T&D* 56 (December 2002): 26–31.
85. Maureen Smith, "Getting Value from Exit Interviews," *Association Management* 52 (April 2000): 22.
86. Andrea C. Poe, "Make Foresight 20/20," *HRMagazine* 45 (February 2000): 74–80.
87. R. S. Dreyer, "Keeping 'Em Down on the Farm," *Supervision* 62 (November 2001): 20–22.
88. Wanda R. Embrey, R. Wayne Mondy, and Robert M. Noe, "Exit Interview: A Tool for Personnel Development," *Personnel Administrator* 24 (May 1979): 46.
89. Theodore Kunin, "The Construction of a New Type of Attitude Measure," *Personnel Psychology* 51 (Winter 1998): 823.
90. Paul Falcone, "Resignations," *HRMagazine* 44 (April 1999): 125.
91. Robin Kessler, "Employee Relations Say Good-Bye with Style When Employers and HR Professionals Don't Leave Departing Employees with a Good Feeling, the Cost to the Organization Can Be Surprisingly High," *HRMagazine* 43 (June 1998): 171–174.

92. Falcone, "Resignations."
93. Carlos Tejada, "A Special News Report About Life on the Job—And Trends Taking Shape There," *Wall Street Journal* (July 31, 2002): B9.
94. "Services Brief—U.S. Postal Service: Approval Is Sought to Offer Early Retirement to Employees," *Wall Street Journal* (January 30, 2003): B2.
95. Therese Poletti, "Hewlett-Packard to Cut 15,000 Jobs, Downgrades Sales Forecast," *San Jose Mercury News* (June 5, 2002).
96. Tejada, "A Special News Report About Life on the Job."
97. Ibid.
98. "SHRM Exploring Ways to Develop a Universal Cost-Per-Hire Method," *HR Focus* 79 (November 2002): 8–9.
99. "A Growing Trend: Measuring Employees' Bottom-Line Value," *HR Focus* 79 (September 2002): 8.
100. "Is It Time to Try an Employment Practice Audit?" *HR Focus* 77 (June 2000): 9.
101. Nancy Sorensen, "Measuring HR for Success," *Training & Development* 49 (November 1995): 49.
102. "How Much Does Turnover Really Cost?" *HR Focus* 77 (May 2000): 9.
103. Lori Tansey Martin and Amber Crowell, "Whistleblowing: A Global Perspective" (Part I), *Ethikos* (May 1, 2002): 6.
104. Ibid.
105. Ibid.

PART EIGHT

Operating in a Global Environment

CHAPTER OBJECTIVES

After completing this chapter, students should be able to

1. Describe the use of virtual teams in a global environment.
2. Describe the evolution of global business and global human resource management.
3. Explain global staffing.
4. Describe global human resource development.
5. Explain global compensation and benefits.
6. Describe global safety and health.
7. Explain global employee and labor relations.
8. Describe political and legal factors affecting global human resource management.
9. Describe cultural differences affecting global human resource management.

CHAPTER 15

Global Human Resource Management

HRM IN *Action:*

Virtual Teams in a Global Environment

OBJECTIVE

Describe the use of virtual teams in a global environment.

In the wake of the 9/11 terrorist attacks, many corporations have responded to employees' fears by reducing air travel to an absolute minimum. There has been an increased use of virtual global teams where members located in several countries work together effectively in the absence of face-to-face interactions.[1] In all other ways, virtual teams emulate traditional teams.[2] Virtual teams have been defined in many ways, with the virtual component ranging from occasional to total reliance on technology as the medium for interaction.[3] In the past, people thought that teams needed to meet face-to-face to discuss issues and resolve problems, but in a number of functions, virtual teams have outperformed face-to-face teams.[4]

Virtual teams enable companies to accomplish things more quickly and efficiently. For example, Texas Instruments found that virtual meeting software such as WebEx reduced travel costs and saved time. With WebEx, participants see a slide presentation on their computers and can instant-message questions and comments throughout the presentation. This software also produced a higher level of feedback from workers who spoke English as a second language. Virtual teams frequently communicate via e-mail, with some managers estimating it amounts to 75 to 80 percent of their communication.[5]

The times when virtual team members are in one place are scarce, especially when members are headquartered or stationed all across the globe. This often makes global teams more difficult to manage effectively. Communication is the key to keeping teams working effectively together. Some of the difficulties that virtual teams confront with regard to communication are discussed next. First, dispersed team members often do not feel as connected or committed to the team. "Out of sight, out of mind" may apply. Second, communication problems between team members appear to be directly proportional to the number of time zones that separate them. If it is only a couple of zones, teammates will be in their offices earlier or later than one another, but their workdays still overlap enough to allow phone calls. If the distance stretches from nine to twelve time zones, workdays do not overlap at all, and e-mail and voice mail must be used. Third, there is the language problem. Since English is slowly becoming the world language, those for whom English is a second language may be placed at a disadvantage. Many Asians are concerned with saving face if they do not understand something. They may be hesitant to ask questions that would reveal their ignorance, thus widening the communication gap. Leading global virtual teams is certainly challenging.[6]

Countless tools are available these days to help dispersed teams stay in close communication. They include e-mail, voice mail, video- and teleconferencing, groupware, and various aids to communication and decision making. No single tool is best for all situations. Some tools, such as phone calls or face-to-face meetings, provide real-time communication. Others, such as e-mail or voice mail, have an inherent delay.[7]

We first described the use of virtual teams in a global environment. Next, we describe the evolution of global business and global human resource management. Then we explain global staffing and describe global human resource development. Global compensation and benefits and global safety and health are discussed. This is followed by a discussion of global employee and labor relations. This chapter ends with a discussion of political and legal factors affecting global human resource management and cultural differences affecting global human resource management.

2 OBJECTIVE

Describe the evolution of global business and global human resource management.

The Evolution of Global Business

"Organizations must either globalize or they die" accurately describes the twenty first-century economy. Almost 50 percent of the U.S. economy is based on exports and imports. U.S. corporations have invested more than $1 trillion abroad and employ more than 100 million overseas workers.[8] For many companies to grow in today's domestic economic environment, they must expand overseas because often the market has been saturated at home.[9]

Years ago, many U.S. multinational corporations had operations in Canada or perhaps Mexico, but not in many other countries. American companies still regularly do business in Canada and Mexico, but many now have operations in Hong Kong, Singapore, Japan, the United Kingdom, France, Germany, and Southeast Asia, to name only a few. More and more U.S. global corporations are doing business in former Eastern Bloc countries. Vietnam, a country that the United States was at war with only 25 years ago, is now viewed as a potential marketplace. The globalization of the marketplace has created special human resource challenges that will endure well into this century.

Exporting:
Selling abroad, either directly or indirectly, by retaining foreign agents and distributors.

Licensing:
A global arrangement whereby an organization grants a foreign firm the right to use intellectual properties such as patents, copyrights, manufacturing processes, or trade names for a specific period of time.

Franchising:
A multinational option whereby the parent company grants another firm the right to do business in a prescribed manner.

Normally, companies evolve to the point of being truly global over an extended period. Most companies initially become global without making substantial investments in foreign countries, by exporting, licensing, or franchising. **Exporting** entails selling abroad, either directly or indirectly, by retaining foreign agents and distributors. It is a way that many small businesses enter the global market.[10] **Licensing** is an arrangement whereby an organization grants a foreign firm the right to use intellectual properties such as patents, copyrights, manufacturing processes, or trade names for a specific period of time. **Franchising** is an option where the parent company grants another firm the right to do business in a prescribed manner. Franchisees must follow stricter operational guidelines than do licensees. Licensing is usually limited to manufacturers, while franchising is popular with service firms, such as restaurants and hotels. Tricon Restaurants International reports a record-breaking 1,041 new international restaurant openings for its KFC, Pizza Hut, and Taco Bell brands.[11] Franchising possibilities are even available in China, where the rapid emergence of a middle class, led by a growing population of educated professionals, is paving the way for franchise development.[12]

Although exporting, licensing, and franchising are good initial entry options, in order to take full advantage of global opportunities, companies must make a substantial investment in another country. Companies can vary greatly in their degree of global involvement. A **multinational corporation (MNC)** is a firm that is based in one country (the parent or home country) and produces goods or provides services in one or more foreign countries (host countries). A multinational corporation directs manufacturing and marketing operations in several countries; these operations are coordinated by a parent company, usually based in the firm's home country.

Multinational corporation (MNC):
A firm that is based in one country (the parent or home country) and produces goods or provides services in one or more foreign countries (host countries).

General Motors and Ford have evolved beyond being a multinational corporation to becoming a **global corporation (GC)**; an organization that has corporate units in a number of countries that are integrated to operate as one organization worldwide. The global corporation operates as if the entire world were one entity. Global corporations sell essentially the same products in the same manner throughout the world with components that may be made and/or designed in different countries. Expectations are that as the world becomes more globally open, the globalization of corporations will become much more commonplace. Not many years ago Procter & Gamble was still primarily a U.S. business investing heavily in food brands. Now it is a truly global corporation with operations in 140 countries and a tremendous variety of product categories. Its 30 corporate leaders are an extremely diverse group representing many cultures and backgrounds.[13]

Global corporation (GC):
An organization that has corporate units in a number of countries; the units are integrated to operate as one organization worldwide.

The importance of human resource management in the global environment is illustrated by the fact that the first international HR certification exam will be administered at the SHRM Global Forum Conference in 2004. Six areas of international human resource management have been identified for the examination. These are: strategic international HR management, organizational effectiveness and employee development, global staffing, international assignment management, global compensation and benefits, and international employee relations and regulations. These topics form the basis for this chapter.[14]

Global Human Resource Management

HR Web Wisdom

SHRM HR Links

www.shrm.org/hrlinks/Links.asp?Category=34

This SHRM link provides information on International HR.

Global human resource problems and opportunities are enormous and are expanding. **Global human resource management (GHRM)** is the utilization of global human resources to achieve organizational objectives without regard to geographic boundaries. Consequently, global managers are no longer able to simply strategize from the standpoint of domestic considerations but must think globally. Individuals dealing with global human resource matters face a multitude of challenges beyond that of their domestic counterparts. These considerations range from cultural barriers to political barriers to international aspects such as compensation. Before upper management decides on a global move, it is vitally important that the critical nature of human resource issues be considered.

Global human resource management (GHRM):
The use of global human resources to achieve organizational objectives without regard to geographic boundaries.

Companies that engage in the global economy place even greater emphasis on strategic HR. General Motors, the world's largest automobile manufacturer, has completely reshaped the way its HR operates. At GM, the corporate HR function has evolved from a tactical to a strategic role. GM believes it cannot become a truly global corporation without strategic support from HR. To this end, GM CEO Rick Wagoner appointed the head of HR, Kathleen S. Barclay, to the company's overall strategy board. He also gave her the authority to reshape the HR department.[15]

Those engaged in the management of global human resources develop and work through an integrated global human resource management system similar to the one they experience domestically. As Figure 15-1 shows, the functional areas associated with effective global human resource management are the same as those experienced domestically. Although the five areas are the same, how they are implemented may

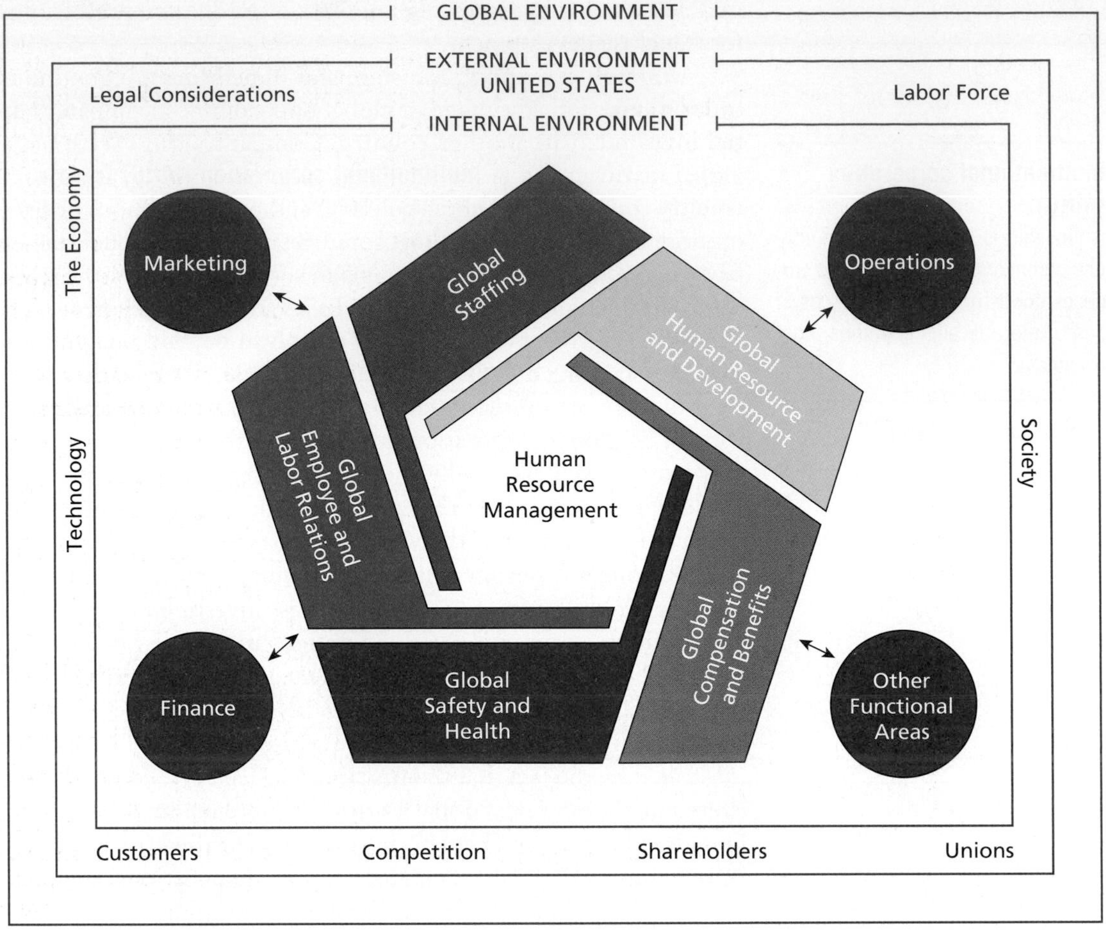

Figure 15-1 Human Resource Management in the Global Environment

differ. Sound global human resource management practices are required for successful performance in each area. As with domestic human resources, the functional areas are not separate and distinct, but are highly interrelated.

3 OBJECTIVE

Explain global staffing.

Global Staffing

Corporations make big investments in global assignments that can cost two to three times what it would to employ the same executive in the United States.[16] Unfortunately, many HR managers have never worked abroad and are not adequately prepared to cope with the global environment.[17] Before the staffing process for an international assignment begins, a thorough understanding of what is involved in the job should be developed (job analysis). A global organization must have qualified individuals in specific jobs at specific places and times in order to accomplish its goals (human resource planning). Individuals should be recruited and selected based upon the specific qualifications identified. Without proper identification of the qualities needed for an overseas assignment, an outstanding worker in the United States may fail on a global assignment.[18]

Expatriate:
An employee who is not a citizen of the country in which the firm's operation (or subsidiary) is located but is a citizen of the country in which the organization is headquartered.

Types of Global Staff Members

Companies must choose from various types of global staff members and may employ specific approaches to global staffing. Global staff members may be selected from among three different types: expatriates, host-country nationals, and third-country nationals. An **expatriate** is an employee who is not a citizen of the country in which the firm's operation (or subsidiary) is located, but is a citizen of the country in which the

Host-country national (HCN): An employee who is a citizen of the country where the subsidiary is located.

organization is headquartered. A **host-country national (HCN)** is an employee who is a citizen of the country where the subsidiary is located. An example would be a U.S. citizen working for a Japanese company in the United States. Normally, the bulk of employees in international offices will be host-country nationals. Not only are companies staffed by locals less expensive; they also offer advantages from a cultural and business standpoint.[19] In most industries, local nationals comprise more than 98 percent of the workforce in the foreign operations of North American and Western European multinational companies.[20] According to Roberta Davis, expatriate services manager at Chubb & Son Inc., "As a company develops its presence in a foreign market . . . it's a wise strategy to be seen as a local company with a local staff."[21] This means that hiring local people and operating the company like local companies whenever possible is good business. The ultimate goal of most foreign operations is to turn over control to local management.[22] However, relying totally on local employees may, at times, pose problems. Chinese officials often think a foreign company (particularly a large multinational) is not taking them seriously if a local represents them with no links to the decision makers in the home country.[23] A **third-country national (TCN)** is a citizen of one country, working in a second country, and employed by an organization headquartered in a third country. An example would be an Italian citizen working for a French company in Algeria.

Third country national (TCN): A citizen of one country, working in a second country, and employed by an organization headquartered in a third country.

International Public Management Association for Human Resources

www.ipmaac.org

This Web site provides information on an international HR organization.

Approaches to Global Staffing

Using the three basic types of global staff, there are four major approaches to global staffing:[24] ethnocentric, polycentric, regiocentric, and geocentric staffing. These reflect how the organization develops its human resource policies and the preferred types of employees for different positions.

Ethnocentric staffing: A staffing approach in which companies primarily hire expatriates to staff higher-level foreign positions.

Ethnocentric Staffing. With **ethnocentric staffing,** companies primarily hire expatriates to staff higher-level foreign positions. This strategy assumes that home-office perspectives and issues should take precedence over local perspectives and issues and that expatriates will be more effective in representing the views of the home office. Corporate human resources is primarily concerned with selecting and training managers for foreign assignments, developing appropriate compensation packages, and handling adjustment issues when managers return home. Generally, expatriates are used to ensure that foreign operations are linked effectively with parent corporations. However, the use of expatriate employees must be carefully considered since the cost of an international assignment may be high both in terms of financial compensation and resentment on the part of the host-country employees.[25]

Expatriates are often selected from those already within the organization and the process involves four distinct stages: self-selection, creating a candidate pool, technical skills assessment, and making a mutual decision. In the self-selection stage, employees determine if they are right for a global assignment, if their spouses and children are interested in relocating internationally, and if this is the best time for a move.[26] There is growing evidence that keeping an expatriate's spouse happy is extremely important.[27] In the case of self-selection, the candidate will assess himself or herself on all of the relevant dimensions for a job and then decide whether to pursue a global assignment. The self-assessment extends to the entire family.[28] Basically, candidates must decide whether to go to the next step in the selection process.[29] "Self-nomination is helpful. Someone who is interested in a country and a culture has a better chance to succeed. They're appreciative of being sent and aren't looking for other kinds of perks to make it worthwhile to go," says Melanie Young, director of global talent management at NCR.[30]

Stage two involves creating a candidate database organized according to the firm's staffing needs. Included in the database is information such as the year the employee is available to go overseas, the languages the employee speaks, the countries the employee prefers, and the jobs for which the employee is qualified. During stage three, the database is scanned for all possible candidates for a given global assignment;

then the list is forwarded to the assigning department. There, each candidate is assessed on technical and managerial readiness relative to the needs of the assignment. In the final stage, one person is identified as an acceptable candidate based on his or her technical or managerial readiness and is tentatively *selected*.

If the decision is made to employ expatriates, certain selection criteria should be carefully considered in stages two and three. Expatriate selection criteria should include cultural adaptability, strong communication skills, technical competence, professional or operational expertise, global experience, country-specific experience, interpersonal skills, language skills, family flexibility, and country- or region-specific considerations.[31]

Polycentric staffing:
When more host-country nationals are used throughout the organization, from top to bottom.

Polycentric Staffing. When more host-country nationals are used throughout the organization, from top to bottom, it is referred to as **polycentric staffing.** The ultimate goal of most foreign operations is to turn over control to local management. Not only are locally run businesses less expensive; they also offer advantages from a cultural and business standpoint.[32] The use of the polycentric staffing model is based on the assumption that host-country nationals are better equipped to deal with local market conditions. Organizations that use this approach will usually have a fully functioning human resource department in each foreign subsidiary responsible for managing all local human resource issues. Corporate human resource managers focus primarily on coordinating relevant activities with their counterparts in each foreign operation. Most global employees are usually host-country nationals because this helps to clearly establish that the company is making a commitment to the host country and not just setting up a foreign operation. Host-country nationals often have much more thorough knowledge of the culture, the politics, and the laws of the locale, as well as how business is done. There is no standard format in the selection of host-country nationals.

Regiocentric staffing:
Similar to the polycentric staffing approach, but regional groups of subsidiaries reflecting the organization's strategy and structure work as a unit.

Regiocentric Staffing. **Regiocentric staffing** is similar to the polycentric approach, but regional groups of subsidiaries reflecting the organization's strategy and structure work as a unit. There is some degree of autonomy in regional decision making, and promotions are possible within the region but rare from the region to headquarters. Each region develops a common set of employment practices.

Geocentric staffing:
A staffing approach that uses a worldwide-integrated business strategy.

Geocentric Staffing. **Geocentric staffing** is a staffing approach that uses a worldwide integrated business strategy. The firm attempts to always hire the best person available for a position, regardless of where that individual comes from. The geocentric staffing model is most likely to be adopted and used by truly global firms such as General Motors and Ford. Usually, the corporate human resource function in geocentric companies is the most complicated, since every aspect of HR must be dealt with in the global environment.

OBJECTIVE

Describe global human resource development.

International Personnel Management Association

www.ipmaac.org

This Web site is for an organization for applied personnel assessment professionals.

Global Human Resource Development

Many U.S. businesses operate under the assumption that American ways and business practices are standard across the globe. Similarly, many T&D professionals believe that training and consulting principles and strategies that work for a U.S. audience can be equally effective abroad. Unfortunately, nothing could be further from the truth.[33] Global training and development is needed because people, jobs, and organizations are often quite different globally.[34] Next, various aspects of global HRD will be discussed.

Expatriate Development

In a recent study, nearly 40 percent of expatriates said they were not prepared adequately for an international assignment, 56 percent cited poor coordination between local-country and home-office HR departments, and 35 percent said they expect to leave their current employer within five years.[35] The development process should start as soon as workers are selected, definitely before beginning the global assignment.

Global expansion into China has been particularly difficult for McDonald's because the cultural revolution of the 1960s and 1970s closed most schools in China. As a result, an entire generation did not receive much education. McDonald's has had to personally develop its workforce. Bob Wilner, McDonald's director of international HR, says that McDonald's tries to develop local people in Asia, finding them more effective than expatriates because they better understand the Asian marketplace and customers.[36] David Hoff of Anheuser-Busch in Asia hires host-country nationals, develops their talents in the United States, and reassigns them abroad as local managers.[37]

Organizations are recognizing that expatriate employees and their families face special situations and pressures that training and development activities must prepare them to deal with.[38] Employees and their families must have an effective orientation program and a readjustment-training program. In addition, the employee must have a program of continual development. Figure 15-2 illustrates the ideal expatriate preparation and development program, which includes pre-move orientation and training, continual development, and repatriation orientation and training.

Pre-move orientation and training of expatriate employees and their families are essential before the global assignment begins. The pre-move orientation involves training and familiarization in language, culture, history, living conditions, and local customs and peculiarities.[39] Continuing employee development, in which the employee's global skills are fitted into career planning and corporate development programs, makes the eventual transition to the home country less disruptive. Continual development involves expanding both professional and operational skills when appropriate, comprehensive career planning, and involvement in home-country development programs.

On-Site Assistance and Training

Companies are now offering Internet service in the areas of career services, cross-cultural training, and employee assistance programs (EAP). The Internet offers troubled global employees assistance 24 hours a day, seven days a week. Technology is a time-saving and cost-effective solution for the stress experienced by employees who are on assignment or doing business travel. Even if the assignment is a short-term business trip, technology can be used to provide ongoing contact and support. For example, online career services can give expatriates and their spouses the opportunity to upgrade skills while on assignment.[40]

Repatriation Orientation and Training

Repatriation: The process of bringing expatriates home.

Orientation and training are also necessary prior to **repatriation,** which is the process of bringing expatriates home. Repatriation orientation and training are needed to prepare the employee and the family for a return to the home-country culture and to prepare the expatriate's new subordinates and supervisor for the return. According to a

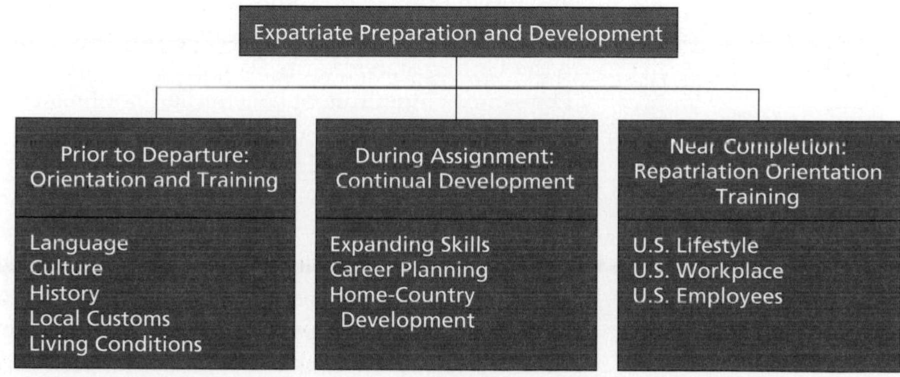

Figure 15-2 The Expatriate Preparation and Development Program

Trends & Innovations

E-learning

Globalization has created a special need for e-learning. In the past, a program for a *Fortune* 200 company in the Far East would likely cost between $250,000 and $500,000 for travel and related expenses. Many believe that live, instructor-led training is still more effective, but the question that must be asked is "how much more effective?" The costs of a training program include the instructor's salary, materials costs, travel costs, meeting room expenses, and the salaries and benefits of the people attending the program, in addition to the costs of the program.[41] E-learning allows companies to keep the money and still receive a good training product.[42]

The most obvious challenges for any global e-learning implementation are language and localization issues. Many companies offer courses only in English or in English and one other language, usually Spanish. An English-only focus works for firms that routinely conduct their business all over the world in English. But others need courses in more than one language. Companies that want to offer courses in several languages usually turn to translators. Financial services provider GE Capital relies on translation companies to offer Web-based courses in English, French, German, and Japanese.[43]

survey of leading *Fortune* 1000 companies, while nearly half of respondents state that they select their best employees for international assignments, only 35 percent state that their respective companies manage the repatriation process successfully.[44] In fact, 68 percent of companies do not even guarantee expatriates a job upon their return.[45] Approximately 50 percent of repatriates leave their companies within two years of repatriation because most companies do a poor job of repatriating employees.[46] Adjustments involve preparing the individual and the family, when appropriate, for returning to the U.S. lifestyle.[47]

OBJECTIVE

Explain global compensation and benefits.

International Foundation of Employee Benefit Plans

www.ifebp.org

This Web site provides insight into international employee benefit plans.

Global Compensation and Benefits

Companies that are successful in the global environment align their human resources programs in support of their strategic business plans. A major component is the manner in which the human resources total compensation program supports the way the business is structured, organized, and operated both globally and regionally.[48]

Compensation for Host-Country Nationals

Certainly, in compensation-related matters, organizations should think globally but act locally. One reason that organizations relocate to other areas of the world is probably the high wage pressures that threaten their ability to compete on a global basis. Globally, the question of what constitutes a fair day's pay is not as complicated as it is in the United States; normally, it is slightly above the prevailing wage rates in the area. The same is often true of benefits and nonfinancial rewards. Variations in laws, living costs, tax policies, and other factors all must be considered when a company is establishing global compensation packages.

The company will want to create a precise picture of employment and working conditions in order to establish appropriate practices in each country. Some of the factors that should be considered include: minimum wage requirements, which often differ from country to country and even from city to city within a country;[49] working time information such as annual holidays, vacation time and pay, paid personal days, standard weekly working hours, probation periods, and overtime restrictions and payments; and hiring and termination rules and regulations covering severance practices.[50]

Expatriate Compensation

On average, expatriates cost two to three times more than they would in an equivalent domestic position.[51] For expatriate managers and professionals, the situation is more complex than simply paying at or slightly above local host-country compensation rates. Even minor changes in the value of the U.S. dollar may result in compensation adjustments for expatriates. Also, expatriate compensation packages must cover the extra costs of housing, education for children, and yearly transportation home for themselves and their family members. Additionally, compensation packages may include foreign service and hardship premiums, relocation and moving allowances, cost-of-living adjustments, and tax equalization payments. Regarding tax equalization payments, U.S. citizens living overseas can exclude up to $70,000 of income earned abroad. Also, credits against U.S. income taxes are given for a portion of the foreign income taxes paid by U.S. expatriates beyond the $70,000 level.[52] All these factors make global compensation extremely complex.

A country's culture can also impose significant constraints on the globalization of pay.[53] Including bonus and long-term incentives, total compensation of a chief executive of a U.S company typically exceeds the pay of that company's lowest-paid employee by a ratio of more than 60 to one. In Sweden, the spread is likely to be closer to eight to one. While people in the United States derive great status from high pay, nations in large parts of Europe and Asia shun conspicuous wealth. In Italy, where teamwork is more valued than individual initiative, sales incentives for top sales professionals working in small teams can be demotivational. The recipient of a large award may feel awkward when receiving larger than a *fair share* of the reward pie.[54]

Global HR professionals must constantly strive to reduce costs associated with expatriate programs.[55] Paul Patt, director of business development at Runzheimer International, believes that companies should "try not to start out overly generous, because it is very, very difficult to scale back packages once they're in place."[56] "Companies invest an average of $1.3 million for each expatriate during the course of a typical three-year assignment," says Bill Sheridan, senior director of the National Foreign Trade Council.[57] The cost of an overseas assignment becomes even higher when the usual 25 percent attrition rate is factored in.[58]

One cost-saving trend that experts see is the move away from foreign service premiums, which companies have given nearly all assignees in the past and which traditionally run 10 percent to 15 percent of the employee's base salary.[59] Living as an expatriate is no longer considered a hardship tour. Companies are finding out that they do not need to provide incentives for people to go abroad to work any more. International experience is now becoming more and more crucial for people to move up within a company. Today only 15 percent of chief executives in the United States currently have international experience, but that is expected to increase dramatically in the next few years as companies focus on finding global leaders.[60]

American concepts such as employee stock ownership and linking executive compensation to corporate performance through equity and equity-based compensation techniques have caught on in an increasingly globalized marketplace.[61] Successful companies around the world realize the importance of using long-term incentives and are making stock options a central feature of their remuneration programs.[62] Several Japanese companies, including Sony, have introduced radical foreign compensation practices such as employee stock options for their employees in Japan. In a like manner, many U.S.-based companies have adopted equally radical foreign approaches such as profit sharing and team-based and skill-based pay. No one country has a monopoly on the best practices.[63]

 OBJECTIVE

Describe global safety and health.

Global Safety and Health

Safety and health aspects of the job are important because employees who work in a safe environment and enjoy good health are more likely to be productive and yield long-term benefits to the organization than those in less desirable circumstances. U.S.-based global operations are often safer and healthier than host-country operations, but frequently not as safe as similar operations in the United States.[64] Safety and health laws and regulations often vary greatly from country to country. Such laws can range from virtually nonexistent to more stringent than those in the United States.[65] Also, health-care facilities across the globe vary greatly in their state of modernization. Companies are attempting to overcome this problem. For example, at CIGNA International, a division of CIGNA Corp., expatriate employees and their families on international assignment have instant access to an expanded global network of physicians and care facilities accessible by Internet and available in-person around the world.[66]

Additional considerations specific to global assignments are emergency evacuation services and global security protection. An international firm was preparing to evacuate 15 expatriate employees and dependents from a country that had suffered an earthquake. When it came time to meet at the departure point, 25 people showed up. Those arranging for the evacuation had not known that two technical teams were in the country supporting clients at the time.[67] Often, evacuation and care of injured employees is done through private companies. Medical emergencies are frightening under any circumstances, but when an employee becomes sick or injured abroad, it can be a traumatic experience. If the travelers are assigned to more remote or less developed areas, companies should be aware that in many medical facilities needles are often reused, equipment is not properly used, and there is a lack of basic medical supplies.[68] Also, employees and their families living abroad must constantly be aware of security issues. Many firms provide bodyguards who escort executives everywhere. Some firms even have so-called "disaster plans" to deal with evacuating expatriates if natural disasters, civil conflicts, or wars occur. This was certainly the case during the 2003 Iraqi War.

 OBJECTIVE

Explain global employee and labor relations.

Global Employee and Labor Relations

While unionism has waned in the United States, it has maintained much of its strength abroad. In Sweden, 96 percent of its employees are union members; it is 50 percent in the United Kingdom, 43 percent in Germany, and 28 percent in Japan and France.[69] There are 12.8 million working Canadians and 30.3 percent are in a union.[70] Foreign unions are generally less adversarial with management and less focused on wage gains and yet they are still quite influential around the globe. For this reason, HR policies and practices must be geared toward dealing with the global differences in collective bargaining.

Obviously, the strength and nature of unions differ from country to country, with unions ranging from nonexistent to relatively strong. Codetermination, which requires firms to have union or worker representatives on their boards of directors, is very common in European countries. Even though they face global competition, unions in several European countries have resisted changing their laws and removing government protections. Laws make it hard to fire workers, so companies are reluctant to hire.[71] Generous and lengthy unemployment benefits discourage the jobless from seeking new work. Wage bargaining remains centralized and companies have little flexibility to fashion contracts that fit their needs. High payroll taxes raise labor costs.[72] Recently, labor unions in Italy virtually shut down the entire country, protesting the government's plan that would, for the first time, allow companies to lay off workers.[73]

On the other hand, in some South American countries such as Chile, collective bargaining for textile workers, miners, and carpenters is prohibited. All negotiations are limited to the individual company. And unions are generally allowed only in companies of 25 workers or more. This practice has encouraged businesses to split into small companies to avoid collective bargaining, leaving workers on their own.[74]

The North American Free Trade Agreement (NAFTA) between Canada, Mexico, and the United States facilitated the movement of goods across boundaries within North America. Labor relations took a major step forward, with a *side agreement* on labor designed to protect workers in all three countries from the effects of competitive economic pressures. NAFTA established a Commission for Labor Cooperation with offices in each country, which is governed by a council made up of labor ministers of Canada, Mexico, and the United States. Each country is accountable for complying with its *own* labor laws when dealing with occupational safety and health; child labor; migrant workers; human resource development; labor statistics; work benefits; social programs for workers; productivity improvements; labor–management relations; employment standards; the equality of men and women in the workplace; and forms of cooperation among workers, management, and government. A country that consistently fails to enforce its own labor laws could be fined up to $20 million per violation. There are also a number of principles identifying broad areas of common agreement to protect the rights and interests of each workforce. Since NAFTA was implemented over 10 years ago, trade between the United States, Canada, and Mexico has grown dramatically.[75]

8 OBJECTIVE

Describe political and legal factors affecting global human resource management.

Political and Legal Factors Affecting Global Human Resource Management

Legal and political forces are unique for each country.[76] The nature and stability of political and legal systems vary throughout the globe. U.S. firms enjoy a relatively stable political and legal system. The same is true in many of the other developed countries. In other nations, however, the political and legal systems are much less stable. Some governments are subject to coups, dictatorial rule, and corruption, which can substantially alter the business environment, as well as the legal environment. Legal systems can also become unstable, with contracts suddenly becoming unenforceable because of internal politics.

International Law Affecting HR

www.lir.msu.edu/hotlinks/igo.htm

This Web site provides links to numerous international law sites.

There is a seemingly unstoppable force of unethical behavior in global business transactions.[77] However, since 1977, U.S. firms have been prohibited from bribing foreign officials under the Foreign Corrupt Practices Act. While unacceptable to most American multinational firms, paying bribes to foreign public officials is a generally accepted marketing ploy on the part of the traditional competitors of U.S. companies—multinational firms from other developed nations.[78] Countries most likely to pay bribes to win business were Russia, China, Taiwan, South Korea, and Italy. Australia, Sweden, and Switzerland were identified as least likely to make corrupt payments.[79]

HR regulations and laws vary greatly among countries. Merely conducting a background check is different from one country to another. For instance, Japanese law covers a person working at the Tokyo office of a U.S.-based company, including privacy statutes that prohibit criminal checks on Japanese citizens.[80] In many Western European countries, laws on labor unions and employment make it difficult to lay off employees.[81] Because of political and legal differences, it is essential that a comprehensive review of the political and legal environment of the host country is conducted before beginning global operations.[82]

Americans may encounter laws that are routinely ignored by host countries, creating somewhat of a dilemma. For example, the laws in some countries that require a minimum age for factory workers are not enforced. The U.S. Department of Labor report revealed continued child labor abuses in the apparel and textile industries. The report identified several countries such as Pakistan, the Philippines, Brazil, Bangladesh, Egypt, Cambodia, India, Indonesia, and Lesotho as the greatest abusers.[83] In addition, a form of indentured servitude exists for many foreign workers in Asian factories. Here, foreign workers are grossly overcharged by labor brokers just for the privilege of working.[84]

Ethical Dilemma

Mordita

Your company, a distributor of heavy mining equipment, wants to trade in the Mexican market where cash under the table—mordita (a little bit)—is part of doing business. This payoff practice is so ingrained in the Mexican culture that a business virtually cannot open a Mexican operation without going along. You have observed many companies that did not pay and they failed to enter the Mexican market, as well as those that paid and entered the market, and overall, did fairly well. You can continue to raise your stature with mining companies, farmers, and contractors, and encourage them to lobby the government to freely open the market, or you can pay the bribe.

What would you do?

Tariffs: Taxes collected on goods that are shipped across national boundaries.

Quotas: Policies that limit the number or value of goods that can be imported across national boundaries.

Also affecting the environment in which global companies operate are certain tariffs and quotas that can greatly impact business profitability. **Tariffs** are taxes collected on goods that are shipped across national boundaries. In 2001, the U.S. chemical industry's $80 billion worth of exports were subject to $3.8 billion in tariffs around the globe. These tariffs make U.S. chemical products more expensive for foreign customers and effectively close some markets to U.S. goods. A U.S. proposal to the World Trade Organization has called for the elimination of global tariffs on all industrial goods by 2015.[85] **Quotas** limit the number or value of goods that can be imported across national boundaries.

 **OBJECTIVE**

Describe cultural differences affecting global human resource management.

Country's culture: The set of values, symbols, beliefs, languages, and norms that guide human behavior within a country.

Cultural Differences Affecting Global Human Resource Management

Cultural differences vary from country to country, with corresponding differences in HR practices. A **country's culture** is the set of values, symbols, beliefs, languages, and norms that guide human behavior within a country. The cultural norms of Asia promote loyalty and teamwork. In Japan, most management personnel tend to remain with the same company for life. In the United States, senior executives often change companies but there are few second chances in Japan. The Japanese believe strongly that leaving a job is to be avoided out of respect to the business team.[86] Knowing the cultural differences present in a diverse workplace can help HR practitioners understand how to achieve maximum effectiveness.[87]

Americans going overseas need to understand that other cultures view us differently. Philip R. Harris and Robert T. Moran, in their book, *Managing Cultural Differences,* summarize feedback from Arab businesspeople regarding how they perceive many Westerners. To them, Westerners act superior, as if they know the answer to everything; are not willing to share credit for joint efforts; are unable or unwilling to respect and adjust to local customs and culture; prefer solutions based on their home cultures rather than meeting local needs; resist working through local administrative and legal channels and procedures; manage in an autocratic and intimidating way; and are too imposing and pushy.[88] Successful international assignees find the important balance between maintaining their own cultural values while at the same time accepting those of the host country, creating a "third culture" style of doing business. In this "third culture," expatriates do not have to abandon their own values or totally adopt the host country's value system.[89]

Culture often plays a part in determining compensation. North American compensation practices encourage individualism and high performance; continental

European programs typically emphasize social responsibility; the traditional Japanese approach considers age and company service as primary determinants of compensation. There is no guarantee that additional compensation will ensure additional output. Some have found that, in some countries, additional pay has resulted in employees' working less. As soon as employees have earned enough to satisfy their needs, time spent with family or on other noncompany activities is perceived as more valuable than additional cash.

Maintaining an effective corporate culture that reflects the culture of the home country is essential for continuity worldwide. When a U.S. company hires too many local people in its foreign offices, it risks losing the unique set of values and operating procedures that define its corporate culture. According to Bill Fontana, a veteran of many foreign assignments for Citibank and now vice president of NFTC, "If you rely too heavily on locals, you're going to have a local culture, not the corporate culture you want . . . and the local culture may be totally foreign to the way you operate." To ensure a parallel corporate culture, firms should bring in a critical mass of expatriates who carry the culture with them at the beginning of the start-up. It is also critical that global corporations leave at least one or two expatriates behind to oversee the locals and ensure that they are following corporate policies.[90]

Summary

1. Describe the use of virtual teams in a global environment.

In the wake of the 9/11 terrorist attacks, many corporations have responded to employees' fears by reducing air travel to an absolute minimum. There has been an increased use of virtual global teams where members located in several countries work together effectively in the absence of face-to-face interactions. In all other ways, virtual teams emulate traditional teams.

2. Describe the evolution of global business and global human resource management.

Most companies initially become global without making substantial investments in foreign countries by either exporting, licensing, or franchising. A multinational corporation (MNC) is a firm that is based in one country (the parent or home country) and produces goods or provides services in one or more foreign countries (host countries). A global corporation (GC) has corporate units in a number of countries that are integrated to operate as one organization worldwide. The functions are global human resource planning, recruitment, and selection; global human resource development; global compensation and benefits; global safety and health; and global employee and labor relations.

3. Explain global staffing.

Companies must choose from various types of global staff members and may employ specific approaches to global staffing. Global staff members may be selected from among three different types: expatriates, host-country nationals, and third-country nationals.

4. Describe global human resource development.

Many T&D professionals believe that training and consulting principles and strategies that work for a U.S. audience can be equally effective abroad. Nothing could be further from the truth. Global training and development is needed because people, jobs, and organizations are often quite different globally.

5. Explain global compensation and benefits.

Companies that are successful in the global environment align their human resources programs in support of their strategic business plans. A major component is the manner in which the human resources total compensation program supports the way the business is structured, organized, and operated both globally and regionally.

6. Describe global safety and health.
U.S.-based global operations are often safer and healthier than host-country operations, but frequently not as safe as similar operations in the United States. Safety and health laws and regulations often vary greatly from country to country. Such laws can range from virtually nonexistent to more stringent than those in the United States.

7. Explain global employee and labor relations.
While unionism has waned in the United States, it has maintained much of its strength abroad.

8. Describe political and legal factors affecting global human resource management.
Legal and political forces are unique for each country.

9. Describe cultural differences affecting global human resource management.
Cultural differences vary from country to country, with corresponding differences in HR practices. A country's culture is the set of values, symbols, beliefs, languages, and norms that guide human behavior within a country.

Key Terms

- **Exporting, 482**
- **Licensing, 482**
- **Franchising, 482**
- **Multinational corporation (MNC), 483**
- **Global corporation (GC), 483**
- **Global human resource management (GHRM), 483**
- **Expatriate, 484**
- **Host-country national (HCN), 485**
- **Third-country national (TCN), 485**
- **Ethnocentric staffing, 485**
- **Polycentric staffing, 486**
- **Regiocentric staffing, 486**
- **Geocentric staffing, 486**
- **Repatriation, 487**
- **Tariffs, 492**
- **Quotas, 492**
- **Country's culture, 492**

Questions for Review

1. How are virtual teams used in the global environment?
2. How has global business evolved?
3. Define the following terms:
   a. exporting
   b. licensing
   c. franchising
4. What is the difference between a multinational corporation and a global corporation?
5. What are the various types of global staff members?
6. What are the approaches to global staffing?
7. Why is repatriation orientation and training needed?
8. What is meant by the statement "Organizations should think globally but act locally"?
9. What is the state of affairs for international unions?
10. What are some political and legal factors affecting global human resource management?
11. What are some cultural differences affecting global human resource management?

The Overseas Transfer

In college, Pat Marek majored in industrial management and was considered by his teachers and peers to be a good all-around student. Pat not only took the required courses in business, but he also learned French. After graduation, Pat took an entry-level management training position with Tuborg International, a multinational corporation with offices and factories in numerous countries, including the United States. His first assignment was in a plant in Chicago. His supervisors quickly identified Pat for his ability to get the job done and still maintain good rapport with subordinates, peers, and superiors. In only three years, Pat had advanced from a manager trainee to the position of assistant plant superintendent.

After two years in this position, he was called into the plant manager's office one day and told that he had been identified as ready for a foreign assignment. The move would mean a promotion. The assignment was for a plant in Haiti, a predominantly French-speaking country; but Pat wasn't worried about living and working there. He was excited and wasted no time in making the necessary preparations for the new assignment.

Prior to arriving at the plant in Haiti, Pat took considerable time to review his French textbook exercises. He was surprised by how quickly the language came back to him. He thought that there wouldn't be any major difficulties in making the transition from Chicago to Haiti. However, Pat found, on arrival, that the community where the plant was located did not speak the pure French that he had learned. There were many expressions that meant one thing to Pat but had an entirely different meaning to the employees of the plant.

When meeting with several of the employees a week after arriving, one of the workers said something to him that Pat interpreted as uncomplimentary. Actually, the employee had greeted him with a rather risqué expression but in a different tone than Pat had heard before. All of the other employees interpreted the expression to be merely a friendly greeting. Pat's disgust registered in his face.

As the days went by, this type of misunderstanding occurred a few more times, until the employees began to limit their conversation with him. In only one month, Pat managed virtually to isolate himself from the workers within the plant. He became disillusioned and thought about asking to be relieved from the assignment.

Questions

1. What problems had Pat not anticipated when he took the assignment?
2. How could the company have assisted Pat to reduce the difficulties that he confronted?
3. Do you believe the situation that Pat confronted is typical of an American going to a foreign assignment? Discuss.

HRM Incident 2

Boundless Technologies Venture Overseas

Not many years ago, Boundless Technologies, headquartered in Hauppauge, Long Island, moved its network computer manufacturing operation to Hong Kong. Moving production to Hong Kong meant dealing with a new workforce, a new work environment, new pay structures, and a multitude of other global HR issues. High wage rates were the driving force behind the relocation decision, because Hong Kong wages were much lower than those in Long Island. Unfortunately, the move was made primarily to escape high wage pressures, without regard to other HR issues.

Surprisingly, only a few years after moving to Hong Kong, Boundless returned to the United States, creating even more HR problems and requiring another massive HR effort. Failure to consider all of the problems that could result when relocating globally caused major disruptions in Boundless Technologies' operations. Basically, Boundless returned to the United States to be closer to its consumer base and because the company could achieve high productivity rates here that could nearly offset the higher wage expense.

Globalization is multidimensional and must be considered with a strategic vision, taking into account all factors that impact business performance. Currently, management decisions focus on accomplishing the corporate mission rather than just zeroing in on factors such as cost savings. In line with that approach, Boundless recently bought a 70,000-square-foot manufacturing plant in Boca Raton, Florida. Having two U.S. plants diversifies its production capabilities and expands its geographic manufacturing base, while further complicating HR. Even with the expansion, Boundless will remain small and nimble, with the ability to quickly adapt to global market conditions.[91]

Question

1. Boundless Technologies is a real company that actually did return to the United States and has been able to compete, even with higher U.S. wage rates, to the point of expanding by buying another plant in Boca Raton. What issues should have been considered prior to the overseas move?

Notes

1. Lionel Laroche and Catherine Mercer Bing, "Technology, Protocol Keep Global Teams Going Without Face-to-Face Meetings," *Canadian HR Reporter* (October 22, 2001): 17, 19.
2. Deborah Britt Roebuck and Aubrey Clarence Britt, "Virtual Teaming Has Come to Stay—Guidelines and Strategies for Success," *Southern Business Review* 28 (Fall 2002): 29–39.
3. Elizabeth Kelley, "Keys to Effective Virtual Global Teams," *The Academy of Management Executive* 15 (May 2001): 132–133.
4. Roebuck and Britt, "Virtual Teaming."
5. Christine Uber Grosse, "Managing Communication Within Virtual Intercutlural Teams," *Business Communication Quarterly* 65 (December 2002): 22–38.
6. Preston G. Smith, "Communication Holds Global Teams Together," *Machine Design* (July 26, 2001): 70–74.
7. Ibid.
8. Sabrina Hicks, "Successful Global Training," *Training & Development* 54 (May 2000): 95.
9. Milford Prewitt, "Global Expansion Requires World of Planning, Panelists Agree," *Nation's Restaurant News* (October 21, 2002): 58.
10. John D. Mittelstaedt, George N. Harben, and William A. Ward, "How Small Is Too Small? Firm Size as a Barrier to Exporting from the United States?" *Journal of Small Business Management* 41 (January 2003): 41.
11. Polly Larson, "International Growth Patterns Remain Strong," *Franchising World* 34 (April 2002): 6–8.
12. Russell J. Frith, "Going Global: Franchising International Development," *Franchising World* 35 (April 2003): 6.
13. Kevin T. Higgins, "P&G Reinvents Itself," *Marketing Management* 11 (November/December 2002): 12–15.
14. Beth McConnell, "HRCI to Offer Global HR Certification in 2004," *HRMagazine* 48 (March 2003): 115, 117.
15. Bill Leonard, "GM Drives HR to the Next Level," *HRMagazine* 47 (March 2002): 46–50.
16. Bill Ching, "Home Truths About Foreign Postings: To Make an Overseas Assignment Work, Employers Need More Than an Eager Exec with a Suitcase. They Must also Motivate the Staffer's Spouse," *BusinessWeek* (July 16, 2002).
17. Mark Wolfendale, "Doing Business in the Asia Pacific," *Strategic Finance* 84 (December 2002): 26–30.
18. Herbert Greenberg, "The People Connection to Global Expansion: The Quality of People Is Critical to the Success of a Corporation," *Franchising World* 35 (April 2003): 28.
19. Frank Jossi, "Successful Handoff," *HRMagazine* 47 (October 2002): 48–52.
20. Calvin Reynolds, "Global Compensation and Benefits in Transition," *Compensation and Benefits Review* 32 (January/February 2000): 28.
21. Donald J. McNerney, "Global Staffing: Some Common Problems—And Solutions," *HR Focus* 73 (June 1996): 1–5.
22. Jossi, "Successful Handoff."
23. Pauline Loong, "The Search for New Rainmakers," *Asiamoney* 13 (October 2002): 38–41.
24. This section was developed based on Anne Marie Francesco and Barry Allen Gold, *International Organizational Behavior* (Upper Saddle River, NJ: Prentice Hall, 1998): 165.
25. Carla Joinson, "No Returns," *HRMagazine* 47 (November 2002): 70–77.
26. Valerie Frazee, "Selecting Global Assignees," *Workforce* 3 (July 1998): 28–30.
27. Ching, "Home Truths About Foreign Postings."
28. Stan Lomax, "So You Want to Work Abroad?" *Business and Economic Review* 48 (April-June 2002): 12.
29. Paula Caligiuri, "Legal Issues in Selecting Global Assignees," *Workforce* 3 (July 1998): 29.
30. Andrea C. Poe, "Selection Savvy," *HRMagazine* 47 (April 2002): 77–83.
31. Charlene M. Soloman, "Success Abroad Depends on More than Job Skills," *Personnel Journal* 73 (April 1994): 51–59.
32. Jossi, "Successful Handoff."
33. Gary Wederspahn, "Expatriate Training: Don't Leave Home Without It," *T&D* 56 (February 2002): 67.
34. Karen Roberts, Ellen Ernst, and Cynthia Ozeki, "Managing the Global Workforce: Challenges and Strategies" (Special Issue: Competitiveness and Global Leadership in the 21st Century), *The Academy of Management Executive* (November 1, 1998): 93.
35. Julie Britt, "Expatriates Want More Support from Home," *HRMagazine* 47 (July 2002): 21.
36. Clifford C. Hebard, "Managing Effectively in Asia," *Training & Development* 50 (April 1996): 34.
37. Ibid.
38. Britt, "Expatriates Want More."
39. Mark E. Mendelhall and Carolyn Wiley, "Strangers in a Strange Land: The Relationship between Expatriate Adjustment and Impression Management," *American Behavioral Scientist* (March/April 1994): 605–621.
40. Louise O'Grady, "Using Technology to De-Stress on International Assignment," *Canadian HR Reporter* (September 24, 2001): 8, 12.
41. Paul Goldner, "Six Ways to Implement e-learning in Your Business," *Agency Sales* 31 (October 2001): 22–23.
42. Ibid.
43. Dawn Gareiss, "E-Learning Around the World," *Information Week* (February 26, 2001): 63–64.

44. "Top Employees Get Overseas Jobs," *Westchester County Business Journal* (August 26, 2002): 15.
45. O'Grady, "Using Technology."
46. Andrea C. Poe, "Welcome Back," *HRMagazine* 45 (March 2000): 94.
47. Charlene Mramer Solomon, "Global HR: Repatriation Planning," *Workforce* (2001): 22–23.
48. Neil B. Krupp, "Global Compensation Planning—Establishing and Maintaining a Competitive Edge in the International Marketplace," *Compensation & Benefits Management* 18 (Spring 2002): 54–56.
49. Robert J. S. Ross and Anita Chan, "From North-South to South-South," *Foreign Affairs* 81 (September/October 2002): 8–13.
50. Krupp, "Global Compensation Planning."
51. Richard G. Knator, "Multinational Employees: Compensation Must Balance Flexibility and Consistency," *Compensation & Benefits Report* 16 (October 2002): 4–6.
52. Bent M. Longnecker and Wendy Powell, "Executive Compensation in a Global Market," *Benefits & Compensation Solutions* (April 1996): 40–43.
53. Krupp, "Global Compensation Planning, 54–56.
54. Steven E. Gross and Per L. Wingerup, "Global Pay? Maybe Not Yet!" *Compensation and Benefits Review* 31 (July/August 1999): 25–34.
55. Carla Joinson, "Save Thousands Per Expatriate," *HRMagazine* 47(July 2002): 73–77.
56. Ibid.
57. Britt, "Expatriates Want More Support from Home."
58. Robert O'Connor, "Plug the Expat Knowledge Drain," *HRMagazine* 47 (October 2002): 101–107.
59. Joinson, "Save Thousands Per Expatriate."
60. Suh-kyung Yoon, "Forget the Ferrari," *Far Eastern Economic Review* (October 10, 2002): 64.
61. Arthur H. Kroll, "Equity Compensation in the Global Marketplace," *HR Focus* 61 (August 1999): S4.
62. Fabrizio Alcobe-Fierro, "Global Human Resource Management: Stock Options in Remuneration Programs," *Chemical Market Reporter* (July 16, 2001): 31–33.
63. Reynolds, "Global Compensation and Benefits in Transition," 28–38.
64. M. Janssens, J. M. Brett, and F. J. Smith, "Confirmatory Cross-Cultural Research Testing the Viability of a Corporation-Wide Safety Policy," *Academy of Management Journal* 38 (June 1995): 364–380.
65. R. B. Palchak and R. T Schmidt, "Protecting the Health of Employees Abroad," *Occupational Health & Safety* 65 (February 1996): 53–56.
66. Wayne Adams, "CIGNA Teams with International SOS to Launch World's First Online Physician-Led Health Care Network for Employees on Global Assignments, Improves Expatriates' Access to Quality Health Care Around the World; Helps Companies Maximize Their Multimillion-Dollar Investments in Expatriate Assignments," *Internet Wire* (February 14, 2002): 1008045.
67. Moray J. Taylor-Smith, "Do You Know Where Your Employees Are?" *Security Management* 46 (July 2002): 74–80.
68. "Global Protection," *Occupational Health & Safety* 67 (October 1998): 182.
69. M. E. Sharpe, "Labor's Future," *Challenge* 39 (March 1996): 65.
70. "Unions Show Slight Growth in 2002," *Canadian HR Reporter* (September 23, 2002): 2.
71. Neal E. Boudette, "Searching for Solutions, Germany May Tackle Taboo—Economic Woes Lead Some to Say Beloved Job Law Is Ripe for Rethinking," *Wall Street Journal* (February 28, 2003): A7.
72. Robert J. Samuelson, "The (New) Sick Man of Europe," *Newsweek* (November 18, 2002): 59.
73. Ken Rankin, "European Labor Laws No Solution to American Retail Struggles," *DSN Retailing Today* (June 24, 2002): 14.
74. Howard LaFranchi, "Protecting Workers in a Global Economy," *Christian Science Monitor* (May 6, 1998): 5.
75. Ken Cottrill, "New Roads to NAFTA," *Planning* 68 (February 2002): 32–34.
76. Gerald L. Maatmann, Jr., "Harassment, Discrimination Laws Go Global," *National Underwriter* (September 11, 2000): 34–35.
77. Judith Scott, Debora Gilliard, and Richard Scott, "Eliminating Bribery as a Transnational Marketing Strategy," *International Journal of Commerce & Management* 12 (2002): 1–17.
78. Ibid.
79. D. Salierno, "Bribery Gauged Worldwide," *Institute of Internal Auditors, Inc.* 59 (August 2002): 141.
80. Ron Lashier, "Global Challenges of Background Checks," *Security Management* 47 (March 2003): 105–108.
81. Samuelson, "The (New) Sick Man of Europe," 59.
82. Krupp, "Global Compensation Planning."
83. Kristi Ellis, "Child Labor Report the Good and Bad," *Fairchild Publications, Inc.* (August 2, 2002): 14.
84. Nicholas Stein, "No Way Out," *Fortune* (January 20, 2003): 102–108.
85. "Administration Supports Move to Zero Global Tariffs," *Chemical Market Reporter* (December 2, 2002): 3.
86. Mark Wolfendale, "Doing Business in the Asia Pacific," *Strategic Finance* 84 (December 2002): 26–30.
87. Patricia Digh, "One Style Doesn't Fit All," *HRMagazine* 47 (November 2002): 79–83.
88. Wederspahn, "Expatriate Training."
89. Dana Breitenstein, "Helping New Assignees Swim When They're Thrown in the Cultural Deep End," *T&D* 8 (September 2002): 9.
90. McNerney, "Global Staffing: Some Common Problems—And Solutions."
91. This is an adaptation of the actual experiences of Boundless Technologies. Paul Krugman, "Lower Wages Weren't Enough to Keep U.S. Company Abroad," *USA Today* (June 16, 1997): 19A; Mark Harrington, "Boundless Buys Florida for Undisclosed Sum," *Newsday* (January 26, 2000): A49; "Boundless Corporation," *Hoover's Company Capsules* Bm-Bz (January 15, 2003): 45084.

Glossary

Acceleration pools: A management succession planning system that develops a group of high-potential candidates for undefined executive jobs and focus on increasing their skills and knowledge rather than targeting one or two people for each senior management position.

Adverse impact: A concept established by the *Uniform Guidelines*; it occurs if women and minorities are not hired at the rate of at least 80 percent of the best-achieving group.

Advertising: A way of communicating the firm's employment needs to the public through media such as radio, newspaper, or industry publications.

Affirmative action: Stipulated by Executive Order 11246, it requires employers to take positive steps to ensure employment of applicants and treatment of employees during employment without regard to race, creed, color, or national origin.

Affirmative action program (AAP): A program that an organization develops to employ women and minorities in proportion to their representation in the firm's relevant labor market.

Agency shop: A labor agreement provision requiring, as a condition of employment, that each nonunion member of a bargaining unit pay the union the equivalent of membership dues as a service charge in return for the union acting as the bargaining agent.

AIDS (acquired immune deficiency syndrome): A disease that undermines the body's immune system, leaving the person susceptible to a wide range of fatal diseases.

Alcoholism: A a medical disease characterized by uncontrolled and compulsive drinking that interferes with normal living patterns.

Alternative dispute resolution (ADR): A procedure agreed to ahead of time by the employee and the company for resolving any problems that may arise.

Applicant tracking system (ATS): A system that automates online recruiting and selection processes.

Apprenticeship training: A combination of classroom instruction and on-the-job training.

Arbitration: A process in which a dispute is submitted to an impartial third party for a binding decision.

Assessment center: A selection technique that requires individuals to perform activities similar to those they might encounter in an actual job.

Attitude survey: A survey that seeks input from employees to determine their feelings about topics such as the work they perform, their supervisor, their work environment, flexibility in the workplace, opportunities for advancement, training and development opportunities, and the firm's compensation system.

Authorization card: A document indicating that an employee wants to be represented by a labor organization in collective bargaining.

Autonomy: The extent of individual freedom and discretion employees have in performing their jobs.

Availability forecast: A process of determining whether a firm will be able to secure employees with the necessary skills from within the company, from outside the organization, or from a combination of the two sources.

Baby boomers: People born between just after World War II and 1964.

Bargaining unit: A group of employees, not necessarily union members, recognized by an employer or certified by an administrative agency as appropriate for representation by a labor organization for purposes of collective bargaining.

Beachhead demands: Demands that the union does not expect management to meet when they are first made.

Behavioral interview: A structured interview where applicants are asked to relate actual incidents from their past that are relevant to the target job.

Behaviorally anchored rating scale (BARS) method: A performance appraisal method that combines elements of the traditional rating scale and critical incident methods.

Behavior modeling: A training method that utilizes videotapes to illustrate effective interpersonal skills and the ways managers function in various situations.

Benchmark job: A well-known job in the company and industry and one performed by a large number of employees.

Benefits: All financial rewards that employees generally receive indirectly.

Biofeedback: A method of learning to control involuntary bodily processes, such as blood pressure or heart rate.

Board interview: A meeting in which several representatives of a company interview a candidate in one or more sessions.

Bonus (lump-sum payment): A one-time award that is not added to employees' base pay.

Bottom-up approach: A forecasting method beginning with the lowest organizational units and progressing upward through an organization ultimately to provide an aggregate forecast of employment needs.

Boycott: Refusal by union members to use or buy their firm's products.

Broadbanding: A compensation technique that collapses many pay grades (salary grades) into a few wide bands in order to improve organizational effectiveness.

Burnout: An incapacitating condition in which individuals lose a sense of the basic purpose and fulfillment of their work.

Business games: Simulations, computer-based or non-computer-based, that attempt to duplicate selected factors in a particular business situation, which the participants manipulate.

Byline strike: Newspaper writers withhold their names from stories.

Capitation: The reimbursement method typically used by primary care physicians where providers negotiate a rate for health care for a covered life over a period of time.

Career: A general course that a person chooses to pursue throughout his or her working life.

Career development: A formal approach used by the organization to ensure that people with the proper qualifications and experiences are available when needed.

Career development tools: Skills, education, and experiences, as well as behavioral modification and refinement techniques that allow individuals to work better and add value.

Career path: A flexible line of progression through which an employee may move during his or her employment with a company.

Career planning: An ongoing process whereby an individual sets career goals and identifies the means to achieve them.

Career security: Requires developing marketable skills and expertise that help ensure employment within a range of careers.

Carpal tunnel syndrome: A condition caused by repetitive flexing and extension of the wrist.

Case study: A training method in which trainees are expected to study the information provided in the case and make decisions based on it.

Cash balance plan: A plan with elements of both defined benefit plans and defined contribution plans.

Central tendency: A common error in performance appraisal that occurs when employees are incorrectly rated near the average or middle of a scale.

Checkoff of dues: An agreement by which a company agrees to withhold union dues from members' paychecks and to forward the money directly to the union.

Classification method: A job evaluation method in which classes or grades are defined to describe a group of jobs.

Closed shop: An arrangement making union membership a prerequisite for employment.

Coaching: Often considered a responsibility of the immediate boss and provides assistance much the same as a mentor.

Cognitive aptitude tests: Tests that measure an individual's ability to learn as well as to perform a job.

Collective bargaining: The performance of the mutual obligation of the employer and the representative of the employees to meet at reasonable times and confer in good faith with respect to wages, hours, and other terms and conditions of employment; or the negotiation of an agreement, or any question arising thereunder; and the execution of a written contract incorporating any agreement reached if requested by either party. Such obligation does not compel either party to agree to a proposal or require the making of a concession.

Comparable worth: A determination of the values of dissimilar jobs (such as company nurse and welder) by comparing them under some form of job evaluation, and the assignment of pay rates according to their evaluated worth.

Compensation: The total of all rewards provided employees in return for their services.

Compensation policy: Policies that provide general guidelines for making compensation decisions.

Compensation survey: A means of obtaining data regarding what other firms are paying for specific jobs or job classes within a given labor market.

Competencies: Include a broad range of knowledge, skills, traits and behaviors that may be technical in nature, relate to interpersonal skills, or be business oriented.

Competency-based pay: A compensation plan that rewards employees for their demonstrated expertise.

Compressed workweek: Any arrangement of work hours that permits employees to fulfill their work obligation in fewer days than the typical five-day workweek.

Computer-based training: A teaching method that takes advantage of the speed, memory, and data manipulation capabilities of the computer for greater flexibility of instruction.

Concurrent validity: A validation method in which test scores and criterion data are obtained at essentially the same time.

Conspiracy: The combination of two or more persons who band together to influence the rights of others or of society (such as by refusing to work or demanding higher wages).

Construct validity: A test validation method to determine whether a selection test measures certain traits or qualities that have been identified as important in performing a particular job.

Content validity: A test validation method whereby a person performs certain tasks that are actual samples of the kind of work a job requires or completes a paper-and-pencil test that measures relevant job knowledge.

Contingency search firms: A search firm that receives fees only upon successful placement of a candidate in a job opening.

Contingent workers: Described as the "disposable American workforce" by a former Secretary of Labor, work as part-timers, temporaries, or independent contractors.

Corporate homepage: The initial page of the Web site used by an organization to present itself to viewers on the Internet.

Corporate labor campaigns: Labor maneuvers that do not coincide with a strike or organizing campaign to pressure an employer for better wages, benefits, and the like.

Corporate social responsibility (CSR): The implied, enforced, or felt obligation of managers, acting in their official capacity, to serve or protect the interests of groups other than themselves. It is how a company as a whole behaves toward society.

Corporate Web site: A virtual medium that presents information about the company, often including human resources information, and possibly even allowing individuals to apply for jobs.

Cost-of-living allowance (COLA): An escalator clause in a labor agreement that automatically increases wages as the U.S. Bureau of Labor Statistics' cost-of-living index rises.

Country's culture: The set of values, symbols, beliefs, languages, and norms that guide human behavior within a country.

Craft union: A bargaining unit, such as the Carpenters and Joiners union, which is typically composed of members of a particular trade or skill in a specific locality.

Criterion-related validity: A test validation method that compares the scores on selection tests to some aspect of job performance determined, for example, by performance appraisal.

Critical incident method: A performance appraisal technique that requires a written record of highly favorable and highly unfavorable employee work behavior.

Cyberwork: A possibility of a never-ending workday created through the use of technology.

Decertification: Election by a group of employees to withdraw a union's right to act as their exclusive bargaining representative; the reverse of the process that employees must follow to be recognized as an official bargaining unit.

Defined benefit plan: A retirement plan that provides the participant with a fixed benefit upon retirement.

Defined contribution health-care system: A system where companies give each employee a set amount of money annually with which to purchase health-care coverage.

Defined contribution plan: A retirement plan that requires specific contributions by an employer to a retirement or savings fund established for the employee.

Demotion: The process of moving a worker to a lower level of duties and responsibilities, which typically involves a reduction in pay.

Development: Learning that goes beyond today's job and has a more long-term focus.

DirectEmployers.com: A search engine that was developed by a group of corporations that enables job candidates to search member companies' job listings and be taken directly to a member company Web site once a desired position is identified.

Direct financial compensation: Pay that a person receives in the form of wages, salary, bonuses, and commissions.

Disciplinary action: The invoking of a penalty against an employee who fails to meet established standards.

Disciplinary action without punishment: A process in which a worker is given time off with pay to think about whether he or she wants to follow the rules and continue working for the company.

Discipline: The state of employee self-control and orderly conduct; indicates the extent of genuine teamwork within an organization.

Disparate impact: Occurs when certain actions in the employment process work to the disadvantage of members of protected groups.

Diversity: Any perceived difference among people: age, functional specialty, profession, sexual orientation, geographic origin, lifestyle, tenure with the organization, or position.

Diversity management: Ensuring that factors are in place to provide for and encourage the continued development of a diverse workforce by melding these actual and perceived differences among workers to achieve maximum productivity.

Diversity training: Attempts to develop sensitivity among employees about the unique challenges facing women and minorities and strives to create a more harmonious working environment.

Downsizing: A reduction in the number of people employed by a firm (also known as *restructuring*, and *rightsizing*); essentially the reverse of a company growing, and suggests a one-time change in the organization and the number of people employed.

Dual-career family: A situation in which both husband and wife have jobs and family responsibilities.

Dual career path: A career path that recognizes that technical specialists can and should be allowed to contribute their expertise to a company without having to become managers.

E-learning: An umbrella term describing online instruction.

Employability doctrine: Employees owe the company their commitment while employed and the company owes its workers the opportunity to learn new skills—but that is as far as the commitment goes.

Employee assistance program (EAP): A comprehensive approach that many organizations have taken to deal with burnout, alcohol and drug abuse, and other emotional disturbances.

Employee equity: A condition that exists when individuals performing similar jobs for the same firm are paid according to factors unique to the employee, such as performance level or seniority.

Employee requisition: A document that specifies job title, department, the date the employee is needed for work, and other details.

Employee stock option plan (ESOP): A defined contribution plan in which a firm contributes stock shares to a trust.

Employment agency: An organization that helps firms recruit employees and at the same time aids individuals in their attempt to locate jobs.

Employment at will: An unwritten contract created when an employee agrees to work for an employer but no agreement exists as to how long the parties expect the employment to last.

Employment interview: A goal-oriented conversation in which an interviewer and an applicant supposedly exchange information.

Equity: The perception by workers that they are being treated fairly.

Ergonomics: The study of human interaction with tasks, equipment, tools, and the physical environment.

Essay method: A performance appraisal method in which the rater writes a brief narrative describing an employee's performance.

Ethics: The discipline dealing with what is good and bad, or right and wrong, or with moral duty and obligation.

Ethnocentric staffing: A staffing approach in which companies primarily hire expatriates to staff higher-level foreign positions.

Exclusive provider organization (EPOs): A managed care option that offers a smaller preferred provider network and usually provides little, if any, benefits when an out-of-network provider is used.

Executive: A top-level manager who reports directly to a corporation's chief executive officer or to the head of a major division.

Executive order (EO): Directive issued by the president that has the force and effect of law enacted by the Congress.

Executive search firms: Organizations used by some firms to locate experienced professionals and executives when other sources prove inadequate.

Exempt employees: Those categorized as executive, administrative, or professional employees and outside salespersons.

Exit interview: A means of revealing the real reasons employees leave their jobs, providing the organization with information on how to correct the causes of discontent, and reducing employee turnover.

Expatriate: An employee who is not a citizen of the country in which the firm's operation (or subsidiary) is located but is a citizen of the country in which the organization is headquartered.

Exporting: Selling abroad, either directly or indirectly, by retaining foreign agents and distributors.

External environment: The factors that affect a firm's human resources from outside the organization's boundaries.

External equity: Payment of employees at rates comparable to those paid for similar jobs in other firms.

Factor comparison method: A job evaluation method in which raters need not keep an entire job in mind as they evaluate it; instead, they make decisions based on separate aspects or factors of the job.

Feedback: The amounts of information employees receive about how well they have performed the job.

Flexible compensation plan: A method that permits employees to choose from among many alternatives in deciding how their financial compensation will be allocated.

Flextime: The practice of permitting employees to choose, with certain limitations, their own working hours.

Flooding the community: The process of the union inundating communities with organizers to target a particular business.

Forced-choice performance report: A performance appraisal technique in which the rater is given a series of statements about an individual and indicates which items are most or least descriptive of the employee.

Forced distribution method: An appraisal approach in which the rater is required to assign individuals in a workgroup to a limited number of categories similar to a normal frequency distribution.

401(k) plan: A defined contribution plan in which employees may defer income up to a maximum amount allowed.

Franchising: A multinational option whereby the parent company grants another firm the right to do business in a prescribed manner.

Free agents: People who take charge of all or part of their careers, by being their own bosses or by working for others in ways that fit their particular needs or wants.

Functional job analysis (FJA): A comprehensive approach to formulating job descriptions that concentrates on the interactions among the work, the worker, and the work organization.

Gainsharing: Plans designed to bind employees to the firm's productivity and provide an incentive payment based on improved company performance.

Generalist: A person who performs tasks in a variety of human resource–related areas.

Generation I: Internet-assimilated children, born after 1994.

Generation X: The label affixed to the 40 million American workers born between 1965 and 1976.

Generation Y: The sons and daughters of boomers; people who were born between 1979 and 1994.

Genetic testing: Testing that can determine whether a person carries the gene mutation for certain diseases, including heart disease, colon cancer, breast cancer, and Huntington's disease.

Geocentric staffing: A staffing approach that uses a worldwide-integrated business strategy.

Glass ceiling: The invisible barrier in organizations that prevents many women and minorities from achieving top-level management positions.

Global corporation (GC): An organization that has corporate units in a number of countries; the units are integrated to operate as one organization worldwide.

Global human resource management (GHRM): The use of global human resources to achieve organizational objectives without regard to geographic boundaries.

Golden parachute contract: A perquisite provided for the purpose of protecting executives in the event their firm retires them or they are forced to leave for other reasons.

Grievance: An employee's dissatisfaction or feeling of personal injustice relating to his or her employment.

Grievance procedure: A formal, systematic process that permits employees to express complaints without jeopardizing their jobs.

Group interview: A meeting in which several job applicants interact in the presence of one or more company representatives.

Guidelines-oriented job analysis (GOJA): A method that responds to the growing amount of legislation affecting employment decisions by utilizing a step-by-step procedure to describe the work of a particular job classification.

Halo error: The perception by an evaluator that one factor is of paramount importance and who then gives a good or bad overall rating to an employee based on this particular factor.

Hay Guide chart-profile method (Hay Plan): A highly refined version of the point method of job evaluation that uses the factors of know-how, problem solving, accountability, and additional compensable elements.

Hazard pay: Additional pay provided to employees who work under extremely dangerous conditions.

Health: An employee's freedom from physical or emotional illness.

Health maintenance organizations (HMOs): Insurance programs provided by companies that cover all services for a fixed fee, but control is exercised over which doctors and health facilities may be used.

Host-country national (HCN): An employee who is a citizen of the country where the subsidiary is located.

Human capital management (HCM): The task of measuring the cause and effect relationship of various HR programs and policies on the bottom line of the firm.

Human resource development (HRD): A major HRM function that consists not only of T&D but also individual career planning and development activities and performance appraisal.

Human resource ethics: The application of ethical principles to human resource relationships and activities.

Human resource information system (HRIS): Any organized approach for obtaining relevant and timely information on which to base human resource decisions.

Human resource management (HRM): The utilization of a firm's human resources to achieve organizational objectives.

Human resource manager: An individual who normally acts in an *advisory* or *staff* capacity, working with other managers regarding human resource matters.

Human resource planning (HRP): The process of systematically reviewing human resource requirements to ensure that the required numbers of employees, with the required skills, are available when and where they are needed.

Hypnosis: An altered state of consciousness that is artificially induced and characterized by increased receptiveness to suggestions.

In-basket training: A simulation in which the participant is asked to establish priorities for and then handle a number of business papers such as memoranda, reports, and telephone messages, that would typically cross a manager's desk.

Indexed stock option plan: A stock option plan that holds executives to a higher standard and requires that increased stock compensation be tied to outperforming peer groups or a market index.

Indirect financial compensation: All financial rewards that are not included in direct compensation.

Individual representation: A situation in which people prefer to bargain for themselves and ignore the interests of the collective members of the workforce.

Industrial union: A bargaining unit that generally consists of all the workers in a particular plant or group of plants.

Informational picketing: The use of union members to display place cards and hand out leaflets, usually outside their place of business, depicting information the union wants the general public to see.

Injunction: A prohibiting legal procedure used by employers to prevent certain union activities, such as strikes and unionization attempts.

Interest arbitration: Arbitration that involves disputes over the terms of proposed collective bargaining agreements.

Internal employee relations: Those human resource management activities associated with the movement of employees within the organization.

Internal equity: Payment of employees according to the relative values of their jobs within the same organization.

Internet: The large system of many connected computers around the world that individuals and businesses use to communicate with each other.

Internet recruiter: Also called cyber recruiter, is a person whose primary responsibility is to use the Internet in the recruitment process.

Internship: A special form of recruitment that involves placing a student in a temporary job with no obligation either by the company to hire the student permanently or by the student to accept a permanent position with the firm following graduation.

Intranet: A system of computers that enables people within an organization to communicate with each other.

Job: A group of tasks that must be performed if an organization is to achieve its goals.

Job analysis: The systematic process of determining the skills, duties, and knowledge required for performing specific jobs in an organization.

Job analysis schedule (JAS): A systematic method of studying jobs and occupations; developed by the U.S. Department of Labor.

Job bidding: A technique that permits individuals in an organization who believe that they possess the required qualifications to apply for a posted job.

Job characteristics theory: Employees experience intrinsic compensation when their jobs rate high on five core job dimensions: skill variety, task identity, task significance, autonomy, and feedback.

Job description: A document that provides information regarding the tasks, duties, and responsibilities of a job.

Job design: A process of determining the specific tasks to be performed, the methods used in performing these tasks, and how the job relates to other work in an organization.

Job enlargement: A change in the scope of a job so as to provide greater variety to a worker.

Job enrichment: The restructuring of the content and level of responsibility of a job to make it more challenging, meaningful, and interesting to a worker.

Job evaluation: That part of a compensation system in which a company determines the relative value of one job in relation to another.

Job evaluation ranking method: A method in which the raters examine the description of each job being evaluated and arrange the jobs in order according to their value to the company.

Job fair: A recruiting method engaged in by a single employer or group of employers to attract a large number of applicants for interviews.

Job hazard analysis (JHA): A multi-step process designed to study and analyze a task or job and then break down that task into steps that provide a means of eliminating associated hazards.

Job knowledge tests: Tests designed to measure a candidate's knowledge of the duties of the job for which he or she is applying.

Job overload: A condition that exists when employees are given more work than they can reasonably handle.

Job posting: A procedure for communicating to company employees the fact that a job opening exists.

Job pricing: Placing a dollar value on the worth of a job.

Job rotation: A form of OJT where employees move from one job to another to broaden their experience.

Job security: Implies security in one job, often with one company.

Job sharing: The filling of a job by two part-time people who split the duties of one full-time job in some agreed-on manner and are paid according to their contributions.

Job specification: A document that outlines the minimum acceptable qualifications a person should possess to perform a particular job.

Job underload: Occurs when employees are given menial, boring tasks to perform.

Just-in-time training: Training provided anytime, anywhere in the world and just when it is needed.

Keyword résumé: A resume that contains an adequate description of the job seeker's characteristics and industry-specific experience presented in keyword terms in order to accommodate the electronic/computer search process.

Keywords: Those words or phrases that are used to search databases for résumés that match.

Labor market: The geographic area from which employees are recruited for a particular job.

Lateral skill path: A career path that allows for lateral moves within the firm that are taken to permit an employee to become revitalized and find new challenges.

Learning organizations: Firms that recognize the critical importance of continuous performance-related training and development and take appropriate action.

Leniency: Giving an undeserved high performance appraisal rating to an employee.

Licensing: A global arrangement whereby an organization grants a foreign firm the right to use intellectual properties such as patents, copyrights, manufacturing processes, or trade names for a specific period of time.

Likes and dislikes survey: A procedure that helps individuals recognize restrictions they place on themselves.

Line managers: Individuals directly involved in accomplishing the primary purpose of the organization.

Local union: The basic element in the structure of the U.S. labor movement.

Lockout: A management decision to keep employees out of the workplace and to operate with management personnel and/or temporary replacements.

Management development: Learning experiences provided by an organization for the purpose of upgrading skills and knowledge required in current and future managerial positions.

Management position description questionnaire (MPDQ): A form of job analysis designed for management positions that use a checklist method to analyze jobs.

Mandatory bargaining issues: Bargaining issues that fall within the definition of wages, hours, and other terms and conditions of employment; refusal to bargain in these areas is grounds for an unfair labor practice charge.

Market (going) rate: The average pay that most employers provide for the same job in a particular area or industry.

Mediation: A process in which a neutral third party enters and attempts to resolve a labor dispute when a bargaining impasse has occurred.

Medical savings accounts: A system that allows employees to set aside pretax money (taken out through payroll deductions throughout the year) to pay for medical bills in the coming year that aren't covered by their regular health insurance, including costs like deductibles and co-payments.

Mentoring: An approach to advising, coaching, and nurturing, for creating a practical relationship to enhance individual career, personal, and professional growth and development.

Merit pay: Pay increase given to employees based on their level of performance as indicated in the appraisal. The increase is added to the employee's base pay.

Modified retirement: An option that permits older employees to work fewer than their regular hours for a certain period of time preceding retirement.

Multinational corporation (MNC): A firm that is based in one country (the parent or home country) and produces goods or provides services in one or more foreign countries (host countries).

NACElink is the result of an alliance between two nonprofit associations—the National Association of Colleges and Employers (NACE) and DirectEmployers Association, Inc.—and an initial collaborating group of career centers.

National union: An organization composed of local unions, which it charters.

Negligent hiring: The liability an employer incurs when it fails to conduct a reasonable investigation of an applicant's background, and then assigns a potentially dangerous person to a position where he or she can inflict harm.

Negligent referral: When a former employer fails to offer a warning about a particularly severe problem with a past employee.

Negligent retention: When a company keeps persons on the payroll whose records indicate strong potential for wrongdoing and fails to take steps to defuse a possible violent situation.

Network career path: A method of job progression that contains both a vertical sequence of jobs and a series of horizontal opportunities.

Niche sites: Web sites that cater to a specific profession.

Nonfinancial compensation: The satisfaction that a person receives from the job itself or from the psychological and/or physical environment in which the job is performed.

Norm: A frame of reference for comparing an applicant's performance with that of others.

Objectivity: The condition that is achieved when all individuals scoring a given test obtain the same results.

On-the-job training (OJT): An informal approach to training in which an employee learns job tasks by actually performing them.

Open shop: Employment that is open on equal terms to union members and nonmembers alike.

Operative employees: All workers in a firm except managers and professionals, such as engineers, accountants, and professional secretaries.

Organizational career planning: The planned succession of jobs worked out by a firm to develop its employees.

Organizational fit: Management's perception of the degree to which the prospective employee will fit in with the firm's culture or value system.

Organizational stakeholder: An individual or group whose interests are affected by organizational activities.

Organization development (OD): The planned process of improving an organization by developing its structures, systems, and processes to improve effectiveness and achieve desired goals.

Orientation: The initial T&D effort for new employees that strives to inform them about the company, the job, and the workgroup.

Outplacement: A company procedure that assists a laid-off employee in finding employment elsewhere.

Outsourcing: The process of transferring responsibility for an area of service and its objectives to an external provider.

Paid time off (PTO): A means of dealing with the problem of unscheduled absences by providing a certain number of days each year that employees can use for any purpose they deem necessary.

Paired comparison: A variation of the ranking method of performance appraisal in which the performance of each employee is compared with that of every other employee in the group.

Passive job-seekers: Individuals who are willing to change jobs if the right opportunity comes along.

Pay compression: A situation that occurs when workers perceive that the pay differential between their pay and that of employees in jobs above or below them is too small.

Pay-equalization rules: Rules under which every worker is rewarded equally when pay or benefit gains are realized, based on seniority rather than worker productivity.

Pay followers: Companies that choose to pay below the going rate because of a poor financial condition or a belief that they simply do not require highly capable employees.

Pay grade: The grouping of similar jobs to simplify the job-pricing process.

Pay leaders: Those organizations that pay higher wages and salaries than competing firms.

Pay range: A minimum and maximum pay rate for a job, with enough variance between the two to allow for a significant pay difference.

Perception set: A fixed tendency to interpret information in a certain way.

Performance appraisal (PA): A formal system of review and evaluation of individual or team task performance.

Performance management: A process that significantly affects organizational success by having managers and employees work together to set expectations, review results, and reward performance.

Permissive bargaining issues: Issues that may be raised by management or a union; neither side may insist that they be bargained over.

Perquisites (perks): Any *special benefits* provided by a firm to a small group of key executives and designed to give the executives something extra.

Personality tests: Self-reported measures of traits, temperaments, or dispositions.

Piecework: An incentive pay plan in which employees are paid for each unit produced.

Point method: An approach to job evaluation in which numerical values are assigned to specific job components, and the sum of these values provides a quantitative assessment of a job's relative worth.

Point-of-service (POS): A managed care option that requires a primary care physician and referrals to see specialists, as with HMOs, but permits out-of-network health-care access.

Polycentric staffing: When more host-country nationals are used throughout the organization, from top to bottom.

Position analysis questionnaire (PAQ): A structured job analysis questionnaire that uses a checklist approach to identify job elements.

Position: The tasks and responsibilities performed by one person; there is a position for every individual in an organization.

Predictive validity: A validation method that involves administering a selection test and later obtaining the criterion information.

Preferred provider organizations (PPOs): A flexible managed-care system in which incentives are provided to members to use services within the system; out-of-network providers may be utilized at greater cost.

Premium pay: Compensation paid to employees for working long periods of time or working under dangerous or undesirable conditions.

Profession: A vocation characterized by the existence of a common body of knowledge and a procedure for certifying members of the profession.

Professional employer organization (PEO): Firms that work with company clients in a co-employment relationship to provide human resource administration, comprehensive employee benefit programs, assumption of employer risk, tax filing, and compliance with employment laws.

Profit sharing: A compensation plan that results in the distribution of a predetermined percentage of the firm's profits to employees.

Progressive disciplinary action: An approach to disciplinary action designed to ensure that the minimum penalty appropriate to the offense is imposed.

Prohibited bargaining issues: Issues that are statutorily outlawed from collective bargaining.

Promotion: The movement of a person to a higher-level position in an organization.

Promotion from within (PFW): The policy of filling vacancies above entry-level positions with employees presently employed by a company.

Psychomotor abilities tests: Aptitude tests that measure strength, coordination, and dexterity.

Quality circles: Groups of employees who voluntarily meet regularly with their supervisors to discuss problems, investigate causes, recommend solutions, and take corrective action when authorized to do so.

Quotas: Policies that limit the number or value of goods that can be imported across national boundaries.

Ranking method: A job evaluation method in which the rater simply places all employees from a group in rank order of overall performance.

Ranking method of performance appraisal: A performance appraisal method in which the rater simply places all employees from a group in rank order of overall performance.

Rating scales method: A widely used performance appraisal method that rates employees according to defined factors.

Realistic job preview (RJP): A method of conveying both positive and negative job information to an applicant in an unbiased manner.

Recruitment: The process of attracting individuals on a timely basis, in sufficient numbers, and with appropriate qualifications, and encouraging them to apply for jobs with an organization.

Recruitment methods: The specific means by which potential employees are attracted to an organization.

Recruitment sources: Various locations in which qualified individuals are sought as potential employees.

Reengineering: The fundamental rethinking and radical redesign of business processes to achieve dramatic improvements in critical, contemporary measures of performance such as cost, quality, service, and speed.

Reference checks: Validations that provide additional insight into the information furnished by the applicant and allow verification of its accuracy.

Regiocentric staffing: Similar to the polycentric staffing approach, but regional groups of subsidiaries reflecting the organization's strategy and structure work as a unit.

Reliability: The extent to which a selection test provides consistent results.

Relocation benefits: Company-paid shipment of household goods and temporary living expenses, covering all or a portion of the real estate costs associated with buying a new home and selling the previously occupied home.

Repatriation: The process of bringing expatriates home.

Requirements forecast: An estimate of the numbers and kinds of employees an organization will need at future dates to realize its stated objectives.

Résumé management systems: Systems that scan résumés into databases, search the databases on command, and rank the résumés according to the number of resulting hits they receive.

Retained search firms: Search firms that are considered as consultants to their client organizations, serve on an exclusive contract basis, and typically recruit top business executives.

Reverse mentoring: A process where the older employees learn from the younger ones.

Rights arbitration: Arbitration involving disputes over the interpretation and application of the various provisions of an existing contract.

Right-to-work laws: Laws that prohibit management and unions from entering into agreements requiring union membership as a condition of employment.

Role ambiguity: A condition that exists when employees do not understand the content of their job.

Role conflict: A condition that occurs when an individual is placed in the position of having to pursue opposing goals.

Role playing: A training method in which participants are required to respond to specific problems they may actually encounter in their jobs.

Sabbaticals: Temporary leaves of absence from an organization, usually at a reduced amount of pay.

Safety: The protection of employees from injuries caused by work-related accidents.

Scanlon plan: A gainsharing plan that provides a financial reward to employees for savings in labor costs that result from their suggestions.

Secondary boycott: A union's attempt to encourage third parties (such as suppliers and customers) to stop doing business with a firm.

Selection: The process of choosing from a group of applicants those individuals best suited for a particular position and organization.

Selection ratio: The number of people hired for a particular job compared to the total number of individuals in the applicant pool.

Self-assessment: The process of learning about oneself.

Seniority: The length of time that an employee has worked in various capacities with the firm.

Sensitivity training: An organization development technique that is designed to help individuals learn how others perceive their behavior (also know as T-group training).

Severance pay: Compensation designed to assist laid-off employees as they search for new employment.

Shared service center (SSC): A center that takes routine, transaction-based activities dispersed throughout the organization and consolidates them in one place.

Shareholders: The owners of a corporation.

Shift differential: Additional money paid to reward employees for the inconvenience of working undesirable hours.

Simulation: A technique for experimenting with a real-world situation by means of a mathematical model that represents the actual situation.

Simulators: Training devices of varying degrees of complexity that duplicate the real world.

Skill-based pay: A system that compensates employees on the basis of job-related skills and the knowledge they possess.

Skill variety: The extent to which work requires a number of different activities for successful completion.

Social audit: A systematic assessment of a company's activities in terms of its social impact.

Social contract: The set of written and unwritten rules and assumptions about acceptable interrelationships among the various elements of society.

Social responsibility: The implied, enforced, or felt obligation of managers, acting in their official capacity, to serve or protect the interests of groups other than themselves.

Specialist: An individual who may be a human resource executive, a human resource manager, or a nonmanager, and who is typically concerned with only one of the five functional areas of human resource management.

Staffing: The process through which an organization ensures that it always has the proper number of employees with the appropriate skills in the right jobs at the right time to achieve the organization's objectives.

Standardization: Uniformity of the procedures and conditions related to administering tests.

Status symbols: Organizational rewards that take many forms such as office size and location, desk size and quality, private secretaries, floor covering, and title.

Stock option plan: An incentive plan in which managers can buy a specified amount of stock in their company in the future at or below the current market price.

Strategic planning: The determination of overall organizational purposes and goals and how they are to be achieved.

Strength/weakness balance sheet: A self-evaluation procedure, developed originally by Benjamin Franklin that helps people to become aware of their strengths and weaknesses.

Stress: The body's nonspecific reaction to any demand made on it.

Stress interview: A form of interview that intentionally creates anxiety to determine how a job applicant will react in certain types of situations.

Strictness: Being unduly critical of an employee's work performance.

Strike: An action by union members who refuse to work in order to exert pressure on management in negotiations.

Structured interview: A process in which an interviewer consistently presents the same series of job-related questions to each applicant for a particular job.

Succession planning: The process of ensuring that qualified persons are available to assume key managerial positions once the positions are vacant.

Survey feedback method: A process of collecting data from an organizational unit through the use of questionnaires, interviews, and objective data from other sources such as records of productivity, turnover, and absenteeism.

Talent auction: The act of a person or persons placing their qualifications on a Web site and having organizations bid on their services.

Tariffs: Taxes collected on goods that are shipped across national boundaries.

Task identity: The extent to which the job includes an identifiable unit of work that is carried out from start to finish.

Task significance: The impact that the job has on other people.

Team building: Achieved when teams are rewarded based on their *group's productivity*.

Team equity: Payment of more productive teams in an organization at a higher rate than less productive teams.

Telecommuting: A work arrangement whereby employees, called *teleworkers* or *telecommuters*, are able to remain at home (or otherwise away from the office) and perform their work using computers and other electronic devices that connect them with their offices.

Third country national (TCN): A citizen of one country, working in a second country, and employed by an organization headquartered in a third country.

360-degree feedback evaluation method: An increasingly popular appraisal method that involves evaluation input from multiple levels within the firm and external sources as well.

Traditional career path: A vertical line of career progression in which an employee progresses vertically upward in the organization from one specific job to the next.

Training: Activities designed to provide learners with the knowledge and skill needed for their present jobs.

Training and development (T&D): The heart of a continuous effort designed to improve employee competency and organizational performance.

Transcendental meditation (TM): A stress-reduction technique in which an individual, comfortably seated, mentally repeats a secret word or phrase (mantra) provided by a trained instructor.

Transfer: The lateral movement of a worker within an organization.

Type I ethics: The strength of the relationship between what an individual or an organization believes to be moral and correct and what available sources of guidance suggest is morally correct.

Type II ethics: The strength of the relationship between what one believes and how one behaves.

Union: Comprised of employees who have joined together for the purpose of dealing with their employer.

Union salting: The process of training union organizers to apply for jobs at a company and, once hired, work to unionize employees.

Union shop: A requirement that all employees become members of the union after a specified period of employment (the legal minimum is 30 days) or after a union shop provision has been negotiated.

Unstructured interview: A meeting with a job applicant during which the interviewer asks probing, open-ended questions.

Utilization review: A process that scrutinizes medical diagnoses, hospitalization, surgery, and other medical treatment and care prescribed by doctors.

Validity: The extent to which a test measures what it claims to measure.

Vestibule training: Training that takes place away from the production area on equipment that closely resembles the actual equipment used on the job.

Virtual reality: A unique computer-based approach that permits trainees to view objects from a perspective otherwise impractical or impossible.

Vocational interest tests: A method of determining the occupation in which a person has the greatest interest and from which the person is most likely to receive satisfaction.

Wage curve: The fitting of plotted points on a curve to create a smooth progression between pay grades (also known as the *pay curve*).

Web (World Wide Web): The system of connected documents on the Internet, which often contains color pictures, video, and sound and can be searched for information about a particular subject.

Weighted checklist performance report: A performance appraisal technique in which the rater completes a form similar to a forced-choice performance report except that the various responses have been assigned different weights.

Workload variance: Involves dealing with both job overload and job underload.

Work-sample tests: Tests requiring the identification of a task or set of tasks that are representative of a particular job.

Work standards method: A performance appraisal method that compares each employee's performance to a predetermined standard or expected level of output.

Yellow-dog contract: A written agreement between an employee and a company made at the time of employment that prohibits a worker from joining a union or engaging in union activities.

Zero-base forecasting: A method for estimating future employment needs using the organization's current level of employment as the starting point.

Name Index

Company Index

Subject Index